Nevada Real Estate

PRINCIPLES AND PRACTICES

Nevada Real Estate

PRINCIPLES AND PRACTICES

Harry V. Eastlick

SOUTH-WESTERN
CENGAGE Learning~

Australia • Brazil • Japan • Korea • Mexico • Singapore • Spain • United Kingdom • United States

SOUTH-WESTERN
CENGAGE Learning™

Nevada Real Estate Principles and Practices

Harry V. Eastlick

Vice President of Editorial, Business: Jack W. Calhoun

Vice President/Editorial Director: Dave Shaut

Executive Editor: Scott Person

Acquisitions Editor: Sara Glassmeyer

Developmental Editor: Arlin Kauffman

Editorial Assistant: Michelle Melfi

Senior Marketing and Sales Manager: Mark Linton

Production Technology Analyst: Starratt Alexander

Production Manager: Jennifer Ziegler

Content Project Management: Pre-Press PMG

Senior Manufacturing Buyer: Charlene Taylor

Production Service: Pre-Press PMG

Copyeditor: Sarah Wales McGrath

Compositor: Pre-Press PMG

Senior Art Director: Jennifer Wahi

Cover Designer: Kathy Heming

Cover Image: ©iStock

Image Permissions Acquisitions Manager: Amanda Groszko

Text Permissions Acquisitions Manager: Arlin Kauffman

For product information and technology assistance, contact us at **Cengage Learning Customer & Sales Support, 1-800-354-9706**

For permission to use material from this text or product, submit all requests online at **www.cengage.com/permissions**
Further permissions questions can be emailed to **permissionrequest@cengage.com**

Library of Congress Control Number: 2009926308

ISBN-13: 978-0-324-65354-0

ISBN-10: 0-324-65354-9

South-Western Cengage Learning
5191 Natorp Boulevard
Mason, OH 45040
USA

Cengage Learning products are represented in Canada by Nelson Education, Ltd.

For your course and learning solutions, visit **www.cengage.com**

Purchase any of our products at your local college store or at our preferred online store **www.ichapters.com**

Printed in the United States of America
1 2 3 4 5 6 7 13 12 11 10 09

Brief Contents

Contents

25 INVESTING IN REAL ESTATE AND INCOME TAX ASPECTS OF REAL ESTATE 408

Preface

Nevada Real Estate Principles and Practices, a comprehensive text for students entering the real estate profession, uniquely combines national and Nevada real estate principles and practices into one book. It is derived from a text originally written in the 1980s that thousands of real estate professionals have used in the successful completion of the 90-hour licensing education. The author's vision is to provide a single text that includes the subjects set forth in the Nevada Real Estate Division course outlines for the broker and salesperson prelicensure courses.

Each chapter is consistently organized with the following sections:

- **Learning Objectives**

    Provide focus for the reader at the beginning of each chapter

    Are measurable and based on the Division course requirements

- **Important terms and concepts**

    Are listed at the beginning of each chapter

    Afford a quick reference of professional terminology

- **Chapter Content**

    Is presented in the order of the objectives

    Is written in a clear and concise style

    Follows easy-to-use headings

    Presents key terms in boldface print

- **Chapter Summary**

    Assists the reader in identifying key chapter concepts

- **Checking Your Comprehension**

    Asks questions related to the chapter's learning objectives

    Is provided in discussion and multiple-choice question format

- **Reviewing Your Understanding**

    Enables the reader to check understanding of chapter content

    Aids the student in preparing for the state examination

Other features include:

- A complete glossary
- State examination study guide
- Practice state examination
- Practice real estate mathematics section

The author believes that the text provides all of the information and study tools necessary to enable a real estate student to pass the state of Nevada licensing examinations. In addition, the text can help a prospective licensee establish a foundation for a successful career as a real estate professional.

ABOUT THE AUTHOR

HARRY V. EASTLICK is the Chairman and Chief Executive Officer of LRNN Corporation, a developer of online course materials for the real estate profession. Harry graduated from the University of Arizona with a Bachelor of Science degree in Accounting. After 20 years practicing as a Certified Public Accountant, with extensive experience with real estate clients, he retired as a partner in an international accounting firm as the National Director of Human Resources and Continuing Education. In 1973, Harry acquired an Arizona real estate school and has been involved since then in the operation of real estate schools and/or the development of course materials.

ACKNOWLEDGMENTS

It is impossible to specifically acknowledge the numerous contributions from students, instructors, and associates; however, I have attempted to weave their valuable suggestions into the text, and I thank them for their assistance. Comments and suggestions from students, readers, and instructors who use this text are welcome as the author desires to enhance future editions.

Special recognition is given to the staff of LRNN Corporation for their invaluable assistance, especially to Whipple H. Manning, who provided updates to the mortgage financing chapters and to Debra Prevost, Chief Operating Officer of ReNewal Education Corporation, the owner of The Academy for Real Estate Professionals, a Nevada real estate school. Finally, a sincere "thank you" to the editorial staff of Cengage Learning, especially Scott Person and Sara Glassmeyer, Arlin Kauffman of LEAP, and Jared Sterzer of PrePress PMG who have led us from the original concept to publication. We also value the feedback from the following reviewers: Nancy Scobee, American Career Institute, and Don Braselton, Northern Nevada Real Estate School. Thank you all.

Harry V. Eastlick

Nevada Real Estate

PRINCIPLES AND PRACTICES

Chapter 1

IMPORTANT TERMS AND CONCEPTS

accretion

air rights

alluvion

appurtenances

avulsion

common law

economic characteristics of real estate

erosion

improvements

land

littoral rights

navigable waterways

non-navigable waterways

physical characteristics of real estate

prior appropriation

real estate

reasonable use

riparian rights

situs

statutory law

subsurface rights

tenements

topography

water rights

CHAPTER OBJECTIVES

After completing this chapter, you should be able to:

- Identify the sources of real estate law.
- Explain that Nevada real estate law consists of statutory law and common law.
- Define land and real estate.
- Discuss the ownership of air rights and subsurface rights, including access rights to minerals.
- Identify and explain various terms and definitions used to discuss water law and rights.
- Describe the riparian doctrine of water rights and its application to Nevada.
- Describe the doctrine of prior appropriation.
- List and explain the economic and physical characteristics of real estate.

Land and Real Estate

1.1 REAL ESTATE LAW SOURCES

Students of real estate need to understand the extent to which federal, state, and local laws affect real estate.

Real estate law is based on both statutory law and common law.

Statutory Law

Statutory law can be divided into federal, state, and local classifications, as follows:

- The U.S. Constitution establishes the limits of governmental power and states the rights of citizens.
- Congress passes laws that are binding in all states (for example, federal fair housing laws).
- The federal bureaucracy is comprised of departments, boards, and commissions. The Code of Federal Regulations contains the administrative rules developed by federal administrative agencies to implement federal statutes. For example, the Department of Housing and Urban Development (HUD) administers laws and announces federal regulations. HUD is an agency that developed administrative rules to implement the Federal Fair Housing Amendments Act of 1988.
- The state constitution establishes the limits of governmental power within the state.
- The state legislature enacts bills (also known as statutes), which become law when signed by the governor. Chapter 645 of the Nevada Revised Statutes (NRS) includes the set of statutes that established the Real Estate Division of the Nevada Department of Business and Industry and real estate licensing law and governs real estate transactions and licensees in Nevada.
- The state bureaucracy, like the federal bureaucracy, is made up of departments, boards, and commissions, such as the Real Estate Commission and

the Real Estate Division. The Commission adopts the Nevada Administrative Code as it relates to real estate and real estate licensees. The Real Estate Division administers the relevant statutes and administrative code.

• Local governments have the power to adopt laws affecting the city or town. Local government laws are known as *ordinances*.

Common Law

Common law is based on tradition, customs, and usage and is generally unwritten in statute or code. Common law was developed in England and transferred to the United States with the early colonists.

Common law is also derived from judicial decisions. Court decisions interpret statutory law and set precedents with the same force as law. Only the published decision of an appellate court (that is, the Nevada Court of Appeals or the Nevada Supreme Court) establishes a legal precedent; trial court decisions, while important to the litigants involved in that case, do not establish a legal precedent.

Common law is the basis for the legal system throughout the United States, with the exception of Louisiana. In Nevada, common law has the same effect as statutory law, unless a statute has been passed to the contrary. For example, the Nevada Revised Statute 645.251 reads as follows:

"A licensee is not required to comply with any principles of common law that may otherwise apply to any of the duties of the licensee..."

A discussion of the duties of the licensee is included in Chapter 13.

1.2 LAND AND REAL ESTATE

Understanding property ownership and its implications represents some of the most basic principles and aspects of real estate. To gain an understanding of property rights, one must first learn the definitions of land and real estate.

Land

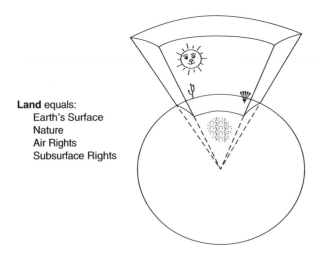

Land equals:
  Earth's Surface
  Nature
  Air Rights
  Subsurface Rights

Earth's Surface and Nature

When using the term *land*, most people think only of surface rights. However, **land** is legally defined as the earth's surface, down to the center of the earth, up to infinity, and including all things permanently attached by nature. Trees and cultivated perennial plants are also part of the land. In addition to surface rights and perennial plants, land includes air rights and subsurface rights, such as minerals, oil, and gas.

It is possible to have different owners for the earth's surface or the air and subsurface rights.

Air Rights

The surface owner also owns the **air rights**, which give the owner the right to reasonable use of the airspace for light and air. It is possible to have separate ownership of the land surface and air rights. In some metropolitan areas, railroads have sold the air rights over their terminals and tracks to allow the development of high-rise office complexes. When a unit in a high-rise condominium is purchased, a portion of the airspace is also acquired.

Until the development of air travel, the legal definition of surface ownership included the area above the surface, and that definition was sufficient to resolve most legal disputes. Now, the courts generally permit reasonable use of the airspace by aircraft, provided that it does not interfere with the right to use and occupy the land. In some cases, governments and airport authorities have purchased air rights adjacent to airports for glide patterns.

Subsurface Rights

The owner of the land surface rights also owns the subsurface rights, unless those rights have been previously sold or reserved by a prior landowner. The owner of the **subsurface rights** is allowed to remove the underlying minerals, oil, or gas. The laws related to the acquisition or sale of subsurface rights vary by state, and often differences exist between the transfer of rights for minerals, such as copper, and for oil or for gas.

When acquiring or selling land in an area known to include oil, gas, or minerals, the property's deed and other public records need to be examined to see if

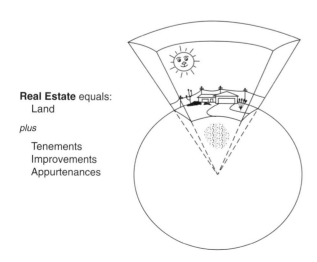

Real Estate equals:
Land

plus

Tenements
Improvements
Appurtenances

reservations concerning the transfer or retention of subsurface rights have been made.

Real Estate

Real estate is defined as the "land" (as defined previously), plus man-made additions permanently attached to the earth. These additions are called improvements, tenements, and appurtenances.

Tenements include any buildings on the land (for example, a house, barn, garage, warehouse, office, or apartment).

Improvements include sewers, sidewalks, streets, and utilities.

Appurtenances are rights, privileges, or improvements that belong to and pass with a property. For example, easements, rights of way, water rights, and mineral rights are all appurtenances.

1.3 WATER RIGHTS

Water rights and efficient use of water are vital to the growth and future development of Nevada. The common law doctrine, called riparian rights, governs many states' water rights. In Nevada, riparian rights apply only to the land rights of properties that border a waterway.

Land Rights under Riparian Doctrine

The ownership of land along a waterway depends on whether the waterway is navigable or non-navigable.

Navigable Waterways

If the waterway is navigable, the landowner owns the land to the water's edge at the high watermark, but no land below the water. The classification of a waterway as **navigable** is made by the federal government and is based on whether the waterway is used for commerce. The only navigable waters in Nevada are the Colorado River, the Virgin River, and Winnemucca Lake. In the case of navigable waters, the bed itself is owned by the state.

Non-Navigable Waterways

If the waterway is **non-navigable**, the landowner owns the land beneath the surface of the water to the center of the streambed at the low watermark.

Riparian Rights vs. Littoral Rights

Riparian rights are granted to owners of land located along a stream, river, or lake. They generally apply to non-navigable waters. Consequently, someone with riparian rights owns the land beneath the surface of the water.

Littoral rights are similar to riparian rights. Littoral rights are granted to owners of land that borders navigable lakes or oceans. These property owners may have full enjoyment of the water, but they own only the land to the water's edge at the average high watermark.

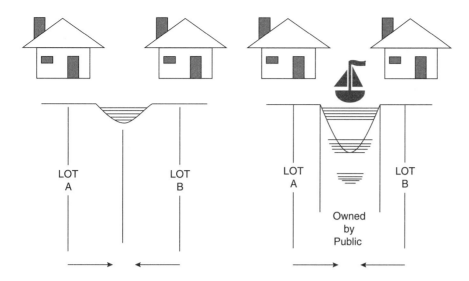

Erosion, Accretion, and Avulsion

A property owner may lose land through erosion or avulsion. **Erosion** is the gradual wearing away of land through processes of nature. **Avulsion** is a sudden loss of land, which may occur as a result of a sudden shift in a riverbed, volcanic action, an earthquake, or another cause. A property owner may also gain land through **accretion**, which is a slow buildup of land by natural forces such as wind or water. The surface land gained by accretion is known as **alluvion**.

Water Use Rights

Water use rights are governed by two primary doctrines:

*   The riparian doctrine is generally the basis for water rights laws in states where there is abundant surface water.
*   The doctrine of prior appropriation applies to arid regions of the country.

Riparian Doctrine

Under the riparian doctrine, the owners of land bordering the surface waters of a stream or river are granted water use rights. The landowner has unrestricted use of the water; however, the owner may not contaminate or disrupt the flow of the water. Only the riparian doctrine that relates to ownership of land next to a waterway relates to Nevada; the riparian doctrine related to water use is not applicable in Nevada.

Prior Appropriation and Reasonable Use

In Nevada, all water rights are governed by the doctrine of prior appropriation and reasonable use. **Prior appropriation** is often translated to mean "first in time, first in use." The policy of **reasonable use** declares that users must show beneficial use of water requested and secure a permit. Requests for permits may be made for surface water or groundwater. The State Engineer controls the use of water in the state.

The State Engineer enforces the groundwater laws. Except for areas for which a waiver of the requirements has been issued or for certain domestic wells, every person desiring to sink or bore a well in any basin or portion therein in the state of Nevada must first make application to and obtain from the State Engineer a permit to appropriate the water before performing any work in connection with the boring or sinking of the well. Surface water permits must be obtained to be sure that there is sufficient water to satisfy the needs of all potential users. The user holding the recorded permit with the oldest date has the legal right to first use the water. Then, the second oldest permit may use the water to satisfy his or her needs, and so on, until all of the water is used.

Irrigation water permits must be obtained from the State Engineer for irrigation water, whether for surface or groundwater. The date the permit was recorded determines the order of priority for use.

1.4 CHARACTERISTICS OF REAL ESTATE

The characteristics of real estate can be divided into two main classifications: economic and physical.

Economic Characteristics of Real Estate

There are four **economic characteristics of real estate:** scarcity, improvements, fixed investments, and situs.

Scarcity

There is no shortage of land on Earth, even though there is a fixed amount of it. *Scarcity* means a lack of land in a given area that is suitable for desired development. In Nevada, for instance, there is plenty of land for development if there is sufficient water. As Nevada's population continues to grow, more and more land is converted to urban use, which demonstrates the theory of supply and demand and the economic change in the land's value due to scarcity.

Improvements

After improvements are made to a parcel of land, an economic ripple effect may be noticed on the neighboring properties. If a major shopping center is developed in an area of directional growth, it will not be long until apartments, offices, residences, motels, and business services will follow in that area.

Fixed Investments

Because a real estate investment in a business complex or industrial site usually takes 20 to 30 years to pay for itself, investment in real estate must include long-range planning. Fixed investments include capital investments, labor, improvements such as utilities and sewers, and maintenance. Even a private residence usually represents the largest individual investment of a lifetime and is a fixed investment for a long period of time.

Situs

Considered the most important economic characteristic in real estate, **situs**, or area preference, is defined as the people's choice of a given area. Situs can be based on a beautiful view or on the proximity of employment, schools, or cultural centers. It may also be completely subjective and based on personal preferences. Transportation, labor, market, highway, or rail access could also be reasons for preference in a commercial or industrial site.

Physical Characteristics of Real Estate

There are three **physical characteristics of real estate**: immobility, indestructibility, and non-homogeneity.

Immobility

All real estate is immobile because it has a fixed location. Some soil may be lost through erosion or flood damage, but there is always more land beneath it.

Indestructibility

Land is said to be indestructible. Even though few structures remain of the early Native American inhabitants of this area, the land and the natural landmarks are virtually the same as in the days of Frémont and other early explorers in Nevada. This characteristic of durability is one of the reasons people think investments in real estate are preferable to stocks and bonds, metals, and commodities.

Non-homogeneity

Sometimes called *heterogeneity*, the term *non-homogeneity* means that no two parcels of real estate are alike. If for no other reason, every parcel of real estate is in a different location, each with its own legal description and identity. Often, properties will differ in size or topography, or the improvements will be different.

Because no two parcels are alike, the courts of law recognize this characteristic of land as non-fungible, which means "cannot be substituted for."

Physical and Economic Factors Affecting Land Use

The following are examples of physical and economic factors that affect land use.

- Contour and elevation of land. For example, rolling hills are considered ideal for residences, while a level area is preferable for commercial or industrial property. The contours of land are referred to as **topography**.
- Prevailing winds are important in relation to locations of industrial centers and residences. For example, even though copper smelters are located miles away from Ely, Nevada, the air quality in Ely is affected due to air currents.
- Transportation is an important factor in considering the location of a commercial or an industrial business.
- Public improvements, such as parks and airports, will be a factor in site selection whether residential, commercial, or industrial.
- Natural resources such as water, mineral deposits, and soil all affect land use.

- Weather conditions such as extreme heat and cold have a great effect on land use. Extreme weather conditions can be beneficial to an area, as evidenced by the ski resorts operating in northern Nevada. The development of air conditioning in Nevada is partially responsible for Nevada's population growth. Air conditioning has changed the negative effect of the summers in southern Nevada, which experience average high temperatures of 104°F.

- Employment opportunities—if an area has all the positive effects of the previously mentioned factors and no employment opportunities, there would be little desire for the land.

- Population growth has perhaps the greatest effect on land use.

CHAPTER SUMMARY

Real estate law is based on statutory law and common law. Statutory law includes the U.S. Constitution and state constitutions, laws enacted by Congress and the state legislature, departments of the federal and state bureaucracies, and ordinances adopted by local governments. Common law is the basis for the legal system in all states, except Louisiana.

Land is legally defined as the earth's surface including down to the center of the earth and up to infinity, as well as all things permanently attached to the surface by nature. Land includes surface rights, perennial plants, air rights, and subsurface rights, such as minerals, oil, and gas.

Real estate is defined as the land, plus man-made additions permanently attached to the earth. These additions are called improvements, tenements, and appurtenances. Tenements include any buildings on the land. Improvements include sewers, sidewalks, streets, and utilities. Appurtenances are rights, privileges, or improvements that belong to and pass with a property.

Riparian rights related to the ownership of land along a waterway depend on whether the waterway is navigable or non-navigable. If the waterway is navigable, the landowner owns the land to the water's edge at the high watermark, but no land below the water. If the waterway is non-navigable, the landowner owns the land beneath the surface of the water to the center of the streambed at the low watermark.

Littoral rights are granted to owners of land that borders navigable lakes or oceans. Property owners may lose land through erosion or avulsion. Property owners may also gain land, through the process of accretion.

In the United States, water use rights are governed by two primary doctrines: the riparian doctrine and the doctrine of prior appropriation. In Nevada, all water rights are governed by the doctrine of prior appropriation and reasonable use. Prior appropriation is often translated to mean "first in time, first in use." The policy of reasonable use declares that users must show beneficial use of water requested and secure a permit. A completed and perfected water right is appurtenant to the land and passes with the title.

Real estate has both economic and physical characteristics. Economic characteristics include scarcity, improvements, fixed investments, and situs. Physical characteristics include immobility, indestructibility, and non-homogeneity. Certain physical and economic factors may combine to affect land use and value, including but not limited to natural resources, weather conditions, employment opportunities, and population growth.

CHECKING YOUR COMPREHENSION

1. Define *land* and *real estate* and all the terms included in the definitions.

2. Describe the riparian doctrine and its applicability in Nevada. Also, define the following terms:
   - Littoral rights
   - Erosion
   - Accretion
   - Avulsion
   - Alluvion

3. Describe the Nevada water use rights doctrine.

4. The economic characteristics of real estate are scarcity, improvements, fixed investments, and situs. Define each of these.

5. The physical characteristics of real estate are immobility, indestructibility, and non-homogeneity. Define each of these.

REVIEWING YOUR UNDERSTANDING

1. Real estate is **BEST** defined as:
   a. land and the air above it
   b. land, the air above it, and everything above and below the ground
   c. land, the buildings on it, anything permanently attached to the land and/or buildings, and all appurtenances
   d. land and all rights in the land

2. Physical characteristics of real estate include:
   a. indestructibility
   b. scarcity
   c. improvements
   d. situs

3. All of the following are separable ownerships in land, **EXCEPT**:
   a. surface of the land
   b. area below the surface
   c. non-homogeneity
   d. air rights

4. Which economic characteristic has the greatest effect on real property value?
   a. tax rates
   b. situs
   c. availability
   d. indestructibility

5. Rights, privileges, or improvements that belong and pass to a new landowner are known as:

   a. tenements

   b. appurtenances

   c. improvements

   d. land

6. Physical characteristics of real estate include all of the following, **EXCEPT**:

   a. situs

   b. immobility

   c. indestructibility

   d. non-homogeneity

7. Land includes all of the following, **EXCEPT**:

   a. the earth's surface

   b. trees

   c. air above the surface

   d. street improvements

8. In Nevada, the doctrine for use of water is the:

   a. riparian doctrine

   b. littoral doctrine

   c. doctrine of prior appropriation and reasonable use

   d. Colorado River doctrine

9. The sudden loss of land due to a shift in a riverbed is called:

   a. erosion

   b. avulsion

   c. accretion

   d. alluvion

10. The ownership of land next to a stream or river is determined by:

    a. littoral doctrine

    b. prior appropriation

    c. riparian doctrine

    d. reasonable use

11. The quality of the location of land and consequently the value of the land can be changed by:

    a. the principle of non-homogeneity

    b. relocation of the land

    c. changes in the national scope of the real estate business

    d. improvements to the land that result in accessibility not previously available

12. Which of the following has the **GREATEST** effect on real estate value?

    a. tax rates

    b. location

    c. availability

    d. indestructibility

13. The non-homogeneity of land:

    a. results from the uniqueness of every parcel of real estate

    b. considers all real estate to be similar

    c. prevents buyers from suing for specific performances

    d. enables brokers to substitute any one parcel for another

14. The characteristic of land that causes the real estate market to be essentially a local market is the physical characteristic of:

    a. indestructibility

    b. immobility

    c. availability

    d. natural features

15. Water rights in Nevada are:

    a. a constitutional right of property owners

    b. indefeasible by right of law

    c. a federal right granted by Congress

    d. first in time, first in right

16. Utilities and streets added to land are called:

    a. improvements

    b. appurtenances

    c. tenements

    d. land

17. A pine tree planted in the front yard of a residence is considered to be:

    a. an emblement

    b. fructas industrials

    c. real estate

    d. a physical characteristic

18. A building added to the land is known as:

    a. a tenement

    b. an improvement

    c. an appurtenance

    d. a fixture

19. The body of law that traces its origins to England and prevails unless superceded by other laws is called:

    a. statutory law

    b. agency law

    c. contract law

    d. common law

20. The doctrine that regulates the ownership of lands next to navigable lakes and the ocean is known as the:

    a. riparian doctrine

    b. littoral doctrine

    c. doctrine of prior appropriation

    d. doctrine of reasonable use

Chapter

2

allodial system

asset

bundle of rights

condemnation

confiscation

emblements

eminent domain

escheat

feudal system

fief

fixture

fructus industriales

fructus naturales

government rights

hereditament

intangible assets

MARIA

personal property

police power

property

real property

rights of others

tangible assets

taxation

trade fixtures

Uniform Commercial
   Code (UCC)

CHAPTER OBJECTIVES

After completing this chapter, you should be able to:

- Discuss the history of ownership systems.
- Define property and the bundle of rights.
- Describe private, non-governmental limitations on the bundle of rights.
- List and explain the four government powers.
- Define hereditaments, real property, and personal property.
- Define and give examples of fixtures, trade fixtures, and emblements.

Real and Personal Property

2.1 OWNERSHIP SYSTEMS

Two basic systems of land ownership have evolved over the centuries:

- In a **feudal system**, all the land belongs to the sovereign king (or queen) and everyone owes rent or services to a superior.
- The **allodial system** establishes absolute ownership, which means there is no obligation to pay rent or services.

Absolute ownership formed the basis of Roman property laws. After the fall of the Roman Empire, the feudal system became more popular in most parts of Europe. In the area that continued to be influenced by Roman law, the allodial system prevailed, and landowners had absolute title with few limitations.

History of Feudalism

After the fall of the Roman Empire, the people of Western Europe turned to local leaders to protect their lands. They turned their lands over to the local leaders, who in turn protected them and granted them certain rights in the land. This practice survived several generations and resulted in ownership that was no longer absolute—one person owned the land and another or many others had an interest in it. The person holding the land or in possession of it was similar to a tenant who owed goods or services to the overlord for the use of the land, as did the overlord to his authorities.

Fiefdoms

In 1066, the Norman Conquest brought a more sophisticated form of feudalism to England. In an effort to consolidate his power and keep his fellow Normans in England, William the Conqueror declared all English lands forfeited to him. Then as supreme lord of all lands, he distributed land as fiefs. A **fief** is an estate held as a condition of service to another. Holders of fiefs were not given absolute ownership; they owed a service to the king, which could be military, supplies, food, or personal.

Land was also given to religious leaders in return for religious support of the king. This practice resulted in a system of tenancy in land as opposed to ownership.

Because the land always belonged to the king, if a tenant died and the heirs were minors, the king became guardian of both the heirs and the land and retained the profits. If a tenant died and had no heirs, his land or claim escheated, which means that his land or claim transferred to the sovereign power. This part of the feudal system still exists today in the United States. Later in this chapter, the current governmental limitation on property rights of escheat will be explained.

The Statute of Quia Emptores, passed by Edward I of England in 1290, enabled a tenant to sell his land, but it required the new owner of the land to continue to pay the goods, services, or feudal duties connected to that tenancy. This statute—along with the changes in the economic and political conditions—led to the payment of money rather than services and eventually caused the end of the tenure system of landholdings.

U.S. Ownership

In the time of the early U.S. settlers, land was held in tenure by the colonists and a small payment of money called a *quitrent* was paid to the king. The holder of a large section of land would subdivide it into smaller sections; however, because so much land was available on the frontier, this system was virtually ignored.

After the American Revolution, the quitrent system was abolished and people were given absolute ownership of the land, known also as allodial ownership. In the United States, the Bill of Rights established the right of individuals to own land free from government control.

2.2 OWNERSHIP RIGHTS

In law, **property** usually refers to rights that people have to use what they legally own, such as furniture, cars, and so on. The item itself is not as important as the right to use that item as you choose, so long as it does not infringe on the law.

The **bundle of rights**, also called property rights, in the Bill of Rights refers to both real and personal items. The differences between real and personal property will be explained later in this section. The five rights included in the bundle of rights are:

1. *Control*—total control within the framework of the law.
2. *Possession*—the right to have and to hold.
3. *Quiet and peaceful enjoyment*—the right to use the property; no one has superior rights.
4. *Disposition*—the right to sell, will, lease, barter, or destroy.
5. *Encumbrance*—the right to mortgage, grant easement, or burden title.

Limitations on Ownership Rights

Although the bundle of rights gives the individual property owner the greatest amount of control and freedom possible, there are limitations on the owner's rights. These limitations are classified as the **rights of others** and **government rights**.

Individual	Private Ownership	Government
Property Rights of Other Persons	Bundle of Rights: Control Possession Enjoyment Disposition Encumbrance	Police Power Eminent Domain Taxation Escheat

Rights of Others

The rights of others are private, non-governmental limitations on the bundle of rights. These non-governmental limitations are formally referred to as encumbrances, which can be classified as either non-monetary or monetary. Encumbrances will be examined in more detail in Chapter 6. The rights of others include the following:

- *Deed restrictions*—clauses in a deed limiting future use of a property.
- *Easements*—the right, privilege, or interest that one party has in the land of another.
- *Tenants*—the right of possession and use of an owner's property pursuant to a lease or rental agreement.
- *Lenders*—a charge, known as a lien, against property making it security for the payment of a debt, judgment, or mortgage; a lien is a monetary encumbrance.

Government Rights

Government powers designed to protect public health, safety, and welfare include the following:

- *Police power*
- *Taxation*
- *Eminent domain*
- *Escheat*

The State Enabling Acts granted these powers to cities and counties.

Police power is the government's right to enact laws for the common good. Usually one thinks of police power as the operation of police, fire, sanitation, and the health departments of a city. Other responsibilities of police power that have a distinct bearing on real estate are planning, subdivision regulations, zoning ordinances, and building codes. The Enabling Acts generally require that the zoning codes adopted by the local governing body be consistent with a plan for development. In Chapter 4, we will cover local zoning regulations in more detail.

Taxation is the government's right to levy taxes against real and personal property in order to provide city, county, and state governmental services for the benefit of the people. The following are taxes on real estate:

- *Ad valorem taxes*—taxes according to the value of the property.
- *Special assessments*—improvements to property such as street paving, curbs, sidewalks, sewers, or street lighting.

These topics will be discussed in detail in Chapter 6.

Eminent domain is the government's right to take private property for public use without the owner's consent, after paying the owner fair compensation. Local, state, and federal governments can use the right of eminent domain. The property is appraised, and fair market value is offered for the property. The government will attempt to negotiate and reach an agreement without initiating court action. If the owner refuses the offer, a court hearing is held to exercise the right of eminent domain. This process is called **condemnation**.

Escheat refers to the right of the state to take property from a deceased person's estate when there is no will and no heirs can be located.

In addition to the government powers described previously, the federal government also has a wartime power called **confiscation**, which gives it the right to seize property without compensation in the interest of national security.

2.3 REAL AND PERSONAL PROPERTY

Property can be classified in two groups: real property and personal property. An overall classification, called a hereditament, is the most inclusive classification of property. A **hereditament** includes anything capable of being inherited, both real and personal property.

In some countries, possessing and owning land was much more important than amassing money or personal items because land ownership carried with it voting rights. If a land owner was removed from his land, he could bring immediate action in the courts to recover that land. Legal actions to reinstate rights of possession were called *real actions*, and, therefore, we refer to land as *real property*. Actions to settle claims for money and goods were called *damages* and were considered *personal actions*; therefore, we refer to goods as *personal property*.

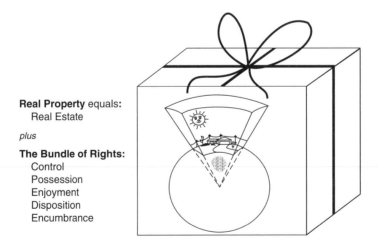

Real Property equals:
Real Estate

plus

The Bundle of Rights:
Control
Possession
Enjoyment
Disposition
Encumbrance

Real Property

Real property, or *realty*, is defined as real estate that is owned, meaning that the owner of the real estate has property rights referred to as the bundle of rights. In Chapter 1, real estate was defined as land, plus tenements, improvements, and appurtenances. As a reminder, the bundle of rights includes the rights of control, possession, quiet and peaceful enjoyment, disposition, and encumbrance.

Personal Property

Personal property is moveable. Everything that is not real property is classified as personal property. Examples include furniture, cars, tractors, clothes, money, stocks and bonds, jewelry, leases, mortgages, and trust deeds. Personal property is also called *personalty* or *chattel*. Personal property can be conveyed, encumbered, or assessed for taxes.

Growing Crops and Their Transfer

Courts divide growing crops (called **emblements**) into two categories. Annual crops, called *fructus industriales* or fruits of the industry, include such things as wheat, cotton, oats, and corn, and they are considered personal property. Crops that grow on perennial roots, such as trees, bushes, and vines, are called *fructus naturales*, and they are generally considered real property.

The **Uniform Commercial Code (UCC)**, adopted in all U.S. states, defines annual crops as goods, which are considered personal property. An effective salesperson makes provisions in the listing agreement as well as in the purchase contract that eliminate the need to discuss what land or crops will transfer.

2.4 FIXTURES

A **fixture** is an item that was once tangible, personal property that has been attached to and made a part of the land or improvements. Real property is immovable and includes everything permanently attached to the land. Therefore, fixtures that were once personal property become real property when they are permanently attached. Examples of fixtures include air-conditioning systems, furnaces, kitchen cabinets, and garbage disposals.

One way to test whether the item is real property (a fixture) or personal property is to remember the acronym **MARIA**:

M   *Method of attachment.* A refrigerator is not usually a fixture because it is simply plugged in, whereas bookshelves could be either real or personal property, depending on whether they are permanently attached. A dishwasher is generally a fixture because it is secured to the wall and/or surrounding cabinets and connected to the plumbing.

A   *Adaptability.* If an item such as a sunscreen were manufactured to fit an irregularly sized window, it should be classified as a fixture and remain with the property in the event of a sale. Other examples include custom drapes, custom Venetian blinds, and custom window shutters. Typically, whenever the description of personal property is modified by the word *custom*, it suggests that the item was specially adapted for the subject property and, therefore, is considered a fixture.

R   *Relationship of parties.* If a tenant installs a ceiling fan, he or she no doubt considered it personal property and hopes to remove it when he or she leaves. If an owner installed the same item, it could be classified as a fixture.

I   *Intent of annexor.* The intent of the annexor is considered the most important test of a fixture. The other four tests given here are used to clarify the intent of the annexor.

A *Agreement of parties.* To avoid disputes over whether an item is a fixture or personal property, it is wise to delineate in the contract any item that could be considered in either classification, for example, TV antenna, pool equipment, drapes, and so on.

Cost is not a factor in determining whether an item is classified as a fixture or personal property.

Trade Fixtures

Trade fixtures are items that are the personal property of a tenant or owner and are used to carry on his or her business. Even though attached to a building, they may be removed by the tenant or owner, provided they are removed before the lease expires or the sale of the property is completed. If they are not removed in time, the trade fixtures become the property of the landlord or the new owner. If removing the trade fixture causes any damage to the building, the building must be repaired. Examples of trade fixtures include restaurant equipment, store shelves, display cases, and beauty shop equipment.

Changing Classification

With the exception of trade fixtures, fixtures become real property by attachment and the other **MARIA** test factors. It is also true that real property can become personal property. For example, if a pine tree is cut down, it becomes personal property when it is removed from the earth because it is now moveable and unattached. The pine tree is then taken to a mill and made into lumber (still personal property). Then it is sold and used in building a home; the pine tree is attached, and so it becomes real property.

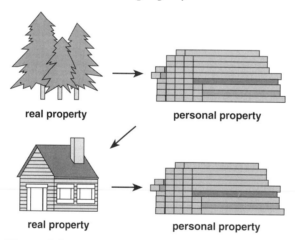

real property   personal property

real property   personal property

Tangible vs. Intangible Assets

Real and personal property are also assets. An **asset** is something of value, a useful item of property, owned by a person. Assets can be classified as tangible or intangible. **Tangible assets** are corporeal, which means *having a body.* Tangible assets are visible. **Intangible assets** are incorporeal, which means *without a body.* You cannot see intangible assets.

Real property is generally a tangible asset. Personal property is either tangible, such as a car, or intangible, such as a patent, copyright, or trademark.

CHAPTER SUMMARY

The two historic systems of land ownership are the feudal system and the allodial system. In a feudal system, all the land belongs to a king or queen and everyone owes rent or services to a superior. The allodial system established absolute ownership. In early U.S. history, land was held in tenure by the colonists, who had to pay a quitrent to the king. After the American Revolution, the quitrent system was abolished, and the allodial system prevailed. The Bill of Rights established the right of citizens to own land free from government control.

The Bill of Rights also established property rights, known as the bundle of rights. The bundle of rights includes the rights of control, possession, quiet and peaceful enjoyment, disposition, and encumbrance.

Although the bundle of rights grants as much freedom as possible, there are limitations on an owner's rights. These limitations are the rights of others and government rights. The rights of others include deed restrictions, easements, tenants, and lenders. Government rights include police power, taxation, eminent domain, and escheat. Police power is the government's right to enact laws for the common good. Eminent domain is the government's right to take private property for public use, after paying fair compensation to the owner. Taxation is the government's right to levy taxes against real and personal property. Taxes on real estate include ad valorem taxes and special assessments. Escheat refers to the right of the state to take property from a deceased person's estate when there is no will.

There are two main classifications of property: real property and personal property. A hereditament is anything capable of being inherited, which includes real and personal property. Real property is real estate that is owned, which means that the owner has property rights. Personal property is moveable. Everything that is not real property is classified as personal property.

Growing crops are called emblements, and they are divided into two categories. *Fructus industriales* consists of annual crops, which are considered personal property. *Fructus naturales* consists of perennial crops, which are considered real property.

A fixture is an item that was once tangible personal property but has since been permanently attached to and made a part of the land or improvements. Trade fixtures are personal property items used by a tenant or owner to carry on his or her business. Even though trade fixtures are attached to a building, the tenant or owner may remove them, provided they are removed before the lease expires or the sale of the property is completed.

Real and personal property are also considered assets. An asset is something of value owned by a person. Assets can be classified as tangible or intangible. Tangible assets are visible and corporeal, which means having a body. Real property is generally a tangible asset. Intangible assets cannot be seen and are incorporeal, which means without a body.

CHECKING YOUR COMPREHENSION

1. Define *property* and list and explain the meaning of the five components of the bundle of rights.

2. List and explain the meaning of the four government powers that limit private property rights.

3. Describe private, non-governmental limitations on the bundle of rights and list some of the private limitations.

4. Define *hereditament, real property*, and *personal property*.

5. Define a fixture and describe the purpose and components of a MARIA test. Also, describe what type of fixture is considered personal property.

REVIEWING YOUR UNDERSTANDING

1. Real property includes:
   a. fixtures
   b. trade fixtures
   c. emblements
   d. *fructus industriales*

2. What **BEST** describes chattel?
   a. a fixture
   b. personal property
   c. personal property that has been converted to real estate
   d. a mortgage on personal property

3. Which of the following would **NOT** be an appurtenance?
   a. easement rights
   b. mineral rights
   c. water rights
   d. trade fixtures

4. Articles of personal property owned by a tenant and solidly installed in his or her rented space for use in the business he or she conducts are known as:
   a. fixtures
   b. real estate
   c. leasehold fixtures
   d. trade fixtures

5. The government may acquire private land for the public welfare through the right of:
   a. eminent domain
   b. planning and zoning
   c. escheat
   d. police power

6. The property of a person who dies intestate and has no heirs will escheat to the:
   a. federal government
   b. state government
   c. county government
   d. city government

7. Which of the following is **NOT** a function of police power?
   a. control land use
   b. control rents
   c. collect taxes
   d. condemn as unfit for occupancy

8. Which of the following is **NOT** an "improvement" to land?
   a. building
   b. driveway
   c. orchard
   d. tomato crop

9. Which of the following is **NOT** included in the bundle of rights?
   a. encumbrance
   b. quiet enjoyment
   c. freedom
   d. control

10. In the absence of any agreement in the sales contract, which of the following would **MOST** likely be considered personal property?
    a. wall-to-wall carpeting
    b. an ornamental hedge
    c. fuel in an underground storage tank
    d. custom-made window shades

11. Patents, copyrights, and trademarks are **BEST** described as:
    a. corporeal
    b. bilateral
    c. incorporeal
    d. tangible

12. All of the following are methods for regulating land for use, **EXCEPT**:
    a. building codes
    b. zoning laws implemented by county or city government
    c. deed restrictions listed in a subdivision's restrictive covenants
    d. resolutions passed by local REALTOR associations

13. Police power is the government's right to:
    a. take private land for public use
    b. enact laws for the common good
    c. condemn property for the good of the public
    d. tax property to pay for government services

14. Which of the following is an example of the private control of land use?
    a. zoning
    b. restrictive covenants
    c. building codes
    d. environmental controls

15. The purchase agreement **DOES NOT** specify it, but a home seller can most likely remove:
    a. sprinkler heads that unscrew from the underground system
    b. prize rosebushes
    c. the freestanding fireplace screen
    d. the almost new garbage disposal

16. "It would **NOT** be an appurtenance" describes which of the following?
    a. easement rights
    b. mineral rights
    c. water rights
    d. trade fixtures

17. Taking property for public use by utilizing the condemnation process is allowed due to the:
    a. police power of the state
    b. power of eminent domain
    c. power of adverse possession
    d. dedication rights of the state

18. Which of the following is **NOT** used to determine whether an item is a fixture?
    a. method of attachment
    b. intent of the annexor
    c. cost of item
    d. adaptability of item

19. Which of the following is personal property?
    a. fixture
    b. mortgage note
    c. cesspool system
    d. perennial shrubs

20. Any property, whether real or personal, tangible or intangible, that may be inherited is classified as:
    a. land
    b. tenements
    c. fixtures
    d. hereditaments

Chapter

3

IMPORTANT TERMS AND CONCEPTS

air lots

base lines

bench mark

caissons

datum

fractional sections

government checks

guide meridians

map and plat description,
    or lot and block
    survey

meridians

metes and bounds
    descriptions

monuments

Mt. Diablo Base Line
    and Meridian

plat

point of beginning

principal meridian

range lines

rectangular survey or
    government survey

section

standard parallels

tiers

townships

township lines

CHAPTER OBJECTIVES

After completing this chapter, you should be able to:

* Explain the three basic methods of real estate legal description.
* Locate a parcel based on the legal description.
* Calculate acreage based on the legal description.

Legal Descriptions

3.1 INTRODUCTION

Legal descriptions are essential for identifying any parcel of property in such a specific manner that the description is acceptable in a court of law. A legal description is considered adequate if a competent surveyor can locate the real estate as described.

A legal description is one of the elements required of a valid real estate contract. Therefore, all listings, purchase contracts, deeds, mortgages, and so on require legal descriptions; leases generally do not require a legal description. Consequently, it is important to understand the different legal description methods used in Nevada.

The following are the basic methods used in legal descriptions:

1. Metes and bounds description
2. Rectangular survey (also called government survey)
3. Map and plat description (also known as lot and block description)

3.2 METES AND BOUNDS DESCRIPTIONS

Metes and bounds descriptions are the oldest form of legal descriptions used in the United States. This type of description was used in England and by all 13 original colonies.

Metes and bounds descriptions are still used exclusively in the eastern United States (19 states) and Texas. In other sections of the country, metes and bounds descriptions are used as a secondary method (along with the rectangular survey) to describe irregularly shaped or very small parcels of property.

In the early days of the United States, metes and bounds descriptions used landmarks for the point of beginning and boundaries. These natural and man-made landmarks, known as **monuments**, were trees, banks of streams, fences, and roads. The **point of beginning** indicates the place where the surveyor begins to describe the parcel in terms of the distance and direction from that point.

An example of this type of informal survey, a description dated 1665 in New London, Connecticut, follows:

1665. Laid out for George Geer one hundred acres of upland, granted to him by the town of New London, July ye 24, 1665, and is laid out as follows: Beginning upon the side of the hill at a white oak tree marked of four sides, standing about a mile from his own house, and from thence southerly upon a straight line running one hundred rods to a white oak tree marked on four sides; and from thence westerly and straight line one hundred and sixty rods to a white oak tree marked on four sides; and from thence northerly upon a straight line one hundred rods, running down a hill to a large tree standing by a run of water marked on four sides, and easterly to the first bound mark here we did begin upon a straight line. This laid out as above written, highways included. Per us,

ALEXANDER PYGAN,
JAMES MORGAN,   Surveyors
JOHN B STUBBINS

A true copy of the record examined. Per EDWARD HALLAM, Recorder.

These early descriptions were not entirely accurate because natural landmarks could change or be lost as years passed. Consequently, metes and bounds descriptions now use permanent monuments, such as iron posts, and surveying instruments to give accurate distance and direction.

Formal Metes and Bounds

The formal metes and bounds survey uses a permanent man-made monument that is placed in the ground by the surveyor at one corner of the parcel. This monument is typically an iron pin one to two inches in diameter driven several feet into the ground. Starting from this point of beginning, the surveyor creates a metes and bounds legal description, which indicates distance (metes) and direction (bounds). From the point of beginning, the surveyor describes the parcel's outside lines by compass and distance until the description returns to the point of beginning.

Distances and Descriptions

Distances are measured in feet, usually to the nearest tenth or one-hundredth of a foot. Directions are compass readings shown in degrees, minutes, and seconds. There are 360 degrees (°) in a circle, 60 minutes (′) in a degree, and 60 seconds (″) in a minute. When we refer to a southwest direction, it indicates that south is the first direction and west is the direction of the departure from south.

If a description is N 30° E, the line we are looking for is 30° east of due north. If we located N 45° W, we would face north and the line would be halfway between due west and due north, because 90° is always at right angles and the compass is divided into 360 degrees.

EXERCISE: Find the compass readings described:

N 24° E _____   N 35° W _____
S 30° W _____   E 20° S _____
S 70° E _____   W 80° N _____

Preparing a Metes and Bounds Description

In preparing a metes and bounds description, we simply add distance to our directional points. This tells the number of feet in that direction we must go. If we were measuring to a point 1000 ft. away in the direction W 25° S, we would write W 25° S 1000 ft. A line that is not exactly 45° would be shown as 45° 15′ and 30″ west of south.

Let's find this subject property:

Beginning at a point 400 ft. due east of the center of the intersection of Cottontail and Saddlecreek Run:

Thence N 0° E	2640 ft.
Thence N 90° E	5280 ft.
Thence S 0° W	2640 ft.
Thence S 90° W	5280 ft. to a point of beginning

We have described a rectangular tract of land 5280 ft. wide by 2640 ft. deep, or 13,939,200 square feet divided by 43,560, which is 320 acres.

EXERCISE: In the following space, draw the parcel described in the preceding section.

Let's try one more:

From a point of beginning thence S 45° W 1000 ft. to a metal stake thence S 90° W 2000 ft. to a metal stake, thence N 45° E 1000 ft. to a metal stake, thence N 90° E 2000 ft. to a point of beginning.

EXERCISE: In the following space, draw the parcel described in the preceding section.

3.3 RECTANGULAR SURVEY

In 1785, the Continental Congress passed a land ordinance that established a plan for surveying the abundance of public land west of the Appalachians and north of the Ohio River. At that time, the country was "land rich" and needed a way to use the land to fund public services. The Land Ordinance of 1785 contained a plan for dividing the land to create small, affordable parcels so that land ownership could become a reality for people of average means, not just the wealthy. The Ordinance divided the land into **townships** of 36 square miles and then divided each township into 36 sections of one square mile (640 acres) each. Each section could be purchased and divided further by the purchaser. Section 16, which was centrally located in each township, was set aside for school buildings. This method helped settlements spread in an orderly way across the western territories. This system of description is known as **rectangular survey or government survey**.

Meridians and Base Lines

The rectangular survey is based on imaginary north-south lines called **meridians**, which are parallel to the longitudinal lines, and east-west lines called **base lines**, which are parallel to the latitudinal lines.

This system is based on mathematics and a standard land unit (a **section**) of uniform shape and area with the boundaries physically marked on the ground.

The Land Office in Washington, D.C., was responsible for the establishment of the 35 principal meridians and base lines throughout the United States (Figure 3.1).

FIGURE 3.1 Principle Meridians and Base Lines

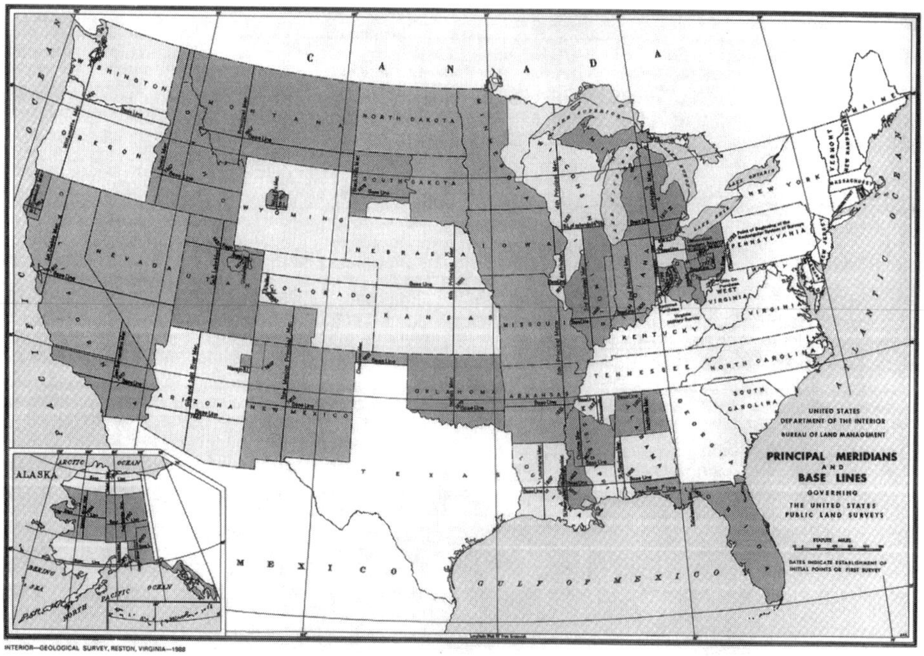

INTERIOR—GEOLOGICAL SURVEY, RESTON, VIRGINIA—1988

Source: Bureau of Land Management

Mt. Diablo Base Line and Meridian

The first step in putting this type of survey system into operation is determining an initial point. In Nevada, the initial point is called the Mt. Diablo Base Line and Meridian. The Mt. Diablo point of beginning is used for describing land in the central and northeastern parts of California plus all of the state of Nevada. The actual intersection of the Mt. Diablo Base Line and Meridian is on Mt. Diablo, near Walnut Creek, California (Figure 3.2).

Ranges and Township Lines

Every six miles, parallel to the principal meridian, there are north-south lines called **range lines**. They run north and south, but they measure the space east and west of the principal meridian. The ranges are coded R1E, R2W, and so on.

Every six miles, parallel to the base line, there are east-west lines called **township lines**. These strips, also called **tiers**, measure the space north and south. They are numbered north and south of the base line as T1N, T4S, and so on (Figure 3.3).

Correction Lines—Government Checks

Due to the curvature of the earth, it is necessary to make corrections every 24 miles on the meridian lines. To accomplish this, **guide meridians** and **standard parallels** have been established every 24 miles. The guide meridians are called "1st Guide Meridian, East or West," and so on, according to the distance from the principal meridian. The standard parallels are called "1st or 2nd Standard Parallel, North or South," and so on, according to the distance from the base line.

FIGURE 3.2 Mt. Diablo Base Line and Meridian

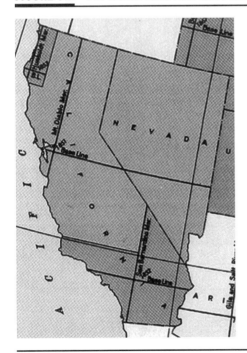

Source: Bureau of Land Management

FIGURE 3.3   Ranges and Township Lines

	Ranges West				Ranges East			
	T4N R4W	T4N R3W	T4N R2W	T4N R1W	T4N R1E	T4N R2E	T4N R3E	T4N R4E
Townships North	T3N R4W	T3N R3W	T3N R2W	T3N R1W	T3N R1E	T3N R2E	T3N R3E	T3N R4E
	T2N R4W	T2N R3W	T2N R2W	T2N R1W	T2N R1E	T2N R2E	T2N R3E	T2N R4E
Base Line	T1N R4W	T1N R3W	T1N R2W	T1N R1W	T1N R1E	T1N R2E	T1N R3E	T1N R4E
	T1S R4W	T1S R3W	T1S R2W	T1S R1W	T1S R1E	T1S R2E	T1S R3E	T1S R4E
Townships South	T2S R4W	T2S R3W	T2S R2W	T2S R1W	T2S R1E	T2S R2E	T2S R3E	T2S R4E
	T3S R4W	T3S R3W	T3S R2W	T3S R1W	T3S R1E	T3S R2E	T3S R3E	T3S R4E
	T4S R4W	T4S R3W	T4S R2W	T4S R1W	T4S R1E	T4S R2E	T4S R3E	T4S R4E

←————24 miles————→

Principal Meridian

FIGURE 3.4   Government Check

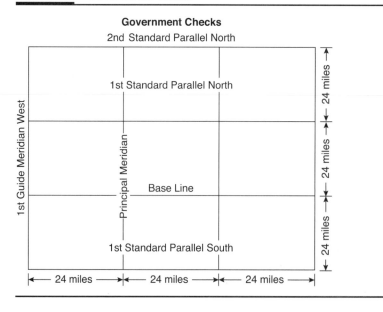

Government Checks

These 24-mile squares are called **government checks**. They each contain 16 townships. Because the range lines follow the curvature of the earth, there is an almost 200-foot difference in the east-west measurement from the first township in each government check. Therefore, at each standard parallel, the guide meridian is adjusted 200 feet to keep the townships more accurately six miles square (Figure 3.4).

Township Practice Problem

Use the following graph to answer the following questions.

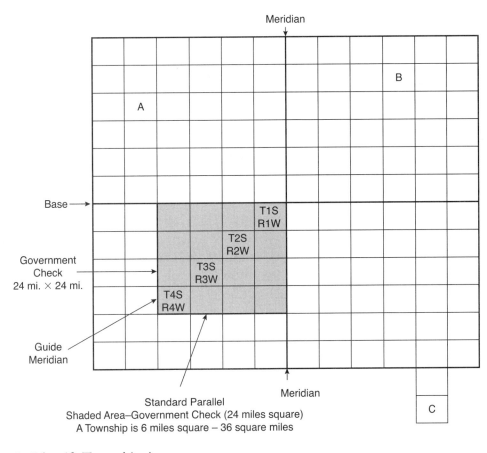

Shaded Area–Government Check (24 miles square)
A Township is 6 miles square – 36 square miles

1. Identify Township A. _____
2. Identify Township B. _____
3. Identify Township C. _____
4. How far north of the base line and east of the principal meridian is the southwest corner of Township B? _____
5. An area 8 miles north of the base line and 69 miles east of the meridian would be in what township? _____

Sections

Townships are divided into sections as follows:

- Each township has 36 sections. Each section is one square mile and contains 640 acres.

FIGURE 3.5   Township Divided into 36 Sections

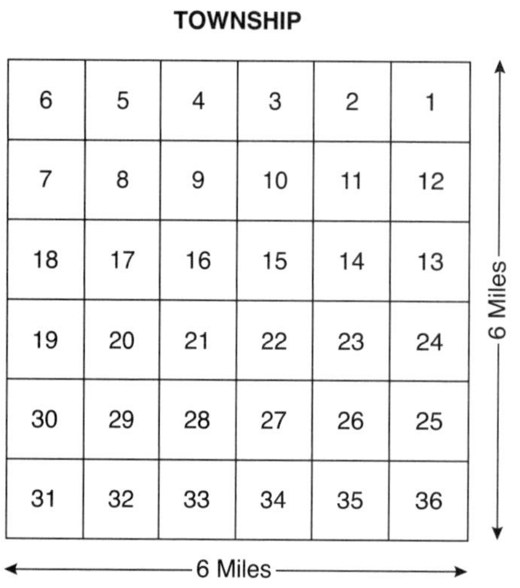

TOWNSHIP

6	5	4	3	2	1
7	8	9	10	11	12
18	17	16	15	14	13
19	20	21	22	23	24
30	29	28	27	26	25
31	32	33	34	35	36

6 Miles

←——————— 6 Miles ———————→

- Sections in a township are always numbered in the same way, with section 1 in the NE corner and section 36 in the southeast corner.
- The township in Figure 3.5 is designated as T4N, R4W. Township 4 North, Range 4 West.

When a township is adjusted for the government check, the corrections are confined to Sections 1, 2, 3, 4, 5, 6, 7, 18, 19, 30, and 31. These are known as **fractional sections**. There are 11 fractional sections and 25 full sections in a township. The corrections are 49.5 feet (3 rods).

Describing Part of a Section

Most often, less than a section of land is owned. A legal description of a portion of a section follows these principles:

- Individual sections break down into halves and quarters, and those quarters break down into still smaller halves and quarters, and so on.
- A section is the smallest area surveyed by the government survey system.
- Usually, 2.5 acres is the smallest subdivision of a section.

A written legal description starts with the smallest portion, with each successively larger parcel described until the initial point is reached, which in Nevada is the Mt. Diablo Base Line and Meridian. When locating a parcel of land from a written description, start with the largest portion first, reading from right to left. Figure 3.6 shows the descriptions for various divisions of section:

FIGURE 3.6 Description of Partial Sections

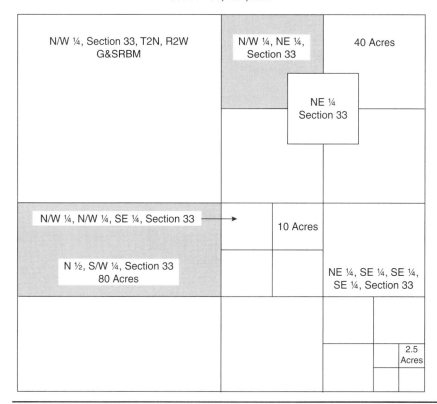

Legal Description Math Problems

An easy method to convert a legal description to acreage is described in calculating acreage followed by three practice problems.

Calculating Acreage

The following example provides step-by-step instructions for converting a legal description to acreage.

> **Example—Converting Legal Description to Acreage**
>
> The N½ of the W½ of the W½ of the NW¼ of section **4 and** the E½ of the NE¼ of the NE¼ of section 5 together contain how many acres?
>
> **Step 1**: Multiply the denominators of the legal description until you come to the word *and.*
>
> $$2 \times 2 \times 2 \times 4 = 32$$
>
> **Step 2**: Divide that number into **640** acres (for a section).
>
> $$32\overline{)640} \quad 20$$
>
> **Step 3**: Start over after the word "and" by multiplying denominators until the end of the description.
>
> $$2 \times 4 \times 4 = 32$$
>
> **Step 4**: Divide that number into 640 acres.
>
> $$32\overline{)640} \quad 20$$

Step 5: Add the two quotients to get the number of acres.

$$20 + 20 = 40 \text{ acres}$$

Practice Problems

EXERCISE 1: How many acres are in a plot of ground whose legal description is NW¼ of the SE¼ and the S½ of the SW¼ of the NE¼ of Section 6?

EXERCISE 2: A parcel of land is sold for $4800 per acre, and the legal description reads the SW¼ of the NE¼ of the SE¼. What would the sales price be?

EXERCISE 3: A legal description reads the N½ of the NW½ of the SE¼ of the SW¼ of the NW¼ of Section 2. This parcel of land contains how many acres?

3.4 MAP AND PLAT DESCRIPTIONS

The rectangular survey system is not suitable for describing small properties in urban areas. For describing these types of subdivided properties, the **map and plat description** (also known as **lot and block survey**) is the preferred method.

A **plat** is a survey that shows the location and boundaries of individual properties, dedicated streets, parks, and so on.

A surveyor or land engineer divides the plat into lots, streets, and blocks. Each block is given a number. The surveyor then assigns each lot a number, and notes the dimensions and exact size of each lot. The plat map usually also includes the surveyor's name, the owner's name, the date of the survey, and the date of approval.

The plat map is recorded in the county where the property is located and given a name and page number in the recorder's map book.

Property is described by giving the lot number, block number, tract name, map book reference, county, and state. For instance, Lot 180, Block 100, Wrigley Terrace, Plat 3, according to the plat map for block 5 of the Jones Tract 3 follows on the next page.

The shaded portion in Figure 3.7 might be legally described by lot and block number as follows:

"The north 25 feet of Lot 10 and all of Lots 1, 2, and 9, in block 5, Jones Tract 3, on page 67, Book of Maps #3, as recorded in Clark County."

The lot and block number description is most often used when describing urban property.

FIGURE 3.7   Plat Map

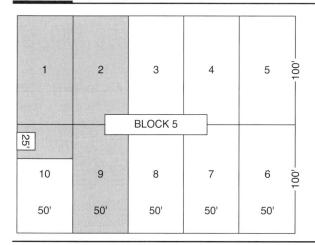

Helpful Hints for Solving Legal Description Problems

In working with land description problems, a few simple reminders are helpful:

1. The top of a map is always north unless otherwise marked.
2. When you are looking at a map and have difficulty remembering which direction is east or west, just write the word *WE*. This shows *W*, or west, to the left, and *E*, or east, to the right.
3. When working on a written land description problem, it is a good idea to draw a sketch first, placing all necessary values on the sketch, and then work out the problem onto the sketch. This avoids careless errors and gives you a way to check your answer.

Terms Related to Legal Descriptions

Air lots consist of air-specific elevation boundaries using a local datum over a parcel of land. In addition to the airspace, small parcels of land must be purchased for support. These support foundations are called **caissons**. The Pan Am Building in New York City and the Merchandise Mart in Chicago, both built over railroads, are examples of the use of air lots.

Condominiums sell the airspace along with common areas, such as elevators, stairs, halls, grounds, and any recreational facilities, such as a swimming pool, meeting room, or other amenity. Chapter 7 provides more information about condominiums.

Datum is a point of reference to which heights and depths are referred. The national datum is located at the mean (average) sea level in New York Harbor. Almost all cities have established a local datum to which surveyors can refer. Datum is used in reference to air lots for descriptions.

A **bench mark** is a brass marker embedded in a road or permanently attached to a tree or iron post to give the elevation based on the official datum. Therefore, a surveyor can start at any bench mark to set elevations for a given area. If no local datum is established, the U.S. Geodetic Survey datum is used, which covers the whole nation.

CHAPTER SUMMARY

There are three basic methods used in legal descriptions—metes and bounds descriptions, rectangular survey (also called government survey), and map and plat descriptions (also known as lot and block descriptions).

Metes and bounds descriptions are used in 20 states. In other sections of the country, metes and bounds descriptions are used as a secondary method of describing property. Early metes and bounds descriptions used natural landmarks called monuments for the point of beginning and boundaries. The point of beginning indicates the place where the surveyor begins to describe the parcel. Metes and bounds descriptions now use surveying instruments and permanent monuments.

The formal metes and bounds survey uses a permanent monument that is placed in the ground by the surveyor at one corner of the parcel. Starting from this point of beginning, the surveyor creates a metes and bounds legal description, which indicates distance (metes) and direction (bounds). From the point of beginning, the surveyor describes the parcel's outside lines by compass and distance until the description returns to the point of beginning.

Distances are measured in feet. Directions are compass readings shown in degrees, minutes, and seconds. There are 360 degrees (°) in a circle, 60 minutes (′) in a degree, and 60 seconds (″) in a minute. To prepare a metes and bounds description, simply add the distance to the directional points.

The system of description known as rectangular or government survey started with the Land Ordinance of 1785, which contained a plan for dividing the land, creating small, affordable parcels. The Ordinance divided the land into townships of 36 square miles, and then divided each township into 36 sections of one square mile (640 acres) each. Each section could be purchased and divided further by the purchaser.

The rectangular survey is based on imaginary lines called meridians and base lines. Meridians are north-south lines parallel to the longitudinal lines. Base lines are east-west lines parallel to the latitudinal lines. This system is based on mathematics and sections of uniform shape and area, with the boundaries physically marked on the ground.

The Land Office in Washington, D.C., established 35 principal meridians and base lines throughout the United States. In Nevada, the initial point is called Mt. Diablo Base Line and Meridian.

Every six miles, parallel to the principal meridian, there are north-south lines called range lines. They measure the space east and west of the principal meridian. The ranges are coded R1E, R2W, and so on.

Every six miles, parallel to the base line, there are east-west lines called township lines. These strips, also called tiers, measure the space north and south of the base line. They are numbered north and south of the base line as T1N, T4S, and so on.

Due to the curvature of the earth, it is necessary to make corrections every 24 miles on the meridian lines. To accomplish this, guide meridians and standard parallels were established every 24 miles. These 24-mile squares are called government checks. They each contain 16 townships. Each township has 36 sections. Each section is one square mile and contains 640 acres. The sections in a township are always numbered in the same way, with section 1 in the NE corner and section 36 in the SE corner. When a township is corrected, the corrections are confined to Sections 1, 2, 3, 4, 5, 6, 7, 18, 19, 30, and 31. These are known as fractional sections.

A section is the smallest area surveyed by the government survey system, but most often, less than a section of land is owned. In a legal description of a portion of a section, individual sections break down into halves and quarters, and those quarters break down into still smaller halves and quarters. Usually, 2.5 acres is the smallest subdivision of a section.

A written legal description starts with the smallest portion, with each successively larger parcel described until the initial point is reached. When locating a parcel of land from a written description, start with the largest portion first, reading from right to left.

To calculate acreage in a legal description, multiply the denominators of the legal description until you come to the word *and*. Then divide that number into 640 acres. Start over after the word *and* by multiplying denominators until the end of the description. Divide the denominator into 640 acres and then add the two quotients to get the number of acres.

The map and plat description is the best system for describing small, subdivided properties in urban areas. The map and plat description is also known as a lot and block survey. A plat is a survey that shows the location and boundaries of individual properties, dedicated streets, parks, and so on. All developers who subdivide tracts of land into six or more parcels, each containing less than 36 acres, must file a subdivision plat map before any parcels can be sold.

A surveyor or land engineer surveys the plat into lots, streets, and blocks. Each block is given a number, and each lot is also numbered. Dimensions and exact sizes of each lot are given as well. After receiving approval, the plat map will then be recorded in the county where the property is located and given a name and page number in the recorder's map book.

CHECKING YOUR COMPREHENSION

1. List and define the three basic methods used to describe land.

2. Explain when each of the three methods is most applicable.

PRACTICAL APPLICATION

1. What section is due north of Section 4?

2. The shortest distance between the southern boundary of Section 9 and the northern boundary of Section 33 in the same township is how many miles?

3. Part of a legal description reads T6N, R3W.
   a. The southern boundary of the township is how many miles north of the base line?
   b. The western boundary of the township is how many miles west of the principal meridian?

4. One half of a township equals how many acres?

5. A subdivider owns the NW¼ of the NW¼ of the SW¼ of Section 4. The land in Section 4 is selling at $2000 per acre. To own all of the SW¼ of Section 4 would cost the subdivider how much?

6. How many square-acre lots can be developed along a road on the west side of a ¼-section parcel of land?

REVIEWING YOUR UNDERSTANDING

1. To fence the N½ of the N½ of the SE¼ of a section, how much fencing is required?
   a. 1 mile
   b. 1¼ mile
   c. 2 miles
   d. 3960 feet

2. A metes and bounds legal description reads, "From the point of beginning 1200 ft. south then 1500 ft. west then 600 ft. north then back to the point of beginning." The parcel of land contains how many square feet?
   a. 900,000
   b. 1,350,000
   c. 1,800,000
   d. 1,125,000

3. A range is a strip of land:
   a. six miles wide running north and south
   b. one mile wide running east and west
   c. six miles wide running east and west
   d. one mile wide running north and south

4. Assume a metes and bounds description starts in the center of a section and thence goes in a straight line to the northwest corner of the section, thence south 2640 ft. along the west section line and thence in a straight line to the point of beginning. The parcel so described would contain:
   a. 40 acres
   b. 80 acres
   c. 180 acres
   d. 320 acres

5. The shortest distance between Sections 5 and 32 of the same township would be:
   a. 4 miles
   b. 5 miles
   c. 6 miles
   d. 7 miles

6. The W½ of the NW¼ of the NW¼ of the SE¼ of the SW¼ of a section is to be paved for parking at a cost of $1.20 per square foot. The total paving cost will be:
   a. $16,336
   b. $32,668
   c. $65,340
   d. $130,677

7. A farmer owns the W½ of the NW¼ of the NW¼ of a section. The adjoining property can all be purchased at $2300 per acre. To own all of the NW¼ of the section, the farmer would have to pay:
   a. $46,000
   b. $92,000
   c. $322,000
   d. $368,000

8. A legal description reads, "Starting at the northwest corner of Section 3 and proceeding in a straight line to the southwest corner of Section 8, thence in a straight line due east for two miles, thence north to the point of beginning." How many acres are represented by the legal description?
   a. 320
   b. 640
   c. 960
   d. 1280

9. Correction lines are 24 miles apart and were established to:
   a. overcome surveyors' mistakes
   b. make township lines accurate
   c. overcome the effect of the earth's curvature
   d. make township lines even

10. A metes and bounds legal description includes all of the following, **EXCEPT**:
    a. metes as lengths
    b. a point of beginning
    c. bounds as directions
    d. identification of lot and block

11. Which sections are contiguous to Section 7 of a township?
    a. 12 and 17
    b. 6 and 19
    c. 8 and 16
    d. 8 and 14

12. A datum plane is used by:
    a. appraisers
    b. bankers
    c. surveyors
    d. carpenters

13. One quarter of a township equals:
    a. 160 acres
    b. 320 acres
    c. 5760 acres
    d. 23,040 acres

14. Part of a legal description reads "T7NR4W." The south boundary of the township so described would be how far north of the base line?
    a. 6 miles
    b. 36 miles
    c. 42 miles
    d. 60 miles

15. A four-sided parcel of land has 2640 feet on one side. At a right angle to this side is a side 5280 feet long. Parallel to the shorter side is a side of 5280 feet. The ends of the two parallel sides of 2640 feet and 5280 feet are connected. The resulting acreage is:
    a. 320 acres
    b. 460 acres
    c. 480 acres
    d. 640 acres

16. The following is **NOT** a description of a section:
    a. one square mile
    b. one mile square
    c. 5280 feet on each side
    d. 160 acres

17. The S½ of NW¼ of SE¼ of SW¼ of NW¼ of a section contains:
    a. 1¼ acres
    b. 2½ acres
    c. 5 acres
    d. 10 acres

18. Section 13 in a township is located in what quarter of the township?
    a. NW¼
    b. NE¼
    c. SW¼
    d. SE¼

19. The rectangular survey system:
    a. covers all the land in the continental United States
    b. is used primarily in the northeast
    c. is used primarily in the west and midwest
    d. is used in 20 states

20. The primary survey line running east and west in the rectangular survey is the:
    a. township line
    b. base line
    c. range line
    d. principal meridian

IMPORTANT TERMS AND CONCEPTS

buffer zone

certificate of occupancy

cluster zoning

comprehensive development plan

down zoning

Environmental Impact Statement (EIS)

master plan

master planned community

non-conforming use

planning commission

police power

real property classifications

special use permit

spot zoning

State Land Office

zoning changes

zoning variance

CHAPTER OBJECTIVES

After completing this chapter, you should be able to:

- Summarize the history of land owned by the state of Nevada, including School Trust Lands.
- Discuss the government right of police power.
- Discuss community planning and planning requirements.
- Describe the nature and scope of Environmental Impact Statements.
- Explain zoning regulations and various zoning terminology and concepts.

Government Land Ownership and Use Controls

4.1 PUBLIC OWNERSHIP

Public ownership provides land control for public use and benefit. Based on reports from the U.S. General Services Administration and the state of Nevada, the percentage of land in Nevada that is privately owned could be as low as 7.7%, but not higher than 11.5%.

Types of public ownership in Nevada include the following:

- Government buildings—municipal, county, state, and federal
- Schools—elementary, junior high, senior high, colleges, and universities
- Parks—city, state, and federal
- U.S. Bureau of Land Management
- State of Nevada School Trust Land
- U.S. Forests
- Indian Trust land
- Streets and highways

The percentage of U.S. government land ownership in Nevada appears to be increasing because of the federal government's program for sales of federal lands that is more than offset by purchases of private land primarily for conservation purposes.

The Nevada Legislature believes it has a strong moral claim upon the public land retained by the federal government that is within its borders and has adopted Nevada Revised Statute 321.596, which reads as follows:

NRS 321.596 Legislative findings. The Legislature finds that:

1. The State of Nevada has a strong moral claim upon the public land retained by the Federal Government within Nevada's borders because:

   (a) On October 31, 1864, the Territory of Nevada was admitted to statehood on the condition that it forever disclaim all right and title to unappropriated public land within its boundaries;

(b) From 1850 to 1894, newly admitted states received 2 sections of each township for the benefit of common schools, which in Nevada amounted to 3.9 million acres;

(c) In 1880 Nevada agreed to exchange its 3.9-million-acre school grant for 2 million acres of its own selection from public land in Nevada held by the Federal Government;

(d) At the time the exchange was deemed necessary because of an immediate need for public school revenues and because the majority of the original federal land grant for common schools remained unsurveyed and unsold;

(e) Unlike certain other states, such as New Mexico, Nevada received no land grants from the Federal Government when Nevada was a territory;

(f) Nevada received no land grants for insane asylums, schools of mines, schools for the blind and deaf and dumb, normal schools, miners' hospitals or a governor's residence as did states such as New Mexico; and

(g) Nevada thus received the least amount of land, 2,572,478 acres, and the smallest percentage of its total area, 3.9 percent, of the land grant states in the Far West admitted after 1864, while states of comparable location and soil, namely Arizona, New Mexico and Utah, received approximately 11 percent of their total area in federal land grants.

2. The State of Nevada has a legal claim to the public land retained by the Federal Government within Nevada's borders because:

(a) In the case of the State of Alabama, a renunciation of any claim to unappropriated lands similar to that contained in the ordinance adopted by the Nevada constitutional convention was held by the Supreme Court of the United States to be "void and inoperative" because it denied to Alabama "an equal footing with the original states" in *Pollard v. Hagan,* 44 U.S. (3 How.) 212 (1845);

(b) The State of Texas, when admitted to the Union in 1845, retained ownership of all unappropriated land within its borders, setting a further precedent which inured to the benefit of all states admitted later "on an equal footing"; and

(c) The Northwest Ordinance of 1787, adopted into the Constitution of the United States by the reference of Article VI to prior engagements of the Confederation, first proclaimed the "equal footing" doctrine, and the Treaty of Guadalupe Hidalgo, by which the territory including Nevada was acquired from Mexico and which is "the supreme law of the land" by virtue of Article VI, affirms it expressly as to the new states to be organized therein.

3. The exercise of broader control by the State of Nevada over the public lands within its borders would be of great public benefit because:

(a) Federal holdings in the State of Nevada constitute 86.7 percent of the area of the State, and in Esmeralda, Lincoln, Mineral, Nye and White Pine counties the Federal Government controls from 97 to 99 percent of the land;

(b) Federal jurisdiction over the public domain is shared among 17 federal agencies or departments which adds to problems of proper management of land and disrupts the normal relationship between a state, its residents and its property;

(c) None of the federal lands in Nevada are taxable and Federal Government activities are extensive and create a tax burden for the private property owners of Nevada who must meet the needs of children of Federal Government employees, as well as provide other public services;

(d) Under general land laws only 2.1 percent of federal lands in Nevada have moved from federal control to private ownership;

(e) Federal administration of the retained public lands, which are vital to the livestock and mining industries of the State and essential to meet the recreational and other various uses of its citizens, has been of uneven quality and sometimes arbitrary and capricious; and

(f) Federal administration of the retained public lands has not been consistent with the public interest of the people of Nevada because the Federal Government has used those lands for armament and nuclear testing thereby rendering many parts of the land unusable and unsuited for other uses and endangering the public health and welfare.

4. The intent of the framers of the Constitution of the United States was to guarantee to each of the states sovereignty over all matters within its boundaries except for those powers specifically granted to the United States as agent of the states.

5. The attempted imposition upon the State of Nevada by the Congress of the United States of a requirement in the enabling act that Nevada "disclaim all right and title to the unappropriated public lands lying within said territory," as a condition precedent to acceptance of Nevada into the Union, was an act beyond the power of the Congress of the United States and is thus void.

6. The purported right of ownership and control of the public lands within the State of Nevada by the United States is without foundation and violates the clear intent of the Constitution of the United States.

7. The exercise of such dominion and control of the public lands within the State of Nevada by the United States works a severe, continuous and debilitating hardship upon the people of the State of Nevada.

(Added to NRS by 1979, 1362)

4.2 NEVADA DIVISION OF STATE LANDS[1]

The Division of State Lands provides land and land use planning services to the state, its agencies, and its people. This division has three program areas. It also

---

[1] Information on the Nevada Division of State Lands is taken from its website: www.lands.nv.gov.

administers other special programs as well as provides staff assistance to the Nevada Tahoe Regional Planning Agency and the State Land Use Planning Advisory Council. The **State Land Office** serves as the state's "real estate" agency for all agencies except the legislature, the university system, and the Department of Transportation. The agency holds title to state lands and interests in land. The agency buys land needed by the state and sells excess land. The agency issues leases, easements, permits, and other authorizations for the use of state land. The land office also keeps records of all lands that have ever been owned by the state and provides land records information upon request.

Agency Lands

The Division of State Lands holds title to the lands used by most state agencies, including the Division of Buildings and Grounds, the Department of Prisons, the Division of State Parks, and the Department of Wildlife. Day-to-day management of these lands is the responsibility of the agency using the land. There are currently approximately 139,000 acres of "agency lands" statewide. The State Land Office has copies of all land records and will provide information and assistance regarding all state agency lands. All leases, easements, and other interest in theses lands must be issued through the Division of State Lands.

Sovereign Lands

Upon statehood, Nevada received title to all sovereign lands that are submerged beneath navigable bodies of water. At the present time, the following bodies of water are considered to be navigable:

- Lake Tahoe
- Carson River
- Washoe Lake
- Colorado River
- Walker Lake
- Virgin River
- Truckee River

The state owns the beds and banks of these bodies of water, generally up to the ordinary and permanent high water mark. At Lake Tahoe, the state owns the bed of the lake to elevation 6223.0. The state's ownership does not generally extend to wetlands, tributaries, ditches, or flood overflows. Any use or disturbance of these lands requires agency authorization. Upon request, the agency will assist the public to locate the state's ownership boundaries.

School Trust Lands

At statehood, Nevada received several grants of trust lands from the federal government. Most of those lands have been sold and now make up a large part of the state's private land base. The state still holds approximately 3000 acres of original School Trust Lands. These lands are assets of the Permanent School Fund and are required by the state constitution to be managed or disposed of to generate revenue for the Fund.

4.3 LAND USE CONTROLS

Land use controls are divided into several classifications: public ownership of land, public land use control, and private land use control (see Chapter 6). Public land use control is derived from the police power limitation on private property rights.

Police power (one of the government powers) allows the government to adopt laws that limit private property land use through planning requirements, zoning ordinances, subdivision regulations, building codes, and environmental protection. The main purpose of police power is to protect the public health, safety, and welfare of the community. Police power, which is granted by the 14th Amendment to the U.S. Constitution, passes the rights to the cities and counties through the State Legislative Enabling Acts. Subdivision regulations and environmental protection will be covered in later chapters.

Community Planning

The first city in the nation to develop a community plan was Washington, D.C., with the McMillan Plan in 1901. The second city to do so was Chicago, with the Burnham Plan.

Cities and counties in Nevada are required to complete and adopt a comprehensive long-term general plan to be known as a **Master Plan**. Also, counties where population exceeds 100,000 are required to form Regional Planning Commissions, and the Master Regional Plans must be coordinated with similar plans of adjoining regions along with Master County and City Plans within each region.

Community planning is a continuous process intended to guide the preservation, development, or redevelopment of a neighborhood, community, or region, and to promote the goals and ambitions of its residents. Quality of life, infrastructure, and land use are typically key considerations in the process. Communities need to prudently manage and direct their growth-strained resources to ensure an economic future consistent with their goals. Communities appoint planning commissions and employ urban planners to aid in the completion of the planning process. The State Land Use Advisory Council of the Nevada Division of State Lands is also available to provide statewide technical assistance and training to Nevada's municipalities and counties.

Nevada's planning legislation establishes the Master Plan requirements for Nevada municipalities, counties, and regional planning commissions. Some required elements of a plan include:

* Planning for land use, including uses for housing, business, industry, and agriculture.

- Establishing standards for population density and building intensity for each land use category.
- Planning for circulation, including the general location and extent of roads, freeways, bicycle routes, and other modes of transportation, all in correlation to the land use plan.
- Planning for open space acquisition and preservation, including the following:

    a. Inventory of open space areas, recreational resources, and access points.
    b. Analysis of future needs, policies for managing and protecting open space areas, and strategies for acquiring additional open space and establishing new recreational resources.
    c. Policies and strategies to promote a regional system of integrated open space and recreational resources.

- Planning for growth areas, including identifying any suitable areas for planned multimodal transportation, infrastructure expansion, and improvements designed to support a variety of land uses.
- Environmental planning that contains analysis, policies, and strategies to address any anticipated effects on air and water quality and natural resources.
- Cost of development element that identifies policies and strategies that require development to pay its fair share toward the cost of additional public service needs.

The required elements of a Master Plan vary for municipalities, counties, and regional planning commissions. The plan is in place for 20 years from adoption with annual reviews and a plan update not less than every 5 years.

Environmental Impact Statement (EIS)

The purpose of an **Environmental Impact Statement (EIS)** is to gather information that will demonstrate a positive or negative impact of a proposed project on the physical, economic, and social environment of the area.

The EIS is presented to the **Planning Commission**, along with the development application for approval. The statement is made available to the public and becomes a part of the discussion at the public hearing.

The report includes information on the effects of the project on the following areas:

- Population, demographic density, growth, and so on
- Traffic congestion
- Pollution (air, water, noise)
- Recreation, wildlife, vegetation, conservation
- Energy requirements
- Public school enrollments
- Health and safety (sanitation, water, and sewer systems)
- Employment opportunities

Preparing an EIS is time-consuming and costly—and the cost is usually passed on to the consumer. However, the environmental study's positive effects far outweigh these disadvantages.

4.4 ZONING

Local communities and counties pass zoning ordinances to regulate use and control of land. The first zoning laws were passed in New York City in 1916 to restrict the garment industry from encroaching on the fashionable Fifth Avenue business and residential area. Today, most cities with populations of more than 10,000 have zoning restrictions.

Zoning regulations are considered restrictions rather than encumbrances because their purpose is to improve and maintain property values and provide for orderly growth of the community. They must be reasonable and are enacted to ensure the health, safety, and general welfare of the public. These regulations usually include the following:

- Dividing property into zones
- Setting limits on the height and bulk of buildings
- Designating use of buildings
- Determining use of land
- Limiting population density
- Establishing setback lines

Classifications of Real Property

The zones are established according to five general classifications: residential, agricultural and raw land, industrial and manufacturing, commercial, and special purpose (hospitals, airports, and schools).

Real Property

Residential   Agricultural   Industrial   Commercial   Special Purpose

There are numerous divisions within each classification. The divisions are referred to by codes such as R1 (single family), R2 (duplex), and so on. No standard code is used throughout the United States or in Nevada; each community uses its own coding system.

Zoning Concepts

One popular zoning concept is the **comprehensive development plan**, which provides housing, recreation, and commercial development in one self-contained development or in urban high-rise facilities where individuals can live, work, and play within the same area.

A **master planned community** is a development consisting of two or more separately platted subdivisions and is subject to either (1) a master declaration of covenants, conditions, or restrictions; (2) restrictive covenants that clearly indicate a general scheme for improvement or development of real property; or (3) a master owner's association that governs or administers the development.

Another popular development is **cluster zoning**. This type of zoning changes street patterns and reduces the size of individual lots but provides for the same number of residences with more open recreational space and less traffic congestion than on a regular grid pattern of subdivision. Cluster zoning is favored in parts of the country where people desire an outdoor, recreational lifestyle.

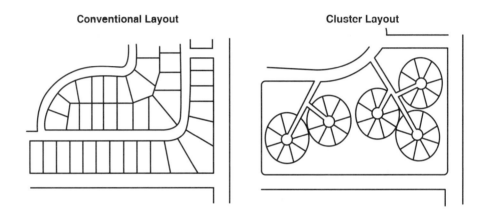

Zoning Terms

Non-conforming use is a building or land use that does not conform to a current zoning ordinance. Any building or land use that was in existence prior to the zoning ordinance may be continued under a *grandfather clause*. Generally, a nonconforming property cannot be remodeled, enlarged, or rebuilt (if it has been destroyed), nor can the use of the property be changed, unless it complies with the current zoning. In the event of fire or other destruction, the grandfather clause expires and the property will have to conform to present zoning restrictions.

A **zoning variance** represents a minor change in zoning for one specific property. A variance requires a hearing at which the property owner must show that the current zoning presents a hardship. An example would be a backyard pool that needs to be closer to the side property lines than the zoning setback lines allow. A second example would be property that, due to terrain or lot size, could not accommodate a house unless front setback lines were minimally adjusted.

A **special use permit** may be given by approval of the Planning and Zoning Commission for a property owner to develop a property in the public interest, as long as it does not interfere with the intent of the existing zoning. An example could be a site for a new church. Another example would be a small restaurant in an industrial area to provide meals for workers.

Zoning changes may be initiated by a property owner or by the local government. In either case, the zoning changes must be presented in a petition and at a formal hearing before the Planning and Zoning Commission. All property owners in the area must be notified of the public hearing. The Planning and Zoning Commission approves or rejects the changes and forwards its opinion to the city council for final action. Approval by the city council makes the change permanent. If the request for a zoning change is denied, property owners may go directly to the city council.

When a zoning change is requested for an individual piece of property, as opposed to a change for an area, it is called **spot zoning**. The procedures are the same for all zoning changes.

Down zoning occurs when a property zoned for higher-density uses is rezoned for lower-density uses. For example, when land zoned for apartments is rezoned to single-family residential, the parcel is considered "down zoned."

A **buffer zone** is a strip of land that separates one land use from another. An example of a buffer zone is a park or greenbelt that a developer has left between a commercial office center and a single-family residential subdivision.

Building Codes

Building codes regulate building construction for safety and public welfare. They establish minimum construction standards and materials for all types of buildings. These include protection, electrical, plumbing, heating, cooling, lighting, sanitation, and design and architectural standards.

A building permit is required before building begins. During construction, the building is inspected as various phases of construction are completed. When the building is completed, a **Certificate of Occupancy** must be issued before the building can be occupied.

CHAPTER SUMMARY

The percentage of land that is privately owned in Nevada could be as low as 7.7%, but no higher than 11.5%. The state legislature has adopted a statute expressing the belief that Nevada has a strong moral claim upon the public land retained by the federal government. A restatement of NRS 321.596 is included in this chapter. Types of public ownership in Nevada include government buildings, schools, and parks. Public ownership provides land control for public use and benefit.

The Nevada Division of State Lands provides land and land use planning services to the state and local governments. The agency holds title to state lands. Nevada holds title to sovereign lands that are submerged beneath navigable bodies of water in the state. Most of the Nevada School Trust Lands have been sold, with about 3000 acres of the original trust lands remaining unsold. These lands are assets of the Permanent School Fund and are required by the state constitution to be managed or disposed of to generate revenue for the Fund.

Land use controls are divided into several classifications: public land use control, private land use control, and public ownership of land. Police power allows the government to adopt laws that limit private property land use through planning requirements, zoning ordinances, subdivision regulations, building codes, and environmental protection.

Cities and counties in Nevada are required to complete community plans known as Master Plans. Community planning guides the preservation, development, or redevelopment of neighborhoods, communities, and regions. Communities appoint planning commissions and employ urban planners to aid in the completion of the planning process. The required elements of a Master Plan vary for municipalities and counties. The plan is effective for up to 20 years from adoption with annual reviews and a plan update not less than every 5 years.

An Environmental Impact Statement (EIS) demonstrates a positive or negative impact of a proposed project on the physical, economic, and social environment of the area. An Environmental Impact Statement usually includes information on population, traffic congestion, pollution, energy requirements, employment opportunities, and more.

Zoning ordinances regulate the use and control of land. Most cities with a population of more than 10,000 have zoning restrictions. Zoning regulations are considered restrictions rather than encumbrances.

Zones are established according to five general classifications: residential, commercial, industrial and manufacturing, agricultural and raw land, and special purpose.

One popular zoning concept is the comprehensive development plan, which provides housing, recreation, and commercial development in one self-contained development.

A master planned community consists of two or more separately platted subdivisions that are governed by a master owner's association or subject to a master declaration or restrictive covenants.

Cluster zoning changes street patterns and reduces the size of individual lots but provides for the same number of residences with more open recreational space and less traffic congestion.

Non-conforming use is a building or land use that does not conform to zoning ordinances.

A zoning variance represents a minor change in zoning for one specific property.

A special use permit may be given by approval of the Planning and Zoning Commission for a property owner to develop a property in the public interest, as long as the property does not interfere with the intent of the existing zoning.

Zoning changes may be initiated by a property owner or by the local government, and the changes require approval by the Planning and Zoning Commission. After a public hearing, the Commission either approves or rejects the changes and forwards its opinion to the city council for final action. Approval by the city council makes the change permanent.

Down zoning occurs when a property zoned for higher-density uses is rezoned for lower-density uses.

A buffer zone is a strip of land that separates one land use from another.

Building codes regulate building construction for safety and public welfare. A building permit is required before construction begins. Inspections are conducted during construction and, when the building is completed, a Certificate of Occupancy must be issued before the building can be occupied.

CHECKING YOUR COMPREHENSION

1. Summarize the purpose of the Nevada Division of State Lands.

2. Describe the meaning of the government right of police power.

3. Summarize the purpose and requirements for community planning.

4. Describe an Environmental Impact Statement.

5. Define the following terms:
   - Comprehensive development plan
   - Master Plan
   - Master planned community
   - Cluster zoning
   - Non-conforming use
   - Zoning variance
   - Special use permit
   - Zoning changes
   - Spot zoning
   - Buffer zone

REVIEWING YOUR UNDERSTANDING

1. The use of property that continues in contravention of new zoning is:
   a. a variance
   b. incentive zoning
   c. a non-conforming use
   d. illegal

2. Which of the following is an example of down zoning?
   a. height limitation
   b. zoning from single-family to multiple-family use
   c. zoning from multiple-family to single-family use
   d. zoning designed to encourage redevelopment

3. A man wants to build a garage next to his home, but the side setback from the zoning does not allow the construction. He should obtain a:
   a. zoning variance
   b. change in zoning
   c. partition action
   d. severance permit

4. A city can originate zoning and building codes to control the use of land for the welfare of the greatest number of people through the:
   a. right of escheat
   b. right of situs
   c. right of police power
   d. principle of highest and best use

5. Buildings that were erected before the enactment of a zoning ordinance and that do not comply with zoning limitations are called:
   a. outlawed classifications
   b. non-conforming uses
   c. dilapidated structures
   d. depreciated improvement

6. Which remedy would be most effective for a property owner whose request for rezoning has been refused by the city planning commission?
   a. ask the court for a writ requiring the planning commission's approval of the request
   b. sue the planning commission for damages
   c. disregard the planning commission's ruling because they acted arbitrarily
   d. make a presentation to the city council in spite of the planning commission

7. Before a person can move into a newly completed building:
   a. the builder must supply lien waivers
   b. the lender must approve the construction
   c. a Certificate of Occupancy must be obtained
   d. all work must be completed

8. A planning commission is generally concerned with all of the following, **EXCEPT**:
   a. parks
   b. streets
   c. construction methods
   d. land use

9. The State Land Office:
   a. adopts laws that limit private property land use through planning requirements
   b. manages the School Trust Lands and tries to maximize its revenues for the beneficiaries
   c. establishes community planning requirements for Nevada municipalities and counties
   d. conducts inspections on buildings under construction

10. The information included in an Environmental Impact Statement (EIS) usually includes all of the following, **EXCEPT**:
    a. population
    b. public school enrollments
    c. traffic congestion
    d. topographical survey

11. Treatment of non-conforming uses under new zoning does **NOT** include:
    a. a prohibition on expansion
    b. a prohibition on rebuilding
    c. a limitation on remodeling
    d. immediate closure

12. The exercise of police power in regulating, enforcing, and controlling the character and use of a municipality's property is a:

a. zoning ordinance

b. penal code

c. building code

d. matter of common law

13. A line fixed by law in front of which nothing can be built is referred to as:

a. 25 feet

b. a setback line

c. a lot line

d. 10 feet

14. A property use that violates the zoning ordinance but may continue because the use predates the zoning ordinance, is:

a. a variation

b. non-conforming use

c. illegal

d. obsolete

15. The right of government to enact laws for the general health, welfare, and safety of the public is known as:

a. eminent domain

b. police power

c. zoning ordinances

d. covenants and restrictions

16. Which of the following would be an example of a zoning variance?

a. a building excepted from setback requirements

b. grandfather clause

c. deed restrictions

d. non-conforming use

17. Which of the following is **NOT** done under police power?

a. control land use

b. control rents

c. collect taxes

d. condemn as unfit for occupancy

18. Zoning of a property for a specified purpose, which is different from that of surrounding properties, is:

a. non-conforming use

b. an easement

c. spot zoning

d. strip zoning

19. Which of the following is **NOT** a classification of real estate under zoning regulations?

a. industrial

b. residential

c. commercial

d. rental

20. The right of _____ enables a government to adopt building codes.

a. eminent domain

b. caveat emptor

c. special assessment

d. police power

Chapter

5

IMPORTANT TERMS AND CONCEPTS

common elements

Common Promotional
   Plan

condominium

contract rescission

cooperatives

developer

exempt sales

homeowners'
   association (HOA)

Interstate Land Sales
   Full Disclosure Act

membership camping

planned community

planned unit
   developments

property report

statement of record

subdivider

subdivision

time-shares

unit

CHAPTER OBJECTIVES

After completing this chapter, you should be able to:

- Describe the requirements, process, and exemptions for a property report for any division of land.
- Explain the specific advertising requirements for subdivisions and time-shares.
- Describe the Land Sales Full Disclosure Act requirements for registration of unimproved lots.
- Explain the nature, advantages, and disadvantages of common-interest developments, such as cooperatives, condominiums, planned unit developments, time-shares, and membership camping.

Subdivisions

5.1 NEVADA SUBDIVISION LAW

Local and state governments can adopt subdivision regulations because of the government's police power limitations on private property rights. As Nevada continues to grow, subdivision regulations have become a major factor in community planning and real estate developments. Subdivision law and regulations are established at both the local and state government level.

Local Government Subdivision Regulation

Except for certain divisions of land parcels, all subdivisions of land must receive approval of the county government or the municipal government if located within the boundaries of the city or town. Local subdivision regulations include setting standards for streets; easements for utilities, sewers, water mains, and rights of way (including irrigation); lot sizes; setback lines; and areas reserved for schools, parks, and other recreational facilities, such as swimming pools, activity centers, golf courses, or tennis courts.

Subdividers work with the local planning commission to submit a proposed subdivision for approval, which includes recording a survey, a detailed map and plat, and a detailed proposal.

Statewide Subdivision Law

The Nevada Revised Statutes (Chapter 119) provide for the licensing and regulation of any division of land into 35 or more lots, parcels, units, or interests being offered for sale or lease in a common promotional plan, including subdivisions permitted by Housing and Urban Development. This law was enacted to prevent dishonest practices when subdividing and selling undeveloped land. The statutes require that a property report be obtained prior to offering any of the land parcels for sale. The purpose is to ensure that purchasers receive complete and accurate disclosure of all material facts related to the subdivision.

Definitions to Know

A **property report** is defined as a report, issued by the Real Estate Administrator in accordance with Chapter 119 of the Nevada Revised Statutes, which authorizes a developer to offer to sell or sell an interest in a subdivision. The report is to contain the disclosures required in Chapter 119 of the statutes.

A **developer** is defined as (1) the owner of subdivided land who, on his or her own behalf or through an agent or subsidiary, offers it for sale, or (2) the principal agent of an inactive owner.

A **subdivision** is defined as any land or tract of land in another state, in this state (Nevada), or in any foreign country from which a sale is attempted, which is divided or proposed to be divided over any period into 35 or more lots, parcels, units, or interest, including but not limited to undivided interests, which are offered, known, designated, or advertised as a common unit by a common name or as a part of a common promotional plan of advertising and sale.

A **Common Promotional Plan** is defined as any offering, sale, or lease of subdivided land by a developer or a group of developers acting in concert, and the land is contiguous or is known, designated, or advertised as a common unit or development or by a common name.

Required Approval

Any person or broker proposing to sell any subdivision, lot, or parcel in Nevada must file a **statement of record** with the Nevada Real Estate Division. The administrator will examine the notice and then issue a property report authorizing the sale or lease of the lots, parcels, or interests.

Statement of Record

A developer, who is not exempt, shall file a Nevada statement of record on a form furnished by the Real Estate Division. The statement of record will include the following:

- Information about the applicant and his ownership, if any, in the proposed subdivision.
- A list of places, dates, and material facts pertaining to each permit or license to sell or promote the sale.
- A list of all current litigation in which the applicant is a party.
- The name, location, acreage, and number of lots, parcels, units, or interests in the subdivision to be offered.
- The location of subdivision records.
- The methods by which prospective purchasers may locate and identify individual lots, parcels, units, or interests.
- The recording and any governmental approval of the subdivision.
- A description of the geology, climate, and physical conditions of the subdivision and its surroundings.
- A description of all completed or promised improvements at or away from the subdivision and a description of financial arrangements for the completion of improvements.

- A list of all applicable taxes and assessments and their current status.
- A description of facilities and services that are available in the area surrounding the subdivision.
- A description of common facilities within the subdivision that are furnished by the developer.
- Any filings with any federal, state, or local governmental authority pertaining to the subdivision.
- A description of all promotional activities in connection with the subdivision.

The Division may require other documents and certifications as necessary for the complete disclosure of the nature of the subdivided land to be offered. The information required in the Nevada Statement of Record must be supplemented by specific exhibits set forth in the Nevada Administrative Code. The required exhibits include evidence of title to the property, a legal description of each lot, documents that indicate any improvements (including the installation of utilities and the financial arrangements made for them), and copies of all contracts, deeds, agreements, and leases that affect the subdivision. A complete listing of the exhibits is included with the Statement of Record form obtained from the Real Estate Division.

Exempt Sales

Any developer who over any period divides or proposes to divide any land into 35 or more lots, parcels, units, or interests must apply to the Division to register his or her subdivision in accordance with the Chapter 119 of the Nevada Revised Statutes and the Nevada Administrative Code, unless he or she is exempted from registration by the statute and code. A developer must make a written request to the Division, specify the class of exemption for which he or she is applying, and submit the information and documents set forth in each type of exemption. The following exemptions are available:

1. The parcels are at least 40 acres in area.
2. The property is free and clear of all liens.
3. The construction consists of residential buildings built by a licensed contractor who owns the land.
4. The registration is not necessary in the public interest.
5. The parcels are greater than 80 acres in area.
6. The disposition is to persons engaged in the business of constructing residential, commercial, or industrial buildings for disposition.

Examination by the Real Estate Division

Before issuing a license, the Real Estate Division shall fully investigate all information included in the Statement of Record and, if in the judgment of the Division it is necessary, inspect the property that is the subject of the application. All reasonable expenses incurred by the Division in carrying out the investigation or inspection must be paid by the applicant and no license may be issued until those expenses have been fully paid.

Issuing the Property Report

After examining a subdivision, the administrator of the Real Estate Division shall, unless there are grounds for denial, issue to the subdivider a property report authorizing the sale or lease, or the offer for sale or lease, in this state of the lots or parcels in the subdivision. The administrator may publish the report. The property report must contain the following:

1. The name and address of each person owning or controlling an interest of 10% or more.
2. The name, principal occupation, and address of every officer, director, partner, owner, associate, or trustee of the subdivider.
3. The legal description and area of lands.
4. A true statement of the condition of the title to the land, including all encumbrances thereon.
5. A true statement of the terms and conditions on which it is intended to dispose of the land and copies of the instruments that will be delivered to a purchaser to evidence his or her interest in the subdivision and of the contracts and other agreements that a purchaser will be required to agree to or sign.
6. A true statement of the provisions, if any, that have been made for public utilities in the proposed subdivision, including water, electricity, gas, telephone, and sewerage facilities.
7. A true statement of the use for which the proposed subdivision will be offered.
8. A true statement of the provisions, if any, limiting the use or occupancy of the parcels in the subdivision.
9. A true statement of the maximum depth of fill used, or proposed to be used on each lot, and a true statement of the soil conditions in the subdivision supported by engineering reports showing the soil has been, or will be, prepared in accordance with the recommendations of a licensed civil engineer.
10. A true statement of the amount of indebtedness that is a lien upon the subdivision or any part thereof, and that was incurred to pay for the construction of any on-site or off-site improvement, or any community or recreational facility and the names and addresses of the holders of the indebtedness together with an indication of their relationship, if any, to the owner and subdivider.
11. A true statement or reasonable estimate, if applicable, of the amount of any indebtedness that has been or is proposed to be incurred by an existing or proposed special district, entity, taxing area, or assessment district, within the boundaries of which the subdivision, or any part thereof, is located, and which is to pay for the construction or installation of any improvement or to furnish community or recreational facilities to the subdivision and which amounts are to be obtained by ad valorem tax or assessment, or by a special assessment or tax upon the subdivision, or any part thereof.
12. A true statement describing any agricultural activities or conditions in the area that may adversely affect residents of the subdivision, including any odors, cultivation and related dust, agricultural burning, application of pesticides, or irrigation and drainage.

13. Such other information as the owner, his or her agent, or subdivider may wish to present.

(Source: Chapter 119.140 of the Nevada Revised Statutes)

Property Report Cover Sheet

The property report issued by the division pursuant to NAC 119.160 will have a cover sheet as follows, with the language "CONSUMER SHOULD READ THIS REPORT BEFORE SIGNING ANY PAPER" printed in red. The Administrative Code Chapter further requires that the cover sheet read as follows:

"THE PROPERTY REPORT OF THE NEVADA LAW REGULATING
SUBDIVISION SALES REQUIRES THAT:

FIRST: A prospective purchaser or lessee MUST BE GIVEN this subdivision
            Property Report;

SECOND: The broker or salesman MUST REVIEW the contents of this Property
            Report with you;

THIRD: If you purchase any property you MUST SIGN A RECEIPT indicating
            you have received this Property Report;

IT IS RECOMMENDED THAT:

FIRST: You DO NOT SIGN ANY CONTRACT OR AGREEMENT before you have
            thoroughly read and understood it and this Property Report;

SECOND: You SEE THE EXACT PROPERTY you may be considering BEFORE
            SIGNING any agreement for a reservation, option, lease or purchase.

NEVADA LAW STATES:

You may cancel this contract of sale, by written notice, until midnight of the 5th calendar day following the date of execution of the contract. The right of cancellation may not be waived. Any attempt by the developer to obtain such a waiver results in a contract which is voidable by the purchaser.

The notice of cancellation must be delivered personally to the developer or sent by certified mail or telegraph to the business address of the developer.

The developer shall, within 15 days after receipt of the notice of cancellation, return all payments made by the purchaser.

1. The property report may contain any of the information submitted to the division in the Nevada statement of record. In addition, if the administrator determines that:

   a. A property report would be misleading without the inclusion of general or specific cautionary statements directed to prospective purchasers, he will include those statements which he deems to be material to an offer.

   b. Certain information in the property report should be emphasized in order to avoid misleading purchasers, he will emphasize that information.

2. The property report will also include:

   a. A form to be completed by the purchaser indicating his receipt of the property report.

   b. A form with which the purchaser may revoke his purchase."

Property Report Denial

The administrator may deny the issuance of a property report on any of the following grounds:

1. Failure to comply with subdivision law or the rules of the Division.

2. The sale or lease would constitute misrepresentation to or deceit or fraud of the purchasers or lessees.

3. Inability to deliver title or other interest contracted for.

4. Inability to demonstrate that adequate financial arrangements have been made for completion of all off-site improvements, community, recreational, or other facilities included in the offering.

5. Failure to show that the parcels can be used for the purpose for which they are offered.

6. Failure to provide in the contract or other writing the use or uses for which the parcels are offered, together with any covenants or conditions relative thereto.

7. Agreements or bylaws to provide for management or other services pertaining to common facilities in the offering that fail to comply with the regulations of the Division.

8. Failure to demonstrate that adequate financial arrangements have been made for any guaranty or warranty included in the offering.

Marketing

No subdivision or lot, parcel, or unit in any subdivision may be sold:

1. Until the Division has approved a written plan or methods proposed to be employed for the procurement of prospective purchasers, the sale to purchasers, and the retention of purchasers after sale. The plan or methods must describe:
   a. The form and content of advertising to be used.
   b. The nature of the offer of gifts or other free benefits to be extended.
   c. The contracts, agreements, and other papers to be used in the sale of the property.
   d. Any other reasonable details as the Division requires.

   The written plan, or the methods proposed may be filed as a part of the Statement of Record application.

2. Only through a licensed broker, and before any offering, the name of the broker must be placed on file with the Division. Only that broker or his or her real estate salesperson may offer or sell the subdivided property or any

interest therein. The broker and salesperson, if any, shall complete the application on a form prescribed by the Division and pay the prescribed fees. Before a broker applies to become a broker of record, the broker must make a personal inspection of the subdivision.

A broker and a salesperson may represent one or more developers only after completing an application and the payment of the prescribed fees with respect to each developer.

No person, except a registered representative of the developer or the broker of record and his or her salespersons, may induce, solicit, or attempt to have any person attend any offer or sale of subdivision property. A broker is responsible for the inducing and soliciting activities of his or her registered representative. The registered representative and the developer must comply with the same standards of business ethics as apply to licensed real estate brokers and salespersons. A registered representative shall not make statements of any kind concerning prices, interests, or values of the subdivision property. The representatives' activities must be limited to inducing and soliciting persons to attend an offer or sale of subdivision property and handing out information approved by the Division, and the representative shall strictly conform to the written plan. Each registered representative must complete an application and pay the required fees before engaging in any of the allowed activities.

The property report must be given to and reviewed with each purchaser by the broker or salesperson before the execution of any contract for the sale of any subdivision property. The broker shall obtain from the purchaser a signed receipt for a copy of the report and, if a contract is entered into, the receipt and a copy of all contracts and agreements must be kept in the broker's files within the State of Nevada for three years, or one year after final payment has been made on any contract, whichever is longer. The files of the broker are subject to inspection and audit by the Division.

The purchaser of any subdivision or any lot, parcel, or unit in any subdivision may cancel, by written notice, the contract of sale until midnight of the fifth calendar day following the date of signing of the contract. The right of cancellation may not be waived, and any attempt by the developer to obtain such a waiver results in a contract which is voidable by the purchaser. The notice of cancellation may be delivered personally to the developer or sent by certified mail to the business address of the developer. The developer shall, within 15 days after receipt of the notice of cancellation, return all payments made by the purchaser.

Owner-Developer Registration

An owner-developer who is registered with the Real Estate Division may employ one or more licensed real estate salespersons to sell any single-family residence that is owned by the owner-developer, that has not been previously sold, and that is located in the area of the current registration. The owner-developer may not sell any lot in the subdivision unless one of the following conditions applies:

a. The lot contains a single-family residence not previously sold.
b. A single-family residence is to be constructed upon the lot, and the residence is purchased under the same agreement as the sale of the land.

The owner-developer must employ a licensed broker-salesperson as the sales manager before employing any licensed real estate salespersons. The area covered by an owner-developer's registration may be enlarged from time to time upon application and payment of the required fees.

The application for original registration as an owner-developer shall be made on a form provided by the Division. The application must be completed by the owner-developer, unless the applicant is a partnership or corporation, and in that case the application must be completed by a partner or principal officer. The application must be filed with an office of the Division and must be accompanied by fingerprint cards. The applicant's fingerprints must be taken by law enforcement agency personnel or other authorized entity acceptable to the Division. If a search of criminal records has been requested by the Division, an application for registration is not complete until the Division has received the appropriate information. The application shall set forth or include the following:

a. The limits of the area within which the applicant owns the residences proposed to be sold, including the legal description of the property to be covered by the registration, as shown on a recorded map.

b. The location of the applicant's principal place of business and the location of each of his or her sales offices.

c. A statement of his or her arrests and convictions, if any, and any proceedings against the owner-developer brought by governmental agencies.

d. A brief business history.

e. A statement that shows the financial condition of the owner-developer and a history, if applicable, of any bankruptcies.

The application must be accompanied by both of the following items:

1. The applicant's sworn verification of the truthfulness of the matters stated in the application and its attachments.

2. A statement that the owner-developer applicant understands the responsibilities of an owner-developer pursuant to Chapter 645 of the Nevada Revised Statutes and Administrative Code and that he or she could be subject to disciplinary action allowed under that chapter of the statutes and code.

The regulations adopted by the Real Estate Commission shall not establish any education qualification or require any examination of an owner-developer, but shall provide appropriate standards of good moral character and financial stability.

The Division's registration of a person as an owner-developer does not constitute licensure. The registered owner-developer may not use the term *licensed* either in advertising or oral presentations to prospective purchasers. However, this does not preclude the use of the term *licensed contractor*, if appropriate. An owner-developer shall keep at each of the sales offices a copy of the letter of registration and shall within 10 days give written notice to the Division of any change of the name, address, or status affecting the owner-developer, or any licensed real estate broker-salesperson or salesperson in his or her employ. The registration of an owner-developer will be annulled at such time as licensed real estate broker-salespersons or salespersons are no longer employed. Inactive status is not available for owner-developers.

A registration for an owner-developer is effective for one year after the date of issuance. An owner-developer may renew the registration by paying the required fee and submitting the appropriate form to the Division. There is no limit on the number of annual renewals. If an owner-developer fails to renew his registration, the licenses of all broker-salespersons and salespersons will immediately be placed on inactive status. If the registration of an owner-developer is cancelled, suspended, or revoked, all activities pursuant to the registration shall immediately terminate, and all licenses of the employees of the owner-developer shall be delivered to the Division.

The licensed broker-salesperson acting as the sales manager for an owner-developer must comply with the following requirements:

- Have at least two years of experience during the immediately preceding four years as a real estate broker-salesperson or salesperson licensed in Nevada or any other state.
- Notify the Division on the prescribed form that he or she will be acting as the sales manager for the owner-developer.
- Notify the Division upon termination of the association with the owner-developer.

A licensee associated with an owner-developer may only sell, lease, rent, or offer and negotiate for the registered development of the owner-developer. The licensee cannot engage in any other activity for which a real estate license is authorized to conduct. The licensee may not be associated with a real estate broker when the licensee is employed by an owner-developer, and real estate brokers working for owner-developers must change their status to real estate broker-salesperson.

An employee of an owner-developer is prohibited from erecting, displaying, or maintaining any sign or billboard or advertising under the employee's name unless the advertisement is located at the office of the employing owner-developer. The name of the employee may not dominate the owner-developer's sign in any way.

The time during which a licensee is employed by an owner-developer does not satisfy the requirement for full-time experience to qualify for a real estate broker license. However, the Real Estate Commission may count the experience of an individual working as a licensed salesperson for an owner-developer if the applicant performs both of the following actions:

a. Files a petition with the Commission.
b. At the meeting of the Commission, demonstrates the quality, quantity, and variety of experience that the applicant received during employment with an owner-developer. The experience must be substantially equivalent to the experience of an individual who has been actively engaged as a full-time licensee in private practice.

All records pertaining to the sale of any single-family residence in the registered owner-developer's subdivision must be maintained at the principal place of business and be available for inspection by the Division. Upon request the owner-developer shall send copies of the records to the appropriate office of the Division.

Advertising

All unapproved advertising of a subdivision and all previously approved advertising that has been modified in any way must be submitted to and approved by the Division before being used. A subdivision may not be advertised for sale until the advertising is approved in writing by the Division. The Division will render a decision on the advertising within 60 days from the date it is submitted in final form. An approval number will be issued when the advertising is approved by the Division. The approval number and the developer's name must appear on the approved item and must be visible or audible to the intended audience when it is published or circulated, unless the Division specifically provides otherwise. A bona fide press release is exempted from the approval regulations and need not be submitted to the Division for approval if no advertising fee will be charged and if both of the following conditions are met:

a. It is intended for publication without any payment of any consideration
b. It does not contain statements about any of the following:
    1. The sales volume of the subdivision
    2. The financial status of the developer
    3. The nature of the subdivision or its investment potential

Some general advertising standards follow:

1. Statements and representations contained in the advertising must be accurate and true.
2. Advertising must fully state factual material so as not to misrepresent the facts or create misleading impressions.
3. All advertising must be consistent with the information contained in the property report filed with the Division.

Advertising that refers to the purchase price of any lot, parcel, or unit must also clearly disclose any additional compulsory assessments or costs to the prospective purchaser. Advertising that refers to predevelopment sales being at a lower price, because the property has not yet been developed in some manner, must disclose whether there is a bona fide plan for development, and if there is such a plan, the prospective completion date must be stated. Advertising may offer a discount that effects a reduction of the advertised price only if the discount is offered for a purchase in quantity, payment in cash, large or accelerated payment, or on other reasonable grounds. The purpose of this standard is to eliminate the use of fictitious pricing and illusory discounts. The advertising must not contain statements concerning future price increases by the developer that are not specific as to the amount and the date of the increase, and such future price increases may not be alluded to unless they are bona fide. Finally, the advertising must not state that land or unit values have increased in the subdivision or the area unless the land or unit used for comparison is directly comparable to the property being advertised for sale.

When the size of a parcel or parcels offered is stated in the advertising, any easement to which any parcel is subject and the nature of the easement must be disclosed. Improvements, facilities, or utility services may not be advertised unless either of the following conditions is met:

1. They have been completed or installed and are available for use.
2. The completion and availability for use is ensured through adequate financial arrangements approved by the Division.

Advertising that refers to promised improvements for which the prospective purchaser will be assessed must clearly and fully disclose the assessments.

Additional advertising standards include the following:

1. Distance and mileage advertisements must state the mileage from a specific point in the subdivision in road miles to a specific point in that community or area, together with the types of roads traversed. The description of roads or streets must disclose the nature of those roads or streets, including whether they are (a) paved, gravel, or dirt and (b) traversable year-round by a conventional automobile.
2. An advertisement must not imply a use or other reason for purchase that is not set forth in the Nevada Statement of Record.
3. An advertisement that refers to facilities for recreation, sports, or other conveniences that are away from the subdivision and not in existence may be included only if it is clearly and prominently disclosed that the facilities are only proposed and are not in the subdivision, with a disclosure of the distance to them. Advertising that refers to a public facility must fully disclose the financial arrangements and the completion date for the facility.
4. Advertisement should not include pictures or sketches of proposed improvements without a clear indication that the scenes do not yet exist.

Before a developer uses promotional meetings, a statement of the nature and manner of conducting the meetings must be submitted in writing as a part of the written plan that must be approved by the Division. Standards for promotional meetings include:

1. All advertising in promotional meetings is subject to the standards of advertising.
2. No use may be made of shills or false or dummy buyers in promotional meetings to initiate sales or for any other purpose.
3. Oral statements made to prospective purchasers at promotional meetings must be completely consistent with written advertising or other material filed with and approved by the Division.
4. Any prospective purchaser who expresses a desire to leave a promotional meeting at any time during or after the sales presentation may not be impeded in any manner from departing or coerced or pressured to remain.
5. Investigators and other employees of the Division may attend any promotional meeting.
6. Excessively loud music must not be played during promotional meetings, and Division employees who are present at the meeting may request that music be turned down or off.

7. A Division employee who is present at a sales presentation may not be identified, singled out, or asked questions in such a way that potential purchasers might hear the questioned employee's remarks.

8. If a broker or developer at any time before, during, or after a promotional meeting uses any electronic surveillance, recording, eavesdropping, or listening device, its use must be disclosed orally at the beginning of the meeting and also by means of a sign or placard prominently displayed in the meeting room, fully disclosing the use of the devices in the meeting.

A complete description of the Advertising and Promotional Meeting Standards is included in Chapter 119 of the Nevada Administrative Code.

5.2 INTERSTATE LAND SALES FULL DISCLOSURE ACT

When developers of 25 or more unimproved lots in a subdivision sell or lease to citizens of another state as part of a Common Promotional Plan, the **Interstate Land Sales Full Disclosure Act** regulates the sale or lease. Unless exempt, the act requires registration with Housing and Urban Development (HUD) that should include the following disclosures:

- Reports on environmental factors.
- Assurances on the developer's commitments to provide promised improvements.
- The availability of utilities and sewage facilities.
- Audited financial statements.

Exemptions from the act's registration requirements are granted in the following situations:

- The plan offers fewer than 25 lots or lots consisting of at least 20 acres each.
- The lots contain an existing building on improved land, or the seller is obligated to erect such a building within two years.
- A professional builder purchases the lots for the purpose of constructing residential, commercial, or industrial buildings.
- The lot is free and clear of all liens and encumbrances at the time of the sale, and the purchaser has personally inspected the property.

Any subdivision that has been registered under the Interstate Land Sales Full Disclosure Act is subject to all of the requirements of Chapter 119, "Sale of Subdivided Land" of the Nevada Revised Statutes. The developer, however, may file with the Division a copy of an effective statement of record filed with the secretary of the Department of Housing and Urban Development. To the extent that the information contained in the effective statement of record provides the Division with information required in the Nevada Statutes, the effective statement of record may substitute for information otherwise required.

5.3 COMMON-INTEREST COMMUNITIES

The rapid growth of Nevada's population has caused an increase in land value. As a result, housing developments require more living units per acre. Cooperatives, condominiums, planned unit developments, and time-shares are all types of ownership designed to provide more affordable housing and other benefits derived from increased living units per acre of land. All of these developments are considered subdivisions and are regulated by state law.

Cooperatives

Cooperatives are generally organized as corporations, with the tenants owning the stock. A cooperative is usually financed by a combination of a mortgage on the land and improvements, plus the proceeds from the sale of stock to the cooperative owners.

In cooperative ownership, there is one mortgage and title for the building held in the name of the cooperative corporation. The individual purchaser of an apartment receives stock in the corporation and has a personal property interest in the form of a proprietary lease.

In a cooperative, the board of directors of the corporation develops a budget, which covers anticipated expenses for principal and interest on the mortgage, taxes, insurance, operating, and maintenance of the common areas and grounds. Sometimes the budget also includes a contingency amount for unexpected or long-term maintenance. The funds for the budget are then collected from the leaseholders in the form of an annual assessment, which is paid in monthly installments.

Advantages and Disadvantages of Cooperatives

Advantages of cooperative ownership include the association of stockholders, controlling the rent, and approving new purchasers.

One disadvantage of cooperative ownership is that there is no income tax deduction for mortgage interest or property taxes. Also, the mortgage could go into default if enough individuals fail to pay their monthly assessments.

Condominiums

Starting in the late 1950s and 1960s, condominium ownership became popular in the United States due to population increases in metropolitan areas.

Technically, ownership in a **condominium** is individual fee simple ownership of a fractional interest, plus a share of the common elements and grounds of the property. The apartment may be held in severalty, joint tenancy, tenants in common, or community property. The common elements are held as tenants in common with other unit owners of apartments. If there were 300 units, the unit owner would own his or her unit and 1/300th of the common elements.

This type of ownership is most often apartment-style housing, but it could also include office or commercial space.

Common Elements

The owner of a condominium purchases space referred to as a unit. A **unit** is a portion of a condominium designated for separate ownership. Each unit owner receives a separate deed. The owner can mortgage his or her unit and claim the interest and taxes as a tax deduction. **Common elements** are all portions of a condominium other than units. Limited common elements are the portions of common elements specifically designed in the declaration and allocated for the exclusive use of one or more but fewer than all units.

Homeowners' Association for Condominiums

All owners of condominium units must be members of the **homeowners' association (HOA)**. The HOA manages the common elements of the condominium development and ensures compliance with the HOA rules and the development's deed restrictions.

Planned Unit Development (PUD)

Planned unit developments (PUDs) are usually high-density, single-family structures that use the land area to the greatest possible extent. Ownership of a PUD is similar to that of a condominium in that the single-family residence is fee simple ownership, in which the owner holds an undivided interest in the common elements with the other owners in the PUD as tenants in common. The major difference between a PUD and a condominium is that the PUD is a single-family residence, whereas a condominium is an apartment, often in a multistory structure.

Similar to a condominium, a PUD has a homeowners' association to manage the common elements of the development.

Homeowners' Associations

All owners in a development with common elements are members of their homeowners' association. The association has the power to:

- Adopt and amend bylaws and rules.
- Select a board of directors and officers with the power to act on behalf of the association within the limits of bylaws and Nevada law.
- Adopt and amend annual budgets for revenues, expenditures, and reserves for common areas.
- Collect assessments.
- Employ and discharge necessary personnel to manage the complex.
- Sign contracts and incur liabilities.

For a summary of all HOA powers, see Nevada Revised Statutes, Chapter 116.

Each owner receives an individual property tax bill and a bill from the homeowners' association for the pro rata share of the association's operating expenses. The assessments bill from the homeowners' association is usually a monthly bill and often includes a prorated share of insurance, plus the cost of operating and maintaining the common and exterior areas. Monthly assessments may also include utilities. In addition, the assessments could include a reserve fund for long-range maintenance (such as new roofs or air conditioning systems for the whole complex), provided the HOA membership approves.

Community Manager Certificate

A Community Manager Certificate must be obtained from the Real Estate Division before an individual is allowed to manage a Common-Interest Community. An applicant for a certificate must complete and submit to the Real Estate Division the following:

- Written application.
- Sixty hours of instruction in the management of Common-Interest Communities.
- Pass the Nevada state examination with a grade of 75% or better.

An applicant must be 18 years of age when the certificate is issued and does not need to hold a real estate license or a property management permit. An applicant must complete and submit the application along with the following:

- Two fingerprint cards completed at an authorized law enforcement facility.
- Documentation of the required experience.
- Certificates demonstrating completion of the required education.
- Certificate demonstrating passage of the state examination.
- Application fees.

An applicant must have been engaged in the management of a common-interest community or have held a management position in a related area for either of the following:

1. The 12 months immediately preceding the date of the application.
2. At least two of the four years immediately preceding the date of the application.

The applicant must have successfully completed at least 60 hours of instruction in courses covering the management of a common-interest community, and these courses must have been approved by the Commission for Common-Interest Communities. The courses shall include:

a. At least 20 hours of instruction relating to federal, state, and local laws applicable to the management of a common-interest community, including:
   (1) Not less than two hours of instruction relating to federal laws applicable to common-interest communities that includes the Americans with Disabilities Act of 1990, the Fair Housing Acts, and the Fair Debt Collection Practices Act of 1996.
   (2) Not less than 18 hours of instruction relating to the Uniform Common-Interest Ownership Act.
b. At least 40 cumulative hours of instruction in specified subjects ranging from accounting and business ethics to risk management. A complete listing of the required subjects is set forth in the Nevada Administrative Code Section 116.120.

The Community Manager Certificate is valid for a two-year period. Renewal notices are sent approximately six weeks prior to certificate expiration. Certificate renewal must be accomplished within the 30 days prior to expiration.

Proof of completing at least 18 hours of community manager designated continuing education during the two-year certificate period must be submitted with the renewal application. At least three hours of the continuing education must be designated as relating to Chapter 116 of the Nevada Revised Statutes and Administrative Code.

Resale of Units

A common-interest community, including cooperatives, condominiums, and planned unit developments, is a real estate development that includes real estate owned by an association created for the purpose of managing, maintaining, or improving the property, and in which the owners of units are mandatory members and are required to pay association assessments.

When a unit in a **planned community** is resold, the seller has an obligation to make disclosures to the potential buyer. Furthermore, the potential buyer should understand the following factors:

- Extent of the covenants, conditions, and restrictions.
- Financial status of the homeowners' association.
- Obligation for monthly or other periodic assessments.

Disclosure Requirements for Common-Interest Communities

The Nevada Revised Statutes require that a buyer of a unit in a common-interest community be provided by the unit owner or his or her authorized agent the following information:

1. A copy of the bylaws and rules or regulations of the association.
2. A copy of the declaration of covenants, conditions, and restrictions (CC&Rs).
3. A statement setting forth the amount of the monthly assessment for common expenses and any unpaid assessment of any kind currently due from the selling unit's owner.
4. A copy of the current operating budget of the association and current year-to-date financial statement for the association. The information must include a study of the adequacy of the reserves and potential for assessments for the maintenance and upkeep of the common elements.
5. A statement of any unsatisfied judgments or pending legal actions against the association and the status of any pending legal actions relating to the common-interest community of which the unit's owner has actual knowledge.
6. The following information statement is required by Nevada Revised Statutes:

BEFORE YOU PURCHASE PROPERTY IN A COMMON-INTEREST COMMUNITY DID YOU KNOW ...

I. YOU GENERALLY HAVE 5 DAYS TO CANCEL THE PURCHASE AGREEMENT?

When you enter into a purchase agreement to buy a home or unit in a common-interest community, in most cases you should receive either a public offering statement, if you are the original purchaser of the home or unit, or a resale package, if you are not the original purchaser. The law generally provides for a 5-day period in which you have the right to cancel the purchase agreement. The 5-day period begins on different starting dates, depending on whether you receive a public offering statement or a resale package. Upon receiving a public offering statement or a resale package, you should make sure you are informed of the deadline for exercising your right to cancel. In order to exercise your right to cancel, the law generally requires that you hand deliver the notice of cancellation to the seller within the 5-day period, or mail the notice of cancellation to the seller by prepaid United States mail within the 5-day period. For more information regarding your right to cancel, see Nevada Revised Statute 116.4108, if you received a public offering statement, or Nevada Revised Statute 116.4109, if you received a resale package.

2. YOU ARE AGREEING TO RESTRICTIONS ON HOW YOU CAN USE YOUR PROPERTY?

These restrictions are contained in a document known as the Declaration of Covenants, Conditions, and Restrictions. The CC&Rs become a part of the title to your property. They bind you and every future owner of the property whether or not you have read them or had them explained to you. The CC&Rs, together with other "governing documents" (such as association by-laws and rules and regulations), are intended to preserve the character and value of properties in the community, but may also restrict what you can do to improve or change your property and limit how you use and enjoy your property. By purchasing a property encumbered by CC&Rs, you are agreeing to limitations that could affect your lifestyle and freedom of choice. You should review the CC&Rs and other governing documents before purchasing to make sure that these limitations and controls are acceptable to you.

3. YOU WILL HAVE TO PAY OWNERS' ASSESSMENTS FOR AS LONG AS YOU OWN YOUR PROPERTY?

As an owner in a common-interest community, you are responsible for paying your share of expenses relating to the common elements, such as landscaping, shared amenities, and the operation of any homeowners' association. The obligation to pay these assessments binds you and every future owner of the property. Owners' fees are usually assessed by the homeowners' association and due monthly. You have to pay dues whether or not you agree with the way the association is managing the property or spending the assessments. The executive board of the association may have the power to change and increase the amount of the assessment and to levy special assessments against your property to meet extraordinary expenses. In some communities, major components of the common elements of the community such as roofs and private roads must be maintained and replaced by the association. If the association is not well managed or fails to provide adequate funding for reserves to repair, replace, and restore common elements, you may be required to pay large, special assessments to accomplish these tasks.

4. IF YOU FAIL TO PAY OWNERS' ASSESSMENTS, YOU COULD LOSE YOUR HOME?

If you do not pay these assessments when due, the association usually has the power to collect them by selling your property in a nonjudicial foreclosure sale. If fees become delinquent, you may also be required to pay penalties and the association's costs and attorney's fees to become current. If you dispute the obligation or its amount, your only remedy to avoid the loss of your home may be to file a lawsuit and ask a court to intervene in the dispute.

5. YOU MAY BECOME A MEMBER OF A HOMEOWNERS' ASSOCIATION THAT HAS THE POWER TO AFFECT HOW YOU USE AND ENJOY YOUR PROPERTY?

Many common-interest communities have a homeowners' association. In a new development, the association will usually be controlled by the developer until a certain number of units have been sold. After the period of developer control, the association may be controlled by property owners like yourself who are elected by homeowners to sit on an executive board and other boards and committees formed by the association. The association, and its executive board, are responsible for assessing homeowners for the cost of operating the association and the common or shared elements of the community and for the day-to-day operation and management of the community. Because homeowners sitting on the executive board and other boards and committees of the association may not have the experience or professional background required to understand and carry out the responsibilities of the association properly, the association may hire professional community managers to carry out these responsibilities.

Homeowners' associations operate on democratic principles. Some decisions require all homeowners to vote, some decisions are made by the executive board or other boards or committees established by the association or governing documents. Although the actions of the association and its executive board are governed by state laws, the CC&Rs, and other documents that govern the common-interest community, decisions made by these persons will affect your use and enjoyment of your property, your lifestyle and freedom of choice, and your cost of living in the community. You may not agree with decisions made by the association or its governing bodies even though the decisions are ones which the association is authorized to make. Decisions may be made by a few persons on the executive board or governing bodies that do not necessarily reflect the view of the majority of homeowners in the community. If you do not agree with decisions made by the association, its executive board, or other governing bodies, your remedy is typically to attempt to use the democratic processes of the association to seek the election of members of the executive board or other governing bodies that are more responsive to your needs. If you have a dispute with the association, its executive board, or other governing bodies, you may be able to resolve the dispute through the complaint, investigation, and intervention process administered by the Office of the Ombudsman for Owners in Common-Interest Communities and Condominium Hotels, the Nevada Real Estate Division, and the Commission for Common-Interest Communities and Condominium Hotels. However, to resolve some disputes, you may have to mediate or arbitrate the dispute and, if mediation or arbitration is unsuccessful, you may have to file a lawsuit and ask a court to resolve the dispute. In addition to your personal cost in mediation or arbitration, or to prosecute a lawsuit, you may be responsible for paying your share of the association's cost in defending against your claim.

6. YOU ARE REQUIRED TO PROVIDE PROSPECTIVE PURCHASERS OF YOUR PROPERTY WITH INFORMATION ABOUT LIVING IN YOUR COMMON-INTEREST COMMUNITY?

The law requires you to provide a prospective purchaser of your property with a copy of the community's governing documents, including the CC&Rs, association bylaws, and rules and regulations, as well as a copy of this document. You are also required to provide a copy of the association's current year-to-date financial statement, including, without limitation, the most recent audited or reviewed financial statement, a copy of the association's operating budget, and information regarding the amount of the monthly assessment for common expenses, including the amount set aside as reserves for the repair, replacement, and restoration of common elements. You are also required to inform prospective purchasers of any outstanding judgments or lawsuits pending against the association of which you are aware. For more information regarding these requirements, see Nevada Revised Statute 116.4109.

7. YOU HAVE CERTAIN RIGHTS REGARDING OWNERSHIP IN A COMMON-INTEREST COMMUNITY THAT ARE GUARANTEED YOU BY THE STATE?

Pursuant to provisions of chapter 116 of Nevada Revised Statutes, you have the right:

a. To be notified of all meetings of the association and its executive board, except in cases of emergency.

b. To attend and speak at all meetings of the association and its executive board, except in some cases where the executive board is authorized to meet in closed, executive session.

c. To request a special meeting of the association upon petition of at least 10 percent of the homeowners.

d. To inspect, examine, photocopy, and audit financial and other records of the association.

e. To be notified of all changes in the community's rules and regulations and other actions by the association or board that affect you.

8. QUESTIONS?

Although they may be voluminous, you should take the time to read and understand the documents that will control your ownership of a property in a common-interest community. You may wish to ask your real estate professional, lawyer, or other person with experience to explain anything you do not understand. You may also request assistance from the Office of the Ombudsman for Owners in Common-Interest Communities and Condominium Hotels, Nevada Real Estate Division, at (telephone number).

Buyer or prospective buyer's initials: _____

Date: _____

Time-shares

This type of common-interest community (time-share) is usually at a resort or recreational area where the use of the property is desired for a short period of time each year. People sometimes own several time-shares at their favorite resorts in different states or countries.

The Nevada Revised Statutes define time-share as the right to use and occupy a unit on a recurrent periodic basis according to an arrangement allocating this right among various owners whether or not there is an additional charge to the owner for occupying the unit.

Each developer, through the project broker and sales agents, shall provide each prospective purchaser with a copy of the public offering statement, which must contain a copy of the permit to sell time-shares. The Real Estate Division is authorized to issue a salesperson license that is restricted to the time-share units that are for sale. The time-share sales agent may work for only one project broker.

Rescission

The statutes also provide for the rescission of contracts or agreements for a time-share. The statutes state:

> *The purchaser of a time-share may cancel, by written notice, the contract of sale until midnight of the fifth calendar day following the date of execution of the contract. The contract of sale must include a statement of this right.*

Membership Camping

Membership camping is covered in Chapter 119B of the Nevada Revised Statutes. When purchasing a membership, a person buys a license to use a recreational facility. There is no real property interest involved; it is simply a right to use the operator's campground land.

Land for a campground may be owned or leased by the operator. The original purchaser of a membership cannot rent or lend his or her membership to someone else, but he or she may sell the contract.

Membership campgrounds may not sell any memberships until the administrator has approved the site in a manner similar to a subdivision.

Rescission

A contract of membership may be cancelled at the option of the member if he or she sends notice of the cancellation by certified mail, return receipt requested, to the developer, posted not later than midnight of the fifth calendar day following the day on which the contract was signed. This right must be set forth in the contract of membership in close proximity to the member's signature line. Within 20 days after the developer receives a notice of cancellation, the contract of membership, the membership card, and other evidence of the membership, the developer shall refund to the former member any money paid as a deposit, down payment, or other consideration.

CHAPTER SUMMARY

Subdivision laws and regulations are established at both the local and state level.

With few exceptions, all subdivisions of land must receive approval of the county government or the municipal government if located within the boundaries of the city or town. Nevada statutes allow counties or municipalities to adopt ordinances and regulations for the review of land divisions.

Local subdivision regulations include setting standards for streets, easements for utilities, lot sizes, and more. Subdividers work with the local planning commission to submit a proposed subdivision for approval, which includes recording a survey, detailed map and plat, and a detailed proposal.

Chapter 119 of the Nevada Revised Statutes was enacted to prevent dishonest practices in the subdividing and sale of subdivided land. The statute requires that a developer obtain a property report prior to offering any of the land parcels for sale.

A non-exempt developer must file a statement of record with the Real Estate Division before offering a subdivision lot or parcel. The administrator will examine the statement and then issue a property report authorizing the sale or lease of the lots, parcels, or fractional interests.

The statute provides for several exemptions from the requirements for a developer to register a subdivision. The exemptions are listed in this chapter's text.

Before issuing the property report, the Real Estate Division investigates information included in the statement of record and, if deemed necessary, inspects the property. All fees and expenses must be paid before the license can be issued.

After examining a subdivision, the administrator will issue a property report to the subdivider authorizing the sale or lease of the lots, parcels, or fractional interests within the subdivision. The content of a property report is described in this chapter's text. Prospective purchasers of subdivided property must sign a receipt that states they have been given a copy of the property report prior to signing any contract.

The administrator may suspend, revoke, or deny issuance of a public report on grounds such as failure to comply with subdivision statute or the code. A listing of these grounds is included in this chapter's text.

A subdivision or lot, parcel, or unit in any subdivision may not be sold until the proposed marketing plan has been approved by the Division. The written plan can be filed as a part of the statement of record application. Sales can be made only through a licensed broker. Alternatively, the subdivider can, if he or she is qualified, register as an owner-developer and can then hire a licensed broker-salesperson as the sales manager.

The property report must be given to and reviewed with each purchaser before execution of any contract for the sale of subdivision property. The broker must obtain it as a signed receipt. The receipt and a copy of all contracts and agreements must be kept in the broker's files, within the state of Nevada, for three years, or one year after final payment has been made on any contract, whichever is longer.

All advertising not approved in the written plan and previously approved advertising that is modified must be submitted to and approved by the Division before it is used. The advertising and promotion regulations are described in this chapter's text.

When developers of 25 or more unimproved lots in a subdivision sell or lease to citizens of another state as part of a common promotional plan, the Interstate Land Sales Full Disclosure Act regulates the sale or lease. The act requires registration with HUD that should include certain disclosures and also specific exemptions detailed in the text.

Cooperatives, condominiums, planned unit developments, and time-shares are all types of ownerships designed to provide more affordable housing. All of these developments are considered subdivisions and are regulated by state law.

Cooperatives are generally organized as corporations, with the tenants owning the stock. In cooperative ownership, there is one mortgage and title for the building held in the name of the cooperative corporation. The individual purchaser of an apartment receives stock in the corporation and has a personal property interest in the form of a proprietary lease.

Ownership in a condominium is individual fee simple ownership of a unit, plus a share of the common elements and grounds of the property. The apartment may be held in severalty, joint tenancy, tenants in common, or community property. The common elements are held as tenants in common with other unit owners of apartments. The owner of a condominium purchases space referred to as a unit. A unit is a portion of a condominium designated for separate ownership.

Planned unit developments (PUDs) are usually high-density, single-family structures that use the land area to the greatest possible extent. The ownership of a PUD is similar to a condominium. The major difference is that the PUD is a single-family residence, whereas a condominium is an apartment, often in a multistory structure.

All owners in a development with common elements are members of their homeowners' association. The association has the power to adopt and amend bylaws and rules, select a board of directors and officers, and more. In Nevada, managers of a common-interest community must obtain a Community Manager Certificate from the Real Estate Division.

When a unit in a planned community is resold, the seller has an obligation to make disclosures to the potential buyer. Furthermore, the potential buyer should understand the following factors: the extent of the CC&Rs, the financial status of the homeowners' association, and the obligation for monthly or other periodic assessments. Nevada Revised Statutes require the disclosure of specific information, which is listed in this chapter's text. Also, a specific information statement is required to be provided to a buyer of a common-interest development. A copy of the required statement is included in this chapter's text. Time-shares are a type of condominium ownership and are usually located at a resort or recreational area where the use of the property is desired for a short period each year. The Nevada Revised Statutes define time-share as the right to use and occupy a unit on a recurrent periodic basis according to an arrangement allocating this right among various owners, whether or not there is an additional charge to the owner for occupying the unit.

Each developer, through the project broker and sales agents, shall provide each prospective purchaser with a copy of the public offering statement, which must contain a copy of the permit to sell time-shares. The Real Estate Division is authorized to issue a salesperson license that is restricted to the sale of time-share units. The time-share sales agent may work for only one project broker. The statutes also provide for the rescission of contracts or agreements for time-shares. The purchaser may rescind the contract without cause by delivering written notice of rescission by midnight of the fifth day following the date on which the contract was signed.

Membership camping is covered in Chapter 119B of the Nevada Revised Statutes. When purchasing a membership, a person buys a license to use a recreational facility. Membership campgrounds may not sell any memberships until the administrator has approved the site in a manner similar to a subdivision. A membership camping contract may be canceled by a purchaser for any reason before midnight on the fifth calendar day following the date on which the contract was signed.

CHECKING YOUR COMPREHENSION

1. Summarize the process for obtaining a property report.

2. Define a subdivider and a subdivision.

3. List the exemptions from the requirement to obtain a property report.

4. Describe the Interstate Land Sales Full Disclosure Act requirements for registration.

5. Describe the various types of common-interest developments and their advantages and disadvantages.

REVIEWING YOUR UNDERSTANDING

1. A person who buys undeveloped acreage, divides it into 10 five-acre lots, and sells the lots is called a:
   a. land developer
   b. subdivider
   c. speculator
   d. city planner

2. The creation of eight equally sized parcels from a 320-acre parcel would be regulated as:
   a. a subdivision
   b. unimproved acreage
   c. condominium units
   d. membership campgrounds

3. A subdivision can be restricted by a developer in the deed restriction for all of the following reasons, **EXCEPT**:
   a. size and shape of buildings
   b. age of owners
   c. zoning changes
   d. physical lot size

4. To manage a homeowner's association the manager must have all of the following, **EXCEPT**:
   a. Community Manager Certificate
   b. 12 months' experience managing a common-interest community
   c. a real estate broker license
   d. 60 hours of specified education

5. An owner of a condominium apartment holds:
   a. a fee simple title
   b. a leasehold interest
   c. title the same as a cooperative apartment
   d. only a life estate

6. The rights of occupancy of owners in a cooperative are based on:
   a. a proprietary lease
   b. the articles of incorporation
   c. the bylaws of the association
   d. individual deeds to each unit

7. In terms of real estate ownership, time-sharing is **BEST** described as:
   a. stock ownership in a corporation that owns the building and the exclusive right to possession of a particular unit
   b. individual ownership of portions of a building and joint ownership of common elements
   c. fee simple ownership of a property with exclusive individual rights to use a specific portion
   d. the right to use and occupy a unit on a recurrent periodic basis according to an arrangement with various owners

8. When must the buyer receive a copy of the property report?
   a. at the close of escrow
   b. within five days of signing the contract
   c. prior to signing the contract
   d. five days prior to signing the contract

9. Which of the following about a registered owner-developer is true:
   a. must have a real estate license
   b. must complete the 90-hour pre-licensing education
   c. must hire a real estate broker-salesperson as the sales manager
   d. owner-developer registration is good for two years

10. Which of the following statements is **NOT** true concerning a membership camping purchaser?
    a. has a real property interest
    b. may sell the membership camping contract
    c. has a license to use a recreational facility
    d. may rescind the contract before midnight of the fifth calendar day following contract signing

11. Which of the following would **NOT** appear on a property report?
    a. utilities
    b. title condition
    c. market value
    d. legal description

12. The administrator may deny a public report for all of the following reasons, **EXCEPT**:
    a. the property is without ingress or egress
    b. the owners have previously declared bankruptcy
    c. the owner cannot produce perfect title
    d. the owner cannot produce marketable title

13. A written marketing plan:
    a. does not include the form and content of advertising to be used
    b. cannot be submitted with the Statement of Record
    c. is not required
    d. must be approved by the Real Estate Division before any sale

14. All of the following are correct about a subdivision advertisement, **EXCEPT**:
    a. must be approved in writing by the Division
    b. all press releases must be approved in writing by the Division
    c. an approval number and developer's name must appear on the advertisement
    d. modifications to approved advertisements must be submitted to the Division for approval

15. Time-sharing is associated with which of the following?
    a. cooperatives
    b. profits
    c. joint ventures
    d. condominiums

16. All of the following statements about a unit in a condominium building are true, **EXCEPT**:
    a. it can be individually mortgaged
    b. it is eligible for title insurance as a separate piece of property
    c. it is assessed for real estate tax purposes
    d. it is part of the common elements of the condominium

17. Which of the following requires unit owners to be stockholders in the corporation that owns the building?
    a. a cooperative
    b. a condominium
    c. a syndication
    d. a time-share

18. One's ownership interest in a condominium is distinguishable from other types of real estate by:
    a. a divided interest in the common area
    b. an undivided interest in the common area
    c. no interest in limited common area
    d. an undivided interest in the master deed areas

19. An owner-developer can sell all of the following, **EXCEPT**:
    a. a lot with the sales contract including the construction of a single-family residence
    b. a lot on which a single-family residence has been constructed and never been sold
    c. a lot on which a mobile home has been installed
    d. a lot with all off-site improvements completed

20. How long does the buyer of a subdivision parcel have to cancel the contract of sale?
    a. seven calendar days
    b. seven business days
    c. five calendar days
    d. five business days

Chapter 6

IMPORTANT TERMS AND CONCEPTS

15-day notice

ad valorem tax

appurtenant easements

assessed value

Certificate of Purchase

Covenants, Conditions, and Restrictions (CC&Rs)

deed restrictions

dominant tenement

easement

easement in gross

egress

encroachment

encumbrance

ingress

judgment

laches

license

lien

lien claimant

lis pendens

mechanic's lien or materialman's lien

mill

monetary encumbrances

non-monetary encumbrances

prescription

priority of liens

profit or profit a prendre

servient tenement

special assessments

Special Improvement Districts

taxable value

writ of attachment

writ of execution

CHAPTER OBJECTIVES

After completing this chapter, you should be able to:

- Define, differentiate, and identify the types of non-monetary and monetary encumbrances.
- Summarize the Nevada real property tax laws and procedures and calculate property taxes.
- Discuss mechanic's liens and the lien holder's foreclosure rights.
- Summarize the creation, enforcement, and renewal of judgments.

Encumbrances

INTRODUCTION

An **encumbrance** is any claim, lien charge, or liability attached to and binding on real property that may lessen the value, burden, obstruct, or impair the use of a property but not necessarily prevent transfer of title. An encumbrance is a right or interest in a property held by someone who is not the legal owner of the property.

The two types of encumbrances are non-monetary and monetary.

6.1 NON-MONETARY ENCUMBRANCES

Non-monetary encumbrances affect the physical condition or use of property. Examples of this type of encumbrance are deed restrictions, easements, and encroachments.

Deed Restrictions

Deed restrictions are private limitations placed on land use. They are established at the time a subdivision is developed, or when a property owner sells the land, and are included in each deed. When the deed restrictions uniformly affect all of the subdivision, they are itemized in a document called the "Uniform Declaration of Restrictions," or "**Covenants, Conditions, and Restrictions (CC&Rs)**," and the deed will refer only to that document.

A deed restriction usually relates to land use, such as the type of building, square footage, setbacks, color, or style. Deed restrictions cannot be used to discriminate on the basis of race, color, religion, sex, or national origin; if they do, they are unenforceable by the courts. Also, deed restrictions limiting the owner's rights (such as participation in zoning hearings) are unenforceable.

Deed restrictions take precedence over zoning ordinances if the deed restrictions are more limiting. They have time limitations but will renew if not voted down. If the current owners in the subdivision agree by 100%, a deed restriction may be changed. Violations of deed restrictions can lead to a court action. If a person violates one of the CC&Rs, the homeowners must, at their own expense, bring a court action to enforce their deed restriction. If the homeowners delay action, they may lose their rights. The delay in asserting one's right is called **laches**.

Easements

An **easement** is an interest that entitles one party to some limited use of another party's land. It is created for a designated use only, such as a roadway for **ingress** (entrance) and **egress** (exit) to otherwise landlocked property. It is a non-possessory interest and not an estate in land. An easement creates a legal right to use someone else's real property and must be written and recorded with the county recorder to satisfy the Statute of Frauds. It is an intangible right and, once it is created, remains in effect until some specific action is taken to terminate it. An easement is not terminated by sale of property.

Types of Easements

Appurtenant easements and *easements in gross* are the two types of easements.

1. **Appurtenant easements** are attached to the land and if the property is sold, the easement is transferred to the new owner. Appurtenant easements are said to "run with the land." Examples of appurtenant easements include a driveway, road, party wall, or common wall, as in a condominium or townhouse.

   - The land on which the easement runs is the **servient tenement** or the "one who serves." (See Property A in Figure 6.1.)
   - The landowner who benefits from the easement is said to be the **dominant tenement**. (See Property B in Figure 6.1.) For example, A owns a very large lot and decides to sell the back half of the property to B. There is a road only along the front of A's property. Because it is illegal to sell landlocked land, A must provide a road for B so that B can get to his property. In this case, A is the servient tenement and B is the dominant tenement. A still has title to the road and must pay taxes on it. B has an interest in the road, and the easement is considered to belong to him or her (dominant tenement). B must pay for the maintenance of the road.

FIGURE 6.1   Servient Tenement and Dominant Tenement

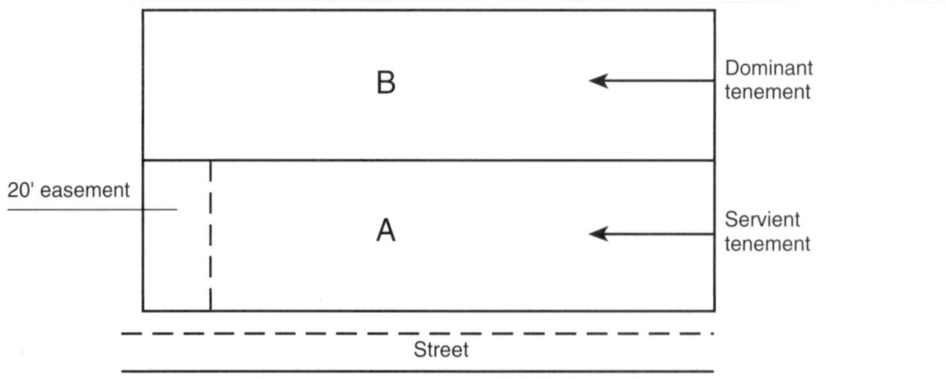

- An easement such as a party wall, when a fence is built on the property line with half on each person's property, is an example of an appurtenant easement. Each person owns half of the fence on his or her property, and each owner has an easement on the other's property.

2. An **easement in gross** is the right to use the land of another. It is not appurtenant, which means it is not attached to the land. There is no dominant tenement in an easement in gross. The two types of easements in gross are:

   - *Commercial easement in gross*—These easements can be assigned or transferred. The sale of the property usually does not affect this type of easement. Examples include railroad for right of way, utility company for water and gas mains and/or for power, and telephone or cable television lines.
   - *Personal easement in gross*—A personal easement in gross cannot be assigned or transferred and terminates with the death of the person to whom the easement was granted or upon transfer (sale) of the subject property. An example is to give an easement in gross to allow a person to cross the owner's land to reach a lake.

Creating Easements

Four main methods are used to create easements:

1. *Express grants*—Most easements are created by an express grant, which is usually executed by a separate deed. The rights, privileges, and duties would be clearly stated in the deed.
2. *Reservation in a deed*—For example, the owner of a property maintains for himself the use of a strip of land being sold as a driveway. The driveway easement is created by reservation in the deed, which transfers ownership to the new buyer.
3. *Necessity*—Because it is illegal to sell landlocked land, an owner would have to grant an easement to allow ingress and egress to the property.
4. *Prescription*—A method of acquiring an easement by continuous, open, hostile, and notorious use for a period of 10 years without the consent of the owner.

Terminating Easements

Easements may be terminated by agreement of the parties. A quitclaim deed can be used to terminate the easement. The quitclaim deed must be recorded to remove the easement from the county records.

A merger of the two properties can terminate the easement, for there is no longer any need for it. A merger occurs when the same person or entity owns two parcels. To continue with the earlier example (shown in Figure 6.1), if Lot B is acquired by the owner of Lot A, then the driveway easement for Lot B is terminated by merger.

An easement can also be terminated by abandonment or adverse possession. The termination of an easement through adverse possession requires continuous,

FIGURE 6.2   Encroachments

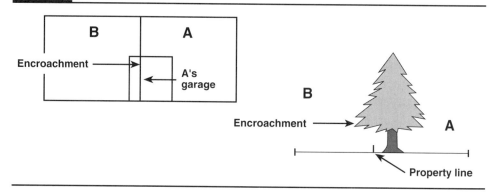

open, hostile, and notorious use for a prescribed period of time that varies by state and the facts related to a specific claim. Abandonment of an easement involves an intention to abandon with an act or an omission to act through which the abandonment intention is carried into effect.

Important Terms

The following terms also relate to land use and property rights.

- **Profit** or **profit a prendre**, generally considered a type of easement, is a right to remove soil, minerals, fruit, timber, or some product of the land with compensation to the surface owner of the land. It is a non-possessory interest in the land, limited to a particular purpose, and can be created only by a written clause.

- **License** is a personal privilege to use the land of another for a limited purpose. It can be revoked at any time. A license is not an interest in land. Permission given to go hunting on someone's property grants a license to use the land. The use of a parking garage is also generally a license.

Encroachments

An **encroachment** is an intrusion upon another person's property without a right to use it. Encroachments can include structures, eaves, fences, overhanging branches, and so on (see Figure 6.2). If the encroachment is a structure, it is called *trespassing*. In the case of overhanging branches, it is known as a *nuisance*. The owner of the property being encroached upon has the right to force the removal of the encroachment. Failure to do so may eventually damage the owner's title through the concept of laches that was described earlier in this chapter.

6.2 MONETARY ENCUMBRANCES

Monetary encumbrances are also called *liens*. A **lien** is a claim or charge against a property as security for the payment of a debt or obligation. Liens affect the title of the property involved. Remember this helpful saying:

"All liens are encumbrances, but not all encumbrances are liens."

Classification of Liens

There are three classifications of liens:

1. *Contractual*—In a contractual lien, the parties enter into a contractual agreement, such as a mortgage or trust deed.
2. *Statutory*—Statutory liens are created by law, such as property taxes or special assessment taxes.
3. *Equitable*—Equitable liens generally occur when the courts declare that justice would be best served by the creation of a lien.

Liens can further be classified as *general* or *specific* and *voluntary* or *involuntary* (see Figure 6.3).

General liens affect all property, both real and personal. Examples of general liens are judgments, internal revenue taxes, debts of a deceased person, and estate taxes.

Specific liens affect only one specific property. These include property taxes, special assessments, mechanic's liens, surety bail bond liens, attachments, and vendor and vendee liens.

Voluntary liens are created by voluntary actions of the individual, such as giving a mortgage or trust deed as collateral for loans on property.

Involuntary liens are created by law without action or consent of the individual. Examples include property taxes and court-ordered judgment liens.

Priority of Liens

Liens with the highest priority are superior to junior liens. The higher-priority lien eliminates junior liens if the higher lien holder forecloses. Real property taxes have the highest priority, followed by special assessments.

The priority of other liens is determined by the order in which the lien is recorded, except for mechanic's and materialman's liens. Priority is established for these liens as of the date the work began.

FIGURE 6.3   Classification of Liens

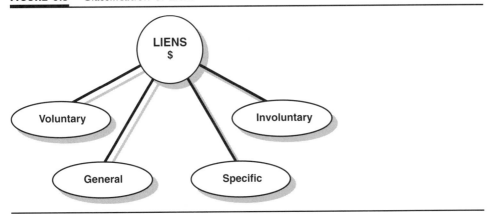

6.3 NEVADA REAL PROPERTY TAXES

One of the government's powers is the right to tax real property. This tax is a lien on a specific property and takes precedence over all other liens and encumbrances.

Nevada uses a single tax bill. The tax bill combines state, county, municipal, school, and other district levies, such as a fire district, into a single statement for payment to the county treasurer.

This property tax is called an **ad valorem tax**, which means "according to value." The principle elements of the property tax consist of the tax rate and the tax base. The tax base is calculated by first appraising the value of property according to statutory requirements to determine "taxable value." Taxable value in turn is multiplied times the level of assessment. The resulting assessed value is the tax base against which a tax rate is applied to determine the total amount of taxes due. Property tax is calculated by applying the elements to the following formula:

$$\text{Taxable Value} \times \text{Level of Assessment} = \text{Assessed Value}$$
$$\text{Assessed Value} \times \text{Tax Rate} = \text{Total Property Tax}$$

Property Tax Elements

The Nevada State Constitution and Statutes prescribe the process and procedures for the determination of the property tax elements of:

- Taxable value
- Level of assessment and assessed value
- Tax rate

Taxable Value

The Constitution of Nevada provides the first guidance in how taxable value will be determined and states:

"The legislature shall provide by law for a uniform and equal rate of assessment and taxation, and shall prescribe such regulations as shall secure a just valuation for taxation of all property, real, personal, and possessory except mines and mining claims, which shall be assessed and taxed only as provided in section 5 of this article."

(Article 10, Section 1, Nevada State Constitution)

In 1981, the legislature determined that a just valuation of real property should no longer be based strictly on the full cash value of the total property. Instead, the value of real property was divided into two components: full cash value of the land and replacement cost new less depreciation of the improvements, with the rate of depreciation set by statute. The resulting "taxable value" must not exceed the full cash value of the entire property. Full cash value is defined as "the most probable price which property would bring in a competitive and open market under all conditions requisite for a fair sale."

Level of Assessment and Assessed Value

The level of assessment is also known as the "rate of assessment" and is generally expressed as the overall ratio of assessed value to taxable value. The Nevada Revised Statutes require that all property subject to taxation be assessed at 35% of the taxable value. The formula set forth in the Statutes is:

$$\text{Taxable Value} \times \text{Level of Assessment} = \text{Assessed Value}$$

For example, if the taxable value of a single-family residence is estimated at $200,000, the assessed value would be $70,000 ($200,000 × .35 = $70,000).

Tax Rate

The State of Nevada Constitution, Article 10, Section 2, limits the property tax rate to $0.05 per $1.00 of assessed value, which translates to $5.00 per $100 of assessed value. In the 1979 session, the Nevada Legislature set the property tax rate at no more than $3.64 per $100 of assessed value, where it remains, plus $0.02 not subject to the cap.

Pursuant to the Nevada Revised Statutes, local government entity property tax revenues are allowed to be increased by a maximum of 6% per year. The previous fiscal year's property tax revenue is multiplied by 106%. This amount is then divided by the projected assessed valuation for the upcoming fiscal year to determine the tax rate necessary to generate that amount of revenue. The Statutes also provide for a "hold harmless" scenario, in which the new calculated tax rate cannot be less than the previous fiscal year's rate.

The tax rate includes, but is not limited to, the following elements:

- School Operating Rate
- General or Special Improvement Districts
- Legislatively Approved Overrides
- Voter Approved Overrides
- State Debt Rate

Pursuant to the Nevada Revised Statutes, the chairman of the county board of commissioners convenes a public meeting of a majority of the governing boards of all affected local governments on or before June 13 of each year for the purpose of establishing a combined tax rate that conforms to the statutory limit. After discussions regarding changes to tax rates, each affected governing board must unanimously approve the changes. Immediately following the meeting, the county clerk advises the Department of Taxation of the results. If no agreement can be reached, or no quorum exists for one or more of the affected local government entities, then the department reviews the record of the discussions and the budgets of the affected entities and makes a recommendation to the Nevada Tax Commission.

The Nevada Tax Commission is mandated statutorily to meet on June 25 each year to certify the property tax rates for the succeeding fiscal year. Prior to the certification vote, the Commission will determine the property tax rates for the entities in any county that exceed the statutory cap, considering any local government testimony and the department's recommendation. Any local government entity affected by a tax rate adjustment made by the Commission files a copy of its revised final budget by July 30.

The Appeal Process

A taxpayer who believes that the valuation is too high or believes an inequity exists may make an appeal to the county board of equalization. It is the responsibility of the landowner to prove why the valuation should be lower. The request for a lower valuation must be evidenced by the valuation of other properties in the area, not simply an owner's desire to reduce his or her tax responsibilities.

A taxpayer may appeal the decision of the county board of equalization to the State Board of Equalization. The appeal to the county board of equalization must be made on or before January 15 of the fiscal year in which the assessment was made.

The property owner may also bring an action in a Nevada court of law; however, no such action may be brought relating to assessed valuations by a county assessor or a county board of equalization unless an appeal was previously made to the State Board of Equalization.

Due Dates

Property taxes become a lien on property on July 1, and the tax is due the third Monday of August. When the taxes assessed on a parcel exceed $100, the tax can be paid in four equal installments. If the taxpayer elects to pay in four installments they are due as follows:

First Installment	Third Monday of August
Second Installment	First Monday of October
Third Installment	First Monday of January
Fourth Installment	First Monday of March

Rate of Tax

The tax rate may be expressed in mills, or an amount per $100 of assessed value. A **mill** is 1/1000 of a dollar, or $0.001.

> **Example**—A residential property with a taxable value of $152,800 is assessed at 35% with a tax rate of $3.00 per $100 of assessed value.
>
> $152,800 × 35% = $53,480 = assessed value
> $53,480 ÷ 100 = $534.80 (100's)
> $534.80 × $3.00 = $1604.40 taxes

1. What will the taxes be for six months on property assessed at $6000 if the tax rate is $3.20 per $100 valuation?
   - Multiply 60 hundreds by the rate per $100 and divide by 2 to get six month's taxes.

2. If the taxable value of a property is $68,000, and the property is assessed at 35% of the appraised value for tax purposes, and the tax rate is $2.80 per $100 of assessed valuation, how much will the taxes be?

   • Multiply the taxable value by the decimal equivalent of 35% to get the assessed valuation. Now, multiply the tax rate by the number of hundreds to get the annual taxes.

Delinquent Taxes

A delinquent notice is mailed to the taxpayer within 30 days after the first Monday of March each year. If the delinquent taxes are not paid by 5 pm on the first Monday in June of the current year, both of the following are true:

1. A certificate will be issued to the county treasurer authorizing the treasurer to hold the property, as trustee for the state and county, subject to redemption within two years after the date of the issuance of the certificate.

2. A tax lien may be sold.

Redemption is accomplished by payment of the taxes and accruing taxes, penalties, and costs, together with interest on the taxes at the rate of 10% per annum accrued monthly from the date due until paid.

The county treasurer may sell a tax lien against a parcel of real property after the first Monday in June after the taxes become delinquent. If a tax lien offered for sale is not sold, the county may collect the delinquent taxes through a suit for delinquent taxes.

The county treasurer issues a **Certificate of Purchase** to the purchaser of a tax lien. The purchaser is entitled to receive:

• The amount of delinquent taxes, penalties, interest, and costs.

• Interest on the amount paid for delinquent taxes, penalties, interest, and costs at the rate established by the board of county commissioners. The rate may not be less than 10% per annum or more than 20% per annum.

If the tax lien is not redeemed within the two-year period, the holder of the Certificate of Purchase may collect the taxes through a suit for delinquent taxes.

Special Assessments

Special Improvement Districts are allowed to be formed by counties, cities, and towns for specific projects within the district. Projects include improvements such as street pavement, curbs and gutters, sidewalks, streetlights, driveways, sewer and water facilities, and other improvements that enhance the value of property. The districts are generally formed to provide a source of funding for eligible improvements.

Chapter 271 of the Nevada Revised Statutes allows the sale of bonds to finance the cost of the improvements with property owners, within the district, being assessed for their benefited share of the improvement. Property owners are responsible for paying back this money all at once or in installments over a

10-year to a 30-year period of time. Assessments not paid at once are due twice a year on June 1 and December 1 of each year.

The improvement costs allocated to the individual property owner are generally assessed on a "front foot" basis. A front foot is the portion of the parcel, expressed in feet, that faces the street as opposed to the depth of the lot. Assessments must be in proportion to the special benefits derived by each property from the improvements being constructed.

Each assessment constitutes a lien on the property and must be paid by the property owner. The lien is prior and superior to all liens, claims, and encumbrances other than the liens of prior assessments and general property taxes.

The assessment remains with the property and should the property be sold during the period that the improvement is financed, the remaining assessment is transferred to the new owner at the time of sale.

Failure to pay any installment when due causes the total whole amount of the unpaid principal to become due and payable immediately with an option to also begin foreclosure proceedings.

6.4 MECHANIC'S AND MATERIALMAN'S LIENS AND JUDGMENTS

Nevada law says that people who provide labor or material to improve someone's property can place liens against and foreclose on that property if they have not been paid for their services or materials. This kind of lien is called a **mechanic's lien** (when it refers to unpaid labor) or **materialman's lien** (when it refers to unpaid materials).

A **lien claimant** has the right to file a mechanic's or materialman's lien and is any person who provides work, material, or equipment with a value of $500 or more to be used in or for the construction, alteration, or repair of any improvement, property, or work of improvement. A lien claimant includes every artisan, builder, contractor, laborer, lessor or renter of equipment, materialman, miner, subcontractor, or other person who provides work, material, or equipment. A lien claimant also includes any person who performs services as an architect, engineer, land surveyor, or geologist in relation to the improvement, property, or work of improvement.

Fifteen-Day Notice

When the work of improvement involves the construction, alteration, or repair of multifamily or single-family residences, including apartment houses, a lien claimant must serve a **15-day notice** of intent to lien. The notice is to include substantially the same information required in a notice of lien and is to be served upon both the owner and the prime contractor before recording the notice of lien. The 15-day notice requirement does not apply to the construction of any non-residential construction project.

Filing, Foreclosure, and Release

A lien claimant must record the notice of lien within 90 days of the completion of work. The time for all parties to record their lien is reduced to 40 days if a notice of completion is recorded. The notice of lien must contain:

(a) A statement of the lienable amount after deducting all credits and offsets.

(b) The name of the owner.

(c) The name of the person by whom the lien claimant was employed.

(d) A brief statement of the terms of payment.

(e) A legal description of the property to be liened.

The priority of the lien dates back to the beginning date of work by the general contractor.

If payment is not made after recording the lien, the contractor must begin collection procedures by filing a foreclosure action. The foreclosure action must be filed within 180 days (six months), or the lien will be terminated.

After payment, the contractor must issue a lien release within 10 days. The owner then records the lien release to give constructive notice that the lien has been removed from the property.

6.5 JUDGMENTS, ATTACHMENTS, AND LIS PENDENS

Judgments

A **judgment** is the result of a court action in which one person brings a suit against another person. The court order is recorded in the county where the debtor lives. This action is attached to any property, real or personal, owned by the debtor. If a person attempts to purchase a property with a new loan, the lender will require the judgment to be satisfied before the new loan will be granted. Because the judgment is against the person, when the deed is recorded, the judgment will attach to the property prior to the new loan and the new loan is considered a junior lien.

Judgments are granted for a six-year period and can be renewed for six-year periods. If a debtor does not satisfy the judgment, Nevada statutes provide for a **writ of execution** to attach one's property and sell it to satisfy the debt.

Nevada law provides that a judgment creditor may (at any time there is a valid judgment lien) bring an action against the debtor for a writ of execution to enforce the lien.

Types of Execution

There are two types of execution: *general execution* and *special execution*.

1. A general execution commands the officer to take the amount of the judgment out of property of the judgment debtor without specifying the particular property.

2. A special execution commands the officer to sell certain specific property or to deliver certain specific real or personal property to the entitled party.

Writ of Attachment

A **writ of attachment** is the legal process of seizing the real or personal property of a defendant in a lawsuit and holding it in the custody of the court as security for satisfaction of a judgment.

A writ of attachment is usually filed prior to the court action for judgment so that the property cannot be sold before the court has acted. In this case, the court has temporarily "seized title."

Process Involved

When a writ of attachment will be used, the creditor seeks a writ of attachment from court and records it, which creates a lien before the entry of a judgment. The plaintiff is then assured that there will be property left to satisfy the judgment.

To obtain attachment, the creditor has to post bond or deposit in order to cover possible loss or damage that the debtor may sustain while the court has custody of the property, if the judgment is not awarded to the creditor.

Lis Pendens

Lis pendens (Latin for *action pending*) is a recorded legal document that gives constructive notice that an action affecting a particular piece of property has been filed in a state or federal court. It does not prevent the sale of a litigant's property, but it does put any potential buyer on notice that the property may be affected by the result of the lawsuit.

CHAPTER SUMMARY

An encumbrance is any claim, lien charge, or liability attached to and binding on real property that may lessen the value, burden, obstruct, or impair the use of a property but not necessarily prevent transfer of title. An encumbrance is a right or interest in a property held by someone who is not the legal owner of the property. There are two types of encumbrances: non-monetary and monetary.

Non-monetary encumbrances affect the physical condition or use of property. Examples of this type of encumbrance are deed restrictions, easements, and encroachments. Deed restrictions are private limitations one places on land use. They are established at the time a subdivision is developed or when a property owner sells the land and are included in each deed. When the deed restrictions uniformly affect all of the subdivision, they are itemized in a document called the "Uniform Declaration of Restrictions," or "Covenants, Conditions, and Restrictions (CC&Rs)." Violations of deed restrictions can lead to a court action. If a person violates one of the CC&Rs, the homeowners must, at their own expense, bring a court action to enforce their deed restriction. If the homeowners delay action, they may lose their rights. The delay in asserting one's rights is called laches.

An easement is an interest that entitles one party to some limited use of another party's land. Appurtenant easements are attached to the land and, if the property is sold, the easement is transferred to the new owner. An easement in gross is the right to use the land of another. It is not attached to the land. A commercial easement in gross can be assigned or transferred. The sale of the property usually does not affect this type of easement. A personal easement in gross cannot be assigned or transferred, and it terminates with the death of the person to whom the easement was granted or upon transfer of the subject property.

Four main methods are used to create easements: express grants, reservation in a deed, necessity, and prescription. Easements may be terminated by agreement of the parties. A quitclaim deed can be used to terminate the easement. The quitclaim deed must be recorded to remove the easement from the county records. A merger of the two properties can also terminate the easement. A merger occurs when the same person or entity owns the two parcels. An easement can also be terminated by abandonment or adverse possession.

An encroachment is an intrusion upon another person's property without a right to use it. If the encroachment is a structure, it is called trespassing. In the case of overhanging branches, it is known as a nuisance. The owner of the property being encroached upon has the right to force the removal of the encroachment. Failure to do so may eventually damage the owner's title.

Monetary encumbrances are also called liens. A lien is a claim or charge against a property as security for the payment of a debt or obligation. Liens affect the title of property involved. The three classifications of liens are contractual, in which the parties enter into a contractual agreement, such as a mortgage or trust deed; statutory, such as property taxes or special assessment taxes, that are created by law; and equitable, which generally occur when the courts declare that justice would be best served by the creation of a lien.

Liens can further be classified as general or specific and voluntary or involuntary. General liens affect all property, both real and personal. Specific liens affect only one specific property. Voluntary liens are created by voluntary actions of the individual. Involuntary liens are created by law, without action or consent of the individual, such as the government's right to tax real property. Involuntary liens are on a specific property and take precedence over all other liens and encumbrances.

Nevada uses a single tax bill. The tax bill combines state, county, municipal, school, and other district levies into a single statement for payment to the county treasurer. This property tax is called an ad valorem tax. The property tax elements are taxable value, level of assessment, assessed value, and tax rate. The taxable value is divided into two components of full cash value for the land and replacement cost new less depreciation of the improvements. The resulting taxable value must not exceed the full cash value of the entire property. The level of assessment is established by statute at 35% of taxable value. The assessed value is computed by multiplying the taxable value by the assessment rate of 35%.

The Nevada Legislature has set the property tax rate at no more than $3.64 per $100 of assessed value plus $0.02 not subject to the cap. Local government entities' property tax revenues are allowed to be increased by a maximum of 6% per year. The previous fiscal year's property tax revenue is multiplied by 106% and the resulting amount is divided by the projected assessed valuation for the upcoming fiscal year to determine the property tax rate. The chairman of the county board of commissioners convenes a public meeting of a majority of the governing boards of all affected local governments on or before June 13 of each year for the purpose of establishing a combined tax rate that conforms to the statutory limit. The Nevada Tax Commission is mandated to meet on June 25 each year to certify the property tax rates for the succeeding fiscal year.

A property owner can appeal the taxable value to the county board of equalization and the decision of the county board can be appealed by the property owner to the State Board of Equalization. The property owner may also bring an action in a Nevada court of law; however, no such action may be brought unless an appeal was previously made to the state board.

Property taxes become a lien on property on July 1, and the tax is due the third Monday of August. When the tax assessed on a parcel exceeds $100, the tax can be paid in four equal installments in August, October, January, and March.

A delinquent notice is mailed to the taxpayer 30 days after the final installment is due in March. If the delinquent taxes are not paid after receiving this notice, a certificate will be issued to the county treasurer authorizing the treasurer to hold the property as trustee for the state and county. The certificate is subject to redemption within two years after the date of the certificate issuance. The tax lien may be sold. The purchaser of the tax lien receives a Certificate of Purchase and is entitled to receive the amount of delinquent taxes, penalties, interest, and costs plus interest on that amount at the rate established by the board of county commissioners. The rate may not be less than 10% or more than 20%.

If the tax lien is not redeemed within the two-year period, the holder of the Certificate of Purchase may collect the taxes through a suit for delinquent taxes.

Special assessments are improvements that enhance the value of property, such as curbs, sidewalks, streets, sewers, and streetlights. Payment for the special assessment may be made in one lump sum or paid in installments. Property may be sold for unpaid special assessment liens.

A person who provides labor or material to improve someone's property can place a lien against and foreclose on that property if he or she has not been paid for his or her services or materials. This kind of lien is called a mechanic's lien or materialman's lien. The priority of the lien dates back to the beginning date of work.

A judgment is the result of a court action in which one person brings a suit against another person. Judgments are granted for a six-year period and can be renewed for six-year periods. If a debtor does not satisfy the judgment, Nevada statutes provide for a writ of execution to attach one's property and sell it to satisfy the debt. There are two types of execution: general execution and special execution. A general execution commands the officer to take the amount of the judgment out of property of the judgment debtor without specifying the particular property. A special execution commands the officer to sell certain specific property or to deliver certain specific real or personal property to the entitled party.

A writ of attachment is the legal process of seizing the real or personal property of a defendant in a lawsuit and holding it in the custody of the court as security for satisfaction of a judgment. A writ of attachment is usually filed prior to the court action for judgment so that the property cannot be sold before the court has acted.

Lis pendens is a recorded legal document that gives constructive notice that an action affecting a particular piece of property has been filed in a state or federal court.

CHECKING YOUR COMPREHENSION

1. Describe a deed restriction and the concept of laches.

2. Describe an easement and summarize the different easement types.

3. Define the three classifications of liens. Then list examples of liens and classify them as *general* or *specific* and *voluntary* or *involuntary*.

4. Summarize the Nevada property tax laws and procedures and list the important dates for payment and delinquency of the property taxes.

5. Define a mechanic's lien and judgment.

PRACTICAL APPLICATION

1. The tax on an owner-occupied residential property is $3.25 per hundred dollars of assessed value. The taxable value of the property is $60,000. What would the taxes be for one-half year?
   a. $682.50
   b. $13,650
   c. $6825
   d. $341.25

2. A house with a taxable value of $128,500 is assessed at 35% of its value. If the tax bill is $1350, what is the rate per $100?
   a. 1.80
   b. 13.50
   c. 4.00
   d. 3.00

3. A home sold for $75,000. The assessed value for taxes was 22% of the sales price. What would the tax bill be if the tax rate were $6.25 per $100 of the assessed value?
   a. $937.50
   b. $975
   c. $1031.25
   d. $1072.50

REVIEWING YOUR UNDERSTANDING

1. Failure to assert a right within a reasonable period may cause the court to determine that the right to assert that right is lost due to:
   a. laches
   b. novation
   c. rescission
   d. reformation

2. An easement in gross:
   a. is attached to a person, not a property
   b. is always a negative easement
   c. must have a definite termination date
   d. is an appurtenant easement

3. An appurtenant easement on the servient tenement's property would:
   a. be lost upon sale of the property
   b. be included in every deed
   c. go with the real property
   d. be lost after one year of non-use

4. A deed restriction would be **BEST** described as a(n):
   a. general lien
   b. specific lien
   c. constructive lien
   d. encumbrance

5. With the permission of Will, Tom has used a shortcut over Will's land for more than 25 years to get to the highway. Tom has a(n):
   a. appurtenant easement
   b. easement by implication
   c. prescriptive easement
   d. license

6. Ann sells property on which a recorded easement exists. Ann makes no mention of the easement during negotiations. Therefore, the easement:
   a. remains with the seller
   b. reverts to whoever created it
   c. runs with the land
   d. terminates

7. To create a lien after a court decision, the instrument recorded is a(n):
   a. writ of attachment
   b. abstract of judgment
   c. order of execution
   d. order of possession

8. Which of the following liens would usually be classified as the priority lien?
   a. a mortgage dated last year
   b. the current real estate tax
   c. a mechanic's lien for work started before the mortgage was recorded
   d. a judgment rendered yesterday

9. The notice of a possible future lien affecting title to real estate and recorded when a suit is filed is:
   a. laches
   b. an attachment
   c. lis pendens
   d. a judgment

10. The successful purchaser at the sale of a property tax lien pays the taxes due and receives a:
    a. Certificate of Sale
    b. Certificate of Purchase
    c. Treasurer's Deed
    d. Sheriff's Deed

11. Which of the following restrictive covenants is **MOST** likely to be enforceable?
    a. prohibits sales to blacks
    b. prohibits resales for 20 years
    c. prohibits use for anything other than single-family dwellings
    d. absolutely prohibits any resales

12. Which of the following would **NOT** terminate an easement?
    a. non-use of an easement for six months
    b. express agreement of the parties
    c. adverse possession of the dominant tenement by the holder of the servient tenement
    d. merger of the dominant and servient tenements

13. What would a landlocked property owner **MOST** likely ask the court to grant?
    a. an easement by prescription
    b. an easement in gross
    c. an easement by necessity
    d. adverse possession of servient tenement

14. When improvements are made accidentally on the land of another:
    a. the owner of the land will probably take title by accession
    b. the improver has the right to buy the property at its tax appraisal value
    c. the improver is allowed to remove the improvements, providing any damage to the property is repaired
    d. the improver is allowed to use the property of the other person by encroachment

15. Nevada property taxes are based on:
    a. the number of closets
    b. assessed value
    c. front footage
    d. transfer value

16. In Nevada, the assessment ratio applied to taxable value of real property is:
    a. 35%
    b. 40%
    c. 45%
    d. 50%

17. Property taxes become a lien on the first day of:
    a. July
    b. June
    c. January
    d. March

18. Which choice below ranks liens in order from highest priority to lowest priority?
    a. IRS liens, property taxes, special assessments
    b. property taxes, special assessments, IRS liens
    c. property taxes, IRS liens, special assessments
    d. IRS liens, special assessments, property taxes

19. When are Nevada property taxes due?
    a. third Monday of August
    b. first Monday of March
    c. first Monday of January
    d. first Monday of October

20. A mechanic's lien is **NOT** available to a person who:
    a. graded the site for construction
    b. supplied the lumber but did not perform any labor
    c. provided the furnishings for a model house
    d. performed labor under a subcontract rather than a direct contract with the owner

7

IMPORTANT TERMS AND CONCEPTS

CLUE report

coinsurance clause

commercial property
insurance

credit report

dwelling insurance

federal flood insurance

foundation

home warranty
contract

homeowners'
insurance

inquiry

insulation

insurance underwriting

R-value

roof

sheathing

stucco

termites

wood frame
construction

CHAPTER OBJECTIVES

After completing this chapter, you should be able to:

* Summarize the advantages and disadvantages of home ownership and renting.

* List the different types of housing.

* Discuss the types of property insurance coverage and the insurance underwriting process.

* Describe home warranty contracts.

* Identify and discuss the fundamentals of construction, including contractor licensing and warranties.

Home Ownership and Home Construction

7.1 HOME OWNERSHIP

According to the U.S. Census Bureau, nearly 70% of people in the United States owned their homes in 2005. The home-ownership percentage continues to increase because of government policies that encourage ownership and because of the significant benefits of home ownership. However, potential buyers should examine the benefits of renting before deciding to buy property.

To Rent or to Buy

Generally, the benefits of owning can be considered the disadvantages of renting, and the benefits of renting can be considered the disadvantages of owning.

Benefits of Home Ownership

- Many people have a *deep longing for ownership*, representative of the "American Dream."
- As homeowners make mortgage payments, their equity grows, which steadily establishes *financial stability*. Home ownership also improves a person's credit rating.
- Psychologically, a person who buys a house will usually feel *pride of ownership*; therefore, he or she will usually take more pride in its care and maintenance than a renter would.
- *Interest in community affairs*. When a person becomes a homeowner, that person tends to become interested in what happens to his or her tax dollars or in what is being done to resolve current community issues.
- Homeowners have the *independence and freedom* to use the property as they wish within the framework of the law. They are also free from landlord restrictions.
- *Creative opportunities*. Homeowners are free to develop their property in accordance with zoning and deed restrictions. The homeowner may remodel and decorate according to his or her artistic and cultural preferences. The renter must take the home or apartment as-is and adjust to its limitations.

- *Tax benefits.* Real property taxes and interest on a mortgage or trust deed are allowable deductions on one's annual income tax return. Gains of up to $250,000 or $500,000 on the sale of a qualified primary residence are exempt from income tax. Tax benefits related to home ownership are covered in Chapter 25.

Benefits of Renting

- *Mobility.* If a person must move from city to city because of his or her job, it is often better to rent than to buy. This also applies if employment is seasonal and one has to move according to the seasons.
- If a person wishes to be *free from the maintenance and management* of property, renting may be more ideal.
- *Financial reasons.* If a person cannot afford the necessary down payment or needs to use his or her funds for other purposes, renting may be the better option. To make home ownership financially advantageous, one must generally own the property for more than three years. The first years of ownership are usually more costly than renting.

Types of Housing

As the population of the United States has become more urban, a greater variety of housing types has become necessary. Affordable housing has also become an important issue as prices for single-family homes continue to increase. Today, people can choose to rent or own units in the following types of housing:

- Single-family residence
- Patio home and town home, usually within a master planned community
- Duplex up to a fourplex
- Apartment complex
- High-rise residential complex
- Mobile home or manufactured housing

7.2 PROPERTY INSURANCE

Insurance is a contractual agreement used to spread the risk of financial loss among a large group. Through the purchase of an insurance policy, a property owner shares the risk of property loss due to various events. The risk of property loss is shared with others insured by the same company and reduces the likelihood of disastrous financial consequences.

Some common types of property insurance include dwelling insurance, homeowners' insurance, commercial property insurance, and federal flood insurance.

Dwelling Insurance

Dwelling insurance is for residential properties, including single-family homes, one- to four-family houses, duplexes, triplexes, and permanently installed mobile homes. A standard dwelling property policy covers losses from fire, lightning, and internal explosion. Additional perils can be covered through the purchase of an extended policy.

Homeowners' Insurance

Homeowners' insurance policies are known as multiline policies, which means that they combine property and casualty coverage in the same policy. The advantage of a multiline policy is that several coverages related to a specific type of exposure are packaged together, which reduces the number of insurance policies that need to be purchased. The package policy provides the same property coverage that is available in a dwelling insurance policy and also includes theft insurance and personal liability coverage. Liability includes personal injuries and expenses sustained by guests or resident employees. It also includes any damage that the homeowner may cause to the property of others.

Commercial Property Insurance

Commercial property insurance is used to cover most types of commercial buildings. Generally, the basic causes of loss that are covered by the commercial property policy are fire, lightning, explosion, windstorm or hail, smoke, aircraft or vehicles, riot or civil commotion, vandalism, accidental sprinkler leakage, sinkhole collapse, and volcanic action. Extending the coverage with special endorsements can also cover additional perils.

Coinsurance Clause

Commercial insurance often includes a **coinsurance clause** that requires the policy owner to insure at least 80% of the value of the property in exchange for a premium discount. If the insured's policy contains this clause and the insured carries less than this amount, a penalty will occur in case of a partial loss. In periods of high inflation, it is important for the property owner to keep track of the property's current value in order to maintain this 80% coverage.

For example, if a person insures a commercial property with an actual market value of $100,000 with a policy containing an 80% coinsurance clause, the insurance required is $80,000 (80% of $100,000). If the insured carried only $60,000 of insurance and there was a loss of $40,000, the insurance policy would cover only $30,000 of the loss. The amount covered is a fraction of the loss, with the amount of insurance as the numerator and the required insurance as the denominator. (In the example, $60,000/$80,000 converts to 75%, and 75% of $40,000 equals $30,000.)

Federal Flood Insurance

Federal flood insurance is a federally subsidized program authorized by Congress in 1968 through the efforts of insurance agents. The program provides aid to victims of disastrous flooding. Floods cause more property damage in the United States than any other form of natural disaster.

There are four situations covered by this insurance:

1. Overflow of inland or tidal waters
2. Run-off of surface waters
3. Mudslides
4. Abnormal erosion caused by floods

Informing the Buyer

The program is administered by the Department of Housing and Urban Development. Flood insurance is mandatory on floodplain properties that the federal government finances, insures, or guarantees.

A broker is responsible for informing the buyer of the flood insurance requirement when negotiating the sale. Many areas in Nevada are in a floodplain, which means the lender will require the buyer to acquire flood insurance. The local broker's office should have a map showing the local floodplain areas.

The flood insurance policy may be purchased through any private insurance agency.

Insurance Underwriting

Insurance underwriting is the process the insurance company uses to ascertain the types of risks it will accept through the issuance of an insurance policy. This includes an evaluation of the property and the individual or entity applying for the insurance. Underwriters use credit reports and Comprehensive Loss Underwriting Exchange (CLUE) reports to evaluate risks.

Credit Reports

When an applicant applies for insurance, the insurance underwriter often orders some type of **credit report** to obtain information concerning the personal habits or financial condition of the potential insured. Credit reports are subject to the Fair Credit Reporting Act, and if an applicant is rejected because of information contained in the report, the applicant can request the name of the reporting agency and contact it directly.

CLUE Reports

CLUE stands for the Comprehensive Loss Underwriting Exchange, which was formed by the insurance industry to better control its losses. CLUE established a national database on claims and inquiries. Almost all large insurance companies and most of the smaller ones are members. Every time an insurance agent is contacted about a claim or any inquiry, it is noted on the Exchange.

Buyers with two or more inquiries or claims during the prior three years may not be insurable at all or might not be insurable with a major insurance company. This means that buyers would have to obtain higher-premium coverage from a smaller company.

An **inquiry** is any call to the insurance agent about an actual or potential loss that would be covered by a homeowner's policy. This also applies to the property being purchased. If the sellers have filed two or more claims or made two or more inquiries, the major insurance companies may not be willing to insure the property. The buyers will be forced to turn to the smaller insurance company and to pay a higher premium.

Only the seller's insurance agent can obtain a CLUE report. Real estate agents should make sure that the CLUE report is obtained during the inspection period so that the buyer's insurance company can determine if the property being purchased is insurable at a premium acceptable to the buyer.

7.3 HOME WARRANTY

As protection against the cost of repairs, the home seller or buyer frequently purchases a **home warranty contract** after the close of escrow. Items usually covered in a home warranty contract include the following:

- Plumbing
- Plumbing stoppages
- Water heaters
- Ductwork
- Electrical
- Kitchen appliances
- Attic and exhaust fans
- Ceiling fans
- Central air-conditioning

Optional coverage is also generally available for the following:

- Pool and spa equipment
- Clothes washer and dryer
- Kitchen refrigerator
- Well pump
- Limited roof leak coverage
- Septic tank pumping

Most contracts cover the cost of repairs to the items covered if the item was in good safe working order at the start of coverage. The contracts also generally provide coverage for unknown defects if the defect or malfunction would not have been detectable to the buyer, seller, or agent through visual inspection or a simple mechanical test.

7.4 HOME CONSTRUCTION

There are many different styles, materials, and finishes used in residential home construction. A basic understanding of construction is vital for those involved in real estate sales. Different methods of construction are used in the eastern and northern United States with their colder climates, as opposed to the South's dampness and the Southwest desert's extreme heat. **Wood frame construction** is the most frequently used in building single-family houses. Because of its cost, block construction is no longer the standard material used in Nevada. Wood frame is less expensive, is easier to heat and cool, and offers a variety of architectural styles.

House Styles

A ranch-style house is far less costly to construct than a "U" or "H" shaped building. While all three styles have the same livable square feet, the "U" and "H" shape could be more costly to construct, heat, and cool due to the greater amount of outside surface. However, the "U" and "H" house shapes do offer more possibilities for interesting architectural designs.

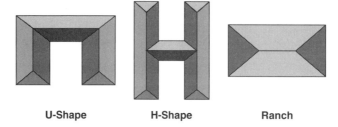

U-Shape   H-Shape   Ranch

Some basic house styles are the ranch, Cape Cod, split-level, and two-story. A split-level house has 1.5 stories with limited attic and basement space. A two-story house has the same living space on both levels. A two-story house can be more economical because the plumbing on each floor can be lined up, and because heat rises, it is easier to heat. A split-level house has a basement a half level below ground level and a second story a half level above ground level. This style allows a larger home to be built in a smaller amount of space.

Architectural styles vary depending on the area of the country. In Nevada, ranch, contemporary, Spanish, and territorial styles are more popular than English Tudor or Southern Colonial. Some styles are not really adaptable to smaller homes, such as a traditional French Provincial or Victorian. The variety of architectural styles is illustrated in Figure 7.1.

Construction Elements

Foundation

The **foundation** is the substructure for the superstructure itself (see Figure 7.2). The foundation includes the footings, foundation walls, columns, and pedestals. Most residences in Nevada are built on a concrete slab. In larger, more expensive homes, cold-air returns are placed in the ground before the slab is poured, offering good circulation.

Before a foundation is poured, the ground is treated for **termites**. Subterranean termites live in the ground and will enter the house through the slab if the ground is not chemically treated beforehand. Some builders treat the entire lot, and some treat only the area inside the footings.

Exterior Structure

Although many different finishes are used to cover the structure, the interior shell frame is the first step. The first step is to place a mudsill around the top of the foundation and then begin the frame, which consists of vertical studs placed at even intervals on top of the mudsill. Walls are most often constructed on the floor in sections, consisting of the mudsill, studding, and top plate, and then they are raised to the upright position and secured in place. Fire-stops, short two-by-fours, are placed horizontally between the studs to retard the spread of fire.

The **roof** consists of rafters, joists, the collar beam, and the ridge board, which gives rigidity and aligns the rafters.

The material used to cover the exterior walls depends on the finish of the house. Some stucco-finished houses use **sheathing** with tarpaper and chicken wire that holds the stucco finish. Sheathing is a 4-foot by 8-foot plywood or other wood exterior covering placed over exterior studding. Some less expensive houses use only tarpaper and chicken wire.

Stucco is one of the most common materials used because it is flexible and inexpensive. Other finishes include brick, stone, or composition board. Brick is usually only a veneer and does not give support, but it does make a durable and desirable finish. However, brick can be used in a double-brick wall or with block backup to form the actual support for the floors and roof, and is used this way in many commercial and industrial buildings and in older homes.

A wide variety of rooflines, such as hip, gable, and shed, are popular in the desert of southern Nevada. Roofing materials vary from the popular composition shingle to cedar shake and tile roof (see Figure 7.3).

Clay mission tile and other forms of tile are popular in the Southwest because they are durable, and the curved design provides good insulation due to the layer of air inside the curved portion.

FIGURE 7.1   Architectural Styles of Homes

New England Colonial
A box-shaped two-story house with a center entrance, wood siding, and shutters.

Georgian Colonial
A brick two-story house with a center entrance and a hip roof.

Southern Colonial
A two-story house with pillars and shutters.

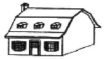

Dutch Colonial
A two-story house with a gambrel roof.

California Bungalow
A small one-story house with a low-pitched roof.

California Ranch
A one-story house with a low-pitched roof and a sprawling floor plan.

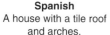

Spanish
A house with a tile roof and arches.

Cape Cod
A house with a second story above the eaves, a high-pitched roof, wood siding, and a large chimney.

French Provincial
A formal house with a high-pitched slate hip roof, a stone or brick exterior, and shutters.

FIGURE 7.1   *(continued)*

Victorian
A house with
ornate gables.

English Elizabethan
A house with a high-
pitched slate roof,
rough half-timbers,
and a plaster exterior.

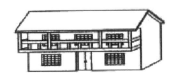

Monterey
A two-story
house with a
front balcony.

French Norman
A house with a tower
as the main entrance
and a steep roof.

English Tudor
A house with a high-pitched
slate roof, a cathedral-
like entrance, and a
masonry exterior.

Mediterranean or Italian
A house with a tile roof,
a stucco exterior, and
rounded decorative work
above the windows.

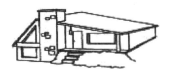

Contemporary
A house of
modern design.

Insulation

No matter what the homeowner is trying to keep in or out, **insulation** is important. Insulation in the walls and ceiling is all rated by the **R-value**. According to the National Association of Homebuilders, a thickness of 4 inches of blanket fiberglass or rock wool is classified as R11 and is equal to 9 inches of lumber or 4 feet of block in its ability to resist heat transfer. Rating on ceilings should be R19, and floors and walls should be R11. The Federal Housing Administration (FHA) and the Department of Veterans' Affairs (DVA) require 6 inches in the ceiling and 3.5 inches in the walls of newly constructed houses.

Insulation materials include fiberglass, rock wool, batts or blown wool, cellulose, poured vermiculite, Celotex or insulating boards, and Styrofoam.

FIGURE 7.2   Construction Elements

CONSTRUCTION DETAILS

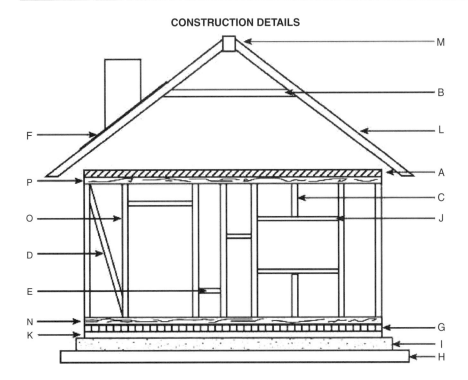

A   CEILING JOIST. Horizontal beams supporting ceiling
B   COLLAR BEAM. A beam that connects opposite rafters above the floor
C   CRIPPLES. Short vertical piece 2 × 4 above or below an opening
D   DIAGONAL BRACE. A brace across corner of structure to prevent
    swaying
E   FIRE STOP. Short board or wall between studs to prevent fire spreading
F   FLASHING. Metal sheet usually around chimney to prevent water
    seepage
G   FLOOR JOIST. Horizontal beams supporting floor
H   FOOTING. Base or bottom of a foundation wall
I   FOUNDATION. The supporting portion of structure resting on footing
J   LINTEL. A horizontal board over a door or window, also called header
K   MUDSILL. Perimeter board anchored directly to foundation
L   RAFTERS. Boards designed to support roof loads
M   RIDGE BOARD. Highest board in the house supporting upper ends
N   SOLE PLATE. Usually 2 × 4 on which wall and studs rest
O   STUDS. Vertical boards 2 × 4 supporting the walls every 16″ (on center)
P   TOP PLATE. A horizontal board fastened to upper end of studs

Other Construction Terms
    Board Foot = used to measure lumber, contains 144 cubic inches
    R–VALUE = ranking of insulation materials
    EER = Energy Efficiency Rating

Interior Walls and Ceilings

Drywall, Sheetrock, plasterboard, and gypsum board are the materials most commonly used to replace lath and plaster to finish ceilings and walls. Sheetrock is nailed over the studs after the insulation has been installed. The seams are butted, mudded, taped, and troweled or sprayed to give the effect of plaster. Ceilings are sometimes sprayed with an acoustical material to absorb sound. Although higher ceilings have become popular, the standard ceiling height is still considered eight feet.

FIGURE 7.3   Roof Styles

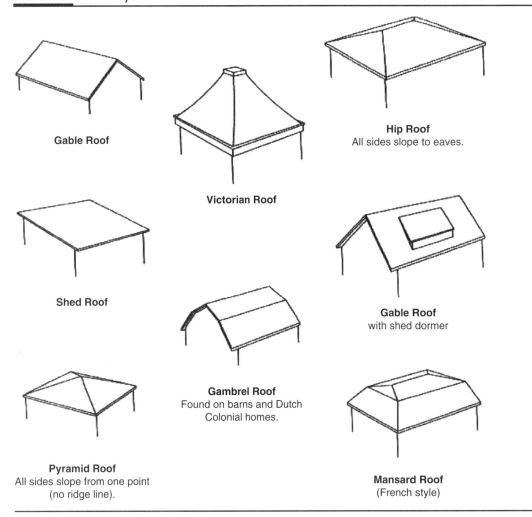

Gable Roof

Victorian Roof

Hip Roof
All sides slope to eaves.

Shed Roof

Gambrel Roof
Found on barns and Dutch
Colonial homes.

Gable Roof
with shed dormer

Pyramid Roof
All sides slope from one point
(no ridge line).

Mansard Roof
(French style)

Heating and Air-Conditioning

Central warm-air heating is found in most houses built today. The system consists of warm air forced through ducts in the ceilings and returned by ducts that intake and recirculate the air. The heating capacity of a furnace is measured in BTUs (British Thermal Units) per hour. A BTU is enough heat to raise one pound of water one degree Fahrenheit. The size of the unit required is determined by calculating the cubic feet to be warmed and taking into account the quality of construction, insulation, windows, and doors.

Air-conditioning units are rated either by BTUs per hour or by tons. A ton of air-conditioning is equal to 12,000 BTUs per hour, which is equivalent to the amount of cooling you would get from melting 1 ton of ice in 24 hours. Like heating units, the size of a unit will depend upon the total cubic feet to be cooled, the quality of construction, and the window placement in relation to the movement of the sun. A rule-of-thumb figure would be about 3200 cubic feet for each ton of equipment for a residence.

Heat Pump

The heat pump is a popular and effective system that uses a natural furnace for heating and may replace an air-conditioning unit. The heat pump is basically a refrigeration unit that reverses the flow of refrigerant so that it can heat as well as cool. It uses electrical energy to move heat from a cooler to a warmer location. This is much more economical than converting electrical energy to heat, which is expensive but cleaner than gas or oil furnaces.

Windows and Doors

Houses in Nevada most often have sliding windows. Other types available are casement or pivot, which swing or crank out, and double hung, with moveable sashes that raise or lower vertically. A sliding window usually has a frame made of aluminum and is the least expensive. Window glass varies in thickness and quality. The quality can be judged by its clarity of view.

Exterior doors are usually of metal or solid wood 1¾″ thick. Interior doors are usually 1⅜″ thick. Flush exterior doors can be hollow-core doors, that is, a wood frame with a wood or molded composition veneer forming a flush or panel door.

Interior Layout

Most houses have separate zones or areas for living, sleeping, and working. The work or kitchen area should be convenient to the dining, storage, and parking areas for easy delivery of groceries and meals. A well-designed kitchen has adequate lighting and storage, and ample work surfaces.

The living area should be near the front door. Its placement should be away from the sleeping areas and closer to the dining room for more comfortable entertainment. If there is no family room, the living or great room should have the best views. The family room, a more active area, is usually away from the sleeping areas and closer to the kitchen for easier access and serving of meals.

The sleeping zone should be farthest away from active living areas and on the cool side of the house. Some popular designs feature a split bedroom plan, with the master bedroom on one side and the smaller bedrooms on the other, each with its own bath. As a general rule, one bath for each two adults and one for each three children is practical. If a house is more than one level, a toilet and lavatory should be on each level. Normally, a bath will require at least 35 square feet of space, but the recent trend is toward much larger bathrooms.

Storage Space

Because most houses in Nevada do not have a basement for storage, ample closet, garage, or other storage space is necessary. A utility area needs to have connections for a washer and dryer, whereas a storage area, usually at the end of a carport, does not. The garage should be placed on the south or west side of the house to absorb the sun and protect the living areas. It should also be close to the kitchen but not block out light to other rooms. A garage should be at least 23 feet deep.

Although you will not be tested on landscaping, a person selling real estate should have a good understanding of the types of grasses and trees grown in the different regions of Nevada, as well as a general knowledge of when flowers bloom and citrus ripens. A trip to the nursery will be a great help to you as you work in the world of selling real estate.

Contractor Requirements

In Nevada, all contractors who perform residential and commercial remodeling and construction must be licensed and bonded. However, this requirement does not apply to work costing less than $1000 (including material and labor) if no building permit is required, the work is not part of a larger project, and the work is not the type performed by a plumbing, electrical, refrigeration, heating, or air-conditioning contractor.

Contractors are licensed to protect the consumer. The Nevada State Contractors Board (NSCB) can order licensed contractors to correct defective work, but no similar recourse exists against unlicensed contractors, who fall outside the jurisdiction of the NSCB.

Contractor's Responsibility

A contractor's responsibility may come in different forms and apply for varying lengths of time. Quality builders typically provide a one-year warranty on a new home and its components and remain responsible for any structural defects. Any defects found in appliances and plumbing and electrical fixtures that were properly installed by the contractor are usually limited to the manufacturer's warranty.

The effective date for the start of coverage generally begins when the buyer occupies the structure or the date of discovery, whichever occurs first. The NSCB has jurisdiction over a contractor's workmanship.

CHAPTER SUMMARY

In the United States, the percentage of people who own homes continues to increase because of government policies that encourage ownership and because of the significant benefits of home ownership, including establishing financial stability, fulfilling a deep longing for ownership, and tax benefits. However, there are benefits to renting as well, including mobility and freedom from management and maintenance.

Some common types of property insurance include dwelling insurance, homeowners' insurance, commercial property insurance, and federal flood insurance. Dwelling insurance is for residential properties, and a standard policy covers losses from fire, lightning, and internal explosion. Homeowners' insurance policies are multiline policies, which means that they combine property and casualty coverage in the same policy. The package policy provides the same property coverage that is available in a dwelling insurance policy and also includes theft insurance and personal liability coverage. The basic causes of loss that are covered by a commercial property policy are listed in the text. Federal flood insurance, a federally subsidized program, is mandatory on floodplain properties with mortgages that the federal government finances, insures, or guarantees. A broker is responsible for informing the buyer of the flood insurance requirement when negotiating the sale.

Insurance underwriting is used by insurance companies to ascertain the types of risks they will accept through the issuance of an insurance policy. Two reports that an insurance underwriter uses to evaluate risks are credit reports and CLUE reports.

The home seller or buyer, as protection against the cost of repairs, frequently purchases a home warranty contract after the close of escrow. Most contracts cover the cost of repairs to the items covered if the item was in good, safe, working order at the start of coverage. The contracts also generally provide coverage for unknown defects if the defect or malfunction would not have been detectable to the buyer, seller, or agent through visual inspection or a simple mechanical test.

Many different styles, materials, and finishes are used in residential home construction. Some basic house styles are the ranch, Cape Cod, split-level, and two-story. In Nevada, ranch, contemporary, Spanish, and territorial styles are more popular than English Tudor or Southern Colonial. The foundation is the substructure for the superstructure itself. The foundation includes the footings, foundation walls, columns, and pedestals. Most residences in Nevada are built on a concrete slab. Wood frame construction, which is less expensive, is easier to heat and cool, and offers a variety of architectural styles, is the most frequently used in building single-family houses. Stucco is one of the most common materials used to cover the exterior walls because it is flexible and inexpensive.

The R-value rates all insulation in the walls and ceiling. Insulation materials include fiberglass, rock wool, batts or blown wool, cellulose, poured vermiculite, Celotex or insulating boards, and Styrofoam. Drywall, Sheetrock, plasterboard, and gypsum board are the materials most commonly used to replace lath and plaster to finish ceilings and interior walls.

Central warm-air heating is found in most houses built today. The system consists of warm air forced through ducts in the ceilings and returned by ducts that intake and recirculate the air. The power of the furnace is measured in BTUs (British Thermal Units). Air-conditioning units are rated either by BTUs or by tons. Like heating units, the size of an air-conditioning unit will depend upon the total cubic feet to be cooled.

In Nevada, all contractors who perform residential and commercial remodeling and construction must be licensed and bonded. This requirement does not apply to work costing less than $1000.

Quality builders typically provide a one-year warranty on a new home and its components, and remain responsible for any structural defects. Any defects found in appliances and plumbing and electrical fixtures that were properly installed by the contractor are usually limited to the manufacturer's warranty. The effective date for the start of coverage generally begins when the buyer occupies the structure or the date of discovery, whichever occurs first.

CHECKING YOUR COMPREHENSION

1. List the advantages and disadvantages of home ownership.

2. Summarize the types of property insurance coverage.

3. Describe the purpose and importance of the CLUE report.

4. Explain the purpose of the federal flood insurance program and a real estate agent's responsibilities.

5. Summarize a contractor's licensing requirements and warranty obligations.

REVIEWING YOUR UNDERSTANDING

1. All of the following are benefits of home ownership, **EXCEPT**:
   a. creative opportunities
   b. mobility
   c. tax benefits
   d. independence

2. A dwelling insurance policy covers losses from all of the following risks, **EXCEPT**:
   a. fire
   b. internal explosion
   c. lightning
   d. theft

3. Terminology such as ranch, contemporary, Spanish, adobe, or Santa Fe, all refer to:
   a. roof lines
   b. siding materials
   c. architectural design
   d. foundation materials

4. A coinsurance clause:
   a. requires reinsurance
   b. requires coverage of a certain percentage of the property's market value
   c. eliminates the need to monitor the adequacy of insurance coverage
   d. is generally included in a homeowners' policy

5. A roof with four sides sloping to eaves is called a:
   a. hip
   b. mansard
   c. gable
   d. gambrel

6. Federal flood insurance covers all of the following, **EXCEPT**:
   a. run-off of surface waters
   b. flooding caused by plumbing failure
   c. mudslides
   d. erosion caused by floods

7. Who is the party responsible for informing a buyer that a property requires flood insurance because it is located in a floodplain?
   a. broker
   b. insurance agent
   c. the buyer has sole responsibility
   d. escrow officer

8. The lowest structural horizontal member of a frame house, resting on top of the foundation is a:
   a. lintel
   b. stud
   c. joist
   d. mudsill

9. A home warranty contract generally covers the cost of all of the following repairs, **EXCEPT**:
   a. kitchen appliances
   b. central air-conditioning
   c. exhaust fans not working at the start of coverage
   d. an unknown defect that was not detectable to the buyer, seller, or agent through visual inspection or a simple mechanical test

10. A CLUE report:
    a. provides a buyer with indications of structural defects
    b. provides investigative data on the condition of title
    c. has no relevance to a real estate transaction
    d. can affect the cost or availability of property insurance coverage

11. The deduction a homeowner has for tax purposes is:
    a. interest expense
    b. insurance cost
    c. depreciation
    d. maintenance expense

12. In frame construction, what is the 4′ × 8′ exterior covering called?
    a. stucco
    b. sheathing
    c. lath
    d. monolithic slab

13. The uprights used in construction, to which drywall is affixed, are called:
    a. joists
    b. studs
    c. beams
    d. headers

14. Home casualty insurance does **NOT** normally cover:
    a. flood damage
    b. vandalism
    c. smoke damage
    d. theft

15. Disadvantages of renting a dwelling include all of the following, **EXCEPT**:
    a. lack of tax benefits
    b. lack of obligations for maintenance and property management
    c. lack of equity growth
    d. lack of credit rating improvements

16. A commercial building with a market value of $100,000 has an insurance policy with an 80% coinsurance clause. The owner carried $60,000 of insurance and sustained a covered loss of $30,000. What amount of the loss would be covered by the insurance company?
    a. $60,000
    b. $40,000
    c. $30,000
    d. $22,500

17. Buyers with the following number of inquiries in the prior three years might not be insurable with a major insurance company:
    a. one
    b. two
    c. three
    d. four

18. A CLUE report can be obtained by the:
    a. listing broker
    b. seller
    c. seller's insurance agent
    d. buyer

19. Contractors who perform residential and commercial remodeling and construction must be licensed unless there is no building permit required and the work costs less than:
    a. $1000
    b. $750
    c. $500
    d. $250

20. New home builders generally remain responsible for structural defects for:
    a. two years
    b. 18 months
    c. one year
    d. six months

Chapter

8

IMPORTANT TERMS AND CONCEPTS

community property

community property
with rights of survi-
vorship (CPWROS)

concurrent ownership
or co-ownership

conventional life estates

curtesy

declaration of
homestead

defeasible

dower

estate

estate in remainder

estate in reversion

estate pur autre vie

fee simple conditional

fee simple determinable

fee simple estate

fee simple on condition
subsequent

freehold estate

homestead exemption

indefeasible fee

joint tenancy

leasehold estate

legal life estate

leagal list estate

life tenant

partition action

qualified fee estate

remainderman

severalty

straw person

tenancy by the entirety

tenants in common

CHAPTER OBJECTIVES

After completing this chapter, you should be able to:

- List and describe freehold estates, including fee estates and life estates.
- Summarize and explain the Nevada homestead exemption.
- List and explain how property can be held, including sole ownership and the forms of concurrent ownership.

Freehold Estates and How Property Is Held

8.1 ESTATES IN LAND

According to *Webster's Dictionary*, an **estate** is "the degree, quantity, nature, and extent of one's interest in land or other property." In other words, an estate equals all of one's possessions.

Because this text primarily emphasizes realty, *estate* in this section refers to the types and classifications of real property estates. There are two general classifications of estates: *freehold* and *leasehold*.

A **freehold estate** is a real property ownership estate of uncertain duration. A **leasehold estate** is an estate that is less than freehold and lasts for a certain duration of time (see Chapter 10). The following table compares the main attributes of freehold and leasehold estates.

Characteristics of Freehold Estates	Characteristics of Leasehold Estates
Actual ownership of the land	Possession of the land, but no ownership
Unpredictable duration	Definite duration
Legal matters tried under real property laws	Legal matters tried under personal property laws

8.2 FREEHOLD ESTATES

The rest of this section will be devoted to freehold estates. There are two kinds of freehold estates: *fee estates* and *life estates* (see Figure 8.1).

Fee Estates

A **fee simple estate** is also known as *fee*, or *fee simple absolute*. A fee simple estate gives the owner the greatest interest possible and is of indefinite duration. Therefore, it is fully transferable and can be sold, leased, exchanged, or given away. A fee simple estate is also inheritable through a will or by the laws of descent. Generally, when people speak of owning property, they are referring to a fee simple estate.

FIGURE 8.1   Freehold Estates

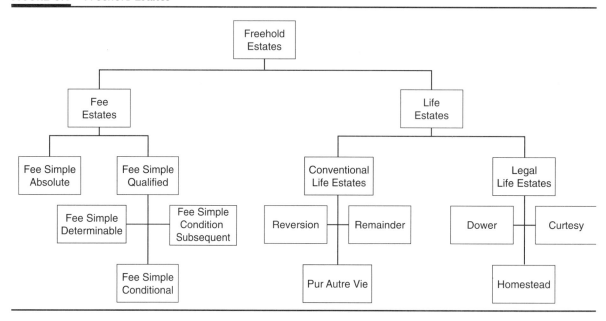

A fee simple estate is also known as an **indefeasible fee**, meaning that it cannot be annulled, forfeited, or terminated without the action of the owner, as long as the owner is not interfering with the rights of others or of the government.

Qualified Fee Estates

There are three types of qualified fees:

1. Fee simple determinable
2. Fee simple on condition subsequent
3. Fee simple conditional

Qualified fees are said to be **defeasible**, which means they can be terminated if certain conditions are met or not met.

Fee simple determinable is subject to a certain restriction that is included in the deed. For example, a fee simple determinable estate could be granted to a church with the words, "as long as it is used as a church." The limiting language (for example, "for so long as," "while," or "during the period") speaks in terms of duration. In other words, the estate is vested in the grantee until such time as the restriction is not observed. In the previous example, in the event the building and land are no longer used as a church, the property will automatically revert to the grantor or the grantor's heirs without any action on their part. The grantor of a fee simple determinable retains a possibility of reverter, meaning a right to retake possession of the land.

Fee simple on condition subsequent places conditions on the grantee. For example, a fee simple on condition subsequent estate could grant property to a person with the words, "provided that you do not smoke on the property." The limiting language (for example, "provided that," "on the condition that," or "if") speaks in terms of an event or a specific condition. In this example, if the condition is violated, the grantor or his or her heirs have a right to regain ownership. However, the property does not revert to the grantor (or heirs) automatically. To get the property back, the grantor must take action, which may include court action. The grantor of a fee simple on condition subsequent retains a possibility of reverter and right of reentry (that is, a right to reenter upon the land and retake possession).

In both fee simple determinable and fee simple on condition subsequent instances, the grantor retains a possibility of reverter, which means that title to the property may, at some future date, revert to the grantor. For fee simple determinable, title will revert to the grantor automatically; for a fee simple on condition subsequent, the grantor (or grantor's successor) must physically retake possession of the property within a reasonable time after the condition subsequent has been violated. Physically retaking possession may require legal action.

To decide whether the fee ownership is fee simple determinable or fee simple on condition subsequent, use these guidelines:

- Usually fee simple determinable states a use limitation, which is usually stated in a positive manner, for example, "as long as used as a school."
- A fee simple on condition subsequent is usually stated in a negative manner, and is frequently a personal condition, for example, "as long as you do not drink alcohol or use drugs."

Fee simple conditional, also known as *fee tail*, is a fee simple with a restriction to the right of inheritance, such as limiting the right of inheritance to a fixed line of succession, such as "to the first-born son in each generation." Fee simple conditional is not legal in Nevada.

Life Estates

Life estates are divided into two classifications: *conventional life estates* and *legal life estates.*

Conventional Life Estates

Conventional life estates are not inheritable. A conventional life estate is a fee simple estate granted for the life of an individual. The estate is terminated upon the individual's death. A property owner uses a deed that names the life tenant and specifies who will receive the property at the death of the life tenant.

The person or organization that is to receive the property after the death of the life tenant has a future interest in the property. There are three variations of life tenancies, each with a difference in the future interest. They are known as:

Estate in reversion. The grantor specifies by reservation in the deed that the property will be returned to the grantor or his or her heirs at the time of the life tenant's death. In Figure 8.2, A deeds a life estate to B for B's life with the provision that when B dies the title reverts to A. B holds a life estate; A holds the estate in reversion.

Estate in remainder. The grantor states in the deed that upon the death of the life tenant, the property will go to a third person. The third person with

FIGURE 8.2 Estate in Reversion

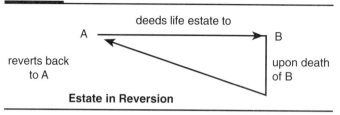

the remainder interest is known as the **remainderman**. In Figure 8.3, A deeds a life estate to B for the life of B. When B dies, the property passes to C. B holds the life estate; C holds the estate in remainder.

Estate pur autre vie (taken from French, meaning "for the life of another"). In this case, the grantor names a life tenant, but the estate is based on the life of a person other than the life tenant. At the death of the third person, the estate reverts to either the grantor or to a remainderman, whomever the grantor has specified in the deed. An estate pur autre vie can be willed by the life tenant, but the estate is still limited by the life of the third person.

For as long as he or she lives, a **life tenant** has all the privileges of ownership. A life tenant can use the property or receive any income from the property. A life tenant can also mortgage, sell, or lease the property; however, because the estate is valid only for the life tenant's lifetime, it would be difficult to find an interested buyer or tenant. A lender might be willing to make a loan on the property, provided that a life insurance policy in the amount of the loan was issued, with the lender named as the beneficiary.

A life tenant must keep the property in repair, plus pay the taxes and assessments. The life tenant must not commit waste—that is, the property must be maintained and kept in good condition so that the property value will not decrease.

Legal Life Estates

State law creates three **legal life estates**: *dower*, *curtesy*, and *homestead*. Dower and curtesy have been enacted as law in 11 states, with a homestead law in effect in 43 states. In Nevada, homestead is the only legal life estate. Dower and curtesy are not necessary in Nevada because of the state's community property laws.

FIGURE 8.3 Estate in Remainder

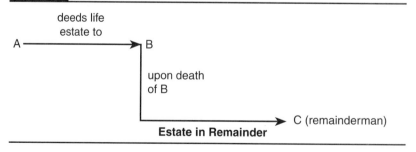

Dower rights come from old English law, wherein any property bought during marriage belongs to the husband, but husband and wife share the use of the property. The wife is said to have *inchoate* (incomplete) rights in the property until the death of her husband. At her husband's death, she has a life tenant's estate.

Curtesy rights are just the reverse of dower rights. Curtesy gives the husband rights to his wife's freehold estate upon her death, in the form of a life estate, provided she owned an estate of inheritance during marriage, and that she also gave birth to children who could inherit the life estate at the death of her spouse. Curtesy rights are also inchoate rights, which do not take effect until the death of the wife.

Homestead means that a person's primary residence or homestead is exempt from attachment, execution, and forced sale from creditors. We will review the homestead exemption in more detail in the next section.

8.3 HOMESTEAD EXEMPTION

Homestead is the only legal life estate in Nevada created by statute. What the homestead law really means is that a person's primary residence or homestead is exempt from attachment, execution, and forced sale from creditors. The equity in an owner's primary residence is protected up to $550,000.

The **homestead exemption** law exempts the homestead of any person 18 years of age or over, married or single, who resides in the state and is the head of the household. The law protects the principal residence, such as a single-family house, a condominium or townhouse, a mobile home in a park, or a mobile home on one's own land. In the latter case, both are protected, the mobile home and the land. The exemption attaches to the homestead property when the owner has recorded a proper **declaration of homestead**.

A married couple or a single person may protect only one homestead. If the home where they both lived as a married couple is claimed as a homestead after they are divorced, the total exemption could not exceed $550,000. If a homestead is claimed before the time of a voluntary or involuntary sale of the property, the cash proceeds from the sale are protected by the homestead law for 18 months or until a new homestead is acquired, whichever is sooner.

Under Nevada homestead law, a married couple may claim the homestead, but both spouses must claim the homestead in community or joint property. If a claimant is married, the homestead exemption may protect community or joint property, or it may protect sole and separate property.

The homestead exemption protects the primary residence from process and from sale under judgment or lien, except for the following:

1. A consensual lien, including a mortgage or trust deed.
2. A mechanic's lien for labor or material.
3. A judgment or other lien exceeding $550,000 that may be satisfied from the equity of the debtor.

Homestead Exemption Removal

A homestead may be removed from the property in a number of ways, including a sale or transfer by deed, moving out of Nevada, or abandonment.

8.4 HOW PROPERTY IS HELD

One or more persons may hold property. When one person holds property, it is held in severalty. When two or more persons hold property, the tenancy is called concurrent ownership, also known as co-ownership. Remember, tenancy means the estate of a tenant, whether in-fee, for life, for years, at will, or otherwise.

Severalty

Severalty is taking title as sole owner, either as a natural person or a legal person. A *natural person* means an individual person, whereas a *legal person* means a legal entity, such as a corporation, an association, or an organization.

All government-owned property, such as streets, buildings, and parks, is owned in severalty. It is owned by the government entity that has jurisdiction over it, such as municipal, county, state, or federal government.

Concurrent Ownership

Concurrent ownership, or **co-ownership**, is a form of ownership in which two or more persons have an undivided interest in the same land. For example, a number of people could each own a fraction of land but share with others a single right of possession.

A number of legal problems can arise from ownership that is too complex. Some of the forms of ownership that were derived from common law are now being replaced with partnerships, corporations, or trusts.

8.5 FORMS OF CONCURRENT OWNERSHIP

There are five basic forms of concurrent ownership:

1. Tenants in common
2. Joint tenancy
3. Community property
4. Community property with rights of survivorship
5. Tenancy by the entirety

Tenants in Common

Tenants in common is probably the most widely used form of ownership between multiple parties. In Nevada, if two single people do not address how they choose to take title, they will automatically become tenants in common. In this form of ownership, each owner or part owner has an undivided interest and rights of possession of the entire parcel. These undivided rights exist even though there may be unequal shares.

For example, if five people owned an acre of ground and one person paid for half of the land and the other four paid for the other half, they still have equal rights of possession. Each person will receive a deed—one for an undivided half-interest and the others each with an undivided $\frac{1}{8}$-interest. Each person has the right to sell, encumber, or will his or her interest in the land. If one of the five owners died, his or her share of the ownership would pass by will or by descent, and the rest of the owners' rights would not be affected.

At times, co-ownership creates problems that cannot be resolved by agreement of the owners. In that situation, it is possible to appeal to the courts to divide the ownership. This is referred to as a **partition action**, which means "to divide."

Joint Tenancy

Joint tenancy is also called *joint tenancy with the right of survivorship (JTWRS)*. In this type of ownership, in the case of death, the survivor automatically acquires ownership of the property. If there are ten owners and one dies, nine owners now share that interest.

There are four common-law unities that must be present to create JTWRS:

1. *Possession*—Equal rights for all.
2. *Interest*—Each has equal percentage of ownership.
3. *Title*—There is only one deed; all owners take title under one deed.
4. *Time*—It must be created at the same time.

These four common-law unities are often referred to as "P.I.T.T."

The distinguishing characteristic of joint tenancy is the right of survivorship, which makes the ownership interest not inheritable. Ownership interest cannot be willed because it ceases with death. This type of ownership is sometimes referred to as a "poor man's will" because taking title as JTWRS eliminates the need to probate. The filing of an estate tax waiver and a copy of the death certificate will suffice.

Deeds to JTWRS must be signed by all grantees to acknowledge that they are in fact creating a tenancy that allows their interest to pass to the survivor.

A joint tenant can sell his or her interest or deed it away without the consent of the other owner or owners. This action breaks the tenancy and establishes a new tenancy depending on the number of owners.

If three people bought a building and took title as JTWRS and one sold his or her interest, the two remaining would still have JTWRS along with the new owner as tenants in common. Because one of the unities (time) is missing, the new owner cannot have a JTWRS. It could be created again by deeding the property to a straw person who would then deed it back on one deed at one time. A **straw person** is an individual or entity, such as an escrow company, that briefly holds title to the real estate and then transfers the interest at one time to the owners that now include the new owner. This allows the unity of time to be met and, therefore, the old joint tenant owners and the new owner can hold the property together as joint tenants.

If owners who hold title as JTWRS sell a property and carry back the equity in the form of a note and trust deed, unless it states in the note and trust deed that they wish to hold title to the paper as JTWRS, it will become either community property, if they are married, or tenants in common, if they are not.

Community Property

Nevada is one of eight states that have enacted **community property** laws. The other states are Arizona, Washington, Idaho, California, New Mexico, Texas, and Louisiana. The origin of community property is in Spanish law and is used in the western United States because of the 1848 treaty signed at Guadalupe Hidalgo. The Spanish law is based on the theory that in marriage the husband and wife are equals, rather than marriage being a combination of the husband and wife into one entity.

Each spouse has ownership of half of the marital property (both real and personal), including wages acquired subsequent to marriage. Because of this law, neither dower nor curtesy rights are recognized in Nevada. For married couples in Nevada, title is automatically taken as community property, unless specifically stated otherwise in the deed.

All community property is used and liable for the debts of either spouse, no matter who created the debts. Each spouse is also liable for the separate debts of a spouse up to his or her share of the community property. Both spouses have equal authority to manage, control, or dispose of all community property. Except for real property, each spouse can create debt, but the total assets of the marital community can be claimed for payment of the debt.

Each spouse is free to will his or her half of the community estate. Upon the death of one of the spouses, one half of the property belongs to the survivor. If there is no will and no children of that marriage, the other half goes to the survivor. If there are heirs and no will, the property will pass by the laws of intestate succession descent. Intestate succession means that the decedent did not have a will. The laws of intestate succession, which will be covered in Chapter 11, are the statutes that identify which heirs of the decedent are to inherit the estate when there is no will.

In community property ownership, one spouse can purchase property without the consent of the other. However, one spouse may not sell, encumber, or convey property without the consent of the other spouse. An easy way to remember this is, "It takes one to buy and two to sell." Both spouses' signatures are required to convey. This is an important aspect for the prospective licensee, because it affects many of the documents involving the selling of real estate.

Separate property brought into the marriage by one of the spouses remains that spouse's separate property. Separate property items, real or personal, stocks, bonds, money, and automobiles should not be commingled with the community property. Money and real property inherited or received as a gift after the marriage remain the separate property of the devisee. One must be careful to keep separate accounts of separate property so that it does not become part of the community property.

Community Property with Rights of Survivorship

Community property with rights of survivorship (CPWROS) was created by the Nevada legislature. Its objective is to allow a married couple to receive benefits under the federal tax code for community property while avoiding probate. A husband and wife may take title to property as CPWROS when the deed expressly states the right of survivorship is desired. The four common-law unities (possession, interest, title, and time) required to create a joint tenancy are not

FIGURE 8.4   Basics of Co-Ownership

	Tenancy in Common	Joint Tenancy	Community Property
Who Can Hold Title?	Any two or more, including married couples	Any two or more, including married couples	Husband and wife only
Ownership Interest	Can be any percent, equal or not	All shares must be equal	Equal shares
Upon Death	Probate usually required	No probate, right of survivorship, no will allowed	Right to will; intestate goes to surviving spouse; optional right of survivorship
Disposition of Title	Convey interest without others' permission	Convey interest without others' permission	Need both signatures to convey title

required when taking title as CPWROS. The legislature specifically states that the husband and wife may create community property with right of survivorship by either deeding to themselves or, when one of them already has title, deeding to him- or herself and the spouse. Straw party deeds are not necessary to create CPWROS. The statute also provides that either spouse may terminate the effect of the right of survivorship provision by recording an affidavit. Furthermore, divorce or annulment terminates the right of survivorship.

Tenancy by the Entirety

Tenancy by the entirety is a type of ownership existing only between husband and wife. This type of co-ownership is based upon the common law that regarded a husband and wife as a single legal person. One result was that if the spouses acquired equal interests in real estate by the same instrument, the property was considered owned as an indivisible legal unit. Upon the death of either, the survivor remained as the parcel's sole owner. Modern law has long accepted this result.

Today, a right of survivorship similar to that existing for the joint tenancy exists for the tenancy by the entirety. In a small estate, this right benefits the surviving spouse because it avoids probate proceedings. A tenancy by the entirety cannot be terminated without the consent of the other party. Tenancy by the entirety does not exist in Nevada because of our community property laws.

The forms of co-ownership allowed by law in Nevada are summarized in Figure 8.4.

Salespeople Dispensing Legal Advice

A salesperson must be very careful not to advise any buyer on how he or she should take title to real property. Real estate salespeople are not licensed to practice law. Always recommend that buyers consult an attorney if they are concerned about which way to hold title. What is right for one could be wrong for someone else.

CHAPTER SUMMARY

There are two general classifications of estates: freehold and leasehold. A freehold estate is a real property ownership estate of uncertain duration. A leasehold estate is an estate that is less than freehold and lasts a certain duration of time.

There are two kinds of freehold estates: fee estates and life estates. A fee simple estate gives the owner the greatest interest possible and is of indefinite duration. It is fully transferable and can be sold, leased, exchanged, or given away. Qualified fees are defeasible. There are three types of qualified fees: fee simple determinable, fee simple on condition subsequent, and fee simple conditional. Fee simple determinable is subject to a certain restriction, which is included in the deed. Fee simple on condition subsequent places conditions on the grantee. Fee simple conditional has a restriction on the right of inheritance and is not legal in Nevada.

There are two kinds of life estates: conventional life estates and legal life estates. Conventional life estates are not inheritable. A conventional life estate is a fee simple estate granted for the life of an individual. The estate is terminated upon the individual's death. A property owner uses a deed that names the life tenant and specifies who will receive the property at the death of the life tenant. There are three variations of life tenancies, each with a difference in the future interest: estate in reversion, estate in remainder, and estate pur autre vie. A life tenant has all the privileges of ownership for as long as he or she lives.

There are three legal life estates: dower, curtesy, and homestead. In Nevada, homestead is the only legal life estate. Dower and curtesy are not necessary because of Nevada's community property laws. With dower rights, any property bought during marriage belongs to the husband. When any property bought during marriage belongs to the wife, it is known as curtesy rights. Homestead means that a person's primary residence or homestead is exempt from attachment, execution, and forced sale from creditors. In reality, the equity (not the property itself) in an owner's primary residence is protected up to $550,000.

The homestead exemption law exempts the homestead of any person 18 years or older who resides in the state and is the head of the household. The law protects the principal residence. A married couple or a single person may protect only one homestead. A married couple may claim the homestead, but both spouses must claim the homestead in community or joint property. If a claimant is married, the homestead exemption may protect community or joint property, or it may protect sole and separate property. A homestead may be removed from the property in a number of ways, including a sale or transfer by deed, or moving out of Nevada.

One or more persons may hold property. When one person holds property, it is held in severalty. When two or more persons hold property, the tenancy is called concurrent ownership. Severalty is taking title as sole owner, either as a natural person or a legal person. All government-owned property, such as streets, buildings, and parks, is owned in severalty. Concurrent ownership, or co-ownership, is a form of ownership in which two or more persons have an undivided interest in the same land. There are five basic forms of concurrent ownership: tenants in common, joint tenancy, community property, community property with rights of survivorship, and tenancy by the entirety. Tenants in common is a widely used form of ownership between multiple parties. In this form of ownership, each owner or part owner has an undivided interest and rights of possession of the entire parcel. These undivided rights exist even though there may be unequal shares.

In joint tenancy, in the case of death, the survivor automatically acquires ownership of the property. There are four common-law unities that must be present to create JTWRS: possession, interest, title, and time (P.I.T.T.). The distinguishing characteristic of joint tenancy is the right of survivorship, which makes the ownership interest not inheritable. A joint tenant can sell his or her interest or deed it away without the consent of the other owner or owners. This action breaks the tenancy and establishes a new tenancy depending on the number of owners. Joint tenancy can be created again by deeding the property to a straw person. A straw person is an individual or entity that briefly holds title to the real estate and then transfers the interest at one time to the group of owners that now includes the new owner.

Nevada is one of eight states that has enacted community property laws. In community property, each spouse has ownership of half of the marital property (both real and personal), including wages acquired subsequent to marriage. For married couples in Nevada, title is automatically taken as community property. Each spouse is free to will his or her half of the community estate. Upon the death of one of the spouses, one half of the property belongs to the survivor. If there is no will and no children of that marriage, the other half goes to the survivor. If there are heirs and no will, the property will pass by the laws of intestate succession descent.

Community property with rights of survivorship allows a married couple to receive benefits under the federal tax code for community property while avoiding probate. The four common-law unities (P.I.T.T.) required to create a joint tenancy are not required when taking title as CPWROS. Either spouse may terminate the effect of right of survivorship provision by recording an affidavit. Divorce or annulment terminates the right of survivorship.

Tenancy by the entirety is a type of ownership existing only between husband and wife. Tenancy by the entirety does not exist in Nevada because of the community property laws.

CHECKING YOUR COMPREHENSION

1. Define a freehold estate and a leasehold estate.

2. Summarize the differences between a fee simple estate and a qualified fee estate.

3. List the three qualified fee estates and describe the attributes of each one.

4. Define each of the following:
   - Life tenant
   - Estate in reversion
   - Estate in remainder
   - Estate pur autre vie

5. List the three legal life estates and explain the purpose and amount of the Nevada homestead exemption.

6. Summarize and explain the five basic forms of concurrent ownership.

REVIEWING YOUR UNDERSTANDING

1. Which of the following is **NOT** a characteristic of a fee simple estate?
   a. it is of indefinite duration
   b. it is free of encumbrances
   c. it is transferable with or without consideration
   d. it is transferable by will or intestate succession

2. Which of the following is a freehold interest?
   a. life estate
   b. estate for years
   c. estate at will
   d. periodic tenancy

3. Alex gave a life estate to Ben based on the life of Chuck. If Ben dies, who is entitled to possession?
   a. Alex
   b. Alex's heirs
   c. Ben's heirs
   d. Chuck

4. The owner of a property with a fee simple on condition subsequent has:
   a. a remainder interest
   b. a defeasible estate
   c. less than a freehold interest
   d. an estate for years

5. If a husband and wife are the owners of real estate in joint tenancy, the kind of title or estate the wife would receive in the event of her husband's death is called a:
   a. life estate
   b. fee simple estate
   c. dower interest
   d. remainder estate

6. One tenant in common may **NOT**:
   a. use the property without paying co-tenants for the use
   b. place an easement over the property
   c. lease his or her interest without approval of other co-tenants
   d. sell his or her interest without approval of other co-tenants

7. Four brothers received title to a large tract of land from their grandfather, who gave each brother a one-fourth undivided interest with equal rights to possession of the land. All four received their title on their grandfather's seventieth birthday. The brothers **MOST** likely hold title in which of the following ways?
   a. in severalty
   b. as remaindermen
   c. tenants by the entirety
   d. joint tenants

8. Two persons own property as joint tenants. The husband has a son by a previous marriage and the wife has a daughter by a previous marriage. The wife dies, leaving the property to both the son and the daughter. Which of the following statements is true?
   a. the son and daughter each have half interest in the property
   b. the son, daughter, and husband each have a one-third interest in the property
   c. the husband is the sole owner of the property
   d. the daughter is the sole owner of the property

9. Ownership in severalty is ownership by:
   a. one person (or legal entity)
   b. two or more persons (or legal entities)
   c. several persons with differing interests
   d. all of the above

10. Which of the following is a correct statement in reference to a tenancy in common?
    a. each party's interest must be equal
    b. each party must have acquired interest at the same time
    c. any party may sell his interest without consent of the other parties
    d. parties may have unequal rights of possession

11. When the word *fee* is used in connection with ownership of real property, it refers to:
    a. commission
    b. a conveyance charge
    c. the price paid
    d. an estate of inheritance

12. A life estate holder purchased the interest of the remainderman. The life tenant now holds:
    a. a fee simple
    b. a life estate for two lives
    c. a tenancy in common
    d. two separate estates

13. Which of the following **CANNOT** be owned in fee simple?
    a. a condominium
    b. property owned as tenants in common
    c. property owned as a joint tenant
    d. leasehold rights

14. The ownership of a parcel of land as long as it is used as a church site is known as a:
    a. fee simple estate
    b. life estate
    c. determinable fee
    d. testamentary trust

15. Susan gives a life estate to Sally and upon the death of Sally the estate will go to Susan's grandchildren. The grandchildren's interest is:
    a. reversionary estate
    b. remainder estate
    c. fee conditional
    d. fee determinable

16. Title is conveyed to two persons who are **NOT** married, and no mention is made of how they are to take title. Ownership is presumed to be as:
    a. community property
    b. tenants in common
    c. joint tenants
    d. a tenancy in the entirety

17. Which of the following types of ownership requires unity of possession, interest, title, and time?
    a. cooperative
    b. tenancy in common
    c. joint tenancy
    d. community property

18. A method of ownership reserved only for husband and wife that does **NOT** exist in Nevada is:
    a. community property
    b. tenancy in common
    c. tenancy by the entirety
    d. joint tenancy

19. When two or more people take title to the same property and there are no directions regarding survivorship, they take title as:
    a. tenants in common
    b. non-surviving tenants
    c. joint tenancy
    d. tenants by the entirety

20. When community property is to be divided because of a divorce, the husband or wife may file an action in court for a:
    a. writ of no excuse
    b. writ of partition
    c. survivor's advantage claim
    d. right of deserving spouse claim

Chapter

9

Articles of Incorporation

Articles of Organization

beneficiary

business trust

corporation

entity taxation

general partnership

limited liability company (LLC)

limited partnerships

living trust

operating agreement

partnership

real estate investment trusts (REIT)

subchapter S corporation

testamentary trust

trust

trustee

trustor

CHAPTER OBJECTIVES

After completing this chapter, you should be able to:

- Describe a corporation, general and limited partnerships, and a limited liability company.
- Summarize the legal liability and income tax considerations related to an entity choice.
- List the requirements and benefits of a subchapter S corporation and a real estate investment trust.
- List and describe the various types of trusts.

Entities for Ownership

9.1 ENTITIES FOR OWNERSHIP

Income taxes and legal liability considerations may make it more desirable to choose one entity over another as a way to hold title to real estate. The choice of entity is generally between a corporation, partnership, or limited liability company. A description of those entities, plus their advantages and disadvantages, follows.

Corporation

A **corporation** (also known as a C corporation) is formed by filing **Articles of Incorporation** in the state in which it is to be incorporated. If the corporation is going to be a Nevada corporation, then the articles are filed with the Office of the Secretary of State of the State of Nevada. The articles establish the corporate entity and describe its purpose, the responsibilities of the directors and officers, and its authorized capital.

After formation, a corporation may own property either in severalty, if the corporation is the sole owner (without regard to how many shareholders actually own the corporation), or as tenants in common, if there is concurrent ownership. A corporation can never hold property as a joint tenant because the corporate legal entity generally has continuous existence and therefore does not die.

Partnerships

A **partnership** includes a group, pool, joint venture, or other unincorporated organization of two or more people (one or more of whom could be a corporation or other business entity) who carry on a business for profit. In real estate, a partnership is created by two or more persons or entities joining together to deal in real estate investments for a profit.

A corporation differs from a partnership in that a corporation is a legal entity separate from its stockholders, whereas a partnership has no legal standing apart from that of its partners.

There are two types of partnerships: *general partnerships* and *limited partnerships*.

A **general partnership** involves an association of two or more persons (natural or legal) who share in the management and operation of the business, as well as the profits and losses. Each partner has unlimited liability for all the debts and obligations of the partnership. Profits or losses are assigned to the individual partner according to the amount of his or her interest in the partnership.

The Nevada Uniform Partnership Act allows a partnership to hold title to real property in the name of the partnership.

Limited partnerships are made up of general partners and limited partners. The general partners are responsible not only for the management but also for the entire operation of the partnership. A general partner has unlimited liability. The limited partners have no voice or responsibility in the management of the partnership. They share in the profits and losses, but their risk is generally limited to the amount of their individual investment. The Uniform Limited Partnership Act establishes the legality of this type of ownership and requires a written limited partnership agreement for it.

Corporations vs. Partnerships—Income Taxes

The choice of entity for the ownership of real estate is significantly influenced by the income tax consequences of the choice. A summary of the tax differences follows:

Entity taxation is the basic difference between a corporation and a partnership. A corporation is taxed on its income, and the shareholders are taxed when they receive dividends from earnings and profits. An S corporation is an exemption to this rule, which will be discussed later in this section.

A partnership is required to file an information return but is not taxed on its taxable income. The partners report their allocated share of the taxable income on their individual returns, even if there is no distribution of assets to the partners by the partnership.

As a result, in order to avoid double taxation, real estate investments are usually not owned by a corporation. An example of the results of double taxation follows:

	Corporation	Partnership
Taxable gain on sale of real estate	$100,000	$100,000
Corporate entity taxes at 39%	$ 39,000	—
Available for distribution	$ 61,000	$100,000
Tax on dividend to shareholders at 15% or partners' share of profits at 35%	$ 9,150	$ 35,000
Gain remaining after taxes	**$ 51,850**	**$ 65,000**

The increased gain of $13,150 is because the partnership is a conduit for tax purposes and, therefore, has no taxes at the entity level.

Corporations vs. Partnerships—Losses

A partnership's losses are reported by the partners on their individual tax returns, whether or not there is an actual distribution. A corporation, however, can deduct its losses against income only at the entity level. Therefore, the corporate shareholder will not benefit from a pass-through of the losses.

The 1986 Tax Reform Act has limited the benefit of losses allocated to partners in real estate partnerships. A discussion of federal income taxes, including passive loss limitations, is included in Chapter 25.

Potential real estate investors should seek the advice of legal and accounting professionals, because the choice of the entity to own real estate can significantly affect returns on the investment.

Limited Liability Companies

With passage of the Nevada Limited Liability Company Act (the LLC Act), Nevada authorized use of the business entity known as a *limited liability company*. The LLC Act not only benefits small and medium-sized businesses, but also offers some particular benefits to professionals and real estate investors.

General Characteristics

A **limited liability company (LLC)** combines some of the best features of corporations, general partnerships, and limited partnerships. LLCs have "members," which are similar to partners in a partnership and shareholders in a corporation. LLCs offer limited personal liability exposure, full management participation and control rights, and, if properly structured, direct pass-through income tax advantages.

The LLC Act extends the benefit of the LLC form of doing business to professionals such as accountants, engineers, appraisers, doctors, lawyers, and brokers. The advantages offered by the LLC Act are substantial and, due to this, LLCs have replaced general and limited partnerships, subchapter S corporations, and some other corporations as the preferred business entity for small and medium-sized businesses.

Organization and Management

The LLC Act authorizes the organization of LLCs for any lawful purpose, except banking or insurance. A limited liability company is formed by filing **Articles of Organization** with the Office of the Secretary of State of the State of Nevada, setting forth the following:

1. The name of the LLC (including the words "Limited Liability Company" or "Limited Company" or the abbreviations "L.L.C." or "L.C.").
2. The address of its registered office and the name and address of its registered agent.
3. The name and address of each of the organizers.
4. Whether management of the LLC is vested in one or more managers or in all of the members, and their names and addresses.

Operating Agreement

A limited liability company is generally governed by an **operating agreement**, which is similar to the bylaws and shareholders' agreement of a corporation or the partnership agreement of a partnership. Although the legal requirements of an operating agreement are deceptively simple, members of an LLC should exercise care to ensure that the operating agreement clearly sets forth the relationship between the members (their rights and duties) and describes the parameters of the daily business operations of the LLC.

Operating agreements generally specify at a minimum:

1. The obligations of LLC members to make capital contributions.
2. The rights of members to receive distributions.
3. The rights of members and/or managers to control the LLC business.
4. The members' right to transfer their interests in the LLC.
5. The terms and conditions on which the LLC will dissolve.

Unless the Articles of Organization provide differently, the LLC is managed directly by its members, subject to any provision restricting or enlarging the management rights of one or more members.

Limited Personal Liability

Probably the most enticing feature of the limited liability company is the combination of allowing business ventures to secure limited personal liability exposure while maintaining full management and control of the LLC business. The LLC Act expressly provides that members, officers, and employees of an LLC are not personally liable to third-party creditors or alleged tort victims solely by virtue of being a member, officer, or employee of the LLC.

With respect to a professional limited liability company (PLLC), each member is personally liable for malpractice or professional misconduct due to his or her own negligence or misconduct and for the misconduct of other members or employees under his or her direct supervision at the time the alleged misconduct occurred.

But professional liability for members of a PLLC will be several only, meaning that a member is not liable as to his or her personal assets due to negligent acts or professional misconduct of other members or employees not under that member's direct supervision.

In other words, in order for a professional to be personally liable for malpractice or misconduct, he or she must have been directly involved in the alleged misconduct either because he or she caused the problem or because he or she was supervising the individual who did. This narrower standard of personal liability constitutes a significant departure and relief from the existing standard of unlimited personal liability for general partners of a partnership and for shareholders of a professional corporation.

Federal Income Tax Advantages

While both an LLC and a corporation generally provide limited liability for their owners, a properly formed LLC may also receive the favorable income tax treatment of general and limited partnerships. If the LLC elects to be treated as a partnership for federal income tax purposes, income, loss, and other tax attributes are "passed through" to the members, and the LLC itself is not subject to income taxation. In contrast, a corporation is subject to double taxation—not only are shareholders taxed on dividend income they receive from the corporation, but the corporation itself pays a separate tax at the corporate level. The election to be treated as a partnership generally requires the advice from legal and accounting professionals.

By definition, all members of an LLC possess limited liability.

The LLC Act also offers considerable flexibility in structuring the management and continuity of an LLC and the transferability of members' "interests." However, as a result of this flexibility, the tax status of each LLC formed under the LLC Act will be determined by how its operating agreement is structured, rather than by the terms of the LLC Act. Therefore, the operating agreement must be carefully drafted to ensure that the LLC is classified as a partnership for federal income tax purposes.

Benefits to the Real Estate Industry

Based on its limited personal liability benefits and partnership tax advantages, the limited liability company results in significant benefits to professionals in the real estate industry. Through the use of an LLC, real estate investors can now participate fully in the management and control of a real estate project, limit the size of the risk, and take advantage of the more flexible tax treatment.

9.2 OTHER CORPORATE ENTITY CHOICES

Other entity choices for real estate ownership exist; some are variations of the corporate form and were established to overcome the problem of double taxation. These entities are described in the following sections.

Subchapter S Corporations

A **subchapter S corporation** is incorporated pursuant to the laws of the state in exactly the same manner as a C corporation. However, the shareholders elect in accordance with subchapter S of the Internal Revenue Code to make the corporation not subject to income taxes imposed by normal corporate rules. As a result, the corporation becomes a conduit similar to a partnership. The taxable income or losses are allocated to the shareholders and reported on their individual returns.

To be able to elect under subchapter S, the corporation must:

- Have 100 or fewer shareholders
- Have no corporation shareholders
- Have no non-resident alien shareholders
- Have only one class of stock

For a more comprehensive list of criteria and instructions, see IRS Form 2553, available at www.irs.gov/pub/irs-pdf/i2553.pdf.

Although a subchapter S corporation is generally taxed like a partnership, there are certain circumstances in which subchapter S corporations and their shareholders may be subject to the same two-tiered tax as regular corporations and their shareholders.

Real Estate Investment Trusts

Real estate investment trusts (REITs) are also known as Massachusetts Trusts or Common Law Trusts.

Congress passed a law in 1960 exempting certain real estate investment trusts from paying corporate tax, as long as they meet certain requirements. A REIT must meet the following requirements to avoid paying corporate tax:

1. Seventy-five percent of the assets must be in real estate.
2. There must be at least 100 owners.
3. Investors transfer legal title and possession of real estate to the trustee, who manages trust property for their benefit.
4. Investors purchase ownership in the trust, which is transferable.
5. Ninety-five percent of the gains must be distributed to investors each year.
6. Income accrues from rent, interest on mortgages, and so on, rather than capital gains from sales of real estate.

Another advantage of REITs is that an investor with a small amount of money can invest in a trust, which offers a tax advantage, is free from management responsibilities, and provides a diversified investment. REIT shares often trade on a stock exchange or in the over-the-counter market and, therefore, it is easier to transfer ownership than it is to sell an actual parcel of real estate.

The choice of a REIT is usually eliminated when smaller real estate investments are involved, due to the need for 100 owners. The REIT requirement for 100 owners generally requires consideration of securities laws (Securities and Exchange Commission and State Blue Sky). An offering to 100 potential owners could require registration pursuant to the Securities Act of 1933. Such a registration is costly and, therefore, eliminates the possibility of smaller real estate projects. However, when the requirements can be met, a REIT allows flexibility and many of the corporate and partnership advantages.

9.3 TRUSTS

A **trust** is an entity created to own assets, including real and personal property, for the benefit of a person, persons, or another entity. The trust is created by a **trustor**, who transfers ownership of the asset or assets to the trust and names a **trustee**, who manages the property for the benefit of one or more beneficiaries. The trustee can be an individual or a corporation, such as a trust department of a bank or a trust company. The trustor sets forth the powers, duties, and responsibilities of the trustee in an instrument, which may be a trust agreement or a will.

During the life of the trust, profits and sometimes a portion of the principal may be distributed to the beneficiaries. After the death of the last trustor, the trustee will distribute any remaining trust assets to the beneficiaries. A trust may take the place of a will and avoid probate by providing for the distribution of all remaining assets of the trust upon the death of the trustors. Additional advantages of a trust are saving estate taxes and providing protection for the beneficiaries (usually the spouse and children).

Types of Trusts

There are many types of trusts, but the three primary types are:

- Living trusts
- Testamentary trusts
- Business trusts

A **living trust**, also known as an *intervivos trust* (Latin for "within one's life"), is created and takes effect during the trustor's lifetime. A living trust relieves the trustor of the responsibility of handling the estate. The property is transferred to the trustee with instructions to manage the estate and distribute the income from the assets according to the trustor's instructions. A living trust generally can be revoked by the trustor at any time until the death of the trustor. While a living trust is a generic name for any trust that comes into existence during the lifetime of the person creating the trust, it is most commonly a trust in which the trustors receive benefits from the profits of the trust during their lifetimes.

A **testamentary trust** is similar to a living trust, except that it is set up in a will and takes effect upon the maker's death. The will can name the trustee and beneficiaries and provides instructions to the trustee for the management and distribution of assets of the trust.

A relatively new entity in Nevada is the **business trust**. The business trust is created by a trust instrument under which a property is held, managed, controlled, invested, and reinvested by a trustee for the benefit of the persons entitled to a beneficial interest in the trust property. This includes the operation of a business or professional services for a profit.

CHAPTER SUMMARY

Income taxes and legal liability considerations may make it more desirable to choose one entity over another as a way to hold title to real estate. The choice of entity is generally between a corporation, partnership, or limited liability company. A corporation is formed by filing Articles of Incorporation in the state in which it is to be incorporated. A corporation may own property either in severalty, if the corporation is the sole owner, or as tenants in common, if there is concurrent ownership. A partnership includes a group, pool, joint venture, or other unincorporated organization of two or more people (one or more of whom could be a corporation or other business entity), who carry on a business for profit. There are two types of partnerships: general partnerships and limited partnerships.

A general partnership involves an association of two or more persons (natural or legal) who share in the management and operation of the business, as well as the profits and losses. Limited partnerships are comprised of general partners and limited partners. The general partners are responsible for the management and also the entire operation of the partnership. A general partner has unlimited liability. The limited partners have no voice or responsibility in the management of the partnership. They share in the profits and losses, but their risk is generally limited to the amount of their individual investment.

Entity taxation is the basic difference between a corporation and a partnership. A corporation is taxed on its income, and the shareholders are taxed when they receive dividends from earnings and profits. A partnership is required to file an information return but is not taxed on its taxable income. The partners report their allocated share of the taxable income and/or losses on their individual returns, whether there is or is not a distribution of assets to the partners by the partnership.

A limited liability company combines some of the best features of corporations, general partnerships, and limited partnerships. LLCs have "members," which are similar to partners in a partnership and shareholders in a corporation. LLCs offer limited personal liability exposure, full management participation and control rights, and, if properly structured, direct pass-through income tax advantages. A limited liability company is formed by filing Articles of Organization with the Nevada Secretary of State. A limited liability company is generally governed by an operating agreement, which is similar to the bylaws and shareholders' agreement of a corporation or the partnership agreement of a partnership. The operating agreement sets forth the rights and duties of the members and describes the daily business operations of the LLC. The Nevada Limited Liability Company Act provides that members, officers, and employees of an LLC are not personally liable to third-party creditors or alleged tort victims solely by virtue of being a member, officer, or employee of the LLC. While both an LLC and a corporation generally provide limited liability for their owners, a properly formed LLC may also receive the favorable income tax treatment of general and limited partnerships. If the LLC elects to be treated as a partnership for federal income tax purposes, income, loss, and other tax attributes are "passed through" to the members, and the LLC itself is not subject to income taxation.

Other possible entity choices to own real estate include subchapter S corporations and real estate investment trusts. A subchapter S corporation is incorporated in exactly the same manner as a C corporation. However, the shareholders elect to make the corporation not subject to income taxes imposed by normal corporate rules. As a result, the corporation becomes a conduit similar to a partnership.

Real estate investment trusts (REITs) are also known as Massachusetts trusts or common-law trusts. An investor with a small amount of money can invest in a REIT, which offers a tax advantage, is free from management responsibilities, and provides a diversified investment. A trust is an entity created to own assets, including real and personal property, for the benefit of a person, persons, or another entity. The trust is created by a trustor, who transfers ownership of the asset or assets to the trust and names a trustee, who manages the property for the benefit of one or more beneficiaries. The trustee can be an individual or a corporation, such as a trust department of a bank or a trust company. The trustor sets forth the powers, duties, and responsibilities of the trustee in an instrument, which may be a trust agreement or a will.

The three primary types of trusts are living trusts, testamentary trusts, and business trusts. A living trust, also known as an intervivos trust, is created and takes effect during the trustor's lifetime. A living trust relieves the trustor of the responsibility of handling the estate. The property is transferred to the trustee with instructions to manage the estate and distribute the income from the assets according to the trustor's instructions. A testamentary trust is similar to a living trust, except that it is set up in a will and takes effect upon the maker's death. In a land trust, real estate is the only asset. The trustor and **beneficiary** are usually the same person. The trustee has full power to sell, mortgage, and manage the property according to the written provisions of the trust agreement. The beneficiary has the rights to possession, income, and proceeds of the sale of the property.

CHECKING YOUR COMPREHENSION

1. Define the following terms:
   - Corporation
   - General partnership
   - Limited partnership
   - Limited liability company

2. Summarize the legal liability and income tax considerations related to each of the entity types in question 1.

3. List the requirements and benefits of a subchapter S corporation.

4. List the requirements and benefits of a real estate investment trust (REIT).

5. List and describe the various types of trusts.

REVIEWING YOUR UNDERSTANDING

1. A limited partner is **ALWAYS**:
   a. an active partner
   b. liable for debts in excess of his or her investment
   c. limited as to profits received
   d. limited as to liability

2. An incorporated developer wants to raise capital for improvements without creating any liens or incurring new debt. The developer could:
   a. sell bonds
   b. use a blanket encumbrance
   c. become a subchapter S corporation
   d. sell stock

3. Which of the following bears the **GREAT-EST** liability for the investor?

    a. a corporation

    b. a limited partnership

    c. a general partnership

    d. a subchapter S corporation

4. What form of financing is controlled by federal securities law?

    a. ARM

    b. REIT

    c. GPM

    d. ARMLS

5. A passive investor in a real estate syndicate would **MOST** likely be a:

    a. beneficiary

    b. trustee

    c. limited partner

    d. general partner

6. Which of the following characteristics would apply to a limited liability company?

    a. stockholders

    b. unlimited liability

    c. members

    d. unlimited duration

7. It always takes a minimum of 100 people to form a:

    a. corporation

    b. limited partnership

    c. real estate syndicate

    d. real estate investment trust

8. Which of the following types of ownership is **LEAST** likely to be subject to securities regulations?

    a. limited partnership

    b. subchapter S corporation

    c. joint tenancy

    d. joint venture

9. A corporate officer's authority to make or accept an offer can be checked in the:

    a. corporate bylaws

    b. corporation code

    c. corporate charter

    d. State Department of Corporation regulations

10. A syndicate for real estate purposes would **MOST** likely be:

    a. a corporation

    b. a limited partnership

    c. a general partnership

    d. unincorporated associations

11. A limited partner may **NOT**:

    a. demand an accounting

    b. participate in management

    c. share in the profits

    d. retain limited liability

12. The owner of a commercial office building transfers his interest to a trustee who manages the office building for the benefit of the trustor. What type of trust has been formed?

    a. REIT

    b. testamentary trust

    c. reconveyance

    d. intervivos trust

13. ABC Corporation with 50 stockholders holds title to its owned office building:

    a. as joint tenants

    b. as tenants in common

    c. in severalty

    d. in trust for its stockholders

14. All of the following are reasons for selecting a real estate investment entity to be treated as a partnership for income tax purposes, **EXCEPT**:

   a. the entity does not pay taxes on its taxable income

   b. entity losses are allocated to partners for inclusion on their individual tax returns

   c. taxable income and cash distributions to the individual partners are taxed only one time

   d. a partnership entity does not file an income tax return

15. A limited liability company provides a real estate investor all of the following, **EXCEPT**:

   a. limited personal liability exposure

   b. full management participation and control

   c. organization without filing with the Nevada Secretary of State

   d. partnership income tax benefits

16. The maximum number of shareholders allowed in a subchapter S corporation is:

   a. 35

   b. 50

   c. 75

   d. 100

17. To avoid paying corporate income tax, a REIT must maintain the following percentage of its assets in real estate:

   a. 25%

   b. 50%

   c. 75%

   d. 95%

18. To avoid paying corporate income tax, a REIT must distribute the following percentage of its gains to investors each year:

   a. 25%

   b. 50%

   c. 75%

   d. 95%

19. The party who manages the property of a trust is known as the:

   a. trustee

   b. trustor

   c. beneficiary

   d. administrator

20. A trust established in a will and taking effect upon the maker's death is a:

   a. living trust

   b. testamentary trust

   c. land trust

   d. business trust

IMPORTANT TERMS AND CONCEPTS

agricultural lease
assignment
cash rent
chattel real
contract rent
defeasance clause
demise
devise
economic rent
estate at sufferance
estate at will
estate for years
freehold
graduated lease
gross lease

ground lease
hold harmless clause
index lease
landlord
leasehold
lease-purchase
lessee
lessor
net lease
novation
oil or gas leases
option clause
option to purchase
option to renew
percentage lease

periodic estates
rent
reversionary rights
rooftop lease
sale and leaseback leases
sale clause
sandwich lease
sharecropping
statute of frauds
sublease
sublessee
sublessor
tenant
variable lease

CHAPTER OBJECTIVES

After completing this chapter, you should be able to:

- Define a leasehold estate and summarize the rights of the lessor and lessee.
- Summarize the requirements for a valid lease.
- Describe the following lease classifications: estate for years, periodic estate, estate at will, and estate at sufferance.
- Describe the types of options that can be included in a lease, and explain the difference between contract rent and economic rent.
- Summarize the different types of lease agreements.
- List and define the common lease clauses.
- Summarize the transfer of leasehold estates.

Leasehold Estates

10.1 LEASEHOLD INTEREST

Estates in land are either **freehold**, which means for an indeterminable amount of time, or *less than freehold*, which means for a definite period of time. This section covers estates in land that are less than freehold, such as leases and rental agreements. A **leasehold** is an interest in someone else's land, which allows the holder of the lease the right of possession.

According to the **statute of frauds**, a lease can be written or oral. However, a lease can be oral only if it is for a period of one year or less *and* can be performed within one year. For example, a lease signed on January 1 for the period January 1 to December 31 of the same year is for exactly one year and is not required to be in writing. On the other hand, a lease for the period January 1 to December 31 but signed the day before the lease commenced (that is, December 31 of the prior year) cannot be performed within one year and a lease for the period January 1 to January 1 of the following year is for more than one year. Therefore, both of the foregoing leases must be in writing.

Rental agreements for one year or less may be oral. Although an oral agreement is legal, it could be difficult to enforce the terms without sufficient proof of an agreement.

Because a lease is a contract, the essential elements of a contract must exist. The lease must identify the property (in most cases a street address is sufficient on a lease, in other cases a legal description may be necessary) and must spell out the terms and conditions in sufficient detail so that a clear understanding exists between the parties and it shows that there was a "meeting of the minds."

The **landlord**, also known as the **lessor**, is the owner of the property, who subordinates the rights of possession. The **tenant**, or **lessee**, gains the rights to possession and quiet enjoyment.

Transfer of Leasehold Interest

A real estate lease is personal property, the same as furniture, common stock, and cars. Personal property is also called *chattel*. Even though the real estate leasehold interest itself is personal property, its roots are in land, and therefore, it is referred to as **chattel real**.

Under the lease, either party may transfer his or her interest in the property unless prohibited in the contract. The lessor, who has given up his or her rights to possession, has **reversionary rights**, which means possession will be returned at the termination of the lease.

The transfer of a leasehold interest is referred to as **demise**. This is not to be confused with **devise**, which is the transfer of real property by will.

10.2 CLASSIFICATION OF LEASES

An **estate for years** is a lease that extends for a definite term. An estate for years can be for three months or three years—there is no minimum or maximum time period for an estate for years. A lease from January 1 to January 31, five years later, and a lease from January 1 to January 31, one month later, are both classified as estates for years because they have definite start and end dates—the hallmarks of an estate for years.

A long-term lease may extend to 10 years and beyond. Because an estate for years has a predetermined ending date, there is no reason for the lessee to give notice that he or she does not intend to renew and will vacate at the expiration of the lease. However, if the lease has such a provision written into the agreement, then the lessee must give notice as agreed.

Periodic estates, also known as estates from period to period, do not have a definite expiration date and renew automatically at the end of each term, unless one party or the other gives notice of termination. For example, a tenancy from year-to-year renews at the end of each year for another year; a tenancy from month-to-month renews at the end of each month for another month.

An **estate at will** is created when the owner permits another to occupy a property without a formal agreement. Sometimes referred to as a *mother-in-law lease*, it applies equally to a lessor who agrees to allow a lessee to retain possession of a property after the more formal agreement has expired. A lessee who stays in possession on a modified rental agreement after the expiration of a previous lease is referred to as a *holdover tenant*. An estate at will is sometimes called a license to use one's property. An estate at will can terminate by verbal notice with reasonable time given to vacate.

An **estate at sufferance** is the lowest type of estate a person can hold. A tenant at sufferance is distinguishable from a trespasser only by the fact that a tenant at sufferance at one time had the consent of the landlord to occupy the subject property, whereas a trespasser never had consent. A tenant under any of the foregoing estates (that is, estate for years, period to period, estate at will), whose right to occupy the subject property has terminated (for whatever reason) and who refuses to vacate the property is a tenant at sufferance. A person who occupies the subject property after a lender has lawfully foreclosed on a defaulted loan is also a tenant at sufferance. See Figure 10.1 for a summary of the classification of leasehold estates.

FIGURE 10.1   Leasehold Estates

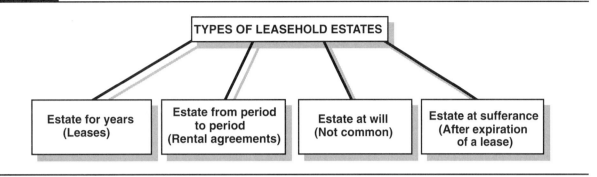

Options

An option may be included as part of a lease. An option may be a right to renew or extend the lease or may be a right to purchase the subject property.

An **option to renew** allows for the renewal or extension of the present lease for another specific period of time. The option will specify the time required to notify the lessor that the lessee intends to exercise the option to renew. A lease may have a provision for an automatic renewal. If it does and the lessee does not intend to renew, the lessee must notify the lessor that he or she will not renew.

Some leases contain an **option to purchase**. An option to purchase is an agreement to enter into a contract to purchase at the option of the lessee, and at a specified time during the lease. Buyers might want to use a lease with a purchase option for the following reasons: (1) they do not have enough money for a down payment, (2) they need to build credit, or (3) they might not stay in the area.

A **lease-purchase** is a simple lease for a specified period of time, after which or during which the lessor agrees to sell and the lessee has the option to purchase at an agreed price and terms. Lease-purchases are sometimes used when buyers are relocating and have not yet sold their other home and/or for the same reasons as an option to purchase. Because a lease-purchase changes the nature of the agreement between the parties from a lease to a purchase, thereby giving the tenant an equitable interest in the subject property, eviction of a tenant in a lease-purchase agreement is more difficult and requires more time. Therefore, a seller/landlord should not enter into a lease-purchase agreement without first seeking competent legal advice.

Rent

Rent is the consideration paid under a leasehold estate for the use and possession of real property. Rent is paid in advance, usually on the first day of each month. Note the contrast between rent, which is paid in advance, and interest (such as interest on a mortgage), which is paid in arrears.

There are different rents that are referred to in the leasing of property, specifically contract rent and economic rent. **Contract rent** is the rental price stated on the lease agreement. **Economic rent** is the amount that a property would bring at current market if it were not under prior contract. Economic rent may be more or less than the contract rent, depending upon whether the market has gone up or down since the beginning of the lease. Generally speaking, but not in all cases, at the beginning of a lease, the contract rent and the economic rent are the same.

10.3 TYPES OF LEASES AND CLAUSES

There are many different types of lease agreements. A simple residential lease form may be only one or two pages, whereas a commercial lease form may entail 20 to 40 pages of provisions regarding the use of the space and payment of rental fees. Lease agreements typically fall into one of the following categories, or may be a combination of more than one of the following categories of leases.

A **gross lease** is a simple lease used in most houses and apartment complexes. It calls for a set rental price, such as $800 per month. Out of that gross amount of rent, the property owner pays the expenses (that is, property taxes, insurance, maintenance, and sometimes even the utilities).

A **net lease** or triple net lease is used in most commercial properties. The lease contains a provision for a square foot fee—for example, $10 per square foot. This amount is multiplied by the total number of square feet to arrive at a yearly rent. For example, the annual rent for 1000 square feet of commercial space at $12 per square foot would be $12,000 per year. The yearly rent is divided by 12 for the monthly rate. The monthly rent on the previous example would be $1000 per month plus expenses. If the rental space consists of only one building and one tenant, then the tenant will pay all expenses for the property (including property taxes, insurance, maintenance, repairs, utilities, and so on). If the rental property has two or more tenants, the tenants are still responsible for all expenses, but the amount of expenses is divided between the tenants.

Typically, the expenses are apportioned according to the amount of space the tenant leases. For example, if there were three tenants occupying a 3000-square-foot building and each tenant occupied 1000 square feet, then each tenant would pay one-third of the total expenses. As a second example, if the same 3000-square-foot building is occupied by two tenants, one occupying 1000 square feet and the other occupying 2000 square feet, then the former will pay one-third of the expenses and the latter will pay two-thirds of the expenses. In this way, the lessor (landlord) receives a specified amount of rent and the lessee(s) pay all of the expenses for the property.

A **ground lease** is a long-term lease for the use of land. Improvements to the land (such as buildings, and so on) become a part of the real property. A ground lease is typically used for a recreational site, agricultural land (that is, to grow crops), or ranching (grazing rights), but it may also be used for a shopping center or commercial building.

A **variable lease** provides that the rent may increase during the term of the lease. Variable leases include an index lease and a graduated lease. An **index lease** allows for periodic increases in base rental fees based on a predetermined guideline, such as the Consumer Price Index (CPI). A **graduated lease** allows for periodic increases in rent at predetermined intervals and predetermined rates. For example, this type of lease may provide that rent increases each year (or some other period of time) by a set amount (for example, $100) or by a percentage (such as 3%).

A **percentage lease** is a commercial lease in which the tenant pays a percentage of the gross income received by the tenant, in addition to rent. Typically, retail centers and shopping malls are triple net leases, meaning that the tenant pays (1) a base amount of rent, (2) a percentage of all of the property expenses, and (3) a percentage of the tenant's gross income as rent.

Oil or gas leases consist of a flat fee for the exploration of gas or oil and a royalty if any is found.

A **rooftop lease** is used to rent the airspace above a piece of real estate. A rooftop lease is typically used for advertising space (such as billboards) or communication towers.

Sale and leaseback leases are used after a person has developed a building and wants his or her working capital available for other developments. In this case, the owner would sell the building and lease it back from the new owner. This type of lease is normally a long-term lease.

Agricultural Leases

Owners of agricultural land generally enter into one of two types of agreements with a tenant: cash rent or sharecropping.

Sharecropping is a lease between an agricultural landowner and a tenant, whereby the landowner provides the land and may also provide equipment in return for the tenant's planting, maintaining, and harvesting a crop. The proceeds are then divided (not necessarily equally) between the tenant and the landowner. The tenant is called a sharecropper.

Cash rent is a lease between an agricultural landowner and a tenant, whereby the tenant pays the landowner a specified amount of money in advance in exchange for the right of the tenant to use the agricultural land to plant, maintain, and harvest a crop upon the land. All of the proceeds from the crop belong to the tenant.

Lease Clauses

A lease may include one or more of the following common lease clauses:

1. An **option clause** may give the tenant the right to extend the lease for a specified period of time (that is, an option to renew/extend) and/or may give the tenant the right to purchase the subject property (that is, an option to purchase).

2. **Hold harmless clause**. State law may restrict a residential landlord's ability to require the tenant to hold the landlord harmless and/or cover the landlord for any liability incurred by the landlord, but a commercial lease typically

transfers all liability for the premises to the tenant and requires the tenant to indemnify (reimburse) the landlord for any and all liability incurred by the landlord.

3. A **sale clause** is typically found only in residential leases. This clause allows the tenant or the landlord to terminate the lease in the event the subject property is sold.

4. A **defeasance clause** in a mortgage or deed of trust renders those documents null and void upon complete payment of the promissory note. Similarly, a defeasance clause in a lease may terminate the lease upon the occurrence of specified events, such as destruction of the premises or condemnation.

10.4 TRANSFER OF LEASEHOLD ESTATES

Unless otherwise stated in the lease, either the tenant or the landlord may freely transfer his or her rights. A landlord may sell the subject property, and the tenant may assign the lease. In practice, however, virtually all leases, residential or commercial, restrict the tenant's right to assign or sublet all or part of the leased premises without the landlord's approval.

Transfer

The landlord/owner may freely transfer ownership rights anytime during the lease. The new owner, however, takes ownership subject to the existing lease. This means the new landlord cannot cancel the lease (unless there is a sale clause, as discussed previously) or change any of the terms of the lease unless the tenant consents.

Assignment

A tenant may freely assign a lease unless the lease prohibits it. Typically, the lease will prohibit assignment by the tenant without landlord approval. Even when assignment is permitted, the original lessee still has liability unless released by the lessor, or unless there is a novation (see later in this chapter). The terms of the lease generally remain unchanged. An assignment is considered a permanent change. Under an assignment, the new lessee pays the rent directly to the lessor. (See Figure 10.2.)

FIGURE 10.2   Lease Assignment

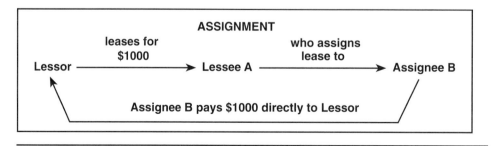

FIGURE 10.3 Sublease

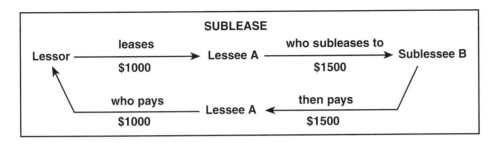

Novation

A **novation** is a complete substitution of parties. A novation, as it applies to leases, makes the new tenant/lessee fully responsible for the lease. In addition, it completely releases the original tenant/lessee from the lease. The same result would be achieved if the original lease were terminated, thereby terminating the original lessee's liability, and a new lease executed by the new lessee, thereby making the new lessee fully responsible for the new lease.

Sublease or Sandwich Lease

As stated previously, a lessee can assign or **sublease** all or part of the leased premises unless the original lease prohibits it. In a sublease, the original lessee remains fully responsible to the lessor under the original lease. The lessee, who becomes the **sublessor**, may sublease all or a portion of the leased premises for any amount of rent (higher or lower) and any amount of the time remaining on the lease. The **sublessee** makes the payments to the sublessor, who in turn pays the lessor according to the original lease. This arrangement is called a **sandwich lease** because the sublessor is "sandwiched" in the middle between the sublessee and the lessor. (See Figure 10.3.)

CHAPTER SUMMARY

A leasehold is an interest in someone else's land, which allows the holder of the lease the right of possession. A lease can be written or oral. However, a lease can be oral only if it is for a period of one year or less and can be performed within one year. Because a lease is a contract, the essential elements of a contract must exist. The landlord, or lessor, is the owner of the property, who gives up the rights of possession. The tenant, or lessee, gains the rights to possession and quiet enjoyment. A real estate lease is personal property, but its roots are in land, so it is referred to as chattel real.

Under the lease, either party may transfer his or her interest in the property unless prohibited in the contract. The lessor, who has given up his or her rights to possession, has reversionary rights, which means possession will be returned at the termination of the lease. The transfer of a leasehold interest is referred to as demise.

An estate for years is a lease that extends for a definite term. Periodic estates do not have a definite expiration date and renew automatically at the end of each term, unless one party or the other gives notice of termination. An estate at will is created when the owner permits another to occupy a property without a formal agreement. A lessee who stays in possession on a modified rental agreement after the expiration of a previous lease is referred to as a holdover tenant.

An estate at sufferance is the lowest type of estate a person can hold. A tenant at sufferance is distinguishable from a trespasser only by the fact that a tenant at sufferance at one time had the consent of the landlord to occupy the subject property, whereas a trespasser never had consent.

An option may be included as part of a lease. An option to renew allows for the renewal or extension of the present lease for another specific period of time. Some leases contain an option to purchase, which is an agreement to enter into a contract to purchase at the option of the lessee, and at a specified time during the lease. A lease-purchase is a simple lease for a specified period of time, after which or during which the lessor agrees to sell and the lessee has the option to purchase at an agreed price and terms.

Rent is the consideration paid under a leasehold estate for the use and possession of real property. Rent is paid in advance. Contract rent is the rental price stated on the lease agreement. Economic rent is the amount that a property would bring at current market if it were not under prior contract.

There are many different types of lease agreements. Most of these are explained in the body of this chapter's text. Some lease agreements are described briefly in the following text:

- A gross lease is a simple lease used in most houses and apartment complexes. It calls for a set rental price. Out of that gross amount of rent, the property owner pays the expenses.
- A net lease or triple net lease is used in most commercial properties. The lease contains a provision for a square foot fee. This amount is multiplied by the total number of square feet in order to arrive at a yearly rent.
- A ground lease is a long-term lease for the use of land.
- Owners of agricultural land generally enter into one of two types of agreements with a tenant: cash rent or sharecropping.

A lease may include one or more of the following common lease clauses: an option clause, a hold harmless clause, a sale clause, or a defeasance clause. These clauses are described in the body of this chapter's text.

Unless otherwise stated in the lease, either the tenant or the landlord may freely transfer his or her rights. The landlord/owner may freely transfer ownership rights anytime during the lease. The new owner, however, takes ownership subject to the existing lease. This means the new landlord cannot cancel the lease or change the terms unless the tenant consents.

A tenant may freely assign a lease unless the lease prohibits it. Typically, the lease will prohibit assignment by the tenant without landlord approval.

A novation, as it applies to leases, makes the new tenant/lessee fully responsible for the lease. In addition, it completely releases the original tenant/lessee from the lease.

In a sublease, the lessee, who becomes the sublessor, may sublease all or a portion of the leased premises for any amount of rent and any amount of the time remaining on the lease. The sublessee makes the payments to the sublessor, who in turn pays the lessor according to the original lease.

CHECKING YOUR COMPREHENSION

1. List the requirements for a valid lease.

2. Define and summarize the lease period and termination provisions for the following lease classifications:
   - Estate for years
   - Periodic estates
   - Estate at will
   - Estate at sufferance

3. Define the following:
   - Option to renew
   - Option to purchase
   - Lease-purchase
   - Contract rent
   - Economic rent

4. List and define the different type of lease agreements and the common lease clauses.

5. Describe the effects of the following:
   - Transfer of the landlord/owner's rights during a lease
   - Assignment of the tenant's leasehold rights
   - Transfer of the tenant's leasehold rights with novation
   - Subleasing

REVIEWING YOUR UNDERSTANDING

1. An estate for years is a:
   a. life estate
   b. fee simple estate
   c. freehold estate
   d. type of lease

2. Definite duration refers to a(n):
   a. life estate
   b. estate for years
   c. estate at will
   d. periodic tenancy

3. Tenant Andrew's lease has expired, and his landlord has indicated that Andrew may remain until the sale of the building is closed. Andrew will be charged rent for the time he occupies the building. Andrew's tenancy is called a:

a. tenancy for years

b. month-to-month tenancy

c. tenancy at will

d. tenancy at sufferance

4. Which of the following contracts does **NOT** have to be in writing to be enforceable?

a. promise to pay a debt of another person

b. one-year lease starting immediately

c. six-month lease starting in seven months

d. contract for sale of real property valued at less than $500

5. The lessee **MOST** likely pays for fire insurance under a:

a. gross lease

b. percentage lease

c. triple net lease

d. commercial lease

6. Under an assignment of a lease, the assignor becomes:

a. responsible for payment of rent

b. secondarily responsible for payment of rent

c. the lessor

d. the sublessee

7. The landlord under a lease:

a. subordinates his or her right of possession

b. subrogates his or her right of possession

c. assigns his or her right of possession

d. alienates his or her right of possession

8. A situation in which the grantor becomes the lessee of the grantee is known as a(n):

a. sublease

b. assignment

c. estate in reversion

d. sale and leaseback

9. A tenant stays in possession without permission of the landlord. The tenant has:

a. tenancy from period to period

b. tenancy at will

c. tenancy at sufferance

d. tenancy for years

10. A gross lease is the type of lease usually:

a. used for leasing space in a shopping center

b. requiring the tenant to pay for taxes and insurance

c. used for leasing apartment rentals

d. requiring the tenant to erect his or her own building and to pay all costs of ownership and maintenance

11. Which of the following **CANNOT** be owned in fee simple?

a. a condominium

b. property owned as tenants in common

c. property owned as a joint tenant

d. leasehold rights

12. A freehold estate would be:

a. an estate in sufferance

b. an estate in reversion

c. an estate for years

d. an estate at will

13. A provision in a lease provided that upon the expiration of its term, the rents increase 250%. The purpose of this clause is to prevent:

    a. an easement by prescription
    b. a tenancy at sufferance
    c. damage to the premises
    d. the removal of fixtures

14. A woman verbally agreed to a six-month lease, but prior to occupancy she changed her mind. Her verbal agreement is:

    a. enforceable
    b. illegal
    c. unenforceable because of the statute of frauds
    d. voidable by her

15. A lessor refused to sign the lease but accepted monthly rent from the lessee who had taken possession. The:

    a. lessee is on a periodic tenancy
    b. lease is valid
    c. lessee is a tenant at sufferance
    d. lessee can be evicted without notice

16. Subordination of right of possession **BEST** describes a(n):

    a. hypothecation
    b. trust deed
    c. lease
    d. exclusive right to sell listing

17. When economic rent exceeds contract rent, an economic decision of the lessee would be to:

    a. sublet
    b. assign the lease
    c. surrender the lease
    d. renegotiate the lease

18. Bill occupies an apartment under written lease for one year, which expired May 1. He has paid his rent each month since then. To cancel this tenancy, the landlord **MUST** serve the tenant with:

    a. one month notice
    b. ten days notice
    c. notice by May 1
    d. no notice required

19. Upon the expiration of the lease, the lessor received the complete bundle of rights by:

    a. reversion
    b. remainder
    c. recovery
    d. redemption

20. Mr. Smith is a tenant under a percentage net lease on commercial property. When the owner sells the real estate to a new buyer who plans to occupy the property, what happens to Mr. Smith's lease?

    a. It is canceled.
    b. It is still binding, and Smith continues to pay his rent to the original owner.
    c. It is still binding, and Smith pays his rent to the new owner under the terms of the original lease.
    d. The new owner may restructure the lease terms unilaterally.

Chapter 11

IMPORTANT TERMS AND CONCEPTS

abstract of title
acknowledgement
actual notice
adverse possession
alienation
alienation by descent
alienation by will
bargain and sale deed
bequest
chain of title
clouds on a title
color of title
constructive notice
conventional (or formal) will
covenants
deed

derivative title
devise
devisee
devisor
disclaimer deeds
electronic will
eminent domain
escheat
exceptions
general warranty deeds
grantee
granting clause
grantor
habendum clause
holographic will
inquiry notice

intestate
intestate succession
involuntary alienation
livery of seisin
nuncupative will
original title
patent
per stirpes
probate
quitclaim deed
reservations
special warranty deed
tack
title
Torrens system
voluntary alienation

CHAPTER OBJECTIVES

After completing this chapter, you should be able to:

- Describe title and the classifications of title.
- Describe constructive, actual, and inquiry notice.
- Describe the chain of title and the methods for documenting the chain of title.
- Define alienation and describe the four alienation methods.
- List and describe the essentials of a valid deed.

Title and Transferring Title

PART 1: TITLE

Title is the right to ownership of property and the evidence of such rights. Title gives evidence of the quality, right, and interest in real property, which allows a government, individual, individuals, or legal entity to retain possession of the property.

11.1 CLASSIFICATIONS OF TITLE

There are two classifications of title: *original title* and *derivative title*.

Original Title

Original title is title held by a country or state. Original title may be gained by conquest, discovery, cession, or purchase. In the early history of the United States, land was taken in the name of the kings by the early explorers of countries such as Spain, France, England, and Russia. The land claimed by the United States following the Revolutionary War is an example of original title by conquest. Examples of original title by purchase would be the Louisiana Purchase, bought by the United States from France, and the purchase of Alaska from Russia.

When an original title is conveyed by a state or federal government to an individual, the instrument used is called a **patent**. The transfer of land through the issuance of a patent by the sovereign owner is different from a patent issued by the U.S. Patent Office, which protects inventions.

Derivative Title

Derivative title is title that belongs to an individual or legal entity and is derived from the government's original title. Derivative title is typically gained by descent, will, purchase, or gift.

11.2 PUBLIC NOTICE

Before England enacted the Statute of Frauds in 1677, private ownership of land was evidenced by its physical possession. A landowner gave notice to everyone of the claim to ownership by visibly occupying the land. When ownership changed, the old owner moved off the land and the new owner then visibly occupied the land.

After enactment of the Statute of Frauds, ownership transfers were required to be documented with a written deed. Because it was difficult to determine who held the most current deed, questions of land ownership still existed. When the holder of the latest deed also occupied the land, there was no problem, but determination of ownership was very difficult when the latest deed holder did not occupy the land.

The solution was to create a government-sponsored, public recording service that allowed a person to record the deed. These public records were open to anyone, and an owner could post notice to all that ownership of the land parcel was claimed.

Two ways are now available to give notice of ownership rights to land. One is by recording documents in the public records (constructive notice), and the other is by visibly occupying or otherwise making use of the land (actual notice).

Constructive Notice

Constructive notice charges the public with the responsibility of examining the public records to gain knowledge of anyone who might claim a right or interest in the property. The legal system assumes that anyone interested in the property has inspected the public records. Constructive notice is also called "legal notice."

Actual Notice

Actual notice is knowledge that is gained from what is seen, heard, read, or observed. When a prospective purchaser reads a deed transferring property from X to Y, the purchaser has actual notice of the deed and Y's claim to the property. If a purchaser goes to the property to be purchased and sees someone in possession, the prospective purchaser has actual notice of that person's claim to be there.

Inquiry Notice

A person interested in acquiring a property is responsible by law for making inquiry of anyone giving actual or constructive notice. This is referred to as **inquiry notice**, which the law presumes a reasonably diligent person would obtain by making further inquiry.

> EXAMPLE 1—A man is considering the purchase of 40 acres of undeveloped desert land. Upon inspecting the land, he observes a dirt road caused by the owner's frequent use of the adjoining land to reach the county highway. The law expects the potential owner to make further inquiry because the road may be a legal easement across the land.

> EXAMPLE 2—When buying rental property, the potential buyer is expected to make inquiry as to the rights of the occupants. In fact, the potential buyer should determine the rights of any occupant of a property to be purchased as he or she may hold substantial rights.

In summary, anyone claiming an interest or right in real property is expected to make it known either by recorded claim or visible use of the property. Anyone who is acquiring a right or interest is expected to look in the public records, go to the property to make a visual inspection for claims, and inquire as to the extent of those claims.

11.3 CHAIN OF TITLE

A **chain of title** shows the linkage of ownership connecting the present owner to each prior owner, all the way back to the original source of title. Generally, the chain starts with the original patent, which grants ownership from the government to a private citizen.

When there is a break or gap in the chain, it must be corrected in order to have marketable title. Marketable title is title that a court will consider so free from defect that it will enforce its acceptance by a purchaser. Marketable title can be easily sold to a reasonably cautious and knowledgeable purchaser. The best evidence of marketable title is through the issuance of a policy insuring the title. The policy is offered by title insurance companies that search the title of the property back to the origin and establish a chain of title.

Title Companies

Title companies employ examiners who search the documents recorded against a property to make sure that the grantor on one deed was the grantee on the previous deed. They check for acknowledgement, and they check for forgery. They also search for liens that have not been released. If there are problems on the title, they can be corrected through the use of a quitclaim or a suit for quiet title. A suit for quiet title is a court action that is used when a previous seller is no longer living in the area or is deceased.

Abstract of Title

An **abstract of title** is a summary of all conveyances and legal proceedings affecting title to a parcel of real estate. The abstract of title will show all liens or encumbrances affecting the property. An abstractor searches the county records and other official sources. The information is then summarized and arranged in order, along with notations of where the information was found.

The abstract of title does not guarantee the validity of the title; it merely discloses items about the property that are of public record. Abstracts of title are usually prepared for or by an attorney who is handling the transaction. In some states, title insurance is available for abstracts. Generally, title abstracts are not used in Nevada because of the use of title insurance.

The Torrens System

The **Torrens system** is a legal system for the registration of land ownership. The Torrens system verifies ownership of land and the status of title, including any encumbrances except tax liens.

With the Torrens system, legal title does not pass, nor is the lien effective against the property, until the conveyance and/or encumbrance is recorded on the certificate. If an error was made through a Registrar of Title, a claim may be made against the state. Title insurance is also available in some cases when using the Torrens system. Under the Torrens system, an owner receives a certificate of title from the office of the Registrar of Titles. The Torrens system is not used in Nevada.

PART 2: TRANSFERRING TITLE

Transferring title is also known as *alienation*. **Alienation** is the act of transferring real property from one person to another. There are four methods of alienation: *voluntary alienation, involuntary alienation, alienation by will*, and *alienation by descent*. Each of these methods will be covered in detail. A full understanding of transfer of title is vital to the success of a real estate professional.

Voluntary alienation is the transfer of ownership with the consent of the owner. Voluntary alienation includes selling, exchanging, or giving away the property. Voluntary alienation also includes the dedication of property. *Dedication* is the voluntary conveyance of private land to the public.

Involuntary alienation is the transfer of property ownership without the consent of the owner. Involuntary alienation is accomplished by operation of the law. Types of involuntary alienation include:

- Mortgage foreclosure
- Escheat
- Adverse possession
- Tax sale
- Judgment
- Eminent domain

Alienation by will takes place according to the individual's last will and testament, which is a legal document executed during the individual's lifetime that takes effect upon the maker's death for the purpose of distributing his or her estate according to his or her desires.

Alienation by descent occurs when a person dies *intestate*. A person dies intestate when he or she dies without a will. The property of the decedent (deceased person) is inherited by his or her heirs according to the state laws of descent.

11.4 VOLUNTARY ALIENATION

In the sale or gift of real property, the seller or giver is known as the **grantor**. The grantor is the owner of the property. The purchaser, or receiver, of the property is the **grantee**. The conveying instrument used for the sale of real property is a deed. A **deed** is "a written legal document by which ownership of real property is conveyed from one party to another." Remember, property rights are known as the "bundle of rights." The bundle of rights are the rights that are conveyed in the deed.

Essentials of a Valid Conveyance Deed

If you remember the essentials of a valid contract, you will recognize some of the essentials of a valid deed:

- Must be in writing, according to the Statute of Frauds
- Competent grantor of sound mind
- Definite grantee (not fictitious person or entity)

- Consideration
- Words of conveyance
- Type of interest being conveyed (fee simple, life estate, and so on)
- Legal description
- Delivery and acceptance
- Grantor's signature
- Grantee's signature (if a joint tenancy deed)
- Exceptions or reservations to the title

Statute of Frauds

When property ownership was transferred prior to the mid-seventeenth century, there was a ceremony called the **livery of seisin**. The parties who were transferring ownership of property would gather on the land with their witnesses. With the exchange of the proper words, the grantor would hand the grantee a clod of earth, or in winter when the turf was frozen, a twig from a tree, as a symbolic transfer of ownership.

Because it was easy for dishonest grantors to commit fraud through this simple oral ceremony, the English court system enacted the Statute of Frauds in 1677, which states that all contracts must be in writing. All states in the United States have enacted a version of the Statute of Frauds. The Nevada statute requires that all deeds must be written to be valid.

Competent Grantor

To convey title, the grantor must be of legal age, 18 years or older. He or she must be of sound mind and deemed mentally competent. There can be no evidence that the grantor was under the influence of drugs, alcohol, or duress.

Definite Grantee

Transfer cannot be made to a fictitious person or nonexistent corporation. Title may not be transferred to John *or* Jane Doe. It may go to one of them or both of them, but not either.

Consideration

Two types of consideration can be used in a deed. *Valuable consideration* means a monetary amount, which is used in the sale of property. *Good consideration* means "for love and affection," which is used in the gift of real property.

Words of Conveyance

The deed must have words of conveyance, which include the granting clause and the habendum clause.

Granting Clause

The words of conveyance include the **granting clause**, which transfers the property rights along with the grantor's covenants (promises). The wording related to the covenants varies depending upon the type of deed.

Type of Deed	Granting Clause Phrasing
General warranty deed	"do hereby convey and warrant"
Special warranty deed	"remise, release, alienate, and convey"
Bargain and sale deed	"grant, bargain, and sell"
Quitclaim deed	"remise, release, and quit claim"

Habendum Clause

The **habendum clause** follows the granting clause and states the manner in which the property is to be held. The habendum clause literally means "to have and to hold." In the case of a joint tenancy deed, it would say, "the grantor hereby conveys to John and Mary Merriweather not as tenants in common, and not as community property, but as joint tenants with right of survivorship the following described property...."

Interest Conveyed

The interest conveyed by the grantor must also be specified in the deed. When a fee simple estate is being conveyed, there is no need to describe any limitations or qualifications of the property rights being transferred. A transfer of a life estate requires a limitation in the deed with words similar to, "John Doe for the duration of his natural life."

Legal Description

A valid conveyance deed must have an accurate legal description. This can be any one of the three accepted types of legal descriptions, although most properties in an urban setting use the map and plat description. A street address is not acceptable as a legal description.

Delivery and Acceptance

Delivery and acceptance actually transfers title to real property. If the closing is an escrow closing, in theory the title company delivers the deed to the grantee on the date of the closing. Escrow closings require recordation of the deed, which the title company handles for the grantor and grantee. The deed is mailed to the grantee by the county recorder within two to three weeks, but it is considered delivered to the grantee at the close of escrow. The delivery, acceptance, and recordation, along with the buyer's payment of funds, fulfill the provisions of the contract, making it an executed contract (that is, a contract that has been completed) as opposed to an executory one (that is, a contract where something remains to be done by one or more parties).

Signatures

The grantor must sign the deed. If property is held in concurrent ownership, both grantors must sign the deed if the interest of all owners is to be conveyed. All deeds have to be acknowledged and should be recorded, although Nevada law does not require recording. Recording the deed gives constructive notice of the ownership of the property.

Acknowledgement

Acknowledgement is the formal declaration by a person executing an instrument that he or she is freely signing it. A public official or a notary public attests to the signing. All deeds must be acknowledged according to the Statute of Frauds. To be recorded, all deeds must be acknowledged; however, deeds do not have to be recorded to be legal in Nevada.

An acknowledgement can be done before a person authorized to take acknowledgements, such as a notary public, county recorder, clerk of the court, or judge.

If property being sold is owned by a corporation, the person(s) signing for the corporation must be an officer. The authority to convey property must be granted by a resolution of the board of directors, which also includes in the resolution the authority of the person(s) designated to sign the deed.

Signatures are always required by the grantor, no matter what type of deed. If the title is taken as joint tenancy or community property with rights of survivorship, the grantee must sign the deed. If a married couple takes title as tenants in common or as joint tenants, they must also sign the deed. This requirement acknowledges that they are not taking title as community property.

Exceptions or Reservations

Exceptions or reservations to the title must be listed on the deed. As mentioned in Chapter 6, these are called "Covenants, Conditions, and Restrictions (CC&Rs)." CC&Rs are limitations placed on the use of the property. They are listed on the deed itself. As part of the recorded deed, CC&Rs are enforceable against any future grantees.

Exceptions are limitations on the title, such as easements, mineral rights or deed restrictions, or other encumbrances on the property.

Reservations are uses that the grantor withholds from the title being conveyed for personal use. The grantor might reserve mineral rights, or, if selling a portion of the land, might reserve an easement for ingress and egress to the portion of land not being sold. A grantor may also reserve a life estate by selling land and reserving a right to live in the house until his or her death.

Exceptions or reservations are usually listed on the deed by a statement similar to the following:

> *Subject to current taxes and other assessments, reservations in patents and all easements, rights of way, encumbrances, liens, covenants, conditions, restrictions, obligations, and liabilities as may appear on record.*

Types of Conveying Deeds

In Nevada, three types of deeds are considered conveyance deeds. Though different names are used, often conveyance deeds differ only in their warranties. The three types of conveyance deeds are:

1. General warranty deeds
2. Special warranty deeds
3. Bargain and sale deeds

General Warranty Deeds

General warranty deeds contain the greatest number of warranties, which are called **covenants** (promises). Therefore, general warranty deeds are used most often in Nevada. They provide the greatest protection to the grantee and impose the greatest responsibility on the grantor.

The following are warranties in a general warranty deed:

- *Covenant of Seisin*, which promises that the grantor is the legal owner of the property and has the right to convey it.
- *Covenant of Quiet Enjoyment* warrants that the grantee's title is good against third parties who might bring court action to establish superior rights.
- *Covenant against Encumbrances*, in which the grantor promises that the property is free from encumbrances, except those listed in the deed.
- *Covenant of Warranty Forever*, in which the grantor promises that if title fails at any time, he or she will compensate the grantee for the loss.
- *Covenant of Further Assurance*, in which the grantor promises to obtain and deliver any instrument needed in order to make the title good.

Special Warranty Deed

A **special warranty deed** offers the same covenants as a warranty deed, except that the covenants are limited to the period of time the grantor was in possession of the property. The words of the granting clause limit all claims and demands made by persons from, through, or under the grantor. This deed is used by trust departments, new homebuilders, or major corporations that wish to sell but only be responsible for claims during their time of ownership.

Bargain and Sale Deed

A **bargain and sale deed** provides the least protection to the grantee of any of the conveying deeds. It contains only two limited warranties, namely that the grantor has the right to convey the property and has not conveyed it to anyone else, and that the property is free of encumbrances, except those listed in the deed. Examples of this deed include the following:

- Treasurer's deed (after tax sale)
- Sheriff's deed (foreclosure on mortgage)
- Trustee's deed (foreclosure on deed of trust)

Quitclaim Deeds

A **quitclaim deed** releases or quits any claim or interest a person has in a property. A quitclaim deed offers no warranties. It simply says, "If I have an interest I give it. If not, I give nothing."

Quitclaim deeds are used in after-ownership situations, such as in a divorce. When one person is awarded sole ownership of property, the other will quit claim by signing a deed.

Clouds on Title

Quitclaim deeds are also used to clear up **clouds on a title**. A *cloud* on the title is an outstanding claim or encumbrance, which, if valid, would affect or impair the owner's title. If there is a defect in a title, an owner or potential owner can go back to the grantor and correct the defect with the use of a quitclaim deed. At that point, because they would possibly not have legal title, only an interest in the property, they cannot transfer legal title. They can only transfer what interest they have.

Quitclaim deeds are also helpful when a "straw person" is used to deed into a joint tenancy situation, when the elements of one time and title are needed.

Disclaimer Deeds

Disclaimer deeds are used when one spouse of a married couple acquires real property and wishes to hold title as separate property from his or her spouse. The spouse must execute and record a disclaimer deed. This places a notice on record that the community property estate between husband and wife is broken on this real property only. If a spouse does not execute and record a disclaimer deed at the time the real property is acquired, that spouse could have a community property interest in the property until a quitclaim deed is executed and recorded.

The exception to this procedure is when one of the married couple inherits real property. In that case, the spouse does not need a disclaimer deed. Nevada law provides that inherited real property is sole and separate.

11.5 INVOLUNTARY ALIENATION

Involuntary alienation is the transfer of ownership without the owner's consent. Involuntary alienation occurs by operation of law. There are two types of involuntary alienation that involve government rights:

- *Escheat*—dying without a will *and* with no heirs.
- *Eminent domain*—taking property for the public welfare by paying fair market value for it.

    Other types of involuntary alienation involve the result of liens on property:

- Tax sale (for delinquent property tax assessment)
- Judgments (court action by creditors)
- Mortgages or trust deeds in default

Adverse Possession

Adverse possession is also a type of involuntary alienation, but it does not involve a government right, nor is it the result of liens on property. The history of adverse possession can be traced back to a time before written deeds were used as evidence of ownership. For a long time, ownership was acquired through occupation, and this practice forms the foundation for what we know today as adverse possession.

A person can acquire ownership by adverse possession through the unauthorized occupation of another person's land. **Adverse possession** is a statute of limitations that prohibits a legal owner from claiming title to land if he or she has done nothing to expel an adverse occupant during the statutory period. Courts demand specific proof before they will rule in favor of someone claiming title by virtue of adverse possession.

Persons claiming ownership by adverse possession must prove that they maintained *actual, visible, continuous, hostile, exclusive*, and *notorious possession* and must have publicly claimed ownership to the property.

This means that the occupant's use must have been consistent, exclusive, and obvious to the legal owner. Also, the occupant's use must have been hostile, which means without permission. Finally, the occupant must prove that he or she has met all the requirements for a specified period of time. When accumulating the required number of years, the adverse claimant may **tack** on his or her period of possession to that of a prior adverse occupant.

Hostile possession does not necessarily connote ill will or evil intent; it merely shows that the occupant claims exclusive right to the property and denies the owner's title. If a possessor fails to realize that he or she is holding property adversely, the possessor can still obtain title by adverse possession.

A person may acquire title by adverse possession under a mistake of fact. Encroachment is a common source of successful adverse possession claims. Even if an occupant had no knowledge that he was encroaching on the owner's property, he still occupied and claimed the property and could acquire title to the property by adverse possession.

Color of Title

To claim title by adverse possession in Nevada, a person must have occupied the property for five years with color of title and the payment of the property taxes. **Color of title** is a believable appearance of ownership interest, such as an improperly prepared deed proclaiming to transfer title to the occupant, or a claim of ownership by inheritance.

11.6 ALIENATION BY WILL

Alienation by will is a form of voluntary alienation, because the maker of the will took the time to specify who should have his or her possessions after the maker's death. The Nevada Revised Statutes state the requirements for a valid will.

A will made during a person's lifetime takes effect upon that person's death. The courts must probate wills. **Probate** is a legal process by which a court determines the assets of the estate and who will inherit the property of the deceased person. A probate court also rules on the validity of the will. If the will is upheld, the estate is distributed according to its provisions.

Property transferred through the use of a joint tenancy deed is not covered by probate. It requires an estate tax waiver, which is a property report by the personal representative of the deceased, and a copy of the death certificate.

Any person who is at least 18 years old can make, alter, or revoke a will. The male maker of a will is called a *testator*; a female maker is a *testatrix*. Its maker must sign the will. Nevada does recognize wills written in other states, and they can be probated here.

The transfer of real property through a will is called "**devise.**" The person who wills the property is the **devisor**; the receiver of the property is the **devisee**. The transfer of personal property through a will is a **bequest**.

Types of Wills

An attorney usually draws a **conventional (or formal) will**. The maker and two witnesses must sign this will. Wills should be dated at the time of the signing. If two or more wills are found, the most recent one will be probated. An amendment to a will is called a "codicil," which must also be dated and signed. When a new will is written, the old will should be destroyed. Wills should not be altered by simply drawing lines through the revised portion; they should be rewritten.

A **holographic will** is a handwritten will that is signed and dated by its maker. A holographic will cannot be typed, but it can be a preprinted form that was filled in by hand. A holographic will requires no witness.

An **electronic will** is written, created, and stored in an electronic record, contains the date and the electronic signature of the maker. The Nevada statutes require other specific authentication and storage requirements and when they are met an electronic will is valid.

A **nuncupative will** or oral will is not valid in Nevada.

11.7 ALIENATION BY DESCENT

Alienation by descent is considered voluntary. The law provides for an orderly transfer of one's property after death when a person dies **intestate**, which means dying without a will. The law assumes that the person agrees with the laws of intestate succession by not making a will to change from the statutory provisions of intestate succession.

Intestate succession passes property to the surviving heirs. Property that is held as joint tenancy will not pass by succession because it is not inheritable.

If a person dies intestate, the probate court will appoint a personal representative. The personal representative acts as the administrator of the estate.

Per stirpes distribution is the distribution of intestate property to a group of people who take a share allocated to a deceased ancestor by representing that person.

EXAMPLE—A couple has three children, who each have two children. One of the couple's children dies, leaving a widow and two children. When the grandparents pass on, the deceased child's share of the grandparents' estate will go to his two children per stirpes or by representation.

CHAPTER SUMMARY

Title gives evidence of the quality, right, and interest in real property. Original title is title held by a country or state. When an original title is conveyed by a state or federal government to an individual, the instrument used is called a patent. Derivative title is title that belongs to an individual or legal entity and is derived from the government's original title. Derivative title is typically gained by descent, will, purchase, or gift.

Two ways are available to give notice of ownership rights to land. One is by recording documents in the public records (constructive notice), and the other is by visibly occupying or otherwise making use of the land (actual notice). Constructive notice, also called legal notice, charges the public with the responsibility of examining the public records to gain knowledge of anyone who might claim a right or interest in the property. Actual notice is knowledge that is gained from what is seen, heard, read, or observed. A person interested in acquiring a property is responsible by law for making inquiry of anyone giving actual or constructive notice. This is referred to as inquiry notice.

A chain of title shows the linkage of ownership connecting the present owner to each prior owner. Generally, the chain starts with the original patent. When there is a gap in the chain, it must be corrected in order to have marketable title. The best evidence of marketable title is through the issuance of a policy insuring the title. Title companies search the documents recorded against a property to make sure that the grantor on one deed was the grantee on the previous deed. They also check for acknowledgement, forgery, and for liens that have not been released. An abstract of title is a summary of all conveyances and legal proceedings affecting title to a parcel of real estate. Generally, title abstracts are not used in Nevada, because of the use of title insurance. The Torrens system is a legal system for the registration of land ownership. The Torrens system is not used in Nevada.

Transferring title is also known as alienation. Alienation is the act of transferring real property from one person to another. There are four methods of alienation: voluntary alienation, involuntary alienation, alienation by will, and alienation by descent.

Voluntary alienation is the transfer of ownership with the consent of the owner and includes selling, exchanging, or giving away the property. Voluntary alienation also includes the dedication of property, which means the voluntary transfer of property to a governmental entity. In the sale or gift of real property, the seller or giver is the grantor. The purchaser or receiver of the property is the grantee. The conveying instrument used for the sale of real property is a deed.

The essentials of a valid deed include, but are not limited to: must be in writing; must have a competent grantor and a definite grantee; must have words of conveyance, which include the granting clause and the habendum clause; and must state the type of interest being conveyed. Delivery and acceptance actually transfers title to real property. The deed must also list any exceptions or reservations to the title. These are called "covenants, conditions, and restrictions (CC&Rs)." CC&Rs are limitations placed on the use of the property.

In Nevada, there are three types of deeds that are considered conveyance deeds: general warranty deeds, special warranty deeds, and bargain and sale deeds. General warranty deeds contain the greatest number of warranties, which are called covenants. General warranty deeds are used most often in Nevada. A special warranty deed offers the same covenants as a warranty deed except that they are limited to the period of time the grantor was in possession of the property. A bargain and sale deed provides the least protection to the grantee of any of the conveying deeds. A quitclaim deed releases or quits any claim or interest a person has in a property. Quitclaim deeds can be used in a divorce or to clear up clouds on a title. Disclaimer deeds are used when one spouse of a married couple acquires real property and wishes to hold title as separate property from his or her spouse.

Involuntary alienation is the transfer of property ownership without the consent of the owner and occurs by operation of law. Two types of involuntary alienation involve government rights: escheat (dying without a will and with no heirs) and eminent domain (taking property for the public welfare by paying fair market value for it). A person can also acquire ownership by adverse possession. Adverse possession is a statute of limitations that prohibits a legal owner from claiming title to land if he or she has done nothing to expel an adverse occupant during the statutory period. Persons claiming ownership by adverse possession must prove that they maintained actual, visible, continuous, hostile, exclusive, and notorious possession, and must have publicly claimed ownership to the property. To claim title by adverse possession in Nevada, a person must have occupied the property for five years with color of title and the payment of the property taxes. Color of title is a believable appearance of ownership interest.

Alienation by will takes place according to the individual's last will and testament and is also a form of voluntary alienation, because the maker of the will took the time to specify who should have his or her possessions after the maker's death. The courts must probate wills. Probate is a legal process by which a court determines the assets of the estate and who will inherit the property of the deceased person. Any person who is at least 18 years old can make, alter, or revoke a will. The transfer of real property through a will is called devise. The person who wills the property is the devisor; the receiver of the property is the devisee. A conventional (or formal) will is usually drawn by an attorney. This will must be signed by the maker and two witnesses. An amendment to a conventional will is called a codicil.

Alienation by descent occurs when a person dies intestate, which means without a will, and is a form of voluntary alienation. The law provides for an orderly transfer of one's property after death when a person dies intestate. Intestate succession passes property to the surviving heirs. Per stirpes distribution is the distribution of intestate property to a group of people who take a share allocated to a deceased ancestor by representing that person.

CHECKING YOUR COMPREHENSION

1. Define the terms *title, original title, derivative title,* and *patent*.

2. Describe and give examples of the following:
   * Actual notice
   * Constructive notice
   * Inquiry notice

3. Summarize the meaning of chain of title and describe the role of title insurance.

4. Define alienation and give examples of the following:
   * Voluntary alienation
   * Involuntary alienation

- Alienation by descent
- Alienation by will

5. List and describe the essentials of a valid deed.

REVIEWING YOUR UNDERSTANDING

1. To be valid, a deed requires:
   a. recording
   b. signature of grantee
   c. a legal street address
   d. delivery

2. Involuntary alienation would include all of the following, **EXCEPT**:
   a. foreclosure sale
   b. adverse possession
   c. eminent domain
   d. dedication

3. The transfer of original title to a private party is accomplished through the issuance of a:
   a. quitclaim deed
   b. bargain and sale deed
   c. special warranty deed
   d. patent

4. The person making an acknowledgement on a deed is **BEST** described as the:
   a. grantor
   b. grantee
   c. broker
   d. notary public

5. A seller who will defend the title she is giving only against others who claim an interest through or under her would give a:
   a. general warranty deed
   b. special warranty deed
   c. bargain and sale deed
   d. quitclaim deed

6. Legal title to real estate is transferred by:
   a. delivery and acceptance of the deed
   b. recordation of the deed
   c. the owner's title insurance
   d. an abstract of title

7. The words, *to have and to hold* **MOST** likely would be included in a(n):
   a. mortgage note
   b. alienation clause
   c. habendum clause
   d. legal description

8. When property is conveyed by devise, the instrument used is a:
   a. deed
   b. will
   c. lease
   d. option

9. An individual who openly, continuously, notoriously, and hostilely occupies property for a specified number of years may acquire title by:
   a. easement by prescription
   b. adverse possession
   c. encroachment
   d. foreclosure

10. When Pete died, a signed and acknowledged, but unrecorded, deed was found in his house, deeding his house to charity. His will provided that his entire estate go to his nephew. The house would **MOST** likely go to:
    a. the charity, because acknowledgement is a presumption of delivery
    b. the charity, because intent was clear
    c. the nephew, because Pete died owning the house
    d. the charity, because delivery is not a requirement as to charitable gifts

11. Tacking on would **MOST** likely refer to:
    a. adding to a structure
    b. adding a third party to a contract or other document
    c. obtaining a fee interest through adverse possession
    d. an amendment on a purchase contract

12. Interest acquired by adverse possession is:
    a. a dominant tenement
    b. personal in nature to the holder
    c. a life interest
    d. a fee

13. Descent refers to:
    a. a formal will
    b. a holographic will
    c. personal property
    d. intestate succession

14. Which of the following actions would **NOT** prevent a claim of adverse possession?
    a. physically barring entry of adverse user
    b. ousting the adverse user
    c. ordering the adverse user to desist
    d. giving the adverse user express permission to use the property

15. Which of the following deeds **WOULD FAIL** to transfer title?
    a. a deed to Henry Jones using his stage name "Mr. Magic"
    b. a deed made to Samuel Smith, et ux
    c. a deed made to Henry or Susan Smith
    d. a deed made to Susan Smith and husband

16. Who has the greatest interest in seeing that a deed is recorded?
    a. a grantor
    b. creditors of the grantor
    c. the grantee
    d. the real estate broker

17. A valid deed does **NOT** require a:
    a. signature of the grantee
    b. statement of consideration
    c. legal description of the property
    d. grantor with legal capacity to execute

18. A deed that conveys property with limited promises, and indicates that the grantor has the right to convey the property, would be a:
    a. quitclaim deed
    b. bargain and sale deed
    c. gift deed
    d. deed of trust

19. An exception in a deed:
    a. excludes part of the property (via easement or encumbrance)
    b. reserves a right for the benefit of a grantor
    c. voids the deed
    d. provides for alternate grantees

20. A deed entailing the **GREATEST** liability for the grantor is a:
    a. special warranty
    b. quitclaim
    c. bargain and sale
    d. general warranty

Chapter 12

IMPORTANT TERMS AND CONCEPTS

American Land Title
  Association (ALTA)
corrective deed
escrow company
escrow instructions
extended coverage

leasehold policy
lender's policy
marketable title
owner's policy
recording acts

standard coverage
subrogation
title commitment/
  preliminary title
  report
title insurance

CHAPTER OBJECTIVES

After completing this chapter, you should be able to:

- Summarize the purpose of recording a document and the procedures involved.
- Describe the role and regulation of escrow companies.
- Explain the purpose and types of title insurance coverage.

Recording Acts and Title Insurance

12.1 RECORDING A DOCUMENT

Every state has adopted **recording acts** to allow certain instruments or documents to be placed in the public record. These recorded instruments and documents provide constructive notice of an estate, interest or right in land, the transfer of rights in land, or the encumbrance of an interest in land.

Within each state, each county has a public recorder's office that is located in the county seat. Each county recorder's office records submitted documents that pertain to real property in that county. Therefore, an individual with a deed to property in Clark County would go to the recorder's office in Clark County for recording. Likewise, a party wanting to know about land ownership in Churchill County would go to the Churchill County recorder's office to review and examine the public records.

Early recordings were usually handwritten accounts of the deed. Later, they were typed and then copied. All documents presented for recording today must have original signatures and acknowledgements. The signer makes the acknowledgement and the notary takes the acknowledgement.

Sequential Recording

Documents are recorded in sequence. Assume a sale to be recorded involves a loan payoff and a new loan. The escrow company positions the document in the correct sequence as follows:

1. The release of the existing mortgage.
2. The deed from the grantor to grantee.
3. The new mortgage lien.

If any of these documents is out of sequence, it must be recorded in the proper position.

Errors

When an error is made in a deed, such as a misspelled name or an inaccurate legal description, and the deed has been recorded, the original deed that was recorded can be corrected by lining through the mistake and typing in the correct information. A clause is then inserted on the deed stating, "This deed is being re-recorded for the sole purpose of ...." The deed is then re-recorded to reflect the correction.

If the original deed containing the error cannot be located, a new deed is prepared with the correct information and a clause that states, "This deed is a corrective deed and is being recorded to replace that certain deed between the same parties dated _____ recorded _____ at Recorder's No. _____." The new deed is marked **"corrective deed"** and is then recorded. (This is also known as a *deed of confirmation*.)

12.2 ESCROW COMPANIES

In your study of recordings and title insurance, an understanding of escrows and escrow companies will prove helpful.

A real estate broker, legal counsel, or the parties to the transaction can complete the closing of a real estate transaction. However, almost all real estate closings in Nevada are escrow closings, done by escrow companies or escrow divisions of title insurance companies.

An **escrow company** orders loan payoffs, prepares escrow instructions, takes signatures, disburses funds, and arranges for the recording of documents. Escrow instructions, which are generally part of the purchase contract, are documents in which buyers and sellers hire escrow companies to work on their behalf. Escrow companies also do the proration and prepare settlement statements, even though the broker is responsible for these reports. At times, escrow companies examine title, but they do not issue the title insurance. In some cases, the escrow department is a division of a large title insurance company that examines and issues its own policies.

Regulation

Escrow agencies, except those that are part of a title insurance company, are licensed and regulated by the Commissioner of Mortgage Lending of the Department of Business and Industry. The Commissioner of Insurance licenses and regulates the escrow departments of title insurance companies.

The rates that are charged for escrow service and title insurance are competitive and are not set by any regulating agency. Each entity establishes its own rate chart for fees and files its rate schedule with the Commissioner of Insurance.

Escrow Instructions

Escrow instructions are generally included in the purchase contract; but sometimes, the escrow company prepares separate instructions. The instructions are the contract through which the escrow company is employed by the buyer and seller to close the escrow according to their instructions.

If there are separate escrow instructions, they should provide the same terms and conditions outlined in the original contract to purchase. It is the broker's responsibility to make sure they are the same. If there is a discrepancy, the terms of the original purchase contract will prevail.

Escrow companies prepare documents as a part of the escrow package, but they may not prepare documents when there is no escrow involved. The escrow company also will take signatures on the closing documents for lenders.

Some of the larger escrow companies and most title companies operate collection departments, which collect payments, provide bookkeeping, and act as trustee in seller-carried trust deeds or vendor/vendee liens. The companies charge a set-up fee and a monthly collection fee.

Marketable Title

A seller is required to provide clear or marketable title when a property is conveyed. **Marketable title** is title that is reasonably free from risk of legal dispute over possible defects. Marketable title is free from undisclosed encumbrances, has no serious defect, is not dependent on doubtful questions of law, and will not expose the purchaser to the hazards of litigation. Last, any reasonably well-informed, careful person, acting upon business principles and willful knowledge of the facts, could in turn mortgage or sell the property at fair market value.

The best evidence of marketable title is title that is covered by a title insurance policy. The title commitment or preliminary title report should be delivered to the buyer during the inspection period to document that marketable title will be delivered by the seller.

Title Commitment/Preliminary Title Report

When an escrow is opened, the title company will begin to search the title and prepare a preliminary title report or a commitment for title insurance. It will state how the property is to be vested, the quality of the estate conveyed, and any requirements that must be resolved, such as back taxes, judgments, or outstanding liens. The buyers should be given a copy of the report for their inspection. The lender will require a copy of the report before the loan will be approved.

When buyers or sellers have common names such as Smith, Jones, or Johnson, they may be asked to sign an identity statement. This information is used to determine whether a judgment that shows on the records against J. Smith could be that particular J. Smith. Many times, it will show that the judgment is against someone else who shares that name.

12.3 TITLE INSURANCE

When acquiring real property, the buyer should protect against financial loss due to title defects with title insurance. Even though the preliminary title report indicates marketable title, there may still be title defects.

A **title insurance** policy requires the insurance company to compensate the insured for financial loss, up to the face amount of the policy, when the loss results from a title defect. A title policy also requires the insurance company to defend against claims, including taking any action necessary to protect the title. The policy protects the insured against title defects that existed at the time the insured received the title.

Exceptions

All title insurance policies contain a list of exceptions. The exceptions are liens, encumbrances, and title problems that the title company will not insure. A title policy will be issued only after a title search that reveals all encumbrances of record, as well as other possible defects in the title.

Several liens and encumbrances do not affect marketable title, and they are not required to be cleared in order to transfer ownership at market value. Examples include current year real estate taxes, utility easements, deed restrictions, and any other lien or encumbrance that the purchaser is willing to accept. On the other hand, mechanic's liens, judgment liens, and overdue taxes need to be resolved before transferring title.

Title that is acceptable to the insurance company is called *insurable title*. The premium paid for the policy is a one-time premium paid when the policy is issued.

Types of Policies

The different types of title insurance policies include *owner's policies*, *lender's policies*, and *leasehold policies*.

Owner's Policy

An **owner's policy** provides protection for the buyer. The face amount of the policy is generally equal to the purchase price. The coverage amount remains the same for the life of the policy. The party that will pay the policy premium should be set forth in the purchase contract; however, the premium is usually paid by the seller.

The insurance in an owner's policy covers the title backward from the time of the recordation of the deed and forward to insure that owner, or the owner's heirs, forever. In other words, if a defect were found 20 years after a property was sold, the title company that issued an owner's policy would still cover the defect.

Owner's policies are structured in two parts: Schedule A and Schedule B. Schedule A lists all of the positive coverage. Schedule B lists the exceptions.

Standard or Extended Coverage

An owner's policy can have either *standard coverage* or *extended coverage*. A **standard coverage** owner's policy is the most common policy used in residential conveyance and is limited to insurance against:

1. Forged documents of incorrect marital status.
2. Documents signed by incompetent parties.
3. Unmarketable property due to defect of title.
4. An improperly delivered deed.

All of these positive assurances are subject to the second page, called Schedule B, which lists standard exclusions and any specific exclusions found by a search of the county records. Some of these exclusions could include:

1. Defects in title known to the owner.
2. Unrecorded easements, mechanic's liens, or other liens.
3. Claims or rights not of public record.
4. Rights of parties in possession (adverse possession).
5. Encroachments or anything that could be found by survey.
6. Legal access to the property.

Extended coverage includes all of the coverage of a standard policy, plus additional insurance against:

1. Anything an inspection of the property might disclose.
2. Discrepancies or conflicts in boundaries.
3. Unrecorded liens, encumbrances, or leases.
4. Not having legal access.

Extended coverage owner's policies are used more often for commercial sales rather than residential sales. Due to the greater coverage they provide, extended coverage policies are more expensive than standard coverage policies. Normally, a seller pays for the owner's policy. If the buyer requests an extended coverage, it should be a condition of the contract, and parties should agree on who will pay for the additional coverage.

Lender's Policy

A **lender's policy** provides protection against defects in the title pledged as security in a mortgage or trust deed note. The lender's insurable interest is only to the extent of the outstanding loan balance at any given time. As a result, the policy coverage amount decreases as the principal balance due on the note is reduced.

The lender's policy insures the lender of his or her security position (that is, first position). Most lenders require an extended coverage policy. The buyer generally pays the premium for the lender's policy.

Leasehold Policy

A **leasehold policy** provides protection to a tenant or a lender to the tenant against defects in the lessor's title. This policy is usually written to protect a lender when the borrower is pledging a leasehold interest instead of a fee simple title.

American Land Title Association (ALTA)

The **American Land Title Association (ALTA)** is an association of land title companies throughout the country. ALTA members use uniform ALTA title insurance forms designed by the association to achieve standardization within the industry.

Claims

The maximum loss for which the insurance company may be liable cannot exceed the face amount of the policy. When a title company makes a payment to settle a claim, the insurance company acquires, by right of subrogation, all the legal remedies and rights that the insured party might have against anyone responsible for the settled claims. **Subrogation** is the substitution of one person in the place of another with reference to a lawful claim, such as when an insurance company pays a claim and then has the right to collect from the party causing the loss.

EXAMPLE—Mr. and Mrs. Cassidy owned a property, and Mr. Cassidy signed his name and forged his wife's name on the deed when they sold to Mr. Rogers. The title being transferred to Mr. Rogers was insured because the title insurance company was not aware of the forgery. Mr. Rogers later sold to Mr. and Mrs. Autry on a warranty deed. Mr. and Mrs. Autry later sold to Mr. and Mrs. Eastwood on a joint tenancy deed that was insured by a title company. Later, Mrs. Cassidy told Mr. Eastwood that she never signed the deed; it was forged, and their title was defective.

The Eastwoods filed a complaint with the title company, who assured them the matter would be cleared. Because the Eastwoods took title on a warranty deed, which says the grantor warrants forever, they have the right to ask that the defect be corrected. Because a title policy covered that title, the title company has the same rights through subrogation as the owner and, in fact, would make the claim on behalf of the Eastwoods. And so it continues all the way back between title insurers and owners until the last title company settles with Mr. Cassidy, who committed the forgery.

Unjustified Claims

An owner must have suffered actual loss before a claim can be paid. Examples of unjustified claims follow:

- Title company report fails to show an easement for public utilities over the south eight feet of a lot, and the right to use the easement was never exercised, nor does the owner suffer any loss when he sells the property. The owner has no claim.

- Property operated as a business in a residential zone is not covered for a loss because of exceptions in Schedule B excluding government regulations or violations thereof.

CHAPTER SUMMARY

Recording acts allow certain instruments or documents to be placed in the public record. These recorded instruments and documents provide constructive notice of an estate, interest or right in land, the transfer of rights in land, or the encumbrance of an interest in land. Each county has a public recorder's office located in the county seat. Each county recorder's office records submitted documents that pertain to real property in that county. Documents are recorded in sequence. If a deed containing an error has been recorded, the original deed can be corrected by lining through the mistake and typing in the correct information. The deed is then re-recorded to reflect the correction. If the original deed with the error cannot be located, a corrective deed is prepared with the correct information.

Almost all real estate closings in Nevada are escrow closings, done by escrow companies or escrow divisions of title insurance companies. An escrow company orders loan payoffs, prepares escrow instructions, takes signatures, disburses funds, and arranges for the recording of documents. Escrow companies also do the proration and prepare settlement statements. The Nevada Commissioner of Insurance regulates the escrow departments of escrow and title insurance companies. The rates that are charged for escrow service or title insurance are competitive and are not set by any regulating agency. Escrow instructions are generally included in the purchase contract, but sometimes, the escrow company prepares separate instructions. If there are separate escrow instructions, they should provide the same terms and conditions outlined in the original contract to purchase.

A seller is required to provide clear or marketable title when a property is conveyed. Marketable title is title that is reasonably free from risk of legal dispute over possible defects. The best evidence of marketable title is title that is covered by a title insurance policy. When an escrow is opened, the title company will begin to search the title and prepare a title commitment or preliminary title report. This report should be delivered to the buyer during the inspection period to document that marketable title will be delivered by the seller.

When acquiring real property, the buyer should protect against financial loss due to title defects with title insurance. A title insurance policy requires the insurance company to compensate the insured for financial loss, up to the face amount of the policy, when the loss results from a title defect. A title policy also requires the insurance company to defend against claims. The policy protects the insured against title defects that existed at the time the insured received the title. All title insurance policies contain a list of exceptions, which are liens, encumbrances, and title problems that the title company will not insure. Several liens and encumbrances do not affect marketable title, such as current year real estate taxes and utility easements. Title that is acceptable to the insurance company is called insurable title.

Title insurance policies include owner's policies, lender's policies, and leasehold policies. An owner's policy provides protection for the buyer, and it can have either standard coverage or extended coverage. A standard owner's policy is the most common policy used in residential conveyance and is limited to insurance against forged documents of incorrect marital status, documents signed by incompetent parties, unmarketable property due to defect of title, and an improperly delivered deed. All of these positive assurances are subject to the second page, Schedule B, which lists standard exclusions and any specific exclusions found by a search of the county records. An extended coverage policy includes all of the coverage of a standard policy, plus additional insurance against anything an inspection of the property might disclose, discrepancies or conflicts in boundaries, unrecorded liens, encumbrances, leases, and not having legal access. Extended coverage policies are used more often for commercial sales rather than residential sales.

A lender's policy provides protection against defects in the title pledged as security in a mortgage or trust deed note and insures the lender of his or her security position. A leasehold policy provides protection to a tenant or a lender to the tenant against defects in the lessor's title. The maximum loss for which the insurance company may be liable cannot exceed the face amount of the policy. When a title company makes a payment to settle a claim, the insurance company acquires, by right of subrogation, all the legal remedies and rights that the insured party might have against anyone responsible for the settled claims. An owner must have suffered actual loss before a claim can be paid.

CHECKING YOUR COMPREHENSION

1. Summarize the purpose of the recording acts.

2. Describe the role of an escrow company and its regulation in the state of Nevada.

3. Explain the meaning of the term *marketable title*.

4. Explain the purpose of title insurance.

5. Summarize the following types of title insurance coverage:
   - Owner's policy
   - Standard coverage
   - Extended coverage
   - Lender's policy
   - Leasehold policy

REVIEWING YOUR UNDERSTANDING

1. Real estate title information is **BEST** found in the records of the:
   a. secretary of state
   b. county recorder
   c. tax assessor
   d. vendor

2. Recording does **NOT** give:
   a. constructive notice
   b. actual notice
   c. a presumption of delivery
   d. priority as to the interest

3. An escrow company does all of the following, **EXCEPT**:
   a. arrange document recording
   b. take signatures
   c. arrange the home inspection
   d. disburse funds

4. Escrow and title insurance rates are:
   a. established by the Commissioner of Insurance
   b. established by the Commissioner of Mortgage Lending
   c. controlled by the Administrator of the Real Estate Division
   d. established by each entity

5. Standard coverage in a title insurance policy does not insure against:
   a. forged documents
   b. incompetent grantor
   c. questions of survey
   d. improperly delivered deed

6. When a claim is settled by a title insurance company, the company acquires all rights and claims of the insured against any other person who is responsible for the loss. This is called:
   a. escrow
   b. surety
   c. subrogation
   d. subordination

7. A title insurance policy may be written to protect all of the following, **EXCEPT** the:
   a. owner
   b. licensee
   c. lessee
   d. mortgagee

8. Marketable title is:
   a. reasonably free from risk of legal dispute over possible defects
   b. not related to any sales price
   c. not evidenced by a title insurance policy
   d. ownership evidence of a grocery store

9. A title insurance commitment provides all of the following, **EXCEPT**:
   a. how the property is to be vested
   b. quality of the estate conveyed
   c. zoning classification
   d. requirements that must be resolved

10. When a buyer desires an extended owner's title insurance policy:

    a. The buyer always pays for the additional premium.

    b. The seller always pays for the owner's policy.

    c. The contract must document who will pay for the coverage.

    d. The seller must agree to and pay for extended coverage if requested by the buyer.

11. A lender's policy is a policy for the lender's protection and generally includes:

    a. actual notice

    b. standard coverage

    c. constructive notice

    d. constructive and actual notice

12. A leasehold title policy is written to protect:

    a. a landlord

    b. a lender with a loan to the landlord

    c. a lender with a loan to a tenant who pledges a leasehold interest

    d. a leasehold title policy cannot be issued

13. A title insurance policy on a new loan would normally be charged to the:

    a. buyer

    b. seller

    c. beneficiary

    d. trustee

14. A disinterested party representing both buyers and sellers is a(n):

    a. broker

    b. salesman

    c. escrow agent

    d. attorney in fact

15. Evidence of ownership that refers to the quality of the estate is:

    a. title

    b. equity

    c. mortgage

    d. trust deeds

16. Notice given by the public record is:

    a. world notice

    b. public notice

    c. actual notice

    d. constructive notice

17. A standard owner's title policy would cover which of the following:

    a. errors in survey

    b. unrecorded IRS liens

    c. forged documents

    d. unrecorded mechanic's liens

18. An extended title insurance policy protects the lender against all of the following title defects **EXCEPT**:

    a. claims of persons in possession

    b. errors a survey would disclose

    c. mechanic's liens yet to be recorded

    d. changes in zoning ordinances

19. A standard owner's policy of title insurance insures a buyer against:

    a. zoning laws

    b. overhangs

    c. rights of individuals in possession

    d. incompetent grantor

20. Searches on title are conducted by:

    a. state law

    b. federal law

    c. title companies

    d. local municipality

IMPORTANT TERMS AND CONCEPTS

accountability
actual notice
agent
caveat emptor
caveat venditor
client
confidentiality
constructive notice
customer
deal fairly
disclosure
dual agency
estoppel agency
exclusive retainer
  agreement

fiduciary relationship
fraudulent
  misrepresentation
general agent
implied agency
in-house sale
latent defects
loyalty
material facts
misrepresentation
Multiple Listing Service
  (MLS)
multiple representation
negligence
negligence per se

negligent
  misrepresentation
obedience
power of attorney
principal
puffing
ratified agency
reasonable care and
  diligence
single agency
special agent
subagent
universal agent

CHAPTER OBJECTIVES

After completing this chapter, you should be able to:

- List the areas of specialization in the real estate business.
- Describe real estate brokerage organization and compensation plans.
- Describe the National Association of REALTORS and the Code of Ethics.
- Define and explain agency relationships.
- Describe the creation of an agency relationship and the parties to an agency.
- Define a fiduciary relationship and explain the specific duties involved.
- Explain the duty to deal fairly with a customer/buyer, describe the disclosure obligations, and define concepts of misrepresentation, negligence, and latent defects.
- Discuss profiles of individuals best served as a customer or client.

Real Estate Business, Agency Law, and Disclosure

13.1 THE REAL ESTATE BUSINESS

Many people think of the real estate profession solely as the business of buying and selling property, including the representation of the buyer or seller by a real estate agent or broker. While this is the major business of real estate professionals, there are many other areas of specialization within the business and numerous other businesses or professions that specialize in real estate. Some of the major divisions of the real estate business are described in the following section.

Brokerages

A **brokerage** is in the business of bringing buyers and sellers together in the marketplace for a fee called a "**commission**." Brokerages may specialize in residential (new homes or resale homes), commercial, industrial, or farm and agricultural properties; property management; leasing; or exchanging. In practice, most brokerages specialize in only two or three of these categories, although nothing restricts a brokerage from being involved in any or all categories. Licensing requirements in the state of Nevada are covered in Chapter 26.

Property Development

Property development includes **subdividers** who take raw land, do the initial planning for its best use by subdividing it into lots, and, after approval of the plan by the proper authorities, do the initial development of the streets, sewers, sidewalks, and so on.

Land developers improve lots by adding buildings and then sell the developed lots. Architects and builders who work for the land developer do the planning and construction of homes or other buildings designed for the use of the subdivided lots. Very often the subdivider and the developer are the same person.

Property Management

Property management is a rapidly growing area of the real estate business, due to increased construction of urban-area large apartment complexes, condominiums, cooperatives, commercial buildings, and industrial parks. All of these income properties require special management to provide the best yield to the investor. Consequently, many brokerages either focus exclusively on property management or form a separate property management division. A property management permit must be obtained from the Real Estate Division before a Nevada real estate broker, broker-salesperson, or salesperson is allowed to engage in property management.

Appraising

In almost all real estate transactions, an opinion of property value must be established. For this reason, **appraising** is an important division of the real estate business. Appraisals are necessary for many purposes, including determining insurance value, assessed value, condemnation value, and so on. **Appraisers** may either be staff appraisers working for county assessors, banks, or the government, or they may work as independent fee appraisers. Appraiser classifications and licensing are covered in Chapter 24.

Other Real Estate Businesses and Professions

In addition to brokers, subdividers, developers, property managers, and appraisers, the business of real estate relies on the services of several other business sectors and professionals, as outlined in the following list.

- *Business brokers* are brokers who sell businesses. Business brokers are required to have a real estate license with a Business Brokerage Permit.
- *Financing and investment service firms* include banks, savings and loans, individual investors, pension funds, and insurance companies.
- *Mortgage brokers and mortgage banking* provide financing and loan processing, and package and service loans for investors.
- *Real estate educators* teach in colleges, universities, and private schools.
- *Urban planning* is defined as planning done for the city, county, state, or federal government.
- *Government divisions*, such as the Bureau of Land Management, Forest Services, and Environmental Protection Agency, affect the business of real estate.
- *Escrow services* fulfill escrow instructions and handle closings.
- *Title companies* complete title analysis and issue title insurance.

In addition, one or more of the foregoing professions may require additional education and/or testing. For example, a Nevada property manager must have a real estate license, attend additional classes, pass an additional test, and obtain a Property Management Permit to manage real property. All of the previously mentioned businesses and professions will be discussed in later chapters.

Real Estate Brokerages

A **real estate brokerage** is engaged in the business of bringing buyers and sellers together for the purpose of completing real estate transactions. This includes buying, selling, exchanging, leasing, or renting real property for others for a commission. A licensed real estate broker operates each brokerage.

When a brokerage is organized as a partnership, limited liability company (LLC), or corporation, the entity must designate its manager, who is qualified to act as its real estate broker. Other requirements to serve as the designated broker for an entity depend on the brokerage entity type as follows:

- *Partnership*—one of its members.
- *Corporation*—an officer of the corporation.
- *Limited liability company*—its manager.

Other individuals who hold broker licenses with a brokerage firm do so as a broker-salesperson.

All licensed salespersons and broker-salespersons are agents of the broker and should have a written employment agreement with the brokerage that indicates their status as employees or independent contractors.

Independent Contractor or Employee

The Tax Equity and Fiscal Responsibility Act (TEFRA) of 1982 provides that licensed real estate agents may be classified as independent contractors exempt from classification as employees by the Internal Revenue Service. A salesperson must meet the following criteria to be eligible as an independent contractor:

1. Be a licensed real estate agent.
2. Receive substantially all income in the form of commissions from his or her designated broker only.
3. Have a written contract giving the agent's status as an independent contractor.

For salespeople classified as independent contractors, the designated broker can tell them what to do but not how to do it. The broker may tell a salesperson that he or she should list and sell houses but generally cannot insist that he or she attend meetings, work a set number of hours, or hold open houses. However, the broker is responsible for the salesperson's actions.

The independent contractor status is helpful to the brokerage because the brokerage does not have to pay Social Security tax or unemployment taxes for its salespersons and brokers. (It may have to pay those expenses for receptionists or other staff who are employees.) Neither does the brokerage have to provide any fringe benefits, such as health insurance.

Compensation

The real estate broker is generally engaged by a seller through a listing agreement, which will be covered in a later chapter. The compensation to the broker is established through negotiations between the seller and the broker. The amount of compensation is set forth in the employment agreement and is often a percentage of the sales price.

Anti-Trust Laws

There are no set commissions between the salesperson and the broker. A set commission for all real estate brokerages would be considered **price fixing**, which is a violation of the **Sherman Anti-Trust Act**. Under this federal law, brokerages cannot establish set commissions or allocate customers and markets. For example, competing brokerages are forbidden from:

- Dividing the market into geographic areas.
- Dividing the market by certain prices of houses, thus avoiding competition.

Commission Sharing

Real estate brokerages are often described as either a commission sharing brokerage or a 100% brokerage. At a *commission sharing brokerage*, a percentage of the commission amount collected by the brokerage is paid to the salesperson. The commission sharing percentages generally range from 50% to 70% depending on the experience and volume of production by the licensed salesperson. For example, if the commission split is 50% and the total commission collected by the brokerage was $5000, the salesperson would receive $2500.

At a *100% brokerage*, the salesperson receives all of the commission collected by the brokerage; however, the salesperson must pay a monthly fee to the brokerage and sometimes a transaction fee as well. The salesperson is also responsible for all of his or her own expenses. The amount of the monthly fee and transaction fee varies depending on the services provided to the salesperson by the brokerage. Newly licensed salespeople most often begin their careers at commission sharing brokerages.

In both commission sharing and 100% brokerages, the commission paid to a real estate salesperson can be paid only by his or her broker.

13.2 THE NATIONAL ASSOCIATION OF REALTORS AND PROFESSIONAL ETHICS

The National Association of REALTORS® (NAR) is the largest trade association in the world. It was founded in 1908 as the National Association of Real Estate Boards and has continued to grow since then. As a member of NAR, an individual also becomes a member of the Nevada Association of REALTORS® and the local board or association of REALTORS.® Even though its membership is large, many licensed real estate persons are not members of the association.

The word *REALTOR*® is a registered trademark. Only members of the association may use the name and logo. *REALTOR*® must always be in capital letters or at least capitalized with the "circle R," as in Realtor.®

NAR is dedicated to the protection and preservation of the free enterprise system and the right of the individual to own real property. Consequently, it opposes intervention of government in the affairs of American businesses and counterproductive taxation, government guidelines, and regulations that increase consumer costs.

The National Association of REALTORS® works locally through local boards, state associations, and state governments, and nationally with the federal government. NAR pays close attention to House and Senate bills, as well as city council activities. NAR does not always work "against" government—it works with governmental bodies to promote actions and beliefs that benefit both the government and NAR's members.

In 1913, NAR adopted the **Code of Ethics** as a guide to ethical practices by which all REALTORS® agree to abide. The code has been amended many times since its inception. Figure 13.1 summarizes the Code and Standards of Practice.

FIGURE 13.1   National Association of REALTORS® Code of Ethics

Duties to Clients and Customers:

- Protect and promote clients' interests while treating all parties honestly.
- Refrain from exaggeration, misrepresentation, or concealment of pertinent facts relating to property or transactions.
- Cooperate with other real estate professionals to advance clients' best interests.
- Make true position or interest known when buying or selling on his or her own account or for his or her family or firm.
- Refrain from providing professional services when he or she has any present or contemplated interest in property without disclosing that interest to all parties.
- Disclose any fee received from recommending related real estate products or services.
- Receive compensation from only one party unless he or she has made full disclosure and has received informed consent from the client.
- Keep entrusted funds of clients and customers in a separate escrow account.
- Make sure that contract details are spelled out in writing and all parties receive copies.

Duties to the Public:

- Give equal service to all clients and customers regardless of race, color, religion, sex, handicap, familial status, or national origin.
- Maintain competence in his or her fields of practice, get assistance from a knowledgeable professional, or disclose any lack of expertise to the client.
- Paint a true picture when advertising.
- Refrain from engaging in the unauthorized practice of law.
- Willingly participate in ethics investigations and enforcement actions.

Duties to Other REALTORS®:

- Make only truthful, objective comments about other real estate professionals.
- Respect the exclusive, professional relationships that other REALTORS® have with their clients.
- Help settle financial disagreements with other REALTORS® and their clients.

Although the Code of Ethics applies only to members of the National Association of REALTORS®, it establishes a professional standard to which all licensees should adhere.

13.3 AGENCY

An **agent** is someone who acts on behalf of others in the sale, purchase, or leasing of real property. All states require that brokers and salespeople be licensed. The agency that is created between a broker and his or her client is the same as those created with clients and their attorneys, accountants, and architects and should not be looked upon lightly.

Types of Agents

A **universal agent** represents the **principal** in all matters. He or she can buy or sell real and personal property with or without permission. A universal agent must have a written document stating that he or she is an attorney in fact, thereby giving him or her the **power of attorney**.

A **general agent** represents the principal in a specific range of matters, such as real estate. General agencies are created by a power of attorney, but general agents are authorized only to buy or sell in a special category such as real estate. A property manager is a general agent for the owner of the managed property. (This is also known as *specific power of attorney*.)

A **special agent** is authorized to represent the principal in one specific transaction, such as in a listing, but is not given the power to bind the principal. The agent is employed to find a ready, willing, and able purchaser but cannot make the decision to sell, reject, or accept any offer to purchase.

13.4 CREATION OF AGENCY

Agency relationships are consensual relationships. One person delegates authority and the agent consents to act. Nevada statutes provide that a real estate agency arises from a brokerage agreement in which the agent agrees to do certain acts on behalf of the principal in dealing with a third party. A brokerage agreement may be either oral or written. The agency does not have to be a contract with offer, acceptance, and consideration. Money or commission is not necessary in the creation of the agency. In fact, a commission or fee may not be paid by the principal or by others, and agency may still exist.

Although a fee is not a necessary part of the agency relationship, if a disagreement related to the agency develops and a lawsuit is filed, the courts will look to see if the injured party paid a fee. If so, this could carry considerable weight in a court's verdict.

The elements necessary for the creation of agency are defined by law. No matter what title one puts on his or her actions, if the actions satisfy the elements of the law, then agency exists. The courts judge agency relationship based upon a licensee's actions. If the actions imply agency, even though a written agreement states that agency does not exist, it may exist in the opinion of a court. Likewise, the licensee's actions could deny the existence of an agency, even if the parties have signed documents upholding the creation of an agency.

If both of the following occur, an agency relationship is created:

1. The principal delegates authority to perform acts on his or her behalf.
2. The agent consents to the authority.

Agency relationships do not require compensation, a contract, or an agreement in writing. The parties to an agency relationship include the following (see Figure 13.2):

1. *Agent*—Someone who acts on behalf of another by that person's authority.
2. *Principal*—Someone who engages the services of an agent (also called *client*).
3. *Customer*—The third party to whom the seller sells or agrees to sell.

Agency Relationships

A number of different agency relationships can be created when dealing with clients. A broker could be in breach of an agency he or she did not know existed without knowledge of what creates the following types of agencies:

1. Subagency
2. Dual agency/multiple representation
3. Single agency (buyer's or seller's)
4. Unintended or implied agency
5. Ratified and estoppel agency

Subagency

The real estate broker is the appointed agent in real estate brokerage transactions, and the licensed salespersons and associate brokers employed by the broker agent are subagents. A **subagent** is a person appointed by the broker agent to assist in the performance of the assignment. The subagent owes the broker the same fiduciary duties that the broker owes to the principal. The subagent is also a fiduciary to the broker's principal.

Dual Agency/Multiple Representation

Nationally **dual agency** exists when a broker represents a buyer and a seller at the same time. Whether that agency is expressed or implied makes little difference.

FIGURE 13.2   Real Estate Agency

The broker owes fiduciary duties to both parties and must walk a very fine line. The buyer and seller must be aware that they will receive less than client-level services because it is difficult, if not impossible, for a licensee to carry out his or her fiduciary duties to both parties. Dual agency, whether or not properly disclosed, is illegal in some states. The creation of dual agency is often unintended and implied, and a broker finds out after the fact that he or she was a dual agent.

Dual agency is a common law term and in 1995 Nevada Revised Statute 645.251 abrogated the common law setting for the following:

"A licensee is not required to comply with any principles of common law that may otherwise apply to any of the duties of the licensee as set forth in NRS 645.252, 645.253, and 645.254 and the regulations adopted to carry out those sections."

Thus, the prevailing law in Nevada regarding agency duties of a licensee is statutory. The term "dual agency" is not used anywhere in Chapter 645 of the Nevada Revised Statutes titled Real Estate Brokers and Salesmen. NRS 645.252.1(d) requires that the representation of more than one party in a real estate transaction may only be undertaken upon licensee's full disclosure to each party that he or she is acting for more than one party in that transaction and with each party's subsequent consent to multiple representation in writing.

An **in-house sale** is a brokerage transaction in which one sales associate obtains the listing and also finds the buyer, or a second associate with the same brokerage procures the buyer. The broker represents the buyer and the seller in an in-house sale.

An in-house sale where one licensee represents the buyer and the seller will result in multiple representation. A Consent to Act form must be reviewed, considered, and approved or rejected by both parties to the transaction. A licensee can legally represent both parties, but only with their knowledge and written informed consent. The written consent must include:

1. A description of the real estate transaction.
2. A statement that the licensee is acting for two or more parties to the transaction who have adverse interests and that in acting for these parties, the licensee has a conflict of interest.
3. A statement that the licensee will not disclose any confidential information for one year after the revocation or termination of any brokerage agreement entered into with a party to the transaction, unless he is required to do so by a court of competent jurisdiction or he is given written permission to do so by that party.
4. A statement that a party is not required to consent to the licensee acting on his behalf.
5. A statement that the party is giving his consent without coercion and understands the terms of the consent given.

See Figure 13.5, Consent to Act.

The broker may assign a separate licensee affiliated with the brokerage to act for each party. When separate licensees are assigned by the broker an additional written consent is not required to be obtained by the assigned licensee. Each assigned licensee shall not disclose, except to the broker, any confidential information related to the client.

Single Agency (Buyer's or Seller's)

Single agency is the practice of representing either the buyer or seller, but not both. If a broker intends to be a single agent, he or she must take special care regarding the subagents within the office. If the broker chooses to be a seller's agent, all of the broker's sales associates are subagents of the seller, and extra care must be taken to disclose to all buyers that they are not represented by anyone in that transaction.

If the broker is a multi-office brokerage, even more problems could arise due to the number of people who must be supervised. Because agency relationships can be created by actions, the agency could exist even though a written understanding says that it does not.

An agent may choose to represent buyers only. Some brokers prefer this type of brokerage because there are fewer problems with listings that do not sell. Representing buyers only eliminates the cost of advertising listed properties and the cost of signs, but a buyer's agent is under pressure to secure buyers. Unlike a seller's agent, a buyer's agent has no ready inventory, so he or she must constantly search for buyers.

Some buyer's agents use an *exclusive right to represent buyer agreement*, which creates an agency relationship with the buyer and is similar to the listing agreement with the seller. In some cases, the buyer pays a retainer fee up front. Then the buyer lists his or her housing requirements and agrees to pay a brokerage fee to the broker, no matter whom the buyer buys from.

At other times, a broker will represent a buyer by declaring a buyer's agency and asking the seller to pay the fee. Information regarding available properties can come from a **Multiple Listing Service (MLS)** if the broker is a member. The purchase contract must also disclose the agency relationships that have been established.

It is not necessary for a broker to choose between always being a buyer's broker and always being a seller's broker. There may be times when a buyer walks into the brokerage and, at that time, the broker may choose to represent that buyer.

Implied Agency

Unintended or **implied agency** exists when the buyer assumes by an agent's actions that the agent is working for the buyer. A broker's desire to make buyers feel comfortable and to assist the buyers in their purchase sometimes leads buyers to believe they are being represented. Simple things done and said to build a rapport can cause this misunderstanding. For example:

- "I'll take care of everything for you."
- "Just give them my card and tell them you are working with me."

- "I'll set aside the next three days to show you homes, if you agree to work only with me."
- "I'll have my mortgage woman call you and set up an interview. She always works hard for my people."

Because an agency is established by one's actions, a broker must take care not to offer client-level services to a customer.

Ratified Agency and Estoppel Agency

Ratified agency is created when a seller or buyer accepts the benefits of an agent's prior and unauthorized actions *after the fact*. When a property is shown without a listing agreement, and later the buyer and seller enter into a sales contract, the seller could be bound by the representation (or misrepresentation) of the agent because on the surface it appears an agency exists. The principal created an agency relationship by accepting the prior unauthorized conduct of the broker.

Estoppel agency is created when a broker allows a seller or buyer to create the illusion that the broker is his or her agent. For example, a broker may agree to finish a transaction for a seller if the seller can no longer handle his or her own sale. As a result, the broker could be responsible for the actions of the seller even before the broker was involved.

Disclosure of Duties Owed and Agent Relationship

Nevada does not recognize "transactional" agency, or limited agency representation. Transactional agency occurs when the broker agrees that he or she is not representing either party but is hired only to facilitate the transaction. Limited agency is a truncated form of agency wherein the broker contractually limits his or her duties and liabilities with the client by agreeing to perform only certain acts of representation. In Nevada, with one exception, no duty of a licensee as found in the Nevada Revised Statutes may be waived. This is true even if a client and broker agree by contract to limit the broker's duties; legally, the broker is always vested with the full duties, responsibilities, and liabilities of representation identified in law. To ensure a client understands the licensee's basic duties, the licensee is required to provide the client and each unrepresented party with a state mandated form, the Duties Owed by a Nevada Real Estate Licensee.

A real estate licensee is required to provide a Duties Owed form that sets forth the duties owed by the licensee to both of the following:

a. Each party for whom the licensee is acting as an agent in the real estate transaction.

b. Each unrepresented party to the real estate transaction, if any.

The Duties Owed form is provided by the Nevada Real Estate Division and a sample is included as Figure 13.3.

The licensee is also required to obtain a confirmation regarding the real estate agent relationship with the seller, buyer, or both the seller and buyer.

FIGURE 13.3 Duties Owed by a Nevada Real Estate Licensee

CONSENT TO ACT
This form does not constitute a contract for services nor an agreement to pay compensation.

DESCRIPTION OF TRANSACTION: The real estate transaction is the ☐ sale and purchase *or* ☐ lease of

Property Address: _____

_____ .

In Nevada, a real estate licensee may act for more than one party in a real estate transaction; however, before the licensee does so, he or she must obtain the written consent of each party. This form is that consent. Before you consent to having a licensee represent both yourself and the other party, you should read this form and understand it.

Licensee: The licensee in this real estate transaction is _____ ("Licensee") whose

license number is _____ and who is affiliated with _____ ("Brokerage").

Seller/Landlord _____
                              Print Name

Buyer/Tenant _____
                              Print Name

CONFLICT OF INTEREST: A licensee in a real estate transaction may legally act for two or more parties who have interests adverse to each other. In acting for these parties, the licensee has a conflict of interest.

DISCLOSURE OF CONFIDENTIAL INFORMATION: Licensee will not disclose any confidential information for one year after the revocation or termination of any brokerage agreement entered into with a party to this transaction, unless Licensee is required to do so by a court of competent jurisdiction or is given written permission to do so by that party. Confidential information includes, but is not limited to, the client's motivation to purchase, trade or sell, which if disclosed, could harm one party's bargaining position or benefit the other.

DUTIES OF LICENSEE: Licensee shall provide you with a "Duties Owed by a Nevada Real Estate Licensee" disclosure form which lists the duties a licensee owes to all parties of a real estate transaction, and those owed to the licensee's client. When representing both parties, the licensee owes the same duties to both seller and buyer. Licensee shall disclose to both Seller and Buyer all known defects in the property, any matter that must be disclosed by law, and any information the licensee believes may be material or might affect Seller's/Landlord's or Buyer's/Tenant's decisions with respect to this transaction.

NO REQUIREMENT TO CONSENT: You are not required to consent to this licensee acting on your behalf. You may
  - Reject this consent and obtain your own agent,
  - Represent yourself,
  - Request that the licensee's broker assign you your own licensee.

CONFIRMATION OF DISCLOSURE AND INFORMATION CONSENT

BY MY SIGNATURE BELOW, I UNDERSTAND AND CONSENT: I am giving my consent to have the above identified licensee act for both the other party and me. By signing below, I acknowledge that I understand the ramifications of this consent, and that I acknowledge that I am giving this consent without coercion.

I/We acknowledge receipt of a copy of this list of licensee duties, and have read and understand this disclosure.					
Seller/Landlord	*Date*	*Time*	*Buyer/Tenant*	*Date*	*Time*
Seller/Landlord	*Date*	*Time*	*Buyer/Tenant*	*Date*	*Time*

Approved Nevada Real Estate Division   Page 1 of 1   **524**
Replaces all previous editions   **Revised 05/01/05**

FIGURE 13.4   Confirmation Regarding Real Estate Agent Relationship

DUTIES OWED BY A NEVADA REAL ESTATE LICENSEE
This form does not constitute a contract for services nor an agreement to pay compensation.

In Nevada, a real estate licensee is required to provide a form setting forth the duties owed by the licensee to:
   a) Each party for whom the licensee is acting as an agent in the real estate transaction, and
   b) Each unrepresented party to the real estate transaction, if any.

Licensee: The licensee in the real estate transaction is _____

whose license number is _____. The licensee is acting for [client's name(s)] _____

_____ who is/are the ☐Seller/Landlord; ☐Buyer/Tenant.

Broker: The broker is _____, whose

company is _____.

Licensee's Duties Owed to All Parties:
A Nevada real estate licensee shall:
   1. Not deal with any party to a real estate transaction in a manner which is deceitful, fraudulent or dishonest.
   2. Exercise reasonable skill and care with respect to all parties to the real estate transaction.
   3. Disclose to each party to the real estate transaction as soon as practicable:
      a. Any material and relevant facts, data or information which licensee knows, or with reasonable care and diligence the licensee should know, about the property.
      b. Each source from which licensee will receive compensation.
   4. Abide by all other duties, responsibilities and obligations required of the licensee in law or regulations.

Licensee's Duties Owed to the Client:
A Nevada real estate licensee shall:
   1. Exercise reasonable skill and care to carry out the terms of the brokerage agreement and the licensee's duties in the brokerage agreement;
   2. Not disclose, except to the licensee's broker, confidential information relating to a client for 1 year after the revocation or termination of the brokerage agreement, unless licensee is required to do so by court order or the client gives written permission;
   3. Seek a sale, purchase, option, rental or lease of real property at the price and terms stated in the brokerage agreement or at a price acceptable to the client;
   4. Present all offers made to, or by the client as soon as practicable, unless the client chooses to waive the duty of the licensee to present all offers and signs a waiver of the duty on a form prescribed by the Division;
   5. Disclose to the client material facts of which the licensee has knowledge concerning the real estate transaction;
   6. Advise the client to obtain advice from an expert relating to matters which are beyond the expertise of the licensee; and
   7. Account to the client for all money and property the licensee receives in which the client may have an interest.

Duties Owed By a broker who assigns different licensees affiliated with the brokerage to separate parties.
Each licensee shall not disclose, except to the real estate broker, confidential information relating to client.

Licensee Acting for Both Parties: You understand that the licensee _____ may *or* _____ may not, in the future act
                                                          (Client Init)   *(Client Init)*
for two or more parties who have interests adverse to each other. In acting for these parties, the licensee has a conflict of interest. Before a licensee may act for two or more parties, the licensee must give you a "Consent to Act" form to sign.

I/We acknowledge receipt of a copy of this list of licensee duties, and have read and understand this disclosure.					
Seller/Landlord	*Date*	*Time*	*Buyer/Tenant*	*Date*	*Time*
Seller/Landlord	*Date*	*Time*	*Buyer/Tenant*	*Date*	*Time*

FIGURE 13.5 Consent to Act

CONFIRMATION REGARDING REAL ESTATE AGENT RELATIONSHIP
This form does not constitute a contract for services

Property Address

In the event any party to the real estate transaction is also represented by another licensee who is affiliated with the same Company, the Broker may assign a licensee to act for each party, respectively. As set forth within the *Duties Owed* form, no confidential information will be disclosed. **This is ☐ is not ☐ such a transaction.**

I/We confirm the duties of a real estate licensee of which has been presented and explained to me/us. My/Our representative's relationship is:

_____ is the AGENT of _____ is the AGENT of

☐ Seller/Landlord Exclusively ② ☐ Buyer/Tenant Exclusively ③   ☐ Buyer/Tenant Exclusively ③ ☐ Seller/Landlord Exclusively ②
☐ Both Buyer/Tenant & Seller/Landlord ①   ☐ Both Buyer/Tenant & Seller/Landlord ①

① IF LICENSEE IS ACTING FOR MORE THAN ONE PARTY IN THIS TRANSACTION, you will be provided a **Consent to Act form for your review, consideration and approval or rejection. A licensee can legally represent both the Seller/Landlord and Buyer/Tenant in a transaction, but ONLY with the knowledge and written consent of BOTH the Seller/Landlord and Buyer/Tenant.**

② A licensee who is acting for the Seller/Landlord exclusively, is not representing the Buyer/Tenant and has no duty to advocate or negotiate for the Buyer/Tenant.

③ A licensee who is acting for the Buyer/Tenant exclusively, is not representing the Seller/Landlord and has no duty to advocate or negotiate for the Seller/Landlord.

by _____ *Seller's/Landlord's Company*   by _____ *Buyer's/Tenant's Company*
Licensed Real Estate Agent   *Licensed Real Estate Agent*

Date   *Time*   *Date*   *Time*

Seller/Landlord   Date   Time   Buyer/Tenant   Date   Time

Seller/Landlord   Date   Time   Buyer/Tenant   Date   Time

Approved Nevada Real Estate Division   **560**
Replaces all previous editions   **Revised 4/1/99**
Century 21 Aadvantage Gold 2279 N Rampart BlvdLas Vegas, NV 89128
Phone: (702) 242 - 4228   Fax: (702) 242 - 0428   Nancy Scobee   Samples
Produced with ZipForm™ by RE FormsNet, LLC 18070 Fifteen Mile Road, Fraser, Michigan 48026   www.zipform.com

The buyer and seller shall elect one of the following arrangements for broker representation:

- The buyer exclusively
- The seller exclusively
- Both the buyer and seller (multiple representation)

The agency election and confirmation should be made before discussions about a real estate transaction are held between the buyer or seller and the licensee. The Confirmation Regarding Real Estate Agent Relationship and Consent to Act forms are included as Figures 13.4 and 13.5, respectively.

13.5 FIDUCIARY DUTY

The **fiduciary relationship** is the relationship created between the principal and the agent and is one of trust and confidence. This aspect of the law of agency is very important. The principal entrusts the agent with confidential information. In addition, the agent is handling other people's money and property.

Whether a broker becomes an agent intentionally or unintentionally, he or she will be deemed a fiduciary. Fiduciary duties are the highest range of duties under the law. As a fiduciary, a real estate broker has agreed, under a listing contract or other brokerage agreement, to these specific duties:

- Loyalty
- Obedience
- Disclosure
- Confidentiality
- Reasonable care and diligence
- Accountability

Loyalty

Loyalty is the most fundamental duty that an agent owes the principal, meaning that the agent has a duty of absolute fidelity to the client's interests. Once a broker has taken a listing, all of his or her salespeople become subagents of the seller and have a duty to represent the seller's best interests. The agent shall seek a sale, purchase, option, rental, or lease of real property at the price and terms stated in the brokerage agreement or at a price acceptable to the client. The broker must place the seller's interest over his or her own and use maximum effort to secure the best possible price and terms for the client. Any broker who does not act accordingly is not acting with the best interest of the client and is in breach of his or her fiduciary duties.

There are two prongs to the duty of loyalty, as follows:

1. The duty to disclose the licensee's interest in the transaction.
2. The prohibition against taking advantage of any situation, even if disclosed, that would harm the client's interest.

Obedience

An agent must follow the instructions of the client as long as the instructions are lawful and ethical. Failure to follow lawful ethical instructions of the client is a violation of the agent's fiduciary duties and subjects the agent to liability for any resulting loss. Unlawful seller's instructions could include directions to not show the property to a minority or to not disclose a material defect in the listed property.

Disclosure

The agent has the duty to disclose to the client material facts of which the licensee has knowledge concerning the transaction. Additional items to be disclosed to the principal include:

1. *Relationship of the agent and buyer.* The failure to disclose an agent's relationship to the buyer (relative, business partner, investor, or close friend) would be a violation of disclosure. If a relationship exists between the buyer and the agent that is more personal than the legal relationship between the client and the agent, the client must be made aware of the situation. Disclosure must be made if the agent and buyer plan on a business arrangement resulting in the purchase of the client's property.

2. *Existence of other offers.* A listing broker must present all offers to a seller. The agent's responsibility to present offers continues until closing because a seller may decide to accept backup offers during escrow. The client can elect to waive the duty of the licensee to present all offers, but the client must sign a waiver of the duty on a form prescribed by the Real Estate Division.

3. *Potential for a higher price.* An agent for the seller must disclose the buyer's potential to pay a higher price. A seller's agent must work with a buyer to secure the highest price and best possible terms for the seller. The agent must never disclose to a buyer the results of any other negotiations indicating that a seller would take a lower price for the property.

4. *Earnest deposit.* Clients must fully understand the nature of earnest deposits. Earnest deposits may be in the form of cash, checks, notes, or partial deposit with additional payments made at a future date. The agent must inform the client of the form of the earnest deposit.

5. *Buyer's financial condition.* The licensee has no duty to conduct an investigation of the financial condition of a party to the real estate transaction. The seller should have some knowledge of a buyer's ability to complete the terms of the contract before he or she accepts an offer to purchase, but the licensee does not have the obligation to complete such an investigation.

6. *True property value.* An agent should express his or her informed opinion of the property value. This opinion must be based on fact. False property value could result in a seller selling for less, or asking too high a price, causing a seller to lose potential purchasers. The agent would be liable for establishing a false value on property.

7. *Commission split.* An agent must disclose any commission paid by the seller that is shared with cooperating brokers. Although the amounts do not need to be spelled out, the disclosure that a fee will be shared should be in writing.

8. *Contract provisions.* An agent should never discourage a client from seeking legal advice. However, it is the broker's responsibility to explain the provisions of the contract prior to a client's signature. In addition, the agent should advise the client to obtain advice from an expert relating to any matters in addition to legal advice that are beyond the expertise of the licensee.

9. *Real Estate Settlement Procedures Act (RESPA).* RESPA prohibits referrals from one business to another business when owned by the same company unless there is full disclosure. The licensee must disclose the ownership interest when there are affiliated business arrangements, such as when a licensee has an ownership interest in a business to which the client is being referred.

Confidentiality

An agent should regard information learned from the client as confidential. An agent must not share any information that could hurt the client's negotiating position. Confidentiality does not prevent an agent from disclosing material facts about the property. This confidentiality is similar to the privileged information concept of doctor-patient and attorney-client relationships. The licensee shall not disclose confidential information relating to a client for one year after the revocation or termination of the brokerage agreement, unless the licensee is required to do so pursuant to an order of a court of competent jurisdiction or he or she is given written permission to do so by the client.

Reasonable Care and Diligence

In offering services to the public as a real estate licensee, the licensee claims to possess the necessary skill and training to perform the employment requirements. When performing duties for the agent's principal, the broker must exercise the **reasonable care and diligence** the public is entitled to expect. If the principal suffers a financial loss because of the agent's negligence or failure to meet the standards of skill and diligence, the agent will be liable for the loss. Also, the principal would not be required to pay compensation to the agent as agreed in the listing.

Accountability

A broker is responsible for holding any monies or property received as a result of a purchase agreement. These are trust funds and are held for the benefit of the seller. A broker may not use these monies or any interest derived for his or her own or the seller's benefit. Likewise, any monies collected as lease payments should be collected and accounted for in regular reporting periods. State law prohibits the commingling of trust monies. Commingling means to mingle or mix, such as depositing client trust funds into the broker's personal account.

13.6 DUTY TO THE BUYER/CUSTOMER

An agent also has responsibility to the buyer/customer. A licensee owes a fiduciary duty to his or her client, and shall protect and promote the interest of the client. The licensee shall also **deal fairly** with the customer and all other parties to the transaction.

Dealing Fairly

Dealing fairly requires that each licensee participating in a real estate transaction shall disclose to all other parties to the transaction any material and relevant facts, data, or information that the licensee knows relating to the property that is the subject of the transaction. The licensee is also responsible for any material and relevant facts, data, or information that should have been known if the licensee exercised reasonable care and diligence.

Disclosure obligations for clients differ from disclosure obligations to non-clients. A licensee owes a fiduciary duty to the client that requires the agent to protect and promote the client's interest. The obligation to non-clients is to "deal fairly."

The concept of "dealing fairly" sometimes creates concern for brokers. The courts have interpreted "deal fairly" in several cases as *honestly and truthfully*. A broker and his or her subagents must exercise great care to ensure that all parties to the transaction are informed in earnest and that their decision to enter into the transaction is based on facts.

An agent is liable for misrepresentations to the buyer/customer. An agent is not responsible for untrue statements made by the seller unless the licensee knew his client made the misrepresentation and failed to inform the person to whom the client made the misrepresentation that the statement was false.

Material Facts

The principal and the principal's agent have a duty to disclose known facts, which are not known to the other parties to the transaction and are not easily observable, that materially affect the value of the property.

Some examples of **material facts** that should be disclosed are included here:

- Leaky roofs
- Termites
- Repairs performed by an unlicensed contractor
- Prior fire in the property
- Property in or near a Superfund site
- Property subject to airport noise

The seller has a responsibility to disclose in writing any material defects that might affect the consideration paid by the buyer/customer. To be sure that the agent and seller are treating all other parties to the transaction fairly, the agent should use due diligence to search for defects in the property. A Residential Disclosure Guide, published by the state of Nevada Real Estate Division, aids sellers in fulfilling their disclosure responsibilities. The guide is available on the Nevada Real Estate Division website, www.red.state.nv.us/forms/622.pdf.

The proper disclosure by the seller of material facts is to be made in writing and in a timely manner and on a format prescribed by the Real Estate Division. The prescribed form 547, entitled Seller's Real Property Disclosure Form (SRPDS), is required for a residential resale, whether the land is improved or unimproved. The following residential resales are exempt from the SRPDS disclosure requirements:

- New homes
- Bank foreclosures
- Government foreclosures
- Transfers between spouses
- Person who takes temporary control
- Seller when relying on information supplied by an officer of the state of Nevada
- Seller when relying on information supplied by a Nevada contractor

The disclosure form must be completed by the seller only at least 10 days before the close of escrow. New defects to which the seller becomes aware after the delivery of the original disclosure must be reported to the buyer before escrow closes.

The seller's failure to properly and honestly complete the SRPDS allows the buyer to:

- Litigate and be entitled to treble damages
- Be entitled to court and legal fees
- Have up to two years from the close of escrow to begin litigation

When the seller, before the close of escrow, informs the purchaser of a defect through the SRPDS or other written document, the purchaser may do either of the following:

a. Rescind the agreement to purchase the property at any time before the conveyance of the property to the purchaser.

b. Close escrow and accept the property with the defect as revealed by the seller without further recourse.

A rescission of the agreement to purchase because of the disclosed defect must be written, notarized, and served on the escrow holder not later than four working days after the date on which the purchaser is informed of the defect.

A sample copy of the Seller's Real Property Disclosure Form is included as Figure 13.6.

A licensee must always be aware of the basis for determining materiality because its determination is a factual matter ultimately decided by a judge or jury. A fact is considered material if a reasonable person would attach importance to it when determining his or her course of action in the transaction at issue. Those making the determination of materiality could be any of the following:

- The judge, jury, or hearing officer in a legal dispute
- The Nevada Real Estate Division
- The consumer, in deciding whether to bring an action

FIGURE 13.6 Seller's Real Property Disclosure Form

SELLER'S REAL PROPERTY DISCLOSURE FORM

In accordance with Nevada Law, a seller of residential real property in Nevada must disclose any and all known conditions and aspects of the property which materially affect the value or use of residential property in an adverse manner *(see NRS 113.130 and 113.140).*

Date _____

Property

address _____

Do you currently occupy or have you ever occupied this property?   YES ☐   NO ☐

☐ Check here if the Seller is exempt from the completion of this form pursuant to NRS 113.130(2).

Purpose of Statement: (1) This statement is a disclosure of the condition of the property in compliance with the Seller Real Property Disclosure Act, effective January 1, 1996. (2) This statement is a disclosure of the condition and information concerning the property known by the Seller which materially affects the value of the property. Unless otherwise advised, the Seller does not possess any expertise in construction, architecture, engineering or any other specific area related to the construction or condition of the improvements on the property or the land. Also, unless otherwise advised, the Seller has not conducted any inspection of generally inaccessible areas such as the foundation or roof. This statement is not a warranty of any kind by the Seller or by any Agent representing the Seller in this transaction and is not a substitute for any inspections or warranties the Buyer may wish to obtain.

Instructions to the Seller: (1) ANSWER ALL QUESTIONS. (2) REPORT KNOWN CONDITIONS AFFECTING THE PROPERTY. (3) ATTACH ADDITIONAL PAGES WITH YOUR SIGNATURE IF ADDITIONAL SPACE IS REQUIRED. (4) COMPLETE THIS FORM YOURSELF. (5) IF SOME ITEMS DO NOT APPLY TO YOUR PROPERTY, CHECK N/A (NOT APPLICABLE). EFFECTIVE JANUARY 1, 1996, FAILURE TO PROVIDE A PURCHASER WITH A SIGNED DISCLOSURE STATEMENT WILL ENABLE THE PURCHASER TO TERMINATE AN OTHERWISE BINDING PURCHASE AGREEMENT AND SEEK OTHER REMEDIES AS PROVIDED BY THE LAW *(see NRS 113.150).*

Systems / Appliances: Are you aware of any problems and/or defects with any of the following:

	YES	NO	N/A		YES	NO	N/A
Electrical system	☐	☐	☐	Shower(s)	☐	☐	☐
Plumbing	☐	☐	☐	Sink(s)	☐	☐	☐
Sewer system & line	☐	☐	☐	Sauna / hot tub(s)	☐	☐	☐
Septic tank & leach field	☐	☐	☐	Built-in microwave	☐	☐	☐
Well & pump	☐	☐	☐	Range / oven / hood-fan	☐	☐	☐
Yard sprinkler system(s)	☐	☐	☐	Dishwasher	☐	☐	☐
Fountain(s)	☐	☐	☐	Garbage disposal	☐	☐	☐
Heating system	☐	☐	☐	Trash compactor	☐	☐	☐
Cooling system	☐	☐	☐	Central vacuum	☐	☐	☐
Solar heating system	☐	☐	☐	Alarm system	☐	☐	☐
Fireplace & chimney	☐	☐	☐	owned ☐ leased ☐			
Wood burning system	☐	☐	☐	Smoke detector	☐	☐	☐
Garage door opener	☐	☐	☐	Intercom	☐	☐	☐
Water treatment system(s)	☐	☐	☐	Data communication line(s)	☐	☐	☐
owned ☐ leased ☐				Satellite dish(es)	☐	☐	☐
Water heater	☐	☐	☐	owned ☐ leased ☐			
Toilet(s)	☐	☐	☐	Other _____	☐	☐	☐
Bathtub(s)	☐	☐	☐				

EXPLANATIONS: Any "Yes" must be fully explained. Attach explanations to form.

_____ _____
Seller(s) Initials   Page 1 of 4   *Buyer(s) Initials*

Nevada Real Estate Division
Replaces all previous versions

Seller Real Property Disclosure Form
Revised 05/01/06   547

Century 21 Aadvantage Gold 2279 N Rampart BlvdLas Vegas, NV 89128   Phone: (702) 242 - 4228   Fax: (702) 242 - 0428   Samples
Nancy Scobee   Produced with ZipForm™ by RE FormsNet, LLC 18070 Fifteen Mile Road, Fraser, Michigan 48026 www.zipform.com

FIGURE 13.6   *(continued)*

Property conditions, improvements and additional information:	YES	NO	N/A

Are you **aware** of any of the following?:

1. **Structure:**
    (a) Previous or current moisture conditions and/or water damage? . . . . ☐ ☐
    (b) Any structural defect? . . . . ☐ ☐
    (c) Any construction, modification, alterations, or repairs made without
        required state, city or county building permits? . . . . ☐ ☐
    (d) Whether the property is or has been the subject of a claim governed by
        NRS 40.600 to 40.695 (construction defect claims)? . . . . ☐ ☐
        (If seller answers yes, FURTHER DISCLOSURE IS REQUIRED)
2. **Land / Foundation:**
    (a) Any of the improvements being located on unstable or expansive soil? . . . . ☐ ☐
    (b) Any foundation sliding, settling, movement, upheaval, or earth stability problems
        that have occurred on the property? . . . . ☐ ☐
    (c) Any drainage, flooding, water seepage, or high water table? . . . . ☐ ☐
    (d) The property being located in a designated flood plain? . . . . ☐ ☐
    (e) Whether the property is located next to or near any known future development? . . . . ☐ ☐
    (f) Any encroachments, easements, zoning violations or nonconforming uses? . . . . ☐ ☐
    (g) Is the property adjacent to "open range" land? . . . . ☐ ☐
        (If seller answers yes, FURTHER DISCLOSURE IS REQUIRED under NRS 113.065)
3. **Roof:** Any problems with the roof? . . . . ☐ ☐
4. **Pool/spa:** Any problems with structure, wall, liner, or equipment? . . . . ☐ ☐ ☐
5. **Infestation:** Any history of infestation (termites, carpenter ants, etc.)? . . . . ☐ ☐
6. **Environmental:** Any substances, materials, or products which may be an environmental
    hazard such as, but not limited to, asbestos, radon gas, urea formaldehyde, fuel or chemical
    storage tanks, contaminated water or soil on the property? . . . . ☐ ☐
7. **Fungi / Mold:** Any previous or current fungus or mold? . . . . ☐ ☐
8. Any features of the property shared in common with adjoining landowners such as walls, fences,
    road, driveways or other features whose use or responsibility for maintenance may have an effect
    on the property? . . . . ☐ ☐
9. **Common Interest Communities:** Any "common areas" (facilities like pools, tennis courts,
    walkways or other areas co-owned with others) or a homeowner association which has any
    authority over the property? . . . . ☐ ☐
    (a) Common Interest Community Declaration and Bylaws available? . . . . ☐ ☐
    (b) Any periodic or recurring association fees? . . . . ☐ ☐
    (c) Any unpaid assessments, fines or liens, and any warnings or notices that may give rise to an
        assessment, fine or lien? . . . . ☐ ☐
    (d) Any litigation, arbitration, or mediation related to property or common area? . . . . ☐ ☐
    (e) Any assessments associated with the property (excluding property taxes)? . . . . ☐ ☐
    (f) Any construction, modification, alterations, or repairs made without
        required approval from the appropriate Common Interest Community board or committee? . . . . ☐ ☐
10. Any problems with water quality or water supply? . . . . ☐ ☐
11. **Any other conditions or aspects of the property which materially affect its value or**
    use in an adverse manner? . . . . ☐ ☐
12. **Lead-Based Paint:** Was the property constructed on or before 12/31/77? . . . . ☐ ☐
    (If yes, additional Federal EPA notification and disclosure documents are required)
13. **Water source:** Municipal ☐   Community Well ☐   Domestic Well ☐   Other ☐
    If Community Well: State Engineer Well Permit # _____ Revocable ☐ Permanent ☐ Cancelled ☐
    Use of community and domestic wells may be subject to change. Contact the Nevada Division of Water Resources for
    more information regarding the future use of this well.
14. **Wastewater disposal:** Municipal Sewer ☐   Septic System ☐   Other ☐

EXPLANATIONS: Any "Yes" must be fully explained. Attach explanations to form.

```
[                                                                              ]
```

_____ _____   _____ _____
       Seller(s) Initials   *Buyer(s) Initials*

Nevada Real Estate Division   Page 2 of 4   **Seller Real Property Disclosure Form**
Replaces all previous versions   **Revised 05/01/06**   547
Produced with ZipForm™ by RE FormsNet, LLC 18070 Fifteen Mile Road, Fraser, Michigan 48026   www.zipform.com

Samples

FIGURE 13.6 Continued.

Buyers and sellers of residential property are advised to seek the advice of an attorney concerning their rights and obligations as set forth in Chapter 113 of the Nevada Revised Statutes regarding the seller's obligation to execute the Nevada Real Estate Division's approved "Seller's Real Property Disclosure Form". For your convenience, Chapter 113 of the Nevada Revised Statutes provides as follows:

CONDITION OF RESIDENTIAL PROPERTY OFFERED FOR SALE

NRS 113.100 Definitions. As used in NRS 113.100 to 113.150, inclusive, unless the context otherwise requires:

1. "Defect" means a condition that materially affects the valu e or use of residential property in an adverse manner.
2. "Disclosure form" means a form that complies with the regulations adopted pursuant to NRS 113.120.
3. "Dwelling unit" means any building, structure or portion thereof which is occupied as, or designed or intended for occupancy as, a residence by one person who maintains a household or by two or more persons who maintain a common household.
4. "Residential property" means any land in this state to which is affixed not less than one nor more than four dwelling units.
5. "Seller" means a person who sells or intends to sell any residential property.

(Added to NRS by 1995, 842; A 1999, 1446)

NRS 113.110 Conditions required for "conveyance of property" and to complete service of document. For the purposes of NRS 113.100 to 113.150, inclusive:

1. A "conveyance of property" occurs:
(a) Upon the closure of any escrow opened for the conveyance; or
(b) If an escrow has not been opened for the conveyance, when the purchaser of the property receives the deed of conveyance.
2. Service of a document is complete:
(a) Upon personal delivery of the document to the person being served; or
(b) Three days after the document is mailed, postage prepaid, to the person being served at his last known address.

(Added to NRS by 1995, 844)

NRS 113.120 Regulations prescribing format and contents of form for disclosing condition of property. The Real Estate Division of the Department of Business and Industry shall adopt regulations prescribing the format and contents of a form for disclosing the condition of residential property offered for sale. The regulations must ensure that the form:

1. Provides for an evaluation of the condition of any electrical, heating, cooling, plumbing and sewer systems on the property, and of the condition of any other aspects of the property which affect its use or value, and allows the seller of the property to indicate whether or not each of those systems and other aspects of the property has a defect of which the seller is aware.
2. Provides notice:
(a) Of the provisions of NRS 113.140 and subsection 5 of NRS 113.150.
(b) That the disclosures set forth in the form are made by the seller and not by his agent.
(c) That the seller's agent, and the agent of the purchaser or potential purchaser of the residential property, may reveal the completed form and its contents to any purchaser or potential purchaser of the residential property.

(Added to NRS by 1995, 842)

NRS 113.130 Completion and service of disclosure form before conveyance of property; discovery or worsening of defect after service of form; exceptions; waiver.

1. Except as otherwise provided in subsections 2 and 3:
(a) At least 10 days before residential property is conveyed to a purchaser:
(1) The seller shall complete a disclosure form regarding the residential property; and
(2) The seller or his agent shall serve the purchaser or his agent with the completed disclosure form.
(b) If, after service of the completed disclosure form but before conveyance of the property to the purchaser, a seller or his agent discovers a new defect in the residential property that was not identified on the completed disclosure form or discovers that a defect identified on the completed disclosure form has become worse than was indicated on the form, the seller or his agent shall inform the purchaser or his agent of that fact, in writing, as soon as practicable after the discovery of that fact but in no event later than the conveyance of the property to the purchaser. If the seller does not agree to repair or replace the defect, the purchaser may:
(1) Rescind the agreement to purchase the property; or
(2) Close escrow and accept the property with the defect as revealed by the seller or his agent without further recourse.
2. Subsection 1 does not apply to a sale or intended sale of residential property:
(a) By foreclosure pursuant to chapter 107 of NRS.
(b) Between any co-owners of the property, spouses or persons related within the third degree of consanguinity.
(c) Which is the first sale of a residence that was constructed by a licensed contractor.
(d) By a person who takes temporary possession or control of or title to the property solely to facilitate the sale of the property on behalf of a person who relocates to another county, state or country before title to the property is transferred to a purchaser.
3. A purchaser of residential property may waive any of the requirements of subsection 1. Any such waiver is effective only if it is made in a written document that is signed by the purchaser and notarized.
4. If a sale or intended sale of residential property is exempted from the requirements of subsection 1 pursuant to paragraph (a) of subsection 2, the trustee and the beneficiary of the deed of trust shall, not later than at the time of the conveyance of the property to the purchaser of the residential property, provide written notice to the purchaser of any defects in the property of which the trustee or beneficiary, respectively, is aware.

(Added to NRS by 1995, 842; A 1997, 349; 2003, 1339; 2005, 598)

_____ _____   _____ _____
Seller(s) Initials   *Buyer(s) Initials*

Nevada Real Estate Division   Page 3 of 4   **Seller Real Property Disclosure Form**
Replaces all previous versions   **Revised 05/01/06   547**

Produced with ZipForm™ by RE FormsNet, LLC 18070 Fifteen Mile Road, Fraser, Michigan 48026   www.zipform.com   Samples

FIGURE 13.6 Continued.

NRS 113.135   Certain sellers to provide copies of certain provisions of NRS and give notice of certain soil reports; initial purchaser entitled to rescind sales agreement in certain circumstances; waiver of right to rescind.

1.   Upon signing a sales agreement with the initial purchaser of residential property that was not occupied by the purchaser for more than 120 days after substantial completion of the construction of the residential property, the seller shall:

(a) Provide to the initial purchaser a copy of NRS 11.202 to 11.206, inclusive, and 40.600 to 40.695, inclusive;

(b) Notify the initial purchaser of any soil report prepared for the residential property or for the subdivision in which the residential property is located; and

(c) If requested in writing by the initial purchaser not later than 5 days after signing the sales agreement, provide to the purchaser without cost each report described in paragraph (b) not later than 5 days after the seller receives the written request.

2.   Not later than 20 days after receipt of all reports pursuant to paragraph (c) of subsection 1, the initial purchaser may rescind the sales agreement.

3.   The initial purchaser may waive his right to rescind the sales agreement pursuant to subsection 2. Such a waiver is effective only if it is made in a written document that is signed by the purchaser.

(Added to NRS by 1999, 1446)

NRS 113.140 Disclosure of unknown defect not required; form does not constitute warranty; duty of buyer and prospective buyer to exercise reasonable care.

1.   NRS 113.130 does not require a seller to disclose a defect in residential property of which he is not aware.

2.   A completed disclosure form does not constitute an express or implied warranty regarding any condition of residential property.

3.   Neither this chapter nor chapter 645 of NRS relieves a buyer or prospective buyer of the duty to exercise reasonable care to protect himself.

(Added to NRS by 1995, 843; A 2001, 2896)

NRS 113.150 Remedies for seller's delayed disclosure or nondisclosure of defects in property; waiver.

1.   If a seller or his agent fails to serve a completed disclosure form in accordance with the requirements of NRS 113.130, the purchaser may, at any time before the conveyance of the property to the purchaser, rescind the agreement to purchase the property without any penalties.

2.   If, before the conveyance of the property to the purchaser, a seller or his agent informs the purchaser or his agent, through the disclosure form or another written notice, of a defect in the property of which the cost of repair or replacement was not limited by provisions in the agreement to purchase the property, the purchaser may:

(a) Rescind the agreement to purchase the property at any time before the conveyance of the property to the purchaser; or

(b) Close escrow and accept the property with the defect as revealed by the seller or his agent without further recourse.

3.   Rescission of an agreement pursuant to subsection 2 is effective only if made in writing, notarized and served not later than 4 working days after the date on which the purchaser is informed of the defect:

(a) On the holder of any escrow opened for the conveyance; or

(b) If an escrow has not been opened for the conveyance, on the seller or his agent.

4.   Except as otherwise provided in subsection 5, if a seller conveys residential property to a purchaser without complying with the requirements of NRS 113.130 or otherwise providing the purchaser or his agent with written notice of all defects in the property of which the seller is aware, and there is a defect in the property of which the seller was aware before the property was conveyed to the purchaser and of which the cost of repair or replacement was not limited by provisions in the agreement to purchase the property, the purchaser is entitled to recover from the seller treble the amount necessary to repair or replace the defective part of the property, together with court costs and reasonable attorney's fees. An action to enforce the provisions of this subsection must be commenced not later than 1 year after the purchaser discovers or reasonably should have discovered the defect or 2 years after the conveyance of the property to the purchaser, whichever occurs later.

5.   A purchaser may not recover damages from a seller pursuant to subsection 4 on the basis of an error or omission in the disclosure form that was caused by the seller's reliance upon information provided to the seller by:

(a) An officer or employee of this state or any political subdivision of this state in the ordinary course of his duties; or

(b) A contractor, engineer, land surveyor, certified inspector as defined in NRS 645D.040 or pesticide applicator, who was authorized to practice that profession in this state at the time the information was provided.

6.   A purchaser of residential property may waive any of his rights under this section. Any such waiver is effective only if it is made in a written document that is signed by the purchaser and notarized.

(Added to NRS by 1995, 843; A 1997, 350, 1797)

The above information provided on pages one (1) and two (2) of this disclosure form is true and correct to the best of seller's knowledge as of the date set forth on page one (1). **SELLER HAS DUTY TO DISCLOSE TO BUYER AS NEW DEFECTS ARE DISCOVERED AND/OR KNOWN DEFECTS BECOME WORSE** *(See NRS 113.130(1)(b)).*

Seller(s): _____   Date: _____

Seller(s): _____   Date: _____

BUYER MAY WISH TO OBTAIN PROFESSIONAL ADVICE AND INSPECTIONS OF THE PROPERTY TO MORE FULLY DETERMINE THE CONDITION OF THE PROPERTY AND ITS ENVIRONMENTAL STATUS. Buyer(s) has/have read and acknowledge(s) receipt of a copy of this Seller's Real Property Disclosure Form and copy of NRS Chapter 113.100-150, inclusive, attached hereto as pages three (3) and four (4).

Buyer(s): _____   Date: _____

Buyer(s): _____   Date: _____

Nevada Real Estate Division   Page 4 of 4   **Seller Real Property Disclosure Form**
Replaces all previous versions   **Revised 05/01/06   547**
Produced with ZipForm™ by RE FormsNet, LLC 18070 Fifteen Mile Road, Fraser, Michigan 48026   www.zipform.com   Samples

Other Required Disclosures

Other required disclosure obligations include the following:

1. Public utility rates
2. Open range
3. Zoning classification and master plan
4. Gaming enerprise district map

Public Utility Rates

A person proposing to sell a previously unsold home or improved lot for which water or sewage services will be provided by a public utility that serves or plans to serve more than 25 customers and presently serves fewer than 2000 customers shall disclose:

a. The current or projected water rates.
b. The current or projected sewer service rates.

Open Range

A seller of a home or improved lot adjacent to an open range shall disclose before the purchaser signs a sales agreement that:

a. The property is adjacent to an open range and unless the purchaser constructs a fence livestock may enter your real property.
b. The purchaser cannot collect damages because the livestock entered the property.
c. It is unlawful to kill, maim or injure livestock that have entered the property, even if the purchaser constructs a fence.

Zoning Classification and Master Plan

Before the purchaser of a previously unsold residence signs a sales agreement or opens escrow, whichever occurs earlier, the seller shall disclose in writing the zoning classification and the designations in the master plan and the general land uses described in the plan for the adjoining parcels of land. The Nevada Revised Statutes require that the written disclosure include the following statement:

> *Zoning classifications describe the land uses currently permitted on a parcel of land. Designations in the master plan regarding land use describe the land uses that the governing city or county proposes for a parcel of land. Zoning classifications and designations in the master plan regarding land use are established and defined by local ordinances. If the zoning classification for a parcel of land is inconsistent with the designation in the master plan regarding land use for the parcel, the possibility exists that the zoning classification may be changed to be consistent with the designation in the master plan regarding land use for the parcel. Additionally, the local ordinances that establish and define the various*

zoning classifications and designations in the master plan regarding land use are also subject to change.

(*NRS 113.070*)

The information contained in the disclosure statement must meet the following requirements:

a. Include updated information not less than every six months, if the information is available from the local government.
b. Advise the initial purchaser that the master plan is for general comprehensive and long-term development of land in the area, and that the designation in the master plan regarding land use provides the most probable indication of future development.
c. Advise the initial purchaser that the master plan and zoning ordinances and regulations are subject to change.
d. Provide the initial purchaser with instructions on how to obtain more current information.

Gaming Enterprise District Map

A copy of the most recent gaming enterprise district map shall be provided to the purchaser of a previously unsold residence by the seller:

• Twenty-four hours before the seller signs the purchase agreement.
• Only required in Nevada counties with a population of 400,000 or more.

The information contained in the disclosure document must:

a. Have been updated not less than once every six months.
b. Advise that gaming enterprise districts are subject to change.
c. Pprovide instructions on how to obtain more current information.

The initial purchaser may waive the 24-hour period if the seller provides the purchaser with the required disclosures. The seller shall retain a copy of the written waiver.

Seller's Other Disclosure Obligations

In addition to disclosing material defects, the seller also has other disclosure obligations, which include the following:

1. The duty to disclose the answer to a buyer's inquiry, regardless of whether or not the fact is material.
2. The duty to disclose any information necessary to prevent a previous statement from becoming a misrepresentation.
3. The duty to disclose an incorrect assumption that the other party is relying on to make the contract.

Defects Not to Be Disclosed

Some defects that are generally considered to materially affect the consideration to be paid for a property are no longer required to be disclosed by the agent. Under a Nevada statute, disclosure of the following information is not required:

- The property is the site of a natural death, suicide, or homicide, except a death that results from a condition of the property.
- The property is the site of any crime punishable as a felony other than a crime that involves the manufacturing of any material, compound, mixture, or preparation which contains any quantity of methamphetamine.
- The property is or was owned or occupied by a person exposed to HIV or diagnosed as having AIDS or any other disease that is not known to be transmitted through common occupancy of real estate.
- The property is located in the vicinity of a sex offender.

Because of this statute, an agent for the seller should not disclose any of the defects described in the law even though they might be of concern to a buyer. To disclose these defects would be a breach of the agent's fiduciary duty to treat information with confidence. Although the seller and seller's agent are not required to disclose this information, the seller or seller's agent cannot give false information. If, for example, the buyer asks if a murder occurred on the premises and the seller/seller's agent knows that it did, then the seller/seller's agent must either answer the question truthfully (that is, *yes*) or respond by stating that such disclosures are not required by law. The seller/seller's agent cannot answer the buyer's question by saying "no" or "I don't know," because that answer would be false.

Naturally, if the seller approves disclosure, the agent can disclose all of these defects, except information about occupancy by a person exposed to HIV or AIDS. An agent is not allowed to disclose any information about occupancy by people exposed to HIV or AIDS, even if authorized by the seller.

A buyer's agent cannot be held responsible for nondisclosure to the buyer of items covered by the statute, but the buyer's agent can disclose the defects without approval of the seller, except for HIV and AIDS.

Taking the foregoing statute into consideration, the following is a list of disclosure examples:

Event	Disclosure Requirement
Murder on the premises	Not a required disclosure
Murder on the next-door property	Must be disclosed
Sex offender lives next door	Not a required disclosure
Occupied by an HIV-positive owner	Must not be disclosed

Duties of the Buyer

For many years, the theory of **caveat emptor**, or "let the buyer beware," was the attitude of the courts in real estate transactions. That theory does not hold true today. More often **caveat venditor**, or "let the seller beware," is appropriate.

The buyer has the responsibility of both *actual notice* and *constructive notice*. **Actual notice** means that the buyer should make an actual inspection of the property. **Constructive notice** means that the buyer should check the public records at the County Recorder's office for any liens, judgments, lis pendens, mortgages, or attachments on the property.

Also, because of the statute eliminating the requirement of the seller or the seller's agent to make certain disclosures, the buyer must assume the responsibility to investigate those areas.

Misrepresentations and Defects

All licensees need to be familiar with the following terms so that all of their actions remain within the framework of the law.

Misrepresentation is a false statement or concealment of a material fact made to someone entitled to the information, by which that person responds with action and thereby suffers damage. In order for a party injured by a misrepresentation to be successful in an action, the party must prove the following:

1. *Reliance*—The injured party relied on the false information, and the reliance was justified. Reliance is not justified if the false information is acquired by the injured party's actions.
2. *Materiality*—To have grounds for suit, the misrepresentation must be material. If the false statement is trivial in relation to the transaction, the statement is not considered material.

Negligent misrepresentation is a statement contrary to fact resulting from failure to exercise reasonable care in obtaining or communicating information. The licensee could be held liable.

Fraudulent misrepresentation is a deceitful practice or material misstatement known to be false and done with intent to deceive. Remedy through the courts is rescission of the contract or actual and punitive damages.

Negligence occurs when an agent fails to exercise a degree of reasonable caution that would be exercised by a person of ordinary prudence under all existing circumstances in view of probable danger or injury.

Negligence per se is conduct that may be declared and treated as negligence without any proof as to the surrounding circumstances, either because it is in violation of a statute or because it is so opposed to the dictates of common prudence.

Latent defects are hidden or dormant structural defects. Latent defects known to the seller must be disclosed, but the seller does not have liability for unknown latent defects.

Puffing occurs when an agent makes an exaggerated statement of opinion, without intending to deceive, such as, "This site has the most beautiful view in the valley." Though it is legal to "puff," it is strongly discouraged as a selling tool.

13.7 CUSTOMER OR CLIENT

A real estate agent's relationship with a customer differs from his or her relationship with a client. Agents work *with* customers; they work *for* clients. It is not always easy to decide whether a prospect would be best served as a customer or a client. In weighing each situation, here are some points that may help you reach that decision with the prospect.

Customer Profile

A prospective buyer may best be served as a **customer** when he or she:

- Needs exposure to property
- Is familiar with real estate practices and procedures
- Knows how to "mentally structure" an offer
- Is capable of negotiating for himself/herself
- Is capable of analyzing the property and legal forms (or capable of engaging the services of someone who can)

  Some of the services to customers could include the following:

- Explaining basic real estate forms
- Explaining real estate terms
- Providing price ranges of specific areas
- Providing information on churches, schools, and so on
- Explaining zoning ordinances
- Explaining MLS and how it works
- Showing properties
- Explaining costs involved in a sale
- Explaining escrow
- Helping to write an offer
- Disclosing material facts about property conditions

Client Profile

A prospective buyer may best be served as a **client** when he or she:

- Is naive regarding real estate purchases and/or business in general
- Has a strong need for help in negotiating
- Has limited funds or restricted terms or types of financing
- Is a prospect who relies heavily on input from the salesperson ("What would you suggest I do?")
- Has a confidentiality that needs to be kept
- Is a very cautious, analytical buyer who constantly probes for every detail

  Some of the services to clients could include the following:

- Preparing and explaining all real estate forms
- Explaining all relevant real estate terms

- Providing price ranges of specific areas and estimates of value for specific properties
- Providing information on churches, schools, and so on
- Explaining zoning ordinances
- Explaining MLS and how it works
- Showing properties
- Explaining costs involved in a sale
- Explaining escrow and handling the transaction while in escrow
- Assisting with locating a lender (bank, mortgage company, mortgage broker, and so on)
- Assisting with locating inspectors (home inspectors, roof inspectors, and so on)
- Assisting with the final walk-through inspection
- Assisting with the closing documents

CHAPTER SUMMARY

The real estate industry is divided into four main categories: brokerages, property development, property management, and appraising. Brokerages provide for the completion of real estate transactions between buyers and sellers. Licensees working for the brokerage are broker-salespersons and licensed salespersons, both of whom have the same privileges and responsibilities. These individuals should have a written employment agreement indicating their status as either employees or independent contractors. Brokerages tend to prefer independent contractors, because brokerages do not have to provide benefits or pay Social Security and unemployment taxes for independent contractors. However, the broker is still responsible for all actions of licensed salespeople and broker-salespersons.

Compensation to the broker is established through negotiations between the seller and the broker. The amount of compensation is set forth in the employment agreement and is often a percentage of the sales price. Under the Sherman Anti-Trust Act, price fixing is illegal. A real estate salesperson generally receives compensation in one of two ways. If the brokerage is a commission-sharing brokerage, then a percentage of the commission amount collected by the brokerage is paid to the salesperson. If the brokerage is a 100% brokerage, the salesperson receives all of the commission collected by the brokerage, but the salesperson must pay a monthly fee to the brokerage. The commission paid to a real estate salesperson can be paid only by his or her broker.

The National Association of REALTORS® is the largest trade association in the world. Members of NAR also become members of the Nevada Association of REALTORS.® NAR created the Code of Ethics as a guide to ethical practices by which all REALTORS® agree to abide and to which all licensees should adhere. The Code of Ethics contains three parts: duties to clients and customers, duties to the public, and duties to other REALTORS.®

A real estate agent is someone who acts on behalf of others in the sale, purchase, or leasing of real property. All states require that brokers and salespeople be licensed. A universal agent represents the principal in all matters. A general agent represents the principal in a specific range of matters, such as real estate. A special agent is authorized to represent the principal in one specific transaction, such as in a listing, but is not given the power to bind the principal.

Agency relationships are consensual relationships. One person delegates authority and the agent consents to act. Agency relationships do not require compensation, a contract, or an agreement in writing. The elements necessary for the creation of agency are defined by law. No matter what title one puts on his or her actions, if the action satisfies the elements of the law, then agency exists. The parties to an agency relationship are the agent, the principal, and the customer.

Other agency relationships include subagency, dual agency (nationally), multiple representation (Nevada), single agency (buyer's or seller's), unintended or implied agency, and ratified and estoppel agency. A subagent is a person appointed by the broker agent to assist in the performance of the assignment. The subagent owes the broker the same fiduciary duties that the broker owes to the principal. Nationally, dual agency exists when a licensee represents a buyer and a seller at the same time. *Dual agency* is a common law term that has been abrogated by the Nevada Revised Statutes. The Statutes specify the duties owed and consents required when there is multiple representation in a real estate transaction. An in-house sale is a brokerage transaction in which one sales associate obtains the listing and also finds the buyer, or a second associate with the same brokerage procures the buyer. Single agency is the practice of representing either the buyer or seller, but never both. Unintended or implied agency exists when the buyer assumes by an agent's actions that the agent is working for the buyer. Ratified and estoppel agency is created when a seller or buyer accepts the benefits of an agent's prior and unauthorized actions "after the fact." The real estate licensee is required to disclose the type of agency relationship or representation they will have with the seller, buyer, or both the seller and buyer.

The fiduciary relationship is the relationship created between the principal (client) and the agent and is one of trust and confidence. As a fiduciary, a real estate broker has agreed, under a listing contract or other employment agreement, to these specific duties: loyalty, obedience, disclosure, confidentiality, reasonable care and diligence, and accountability. With regard to disclosure, the agent has the duty to disclose the following items to the principal: the relationship of the agent and buyer, the existence of other offers, earnest deposit, the buyer's financial condition, the true property value, commission split, and contract provisions.

An agent also has responsibility to and may be liable for misrepresentations to the buyer/customer. An agent must exercise great care to deal fairly with all parties in a transaction. Both the agent and the principal have a responsibility to disclose in writing any material defects existing in the property that might affect the consideration paid by the buyer/customer. To ensure that all parties to the transaction are treated fairly and that disclosure responsibilities are met, the Residential Disclosure Guide is a valuable guide to sellers. Some defects, however, are not allowed to be disclosed. Therefore, agents should thoroughly acquaint themselves with a list of items to be disclosed and those not to be disclosed. Ultimately, because of the statute eliminating the requirement of the seller or the seller's agent to make certain disclosures, the buyer has the responsibility of both actual notice and constructive notice.

All licensees need to be familiar with the following terms so that their actions remain within the framework of the law in regard to the disclosure of defects: *misrepresentation, negligent and fraudulent misrepresentation, negligence and negligence per se, latent defect,* and *puffing.*

In determining whether a prospect would best be served as a customer or a client, an agent should be knowledgeable of the profiles for each. Basically, real estate agents work *with* a customer and *for* a client.

CHECKING YOUR COMPREHENSION

1. Define and explain the following:
   - Agency
   - Universal agent
   - General agent
   - Special agent

2. Explain the requirements for the creation of an agency relationship and describe the roles of the three parties to an agency relationship.

3. Define a fiduciary relationship and explain the meaning of the following:
   - Loyalty
   - Obedience
   - Disclosure
   - Confidentiality
   - Reasonable care and diligence
   - Accountability

4. Summarize the disclosure obligations to a buyer of real property.

5. Summarize the meanings of the following terms:
   - Misrepresentation
   - Negligent misrepresentation
   - Fraudulent misrepresentation
   - Latent defects

6. Describe the following agency relationships:
   - Subagency
   - Multiple representation
   - Implied agency
   - Estoppel agency

REVIEWING YOUR UNDERSTANDING

1. A broker's fiduciary duty to a client includes all of the following, **EXCEPT**:
   a. selling his or her property
   b. care and diligence
   c. loyalty
   d. confidentiality

2. Which phrase **BEST** describes the nature of a broker's duty to keep a principal fully informed?
   a. ethical conduct
   b. continuing responsibility
   c. fiduciary obligation
   d. trustworthy business principles

3. A real estate salesperson advised a prospective buyer that the property the buyer was considering was scheduled for annexation into the city limits. This disclosure constituted which of the following?
   a. disloyalty to principal
   b. misrepresentation
   c. required disclosure to buyer
   d. violation of disclosure of information by agent

4. In a dual agency, the broker:
   a. works with only one buyer at a time
   b. works with both the buyer and seller
   c. must work with another broker
   d. works for both the buyer and seller

5. An intentional misstatement of a material fact that a party relies on to his or her damage is:
   a. misrepresentation
   b. fraud
   c. puffing
   d. exaggeration

6. Which of the following is **NOT** an agency relationship?
   a. attorney-client
   b. broker-seller
   c. trustee-beneficiary
   d. salesperson-buyer

7. To be able to accept compensation from both the buyer and seller, a broker **MUST**:
   a. have a listing agreement
   b. have a buyer broker's agreement
   c. disclose that he or she is a licensed agent
   d. have written permission from both parties

8. A salesperson received two offers for a listed property within a one-minute period. One offer was 2% less than the listed price, and the other was 6% less than the listed price. What should the salesperson present to the seller?
   a. neither offer
   b. both offers
   c. the higher offer
   d. the lower offer

9. The holder of a general power of attorney, in dealing with real property of his or her principal, could **NOT**:
   a. buy the property
   b. sell the property
   c. lease the property
   d. grant an exclusive right to sell listing

10. An agent who can perform any act the principal is capable of delegating would be called a(n):

    a. general agent

    b. specific agent

    c. universal agent

    d. attorney in fact

11. In a subagency, the selling salesperson is responsible to the:

    a. seller

    b. buyer

    c. listing broker

    d. selling broker

12. A broker allowed a person to appear to act as her agent. The broker cannot deny the agency now because of:

    a. ratification

    b. estoppel

    c. subrogation

    d. reformation

13. An offer has been accepted on a 10-acre parcel, when the broker learns that the buyer has been buying up land in the area at a much higher price. The broker should:

    a. notify the seller of the facts

    b. recommend that the seller breach the contract

    c. do nothing, as the seller is obligated to convey

    d. do nothing, as agency has been terminated with the procurement of the buyer

14. Which of the following may a broker disclose to a prospective purchaser without permission?

    a. why the seller must sell now

    b. why the property is not desirable

    c. what the owner actually will accept

    d. what the owner originally paid

15. A broker purchased her own listing because she knew of a purchaser who would pay more than the listing price. The broker:

    a. may never purchase one of her own listings

    b. has done nothing wrong if she never misrepresented the value

    c. acted properly if she revealed the offer was hers

    d. is liable to the seller for the profit she made

16. *Puffing* relates to exaggerations not made as representations of fact. Puffing is:

    a. legal but discouraged

    b. illegal

    c. regulated by the Nevada statutes

    d. unethical

17. A contract in which a property owner employs a broker to market the property creates an agency relationship between which of the following:

    a. buyer and seller

    b. buyer and broker

    c. broker and seller

    d. broker, seller, and buyer

18. John Jamison, a salesman with Taylor Realty, lists the property of Charles and Loretta Simpson for sale at $52,000. The Simpsons have told Jamison that they are pressed to sell and would accept a purchase price of $49,000. Jamison shows the property to Randy Evans and tells Evans he can purchase the property for $49,000. Jamison has:

    a. properly performed his duties to his client

    b. violated his relationship with his client

    c. acted in the best interest of all parties

    d. typically acted as a salesperson is expected to act

19. Which of the following is **TRUE?**
    a. all agency agreements must be in writing
    b. because agency is a contract, there must be consideration
    c. a salesperson cannot create an agency relationship for his or her broker
    d. none of the above

20. A salesperson's position to an owner-client of the broker is closest to that of:
    a. subagent
    b. employee
    c. independent contractor
    d. principal

Chapter 14

IMPORTANT TERMS AND CONCEPTS

90-day clause

agency coupled with an interest

brokerage agreement

cooperating broker

exclusive agency listing

exclusive right to represent buyer

exclusive right to sell listing

listing

listing broker

Multiple Listing Service (MLS)

net listing

open listing

principal

procuring cause

quantum meruit

CHAPTER OBJECTIVES

After completing this chapter, you should be able to:

- Describe the requirements for a real estate brokerage agreement and the information required in a listing.
- Explain the advantages and disadvantages of the four types of listings used in Nevada.
- Summarize how or why a listing can be terminated.
- Describe the objectives and requirements of a Multiple Listing Service (MLS) and the role of a cooperating broker.

Brokerage Agreements

14.1 REQUIREMENTS FOR A REAL ESTATE BROKERAGE AGREEMENT

A **brokerage agreement** is a contract for the employment of a broker by a buyer or a seller. Two types of brokerage agreements exist in real estate. An agreement known as an **exclusive right to represent buyer** is a contract for personal services between a buyer and broker to locate a property. A broker is entitled to compensation for services rendered with this type of contract. The other type of brokerage agreement is a **listing** between the seller and broker. This agreement is both a contract listing a property for sale and a contract for personal services between the broker and the seller to sell the subject property.

A written real estate brokerage agreement is not required for a licensee to represent a party in a transaction. However, a written and signed agreement is required for any exclusive employment agreement. An exclusive real estate brokerage agreement must:

- Be written
- Have a termination date
- Be *signed* by all parties to the agreement

The written agreement cannot require the client to notify the broker of the client's intentions to cancel the exclusive features at termination of the agreement. Other terms of the brokerage agreement are negotiable.

The broker will not be able to collect a commission if:

- An exclusive agreement is not in writing.
- The brokerage agreement does not include a required legal provision.

Failure to include a required legal provision, such as a fixed termination date, makes the brokerage agreement voidable by the client. As a result, the broker cannot claim payment under alternative legal theories of compensation. **Quantum meruit** is a legal theory used to establish the compensation rate when there is no express agreement or when the agreement fails but the court finds it would be inequitable not to give the broker a commission. Quantum meruit allows the broker to be paid the reasonable value of his or her services. The court will look at "established customs" when determining the worth of the broker's services. Quantum meruit cannot be used to collect compensation when there is a faulty exclusive brokerage agreement.

Even though a salesperson may have procured a listing, it does not belong to him or her. The broker owns all of the listings and represents the buyer or seller client. The listings are sometimes called the "broker's business inventory."

Most non-broker licensees (salesperson and broker-salesperson) are independent contractors; nevertheless, by law they cannot enter into their own brokerage agreements with clients. Nevada Revised Statutes restrict a non-broker licensee from being hired independent of a broker. The broker is the entity that represents the client. The non-broker licensees work under the control and supervision of the broker. This does not remove the salesperson's individual responsibilities. Each non-broker licensee has duties toward the client, the broker, professional peers, and the public and may be held personally liable if those duties are breached.

Information Required in a Listing

Standard printed forms for listings are not required and most facts to be included in the listing contract are subject to the negotiations between the broker and client. However, most Multiple Listing Services have developed forms for use in Nevada. A non-member of a Multiple Listing Service may develop his or her own format.

Whether the printed forms are used or not, these material facts should be included in all listings:

- *Price* of property.
- *Amount* of commission (usually a percentage of sales price).
- *Date* of inception and date of expiration.
- *Names and addresses* of the broker and the seller.
- *Legal description.*
- *No-discrimination clause.*
- *Financial terms* the seller is offering.
- *Permission* to place a for-sale sign on the property.
- **90-day clause** *(or broker protection clause)*, which provides for the listing broker to be compensated if a buyer was procured during the period of the listing contract and subsequently agreed to purchase the property within the 90-day period. The number of days of broker protection established in the listing is a matter of negotiation between the seller and the broker (that is, it could be 30, 60, 90, 120, 180 days, or some other amount of time).
- *No blanks*—If something does not apply, write *N/A.*

The broker could be held responsible for any errors or omissions in the listing. All subsequent changes to the original listing must be initialed and dated by all parties generally on an amendment to the listing.

A commission is not payable until the terms of the employment contract have been fulfilled; a ready, willing, and able buyer is found; and a "meeting of the minds" occurs between buyer and seller. There are limitations and exceptions to this statement that are further explained in the following section and in Chapter 17.

Preparing a Listing Agreement

When preparing a listing agreement, it is important for the seller to understand the fine print. The forms deal with the subject of cooperation with buyers, brokers, and subagency. Most sellers do not understand these terms and should be made aware of the provisions of any agreement they are asked to sign.

The broker is responsible for the representation of the client's property and should be certain that a licensee understands how to correctly complete the form. The following list provides some of the information required (shown in *italic print*), followed by where, with whom, or how the information can be found.

1. *Legal description*—Title company, seller's deed, public records (available on MLS), and often the Internet (plat maps).
2. *Assessor number (taxpayer number)*—Title company, Internet, tax valuation notice, or tax bill.
3. *School districts and schools*—Sellers, contact local school board and ask for boundaries or give address, or in some MLS systems.
4. *Size of house or square footage*—Measure outside of building, appraiser, county tax rolls from master appraisal, or builder. Actual measurements are best and appraiser's measurements are next best.
5. *Date of construction*—County records, title company, or MLS systems.
6. *Lot size*—Title company service or copy of plat map. If vacant land, calculate lot size and check deed and maps in county recorder's office.
7. *Room size*—Measure, never copy from expired listing (always use approximate).
8. *Encumbrances and monthly payments*—Loan verification letters to lenders, calculate balance from note and trust deed year-end lender statements.
9. *Assumability of loans, prepayment clauses and due-on-sale clauses*—Loan verification letter to lender, read trust deed or other documents.
10. *Easements and deed restrictions*—Generally found in the title report.
11. *Taxes*—County assessor's office, title company.
12. *Outstanding liens*—Seller, title company, preliminary title report.
13. *Assessment*—Seller, homeowners' association (if applicable).
14. *Price*—Appraisal, comparative market analysis, and competitive market analysis.
15. *Terms of listing*—Price and terms.

FIGURE 14.1   Types of Listings

Types of Listings

Exclusive Right to Sell
Exclusive Agency
Open
Net

14.2 TYPES OF LISTINGS

There are four types of listings used in Nevada (see Figure 14.1):

1. Exclusive right to sell listings
2. Exclusive agency listings
3. Open listings
4. Net listings

Exclusive Right to Sell Listing

The **exclusive right to sell listing** is the most widely used type of listing. An exclusive right to sell listing is given to only one broker who is employed as an exclusive agent. With this type of listing, only the employed broker is entitled to receive a commission, no matter who sells the property. The **listing broker** then pays the selling broker if there is one involved, but if the owner sells the property, the owner must pay a commission to the listing broker, whether or not the broker was the procuring cause. Most listings on a Multiple Listing Service (MLS) are exclusive right to sell listings.

A sample copy of the Greater Las Vegas Association of REALTORS'® Exclusive Authorization and Right to Sell, Exchange, or Lease Brokerage Listing Agreement is included as Figure 14.2, at the end of this chapter.

Exclusive Agency Listing

In an **exclusive agency listing,** the owner employs one broker as an exclusive agent. However, the owner, also known as the **principal**, retains the right to sell the property and does not owe a commission to the agency if the owner sells the property. All other real estate agents deal with the listing agent.

Open Listing

Open listings are generally used with commercial properties rather than residential properties. The owner may employ any number of brokers. The owner retains the right to sell without paying a commission and agrees to pay only the first broker who procures a ready, willing, and able buyer who fulfills the terms of the listing.

This is the least popular type of listing because residential brokers do not want to spend the time, effort, and money for advertising if they are not assured of a commission. Open listings are not accepted by Multiple Listing Services, and a broker would not want to place such a listing on MLS.

Procuring Cause

Procuring cause is the direct or proximate cause. For example, in a real estate transaction, the brokerage that located a potential buyer, who then agreed to purchase the listed property, is considered the procuring cause. Open and agency listings may sometimes create problems when a buyer, after being introduced to a property by one broker, enters into a contract to purchase from another broker or from the seller himself or herself. The introducing broker could be entitled to a commission if he or she can prove that the buyer bought the property because of his or her efforts, even though a second broker was the one who wrote the contract. Procuring cause relates primarily to exclusive agency and open listings.

Net Listing

In a **net listing**, the owner states a required amount of money to be received by the seller, and the broker adds a commission. The broker is free to offer the property at anything over the net price and the amount of any excess represents the compensation to the broker. Because this is simply a different way to establish commission, the listing can be an open or exclusive listing. In Nevada, a net listing is legal but its use is discouraged due to the potential for fraudulent treatment of the public by the licensee. Multiple Listing Services generally will not accept net listings because a cooperating broker's commission is difficult to determine. However, net listings are periodically used for hard to sell properties, such as rural land and environmentally damaged sites.

Exclusive Right to Represent Buyer

Listings are between the broker and the seller of the real property. Frequently, a buyer of real property asks a broker to locate and negotiate the purchase or lease of property. Such an arrangement could be documented in an agreement known as a Buyer-Broker Exclusive Employment Agreement. This exclusive right to represent buyer agreement is a real estate employment agreement and subject to the same requirements for exclusive brokerage agreements previously covered in this chapter.

A copy of the Greater Las Vegas Association of REALTORS' Exclusive Right to Represent Buyer and Agency Agreement is included as Figure 14.3, at the end of this chapter.

14.3 TERMINATION OF LISTINGS

A listing can be terminated through completion of a sale, by agreement between agent and principal, by operation of the law, and by impossibility of performance. Reasons for termination include the following:

- *Sale and the subsequent close of escrow.*
- *Termination date*—The listing has expired.
- *Broker abandonment or renunciation*—A listing can be terminated if the broker has been asked to perform an illegal or unethical act by the principal or due to lack of broker performance.
- *Mutual consent*—The agent and principal mutually agree to terminate the listing.
- *Death or insanity of party*—Either the agent or the principal dies or becomes incompetent.
- *Title cannot be transferred*—Such as when title is seized in a foreclosure or condemnation action.
- *Destruction of property*—Due to a natural disaster.
- *Unilateral revocation by the owner for just cause.*
- *Change in the use of property by an outside force*—Such as a zoning change.

The seller or broker may unilaterally terminate the listing. However, the other party could claim some damages in court. A seller may not unilaterally terminate a listing, without cause, when the agency is coupled with an interest. An **agency coupled with an interest** is more than a personal service contract. Examples follow:

- When a broker pays on the seller's mortgage debt to avoid foreclosure.
- When a broker pays for fix-up costs to make the property more marketable.

14.4 MULTIPLE LISTING SERVICE

The **Multiple Listing Service (MLS)** is an organization formed to share listing information between members. MLS is not a type of listing but a service to member licensees. Almost every Nevada locale is served by a Multiple Listing Service.

Members pool all exclusive right to sell listings and agency listings by reporting the listings to the MLS. These listings are entered into a computer and made available to participating members. Having such wide exposure to the listings is valuable for both the seller and the licensee. The seller benefits from the exposure of the listing to all of the MLS members, who number in the thousands; this exposure often results in the sale of the listed property in the shortest time with the best possible price.

Very often, the sale will be made by an agency other than the brokerage that has the listing. The listing broker, however, handles all offers and negotiations. The listing broker agrees to pay a portion of the commission to the selling broker who procures the buyer. The selling broker is referred to as a **cooperating broker** and almost always represents the buyer.

FIGURE 14.2 Exclusive Authorization and Right to Sell, Exchange, or Lease Brokerage Listing Agreement

---

EXCLUSIVE AUTHORIZATION AND RIGHT TO SELL, EXCHANGE OR LEASE BROKERAGE LISTING AGREEMENT

1. EXCLUSIVE RIGHT TO SELL: I/We, _____ ("Seller")
hereby employs and grants _____ ("Broker") the exclusive and irrevocable
(Company Name)
right, commencing on _____ , and expiring on _____ , to sell, lease or exchange the Real
Property located in the City of _____ , County of _____ Nevada, APN
_____ commonly known as: _____
_____("the Property").

2. TERMS OF SALE: The listing price shall be $ _____ , terms available:
Cash ____ CONV ____ FHA ____ Lease ____ VA ____ Lease Option ____
Owner Will Carry ____ Other _____
(Note: If the Property is offered for lease, then the term "Seller" used in this Agreement includes "Landlord" as applicable.)

3. PROPERTY OFFERED FOR SALE: The listing price noted above includes the Property and all improvements and fixtures permanently affixed and installed.
    a. The following items of Personal Property are **included** in the above price and shall be conveyed unencumbered in escrow by a valid bill of sale: _____
_____
_____
_____
    b. The following items of Personal Property are **excluded** from the above price and not included in the sale: _____
_____
_____
_____

4. MULTIPLE LISTING SERVICE (MLS): Broker is a participant of THE GREATER LAS VEGAS ASSOCIATION OF REALTORS® (GLVAR) Multiple Listing Service, and the listing information will be provided to the MLS to be published and disseminated to its Participants and Subscribers in accordance with its Rules and Regulations and Section 20 herein. Broker is authorized to cooperate with other real estate Brokers, and to report the sale, its price, terms and financing for the publication, dissemination information and use by authorized Association members, MLS Participants and Subscribers.

5. TITLE INSURANCE: Seller agrees to provide Buyer with a policy of title insurance in the amount of the selling price.

6. COMPENSATION TO BROKER: Compensation is solely a matter of negotiation between Broker and Seller and is not fixed, suggested, controlled or recommended by GLVAR, MLS or any other person not a party to this Agreement. Seller agrees to pay Broker as compensation for services _____ % of selling price of the Property or $ _____ amount. If leased, Seller agrees to pay Broker _____ % of the total rental agreed to be paid by lessee or $ _____ . Seller acknowledges that Broker will offer _____% or $ _____ to the cooperating broker who is the procuring cause of the sale. If leased, Broker agrees to pay the cooperating broker _____% or $ _____ . Seller acknowledges that offers of compensation are between brokers and are not negotiable between the Seller and Buyer. Seller will also pay $ _____ for _____ .

Seller acknowledges that he/she has read, understood, and agreed to each and every provision of this page.
SELLER(S) INITIALS: _____ / _____

Exclusive Right Listing Agreement Rev. 2007
Page 1 of 5

FIGURE 14.2   Continued.

49 **Compensation shall be due:**
50   a. if the Property is sold or leased by Broker, or through any other person including Seller, on the above
51 terms or any other price and terms acceptable to Seller during the above time period or any extension of said time
52 period;
53   b. if the Property is transferred, conveyed, leased, rented, or made unmarketable by a voluntary act of
54 Seller without the consent of Broker, during the time period or any extension of said time period;
55   c. if within _____ calendar days of the final termination, including extensions, of this Agreement,
56 the Property is sold, conveyed, or otherwise transferred to anyone with whom the Broker has had negotiations or
57 to whom the Property was shown prior to the final termination. This section (c) shall not apply if Seller enters
58 into a valid Brokerage Listing Agreement with another licensed real estate Broker after the final termination of
59 this Exclusive Brokerage Listing Agreement.
60
61 In the event of an exchange, permission is hereby given to the Broker to represent such parties as Broker may
62 deem appropriate and collect compensation from them provided that there is full disclosure to all parties. If
63 completion of sale is prevented by default of Seller, or the refusal of Seller to accept an offer in accordance with
64 the price and terms of this Agreement, then upon event, Broker is authorized to take any action reasonably
65 necessary to collect said commission. If completion of sale is prevented by a party to the transaction other than
66 Seller, Broker may collect its commission only if and when Seller collects damages by suit or otherwise, and then
67 in an amount not less than one-half of the damages recovered, but not to exceed the above compensation after first
68 deducting title expenses, escrow expenses and the expenses of collections if any. Broker is authorized to
69 cooperate and divide with other brokers the above compensation in any manner acceptable to Broker. Seller
70 hereby irrevocably assigns to Broker the funds and proceeds of Seller in escrow equal to the above compensation.
71 In the event any sum of money due under this Agreement remains unpaid for a period of thirty (30) days, such
72 sum shall bear interest at the rate of (_____) percent per annum from the due date until paid.
73
74 **7. DEPOSIT:** Broker is authorized to accept on Seller's behalf a deposit to be applied toward purchase price or
75 lease.
76
77 **8. AGENCY RELATIONSHIP:**
78   a. Broker warrants that he holds a current, valid Nevada real estate license. Broker shall act as the agent of
79 the Seller and may also assign or designate a licensee of the Broker who shall act as the representative of the
80 seller in any resulting transaction.
81   b. Depending upon the circumstances, it may be necessary or appropriate for the designated licensee to
82 act as agent for both Seller and Buyer, exchange parties, or one or more additional parties. If applicable, Broker
83 and the designated licensee shall disclose to Seller any election to act as an agent representing more than one
84 party and obtain the written Consent To Act Form signed by all parties to the transaction.
85   c. Broker may also have licensees in its company who are agents of the Buyer who may show and
86 negotiate an offer to purchase Seller's Property. In this event the licensees that represent the Buyer will only
87 represent the Buyer in the transaction with all duties owed to the Buyer and not the Seller. This, therefore, does
88 not require a Consent To Act Form.
89
90 **9. REQUIRED DISCLOSURES:**
91   a. Unless exempt under NRS chapter 113, Seller shall truthfully complete and sign a Seller's Real
92 Property Disclosure Statement concerning the condition of the Property. Seller shall update the Seller's Real
93 Property Disclosure as necessary.
94   b. If the Property is or has been the subject of a construction defect claim, whether litigated or not, Seller
95 shall provide the disclosure required by NRS 40.688.
96   c. If the Property was built prior to 1978, Seller shall complete the Disclosure of Information on Lead-
97 Based Paint Hazards in accordance with Federal Regulations.

Seller acknowledges that he/she has read, understood, and agreed to each and every provision of this page.
SELLER(S) INITIALS: _____ / _____

FIGURE 14.2 Continued.

98   d. Seller acknowledges receipt of the Residential Disclosure Guide: [____][____]
99
100 **10. SELLER'S INDEMNIFICATION:** Seller agrees to save, defend, and hold Broker harmless from all claims,
101 disputes, litigation, and/or judgments arising from any incorrect information supplied by Seller or from any
102 material facts which Seller fails to disclose.
103
104 **11. FAIR HOUSING:** Broker shall offer the Property for sale or lease without regard to race, color, sex, creed,
105 religion, national origin, handicap, or familial status in compliance with federal, state, and local anti-
106 discrimination laws.
107
108 **12. COMMON INTEREST COMMUNITY:** If the Property is located within a Common Interest Community,
109 Seller acknowledges and agrees to obtain and/or provide the information required by NRS 116.4109 and
110 116.41095 to Broker for delivery to Buyer.
111
112 **13. SIGN:** Seller authorizes Broker to install a FOR SALE/LEASE sign on the Property.
113
114 **14. KEYBOX:** Seller[___] (does) [___] (does not) authorize Broker to install a keybox in connection with the
115 showing of the Property. Seller acknowledges that they have been advised that:
116   a. The purpose and function of the keybox is to permit access to the interior of the Property by all
117 members of GLVAR's MLS, including certified/licensed appraisers;
118   b. Seller should safeguard Personal Property and valuables located within the Property;
119   c. It is not a requirement of the GLVAR's MLS for a Seller to allow the use of a keybox;
120   d. Where a tenant occupies the Property, the tenant's consent is also required, which shall be obtained by
121 the Seller or his Property Manager;
122   e. Neither the listing nor selling Broker nor the GLVAR is an insurer against the loss of Personal
123 Property. Seller hereby releases Broker and the GLVAR from any responsibility relating to the keybox.
124
125 **15. RENT/LEASE:** The Property_____ is -OR- _____ is not currently occupied by a Tenant. The Property is
126 subject to a management agreement with: (name of Property Manager and phone number): _____ .
127 If the Property is a single family unit, Seller agrees to not rent or lease the Property during the term of this Agreement
128 without fourteen (14) days prior written notice to Broker.
129
130 **16. TAX WITHHOLDING:** Seller agrees to perform any act reasonably necessary to carry out the provisions of
131 FIRPTA (Internal Revenue Code 1445).
132
133 **17. MEDIATION/ARBITRATION:** The Broker and Seller hereby agree that any dispute concerning the terms
134 and conditions of this contract shall be resolved through mediation and/or arbitration proceedings at the GLVAR
135 in accordance with the standards of practice of the National Association of REALTORS® and GLVAR's rules of
136 procedure. If a lawsuit is filed by either party, that lawsuit shall be stayed until the dispute is resolved or
137 terminated in accordance with this paragraph.
138
139 **18. ATTORNEY'S FEES:** In the event suit is brought by either party to enforce this Agreement, the prevailing
140 party is entitled to court costs and reasonable attorney's fees.
141
142 **19. ADVERTISING:** Seller acknowledges that a photo of the Property may be taken by an authorized
143 representative for publication in the MLS computer system. Seller agrees that the Property may be advertised in
144 all formats of media including but not limited to electronic and print advertising.
145

Seller acknowledges that he/she has read, understood, and agreed to each and every provision of this page.
SELLER(S) INITIALS: _____ / _____

FIGURE 14.2 Continued.

146 **20. USE OF LISTING CONTENT:** Seller acknowledges and agrees that all photographs, images, graphics,
147 video recordings, virtual tours, drawings, written descriptions, remarks, narratives, pricing information, and other
148 copyrightable elements relating to the Property provided by to Broker or Broker's agent (the "Seller Listing
149 Content") and any changes thereto, may be filed with MLS, included in compilations of listings, and otherwise
150 distributed, publicly displayed and reproduced in any medium. Seller hereby grants to Broker a non-exclusive,
151 irrevocable, worldwide, royalty-free license to use, sublicense through multiple tiers, publish, display, and
152 reproduce the Seller Listing Content, to prepare derivative works of the Seller Listing Content, and to distribute
153 the Seller Listing Content or any derivative works thereof in any medium. This non-exclusive license shall
154 survive the termination of this Agreement for any reason whatever. Seller represents and warrants to Broker that
155 the Seller Listing Content, and the license granted to Broker for the Seller Listing Content, do not violate or
156 infringe upon the rights, including any copyright rights, of any person or entity.
157
158 **21. NEVADA LAW:** This Agreement is executed and intended to be performed in the State of Nevada, and the
159 laws of Nevada shall govern its interpretation and effect. The parties agree that the State of Nevada, and the
160 county in which the Property is located, is the appropriate judicial forum for any litigation, arbitration or
161 mediation related to this Agreement.
162
163 **22. ENTIRE CONTRACT:** All prior negotiations and agreements between the parties are incorporated in this
164 Agreement, which constitutes the entire contract. Its terms are intended by the parties as a final, complete, and
165 exclusive expression of their agreement with respect to its subject matter and may not be contradicted by evidence
166 of any prior agreement or contemporaneous oral agreement. This Agreement and any supplement, addendum, or
167 modification, including any photocopy or facsimile, may be executed in two or more counterparts, all of which
168 shall constitute one and the same writing. The terms of this Agreement may not be amended, modified or altered
169 except through a written agreement signed by all of the parties hereto. **The parties agree that an MLS Change
170 Order signed by Broker and Seller shall act as a valid written addendum to this Agreement.**
171
172 **23. PARTIAL INVALIDITY:** In the event that any provision of this Agreement shall be held to be invalid or
173 unenforceable, such ruling shall not affect the validity or enforceability of the remainder of the Agreement in any
174 respect whatsoever.
175
176 **24. WARRANTY OF OWNERSHIP:** Seller warrants that Seller is the sole Owner of the Property or has the
177 authority to execute this Agreement. By signing below Seller acknowledges that Seller has read and understands
178 this Agreement, agrees to the terms thereof, and has received a copy.
179
180 **25. ADDITIONAL TERMS:**_____
181 _____
182 _____
183 _____
184 _____
185 _____
186 _____
187 _____
188 _____
189 _____
190 _____
191 _____
192 _____
193 _____
194 _____

Seller acknowledges that he/she has read, understood, and agreed to each and every provision of this page.
SELLER(S) INITIALS: _____ / _____

FIGURE 14.2 Continued.

195 THE PRINTED PORTION OF THIS AGREEMENT HAS BEEN APPROVED BY THE GREATER LAS
196 VEGAS ASSOCIATION OF REALTORS.® NO REPRESENTATION IS MADE AS TO THE LEGAL
197 VALIDITY OR ADEQUACY OF ANY PROVISION OR THE TAX CONSEQUENCES THEREOF. FOR
198 LEGAL OR TAX ADVICE, CONSULT YOUR ATTORNEY OR TAX ADVISOR.
199
200 By signing below, Seller consents to receive transmissions sent from Broker to the fax number(s)
201 and/or e-mail address(es) set forth. Seller agrees to keep Broker advised of his/her address and
202 telephone number (or a number where they may be reached within 24 hours) at all times during
203 the term of this Agreement.
204
205 **SELLER:**
206
207 Date_____, _____ Telephone _____ FAX _____ E-Mail_____
208 Seller's Signature _____ Seller's Signature _____
209 Printed Name: _____ Printed Name: _____
210 Address _____ City _____ State ___ Zip_____
211
212
213 **BROKER:**
214
215 Date_____, _____ Telephone _____ FAX _____ E-Mail_____
216 Company _____
217 Address _____ City _____ State ___ Zip_____
218 Designated Licensee Signature _____ License No. _____
219 Printed Name: _____ Licensee's Telephone: _____
220 Broker's Signature _____ License No. _____
221 Printed Name: _____

Seller acknowledges that he/she has read, understood, and agreed to each and every provision of this page.
SELLER(S) INITIALS: _____ / _____

Exclusive Right Listing Agreement Rev. 2007
Page 5 of 5

FIGURE 14.2   Continued.

WHAT EVERYONE SHOULD KNOW ABOUT EQUAL OPPORTUNITY IN HOUSING

The sale and purchase of a home is one of the most significant events that any person will experience in their lifetime. It is more than the simple purchase of housing, for it includes the hopes, dreams, aspirations, and economic destiny of those involved.

THE LAW - Civil Rights Act of 1866

The Civil Rights Act of 1866 prohibits all racial discrimination in the sale or rental of property.

Fair Housing Act

The Fair Housing Act declares a national policy of fair housing throughout the United States. The law makes illegal any discrimination in the sale, lease or rental of housing, or making housing otherwise unavailable, because of race, color, religion, sex, handicap, familial status, or national origin.

Americans with Disabilities Act

Title III of the Americans with Disabilities Act prohibits discrimination against the disabled in places of public accommodations and commercial facilities.

Equal Credit Opportunity Act

The Equal Credit Opportunity Act makes discrimination unlawful with respect to any aspect of a credit application on the basis of race, color, religion, national origin, sex, marital status, age or because all or part of the applicant's income derives from any public assistance program.

State and Local Laws

State and local laws often provide broader coverage and prohibit discrimination based on additional classes not covered by federal law.

THE RESPONSIBILITIES

The home seller, the home seeker, and the real estate professional all have rights and responsibilities under the law.

For the Home Seller

You should know that as a home seller or landlord you have a responsibility and a requirement under the law not to discriminate in the sale, rental and financing of property on the basis of race, color, religion, sex, handicap, familial status, or national origin. You cannot instruct the licensed broker or salesperson acting as your agent to convey for you any limitations in the sale or rental, because the real estate professional is also bound by law not to discriminate. Under the law, a home seller or landlord cannot establish discriminatory terms or conditions in the purchase or rental, deny that housing is available or advertise that the property is available only to persons of a certain race, color, religion, sex, handicap, familial status, or national origin.

For the Home Seeker

You have the right to expect that housing will be available to you without discrimination or other limitation based on race, color, religion, sex, handicap, familial status, or national origin.

This includes the right to expect:

- housing in your price range made available to you without discrimination
- equal professional service
- the opportunity to consider a broad range of housing choices
- no discriminatory limitations on communities or locations of housing
- no discrimination in the financing, appraising or insuring of housing
- reasonable accommodations in rules, practices and procedures for persons with disabilities
- non-discriminatory terms and conditions for the sale, rental, financing, or insuring of a dwelling
- to be free from harassment or intimidation for exercising your fair housing rights.

For the Real Estate Professional

As a home seller or home seeker, you should know that the term REALTOR® identifies a licensed professional in real estate who is a member of the NATIONAL ASSOCIATION OF REALTORS®. Not all licensed real estate brokers and salespersons are members of the National Association, and only those who are can identify themselves as REALTOR®. They conduct their business and activities in accordance with a strict Code of Ethics. As agents in a real estate transaction, licensed brokers or salespersons are prohibited by law from discriminating on the basis of race, color, religion, sex, handicap, familial status, or national origin. A request from the home seller or landlord to act in a discriminatory manner in the sale, lease or rental cannot legally be fulfilled by the real estate professional.

DEED AND PROPERTY COVENANTS OR RESTRICTIONS OF RECORD

During the history of our country, some persons have placed restrictions on property based on race, color, religion, sex, handicap, familial status, or national origin. Generally, these restrictions are void and unenforceable, with limited exceptions for particular types of religious housing and housing for older persons. The publication of these void restrictions may convey a message that the restrictions continue to be valid. Any time a sales associate or broker is asked to provide a copy of the covenants or restrictions of record relating to the use of a property the following message should be included:

These documents may contain restrictions or covenants based on race, color, religion, sex, handicap, familial status, or national origin.

Such restrictions or covenants generally are void and unenforceable as violations of fair housing laws.

Be assured that all property is marketed and made available without discrimination based on race, color, religion, sex, handicap, familial status, or national origin. Should you have any questions regarding such restrictions, please contact your attorney.

THE EQUAL OPPORTUNITY PROGRAM

The NATIONAL ASSOCIATION OF REALTORS® has developed a Fair Housing Program to provide resources and guidance to REALTORS® in ensuring equal professional services for all people.

The Code of Ethics

Article 10 of the NATIONAL ASSOCIATION OF REALTORS® Code of Ethics requires that "REALTORS® shall not deny equal professional services to any person for reasons of race, color, religion, sex, handicap, familial status, or national origin. REALTORS® shall not be a party to any plan or agreement to discriminate against a person or persons on the basis of race, color, religion, sex, handicap, familial status, or national origin."

A REALTOR® pledges to conduct business in keeping with the spirit and letter of the Code of Ethics. Article 10 imposes obligations upon REALTORS® and is also a firm statement of support for equal opportunity in housing.

Fair Housing Partnership

The Fair Housing Partnership negotiated with the U.S. Department of Housing and Urban Development (HUD) outlines a program of voluntary compliance. REALTORS® voluntarily participate in activities and programs to acquaint the community with the availability of equal housing opportunity, to establish office procedures to ensure that there is no denial of equal professional service, to make materials available which will explain this commitment, and to work with other groups within the community to identify and remove barriers to fair housing.

FURTHER ASSISTANCE

Local Boards of REALTORS® will accept complaints alleging violations of the Code of Ethics filed by a homeseeker who alleges discriminatory treatment in the availability, purchase or rental of housing. Local Boards of REALTORS® have a responsibility to enforce the Code of Ethics through professional standards procedures and corrective action in cases where a violation of the Code of Ethics is proven to have occurred.

Complaints alleging discrimination in housing may be filed with the nearest office of the Department of Housing and Urban Development (HUD), or by calling HUD's Discrimination Hotline at 1-800-669-9777, 1-800-290-1617 (TTY). For information and publications on fair housing, call HUD's Fair Housing Information Clearinghouse at 1-800-343-3442.

Produced with ZipForm™ by RE FormsNet, LLC 18070 Fifteen Mile Road, Fraser, Michigan 48026 www.zipform.com   Samples

FIGURE 14.3   Exclusive Right to Represent Buyer and Agency Agreement

EXCLUSIVE RIGHT TO REPRESENT BUYER
AND AGENCY AGREEMENT

I/We, _____ ("Buyer")
hereby employs and grants _____ ("Broker") the exclusive
(Company Name)
and irrevocable right, commencing on _____, _____ , and expiring at midnight on
_____, _____ , to locate property and negotiate terms and conditions acceptable to
Buyer for purchase, exchange, option, or lease as follows:

1.   **General Nature of Property:** Buyer represents that he intends to acquire an interest in one or more properties meeting the following general description:
Type: _____ Residential _____ Land _____ Commercial _____ Other: _____

2.   **Broker Compensation:** Broker's compensation shall be paid at the time of and as a condition of closing as follows:
     a.   Buyer agrees to pay Broker _____ of the selling price of the Property or the set amount of $ _____ . Buyer authorizes Broker to accept compensation offered by seller or seller's broker, which compensation shall be credited against any compensation owed by Buyer to Broker.
     b.   Buyer agrees to compensate Broker if the Buyer or any other person acting on the Buyer's behalf enters into an agreement to purchase, exchange, option, or lease any property of the general nature described herein.
     c.   If completion of any transaction is prevented by Buyer's Default or with the consent of Buyer, the total compensation due under this Agreement shall be immediately due and payable by Buyer.
     d.   Buyer agrees to pay such compensation if Buyer within _____ calendar days after the termination of this Agreement enters into an agreement to purchase, exchange, option or lease any property shown to or negotiated on behalf of the Buyer by Broker during the term of this Agreement, unless Buyer enters into a subsequent agreement with another Broker.
     e.   Commissions payable for the purchase, exchange, option or lease of property are not set by any Board or Association of REALTORS® or Multiple Listing Service or in any manner other than as negotiated between Broker and Buyer.

3.   **Retainer Fee:** Buyer agrees to pay and Broker acknowledges receipt of a non-refundable retainer fee in the amount of $ _____ payable to Broker for initial counseling, consultation and research, which retainer fee _____ (shall) _____ (shall not be) credited against any other compensation owed by Buyer to Broker as provided above.

4.   **New Home/Lot Sales:** Buyer acknowledges that some sellers (particularly new home subdivisions, open houses and for-sale-by-owner) will compensate Broker only if Broker accompanies Buyer on the first home/lot visit. Buyer agrees that if Buyer makes a first visit without Broker, resulting in a seller's refusal to compensate Broker, that Buyer will compensate Broker as provided above.

Exclusive Right to Represent Buyer and Agency Agreement 6/07

Page 1 of 3

Samples

FIGURE 14.3   Continued.

5.   Buyer's Duties: Buyer agrees to work exclusively with Broker and to provide to Broker or lender, upon request, information necessary to assure Buyer's ability to acquire property described above. Buyer further agrees to view or consider property of the general type set forth in this Agreement, and to negotiate in good faith to acquire such property.

6.   Equal Housing Opportunity: It is the policy of the Broker to abide by all local, state, and federal laws prohibiting discrimination against any individual or group of individuals. The Broker has no duty to disclose the racial, ethnic, or religious composition of any neighborhood, community, or building, nor whether persons with disabilities are housed in any home or facility, except that the agent may identify housing facilities meeting the needs of a disabled buyer.

7.   Other Potential Buyers: Buyer consents and acknowledges that other potential buyers represented by Broker may consider, make offers on, or acquire an interest in the same or similar properties as Buyer is seeking.

8.   Mediation/Arbitration: The Broker and Buyer hereby agree that any dispute concerning the terms and conditions of this contract shall be resolved through mediation and arbitration proceedings at the GLVAR in accordance with local rules of procedure and the standards of practice of the National Association of REALTORS®. If a lawsuit is filed by either party, that lawsuit shall be stayed until the dispute is resolved or terminated in accordance with this paragraph.

9.   Attorneys Fees: In the event suit is brought by either party to enforce this Agreement, the prevailing party is entitled to court costs and reasonable attorneys fees.

10.   Nevada Law Applies: This Agreement is executed and intended to be performed in the State of Nevada, and the laws of the Nevada shall govern its interpretation and effect. The parties agree that the State of Nevada, and the county in which the Property is located, is the appropriate judicial forum for any litigation, arbitration or mediation related to this Agreement.

11.   Capacity: Buyer warrants that Buyer has the legal capacity, full power and authority to enter into this Agreement and consummate the transaction contemplated hereby on Buyer's own behalf or on behalf of the party Buyer represents.

12.   Entire Contract: All prior negotiations and agreements between the parties are incorporated in this Agreement, which constitutes the entire contract. Its terms are intended by the parties as a final, complete, and exclusive expression of their agreement with respect to its subject matter and may not be contradicted by evidence of any prior agreement or contemporaneous oral agreement. This Agreement and any supplement, addendum, or modification, including any photocopy or facsimile, may be executed in two or more counterparts, all of which shall constitute one and the same writing. The terms of this Agreement may not be amended, modified or altered except through a written agreement signed by all of the parties hereto.

13.   Partial Invalidity: In the event that any provision of this Agreement shall be held to be invalid or unenforceable such ruling shall not affect the validity or enforceability of the remainder of the Agreement in any respect whatsoever.

Exclusive Right to Represent Buyer and Agency Agreement 6/07

Page 2 of 3

FIGURE 14.3 Continued.

14.   Acceptance: Buyer hereby agrees to all of the terms and conditions herein and acknowledges receipt of a copy of this Agreement.

15. Additional Terms: _____
_____
_____
_____

THE PRINTED PORTION OF THIS AGREEMENT HAS BEEN APPROVED BY THE GREATER LAS VEGAS ASSOCIATION OF REALTORS®. NO REPRESENTATION IS MADE AS THE LEGAL VALIDITY OF ADEQUACY OF ANY PROVISION OR THE TAX CONSEQUENCES THEREOF. FOR LEGAL OR TAX ADVICE, CONSULT YOUR ATTORNEY OR TAX ADVISOR.

BUYER:

Buyer Signature: _____ Date _____

Buyer Signature: _____ Time: _____

Address: _____ City _____ State _____ Zip _____

Telephone: _____ Fax: _____ Email: _____

BROKER:

Broker Signature: _____ Date _____

Company: _____ Designated Licensee: _____

Address: _____ City _____ State _____ Zip _____

Telephone: _____ Fax: _____ Email: _____

Exclusive Right to Represent Buyer and Agency Agreement 6/07
Page 3 of 3

CHAPTER SUMMARY

Real estate brokerage agreements can be either written or oral; however, exclusive agreements must be written. By law, exclusive agreements must be in writing, be signed by all parties, and include a definite termination date. The broker owns all of the listings and a licensee other than a broker (salesperson or broker-salesperson) cannot contract directly with a client.

The broker is responsible for the representation of the client's property and should be certain that a licensee understands the proper way to complete the listing agreement. Certain facts should be in a listing: price of property, amount of commission, date of inception and expiration, names and addresses of broker and seller, legal description, no-discrimination clause, financial terms, permission for placing a for-sale sign on the property, and a 90-day clause. No sections of the agreement should be left blank; write *N/A* if something does not apply. The broker could be held responsible for any errors and/or omissions in the listing. If any changes are made to the listing through an amendment, they must be signed or initialed and dated by all parties. A commission is not payable until the terms of the employment contract have been fulfilled; a ready, willing, and able buyer is found; and a "meeting of the minds" occurs between buyer and seller.

Some of the information required in a listing includes a legal description of property, assessor number, size and square footage of house, lot size, easements and deed restrictions, taxes, and price. Knowing where, with whom, or how to procure additional information is required.

Four types of listings are used in Nevada: exclusive right to sell listings, exclusive agency listings, open listings, and net listings. An exclusive right to sell listing is the most widely used type of listing. It is given to only one broker, who is then employed as an exclusive agent. Only the employed broker is entitled to receive a commission, no matter who sells the property. In an exclusive agency listing, the owner employs one broker as an exclusive agent. However, the owner, also known as the principal, retains the right to sell the property and does not owe a commission to the agency if the owner sells the property. Open listings are used more often with commercial properties. Open listings are the least popular type of listing because a broker commission is not assured. Procuring cause relates primarily to exclusive agency and open listings. The brokerage that located a potential buyer, who then agreed to purchase the listed property, is considered the procuring cause. In Nevada, a net listing is legal but its use is discouraged. Multiple Listing Services generally will not accept net listings.

A listing can be terminated through completion of a sale, by agreement between agent and principal, by operation of the law, or by impossibility of performance. Reasons for termination include sale of the property, the expiration of the listing, and mutual consent. A seller may not unilaterally terminate a listing, without cause, when the agency is coupled with an interest.

The Multiple Listing Service (MLS) is an organization formed to share listing information between members. Members pool all exclusive right to sell listings and agency listings by reporting them to the MLS. These listings are entered into a computer and made available to participating members. Very often, the sale will be made by a different agency than the brokerage that has the listing. The listing broker, however, handles all offers and negotiations. The listing broker agrees to pay a portion of the commission to the selling broker, who procures the buyer. The selling broker is referred to as a cooperating broker and almost always represents the buyer.

CHECKING YOUR COMPREHENSION

1. List the statutory requirements for a real estate employment agreement.

2. Describe the advantages and disadvantages of the following listing contracts:
   * Exclusive right to sell listing
   * Exclusive agency listing
   * Open listing
   * Net listing

3. Define the term *procuring cause*.

4. List some of the different reasons for termination of a listing contract and describe the risks to the party terminating the agreement.

5. Explain the purpose of a Multiple Listing Service and define a *cooperating broker*.

REVIEWING YOUR UNDERSTANDING

1. Termination of a listing may occur in all of the following situations, **EXCEPT**:
   a. broker abandonment
   b. legal revocation by seller
   c. death by either party
   d. bankruptcy by the buyer

2. An authorization to sell is a mutual agreement between the broker and the principal and it is considered to be:
   a. a contract for sale
   b. a contract for personal and professional services
   c. a contract for purchase
   d. an exclusive listing

3. A listing that requires the seller to pay the listing broker a commission if the property is sold is called a(n):
   a. exclusive agency listing
   b. open listing
   c. exclusive right to sell
   d. net listing

4. An exclusive right to sell agency could **NOT** be terminated prior to the expiration date when the:
   a. agency is coupled with an interest
   b. owner unilaterally declares the agency ended
   c. principal dies
   d. agent becomes incapacitated

5. A commission is earned by a broker when the:
   a. escrow is paid
   b. funds are disbursed at settlement
   c. broker finds a ready, willing, and able buyer
   d. seller is paid

6. An owner sold his home without the services of the broker prior to the expiration of an exclusive agency listing. The broker is entitled to:
   a. the full commission
   b. half of the commission
   c. costs
   d. nothing

7. Upon the death of a broker, his daughter, who is also a broker, wishes to take over his clients. She **MUST**:
   a. inform all of the owners that she is the successor in interest to her father
   b. obtain approval from the probate court
   c. inform the state that she has taken over the responsibility for the listings
   d. renegotiate all of the listings

8. An owner gave an exclusive right to sell listing to broker A, an exclusive agency listing to broker B, and an open listing to broker C. Broker C sold the house and collected a commission while the other listings were still in effect. Which of the following statements is correct?
   a. A and B are entitled to a split of the commission from C.
   b. A and B are entitled to a second commission to be split between them.
   c. A and B are each entitled to a full commission.
   d. Only A is entitled to a full commission.

9. A broker and an owner discussed several types of listing agreements and decided upon an exclusive right to sell. The broker drafted the listing, but the owner did not sign it. The broker subsequently produced a willing buyer and demanded the commission from the owner based upon the exclusive right to sell. The commission is:
   a. not due because the agreement was not signed by the owner
   b. not due because the unsigned agreement amounts to a net listing
   c. due because there is an implied contract between the broker and owner
   d. due because an oral agreement is all that is required for an exclusive right to sell to be enforceable

10. To collect a commission under an exclusive right to sell listing, it is **NOT** necessary for a broker to prove:
    a. The listing was signed by the seller.
    b. The broker was the procuring cause.
    c. The listing was valid.
    d. The broker was licensed at the time.

11. If a commission amount or percentage is **NOT** stated in the listing agreement, which statement is true?
    a. The legal rate of interest would apply.
    b. The normal rate of commission would apply.
    c. The broker would not be entitled to a commission.
    d. The Real Estate Commission would determine the rate to be applied.

12. A Multiple Listing Service deals with:
    a. mostly open listings
    b. only exclusive right to sell listings
    c. member brokers who share information
    d. owners who do not use brokers to sell

13. A broker with an open listing can help protect her commission by:

    a. notifying the other brokers in the area of her prospect's name

    b. notifying the owner in writing that she is negotiating with a particular prospect

    c. notifying the prospect that any purchase must be made through her

    d. registering her prospect with the local real estate board

14. When an open listing is given to six brokers, they:

    a. will share the commission equally in the event of sale

    b. are entitled to expenses if another broker sells

    c. each have the opportunity to earn the entire commission

    d. each have a recordable property interest

15. In the event that two brokers claim a commission under an open listing, the commission should go to:

    a. the broker who listed the property

    b. the broker who advertised the property

    c. the broker who was the procuring cause of the sale

    d. the broker who obtained the first offer

16. Which of the following statements is **FALSE?**

    a. The listing must show a definite expiration date.

    b. An exclusive agency permits the seller to sell without liability to pay a commission to the broker.

    c. In an open listing the broker or salesperson who is the procuring cause receives the commission.

    d. A net listing is illegal in Nevada.

17. Nevada law requires which of the following to appear on the face of an exclusive listing contract?

    a. expiration date

    b. street address

    c. annual taxes

    d. mortgage balance

18. A valid exclusive right to sell listing contract:

    a. requires the seller to sell the property as per the terms of the listing contract

    b. requires the seller to pay the broker a commission if the broker performs in accordance with the terms of the listing contract

    c. allows the seller to sell the property without paying a commission

    d. is the same as an open listing

19. Avery Brown listed his property for sale with broker Steve Bennett, stipulating that he, the seller, wanted to receive $39,000 from a sale after all expenses or charges were deducted. Broker Bennett can sell the property for any amount over the $39,000 and keep the difference. This type of listing is:

    a. discouraged

    b. called an open listing

    c. illegal in all states

    d. illegal in Nevada

20. A broker would be **LEAST** likely to advertise a(n):

    a. exclusive agency listing

    b. exclusive right to sell listing

    c. open listing

    d. listing for a rental with a purchase option

Chapter

15

IMPORTANT TERMS AND CONCEPTS

acre-foot

asbesto

brownfield

clandestine drug laboratories

Comprehensive Environmental Response, Compensation, and Liability Act of 1980 (CERCLA)

electromagnetic field (EMF)

exempt domestic well

groundwater

innocent-purchaser defense

joint and several liability

lead-based paint

lead-based paint disclosure

mold

Phase One Environmental Analysis

potable water

property assessment

radon

releases

retroactive liability

strict liability

Superfund

Superfund Amendments and Reauthorization Act of 1986 (SARA)

surface water

underground storage tank (UST)

unending liability

urea-formaldehyde foam insulation

water table

wetlands

CHAPTER OBJECTIVES

After completing this chapter, you should be able to:

- Describe environmental hazards and preliminary site analysis.
- Summarize the federal environmental laws, the liability standards, and the potential liability and cleanup costs for real estate owners.
- List the major hazardous substances, their dangers, and a real estate agent's responsibilities.
- Summarize the Nevada water laws and regulations.

Environmental Issues and Nevada Water Law

15.1 ENVIRONMENTAL HAZARDS

Real estate transactions are being subjected to increasing scrutiny regarding the presence of hazardous substances and their potential liabilities and cleanup costs. Failure to provide this scrutiny has left many investors, and even lenders, with the cost of addressing conditions of which they were totally unaware and did not cause.

Sites that have a high potential for hazardous materials problems include industrial and manufacturing properties, landfills, railroad yards, oil field and refinery areas, gas stations, dry-cleaning facilities, vehicle maintenance shops, and agricultural land.

Almost any type of property could be contaminated and should undergo at least a preliminary review. A certified or licensed specialist should conduct any type of study that is required beyond a preliminary site analysis.

Types of Hazards

The following categories of hazards can threaten human health and/or the environment:

- Toxics
- Carcinogens
- Radioactivity
- Explosives
- Flammables
- Corrosives
- Ignitables
- Asphyxiates

Property Assessment

A site analysis includes an examination of the site and surrounding properties for indications of the following:

- Solid waste disposal (barreled, loose, buried, dispersed)
- Soil contamination (mixed, absorbed, chemically bound)
- Air pollution (particulate, gas)
- Water pollution (floating, dissolved, suspended, sinking)

In general, looking at on-site and surrounding properties is more important than looking inside buildings. However, abandoned buildings always need to be thoroughly evaluated. A sample list of relevant questions to ask when completing a site analysis follows:

1. Is the subject property an industrial property or is it a property located on land zoned for industrial use?

2. Is the subject property located within close proximity of an industrial area?

3. Is there any indication that the subject property includes an existing or former gas station site, or is the subject property within close proximity of an existing or former gas station site?

4. Does the subject property include an automotive repair facility or a dry-cleaning establishment where the work is done on the premises?

5. Is the subject property immediately adjacent to a railroad track or underground pipeline?

6. Is there any indication that the subject property ever served as a refuse or waste disposal site, or is the subject property within close proximity of a waste disposal site?

7. Is there any indication that the subject property or surrounding properties could have had in the past (or do have in the present) uses that included the storage or usage of hazardous or toxic substances?

8. Is there any indication that the subject property could contain asbestos material that is friable?

9. From your observations, are there any known hazardous conditions that exist on or immediately around the subject property?

10. To your knowledge, is the subject property within close proximity of a state or federal Superfund site?

11. To your knowledge, is the subject property within close proximity of an oil or gas production facility?

15.2 ENVIRONMENTAL LAW

The **Comprehensive Environmental Response, Compensation, and Liability Act of 1980 (CERCLA)**, also known as **Superfund**, was created to provide the authority and a source of funding for cleaning up hazardous materials released into the environment. The **Superfund Amendments and Reauthorization Act of 1986 (SARA)** contains provisions defining who is liable to pay for the cleanup of contamination caused by past activities.

In some cases, the cost of cleaning up a hazardous waste site can far exceed the value of the property, which results in abandoned, idled, or underused industrial and commercial facilities. The expansion or redevelopment of the facilities is complicated by real or perceived environmental contamination; these facilities are referred to as *brownfields*.

Buyers, sellers, and lenders need to be aware of liability provisions outlined under CERCLA/SARA and must take appropriate steps to satisfy the elements of the innocent-purchaser defense or, when contamination is found, to obtain data for negotiating the costs associated with cleanup within the terms of the transaction.

A professional real estate transaction assessment can provide the information needed to satisfy these requirements at a fraction of the cost of the potential liability.

Liability and Innocent-Purchaser Defense

Potential purchasers need to understand the risk for cleanup liability and to review each property for the presence of hazardous substances and other possible hazards.

Liability

CERCLA defines four categories of persons who are financially responsible for hazardous waste cleanup:

1. Present owners and operators
2. Past owners and operators
3. Transporters of hazardous substances
4. Generators of hazardous substances

Current property owners and operators who did not cause contamination may still be financially liable for contamination associated with their land. This concept may extend to financial institutions that manage properties in trust or that receive properties as a result of foreclosure. It applies to property managers, operators, and lessees, as well as owners and lessors.

Standards of Liability

Four liability standards apply to federal and state laws:

1. **Strict liability**—The laws apply regardless of whether intent to pollute or knowledge of the situation was present.
2. **Joint and several liability**—Each party involved with the property can be made responsible for the total cleanup costs or damages, even when other parties are known to have contributed to the problem.
3. **Retroactive liability**—A property owner can be responsible for actions that occurred many years earlier than the passage of the law, regardless of whether the prior actions were the standard practice of the time or had received approval.
4. **Unending liability**—Liability for a problem on a site does not end with the transfer of property but extends as long as the problem exists.

Residential Liability Policy

Residential homeowners are not liable for cleanup at state and federal Superfund sites according to current policies. However, homeowners can be held liable for cleanup when their own actions have led to a release of hazardous substances or the property is used for non-residential purposes. This policy is designed to reduce concerns about cleanup liability for homeowners, as well as parties involved in real estate transactions, such as lenders.

Innocent-Purchaser Defense

SARA amended CERCLA and created an "innocent purchaser" defense to owner responsibility. To claim innocence, the landowner must demonstrate that at the time of property acquisition there was "no reason to know" that the property was contaminated and that "all good commercial or customary practice" was undertaken to detect the potential for property contamination. In most cases, a **Phase One Environmental Analysis** will serve as an adequate defense. This review should be performed by competent professionals who have expertise in evaluating the presence of hazardous substances and other hazards, and who are familiar with the liability implications. It typically involves property surveys, interviews with owners and local government, and reviews of historical records to determine the potential for contamination on the property. Some states have similar or expanded provisions.

Brownfields Cleanup and Redevelopment

Since its inception in 1995, the Environmental Protection Agency's Brownfields Program has grown into a proven, results-oriented program that has changed the way contaminated property is perceived, addressed, and managed. The program is designed to empower states, communities, and other economic development interests to work together in a timely manner to prevent, assess, safely clean up, and sustainably reuse brownfields. As previously described, a **brownfield** is a property, the expansion, redevelopment, or reuse of which may be complicated by the presence or potential presence of a hazardous substance, pollutant, or contaminant. It is estimated that there are more than 450,000 brownfields in the United States. Cleaning up and reinvesting in these properties increases local tax bases, facilitates job growth, utilizes existing infrastructure, takes development pressures off of undeveloped open land, and both improves and protects the environment.

When compared with other real estate development projects, several challenges make brownfields cleanup and redevelopment unique. These challenges include:

- Environmental liability concerns
- Financial barriers
- Cleanup considerations
- Reuse planning

In spite of these challenges, significant opportunities exist for successful brownfields redevelopment. A redevelopment idea that works to bring new life to an area, enhanced by public support for the project, can create the momentum necessary to overcome the challenges associated with brownfields transactions (www.epa.gov/brownfields).

Other Federal and State Legislation

Other federal and state environmental laws also place a significant liability burden on property that is found to have hazardous substances.

These laws and regulations focus on releases of hazardous substances to the environment or people's exposure to these substances. **Releases** are defined broadly and include unintentional as well as intentional acts, and small, chronic releases as well as sudden, major releases.

Common law is also a source of potential liability for problems found on property that has been transferred. Common-law provisions focus on the concepts of nuisance, negligence, nondisclosure, and misrepresentation.

Federal Laws

In addition to CERCLA/SARA, some other federal laws that can affect property are as follows:

- *Resource Conservation and Recovery Act (RCRA) including the Hazardous and Solid Waste Amendments of 1984*—Subtitle C of the Act provides for management of the generation, transport, and disposal of hazardous wastes. The 1984 amendments concern the regulation of underground storage tanks to stop the tanks from leaking, contaminating the soil, or polluting the groundwater. Currently, all underground storage tanks must be equipped with an EPA leak-detector system.

- *Federal Water Pollution Control Act (Clean Water Act)*—This act covers a wide range of issues related to water pollution control, including effluent limits, a priority pollutant list, drinking water standards, and the National Pollutant Discharge Elimination System (NPDES) permitting process. One section of the act regulates the discharge of dredged or fill material into navigable waters of the United States. The Army Corps of Engineers and the Environmental Protection Agency, organizations that are responsible for administering the act, also consider wetlands protected waters. The EPA has defined **wetlands** as "those areas that are inundated or saturated by surface water or groundwater at a frequency and duration sufficient to support, and that under normal circumstances do support, a prevalence of vegetation typically adapted for life in saturated soil conditions." The definition, as interpreted by the EPA, can apply to the filling or altering of Nevada's dry, desert washes or doing site work on lowland vegetated areas and altering artificial lakes and streams.

- *Clean Air Act*—This act addresses a wide range of issues related to air pollution control, including pollutant emissions limitations, air quality criteria and control techniques, and more. The Prevention of Significant Deterioration (PSD) program requires an assessment of air pollution impacts on soil and vegetation. Under National Emissions Standards for Hazardous Air Pollutants (NESHAP), buildings containing asbestos cannot be renovated or demolished unless the asbestos-containing material is removed.

- *Safe Drinking Water Act*—This act provides for regulation of public drinking water systems, establishment of national drinking water regulations, and control of underground injection of waste materials.

- *Toxic Substance Control Act (TSCA)*—TSCA provides for the regulation of the development, testing, manufacture, transportation, and use of toxic chemical substances and mixtures.
- *Federal Insecticide, Fungicide, and Rodenticide Act (FIFRA)*—FIFRA provides for regulation of the use and disposal of pesticides.
- *Asbestos Hazard Emergency Response Act (AHERA)*—AHERA provides for the inspection of schools for asbestos-containing materials and their removal, if found.

15.3 HAZARDOUS SUBSTANCES

Hazardous substances that pollute the air, soil, and water all affect the market value of a real estate site. The known presence of any hazardous substance on a real estate site must be disclosed to a potential buyer. Licensees should be familiar with the following hazardous substances.

Asbestos

Asbestos is a mineral fiber found in rocks. There are several kinds of asbestos fibers, which are all fire resistant and extremely durable. These qualities made asbestos very useful in construction and industry. Asbestos was commonly used until 1980. Since then, the use of asbestos has declined significantly.

Dangers of Asbestos

The inhalation of asbestos fibers can cause various types of cancer, including asbestosis, a serious degenerative lung disease. The breathing of asbestos fibers, which most often escape into the air when surfaces coated with friable asbestos begin to deteriorate, causes the danger posed by asbestos. Asbestos is called *friable* if it crumbles easily when subjected to pressure.

Although the dangers associated with the use of asbestos were known for quite some time, asbestos's superior fire resistance and insulating abilities dictated its use for a long time. Between 1900 and 1980, approximately 30 million tons of asbestos were used in the United States, mostly to cover hot water pipes, ducts, and boilers, and in vinyl floor tiles, siding, and roofing shingles. Up until the late 1970s, asbestos was used extensively as a spray-on insulation material for buildings. By some estimates, 95% of houses that are more than 50 years old and heated with steam or hot water contain asbestos in some form.

Three Types of Asbestos

Three common types of materials can contain friable asbestos, which may signal the need for further investigation.

- The first type is either a fluffy, sprayed-on material used for fireproofing ceilings or walls (it often looks like cotton candy) or a sprayed or troweled-on material resembling a granular, cement-like plaster, usually used for fireproofing and soundproofing on walls and ceilings.

- The second type consists of non-friable asbestos wallboard that presents little threat, unless it is broken and has sprayed or troweled-on friable insulation material behind it.
- The third type of material is asbestos-based pipe or boiler insulation, and it may appear as felt-like, cement-like, or it may resemble a fibrous wrapping paper.

Due to federal legislation that required asbestos inspections to occur in every school in the nation, most local county health officials are knowledgeable regarding asbestos identification. Furthermore, every Environmental Protection Agency (EPA) regional office has a Regional Asbestos Coordinator, who can provide names of local laboratories and contractors to assist in testing for and removing asbestos.

Agent's Responsibility

Potentially significant health threats can be posed by the presence of friable asbestos in buildings and homes. A real estate licensee does not normally possess the knowledge needed to determine the presence of asbestos and whether it represents a health hazard. If licensees have reason to suspect that asbestos may be present, they should exercise due diligence to insure that the material is not disturbed (scraped, sanded, drilled through, and so on), disclose their suspicion to all parties to the transaction, and recommend in writing that an inspection be made.

Radon

Radon is a radioactive gas produced when certain natural radioactive minerals break down or decay. These natural minerals are always present in the environment in slight amounts and are found in increased quantities in particular geologic deposits. Radon gas further decays into smaller particles, which can attach to soil or dust particles in the air. As these particles are inhaled, the smaller particles can be deposited on the lining of the lungs and emit radioactive particles. This radioactive decay damages lung tissues and may cause cancer.

Radon gas can enter a structure by way of slab cracks and leaks and through porous building materials. The highest radon readings are usually found in the lowest levels of a structure and decrease significantly on the first and second floors.

Indoor radon concentrations depend on many factors: the concentration of radon in the underlying soil, the ease with which the radon can move through the soil, and several aspects of the house construction. Testing for the maximum radon reading is done in the lowest level of the building. Various sampling techniques are available through specialized contractors.

A real estate licensee does not possess the technical expertise necessary to predict which homes will have elevated radon levels. Local, state, and federal environmental and health officials, as well as private environmental consultants, can often provide such information.

Lead-Based Paint

The federal government has considerably strengthened its regulation of lead products. Recognizing that lead can be extremely toxic, impair physical and mental development of young children, and can lead to increases in high blood pressure in adults, the Environmental Protection Agency, Department of Housing and Urban Development, and Consumer Product Safety Commission have moved to restrict people's exposure to lead.

Lead Poisoning

The presence of old **lead-based paint** in houses represents the most significant concern for lead poisoning, particularly for young children. The principal means of exposure is through ingestion of peeled and flaking pieces of paint, which is a significant problem in lower-income areas where housing may be older and poorly maintained. At times, even perfectly intact lead-based paint can be the source of lead poisoning. For example, if a stairway banister is painted with intact (non-flaking) lead-based paint, and a young child begins to chew the wood on the banister, the child will ingest lead.

It is estimated that a total of 30 to 40 million older homes around the country contain lead-based paint. Many cities have passed ordinances requiring a seller's certification that no hazards exist or the actual removal of all lead-based paint from any residence or building before the sale of the building. Testing for the presence of lead-based paint can done in two ways—through laboratory analysis of paint chips or by portable x-ray fluorescence analyzers.

Sellers and lessors of most residential properties built before 1978 are required to disclose the presence of known lead-based paint hazards. Figure 15.1 is a sample copy of the Lead-Based Paint Disclosure Form.

Urea-Formaldehyde Foam Insulation (UFFI)

Urea-formaldehyde foam insulation (UFFI) is a thermal insulation material that is pumped into the spaces between the walls of a building, where it hardens to form a solid layer of insulation. Its shaving cream–like quality enables UFFI to fill hard-to-reach places. UFFI has been installed in an estimated half million homes in the United States.

Controversial Ban

In 1982, the Consumer Product Safety Commission (CPSC) banned the future sale and installation of UFFI, having determined that it presented a health hazard due to the formaldehyde gas released from the UFFI product in building interiors. The health problems range from sinus irritations to cancer. The CPSC was not able to identify a level of formaldehyde exposure at which the general population could be assured of no adverse effects.

The CPSC ban was subsequently challenged through litigation, with the court finding that the CPSC did not have sufficient evidence to issue a ban. The court, however, specifically declined to hold that UFFI was a harmless substance.

FIGURE 15.1   Lead-Based Paint Disclosure Form

DISCLOSURE OF INFORMATION ON LEAD-BASED PAINT AND LEAD-BASED PAINT HAZARDS (RENTALS)

Property Address: _____

Lead Warning Statement: Housing built before 1978 may contain lead-based paint. Lead from paint, paint chips, and dust can pose health hazards if not taken care of properly. Lead exposure is especially harmful to young children and pregnant women. Lead poisoning in young children may produce permanent neurological damage, including learning disabilities, reduced intelligence quotient, behavioral problems, and impaired memory. Before renting pre-1978 housing, landlords must disclose the presence of known lead-based paint and lead-based paint hazards in the dwelling. Tenants must also receive a federally-approved pamphlet on lead poisoning prevention.

LANDLORD'S DISCLOSURE (Landlord must complete and initial sections A, B and C below)

A.   Lead-based paint and/or lead-based paint hazards (check A.1 or A.2 below):

A.1   ☐ Landlord is aware that lead-based paint and/or lead-based paint hazards are present in the residence(s) and/or building(s) included in this rental. (Explain)_____

A.2   ☐ Landlord has no knowledge of any lead-based paint and/or lead-based paint hazards in the residence(s) and building(s) included in this rental.

SAMPLE   SAMPLE Landlord's initials required

B.   Records and reports available to the landlord (check B.1 and B.2 below):

B.1   ☐ Landlord has provided the tenant with all available records and reports relating to lead-based paint and/or lead-based paint hazards in the residence(s) and building(s) included in this rental. (List documents).

B.2   ☐ Landlord has no records or reports relating to lead-based paint and/or lead-based paint hazards in the residence(s) and building(s) included in this rental.

SAMPLE   SAMPLE Landlord's initials required

C.   Landlord acknowledges his obligation to disclose to any real estate agent(s) to whom the landlord directly or indirectly is to pay compensation with regard to the transaction contemplated by this disclosure any known lead-based paint or lead-based paint hazards in the premises to be rented, as well as the existence of any reports or records relating to lead-based paint or lead-based paint hazards in the premises to be rented. Landlord further acknowledges that this disclosure accurately reflects the entirety of the information provided by the landlord to the agent(s) with regard to lead-based paint, lead-based paint hazards, and lead-based paint risk-assessment or inspection reports and records.

SAMPLE   SAMPLE Landlord's initials required

TENANT'S ACKNOWLEDGMENT (Tenant must complete and initial sections D and E below):

SAMPLE   D.   Tenant has read the information set forth above, and has received copies of the reports, records, or other materials referenced above, if any.

SAMPLE   E.   Tenant has received the pamphlet *Protect Your Family from Lead in Your Home.*

AGENT'S ACKNOWLEDGMENT (Any real estate agent who is to receive compensation from the landlord or the property manager with regard to the transaction contemplated in this disclosure must initial section F below.)

F.   The agent(s) whose initials appear below has (have) ensured the landlord's compliance under the Residential Lead-Based Paint Hazard 1992 by the landlord's use and completion of this disclosure form.

Agent's initials required: **SAMPLE**   **SAMPLE**
                                            Property Manager/Listing Agent   Leasing Agent

CERTIFICATION OF ACCURACY
By signing below, each signatory acknowledges that he or she has reviewed the above information, and certifies that, to the best of his or her knowledge, the information provided by the signatory is true and accurate.

Landlord: ____**SAMPLE**____   Tenant:____**SAMPLE**____
                                    Date   Date

Landlord: ____**SAMPLE**____   Tenant: ____**SAMPLE**____
                                    Date   Date

Property Manager/Listing Agent: ____**SAMPLE**____   Leasing Agent: ____**SAMPLE**____
                                                          Date   Date

FIGURE 15.1 Continued.

Lead-Based Paint Disclosure Tips for Rentals of Residential Properties

Steps for REALTORS® to follow:

NOTE: The lead-based paint disclosure requirements apply to all real estate agents involved in the transaction except for tenant's agents receiving compensation from the tenant only. The following recommended steps are provided to help REALTORS® meet the law's obligations in a typical residential rental transaction.

1. When entering into an agreement to manage a property, the property manager/listing agent (hereinafter "property manager") should determine if the property is "target housing " (generally, built before January 1,1978). This can generally be accomplished by asking the landlord/owner ("the owner"). If the owner doesn't know, the property manager should consult property records.

   The property manager should also determine if the property falls within an exemption from the lead-based paint disclosure requirements. For example, if a certified inspector has determined that the property is free from lead-based paint and lead-based paint hazards, or if the lease is for less than 100 days with no opportunity for renewal or extension, the disclosure requirements will not apply. Even if an exemption applies, the property manager should have the owner complete and sign the disclosure form, acknowledging in writing the claimed basis for the exemption. If an exemption applies, the disclosure form need not be given to potential tenants.

2. The lead-based paint disclosure requirements became effective for all "target housing" on December 6, 1996. All target housing will require the following steps.

3. If the property is target housing, the property manager must advise the owner of certain obligations, namely the following: 1) disclose to the tenant known lead-based paint or lead-based paint hazards; 2) provide the tenant any existing records, test results, reports, or other known lead-based paint information related to the presence of lead-based paint or lead-based paint hazards in the property, if any; 3) provide the tenant with the pamphlet *Protect Your Family From Lead in Your Home* (EPA approved lead-based paint hazard information pamphlet); and 4) include disclosure and acknowledgment language as part of the rental contract or addenda. (NOTE: The law does not require that all interested tenants must be informed, only the actual tenant).

4. The property manager should have the owner complete, initial and sign the disclosure form. The property manager should obtain from the landlord any records, test results, reports, or other lead-based paint information related to the presence of lead-based paint or lead-based paint hazards in order to be ready to provide copies to a tenant making an offer to rent the property. The property manager should then initial and sign the form.

5. The property manager should disclose to potential leasing agents that the listed property is target housing, probably through the MLS or other offerings to REALTORS®.

6. The leasing agent (the agent working with the tenant who expects to be paid by the property manager or the owner - whether it be tenant's agent, subagent, "facilitator," or whatever) also has an obligation to ensure the owner's compliance. If the disclosure form has not been provided by the property manager, the leasing agent should provide the disclosure form to the property manager for the owner to complete and sign, or directly to the owner if no property manager is involved.

7. When the tenant is ready to make an offer on target housing, the leasing agent should provide the tenant with a copy of the disclosure form signed by the owner and the property manager, together with related test results and records, if any, and a copy of *Protect Your Family From Lead in Your Home*. Ideally, these documents will be obtained by the leasing agent from the property manager before the offer is signed by the tenant, but the signed disclosure form with attachments must be provided to the tenant before the offer to rent is accepted by the owner.

8. The disclosure form must be initialed and signed by the tenant and the leasing agent, which should be done after the owner and the property manager have initialed and signed the form. (By initialing section F of the AAR Disclosure of Information on Lead-Based Paint and Lead-Based Paint Hazards (Rentals) form, signing the Certification, and complying with the other terms of this AAR form, both the property manager and leasing agent will have met their obligations under the law.)

The CPSC ban on UFFI's installation was lifted, although public opinion resulting from this controversy dramatically reduced UFFI's popularity as insulation.

Although a real estate licensee does not possess the technical expertise needed to determine the presence of UFFI and its health risks, local, state, or federal environmental and health officials can often provide information. Additionally, expensive options do exist for those clients who believe further action is warranted. These options include testing indoor air for the presence of formaldehyde and actual removal of UFFI from walls.

Underground Storage Tanks

Underground storage tank (UST) registration is required for all tanks containing regulated substances (all petroleum products) that are not already listed as hazardous "wastes." Look for existing records or registrations with the state UST section. Some guidelines follow:

- Any tank having held a regulated substance needs a site assessment and proper closure. Any materials held in the tank also need to be properly disposed.

- Any tanks brought into current use or already being used will be regulated. This involves the owner's certification of one million dollars in financial responsibility and/or insurance coverage. Owners and operators have to keep responsible records. All tanks must have leak-protection systems of varying degrees of protection, and records must be kept of the operation of that system.

Mold

Mold has been around forever, and it is a rare home that does not have some mold. However, a certain kind of black mold (*stachybotrys*) has been identified as a major contributor to illness. However, not all black mold is toxic, and the presence of stachybotrys can be determined only by a laboratory test. Mold growth can also affect the structural integrity of a building because the surface on which the mold is living serves as its food source. Mold growth requires water and is found underneath materials where water has damaged surfaces or behind walls. By the time mold becomes visible, it has often caused major damage in the wall interior.

Molds can be found in all areas of the nation and they thrive in Nevada in spite of its dry climate. Mold can grow anywhere there is water, including water from leaking pipes, leaking roofs, or humidity.

In recent years there have been numerous awards and settlements related to mold lawsuit claims. Insurance companies have paid millions of dollars to resolve the legal claims. As a result, homebuyers can have difficulty purchasing insurance coverage for a house that has a record of water damage.

Electromagnetic Fields

The movement of electrical current creates an **electromagnetic field** (EMF). This includes the use of small appliances such as televisions, computers, or even hair dryers. However, high-voltage power lines, ordinary distribution lines, and transformers have been suspected of causing cancer and other illnesses. On the other hand, there is some evidence that electromagnetic fields, sometimes referred to as EMFs, do not cause any health hazards. A homebuyer might consider an EMF in the vicinity of a house to be a material defect. Therefore, until there is more evidence regarding the potential health risks of a nearby power line, a licensee must ensure disclosure about a nearby EMF to a potential buyer.

Clandestine Drug Laboratories

Clandestine drug laboratories, often referred to as *meth labs*, utilize chemicals and equipment in the manufacture of illegal substances, such as methamphetamine, ecstasy, or LSD. Meth labs can cause substantial damage to an owner's real property and they are very hazardous and potentially explosive environments. A clandestine drug laboratory becomes an emergency immediately upon discovery. Strong odors and suspicious behavior are often indicators of a laboratory operation.

The fact that the property is or has been the site of a crime that involves the manufacturing of any material, compound, mixture, or preparation which contains any quantity of methamphetamine is not considered a material fact for a real estate transaction if either of the following is the case:

a. All materials and substances involving methamphetamine have been removed from or remediated on the property by an entity certified or licensed to do so

b. The property has been deemed safe for habitation by a governmental entity

15.4 NEVADA WATER[1]

The Nevada Division of Water Resources is responsible for administering and enforcing Nevada water law, which includes the adjudication and appropriation of groundwater and surface water in the state. The appointed administrative head of this division is the State Engineer, whose office was created by the Nevada Legislature in 1903. The purpose of the 1903 legislation was to account for all of the existing water use according to priority. The 1903 act was amended in 1905 to set out a method for appropriation of water not already being put to a beneficial use.

It was not until the passage of the Nevada General Water Law Act of 1913 that the Nevada Division of Water Resources was granted jurisdiction over all wells tapping artesian water or water in definable underground aquifers. The 1939 Nevada Underground Water Act granted the Nevada Division of Water Resources total jurisdiction over all groundwater in the state.

The 1913 and 1939 acts have been amended a number of times, and Nevada's water law is considered one of the most comprehensive water laws in the West. The previously mentioned acts provide that all water within the boundaries of the state, whether above or beneath the surface of the ground, belongs to the public, as referenced in NRS 533.025 and is subject to appropriation for beneficial use under the laws of the state (NRS 533.030 and NRS 534.020).

Water Permit Application Process

To acquire a water permit, an application must be made on an approved form and filed with the State Engineer (NRS 533.325). Pursuant to Nevada water law, the application must be supported by a map prepared in a prescribed form by a water rights surveyor. The supporting map must show the point of diversion and place of use of the water within the proper legal subdivisions. No application shall be for the water of more than one source to be used for more than one purpose (NRS 533.330).

When the application and map are properly completed, a notice must be sent to a newspaper of general circulation in the area where the application was filed. This notice is published for approximately 30 days (NRS 533.360). Interested parties may file a formal protest up until 30 days after the last day of publication, explaining their objections to the application and requesting denial of the application or other appropriate action by the State Engineer (NRS 533.365).

After the expiration of the protest period, the application is ready for action by the State Engineer. When considering an application for approval or denial, the State Engineer must consider the following:

- Is there unappropriated water at the source?
- Will the use of the water under the proposed application conflict with existing rights?
- Will the use of the water under the proposed application prove detrimental to the public interest?
- Will the use of the water under the proposed application adversely impact domestic wells?

In addition to these items, other criteria within NRS 533.370 deal with impacts within irrigation districts, the good faith intent of the applicant to construct the works of diversion and put the water to beneficial use, and the financial ability and reasonable expectation to construct the works of diversion and put the water to beneficial use.

The State Engineer may require any additional information needed prior to approval or rejection of an application (NRS 533.375). The State Engineer also has the discretion to hold a hearing prior to any decision.

The State Engineer reviews any pertinent information and either approves or denies the application. When an application is denied, the State Engineer notifies the applicant of denial, retains the denied application for the record and will not pursue any further action under the application. The denial may be appealed in the appropriate court of jurisdiction within 30 days after the denial action (NRS 533.450). When a water permit is approved, the permit terms and limitations are specified as part of the permit. A fee is also required for any permit issued in accordance with NRS 533.435. Once a permit is issued, the applicant may initiate the work to divert and use the water established as the beneficial use.

Once granted, water rights in Nevada have the standing of both real and personal property, that is, they are conveyed as an appurtenance to real property unless they are specifically excluded in the deed of conveyance. When water rights are purchased or sold as personal property or treated as a separate appurtenance in a real-estate transaction, the water rights are conveyed specifically by a deed of conveyance. It is possible to buy or sell water rights and change the water's point of diversion, manner of use, and place of use by filing the appropriate application with the State Engineer.

Interbasin Transfers

Due to the state's arid climate and limited water resources, transferring water from one basin to another is not new to Nevada. In fact, the first interbasin transfer occurred in 1873, when water from the Hobart Reservoir in the Washoe Valley Hydrographic Basin was conveyed to Virginia City, which is within the Dayton Valley Hydrographic Basin. Many interbasin transfers have been completed since then in nearly every region of the state.

The following table, adapted from the 1999 Nevada State Water Plan, shows interbasin water transfers throughout the state since 1873.

Groundwater Transfers

Basin of Origin	Receiving Basin	Type of Use
Washoe Valley	Eagle Valley	Carson City municipal supply
Goshute Valley	Great Salt Lake Desert	Wendover municipal supply
Pilot Creek Valley	Great Salt Lake Desert	Wendover municipal supply
Long Valley	Cold Springs Valley	Municipal supply
Ralston Valley	Big Smokey Valley	Tonopah municipal supply
Carson Valley	Eagle Valley	Carson City municipal supply
Dayton Valley	Eagle Valley	Carson City municipal supply
L. Meadow Valley Wash	Muddy River Springs Area	Reid Gardner Power Plant
Oreana subarea	Lovelock Valley	Lovelock municipal supply

Surface Water Transfers

Source/Basin of Origin	Receiving Basin	Type of Use
Lake Tahoe Basin	Eagle Valley	Carson City municipal supply
Lake Tahoe Basin	Dayton Valley	Virginia City municipal supply
Truckee River (Tracy Segment)	Carson River (Churchill Valley via Truckee Canal)	Truckee-Carson Irrigation District for irrigation
Newark Valley (spring)	Diamond Valley	Eureka municipal supply
Lake Tahoe Basin (treated effluent)	Carson Valley	Irrigation
Truckee River (Truckee Meadows)	Lemmon Valley	Municipal supply
Carson River (Dayton Valley)	Eagle Valley	Carson City municipal supply
Colorado River (Black Mountain area)	Las Vegas Valley	Las Vegas area municipal supply
Truckee River (Truckee Meadows)	Spanish Springs Valley (via Orr Ditch)	Irrigation
Truckee River (Truckee Meadows)	Sun Valley	Municipal supply

In determining whether an application for an interbasin transfer of water should be approved or rejected, under NRS 533.370 the State Engineer must consider:

- Whether the applicant has justified the need to import the water from another basin

- Whether a conservation plan has been adopted and is being effectively carried out, if the State Engineer determines that such a plan is advisable for the basin into which water is to be imported

- Whether the proposed action is environmentally sound as it relates to the basin from which the water is exported

- Whether the proposed action is an appropriate long-term use that will not unduly limit the future growth and development in the basin from which the water is exported

- Any other factor(s) the Office of the State Engineer determines to be relevant

The applicant may also work with the county from which the water is proposed to be transferred to develop a plan to mitigate adverse economic impacts of the transfer. If a plan cannot be agreed to, the county (with the approval of the State Engineer) has the option to impose an annual fee on the water transferred. The amount of the fee is defined in NRS 533.438.

Environmental Protection

The State Engineer has the authority to require a hydrological, environmental, or any other study necessary prior to final determination of an application (NRS 533.368).

Proof of Completion

As one of the conditions of the permit's approval, the State Engineer requires that a Proof of Completion of the work be filed. This Proof of Completion usually must be filed within two years from the permit issuance. This affidavit provides information on the well construction and other information as requested by the State Engineer.

Proof of Beneficial Use

Beneficial use is the basis, the measure, and the limit of the right to the use of the water. Each water permit issued is limited to the amount that can be applied to beneficial use, not to exceed a specified diversion rate and annual duty. The Proof of Beneficial Use is usually required within five years from the approval of the permit. The Proof of Beneficial Use identifies how the property has been developed and indicates the amount of water placed to beneficial use. Once the Proof of Beneficial Use application has been filed and accepted, the water cannot be used for any additional development.

Extension of Time

The State Engineer may grant an extension of time to comply with the permit requirements such as filing the Proof of Completion or the Proof of Beneficial

Use, provided due diligence and good cause are demonstrated as to why such proofs cannot be submitted as required by the terms of the permit.

Abandonment and Forfeiture of Rights

Surface water rights are subject to abandonment as described in NRS 533.060. Groundwater rights, once granted by the State Engineer, are subject to abandonment and forfeiture as described in NRS 534.090. A water right holder who fails for five consecutive years to use all or any part of a water right for its acquired use runs the risk of forfeiting the water right to the extent of the non-use. In other words, the portion not used could be forfeited. However, a timely filed request for an extension of time may be granted by the State Engineer for good cause shown for a period not to exceed one year for any single extension.

Domestic Wells

A domestic well is one well that serves one home. Domestic wells are exempt from the water-right permitting process when the pumpage does not exceed a daily maximum of 1800 gallons (NRS 534.180) and water cannot be furnished by an entity such as a water district or municipality (NRS 534.120). The domestic well exemption is not subject to forfeiture or revocation, and a homeowner cannot be required to cease pumping as long as the domestic well is operating properly.

(1) Source: Nevada Division of Water Resources website

Other Water Definitions

An **acre-foot** is a volume of water equal to an area of one acre with a depth of one foot (43,560 cubic feet) and equal to 325,850 gallons. **Potable water** is water that can be safely and agreeably used to drink. A **water table** is the natural level at which water will be located, be it above or below the surface of the ground.

CHAPTER SUMMARY

Almost any type of property could be contaminated by an environmental hazard and should undergo a preliminary site analysis. A site analysis includes an examination of the site and surrounding properties for indications of solid waste disposal, soil contamination, air pollution, and water pollution. In general, looking at on-site and surrounding properties is more important than looking inside buildings.

The Comprehensive Environmental Response, Compensation, and Liability Act of 1980 (CERCLA), also known as Superfund, was created to provide the authority and a source of funding for cleaning up hazardous materials released into the environment. The Superfund Amendments and Reauthorization Act of 1986 (SARA) contains provisions defining who is liable to pay for the cleanup of contamination caused by past activities. In some cases, the cost of property cleanup is greater than the value of the property; such properties are called brownfields. Buyers, sellers, and lenders need to be aware of liability provisions outlined under CERCLA/SARA and must take appropriate steps to satisfy the elements of the innocent-purchaser defense or, when contamination is found, to obtain data for negotiating the costs associated with cleanup within the terms of the transaction.

CERCLA defines four categories of persons who are financially responsible for hazardous waste cleanup: present owners and operators, past owners and operators, transporters of hazardous substances, and generators of hazardous substances. In addition, the four liability standards applicable to federal and state laws are strict liability, joint and several liability, retroactive liability, and unending liability. Residential homeowners are not liable for cleanup at state and federal Superfund sites, unless their actions have led to a release of hazardous substances or the property is used for nonresidential purposes. SARA amended CERCLA and created an innocent-purchaser defense to owner responsibility. In most cases a Phase One Environmental Analysis, performed by a hazardous waste professional, will serve as an adequate innocent-purchaser defense.

Other federal laws include, but are not limited to, the Federal Water Pollution Control Act (Clean Water Act), the Clean Air Act, and the Safe Drinking Water Act.

Hazardous substances can pollute the air, soil, and water thereby affecting the market value of a real estate site. The known presence of the following seven hazardous substances on a real estate site must be disclosed to a potential buyer: asbestos, radon, lead, urea-formaldehyde foam insulation, underground storage tanks containing regulated substances, mold, and electromagnetic fields.

The two major categories of water in Nevada are surface water and groundwater. All sources of water supply belong to the public; however, all water may be appropriated for beneficial use as provided in the Nevada Revised Statutes. The Nevada Division of Water Resources is responsible for administering and enforcing Nevada water law. This includes the adjudication and appropriation of groundwater and surface water in the state.

CHECKING YOUR COMPREHENSION

1. Describe the reasons for completing an environmental property assessment.

2. Summarize who can be financially responsible for hazardous waste cleanup and the liability standards applicable to federal environmental laws.

3. List and describe the major hazardous substances.

4. Describe the following legal categories of water:
   - Surface water
   - Groundwater

5. Describe the water permit application process.

REVIEWING YOUR UNDERSTANDING

1. A colorless, odorless gas that is a hazard to health and is found in homes throughout the United States is called:
   a. asbestos
   b. radon
   c. urea formaldehyde
   d. trichloroethylene

2. Which of the following statements does **NOT** describe a Phase One Environmental Analysis?
   a. analyzes the possible presence of hazardous substances
   b. is completed by competent professionals
   c. documents an innocent-purchaser defense
   d. authorizes pollution cleanup

3. A fibrous mineral used for fireproofing, but considered to be an airborne carcinogen, is called:
   a. lead
   b. gypsum
   c. asbestos
   d. copper

4. A site analysis will look for indications of all of the following, **EXCEPT**:
   a. solid waste disposal
   b. water pollution
   c. soil contamination
   d. construction defects

5. Sellers and lessors of residential properties built before 1978 are required to disclose the:
   a. presence of known lead-based paint hazards
   b. results of a test for radon gas
   c. results of a test for asbestos
   d. results of a test for lead-based paint hazards

6. The two types of water categories are:
   a. stagnant and flowing
   b. surface and ground
   c. land and plentiful
   d. exempt and non-exempt

7. An acre-foot of water contains:
   a. 235,851 cubic feet
   b. 43,560 cubic feet
   c. 43,560 gallons
   d. 117,925 gallons

8. All of the following are true for a domestic well, **EXCEPT**:
   a. water right permit not required
   b. pumpage cannot exceed a daily maximum of 1800 gallons
   c. water cannot be furnished by a water district
   d. subject to forfeiture or revocation

9. In Nevada, both ground and surface water:
   a. are appropriated under the riparian doctrine
   b. are appropriated under the littoral doctrine
   c. belong to the public
   d. belong to the federal government

10. To acquire a water permit, an application must be made to the:
    a. Administrator of the Real Estate Division
    b. Environmental Protection Agency
    c. Nevada Division of Water Resources
    d. State Engineer

11. *Water table* is defined as:
    a. annual rainfall
    b. a statement for water usage
    c. depth of river water
    d. depth beneath the ground to usable water

12. The basis for the granting of a water permit is:
    a. beneficial use
    b. riparian doctrine
    c. littoral doctrine
    d. doctrine of prior appropriation

13. Which of the following would be considered an exempt domestic well?
    a. one with a maximum capacity of 500 gallons per day
    b. one with a maximum capacity of 1800 gallons per day
    c. any size pump capacity used for domestic use
    d. any size pump as long as you give notice of intent to drill

14. The Comprehensive Environmental Response, Compensation, and Liability Act of 1980 (CERCLA) is also known as:
    a. Superfund
    b. SARA
    c. Clean Water Act
    d. WQARF

15. A brownfield is:
    a. desert landscape
    b. farmland that is not cultivated due to climate change
    c. abandoned or underused urban area due to issues related to toxic contamination
    d. none of the above

16. All of the following are true about a clandestine drug laboratory, **EXCEPT**:
    a. location for the manufacture of illegal substances, such as methamphetamine
    b. meth labs can cause substantial damage to an owner's real property
    c. meth labs are very hazardous and potentially explosive environments
    d. disclosure that a property was the site of a crime that involved the manufacture of methamphetamine is a material fact that always must be disclosed

17. The contamination of a property from a clandestine drug laboratory is not considered a material fact if:
    a. all materials and substances involving methamphetamine have been removed or remediated
    b. the removal or remediation was completed by an entity certified or licensed to do so
    c. the property has been deemed safe for habitation by a governmental entity
    d. all of the above

18. When altering a Nevada dry desert wash, a developer needs to consider the requirements of the:
    a. CERCLA (Superfund)
    b. Toxic Substance Control Act (TSCA)
    c. Clean Water Act (Wetlands)
    d. Superfund Amendments and Reauthorization Act (SARA)

19. The standards of liability for cleanup under the Superfund legislation include all of the following, **EXCEPT**:
    a. strict liability
    b. retroactive liability
    c. criminal liability
    d. unending liability

20. Residential homeowners are not liable for cleanup at federal Superfund sites, **EXCEPT** when:
    a. the release took place five years earlier
    b. the release took place prior to the purchase by the current homeowner
    c. the release resulted from the actions of the homeowner
    d. all real property owners are liable for cleanup without exception

Chapter 16

CHAPTER OBJECTIVES

After completing this chapter, you should be able to:

- Summarize the history of fair housing in the United States, including a description of the major legislation and court cases.
- List the protected classes and the unlawful acts established by the Fair Housing Acts of 1968 and 1988.
- Summarize the exceptions to the Fair Housing Act of 1968.
- Explain the remedies for violations of the Civil Rights laws.
- Summarize the provisions of the Americans with Disabilities Act.

Fair Housing

16.1 HISTORY OF FAIR HOUSING

The beginning of housing discrimination in America can be traced back to the first colonial settlements. Prior to the Civil War, the courts refused to recognize any rights for persons of African descent, whether they were slaves or free. The federal government did nothing to prohibit discrimination, and even those states that had abolished slavery treated African Americans as inferior.

Legislation and Court Cases

In 1866, the Reconstruction Congress passed the **Civil Rights Act of 1866**, which guaranteed property rights to all citizens regardless of race. This 1866 act specifically provides that all citizens have the same rights as white citizens to inherit, purchase, and sell real and personal property. The 1866 act pertains only to discrimination based upon race.

The 1866 Civil Rights Act guarantee of equal rights to all races was, unfortunately, an empty promise. For more than a century, the courts prohibited racial discrimination only with regard to governmental discrimination. Therefore, the 1866 act was ineffective in combating private discrimination.

In 1896, the U.S. Supreme Court made its infamous ruling in *Plessy v. Ferguson*, which held that the enforcement of racial segregation of private or public facilities did not violate the U.S. Constitution as long as the separate facilities were equal. This *separate but equal* ruling permitted institutionalized segregation in the United States. The Plessy case was not overruled until 1954, almost six decades later.

Finally, in 1954, the U.S. Supreme Court rendered its landmark decision in *Brown v. Board of Education*, reversing the separate but equal decision in Plessy. The Brown case outlawed segregation in schools and marked the beginning of the end of the era of legalized segregation.

Ten years later, Congress enacted the **Civil Rights Act of 1964**, which prohibited discrimination in programs receiving federal financial assistance, but had little impact in the housing market. This act says:

> (N)o person in the United States shall, on the ground of race, color or national origin, be excluded from participation in, be denied the benefits of, or be subjected to discrimination under any program or activity receiving Federal financial assistance.

Birth of Modern Fair Housing

The real change in fair housing came in 1968, a year that is considered the birth of modern fair housing. Two historic events occurred that year that forever changed the housing market.

First, in April, Congress enacted the **Fair Housing Act of 1968** (Title VIII of the Civil Rights Act of 1968). This act bans discrimination on the basis of race, color, religion, and national origin in most types of housing transactions. In 1974, the 1968 act was amended to include the ban on discrimination on the basis of sex. The act also contains a variety of remedies to attack housing discrimination, including private discrimination.

About the same time that Congress approved the 1968 act, the Supreme Court rendered its decision in the case of *Jones v. Mayer*, in which Jones, a black man, complained that the Alfred H. Mayer Co. refused to sell him a house because he was black. The Supreme Court ruled in favor of Jones. This landmark decision resurrected the 1866 Civil Rights Act and held that the act banned governmental and private racial discrimination in housing. This case also noted that the Fair Housing Act allowed some exceptions (discussed later in this chapter). This case, however, was brought under the 1866 Civil Rights Act, which made no exceptions. The final holding of the case is that, where race is involved, no exceptions apply.

Equal Opportunities

The Fair Housing Act was amended in 1972 by a requirement that equal housing opportunity posters be displayed in brokerages, mortgage companies, and new home sites. Failure to display the **equal housing opportunities poster** may, in and of itself, be considered by HUD to be evidence of discriminatory practices.

16.2 FAIR HOUSING ACT

The Fair Housing Act was adopted by Congress in 1968 and amended in 1974 and 1988. The act, as amended, bans housing discrimination for these seven protected classes: race, color, religion, national origin, sex, handicaps, and familial status. The act also establishes unlawful acts, describes exceptions to the act, and defines important terms.

Unlawful Acts

Under the Fair Housing Acts of 1968 and 1988 it is unlawful:

1. To refuse to sell or rent housing to any person because of race, color, religion, sex, national origin, handicap, or familial status.

2. To refuse to negotiate for housing because of race, color, religion, sex, national origin, handicap, or familial status.

3. To discriminate against any person in the terms, conditions, or privileges for sale or rental of housing because of race, color, religion, sex, national origin, handicap, or familial status.

4. To print or publish any notice or advertisement concerning the sale or rental of a dwelling that indicates any preference or discrimination based on race, color, religion, sex, national origin, handicap, or familial status.

5. To falsely deny that housing is available for inspection, sale, or rental because of race, color, religion, sex, national origin, handicap, or familial status.

6. For profit, to persuade any person to sell or rent any dwelling by representation regarding the entry into the neighborhood of a person or persons of a particular race, color, religion, sex, national origin, handicap, or familial status (blockbusting).

Exceptions

The Fair Housing Act of 1968 does not apply to the sale or rental of commercial or industrial properties. The act also exempts:

- Owner-occupied buildings with no more than four units
- Single-family housing sold or rented without the use of a broker
- Housing operated by organizations and private clubs that limit occupancy to their members

The exemption for the sale or rental of single-family homes applies only when these three requirements are met:

1. The home is owned by an individual who does not own more than three such homes at one time, and who does not sell more than one such home every two years.

2. A real estate broker or salesperson is not involved in the transaction.

3. Discriminatory advertising is not used.

The rental of rooms or units is exempted from the Fair Housing Act of 1968 in an owner-occupied one-family to four-family dwelling.

Religious organizations that offer housing only to people of their religion may do so as long as membership is not restricted on the basis of race, color, or national origin.

Also, private clubs that offer room rental (when this is not their main business) may legally discriminate against non-members, provided that membership in the club does not violate the 1968 law.

Advertising material for the sale or lease of real property cannot indicate that the property is available to or not available to people of specific protected class.

Important Terms

Blockbusting is the illegal practice of inducing panic selling in a neighborhood for profit, based on the introduction of minority homeowners into a neighborhood. The Fair Housing Act of 1968 prohibits blockbusting.

Steering is the illegal practice of directing certain persons into or out of areas that are or are not integrated.

Redlining is mortgage credit discrimination based upon the density of minorities in a geographic area. The term *redlining* comes from the practice of certain lenders who used maps with integrated and minority neighborhoods outlined in red, as an indication of a poor risk area.

Fair Housing Amendments Act of 1988

In September of 1988, Congress amended the Civil Rights Act of 1968 (the federal Fair Housing Act) and added handicaps and familial status to the list of protected people.

A **handicapped person** is defined in the amendment as one who has "a physical or mental impairment which substantially limits one or more of such person's major life activities," and has a record of having such an impairment or being regarded as having such an impairment. This does not, however, include current illegal use of or addiction to a controlled substance. It does include those afflicted with AIDS or HIV.

Familial status means one or more individuals (under the age of 18) living with either:

- A parent or legal guardian
- A designee holding written permission of a parent or legal guardian for the child or children to live with him or her

This includes legal custody of a person who is pregnant or in the process of securing legal custody of a minor.

Modifications

It is against the 1988 law to refuse to permit a person with a handicap, at his or her own expense, to make minor modifications to an existing premise. The law also requires owners to make reasonable accommodations necessary to afford a person equal opportunity to use and enjoy a dwelling. If, for example, an apartment complex has a rule that no pets are allowed in the complex, it will be necessary to modify that regulation regarding Seeing Eye dogs or other assistive animals. Assistive animals are not considered pets.

Certain design changes may be necessary in the construction of new multifamily buildings available to make the property accessible for people with handicaps. A multifamily building is defined as four or more units. Therefore, the construction of a two- or three-story housing unit that has elevators must have the floors equipped for wheelchair access. The doors must be wider and light switches and thermostats must be reachable by persons in wheelchairs. Baths must have reinforced walls for grab rails and the kitchen must be large enough to allow wheelchair maneuverability. If, however, there are no elevators, only the first floor must be so equipped.

Senior Housing

Age is not a **protected class**. Instead, the act exempts housing for older persons from the familial status provision provided that the area or facility is intended for and solely occupied by persons 62 years of age or older, or at least one person in

80% of the households is 55 years or older. Also, the facilities and services must be specifically designed to meet the physical and social needs of older persons.

16.3 REMEDIES

Remedies for violations of civil rights laws vary depending on the form of complaint. Most cases, by law, are presented to the **Department of Housing and Urban Development (HUD)**. The complaint must be filed within one year of the violation. HUD has 30 days to investigate the complaint. If the violation is one of race or color, the complaint is filed with a federal district court. HUD may defer a complaint to state authorities. In Nevada, the Nevada Equal Rights Commission investigates and prosecutes fair housing complaints.

If the state has laws substantially the same as the provisions of the 1968 Fair Housing Act laws, HUD will notify the state and turn over the case to the state. If the state acts on the complaint within 30 days, HUD loses jurisdiction unless "justice demands" HUD's continued interest in the matter.

When HUD is involved in the complaint, it seeks relief through conferences, conciliation, and persuasion to satisfy the complaint. HUD will attempt to seek access or similar housing, out-of-pocket expenses, and money for wounded pride. HUD has been successful in negotiating a greater number of complaints in recent years. Also, with the 1988 amendments, HUD can file a formal charge and refer the complaint to an administrative law judge, unless either party elects a jury trial in a civil court. The administrative law judge can impose substantial penalties, ranging from $11,000 for the first offense to $27,300 for a second violation within five years, and $55,000 for further violations within seven years.

A party may elect civil action in federal court at any time within two years of the discriminatory act. For federal court cases, unlimited punitive damages can be awarded in addition to actual damages.

If the attorney general believes there is reasonable cause to suspect that a person or group has engaged in a pattern or practice of resistance to the full enjoyment of any of the rights granted by the federal fair housing laws, the attorney general can file a civil action in any federal district court. Civil penalties may result in an amount not to exceed $50,000 for a first violation and an amount not to exceed $100,000 for a second and subsequent violations.

16.4 AMERICANS WITH DISABILITIES ACT

The **Americans with Disabilities Act (ADA)** was the first comprehensive American civil rights law for people with disabilities, and it affects every employer, business, and public service, including real estate. The ADA attempts to achieve equal treatment, but it does not guarantee equality to all. The ADA differs from other laws because it is aimed at reasonable fairness to each individualized situation rather than a blanket approach to all groups of people with disabilities. For example, an employer does not have to create a job for a person with a disability. However, the employer must give consideration to a reasonable amendment to some existing job requirements for a qualified person with a disability who wants to work.

For many people, Title I, Employment, is the most significant section of the ADA, because it sets the tone and criteria for independence and equality for the disabled. However, Title III, Public Accommodations, causes significant financial concern to business entities, owners of real property, and real estate licensees.

Disability Defined

A person with a disability is defined as a person who meets one of the following three conditions:

1. Has a mental or physical *impairment* that substantially limits one or more major life activities.
2. Has a *record* of a physical or mental impairment that substantially limits one or more major life activities.
3. Is *regarded* as having a physical or mental impairment that substantially limits one or more major life activities.

Impairment

Impairment exists only if the impairment substantially limits one or more life activities. It cannot be simply a minor or temporary impairment. Therefore, the impairment must affect one or more **major life activities**, such as:

- Walking
- Speaking
- Breathing
- Seeing
- Hearing
- Learning
- Working
- Independently caring for oneself

To be covered under ADA, an impairment must substantially limit a person's life activity.

Record

A record of a physical or mental impairment that substantially limits one or more major life activities also meets the definition of disabled under the ADA. By including a record of impairment in the definition, the ADA prohibits discrimination against an individual because of a previous impairment.

An example of someone meeting the definition because of a record would be an individual with a history of cancer. Another example would be someone misdiagnosed as having a particular disability.

Regarded

When others treat an individual as having an impairment, the individual is covered by ADA. For example, an individual with high blood pressure that does not impair major life activities, but the employer treats him as if the condition impairs him, would be covered under this provision of the ADA.

Another example would be if an employer fears there would be a negative reaction if she hires an individual with a visible disfigurement. The individual with the disfigurement is covered under this provision of the ADA.

In the previous examples, the impairments themselves are not limiting, but the negative attitudes of the employers toward the individuals may substantially limit their ability to work. Work is a major life activity.

Examples of Disabilities

A list of disabilities is not set out in the ADA, but disabilities have been established by case law. Examples of disabilities include:

- Cancer
- Cerebral palsy
- Chronic AIDS
- Diabetes
- Emotional illness
- Epilepsy
- Hearing impairment
- HIV infection
- Mental retardation
- Multiple sclerosis
- Muscular dystrophy
- Orthopedic impairment
- Paralysis
- Speech impairment
- Tuberculosis
- Visual impairment

Recovering drug and alcohol users also qualify, provided they are not currently using illegal substances.

Not Considered Impairments

The following is a list of conditions or characteristics that are not considered impairments under ADA.

- Advanced age
- Compulsive gambling
- Current illegal drug use
- Homosexuality or bisexuality
- Normal pregnancy
- Predisposition to illness or disease
- Pyromania or kleptomania
- Sexual behavior disorders
- Short-term illness

Unless associated with a psychological disorder, common traits, such as quick temper, are not considered impairments.

Title I—Employment

The objective of Title I of the ADA is to ensure access to equal employment opportunities for people with disabilities based on merit. The ADA, unlike other civil rights laws, does not set quotas or require special preferences for people with disabilities, nor does it guarantee equal results.

The most significant feature of Title I is the entitlement of an applicant or current employee who has a disability of **reasonable accommodation** to carry out the essential duties of the job function.

All employers with 15 or more full-time employees, including real estate businesses, are covered by the ADA effective July 26, 1994. It is the general consensus that the independent contractor status in the real estate industry does not exempt or prevail over the intent of the ADA to cover employers.

Title I requires reasonable accommodation that does not create an undue hardship on the business involved, provided the essential duties of the job can be performed by the people with disabilities, without a direct threat to the safety of the people with disabilities or others.

Reasonable Accommodation

Reasonable accommodation means modifications or adjustments to a job application process, to the work environment, or to the circumstances customarily performed, and that enable the employee with a disability to enjoy equal benefits and privileges of employment.

A reasonable accommodation involves the alteration of existing facilities and work procedures to make them readily accessible to an employee with disabilities. This could be adjusting a workstation desk height, alternating job requirements, or flexibility in work hours for the disabled employee. However, the ADA is not intended to lower or alter existing required job standards such as police or fire department qualification. People with disabilities should be considered for other positions they are qualified to perform.

Title III—Public Accommodations and Commercial Facilities by Private Entities

Title III of the ADA prohibits all private non-government entities that own, lease, or operate a place of **public accommodation** from discriminating against an individual on the basis of a disability. Accordingly, the ADA requires owners and tenants of public accommodations to (1) remove barriers and (2) make **reasonable modifications**.

The barrier removal and reasonable modifications are required to ensure equal opportunity for access to individuals with disabilities.

The definition of public accommodation includes 12 categories that comprise any business or operation that serves the public such as hotels, restaurants, theaters, and also real estate brokerage offices.

The ADA's nondiscrimination obligations in public accommodations place the emphasis on the public use or operations of the facility. Therefore, if any facility will be used by the public, it must comply with the ADA.

Exceptions

The following facilities are not considered public accommodations under ADA:

1. A model home is not on the 12-category public accommodation list; however, if a public sales office is open in the model home, that portion of the home could be considered a public accommodation and would have to comply with the ADA.

2. The ADA does not apply to private residences. However, if part of the home is operated as a commercial office such as for a real estate broker working in the home, then the ADA would apply to all areas of the home used by clients, including the access areas to the home and bathroom.

3. A vacation time-share property may be under ADA if it resembles a hotel or place of lodging, if its ownership is fee simple, and it is available for short-term rentals of one week or less.

4. The ADA does not apply to a religious entity, but if the church operates a shelter or day-care center that is open for the general public's use, then the facilities must comply with the ADA.

5. The ADA does not apply to a private club, but if the club rents space in a public meeting room to organizations such as the Nevada Association of REALTORS, then the facilities must comply with the ADA.

Commercial Facilities

The definition of *place of public accommodation* refers to "a private entity whose operations affect commerce," or in other words, commercial facilities.

The ADA definition of **commercial facilities** covers those facilities "that are intended for nonresidential use" by a private entity and "whose operations affect commerce."

The ADA covers public nonresidential office buildings, warehouses, factories, shopping malls, and other buildings where employment occurs or operations take place that affect commerce.

The ADA does not apply to residential facilities covered by the Fair Housing Act, but does apply to public services within commercial facilities. Therefore, a residential unit with ground-floor public services such as a restaurant, dry cleaner, or hair salon would be covered by the ADA and the residential unit by the Fair Housing Act.

Enforcement

The ADA allows for civil action by a party subject to discrimination or about to be discriminated against, or the U.S. Attorney General can bring suit if a pattern of discrimination exists or is of public importance.

In the case of public accommodation discrimination, civil awards of $50,000 for a first violation and $100,000 for subsequent violations, plus attorney's fees, are allowed. Also, injunctive relief can be sought requiring the business to modify its facilities or existing policies or practices. The good faith efforts of the non-complying party will be considered in determining a civil penalty.

CHAPTER SUMMARY

The Civil Rights Act of 1866 provided that all citizens have the same rights as white citizens to inherit, purchase, and sell real and personal property. The 1866 act is limited to discrimination based upon race and was an empty promise, because the courts prohibited racial discrimination only with regard to governmental discrimination.

In *Plessy v. Ferguson*, the Supreme Court held that the enforcement of racial segregation of private or public facilities did not violate the U.S. Constitution as long as the separate facilities were equal.

The Supreme Court reversed the separate but equal doctrine in *Brown v. Board of Education*, outlawing segregation in schools and marking the beginning of the end of the era of legalized segregation.

The Civil Rights Act of 1964 prohibited discrimination in programs receiving federal financial assistance. The law had little impact on the housing market.

The Fair Housing Act of 1968 bans discrimination on the basis of race, color, religion, and national origin in most types of housing transactions.

"Sex" was added as a protected class in 1974. The act also contains a variety of remedies to attack housing discrimination, including private discrimination.

In *Jones v. Mayer*, the Supreme Court held that the 1866 Civil Rights Act banned governmental and private racial discrimination in housing.

The Fair Housing Act was amended in 1972 by a requirement that equal housing opportunity posters be displayed in brokerages, mortgage companies, and new home sites.

Under the Fair Housing Acts of 1968 and 1988 it is unlawful:

- To refuse to sell or rent housing to any person because of race, color, religion, sex, national origin, handicap, or familial status.
- To refuse to negotiate for housing because of race, color, religion, sex, national origin, handicap, or familial status.

Other unlawful acts prohibited by the Fair Housing Acts are listed previously in this chapter.

The Fair Housing Act of 1968 does not apply to the sale or rental of commercial or industrial properties. There are other exemptions for religious organizations, private clubs, owner-occupied buildings with no more than four units, and single-family housing, under certain circumstances.

Important terms to know include *blockbusting*, *steering*, and *redlining*.

In 1988, Congress added individuals with handicaps or in a familial status to the list of those protected by the Fair Housing Act. It is against the 1988 law to refuse to permit a person with a handicap, at his or her own expense, to make minor modifications to an existing premise or to refuse to make reasonable accommodations necessary to afford a person equal opportunity to use and enjoy a dwelling.

The Fair Housing Act exempts housing for older persons from the familial status provision provided that the area or facility is intended for and solely occupied by persons 62 years of age or older, or at least one person in 80% of the households is 55 years or older. Also, the facilities and services must be specifically designed to meet the physical and social needs of older persons.

Remedies for violations of civil rights laws vary depending on the form of complaint. Most cases, by law, are presented to HUD. The complaint must be filed within one year of the violation.

The ADA was the first comprehensive American civil rights law for people with disabilities, and it affects every employer, business, and public service, including real estate.

A person with a disability is defined as a person who meets one of the following three conditions: (1) has a mental or physical impairment that substantially limits one or more major life activities, (2) has a record of a physical or mental impairment that substantially limits one or more major life activities, or (3) is regarded as having a physical or mental impairment that substantially limits one or more major life activities.

The objective of Title I of the ADA is to ensure access to equal employment opportunities for the disabled based on merit. The most significant feature of Title I is the entitlement of an applicant or current employee with a disability of reasonable accommodation to carry out the essential duties of the job function.

Title III of the ADA prohibits all private non-government entities that own, lease, or operate a place of public accommodation from discriminating against an individual on the basis of a disability. The ADA requires owners and tenants of public accommodations to remove barriers and make reasonable modifications. Certain facilities are not considered public accommodations.

The ADA allows for civil action by a party subject to discrimination or about to be discriminated against, or the U.S. Attorney General can bring suit if a pattern of discrimination exists or is of public importance.

CHECKING YOUR COMPREHENSION

1. Summarize the following:
   - Civil Rights Act of 1866
   - *Plessy v. Ferguson*
   - *Brown v. Board of Education*
   - Civil Rights Act of 1964
   - *Jones v. Mayer*

2. List the protected classes established by the Fair Housing Acts of 1968 and 1988.

3. List and explain the unlawful acts established by the Fair Housing Act of 1968 and summarize the exceptions to the 1968 act.

4. Explain the remedies available for violation of the civil rights laws and summarize the procedures for investigation and resolution of a complaint.

5. Summarize the provisions of the Americans with Disabilities Act.

REVIEWING YOUR UNDERSTANDING

1. If a minority does not ask to be shown homes located in an all-white neighborhood, a licensee:
   a. has no obligation to show such homes
   b. may automatically assume that the prospect is not interested in those homes
   c. need not service the prospect at all
   d. must select homes for showing as he or she would for any other prospect

2. The practice of making a profit by telling owners that a particular minority group is moving into the neighborhood, thus inducing the owners to sell is called:
   a. blockbusting
   b. racial steering
   c. redlining
   d. puffing

3. Under the Civil Rights Act of 1968 (the Fair Housing Act), discrimination is illegal in the sale and/or rental of property when it is based on:

    a. employment

    b. marital status

    c. sex

    d. family size

4. A broker wants to advertise a property in a black neighborhood in a paper aimed at black readership. To do so, the broker **MUST**:

    a. indicate compliance with the fair housing laws

    b. also advertise in a paper (or papers) of general circulation

    c. include the equal housing opportunity logo in the ad

    d. identify the location in the ad

5. A women's rights organization established a nonprofit housing project with preference to single women with children. Their action is:

    a. proper if the organization is also nonprofit

    b. proper if there is no racial discrimination

    c. improper under the Civil Rights Act of 1866

    d. improper under the 1974 amendment to the Civil Rights Act of 1968

6. Regarding a breach of the Civil Rights Act of 1968, an aggrieved party could do all of the following **EXCEPT**:

    a. bring an action in state court

    b. file a complaint with HUD

    c. bring an action in federal court

    d. file a complaint with the U.S. Attorney General

7. The Civil Rights Act of 1968 protects against discrimination for all of the following classes **EXCEPT**:

    a. age

    b. sex

    c. religion

    d. national origin

8. The landmark case concerning the constitutionality of fair housing was:

    a. *Jones v. Mayer*

    b. *Shelly v. Kramer*

    c. *Brown v. Board of Education*

    d. *Maxwell v. City of Chicago*

9. Which of the following would **MOST** likely be legal under the Civil Rights Act of 1968?

    a. a lender refusing to make loans in areas with more than 25% African American people

    b. a private country club where ownership of homes is tied to club membership, but all members are white

    c. a church, which excludes African Americans from membership, renting its nonprofit housing to church members only

    d. directing prospective buyers away from areas where they are likely to feel uncomfortable because of race

10. Impairment under the Americans with Disabilities Act does **NOT** include:

    a. mental retardation

    b. recovering drug and alcohol addiction

    c. current illegal drug use

    d. inability to care for oneself

11. The Americans with Disabilities Act was adopted for all of the following reasons **EXCEPT**:

    a. to prohibit employment discrimination against those with mental and physical disabilities

    b. to provide accessibility to public accommodations by those with mental and physical disabilities

    c. to provide protection only to American citizens with disabilities

    d. to require the removal by private entities of existing architectural barriers to access

12. A person with a disability who is covered under the ADA has a mental or physical impairment, or a record of such impairment, or is regarded as having such an impairment that:
    a. limits their mobility
    b. affects one or more major life activities
    c. is included on the ADA list of disabilities
    d. has received a certification from the Department of Health that it affects one or more major life activities

13. Title 1 of the Americans with Disabilities Act applies to all employers with:
    a. 15 or more full-time employees
    b. 25 or more full-time employees
    c. 15 or more full-time employees, except that independent contractors such as real estate agents are not counted
    d. 25 or more full-time employees, except that independent contractors such as real estate agents are not counted

14. Reasonable accommodation means modification or adjustment to all of the following **EXCEPT**:
    a. job application process
    b. work environment
    c. job standards that create an undue hardship
    d. circumstances customarily performed

15. All of the following are public accommodations under the Americans with Disabilities Act, **EXCEPT**:
    a. real estate brokerage office
    b. a hotel
    c. a private residence
    d. a private residence in which a room is used as the office for a self-employed real estate broker

16. An apartment complex has a common area where services are available to the public, such as a hair salon. The ADA:
    a. would not cover the facility since it is a residential unit
    b. would cover the public area, and the Fair Housing Act would cover the residential units
    c. would cover the total facility due to the public area
    d. would not cover the facility since the Fair Housing Act covers the total facility

17. The act that specifies **ONLY** race is the:
    a. Equal Credit Opportunity Act
    b. Civil Rights Act of 1968
    c. Real Estate Settlement Procedures Act
    d. Civil Rights Act of 1866

18. The federal Fair Housing Act does **NOT**:
    a. prohibit steering
    b. provide minimum housing standards
    c. prohibit blockbusting
    d. prohibit sex discrimination

19. All of the following are violations of the 1968 federal housing law, **EXCEPT**:
    a. a salesperson assigned to customers on the basis of race
    b. indicating the age of the other homes in the neighborhood
    c. a buyer specifying a religious preference
    d. an owner who instructs a broker to avoid advertising in minority publications

20. When taking a listing, a broker should obtain all of the following information, **EXCEPT**:
    a. age of the building
    b. number of rooms in the property
    c. racial composition of the neighborhood
    d. cost of utilities

Chapter 17

IMPORTANT TERMS AND CONCEPTS

accord and satisfaction

accurate legal
   description

actual damages

assignee

assignment

assignor

bilateral contract

breach of contract

capacity

consideration

contract

damages

deed

discharge of contract

enforceable

executed contract

executory contract

express contract

implied contract

lawful purpose

meeting of the minds

mutual assent

novation

offer

offeree

offeror

parol evidence rule

part performance

punitive damages

real estate purchase
   contract

ready, willing, and able

rescission

specific performance

statute of frauds

"time is of the essence"
   clause

unenforceable

unilateral contract

valid

void

voidable

CHAPTER OBJECTIVES

After completing this chapter, you should be able to:

- Define a contract and explain the various classifications of contracts.
- List and describe the essentials of a valid contract.
- Describe the status of a contract.
- Summarize the various ways a contract can be discharged.
- Explain breach of contract and the actions that can result from a breach.
- Describe the steps in negotiating a "meeting of the minds."

Contract Law

INTRODUCTION

The law of contracts is one of the most complex bodies of law involved in real estate. Contract law plays an important role in the real estate business because a single transaction may require several contracts.

Contracts most commonly used by licensees are listing agreements, sales contracts, land contracts, escrow agreements, options, leases, mortgages, and deeds of trust.

This text will discuss all of these contracts in detail, but first you must know and understand the definition of contracts, classification of contracts, and the essential elements of contracts.

17.1 DEFINITION AND CLASSIFICATION OF CONTRACTS

A **contract** is a legally enforceable agreement between competent parties who agree to perform or refrain from performing certain acts for a consideration.

Contracts may be classified as *express, implied, bilateral, unilateral, executory,* or *executed* (see Figure 17.1).

An **express contract** is expressed in words either written or oral. Each party states his or her terms and intentions in words. A real estate sales contract is an express contract; an oral month-to-month rental agreement is also an express contract.

In an **implied contract**, the agreement of the parties is demonstrated by their acts or conduct. For example, after a lease expires, if the tenant tenders another month's rent and the landlord accepts, then the conduct of the parties implies that they intend to extend tenancy.

In a **bilateral contract**, each party gives a promise to perform in exchange for the other party's promise of performance. A bilateral contract is a two-sided

FIGURE 17.1   Types of Contracts

TYPES		OF CONTRACTS
UNILATERAL	=	PROMISE FOR AN ACT
BILATERAL	=	PROMISE FOR A PROMISE
EXPRESSED	=	VERBAL OR WRITTEN
IMPLIED	=	CREATED BY ACTIONS
EXECUTORY	=	SOME ACTION NEEDED
EXECUTED	=	COMPLETED CONTRACT

Most real estate agreements are expressed bilateral contracts.

contract, with each side making a promise of performance that is binding upon both parties. Most real estate contracts are bilateral contracts.

A **unilateral contract** is a one-sided contract in which one party makes a promise to induce a second party to perform. The second party has no obligation to act; however, if he or she does accept, the first party is obligated to keep the promise. An option is an example of a unilateral contract because it is binding only on the maker of the option (optionor).

An **executory contract** is a contract that is not yet finished (unperformed) and therefore incomplete. If a sales contract has been accepted and is in escrow, it is considered an executory contract.

An **executed contract** is a contract that is completed, meaning both parties have completed their promises. On the day of closing, when the deed is delivered to the buyer and the buyer delivers payment to the seller, the sales contract is an executed contract.

17.2 ESSENTIALS OF A VALID CONTRACT

For a contract to be considered valid and enforceable, certain requirements must be fulfilled:

(C) • *Capacity* or state of mind

(O) • *Offer, acceptance, and notification* (also called mutual assent or meeting of minds)

(V) • *Valid consideration*

(L) • *Lawful* purpose

(A) • *Accurate* legal description

(W) • In *writing*

(S) • *Signed* by all parties

The first four items (COVL) relate to general contract law, and the last three (AWS) pertain to real estate contracts, which are covered by the statute of frauds.

The following descriptions of each of these requirements will help you understand the concept of a valid contract.

Capacity

If a court decides that a person is legally insane, that person has no **capacity** to perform, and any contract entered into by that person is automatically void. On the other hand, a person who is insane but not judged so could enter into a contract that could be voidable. In other words, the party who has the limited capacity may void the contract.

Minors (people who have not reached age 18) in Nevada can also void a contract at their option. For example, if a seller entered into a contract for the sale of a lot and discovered that the adjacent land was being developed and would increase the value of her lot, and also discovered that the buyer was a minor, the seller cannot declare the contract void. The buyer, however, could do so.

A person who was under the influence of liquor or drugs is also considered to lack the capacity to contract. However, the courts may not extend as much sympathy to those incapacitated by alcohol or illegal drugs as they would to a person who was under the influence of extreme medication.

A person who acts under duress, which means being coerced into an agreement through fear or misled trust, will not be held to the contract, and the result could be rescission.

Offer, Acceptance, and Notification

An **offer** is the extension of a proposal to enter into an agreement. The person making the proposal or offer is called an **offeror**. The person considering the offer is the **offeree**.

The proposal may be altered through negotiations between the two parties until a **"meeting of the minds"** or **mutual assent** has been reached. Mutual assent signifies the stage of acceptance. Time is of the essence in all contracts, which means contracts must be acted upon either within the time stated on the contract or within a reasonable time period.

Notification of acceptance is critical to the effectiveness of a contract. Notification of the acceptance requires the same type of communication as the offer. If the offer was mailed, the accepted offer's being deposited into the U.S. mail constitutes acceptance.

In real estate sales contracts, the salesperson is usually responsible for the communication of acceptance or rejection of an offer. An offeror may rescind his or her offer at any time verbally until the agent has notified him or her of acceptance. If a broker is an agent of the buyer, notice to the agent is deemed to be notice to the buyer because the buyer's agent represents him or her in the offer.

Death of an offeror will automatically terminate an offer, whether the offeree knows of the death or not. However, an offer that has been accepted by an offeree before the offeror's death is binding on the estate of the offeror (buyer). The estate of the offeree (seller) is bound to the agreement in the case of the seller's death.

Valid Consideration

Consideration is required to make a contract or agreement enforceable. **Consideration** is the inducement to a contract; specifically it is an act or the forbearance to act or the promise to act that is given by one party in return for the act or promise of another. Consideration is something of value, such as money, property, personal services, or the promise to perform a specific action. Consideration can be an exchange of money for property, a promise for a promise, goods for services, and so on. Forbearance also qualifies as consideration, as does "love and affection." Because love and affection has value, it is a legal type of consideration and is used when property is transferred as a gift.

Lawful Purpose

To be enforceable in court, a contract must have a **lawful purpose** or it is void. One cannot enter into a contract to perform illegal acts and look to the courts to uphold the provisions of the contract. When a contract for legal purpose or object contains a clause that is illegal, that provision may be removed from the agreement, and the court could enforce the rest of the agreement.

Accurate Legal Description

A real estate sales contract must have an **accurate legal description** to be considered valid. A legal description is considered adequate if a surveyor can use it to positively identify the parcel of land. In rural areas of Nevada, a rectangular survey description is most often used, or a combination of rectangular survey and metes and bounds description. In cities and towns, a lot and block (map and plat) subdivision description is usually used.

Contracts Must Be Written

According to the **statute of frauds**, all contracts related to real property (with the exception of leases for one year or less) must be in writing. The statute of frauds was first adopted in England in 1677 and became a part of English law. The purpose of the statute of frauds was to prevent perjury, which is false testimony under oath in a court of law. A party to an oral real estate contract might falsely testify in court to accomplish a fraudulent transaction when there is not a written document.

The **parol evidence rule**, which is part of the statute of frauds, says that a document must stand on the written word; there can be no additional oral testimony. Oral testimony in a written contract dispute can be used only to clarify an ambiguous portion of the document. Oral testimony cannot be used to revise the document or to change the meaning or scope of the written contract.

All states have adopted a version of the statute of frauds. The following table outlines what types of contracts are covered (and not covered) under the statute of frauds.

Covered by Statute of Frauds	Not Covered by Statute of Frauds, May Be Oral
• Listings	• Leases of one year or less for performance
• Real estate sales contract	• General partnership agreements
• Land contracts	• Agreements between brokers or between brokers and their salespeople regarding commission splits
• Options	
• Leases for more than one year	• An agreement to solicit certain types of loans
• Wills	
• Mortgages	
• Trust deeds	
• Promissory notes	
• Deeds	

Signing of Contracts

To be considered a valid contract, the document must be signed by all parties to the agreement.

17.3 STATUS OF CONTRACTS

Contracts are said to be *valid, void, voidable,* and either *enforceable* or *unenforceable* (see Figure 17.2). Let's examine the meaning of these words in relation to real estate contracts.

If a contract is **valid**, it will contain all of the essential elements previously discussed. A valid contract is legal, enforceable, and binding on all parties.

FIGURE 17.2   Legal Effects of Contracts

LEGAL EFFECTS OF CONTRACTS

✓ VALID
  binding and enforceable

✓ VOID
  no legal effect, no contract

✓ VOIDABLE
  one party can cancel due to fraud, duress, or undue influence, but the other side cannot cancel

✓ UNENFORCEABLE
  appears valid, but cannot be enforced in court

If a contract is **void**, it means that one or more of the essential elements are missing. Without all of the essential elements, no contract legally exists and, therefore, it is unenforceable.

If a contract is **voidable**, it seems valid and enforceable on the surface, but it may be voided by one of the parties. This pertains to minors, mentally incompetent or temporarily insane persons, or to persons who were intoxicated or under the influence of drugs. A voidable contract is valid until it is rescinded (cancelled). If the contract is not rescinded, it is considered accepted by ratification.

For example, if a minor enters into a real estate contract, she has a voidable contract. She can force the other party to perform but may choose to reject the contract and call it void at any time during her minority and up to a reasonable time after reaching majority (age 18). On the other hand, she may also continue with the contract and consider it accepted by ratification.

An **unenforceable** contract appears valid on the surface, but for some reason cannot be enforced. One example would be an oral contract covered by the statute of frauds. In an unenforceable contract, neither party can sue to force performance.

An **enforceable** contract is a valid contract with all of the essential elements (COVL) present. The contract is binding on all parties and if a party defaults on the terms of performance, enforcement can be brought through a court of law. A valid contract can become unenforceable because of the statute of limitations.

17.4 DISCHARGE OF CONTRACTS

When performance of the agreed upon actions has been completed, the contract is *discharged*. If one party has not performed, the contract has been *breached*, unless the parties agree not to take action. There are certain conditions in which a contract is discharged even though complete performance has not been accomplished.

Discharge

Completed Contract

The most common **discharge of contracts** is when the contract is fulfilled by complete performance of the parties to the contract. Sometimes there is a question as to how quickly the parties must complete their performance. To remedy this, contracts often set forth a specific time by which the agreed upon acts must be completed.

Contracts frequently include a **"time is of the essence" clause**, which means that the parties will perform within the limits specified. Any party not doing so is considered in breach of contract.

Assignment

Unless the contract states otherwise, it is permissible to assign the rights, duties, and benefits of the contract to a third party without terminating the contract. The third party is called an **assignee**, and the original party to the contract is the **assignor**. Even though the assignee takes over all rights, the assignor is still liable as contracted for the performance of the original contract.

Novation

Under **novation**, a new party is substituted for an existing one with the responsibilities under the old contract completely erased. For example, when a real estate purchaser assumes a seller's existing mortgage loan, the lender would release the seller, and the buyer would become the mortgagor with the responsibility for the mortgage debt. Under novation, the terms remain the same but with a new contract and new parties.

Accord and Satisfaction

Accord and satisfaction occurs when the parties voluntarily agree to complete the contract, even though all of the terms and conditions have not been met.

Discharging of a Contract

The release of contractual obligations to perform by operation of the parties or by operation of law is known as discharging of a contract. Partial performance, substantial performance, unable to perform, and operation of law are examples.

Partial Performance

The doctrine of **part performance** is the major exception to the statute of frauds, which requires certain contracts, including real estate purchase contracts, to be in writing. Performance or substantial performance by one party to an oral real estate purchase contract can be sufficient to allow the enforcement of the oral contract, even though the agreement is subject to the statute of frauds. What defines "sufficient performance" varies from one court jurisdiction to another.

For example, Roger sold a farm to Burke under an oral agreement for $200,000. Burke paid Roger $100,000 and agreed to pay $50,000 each year for two years. Burke made substantial improvements to the farm, paid taxes, and made the first $50,000 payment on time. One month before the final $50,000 payment was due, Roger declared the contract to be void. In this case, the court would hold for Burke on the theory that the statute of frauds does not apply because there was partial performance.

Substantial Performance

A contract may be considered complete and discharged when a party performs most of the required task. For example, a contractor agreed to build a house and makes minor deviations from the plans but still has complied with most of the provisions. The courts would not find the contractor in breach of the entire contract. They may, however, alter the contract and deduct some of the contract price for the portion not in compliance.

Unable to Perform

The terms of the agreement cannot be enforced if they are beyond the control of the parties involved. If a painting contractor enters into an agreement to paint a building and then discovers that fire has gutted the structure, she is unable to perform. Also, if a party to a contract dies and the contract was for personal services, the contract is discharged.

Operation of the Law

An agreement to import or export products to a foreign country could be discharged if the government no longer allowed trade with that country. A contract to construct a home on a site that is suddenly condemned by the city due to contamination could not be enforced.

17.5 BREACH OF CONTRACT

Breach of contract occurs when either party defaults on the contract. Rescission, damages, liquidated damages, or suit for specific performance are actions that may result from a breach of contract.

Rescission

Rescission is a legal remedy of canceling, terminating, or annulling a contract and restoring the parties to their original positions.

Rescission can take place due to mistakes, misrepresentation, or fraud. Contracts can also be rescinded unilaterally if a person entered into a contract while under the influence of drugs, alcohol, or under duress. Contracts can also be rescinded by mutual agreement of both parties. If this happens, there can be no claims for damages or specific performance suits.

Damages

The party who does not breach the contract can seek damages. **Damages** are classified as liquidated damages, actual damages, and punitive damages. An example of liquidated damages is cancellation of a sales contract by the seller when the buyer defaults and acceptance by the seller of the earnest money deposit as the damages. When the injured party sues to recover the actual loss due to a breach of contract, the party is said to be seeking **actual damages**. Seeking **punitive damages** is an attempt to recover amounts over the actual damages suffered as compensation for the breach of the contract.

Suit for Specific Performance

A suit for **specific performance** is a judicial action to force a party to carry out the terms of the contract. For example, under a valid sales contract, if a seller suddenly decides he does not want to sell, the purchaser can force him to carry out the terms of the contract. Likewise, if a buyer has a change of heart after signing a valid sales contract, the seller can sue the buyer to force the buyer to complete the terms of the contract by following through and buying the property.

Statute of Limitations

Statutory law allows a specific time limit during which parties to a contract may file their legal action to enforce their rights. The time limit varies depending on the legal action and the type of contractual terms being enforced. Parties to a contract who do not take steps to enforce their rights within the time limits could lose the rights to do so.

17.6 REAL ESTATE PURCHASE AGREEMENT

The real estate *purchase agreement*, also known as the *contract of sale*, sets out all the details of a sale, states the agreement of buyer and seller, and dictates the contents of the deed. A **deed** is the legal document that transfers ownership of real property.

After being signed, the purchase agreement is binding upon the parties during escrow. The contract also forms the basis for escrow instructions. The signed contract is referred to as an executory contract, which means the terms are agreed upon but not yet completed.

Use of Printed Forms

Using printed forms simplifies the process of handling and negotiating a listing and a sales contract.

Licensees must be thorough when filling out forms. Complete information is absolutely necessary. All blanks must be filled in with the available information or "N/A" if not applicable.

Because the statute of frauds requires contracts to be in writing and signed by all parties, possible conflicts need to be addressed. Any provision that is specific in its terms will take precedence over a more general statement. The use of printed forms also requires some sort of priority to the information added. The general position is that handwritten information takes precedence over printed copy. Also, written amounts (three thousand) take precedence over numerals ($3, 000).

The courts will interpret any errors or incompleteness as the broker's responsibility. Also, remember that in case of litigation, the contract will have to stand on the written word due to the parol evidence rule, which does not allow oral evidence to change or add to the terms of the written contract.

No specific forms are required for a real estate sales contract, lease, listing agreement, or buyer–broker agreement. However, the most-used forms are those developed by local association of REALTORS. A sample Residential Purchase Agreement of the Greater Las Vegas Association of REALTORS is included as Figure 17.3.

Steps in Negotiating a Sale

A description of the typical steps in negotiating and completing a real estate purchase contract follows:

1. A prospective purchaser indicates an interest in a particular property. After a discussion concerning the steps and responsibilities of making an offer, the

FIGURE 17.3   Residential Purchase Agreement

RESIDENTIAL PURCHASE AGREEMENT

(Joint Escrow Instructions and Earnest Money Receipt)

Date: _____

_____ ("Buyer"), hereby offers to purchase
_____ ("Property"),
within the city or unincorporated area of _____ , County of _____ ,
State of Nevada, A.P.N. # _____ for the purchase price of $ _____ ("Purchase Price") on the
following terms and conditions:

Offer & Acceptance

1.   FINANCIAL TERMS & CONDITIONS:

$ _____   A. **EARNEST MONEY DEPOSIT** ("EMD") is☐presented with this offer - OR - ☐ _____

> *(NOTE: It is a felony in the State of Nevada—punishable by up to four years in prison and a $5,000
> fine—to write a check for which there are insufficient funds. NRS 193.130(2)(d).)*

$ _____   B. **ADDITIONAL DEPOSIT** to be placed in escrow on or before (date) _____ .
The additional deposit☐will - OR -☐will not be considered part of the EMD. (Any conditions on the
additional deposit should be set forth in Paragraph 29 herein.)

$ _____   C. **THIS AGREEMENT IS CONTINGENT UPON BUYER QUALIFYING FOR A NEW LOAN
ON THE FOLLOWING TERMS AND CONDITIONS:**
☐ Conventional, ☐ FHA, ☐ VA, ☐ Other (specify) _____ .
Interest: ☐ Fixed rate, _____ years - OR -☐Adjustable rate, _____ years. Initial rate of interest
not to exceed _____ %. Initial monthly payment not to exceed $ _____ , not including
taxes, insurance and/or PMI or MIP.

$ _____   D. **THIS AGREEMENT IS CONTINGENT UPON BUYER QUALIFYING TO ASSUME THE
FOLLOWING EXISTING LOAN(S):**
☐ Conventional,☐FHA,☐VA,☐Other (specify) _____ .
Interest: ☐ Fixed rate, _____ years - OR -☐Adjustable rate, _____ years. Initial rate of interest
not to exceed _____ %. Monthly payment not to exceed $ _____ , not including
taxes, insurance and/or PMI or MIP.

$ _____   E. **BUYER TO EXECUTE A PROMISSORY NOTE SECURED BY DEED OF TRUST PER
TERMS IN "FINANCING ADDENDUM."**

$ _____   F. **BALANCE OF PURCHASE PRICE**   (Balance of Down Payment) in cash or certified funds to be
paid at Close of Escrow ("COE").

$ _____   G. **TOTAL PURCHASE PRICE.** (Total cash, certified funds and/or financing. DOES NOT include
closing costs, prorations, or other fees and costs associated with the purchase of the Property as defined
herein.)

**Each party acknowledges that he/she has read, understood, and agrees to each and every provision of this page unless a
particular paragraph is otherwise modified by addendum or counteroffer.**

Buyer's Name: _____   BUYER(S) INITIALS: _____ / _____

Property Address: _____   SELLER(S) INITIALS: _____ / _____

Rev. 2007   Copyright© Greater Las Vegas Association of REALTORS®   Page 1 of 11

FIGURE 17.3 Continued.

2. **FINANCING CONTINGENCIES:**
    A. NEW LOAN APPLICATION: Buyer agrees to submit a completed loan application with the required information for loan qualification with a lender within _____ business days of Acceptance. Buyer agrees to use Buyer's best efforts to obtain financing under the terms and conditions outlined in this Agreement. If Buyer does not submit the application in the above period, Buyer is in default of this Agreement. Buyer **does☐-OR-☐does not** authorize lender to provide loan status updates to Seller's and Buyer's Brokers, as well as Escrow Officer. Different loan types (i.e., FHA, conventional) have different appraisal and financing requirements, which will affect the parties' rights and costs under this Agreement.

    B. APPRAISAL: If an appraisal is required as part of this agreement, and if the appraisal is less than the purchase price, the transaction will go forward if **(1)** Buyer, at Buyer's option, elects to pay the difference and purchase the Property for the Purchase Price, or **(2)** Seller, at Seller's option, elects to adjust the Purchase Price accordingly, such that the Purchase Price is equal to the appraisal. If neither option (1) or (2) is elected, and the Parties cannot renegotiate, then either Party may cancel this Agreement upon written notice, in which event the EMD shall be returned to Buyer.

3.   **SALE OF OTHER PROPERTY:** This Agreement☐**is not -OR-** ☐**is** contingent upon the sale (and closing) of another property which address is _____.
Said Property☐ **is not -OR-** ☐**is** presently in escrow with   _____.

4.   **ESCROW:**
    A. OPENING OF ESCROW: The purchase of the Property shall be consummated through Escrow ("Escrow"). Opening of Escrow shall take place by the end of one (1) business day after execution of this Agreement ("Opening of Escrow"), at _____ title or escrow company ("Escrow Company" or "ESCROW HOLDER") with _____ ("Escrow Officer") (or such other escrow officer as Escrow Company may assign). Opening of Escrow shall occur upon Escrow Company's receipt of this fully accepted Agreement and receipt of the EMD (if applicable). Escrow Holder will notify the Parties (through their respective Brokers) of the Opening date and the Escrow Number.

    B. EARNEST MONEY: Upon Seller and Buyer signing this Agreement and all counteroffers or addenda, Buyer's EMD as shown in Paragraph 1(A), and 1(B) if applicable, of this Agreement, shall be deposited per the Earnest Money Receipt Notice and Instructions contained herein.

    C. CLOSE OF ESCROW: Close of Escrow ("COE") shall be on (date) _____ . If the designated date falls on a weekend or holiday, COE shall be the next business day.

    D. 1099. Seller is hereby made aware that there is a regulation which became effective January 1, 1987, that requires all ESCROW HOLDERS to complete a modified 1099 form, based upon specific information known only between parties in this transaction and the ESCROW HOLDER. ESCROW HOLDER is hereby authorized and instructed to provide this information to the Internal Revenue Service after the close of escrow in the manner prescribed.

    E. FIRPTA. If applicable, Seller agrees to complete, sign, and deliver to ESCROW HOLDER a certificate indicating whether Seller is a foreign person or a nonresident alien pursuant to the Foreign Investment in Real Property Tax Act (FIRPTA). A foreign person is a nonresident alien individual; a foreign corporation not treated as a domestic corporation; or a foreign partnership, trust or estate. A resident alien is not considered a foreign person under FIRPTA. Seller agrees to comply with IRS reporting requirements. Buyer acknowledges that if the Seller is a foreign person, the Buyer must withhold a tax equal to ten (10) percent of the Purchase Price, unless an exemption applies. 26 USC §1445(a).

Each party acknowledges that he/she has read, understood, and agrees to each and every provision of this page unless a particular paragraph is otherwise modified by addendum or counteroffer.

Buyer's Name: _____   BUYER(S) INITIALS: _____ / _____

Property Address: _____   SELLER(S) INITIALS: _____ / _____

FIGURE 17.3 Continued.

5.   **PRORATIONS, FEES AND EXPENSES (Check appropriate box):**
    A. **TITLE AND ESCROW FEES:**

TYPE	PAID BY SELLER	PAID BY BUYER	50/50	N/A
Escrow Fees	☐	☐	☐	☐
Lender's Title Policy	☐	☐	☐	☐
Owner's Title Policy	☐	☐	☐	☐
Real Property Transfer Tax	☐	☐	☐	☐
Other:	☐	☐	☐	☐

    B. **PRORATIONS:**

TYPE	PAID BY SELLER	PRORATE	N/A
CIC (Common Interest Community) Assessments	☐	☐	☐
CIC Periodic Fees	☐	☐	☐
SIDs / LIDs / Assessments	☐	☐	☐
Sewer Use Fees	☐	☐	☐
Taxes	☐	☐	☐
Other:	☐	☐	☐

All prorations will be based on a 30-day month and will be calculated as of COE. Prorations will be based upon figures available at closing. Any supplementals or adjustments that occur after COE will be handled by the parties outside of Escrow.

    C. **INSPECTIONS AND RELATED EXPENSES:**

Seller will ensure that necessary utilities (gas, power and water) are turned on and supplied to the Property within two (2) business days after execution of this Agreement. (It is strongly recommended that Buyer retain licensed Nevada professionals to conduct inspections.) These elections are for the benefit of Buyer and may be waived at any time by Buyer prior to COE.

TYPE	PAID BY SELLER	PAID BY BUYER	WAIVED
Appraisal	☐	☐	☐
CIC Capital Contribution	☐	☐	☐
CIC Transfer Fees	☐	☐	☐
Fungal Contaminant Inspection	☐	☐	☐
Land Survey	☐	☐	☐
Mechanical Inspection	☐	☐	☐
Pool/Spa Inspection	☐	☐	☐
Roof Inspection	☐	☐	☐
Septic Inspection	☐	☐	☐
Soils Inspection	☐	☐	☐
Structural Inspection	☐	☐	☐
Termite/Pest Inspection	☐	☐	☐
Well Inspection	☐	☐	☐
Other:	☐	☐	☐

    D. **CERTIFICATIONS:**

TYPE	PAID BY SELLER	PAID BY BUYER	WAIVED
Fungal Contaminant	☐	☐	☐
Roof	☐	☐	☐
Septic	☐	☐	☐
Well	☐	☐	☐
Other:	☐	☐	☐

The foregoing expenses for inspections and certifications will be paid outside of Escrow unless the Parties present instructions to the contrary prior to COE (along with the applicable invoice). A certification is not a warranty. All inspections and certifications are to be performed by a company licensed and bonded in Nevada. Notwithstanding the above elections, in the event an inspection reveals

Each party acknowledges that he/she has read, understood, and agrees to each and every provision of this page unless a particular paragraph is otherwise modified by addendum or counteroffer.

Buyer's Name: _____   BUYER(S) INITIALS: _____ / _____

Property Address: _____   SELLER(S) INITIALS: _____ / _____

Rev. 2007   Copyright© Greater Las Vegas Association of REALTORS®   Page 3 of 11

FIGURE 17.3   Continued.

problems with any of the foregoing, Buyer reserves the right to require a certification. This section is for the benefit of Buyer and may be waived hereafter by Buyer prior to COE.

   E.   LENDER'S FEES: In addition to Seller's expenses above, Seller will contribute \$ _____ to Buyer's Lender's Fees and Buyer's Title and Escrow Fees □ **including - OR -** □ **excluding** costs which Seller must pay pursuant to loan program requirements.

   F.   SELLER'S ADDITIONAL COSTS: Seller agrees to pay a maximum amount of \$ _____
to correct defects and/or requirements disclosed by inspection reports and/or appraisals. It is Buyer's responsibility to inspect the Property sufficiently as to satisfy Buyer's use. Buyer reserves the right to request additional repairs based upon the Seller's Real Property Disclosure and/or pursuant to Paragraph 13 herein.

   G.   HOME PROTECTION PLAN: Buyer and Seller acknowledge that they have been made aware of Home Protection Plans that provide coverage to Buyer after COE. **Buyer**□**waives - OR-**□**requires** a Home Protection Plan with _____
_____ . **Buyer** will order the Home Protection Plan.□ **Seller -OR-**□**Buyer**   will pay for the Home Protection Plan at a price not to exceed \$ _____ . Neither Seller nor Brokers make any representation as to the extent of coverage or deductibles of such plans. Escrow Holder is not responsible for ordering the Home Protection Plan.

   H.   OTHER FEES: Buyer will also pay \$ _____ to Buyer's Broker for _____
_____ .

6.   TITLE INSURANCE: Upon COE, Buyer will be provided with the following type of title insurance policy:
□ **CLTA;**□**ALTA-Residential; -OR-** □ **ALTA-Extended (including a survey, if required).**

7.   TRANSFER OF TITLE: Upon COE, Buyer shall tender to Seller the agreed upon purchase price, and Seller shall tender to Buyer marketable title to the Property free of all encumbrances other than (1) current pro-rata Property taxes; (2) covenants, conditions and restrictions (C C & R's) and related restrictions; (3) zoning or master plan restrictions and public utility easements; and (4) obligations assumed and encumbrances accepted by Buyer prior to COE.

8.   COMMON OWNERSHIP INTEREST PROPERTIES: If the Property is subject to a Common Interest Community ("CIC"), Seller or his authorized agent shall request the CIC documents and certificate listed in NRS 116.4109 (collectively, the "resale package") within two (2) business days of Acceptance and provide the same to Buyer within one (1) business day of Seller's receipt thereof. Buyer may cancel this Agreement without penalty until midnight of the fifth (5th) calendar day following the date of receipt of the resale package. If Buyer does not receive the resale package within fifteen (15) calendar days of acceptance, this Agreement may be cancelled in full by Buyer without penalty. If Buyer elects to cancel this Agreement pursuant to this section, he must deliver, via hand delivery or prepaid U.S. mail, a written notice of cancellation to Seller or his authorized agent identified in Paragraph 28 of this Agreement. Upon such written cancellation, Buyer shall promptly receive a refund of the EMD. The parties agree to execute any documents requested by Escrow Holder to facilitate the refund. If written cancellation is not received within the specified time period, the resale package will be deemed approved. Seller shall pay all outstanding CIC fines or penalties at COE.

9.   DELIVERY OF POSSESSION: Seller shall deliver the Property along with keys, alarm codes and garage door opener/ controls outside of Escrow, upon COE. Seller agrees to vacate the Property and leave the Property in a neat and orderly, broom-clean condition and tender possession no later than COE.   In the event Seller does not vacate the Property by COE, Seller shall be considered a trespasser and shall be liable to Buyer for the sum of \$ _____ per calendar day in addition to Buyer's legal and equitable remedies. Any personal property left on the Property after COE shall be considered abandoned by Seller.

Each party acknowledges that he/she has read, understood, and agrees to each and every provision of this page unless a particular paragraph is otherwise modified by addendum or counteroffer.

Buyer's Name: _____   BUYER(S) INITIALS: _____ / _____

Property Address: _____   SELLER(S) INITIALS: _____ / _____

FIGURE 17.3 Continued.

10. **DISCLOSURES: Within five (5) calendar days of Acceptance of this Agreement,** Seller will provide the following Disclosures and/or documents (each of which is incorporated herein by this reference). Check applicable boxes.

☐ **Common Interest Community Information Statement** (Homeowner's Associations) (NRS 116.41095)

☐ **Construction Defect Claims Disclosure**, if Seller has marked "Yes" to Paragraph 1(d) of the Sellers Real Property Disclosure Form (NRS 40.688)

☐ **Fungal (Mold) Disclosure Form** (not required by Nevada law)

☐ **Lead-Based Paint Disclosure and Acknowledgment**, required if constructed before 1978 (24 CFR 745.113)

☐ **Methamphetamine Lab Disclosure**, if applicable (NRS 40.770, NRS 489.776)

☐ **Promissory Note and the most recent monthly statement of all loans to be assumed by Buyer**

☐ **Seller Real Property Disclosure Form** (NRS 113.130)

☐ **Pest Notice Form** (not required by Nevada law)

☐ **Other** (list) _____

In addition, Buyer to be provided with:

☐ **Residential Disclosure Guide** (NRS 645.194)

☐ **Consent to Act**, if applicable (NRS 645.252)

☐ **Duties Owed** (if one party is unrepresented) (NRS 645.252)

☐ **For Your Protection - Get Home Inspection** (HUD 92564-CN) For FHA Loans

In addition, for **NEW CONSTRUCTION**, to the extent applicable, Seller will provide: Public Offering Statement (NRS 116.4108); Electric Transmission Lines (NRS 119.1835); Public Services and Utilities (NRS 119.183); Initial Purchaser Disclosure (NRS 113); Construction Recovery Fund (NRS 624); Gaming Corridors (NRS 113.070); Water/Sewage (NRS 113.060); Impact Fees (NRS 278B.320); Surrounding Zoning Disclosure (NRS 113.070); FTC Insulation Disclosure (16 CFR 460.16); and Other: _____ _____ .

11. **LICENSEE DISCLOSURE OF INTEREST:** Pursuant to NAC 645.640, _____ is a licensed real estate agent in the State(s) of _____ , and has the following interest, direct or indirect, in this transaction: ☐ Principal (Seller or Buyer) -OR- ☐ family relationship or business interest: _____ .

12. **BUYER'S DUE DILIGENCE:**

A. DUE DILIGENCE PERIOD: Buyer shall have _____ calendar days from Acceptance of this offer to complete Buyer's Due Diligence. Buyer shall ensure that all inspections and certifications are initiated in a timely manner as to complete the Due Diligence in the time outlined herein. (If utilities are not supplied by the deadline referenced herein or if the Disclosures are not delivered to Buyer by the deadline referenced herein, then Buyer's Due Diligence period will be extended by the same number of calendar days that Seller delayed supplying the utilities or delivering the Disclosures, whichever is longer.) During this period Buyer shall have the exclusive right at Buyer's discretion to cancel this Agreement. In the event of such cancellation, unless otherwise agreed herein, the EMD will be refunded to Buyer. If Buyer provides Seller with notice of objections, the Due Diligence Period will be extended by the same number of calendar days that it takes Seller to respond in writing to Buyer's objections. If Buyer fails to cancel this Agreement within the Due Diligence Period (as it may be extended), Buyer will be deemed to have waived the right to cancel under this section.

B. PROPERTY INSPECTION/CONDITION: During the Due Diligence Period, Buyer shall take such action as Buyer deems necessary to determine whether the Property is satisfactory to Buyer including, but not limited to, whether the Property is insurable to Buyer's satisfaction, whether there are unsatisfactory conditions surrounding or otherwise affecting the Property (such as

Each party acknowledges that he/she has read, understood, and agrees to each and every provision of this page unless a particular paragraph is otherwise modified by addendum or counteroffer.

Buyer's Name: _____ BUYER(S) INITIALS: _____ / _____

Property Address: _____ SELLER(S) INITIALS: _____ / _____

FIGURE 17.3   Continued.

location of flood zones, airport noise, noxious fumes or odors, environmental substances or hazards, whether the Property is properly zoned, locality to freeways, railroads, places of worship, schools, etc.) or any other concerns Buyer may have related to the Property. During such Period, Buyer shall have the right to have non-destructive inspections of all structural, roofing, mechanical, electrical, plumbing, heating/air conditioning, water/well/septic, pool/spa, survey, square footage, and any other property or systems, through licensed and bonded contractors or other qualified professionals. Seller agrees to provide reasonable access to the Property to Buyer and Buyer's inspectors. Buyer agrees to indemnify and hold Seller harmless with respect to any injuries suffered by Buyer or third parties present at Buyer's request while on Seller's Property conducting such inspections, tests or walk-throughs. Buyer's indemnity shall not apply to any injuries suffered by Buyer or third parties present at Buyer's request that are the result of an intentional tort, gross negligence or any misconduct or omission by Seller, Seller's Agent or other third parties on the Property.

C.   PRELIMINARY TITLE REPORT: Within ten (10) business days of Opening of Escrow, Title Company shall provide Buyer with a Preliminary Title Report ("PTR") to review, which must be approved or rejected within five (5) business days of receipt thereof. If Buyer does not object to the PTR within the period specified above, the PTR shall be deemed accepted. If Buyer makes an objection to any item(s) contained within the PTR, Seller shall have five (5) business days after receipt of objections to correct or address the objections. If, within the time specified, Seller fails to have each such exception removed or to correct each such other matter as aforesaid, Buyer shall have the option to: (a) terminate this Agreement by providing notice to Seller and Escrow Officer, entitling Buyer to a refund of the EMD or (b) elect to accept title to the Property as is. All title exceptions approved or deemed accepted are hereafter collectively referred to as the "Permitted Exceptions."

D.   AIRPORT NOISE: Buyer hereby acknowledges the proximity of various overflight patterns, airports and helipads including, but not limited to, Nellis Air Force Base, McCarran International Airport, the North Las Vegas Airport, and/or the Henderson Executive Airport to the Property. Buyer also fully understands that existing and future noise levels at this location, associated with existing and future airport operations, may affect the livability, value, and suitability of the Property for residential use. Buyer also understands that these airports have been at their present location for many years, and that future demand and airport operations may increase significantly. For further information, contact the Clark County Department of Aviation and/or the Federal Aviation Administration.

E.   CANCELLATION DUE TO INSPECTION REPORT: If Buyer cancels this Agreement due to a specific inspection report, Buyer shall provide Seller at the time of cancellation with a copy of the report containing the name, address, and telephone number of the inspector.

F.   EXPENSES IN THE EVENT OF CANCELLATION: In the event this Agreement is canceled under any provision as set forth herein, neither Buyer nor Seller will be reimbursed for any expenses incurred in conjunction with due diligence, inspections, appraisals or any other matters pertaining to this transaction (unless otherwise provided herein).

G.   FEDERAL FAIR HOUSING COMPLIANCE AND DISCLOSURES: Buyer is advised to consult with appropriate professionals regarding neighborhood or Property conditions, including but not limited to: schools; proximity and adequacy of law enforcement; proximity to commercial, industrial, or agricultural activities; crime statistics; fire protection; other governmental services; existing and proposed transportation; construction and development; noise or odor from any source; and other nuisances, hazards or circumstances. All properties are offered without regard to race, color, religion, sex, national origin, ancestry, handicap or familial status and any other current requirements of federal or state fair housing law.

13.   WALK-THROUGH INSPECTION OF PROPERTY: Buyer is entitled under this Agreement to a walk-through of the Property within _____ calendar days prior to COE to ensure the Property and all major systems, appliances, heating/cooling, plumbing and electrical systems and mechanical fixtures are as stated in Seller's Real Property Disclosure Statement, and that the Property and improvements are in the same general condition as when this Agreement was signed by Seller and Buyer. To facilitate Buyer's walk-through, Seller is responsible for keeping all necessary utilities on. If any systems cannot be checked by Buyer on walk-through due to non-access or no power/gas/water, then Buyer reserves the right to hold Seller responsible for defects which could not be detected on walk-through because of lack of such access or power/gas/water. The purpose of the walk-through is to confirm (a) the Property is being maintained (b) repairs, if any, have been completed as agreed, and (c) Seller has complied with Seller's other obligations.

Each party acknowledges that he/she has read, understood, and agrees to each and every provision of this page unless a particular paragraph is otherwise modified by addendum or counteroffer.

Buyer's Name: _____   BUYER(S) INITIALS: _____ / _____

Property Address: _____   SELLER(S) INITIALS: _____ / _____

FIGURE 17.3   Continued.

14.   **RISK OF LOSS:** Risk of loss shall be governed by NRS 113.040. This law provides generally that if all or any material part of the Property is destroyed before transfer of legal title or possession, Seller cannot enforce the Agreement and Buyer is entitled to recover any portion of the sale price paid. If legal title or possession has transferred, risk of loss shall shift to Buyer.

15.   **ASSIGNMENT OF AGREEMENT:** Unless otherwise stated herein, this Agreement is non-assignable by Buyer.

16.   **CANCELLATION OF AGREEMENT:** In the event this Agreement is properly cancelled in accordance with the terms contained herein, then Buyer will be entitled to a refund of the EMD.

17.   **DEFAULT:**

    A.   MEDIATION: Before any legal action is taken to enforce any term or condition under this Agreement, the parties agree to engage in mediation, a dispute resolution process, through GLVAR in accordance with GLVAR's rules of procedure. Not withstanding the foregoing, in the event the Buyer finds it necessary to file a claim for specific performance, this paragraph shall not apply.

    B.   IF BUYER DEFAULTS: If Buyer defaults in performance under this Agreement,   Seller shall have one of the following legal recourses against Buyer (check one only):

    ☐ As Seller's sole legal recourse, Seller may retain, as liquidated damages, the EMD. In this respect, the Parties agree that Seller's actual damages would be difficult to measure and that the EMD is in fact a reasonable estimate of the damages that Seller would suffer as a result of Buyer's default. Seller understands that any additional deposit not considered part of the EMD in Paragraph 1(B) herein will be immediately released by ESCROW HOLDER to Buyer.

-OR-

    ☐ Seller shall have the right to recover from Buyer all of Seller's actual damages that Seller may suffer as a result of Buyer's default including, but not limited to, commissions due, expenses incurred until the Property is sold to a third party and the difference in the sales price.

    C.   IF SELLER DEFAULTS: If Seller defaults in performance under this Agreement, Buyer reserves all legal and/or equitable rights (such as specific performance) against Seller, and Buyer may seek to recover Buyer's actual damages incurred by Buyer due to Seller's default.

Instructions to Escrow

18.   **ESCROW:** If this Agreement or any matter relating hereto shall become the subject of any litigation or controversy, Buyer and Seller agree, jointly and severally, to hold Escrow Holder free and harmless from any loss or expense, except losses or expenses as may arise from Escrow Holder's negligence or willful misconduct. If conflicting demands are made or notices served upon Escrow Holder with respect to this Agreement, the parties expressly agree that Escrow is entitled to file a suit in interpleader and obtain an order from the Court authorizing Escrow Holder to deposit all such documents and monies with the Court, and obtain an order from the court requiring the parties to interplead and litigate their several claims and rights among themselves. Upon the entry of an order authorizing such Interpleader, Escrow Holder shall be fully released and discharged from any obligations imposed upon it by this Agreement; and Escrow Holder shall not be liable for the sufficiency or correctness as to form, manner, execution or validity of any instrument deposited with it, nor as to the identity, authority or rights of any person executing such instrument, nor for failure of Buyer or Seller to comply with any of the provisions of any agreement, contract or other instrument filed with Escrow Holder or referred to herein. Escrow Holder's duties hereunder shall be limited to the safekeeping of all monies, instruments or other documents received by it as Escrow Holder, and for their disposition in accordance with the terms of this Agreement. In the event an action is instituted in connection with this escrow, in which ESCROW HOLDER is named as a party or is otherwise compelled to make an appearance, all costs, expenses, attorney fees, and judgments ESCROW HOLDER may expend or incur in said action, shall be the responsibility of the parties hereto.

Each party acknowledges that he/she has read, understood, and agrees to each and every provision of this page unless a particular paragraph is otherwise modified by addendum or counteroffer.

Buyer's Name: _____   BUYER(S) INITIALS: _____ / _____

Property Address: _____   SELLER(S) INITIALS: _____ / _____

FIGURE 17.3 Continued.

19. **UNCLAIMED FUNDS:** In the event that funds from this transaction remain in an account, held by ESCROW HOLDER, for such a period of time that they are deemed "abandoned" under the provisions of Chapter 120A of the Nevada Revised Statutes, ESCROW HOLDER is hereby authorized to impose a charge upon the dormant escrow account. Said charge shall be no less than $5.00 per month and may not exceed the highest rate of charge permitted by statute or regulation. ESCROW HOLDER is further authorized and directed to deduct the charge from the dormant escrow account for as long as the funds are held by ESCROW HOLDER.

Brokers

20. **BROKER FEES:** Buyer herein requires, and Seller agrees, as a condition of this Agreement, that Seller will pay Listing Broker and Buyer's Broker, who becomes by this clause a third-party beneficiary to this Agreement, that certain sum or percentage of the purchase price (commission), that Seller, or Seller's Broker, offered for the procurement of ready, willing and able Buyer via the Multiple Listing Service, any other advertisement or written offer. Seller understands and agrees that if Seller defaults hereunder, Buyer's Broker, as a third-party beneficiary of this Agreement, has the right to pursue all legal recourse against Seller for any commission due.

21. **WAIVER OF CLAIMS:** Buyer and Seller agree that they are not relying upon any representations made by Brokers or Broker's agent. Buyer acknowledges that at COE, the Property will be sold AS-IS, WHERE-IS without any representations or warranties, unless expressly stated herein. Buyer agrees to satisfy himself, as to the condition of the Property, prior to COE. Buyer acknowledges that any statements of acreage or square footage by Brokers are simply estimates, and Buyer agrees to make such measurements, as Buyer deems necessary, to ascertain actual acreage or square footage. Buyer waives all claims against Brokers for (a) defects in the Property; (b) inaccurate estimates of acreage or square footage; (c) environmental waste or hazards on the Property; (d) the fact that the Property may be in a flood zone; (e) the Property's proximity to freeways, airports or other nuisances; (f) the zoning of the Property; (g) tax consequences; or (h) factors related to Buyer's failure to conduct walk-throughs or inspections. Buyer assumes full responsibility for the foregoing and agrees to conduct such tests, walk-throughs, inspections and research, as Buyer deems necessary. In any event, Broker's liability is limited, under any and all circumstances, to the amount of that Broker's commission/fee received in this transaction.

Other Matters

22. **DEFINITIONS:** "**Acceptance**" means the date that both parties have consented to and received a final, binding contract by affixing their signatures to this Agreement. "**Agent**" means a licensee working under a Broker. "**Agreement**" includes this document as well as all accepted counteroffers and addenda. "**Bona Fide**" means genuine. "**Buyer**" means one or more individuals or the entity that intends to purchase the Property. "**Broker**" means the Nevada licensed real estate broker listed herein representing Seller and/or Buyer (and all real estate agents associated therewith). "**Business Day**" excludes Saturdays, Sundays, and legal holidays. "**Calendar Day**" means a calendar day from/to midnight unless otherwise specified. "**CFR**" means the Code of Federal Regulations. "**CIC**" means Common Interest Community (formerly known as "HOA" or homeowners associations). "**CIC Capital Contribution**" means a one-time non-administrative fee, cost or assessment charged by the CIC upon change of ownership. "**CIC Transfer Fees**" means the administrative service fee charged by a CIC to transfer ownership records. "**COE**" means the time of recordation of the deed in Buyer's name. "**Default**" means the failure of a Party to observe or perform any of its material obligations under this Agreement. "**Down Payment**" is the Purchase Price less loan amount(s). "**EMD**" means Buyer's earnest money deposit. "**Escrow Holder**" means the neutral party that will handle the escrow. "**FHA**" is the U.S. Federal Housing Administration. "**GLVAR**" means the Greater Las Vegas Association of REALTORS®. "**HPP**" means the Homeowner Protection Plan. "**IRC**" means the Internal Revenue Code (tax code). "**LID**" means Limited Improvement District. "**N/A**" means not applicable. "**NAC**" means Nevada Administrative Code. "**NRS**" means Nevada Revised Statues as Amended. "**Party**" or "**Parties**" means Buyer and Seller. "**PITI**" means principal, interest, taxes, and hazard insurance. "**PMI**" means private mortgage insurance. "**PST**" means Pacific Standard Time, and includes daylight savings time if in effect on the date specified. "**PTR**" means Preliminary Title Report. "**Property**" means the real property and any personal property included in the sale as provided herein. "**Receipt**" means delivery to the party or the party's agent. "**Seller**" means one or more individuals or the entity that is the owner of the Property. "**SID**" means Special Improvement District. "**Title Company**" means the company that will provide title insurance. "**USC**" is the United States Code. "**VA**" is the Veterans Administration.

Each party acknowledges that he/she has read, understood, and agrees to each and every provision of this page unless a particular paragraph is otherwise modified by addendum or counteroffer.

Buyer's Name: _____   BUYER(S) INITIALS: _____ / _____

Property Address: _____   SELLER(S) INITIALS: _____ / _____

Rev. 2007   Copyright© Greater Las Vegas Association of REALTORS®   Page 8 of 11

FIGURE 17.3 Continued.

23. **DELIVERY, FACSIMILE AND COPIES:** Delivery of all instruments or documents associated with this Agreement shall be delivered to the Agent for Seller or Buyer. This Agreement may be signed by the parties on more than one copy, which, when taken together, each signed copy shall be read as one complete form. Facsimile signatures may be accepted as original.

24. **FIXTURES AND PERSONAL PROPERTY:** The following items will be transferred, free of liens, with the sale of the Property with no real value unless stated otherwise herein. Unless an item is covered under Paragraph 5(F) of this Agreement, all items are transferred in an "AS IS" condition.

    A. All EXISTING fixtures and fittings including, but not limited to: electrical, mechanical, lighting, plumbing and heating fixtures, ceiling fan(s), fireplace insert(s), gas logs and grates, solar power system(s), built-in appliance(s), window and door screens, awnings, shutters, window coverings, attached floor covering(s), television antenna(s), satellite dish(es), private integrated telephone systems, air coolers/conditioner(s), pool/spa equipment, garage door opener(s)/remote control(s), mailbox, in-ground landscaping, trees/shrub(s), water softener(s), water purifiers, security systems/alarm(s);

    B. The following additional items: _____

_____

_____

25. **NOTICES:** Except as otherwise provided in Paragraph 8, when a Party wishes to provide notice as required in this Agreement, such notice shall be sent regular mail, personal delivery and/or by facsimile to the Agent for that Party. The notification shall be effective when postmarked, received and/or faxed. Any cancellation notice shall be contemporaneously faxed to Escrow.

26. **IRC 1031 EXCHANGE:** Seller and/or Buyer may make this transaction part of an IRC 1031 exchange. The party electing to make this transaction part of an IRC 1031 exchange will pay all additional expenses associated therewith, at no cost to the other party. The other party agrees to execute any and all documents necessary to effectuate such an exchange.

27. **MISCELLANEOUS:** Time is of the essence. No change, modification or amendment of this Agreement shall be valid or binding unless such change, modification or amendment shall be in writing and signed by each party. This Agreement will be binding upon the heirs, beneficiaries and devisees of the parties hereto. This Agreement is executed and intended to be performed in the State of Nevada, and the laws of that state shall govern its interpretation and effect. The parties agree that the county and state in which the Property is located is the appropriate forum for any action relating to this Agreement. Should any party hereto retain counsel for the purpose of initiating litigation to enforce or prevent the breach of any provision hereof, or for any other judicial remedy, then the prevailing party shall be entitled to be reimbursed by the losing party for all costs and expenses incurred thereby, including, but not limited to, reasonable attorneys fees and costs incurred by such prevailing party.

THIS IS A LEGALLY BINDING CONTRACT. All parties are advised to seek independent legal and tax advice to review the terms of this Agreement.

NO REAL ESTATE BROKER/AGENT MAY SIGN FOR A PARTY TO THIS AGREEMENT UNLESS THE BROKER OR AGENT HAS A PROPERLY EXECUTED POWER OF ATTORNEY TO DO SO.

THIS FORM HAS BEEN APPROVED BY THE GREATER LAS VEGAS ASSOCIATION OF REALTORS® (GLVAR). NO REPRESENTATION IS MADE AS TO THE LEGAL VALIDITY OR ADEQUACY OF ANY PROVISION IN ANY SPECIFIC TRANSACTION. A REAL ESTATE BROKER IS THE PERSON QUALIFIED TO ADVISE ON REAL ESTATE TRANSACTIONS. IF YOU DESIRE LEGAL OR TAX ADVICE, CONSULT AN APPROPRIATE PROFESSIONAL.

This form is available for use by the real estate industry. It is not intended to identify the user as a REALTOR®. REALTOR® is a registered collective membership mark which may be used only by members of the NATIONAL ASSOCIATION OF REALTORS® who subscribe to its Code of Ethics.

Each party acknowledges that he/she has read, understood, and agrees to each and every provision of this page unless a particular paragraph is otherwise modified by addendum or counteroffer.

Buyer's Name: _____ BUYER(S) INITIALS: _____ / _____

Property Address: _____ SELLER(S) INITIALS: _____ / _____

Rev. 2007   Copyright© Greater Las Vegas Association of REALTORS®   Page 9 of 11

FIGURE 17.3 Continued.

28. **CONFIRMATION OF REPRESENTATION: (NOTE: Both sections must be completed per NAC 645.637.)**

The Agents in this transaction are:

Buyer's Broker: _____ **Company:** _____

Agent's Name: _____ Agent's MLS Public ID#: _____

Phone: _____ Fax: _____ E-Mail: _____

Address: _____

Seller's Broker: _____ **Company:** _____

Agent's Name: _____ Agent's MLS Public ID#: _____

Phone: _____ Fax: _____ E-Mail: _____

Address: _____

29. **ADDITIONAL TERMS -AND/OR- ☐ ADDENDUM ATTACHED** _____

_____

_____

_____

_____

_____

_____

_____

_____

_____

_____

_____

_____

_____

_____

_____

_____

_____

_____

_____

Each party acknowledges that he/she has read, understood, and agrees to each and every provision of this page unless a particular paragraph is otherwise modified by addendum or counteroffer.

Buyer's Name: _____ BUYER(S) INITIALS: _____ / _____

Property Address: _____ SELLER(S) INITIALS: _____ / _____

Rev. 2007   Copyright© Greater Las Vegas Association of REALTORS®   Page 10 of 11

FIGURE 17.3 Continued.

Earnest Money Receipt

BUYER'S AGENT ACKNOWLEDGES RECEIPT FROM BUYER HEREIN of the sum of $ _____
evidenced by ☐ Cash,   ☐ Cashier's Check,   ☐ Personal Check, or ☐ Other _____
payable to _____ . Upon Acceptance, Earnest Money to be deposited within ONE (1) business
day, with ☐ Escrow Holder, ☐ Buyer's Broker's Trust Account, - **OR** - ☐ Seller's Broker's Trust Account

Date: _____ Signed: _____ Buyer's Agent.

Buyer's Offer

Upon Seller's acceptance, Buyer agrees to be bound by each provision of this Agreement, and all signed addenda, disclosures, and attachments.

_____	_____	_____	___ : ___ ☐ AM ☐ PM
Buyer's Signature	Buyer's Printed Name	Date	Time
_____	_____	_____	___ : ___ ☐ AM ☐ PM
Buyer's Signature	Buyer's Printed Name	Date	Time

Seller must respond by: _____ ☐ AM ☐ PM on (month) _____ , (day) _____ , (year) _____ .
Unless this Agreement is accepted by execution below and delivered to the Buyer's Broker before the above date and time, this offer shall lapse and be of no further force and effect. (Under NAC 645.632, Seller is required by _law_ to respond in any event.)

Seller's Response

☐ **ACCEPTANCE:** Seller(s) acknowledges that he/she accepts and agrees to be bound by each provision of this Agreement, and all signed addenda, disclosures, and attachments.
☐ **COUNTER OFFER:** Seller accepts the terms of this Agreement subject to the attached Counter Offer #1.
☐ **REJECTION:** In accordance with NAC 645.632, Seller hereby informs Buyer the offer presented herein **is not** accepted.

_____	_____	_____	___ : ___ ☐ AM ☐ PM
Seller's Signature	Seller's Printed Name	Date	Time
_____	_____	_____	___ : ___ ☐ AM ☐ PM
Seller's Signature	Seller's Printed Name	Date	Time

Each party acknowledges that he/she has read, understood, and agrees to each and every provision of this page unless a particular paragraph is otherwise modified by addendum or counteroffer.

Buyer's Name: _____   BUYER(S) INITIALS: _____ / _____

Property Address: _____   SELLER(S) INITIALS: _____ / _____

Rev. 2007   Copyright© Greater Las Vegas Association of REALTORS®   Page 11 of 11

licensee proceeds to complete the purchase agreement, which constitutes the offer by the potential purchaser.

2. The negotiation process between buyer and seller continues until there is a meeting of the minds.

3. All offers to purchase are presented to the seller by the salesperson or broker, regardless of merit. The agent does not have the authority to accept, reject, or modify an offer. The agent acts in the best interest of his principal but cannot bind the principal. The agent's main responsibility is to procure a ready, willing, and able buyer. **Ready, willing, and able** refers to purchasers who have made up their minds to buy a given parcel of property and are financially able to do so according to the price and terms agreed upon with the seller.

4. The seller decides to accept or reject the offer or make a counteroffer. If the seller makes a counteroffer, the original offer is terminated and the seller becomes the offeror.

5. This process continues with offers and counteroffers until both parties agree and a meeting of the minds is achieved. Remember, there is no contract until mutual assent and the notification of both parties.

6. Both parties must initial any changes on the original contract or counteroffer. If there are many changes, it may be best to rewrite the whole contract before the offer is accepted and the contract is placed in escrow. This practice would remove any chance for misunderstanding between the offeror and the offeree.

7. A copy of the signed sales contract is given to the buyer at the time the offer is made. If the seller accepts, she signs the contract, and a copy of the contract is left with the seller.

8. The licensee then officially notifies the buyer of the acceptance by delivering a signed copy to the buyer. If there are counteroffers, a copy is left with each party at each step of the negotiation. In addition to these copies, the original must be kept in the broker's files for a period of five years from the close of the transaction or last activity. Rejected offers must also be kept for a period of five years from the last activity.

If other copies are needed for the lender or escrow, they may be copied from the broker's original copy.

CHAPTER SUMMARY

A contract is a legally enforceable agreement between competent parties who agree to perform or refrain from performing certain acts for a consideration. Contracts may be classified as express, implied, bilateral, unilateral, executory, or executed.

For a contract to be considered valid and enforceable, certain requirements must be fulfilled. These are capacity; offer, acceptance, and notification; valid consideration; and lawful purpose. A real estate sales contract also requires an accurate legal description, must be written, and must be signed by all parties. A person who has limited capacity (insane, minor, under influence of drugs or alcohol, or under duress) may void a contract. An offer is the extension of a proposal to enter into an agreement. Mutual assent signifies the stage of acceptance. Notification of acceptance is critical and requires the same type of communication as the offer. An offeror may rescind her offer at any time verbally until the agent has notified her of acceptance. Consideration, the inducement to contract, is something of value, such as money, property, personal services, or the promise to perform a specific action; consideration makes a contract enforceable. Also, to be enforceable a contract must be for a lawful purpose.

In addition, a valid real estate purchase contract must have an accurate legal description. A legal description is considered adequate if a surveyor can use it to positively identify the parcel of land. According to the statute of frauds, all contracts related to real property (with the exception of leases for one year or less) must be in writing. The parol evidence rule says that a document must stand on the written word.

Contracts may be valid, void, voidable, and either enforceable or unenforceable. A valid contract contains all of the essential elements and is legal, enforceable, and binding on all parties. If a contract is void, one or more of the essential elements is missing, and it is therefore unenforceable. If a contract is voidable, it seems valid and enforceable on the surface, but it may be voided by one of the parties. An unenforceable contract appears valid on the surface, but for some reason cannot be enforced. An enforceable contract is a valid contract with all of the essential elements present. When performance has been completed, the contract is discharged. If one party has not performed, the contract has been breached, unless the parties agree not to take action. The most common discharge of contracts is when the contract is fulfilled by complete performance of the parties to the contract. Contracts frequently include a "time is of the essence" clause, which means that the parties will perform within the limits specified. Any party not doing so is considered in breach of contract. A contract may also be discharged, unless the contract states otherwise, by assigning the rights, duties, and benefits of the contract to a third party without terminating the contract. Even though the assignee takes over all rights, the assignor is still liable as contracted for the performance of the original contract if the assignee does not perform. Under novation, a new party is substituted for an existing one with the responsibilities under the old contract completely erased. Accord and satisfaction occurs when the parties voluntarily agree to complete the contract, even though all of the terms and conditions have not been met.

The doctrine of part performance allows the enforcement of an oral contract covered by the statute of frauds. A contract may be considered complete and discharged when a party performs most of the required task. This is called substantial performance. A contract may also be discharged if one or more of the parties are unable to perform, or if operation of the law makes the contract unenforceable.

Breach of contract occurs when either party defaults on the contract. Rescission, damages, or suit for specific performance are actions that may result from a breach of contract. Rescission is a legal remedy of canceling, terminating, or annulling a contract and restoring the parties to their original positions. The party that did not breach the contract can seek damages. Damages are classified as liquidated, actual, and punitive. A suit for specific performance is a judicial action to force a party to carry out the terms of the contract. Statutory law allows a specific time limit during which parties to a contract may file their legal action to enforce their rights. Parties to a contract who do not take steps to enforce their rights within the time limits could lose the rights to do so.

Typically, negotiating and completing a real estate purchase includes the following steps:

- A prospective purchaser indicates an interest in a particular property.
- The licensee completes the sales contract, which constitutes the offer.
- All offers to purchase are presented to the seller by the salesperson or broker.
- The seller decides to accept or reject the offer, or make a counteroffer.
- If mutual assent is achieved, the seller signs the contract, and a copy of the contract is left with the seller.
- The licensee notifies the buyer of the acceptance by delivering a signed copy to the buyer.

CHECKING YOUR COMPREHENSION

1. Define a contract and explain the following types of contracts:
   - Express and implied contracts
   - Bilateral and unilateral contracts
   - Executory and executed contracts

2. Regarding valid contracts, list and describe each of the following:
   - C
   - O
   - V
   - L
   - A
   - W
   - S

3. Summarize the meanings of the following terms:
   - Completed contract
   - Assignment
   - Novation
   - Part performance

4. Define breach of contract, rescission, actual and punitive damages, and specific performance.

5. Summarize the role and the responsibilities of the real estate agent in negotiating the sale of real estate.

REVIEWING YOUR UNDERSTANDING

1. Lou sells a property to Bud under an oral agreement for $100,000. Bud pays Lou $50,000 and agrees to pay $25,000 each year for two years. Bud makes substantial improvements in the property and makes the first $25,000 payment on time. One month before the final $25,000 payment is due, Lou declares the contract to be void. In this case, which of the following statements is correct?

   a. the contract can be overturned as long as it is done before the last payment is made

   b. the contract can be overturned because it was oral and the agreement is within the statute of frauds

   c. the contract cannot be overturned because the statute of limitations has expired

   d. the contract cannot be overturned due to the doctrine of part performance

2. A property is purchased based on fraudulent statements by the listing broker. The purchase contract, which has not closed escrow, is MOST likely:

   a. void

   b. valid

   c. voidable

   d. illegal

3. Consideration in contract requires:

   a. an earnest money deposit

   b. an exchange of a promise for a promise

   c. an earnest money deposit in escrow and a signed deed in escrow by the seller

   d. full payment of the purchase price

4. A legal procedure brought about by one party to a contract to enforce the terms of the contract is called:

   a. lis pendens

   b. specific performance

   c. punitive damages

   d. exemplary damages

5. The "time is of the essence" clause in a contract means that the contract:

   a. must be presented within 24 hours

   b. must be completed within 30 days

   c. must be accepted within the time stated

   d. should be completed as soon as possible

6. *Voidable* could BEST be described as:

   a. valid unless voided

   b. completely unenforceable

   c. not valid

   d. illegal

7. A valid contract could be unenforceable because of:

   a. lack of contractual capacity

   b. the statute of limitations

   c. the absence of consideration

   d. an illegal purpose

8. Oral testimony can be accepted as evidence for each of the following examples, EXCEPT:

   a. explaining the contract means other than stated

   b. clarifying an ambiguity

   c. showing fraud induced the contract

   d. showing a modified written agreement

9. The person who signs to show acceptance of the sales contract is the:

   a. offeror

   b. offeree

   c. grantor

   d. grantee

10. If, upon receiving an offer to purchase under certain terms and conditions, the seller makes a conditional acceptance, the offeror is:
    a. bound by the original offer
    b. bound to accept the counteroffer
    c. relieved from the original offer at the seller's option
    d. relieved from the original offer unconditionally

11. Assuming that no written provision addresses the death of either party, a purchase contract where the seller dies after the contract is formed, but before settlement:
    a. is void
    b. is binding on the heirs of the seller
    c. is unenforceable by the seller's heirs
    d. is voidable by the buyer

12. "R" submits a purchase agreement to "T," who accepts it and makes minor changes. Then "R" dies. What is the status of the contract?
    a. valid subject to approval of heirs
    b. binding to the heirs
    c. void because the changes were not initialed by the purchaser
    d. unenforceable because a new contract should have been written

13. A new contract is substituted for an existing one and the parties are relieved of responsibility. This is an example of:
    a. executed contract
    b. rescission
    c. assignment
    d. novation

14. An exclusive right to sell listing is an:
    a. executory implied contract
    b. executory bilateral contract
    c. executed bilateral contract
    d. executed implied contract

15. Maria and Don agree that Maria will purchase Don's house for $125,000 cash on June 30. Their agreement has the following characteristics:
    a. unilateral, express, executory
    b. bilateral, express, executory
    c. bilateral, express, executed
    d. unilateral, implied, executed

16. A unilateral contract is enforceable against:
    a. the optionee
    b. the optionor
    c. no one
    d. both the optionee and the optionor

17. Duress applied to a party to a contract makes the agreement:
    a. unilateral
    b. void
    c. voidable
    d. illegal

18. Damages for a breach of contract in excess of the actual loss suffered would be:
    a. liquidated damages
    b. punitive damages
    c. compensatory damages
    d. specific performance

19. Failure to meet the requirement set forth in a contract is a:
    a. waiver
    b. breach
    c. novation
    d. reformation

20. A buyer withdraws her full-price offer prior to acceptance. The earnest money deposit would:
    a. belong to the seller
    b. be split between buyer and seller
    c. be returned to buyer less expenses
    d. be returned in full to buyer

Chapter

18

IMPORTANT TERMS AND CONCEPTS

closing costs

credit

debit

debit and credit
statement

HUD-1 statement

proration

Real Estate Settlement
Procedures Act
(RESPA)

CHAPTER OBJECTIVES

After completing this chapter, you should be able to:

- List and describe buyer's and seller's closing costs.
- Explain the requirements of the Real Estate Settlement Procedures Act (RESPA).
- Calculate settlement prorations.
- Summarize a HUD-1 statement form and complete a debit/credit closing statement problem.

Closing the Transaction

18.1 CLOSING COSTS

Closing costs are the expenses paid by the buyer and seller to complete the transaction. A licensee should prepare an estimate of the closing costs to be paid by the buyer before presentation of an offer, and the estimated amount to be paid by the seller should be determined prior to the presentation of the offer to the seller. Except for certain costs related to government-backed financing, there is no law or regulation stating who should pay the closing costs. Who will pay is a product of the transaction negotiations and should be clearly documented in the purchase contract.

A description of the typical closing costs follows, separated into buyer costs and seller costs, based on the custom for payment responsibility.

Buyer's Closing Costs

The following are closing costs customarily paid by the buyer:

- A *loan origination fee* is charged by the mortgage company to originate a new loan. The fee, often 1% of the loan amount but sometimes waived by the lender, is almost always paid by the buyer.

- *Discount points* are a percentage of the loan amount and are paid by borrowers to buy down the interest rate. The amount of discount charged depends on the availability of mortgage money and the prevailing interest rate.

- An *appraisal fee* is charged for the appraiser's estimate of the fair market value of the property. The appraisal is generally required when the buyer is obtaining new financing.

- A *credit report fee* is charged by a credit bureau to meet the requirements by the lender to obtain the financial background of the buyer.

- A *tax service fee* is charged to order billings that will be mailed to the mortgage company. It also ensures that the mortgage company will be advised of any new assessments and delinquent taxes. This is a one-time charge.

- *Escrow fees* are charged by the escrow agent for handling the escrow. The fee is often split equally between the buyer and the seller.

- *Recording fees* applicable to the buyer are charged by the county recorder's office for recording the documents.

- A *lender's policy* is usually purchased by the buyer to insure the lender that, among other things, the lender's encumbrance is the first lien on the property.

- A *hazard insurance* premium for dwelling insurance coverage against fire, storm, and other risks is paid by the buyer.

- *Tax and insurance reserves* are required when the purchase is financed with a budget mortgage. A *budget mortgage* requires that part of the monthly payment includes additions to the impound account for taxes and insurance. At closing, the lender often requires the buyer to prepay a portion of the required reserve. RESPA (discussed later in this chapter) limits the amount of funds a lender can require the borrower to put into the impound account.

- *Adjusted interest* is prepaid interest collected on new loans from the date of funding to 30 days prior to the due date of the first regular mortgage payment. This allows lenders to conform to their regular amortization schedule.

Seller's Closing Costs

These closing costs are customarily paid by the seller:

- A *real estate brokerage commission* is the fee paid for the employment of the real estate broker for marketing the seller's property. The seller normally pays the brokerage commission, but in the case of a buyer–broker agreement, the buyer could pay a portion or all of the commission.

- A *prepayment penalty* is a fee paid to a lender that is imposed when the existing loan is paid before it is due. Certain loans backed by the federal government do not allow prepayment penalties.

- *Escrow fees* are charged by the escrow agent for handling the escrow. The fees are often split equally between the buyer and the seller.

- *Recording fees* applicable to the seller are charged by the County Recorder's office for recording the documents. An *owner's title policy* premium is charged by the title insurance company to insure the buyer of marketable title up to the date the conveying instrument is recorded. The seller customarily pays the premium for the title insurance.

- A *special assessment payoff* for any sewer, paving, or other improvement district assessment on the property is generally required when the buyer is obtaining a new loan to finance the purchase.

- *Termite inspection* is the examination of the structure for termites or wood-destroying insects. The lender usually requires the inspection, and the seller usually pays the fee.

- *Property tax proration* is a cost charged to the seller, unless the seller paid the current year's property tax in advance. See the section on prorations later in this chapter.

- *Adjusted interest* on loan assumptions requires a proration of the interest for the period that the seller owned the property. Because interest is paid in arrears, the daily interest from the date of the seller's last payment to the date of close must be charged to the seller and credited to the buyer.

- *Real estate transfer tax* is collected by the County Recorder any time an interest in real property is transferred, with some exceptions such as between husband and wife. The tax is based on the sales price of the property, and the tax rate varies from county to county. The real estate transfer tax is customarily paid by the seller; however, depending on the negotiations between the buyer and seller, the tax can be paid by the buyer or split between the buyer and seller.

18.2 REAL ESTATE SETTLEMENT PROCEDURES ACT

Each year, Americans spend nearly $55 billion on loan closing costs, which they sometimes do not fully understand. While the mortgage lending industry has experienced dramatic changes in the past three decades, the disclosure rules regarding closing costs have remained the same.

History of the Real Estate Settlement Procedures Act (RESPA)

The **Real Estate Settlement Procedures Act (RESPA)** was enacted by Congress in 1974 to ensure that borrowers were provided with more abundant and timelier information on the nature and costs of the settlement process, as well as were protected against unnecessarily high settlement costs.

RESPA's requirements apply to loan transactions involving "settlement services" for "federally related mortgage loans." Under the statute, the term *settlement services* includes any service provided in connection with a real estate settlement. *Federally related mortgage loans* is very broadly defined to encompass virtually all purchase money and refinance mortgages. RESPA is administered by the Department of Housing and Urban Development (HUD).

Compliance

Loans that are covered by RESPA must comply with the following:

- The lender must supply the mortgagor with a special booklet, written by HUD, titled *Settlement Costs and You*.

- A good faith estimate of settlement costs must be supplied to the mortgagor at the time of application for the loan or within three business days.

- The lender must use a uniform settlement statement developed by HUD, known as a *HUD-1 statement*.

- No one may charge any fee to the borrower or anyone else for preparation of settlement documents or any disclosures required by the Truth in Lending Act.

- No one may offer and no one may accept any form of fee, kickback, or thing of value for the referral of any real estate settlement service.

- No seller of property may require a buyer to purchase title insurance covering the property from any particular title company as a condition of the sale.
- Undisclosed affiliations are prohibited (that is, between the broker and the mortgage company and/or the escrow company).
- The lender is limited in the amount it can require the borrower to put into the impound account.

Impending Updates

As of 2009, HUD has made a commitment to propose changes to the RESPA regulations that will update, simplify, and improve the disclosure requirements for mortgage settlement costs and help control these costs for consumers. HUD is currently in the process of gathering information and differing views from industry and consumer organizations, as well as other interested parties. Key issues being discussed include changes to the Good Faith Estimate form, disclosure of the compensation to the loan originator, mortgage packages that include interest rate guarantees, and fixed settlement cost prices.

18.3 PRORATION

Proration means allocating taxes, insurance, rents, and interest at settlement to determine the amount of money to be charged or credited to the buyer or seller. In Nevada, the day of closing belongs to the buyer. In other words, beginning on the day of closing, the buyer is charged for interest, taxes, and insurance, and the buyer will receive any rent income generated by the property from that day forward.

Calculating Proration Amounts

There are four steps in the computation of the prorated amount:

1. Compute the cost per day.
2. Calculate the actual number of days to be prorated.
3. Multiply the number of days by the cost per day.
4. Determine whether the amount should be a debit or a credit to the buyer and seller.

When calculating the cost per day and the actual days to be prorated, remember the following:

- Use 360 days for a year.
- Use 30 days for a month (except when prorating rents, in which case you must use the actual number of days in that month).
- The day of closing belongs to the buyer.

If an item is paid by the buyer after the settlement date, there is a charge against the seller for the prorated portion of the total amount paid that represents the expense for the period from the last payment to the day before closing. The same prorated amount is a credit to the buyer, who will pay the total amount due after the settlement date.

If the item was paid before the settlement date and the buyer will benefit from a portion of the payment made, there is a charge against the buyer for the prorated portion of the total amount paid that represents the expense for the period from the date of closing to the end of the prepayment. The same prorated amount is a credit to the seller.

Proration Guidelines

Use the following guidelines for calculating daily amounts for insurance, rent, taxes, or interest:

1. *Taxes and interest*—Divide the annual amount by 360 to find the cost per day.
2. *Insurance*—If a three-year policy, divide by 36 to find the monthly amount. Divide the monthly amount by 30 to find the daily amount.
3. *Rents*—Divide the monthly rent by the actual number of days in the month.

Insurance

Insurance is prorated only when the buyer is assuming the coverage. Insurance is paid in advance and sometimes for one, three, or five years. The premium per day is usually calculated on a 360-day year. To prorate a three- or five-year policy, calculate the yearly, monthly, and daily rate and carry out to three places.

$$\$525 \div 3 \text{ (years)} = \$175.00$$

$$\$175 \div 12 \text{ (months)} = \$14.583$$

$$\$14.583 \div 30 \text{ (days)} = \$0.486$$

or

$$\$525 \div 1080 \text{ (3years)} = \$0.486 \text{ per day}$$

Mortgage Interest

Mortgage interest is usually paid in arrears, so at settlement the seller will be charged with the amount due. If the transaction involves a loan assumption, the buyer will receive a credit for the interest to apply against the next loan payment due.

> **EXAMPLE**—A buyer purchased a home on May 8, 2008, and assumed a loan balance of $67,350 with a 10.5% interest paid to April 1, 2008. What was the buyer's credit at closing?

1. $67,350 × 10.5% = $7071.75 annual interest
   $7071.75 ÷ 360 = $19.644 per day

Now find the exact number of days for settlement:

2. 30 days = April
   + 7 days = May
   37 days × $19.644 = $726.83 charged to the seller at settlement

In this example, 30 days' interest would be paid to the lender, and seven days would be credited to the buyer to apply to the June 1 payment.

Proration Problems

1. A property has been sold for $75,000. The existing $60,000 fire insurance policy is dated May 13, 2006. The three-year premium was $388.00. What is the amount charged to the buyer if settlement is on April 10, 2008?

   • Multiply 3 × 360 (the days in a prorated year) to find the number of days in three years. Divide this into a three-year premium to get daily insurance cost. Calculate the remaining days on the policy by using a 30-day month (including the day of proration). Multiply rate times the number of unused days.

2. The taxes on a property for the year are $645.00. If the sale closed escrow on September 15, 2008, what would the seller's charge be if the taxes were paid to June 30, 2007?

   • Divide the amount of taxes by 360 to find the daily taxes. Determine the number of months and days the seller had possession and multiply by the daily rate.

3. A property is sold and settlement is scheduled for June 3. The buyer is assuming a loan balance of $24,569.20 with 9% interest per annum paid in arrears. The monthly principal and interest payment is $265.42. If the June 1 payment has been made, what would the seller's interest proration be?

   • Multiply the loan balance by the interest rate to compute the annual interest. Then, divide the annual interest by 360 days to get the daily interest expense and multiply that by 2 days to get the seller's interest proration. The monthly principal and interest (P&I) payment is not used in the calculation.

18.4 CLOSING STATEMENTS

A closing statement is a document that accounts for the funds involved in a particular real estate transaction. The closing statement is generally prepared by the escrow agent and must contain:

• The date of closing

• The name of seller and buyer

• The location of the property

• The name of the person who prepared the statement

Each party receives a copy of the closing statement. The broker must retain a copy in the brokerage files.

HUD-1 Statement Form

The closing statement records the distribution of monies involved in the transaction. There are several formats for closing statements, but most residential closings use a **HUD-1 statement** form because the Real Estate Settlement Procedures Act requires that format. A sample HUD-1 statement is included as Figure 18.1. A **debit and credit statement** is a type of settlement statement used for commercial transaction settlements and residential settlements not covered by RESPA.

FIGURE 18.1   Sample HUD-1 Statement Form

A. **Settlement Statement**	U.S. Department of Housing and Urban Development	OMB Approval No. 2502-0265

B. Type of Loan

1. ☐ FHA 2. ☐ FmHA 3. ☐ Conv. Unins. 4. ☐ VA 5. ☐ Conv. Ins.	6. File Number:	7. Loan Number:	8. Mortgage Insurance Case Number:

C. Note: This form is furnished to give you a statement of actual settlement costs. Amounts paid to and by the settlement agent are shown. Items marked "(p.o.c.)" were paid outside the closing; they are shown here for informational purposes and are not included in the totals.

D. Name & Address of Borrower:	E. Name & Address of Seller:	F. Name & Address of Lender:

| G. Property Location: | H. Settlement Agent: | |
| | Place of Settlement: | I. Settlement Date: |

J. Summary of Borrower's Transaction		**K. Summary of Seller's Transaction**	
100. Gross Amount Due From Borrower		**400. Gross Amount Due To Seller**	
101. Contract sales price		401. Contract sales price	
102. Personal property		402. Personal property	
103. Settlement charges to borrower (line 1400)		403.	
104.		404.	
105.		405.	
Adjustments for items paid by seller in advance		**Adjustments for items paid by seller in advance**	
106. City/town taxes to		406. City/town taxes to	
107. County taxes to		407. County taxes to	
108. Assessments to		408. Assessments to	
109.		409.	
110.		410.	
111.		411.	
112.		412.	
120. Gross Amount Due From Borrower		**420. Gross Amount Due To Seller**	
200. Amounts Paid By Or In Behalf Of Borrower		**500. Reductions In Amount Due To Seller**	
201. Deposit or earnest money		501. Excess deposit (see instructions)	
202. Principal amount of new loan(s)		502. Settlement charges to seller (line 1400)	
203. Existing loan(s) taken subject to		503. Existing loan(s) taken subject to	
204.		504. Payoff of first mortgage loan	
205.		505. Payoff of second mortgage loan	
206.		506.	
207.		507.	
208.		508.	
209.		509.	
Adjustments for items unpaid by seller		**Adjustments for items unpaid by seller**	
210. City/town taxes to		510. City/town taxes to	
211. County taxes to		511. County taxes to	
212. Assessments to		512. Assessments to	
213.		513.	
214.		514.	
215.		515.	
216.		516.	
217.		517.	
218.		518.	
219.		519.	
220. Total Paid By/For Borrower		**520. Total Reduction Amount Due Seller**	
300. Cash At Settlement From/To Borrower		**600. Cash At Settlement To/From Seller**	
301. Gross Amount due from borrower (line 120)		601. Gross amount due to seller (line 420)	
302. Less amounts paid by/for borrower (line 220)	( )	602. Less reductions in amt. due seller (line 520)	( )
303. Cash ☐ From ☐ To Borrower		**603. Cash ☐ To ☐ From Seller**	

Section 5 of the Real Estate Settlement Procedures Act (RESPA) requires the following: • HUD must develop a Special Information Booklet to help persons borrowing money to finance the purchase of residential real estate to better understand the nature and costs of real estate settlement services; • Each lender must provide the booklet to all applicants from whom it receives or for whom it prepares a written application to borrow money to finance the purchase of residential real estate; • Lenders must prepare and distribute with the Booklet a Good Faith Estimate of the settlement costs that the borrower is likely to incur in connection with the settlement. These disclosures are mandatory.

Section 4(a) of RESPA mandates that HUD develop and prescribe this standard form to be used at the time of loan settlement to provide full disclosure of all charges imposed upon the borrower and seller. These are third party disclosures that are designed to provide the borrower with pertinent information during the settlement process in order to be a better shopper.

The Public Reporting Burden for this collection of information is estimated to average one hour per response, including the time for reviewing instructions, searching existing data sources, gathering and maintaining the data needed, and completing and reviewing the collection of information.

This agency may not collect this information, and you are not required to complete this form, unless it displays a currently valid OMB control number.

The information requested does not lend itself to confidentiality.

FIGURE 18.1   Continued.

L. Settlement Charges			Paid From Borrower's Funds at Settlement	Paid From Seller's Funds at Settlement
700. Total Sales/Broker's Commission based on price $		@ % =		
Division of Commission (line 700) as follows:				
701. $	to			
702. $	to			
703. Commission paid at Settlement				
704.				
800. Items Payable In Connection With Loan				
801. Loan Origination Fee	%			
802. Loan Discount	%			
803. Appraisal Fee	to			
804. Credit Report	to			
805. Lender's Inspection Fee				
806. Mortgage Insurance Application Fee to				
807. Assumption Fee				
808.				
809.				
810.				
811.				
900. Items Required By Lender To Be Paid In Advance				
901. Interest from to	@$	/day		
902. Mortgage Insurance Premium for		months to		
903. Hazard Insurance Premium for		years to		
904.		years to		
905.				
1000. Reserves Deposited With Lender				
1001. Hazard insurance	months@$	per month		
1002. Mortgage insurance	months@$	per month		
1003. City property taxes	months@$	per month		
1004. County property taxes	months@$	per month		
1005. Annual assessments	months@$	per month		
1006.	months@$	per month		
1007.	months@$	per month		
1008.	months@$	per month		
1100. Title Charges				
1101. Settlement or closing fee	to			
1102. Abstract or title search	to			
1103. Title examination	to			
1104. Title insurance binder	to			
1105. Document preparation	to			
1106. Notary fees	to			
1107. Attorney's fees	to			
(includes above items numbers:		)		
1108. Title insurance	to			
(includes above items numbers:		)		
1109. Lender's coverage	$			
1110. Owner's coverage	$			
1111.				
1112.				
1113.				
1200. Government Recording and Transfer Charges				
1201. Recording fees: Deed $	; Mortgage $	; Releases $		
1202. City/county tax/stamps: Deed $	; Mortgage $			
1203. State tax/stamps: Deed $	; Mortgage $			
1204.				
1205.				
1300. Additional Settlement Charges				
1301. Survey to				
1302. Pest inspection to				
1303.				
1304.				
1305.				
1400. Total Settlement Charges (enter on lines 103, Section J and 502, Section K)				

form **HUD-1** (3/86)
ref Handbook 4305.2

Preparing Closing Statements

The first step in preparing closing statements is to list all items related to the transaction. The items can involve the following:

* Both buyer and seller
* The buyer only
* The seller only

Items that affect both the buyer and seller will appear in both statements.

Credit or Debit

The determination of whether an entry is a debit or credit requires an understanding of those terms as used in a closing statement. **Debit** means that the item will be paid for by the person in whose statement that item appears. A debit is an expense of that party. **Credit** means that the money is received by the person in whose statement it appears. A credit is also given for monies paid against an expense obligation in the transaction.

Table 18.1 outlines some examples of debit and credit entries.

TABLE 18.1   Who Pays for What: Examples of Closing Statement Debit and Credit Entries

Normally Debited to Buyer	Normally Credited to Buyer
Purchase price	Earnest money deposit
Hazard insurance assumption	New loan amounts
Impound account set up at transfer	Prorated property taxes
New loan fees	Prorated interest
Mortgage insurance	
Prepaid interest	
Buyer's share of loan discount	
One half of escrow fees	
Recording fees for deed and trust deed	
Lender's title insurance policy	

Normally Debited to Seller	Normally Credited to Seller
Existing loan amounts	Sales price
Termite inspection	Prorated insurance premium
Title insurance, owner's policy	Impound account
One half of escrow fees	
Brokerage fees	
Seller's share of loan discount	
Affidavit of value fees	

CHAPTER SUMMARY

Closing costs are the expenses paid by the buyer and seller to complete the transaction. A licensee should prepare an estimate of the closing costs to be paid by the buyer before presentation of an offer, and the estimated amount to be paid by the seller should be determined prior to the presentation of the offer to the seller. Closing costs customarily paid by the buyer include a loan origination fee, discount points, an appraisal fee, a credit report fee, a tax service fee, escrow fees, recording fees, a lender's policy, a hazard insurance premium, tax and insurance reserves, and adjusted interest. Closing costs customarily paid by the seller include a real estate brokerage commission, a prepayment penalty, escrow fees, recording fees, an owner's title policy premium, a special assessment payoff, termite inspection, property tax proration, adjusted interest, and real estate transfer tax.

The Real Estate Settlement Procedures Act (RESPA) ensures that borrowers are provided with timely information on the nature and costs of the settlement process, as well as protected against unnecessarily high settlement costs. RESPA's requirements apply to loan transactions involving "settlement services" for "federally related mortgage loans." HUD is currently considering changes to the RESPA regulations that will update, simplify, and improve the disclosure requirements for mortgage settlement costs. Loans that are covered by RESPA must comply with the following (partial list—see the body of this chapter for a full list):

- The lender must supply the mortgagor with a special booklet, written by HUD, titled *Settlement Costs and You*.
- A good faith estimate of settlement costs must be supplied to the mortgagor.
- No one may charge any fee to the borrower for preparation of settlement documents.

Proration means allocating taxes, insurance, rents, and interest at settlement to determine the amount of money to be charged or credited to the buyer or seller. In Nevada, the day of closing belongs to the buyer. Four steps are used in computing the prorated amount: (1) Compute the cost per day. (2) Calculate actual number of days to be prorated. (3) Multiply the number of days by the cost per day. (4) Determine whether the amount should be a debit or a credit to the buyer and seller. Insurance is prorated only when the buyer is assuming the coverage. Mortgage interest is usually paid in arrears, so that at settlement the seller will be charged with the prorated amount due.

A closing statement is a document that accounts for the funds involved in a particular real estate transaction. Each party receives a copy of the closing statement. The broker must retain a copy in the brokerage files. There are several formats for closing statements, but most residential closings use a HUD-1 statement form because the Real Estate Settlement Procedures Act requires that format. A debit and credit statement is a type of settlement statement used for commercial transaction settlements and residential settlements not covered by RESPA.

The first step in preparing statements is to list all items related to the transaction. The items can involve both buyer and seller, the buyer only, or the seller only. Items that affect both the buyer and seller will appear in both statements. As used in a closing statement, debit means that the item will be paid for by the person in whose statement that item appears. A debit is an expense of that party. Credit means that the money is received by the person in whose statement it appears. A credit is also given for monies paid against an expense obligation in the transaction.

CHECKING YOUR COMPREHENSION

1. List and describe closing costs customarily paid by the buyer.

2. List and describe closing costs customarily paid by the seller.

3. Summarize the RESPA compliance requirements.

4. Explain the purpose of a proration in a closing statement.

5. List and explain the sections of a HUD-1 statement.

Escrow Settlement Exercise

James is buying a house from Nancy. Details of the purchase follow:

- Sales price: $256,000
- The sale was handled by XYZ Realty Co., under an exclusive right to sell listing agreement with Nancy, for a commission of 6%.
- James will provide a new mortgage at 80% of the purchase price.
- Nancy will carryback a note and second mortgage in the amount of $25,000.
- Earnest money of $5000 will be deposited to open escrow.
- The sale will close on August 6.
- Property taxes for the current year are $2200 and have been paid through June 30.
- A new hazard insurance policy will cost $380.
- The owner's title insurance policy will be $900.
- An ALTA policy for the new lender is $500.
- Nancy has an existing first mortgage with a payoff due of $66,785.
- Escrow fees will be $450.
- Recording fees will be $85 (Deed: $15, Mortgage: $35, Release $35).

Use the following settlement sheet to allocate the appropriate debits and credits between the buyer and seller. How much cash will James need to close the purchase?

SETTLEMENT CHARGES/CREDITS	BUYER		SELLER	
	Debit	Credit	Debit	Credit
Contract Sales Prices				
Broker's Commission				
Property Taxes:				
Pro Rata				
Title Insurance:				
Lender's Coverage				
Owner's Coverage				
Recording Fees:				
Deed: Mortgage: Release:				
Escrow Fees:				
Earnest Money Deposit				
Principal Amount—New Mortgage				
Principal Amount of Existing Loan Assumed				
Cash Due To/From Buyer/Seller				
Totals				

REVIEWING YOUR UNDERSTANDING

1. A buyer is to assume a seller's existing loan with an outstanding balance of $120,000 as of the date of closing. The interest rate is 9% and payments are made in arrears with the last payment made on October 1. Closing is set for October 11. What will be the entry in the seller's closing statement?
   a. $900 debit
   b. $900 credit
   c. $300 credit
   d. $300 debit

2. On December 6 an escrow closed. The annual taxes of $861 for the current year were paid in full on July 1. If these payments are prorated, what amount will be returned to the seller?
   a. $373
   b. $418
   c. $490
   d. $508

3. A transaction involving a commercial office building will close on June 13. The building has 24 leases with total annual rentals of $2,256,000. Monthly rentals are current as of June 1. Security deposits total $1,804,000. The leases begin to expire in August; all of them must be rewritten by October 1. How much will be charged to the seller at closing for rents collected and security deposits?
   a. $1,880,000
   b. $1,916,800
   c. $1,992,800
   d. $2,068,000

4. What would be violated if a bank required that title insurance be obtained from a particular provider?
   a. REALTOR's Code of Ethics
   b. Federal Fair Housing Act
   c. Equal Credit Opportunity Act
   d. Real Estate Settlement Procedures Act

5. A mortgage assumption on a settlement statement would appear as a:
   a. balance factor
   b. credit to the seller
   c. debit to the buyer
   d. credit to the buyer

6. Which of the following would **MOST** likely be prorated on a closing statement?
   a. income tax liens
   b. rents
   c. loans being assumed
   d. title insurance

7. The primary responsibility for RESPA disclosure rests with the:
   a. buyer
   b. lending institution
   c. selling broker
   d. escrow company

8. The amount of earnest money appears on closing statements as a:
   a. credit to the buyer
   b. debit to the seller
   c. credit to the seller
   d. debit to the buyer

9. Ms. Warner's annual insurance premium was due April 1. She paid a $625 premium for the coming year on that date. If she sells her house on August 15 of this year, what prorated amount will be returned to her?
   a. $234
   b. $392
   c. $417
   d. $625

10. Title insurance on a property is $474.90, the fee for the title search is $175, the cost of preparing papers is $45, and miscellaneous other fees amount to $26.10. If the seller agrees to pay 60% of the total closing expenses and the buyer pays the rest, how much more will the seller pay than the buyer?
    a. $144
    b. $288
    c. $433
    d. $721

11. Under RESPA, a lender **MUST** provide the borrower with a:
    a. good faith estimate of closing costs
    b. home protection warranty
    c. mortgage insurance policy
    d. certified appraisal

12. Under RESPA, when must a lender provide a copy of the HUD information booklet to a borrower?
    a. within three business days of receiving the loan application
    b. when requested by the borrower
    c. at closing
    d. 48 hours prior to closing

13. Which of the following is **NOT** a violation of the Real Estate Settlement Procedures Act?
    a. directing the buyer to a particular lender
    b. accepting a kickback on a loan subject to RESPA
    c. requiring a particular title insurer
    d. accepting a fee or charging for services that were not performed

14. In the settlement of the sale of commercial property, which of the following statements is **CORRECT**?
    a. the seller is charged with prorated property taxes
    b. the buyer is charged with prorated rents
    c. the seller is credited with security deposits
    d. the seller is charged with prorated insurance premiums

15. All of the following insurance premiums are normally charged to the buyer **EXCEPT**:
    a. owner's title insurance policy
    b. ALTA title insurance policy
    c. fire insurance policy
    d. mortgage insurance premium

16. At closing the lender requests a small sum be withheld and be kept in an escrow fund. This money is **MOST** likely:
    a. security deposit
    b. for taxes and insurance
    c. to insure against first payment default
    d. to cover loan discount points

17. For the purchase of a house, a buyer assumes the seller's loan balance of $93,000 with 7.5% interest in arrears. If the September 1 payment has been made and the closing is scheduled for September 20, how much credit for interest is the buyer entitled to at closing?
    a. $388
    b. $368
    c. $213
    d. $581

18. Ms. Warner's annual insurance premium was due April 1. She paid a $625 premium for the coming year on that date. If she sells her house on August 15 of this year, what prorated amount will be returned to her?
    a. $234
    b. $394
    c. $417
    d. $625

19. A list of credits and debits given to both buyer and seller is a(n):
    a. purchase contract
    b. exclusive listing
    c. escrow statement
    d. closing statement

20. Kickbacks from service providers are prohibited by:
    a. RESPA
    b. Truth in Lending
    c. Equal Credit Opportunity Act
    d. FHA

Chapter 19

IMPORTANT TERMS AND CONCEPTS

constructive eviction

distraint

dwelling unit

eviction

finder's fees

investor

Manufactured Home Parks Landlord and Tenant Act

property management agreement

property management trust accounts

property manager

Residential Landlord and Tenant Act

security deposit

CHAPTER OBJECTIVES

After completing this chapter, you should be able to:

- Describe the role of a property manager and the requirements and exceptions for licensing.
- List the essentials of a property management agreement.
- Summarize the requirements for property management trust accounts and property management records.
- Summarize the provisions of the Nevada Residential Landlord and Tenant Act.

Property Management and Nevada Landlord– Tenant Act

19.1 PROPERTY MANAGEMENT

Owning real property and managing real property for profit are two very different aspects of real estate. Investing in real property may be as simple as buying a piece of raw land, holding it for some period of time, and (hopefully) selling it for a profit; "management" is unnecessary for this type of investment. On the other hand, an apartment complex or a single-family home that will be rented to a tenant both require "management" of the real property and of the tenant during the holding period. Real estate investors may not have the skills, time, or desire to manage one or more of the properties that they own.

Property Managers and Investors

Enter the property manager. A **property manager** is a person or company who manages rental property for someone else; property managers may or may not be licensed. An **investor** hires a property manager to efficiently manage the investor's properties and to make a profit for the investor during the holding period. An investor also counts on a property manager to protect, preserve, maintain, and possibly even improve the investment property during the holding period, so that the investor receives the highest possible return when the investment property is ultimately sold.

Investors with many properties sometimes have their own staffs to manage the properties. Typically, investors with few properties either manage the properties themselves, or hire professional property managers (although there are some exceptions). Because of the growth of absentee owners (owners/investors who do not live in the state where the investment property is located), many real estate firms have opened property management divisions.

Categories of Management

As is the case with real estate sales, property management is divided into two categories: *residential* and *commercial*, with each category having several subcategories. Management of a large apartment complex is very different from management of single-family homes, exclusive luxury homes, or furnished seasonal rentals. Similarly, management of a strip mall is very different from management of a shopping center or an industrial building. Nevertheless, all property management is governed by Nevada statutes that set forth the requirements for the following:

1. What must and may be included in a property management agreement.
2. Property management company trust accounts and the handling of the owner's and tenants' money.
3. Record keeping requirements.

Licensing

Negotiating leases, advertising rental property, or otherwise managing real property easily and clearly falls within the definition of a real estate broker, which requires a real estate license. In addition, before a real estate broker may act as a property manager within the state of Nevada the broker or a qualified person appointed by the broker, as the designated property manager, must possess a property management permit. The permit is issued by the Real Estate Division to a real estate broker, broker-salesperson, or salesperson, who meets the following requirements:

- Completion of 24 hours of classroom instruction in property management.
- Pass the Nevada Property Management state examination within one year of the application.

Exceptions

There are some exceptions, however, and not everyone who manages real property has to have a license. A list of persons who are exempt from having a real estate license and property management permit follows:

- The owner or lessor of property, or any of their regular employees who perform management activities for the preservation, increase in income, physical maintenance, and maintenance of high standards of service to the tenants at the property. Management activities do not include sales activities.
- An employee of a real estate broker engaged in the collection of rent for or on behalf of the broker.
- A person performing duties of a property manager for a property, if the person maintains an office on the property and does not engage in property management for any other property.
- A person performing the duties of a property manager for a common-interest community.
- A person performing the property management duties for a property used for residential housing that is subsidized by a federal or state of Nevada governmental unit or agency.

Property Management Agreements

A **property management agreement** is a written agreement between the owner of the property, the client, and the property manager, the broker. It establishes the rights and obligations of the parties.

There is no state-required form that must be used for property management. Most companies develop their own forms, depending on the services offered. For example, a property management firm may collect rents but may not pay the monthly bills and/or the mortgage payment. Although the type of services offered may vary and there is no state-mandated form, Nevada law requires that certain provisions be included in all property management agreements:

1. A description of the subject property and its type, including the number of units managed.
2. The broker's duties to be itemized; that is, collection of rents, holding of deposits, payment of mortgages, physical maintenance, and so on.
3. Broker's compensation.
4. Accounting and reporting requirements.
5. Procedure for repair and payment of repair bills, both emergency and routine.
6. Effective dates of the agreement with a specific termination date, and if the agreement is subject to renewal, provisions clearly setting forth the circumstances under which the agreement may be renewed, and the term of each such renewal.
7. A provision for the retention and disposition of deposits of the tenants of the property during the term of the agreement and, if the agreement is subject to renewal, during the term of each such renewal.
8. If the agreement is subject to cancellation by the broker and/or client, with and/or without cause, provisions stating the circumstances under which the agreement may be cancelled.
9. Names and signatures of the owner(s)/broker(s)/designated property managers.

Property Management Trust Accounts

A broker who is engaged in property management for one or more clients must maintain two separate property management accounts distinct from any trust account that the broker may have for other real estate transactions. One trust account must be used solely for rental operating activities, and the other trust account must be used solely for security deposits.

The following regulation amplifies the record keeping requirements for a broker found in the Nevada Administrative Code regarding property management trust accounts:

1. On or before the date of expiration of his license as a real estate broker, a broker who engages in property management or who associates with a property manager who engages in property management shall provide to the division, on a form provided by the division, an annual accounting that shows an annual reconciliation of each trust account related to property management that he maintains.
2. The reconciliation required must include the 30 days immediately preceding the expiration date of his license as a real estate broker.
3. A broker who engages in property management or who associates with a property manager who engages in property management shall maintain complete accounting records of each trust account related to property management

that he maintains for at least five years after the last activity by the broker which involved the trust account. If the records are maintained by computer, the broker shall maintain an additional copy of the records on computer disc for at least five years after the last activity by the broker which involved the trust account.

Other than the reporting requirements just mentioned, the broker responsibility for the proper maintenance of a property management trust account and trust accounts maintained for other real estate transactions are the same. Trust account responsibilities and record keeping are covered in Chapter 27.

Property Management Records

Records for property management accounts must include at least the property management file, including the management agreement; tax reports and individual tenant/lease files; a cash journal, the chronological record of money received and disbursed; an owner ledger; a tenant ledger; bank statements; and checks. A complete filing system for property management must include the information and documentation of all transactions and business dealings of the manager, owner, vendor, and tenant. A very small property may require only one file, but larger properties need several file folders to maintain this data. The files must include at least the following:

1. Property management agreement
2. Rental/lease agreement
3. Duties Owed
4. Correspondence
5. Invoices and receipts for repairs, purchases
6. Monthly owner reports
7. Other documentation that supports the discharge of the broker's obligation

19.2 LANDLORD/TENANT STATUTE

Entire books have been devoted to a thorough discussion of residential landlord/tenant law. The following is intended merely to familiarize you with the fundamental principles and to cover the issues that most commonly arise.

Nevada Residential Landlord and Tenant Act

The Residential Landlord and Tenant Act is state law. Consequently, if the act applies, unless preempted by federal law, it is applicable statewide. This means that it applies equally in all Nevada communities, both large and small. It also applies equally to a single-family residence rental owned by Mom and Pop Landlord and to a 1200-unit apartment complex owned by Mega Conglomerate Corporation.

Dwelling Units

The act applies to "the rental of dwelling units." A **dwelling unit** is defined as "A structure or the part of a structure that is occupied as, or designed or intended for occupancy as, a residence or sleeping place by one person who maintains a household or by two or more persons who maintain a common household."

Exceptions

The Residential Landlord and Tenant Act applies to most residential rental properties. It also applies to mobile homes if the tenant is renting both the mobile home and the land under it. If a person rents just the mobile home lot, that occupancy is governed by the Landlord and Tenant Act for Manufactured Home Parks. The act also does not apply to hotels, commercial property, or industrial rental property.

To clarify, there are two separate sets of statutes that address the landlord/tenant relationship in Nevada. They are:

- The Residential Landlord Tenant Act, which applies to almost all residential units (see "exclusions," later in this chapter). This is referred to later in this chapter as the "Residential Act."
- The Manufactured Home Parks Landlord and Tenant Act, which applies to the rental of mobile home lots (not the mobile homes themselves).

The Residential Act and the Manufactured Home Parks Act are two separate sets of consumer protection laws, designed to protect residential tenants. You cannot elect, by written agreement or otherwise, to make either act not applicable to the rental of residential property. The legislative intent would be easily frustrated if landlords could merely opt out of the Residential Act or the Manufactured Home Parks Act.

Summary of the Residential Act

The most essential facts to remember about the Residential Act are:

- The Residential Act applies to the rental of residential dwelling units.
- The Residential Act does not apply to:
  - Residences at a public or private facility relating to detention, medical, geriatric education, counseling, religious, or similar services.
  - Occupancy in conjunction with a contract of sale.
  - Occupancy by a member of a fraternal or social organization.
  - Transient occupancy in a hotel, motel, or recreational lodging.
  - On-site managers.
  - Occupancy by an owner of a condominium unit or a holder of a proprietary lease in a cooperative.
  - Occupancy in public housing.
  - Occupancy of a premises used primarily for agricultural purposes
- The Residential Act is state law and applies everywhere in Nevada, unless preempted by federal law.
- A written rental agreement is not required; an oral rental agreement is enforceable. However, rental agreements for more than one year must be

written (a month-to-month rental agreement that continues for more than one year need not be written).

- A written rental agreement must include:
  - Duration of agreement.
  - Amount of rent and the manner and time of its payment.
  - Whether the occupancy by children or pets is allowed.
  - Deposits required and the conditions for their refund.
  - Charges for late payment of rent.
  - Responsibility for the payment of utilities.
  - An inventory and condition of the premises.
  - Inspection rights of the landlord.
  - A listing of the persons or the number of persons who will occupy the premises.
  - Procedures by which the tenant may report a nuisance or a violation of a building, safety, or health code or regulation.
  - Information regarding the right of the tenant to display the flag of the United States.
- Out-of-state owners must have an in-state statutory agent.
- All residential landlords must disclose to the tenant the name and address of the person authorized to manage the premises and the statutory agent.
- An amount equal to three months' rent is the maximum amount of security deposit the landlord may collect as security.
- *Security* includes any reasonable fees for cleaning or repairing damages to the premises.
- Tenant must be shown landlord's rules and regulations before the rental agreement is signed.
- Landlord must give the residential tenant at least 24 hours, advance notice before entering the dwelling, unless an emergency necessitates immediate access.
- If the landlord fails to make a repair after 14 days, written notice, the tenant may:
  a. Terminate the rental agreement.
  b. Recover actual damages.
  c. Apply to the court for relief.
  d. Withhold any rent that becomes due.
- A five-day notice to pay or quit must be served on tenant to start **eviction** of tenant for nonpayment of rent.
- The Residential Act prohibits distraint for rent. **Distraint** is forcing the tenant to pay rent or other financial obligations by seizing the leased premises and/or personal property inside the leased premises.
- Residential landlord cannot "lock out" a residential tenant; instead, the landlord must go to court and get a court order.
- A **constructive eviction** occurs when the tenant moves out because the landlord does not maintain the rental unit.

CHAPTER SUMMARY

A property manager is a person or company that manages rental property for someone else and may or may not be licensed. An investor looks to a property manager to efficiently manage the investor's properties and to make a profit for the investor during the holding period. An investor also counts on a property manager to protect, preserve, and maintain the investment property during this period. Property management is divided into two categories: residential and commercial.

Negotiating leases, advertising rental property, collecting rent, or otherwise managing real property requires a real estate license. The list of persons exempt from needing to have a real estate license includes, but is not limited to, a natural person dealing with his or her own property.

A property management agreement is an agreement between the owner of the property and the property manager. It establishes the rights and obligations of the parties. Nevada law requires that certain provisions be included in all property management agreements. For example, the agreement must state all material terms and conditions of the property management firm's obligations to the property owner, and it must specify a beginning and an ending date. A full list of the requirements is included in the body of this chapter.

Two property management trust accounts are required: one for all owner's monies, such as rents collected, and another for security deposits. There are also many record keeping requirements and mandates that property management firms must follow.

The Nevada Residential Landlord and Tenant Act applies to the rental of dwelling units. Some of the most essential facts to remember about the Residential Act are: The Residential Act applies to the rental of residential dwelling units. An amount equal to three months' rent is the maximum amount of security deposit the landlord may collect as security. The tenant must be shown the landlord's rules and regulations before a rental agreement is signed. The Residential Act prohibits distraint for rent. A residential landlord cannot "lock out" a residential tenant. A complete list of essential facts is included in the body of this chapter.

CHECKING YOUR COMPREHENSION

1. Summarize the purpose and obligations of a property manager.

2. Describe why a real estate license can be required to manage real property and list the exceptions for licensing.

3. List the broker's requirements for:
   - A property management trust account
   - Property management records

4. List the requirements for compliance with the Residential Landlord and Tenant Act.

REVIEWING YOUR UNDERSTANDING

1. What is **NOT** part of the property manager's responsibilities?

    a. ethics

    b. keeping up with rental rates in the area

    c. telling the owner the market value of the building

    d. keeping current with vacancies

2. A property manager **CANNOT** receive:

    a. reimbursement for out-of-pocket expenses

    b. free rent on an apartment unit

    c. a monthly management fee

    d. rebates from suppliers

3. A landlord wishes to show a party your apartment. He may do so with how much notice?

    a. 24 hours

    b. 48 hours

    c. 72 hours

    d. 96 hours

4. Regarding a property management trust account, which of the following is **NOT** true?

    a. multiple properties can be in one trust account

    b. the broker is required to provide an annual accounting to the Real Estate Division

    c. the broker shall maintain property management trust account records for five years after the last activity

    d. a broker engaged in property management activities must maintain one property management trust account

5. Which of the following most accurately describes a property manager?

    a. fiduciary

    b. trustee

    c. escrow agent

    d. resident manager

6. A broker with an ongoing property management contract is required to maintain files that include all of the following, **EXCEPT**:

    a. property management agreement

    b. rental/lease agreement

    c. copy of property management permit

    d. copy of the signed Duties Owed disclosure

7. Before a property management activity can be started, the real estate broker or a qualified person appointed by the broker must obtain a:

    a. property management permit

    b. business broker permit

    c. sales agent license

    d. broker-property manager license

8. Forcing a tenant to pay rent by seizing the leased premises and the personal property inside is called:

    a. seizure

    b. distraint

    c. subrogation

    d. acceleration

9. When a tenant moves from a leased property because the landlord did not maintain the rental unit, what has occurred?

    a. acceleration

    b. distraint

    c. actual eviction

    d. constructive eviction

10. The maximum security deposit that a landlord may collect for a residential rental is equal to:

    a. one month's rent

    b. three months' rent

    c. two months' rent

    d. two and one-half months' rent

11. What is not part of a typical property management agreement?
    a. beginning and ending date
    b. frequency of management reports
    c. cancellation clause
    d. annual budget

12. All of the following are required of property managers, **EXCEPT**:
    a. showing and leasing property
    b. determining the owner's objectives
    c. collecting rent
    d. providing security for the tenants

13. A property manager would be **LESS** likely to:
    a. handle new leases
    b. arrange for repairs and improvements of the property
    c. resolve tenant disputes as to property usage
    d. prepare depreciation schedules for tax purposes

14. A property manager could do all of the following, **EXCEPT**:
    a. provide legal counsel
    b. provide financial management
    c. supervise maintenance workers
    d. market the property

15. A tenant leases a heated apartment, but the landlord fails to provide proper heat within a reasonable period of time. This situation can cause:
    a. actual eviction
    b. a novation to exist
    c. a constructive eviction
    d. a tenancy of sufferance

16. Property managers are usually compensated by:
    a. a percentage of gross rents received
    b. a set fee for leasing
    c. fees for supervising, repairs, and maintenance
    d. rebates from suppliers

17. What is the purpose of the management agreement?
    a. to define the scope of responsibilities and authorities of the manager
    b. to create an opportunity for the manager to earn additional income through solicitation and acceptance of gratuities from supplies of goods and services
    c. to hire the manager to find a buyer for the property
    d. to delegate to the manager the authority to purchase adjacent properties

18. Which of the following would **NOT** be part of the landlord–tenant act?
    a. security deposit regulations
    b. property management agreement regulations
    c. notices for eviction
    d. prohibition of distraint

19. Which of the following acts is **NOT** an example of constructive eviction?
    a. discontinuing required utilities
    b. making modifications that make the property unsuitable for the purpose for which it was rented
    c. making constant unnecessary repairs that interfere with the tenant's quiet enjoyment of the premises
    d. serving the tenant with an unlawful detainer action

20. A security deposit:
    a. does not include a reasonable charge for cleaning
    b. cannot exceed an amount equal to three months' rent
    c. cannot exceed an amount equal to one month's rent
    d. does not include a reasonable charge for repairing damages to the premises

IMPORTANT TERMS AND CONCEPTS

annual percentage rate or APR

commercial banks

Community Reinvestment Act

credit unions

Employee Retirement Income Security Act (ERISA)

Equal Credit Opportunity Act (ECOA)

Fair Credit Reporting Act

Fannie Mae

Federal Deposit Insurance Corporation (FDIC)

Federal Home Loan Bank (FHLB)

Federal Home Loan Mortgage Corporation (FHLMC)

Federal National Mortgage Association (FNMA)

Federal Reserve System (Fed)

Freddie Mac

Ginnie Mae

Government National Mortgage Association (GNMA)

life insurance companies

loan originators

loan servicing

mortgage banker

mortgage broker

mortgage correspondent

mortgage participation certificates (PCs)

mutual savings banks

Office of Thrift Supervision

pass-through certificate

pension and retirement programs

primary mortgage market

Regulation Z

right of rescission

savings and loans

secondary mortgage market

Truth in Lending Act

CHAPTER OBJECTIVES

After completing this chapter, you should be able to:

- Describe the role of the Federal Reserve as the country's money manager.
- Explain the following statutes related to real estate finance: Equal Credit Opportunity Act, Truth in Lending Act (Regulation Z), Fair Credit Reporting Act, and Community Reinvestment Act.
- Identify the sources of real estate financing.
- Explain the purpose of the secondary mortgage market and describe the role of the three major warehousing agencies.

Control of Money and Real Estate Finance

20.1 CONTROL OF MONEY

The **Federal Reserve System (Fed)**, sometimes known as the country's money manager, was originally established as the Federal Reserve Bank in 1913. A number of banking systems have started and failed since the Pennsylvania legislature chartered the Bank of North America in 1781. When President Woodrow Wilson signed the Federal Reserve Act in 1913, its original purpose was to establish facilities for selling or discounting commercial paper and to improve the supervision of banking.

Today, one important function of the Fed is to control the supply and cost of money to member banks. The basic supply of money, called the "*M1*," is cash in circulation, checking accounts, and other demand deposits at commercial banks, credit unions, and thrift institutions. The *M2* money supply includes all M1 money plus time deposits, savings deposits, and all non-institutional money-market funds. The final money supply, *M3*, is all M2 money plus large time deposits, institutional money-market funds, short-term repurchase agreements along with other larger liquid assets.

The primary purpose of the Fed is to maintain the stability of the financial system and contain systemic risk in financial markets resulting in sustainable growth, maximum employment, and stable prices. Inherent responsibilities include regulating and supervising banking institutions and protecting the credit rights of consumers. By controlling the supply of money, the Fed can maintain a hold on the rate of inflation or stimulate growth as necessitated by economic conditions.

Economic Stability

Economic stability is directly linked to the supply and cost of money. As the supply of money increases, an increasing level of economic activity will result. Consider the cost of money as interest charges on borrowed funds. If the cost of money increases, less will be borrowed. As rates come down, borrowing and economic activity will increase. Ideally, control over the supply and cost of money should be used to create an economic balance. The federal agencies empowered to exercise that control are the U.S. Treasury and the Federal Reserve System.

Member banks and all nationally chartered commercial banks must join the Federal Reserve System. Each member bank must buy stock in the Reserve district bank, maintain monetary reserves to meet the Fed requirements, and clear drafts, electronic funds transfers, and bills of exchange (checks) through the system.

Banks may borrow from their district bank and pledge their commercial loans as collateral. The Fed charges interest on its loans at the Fed Funds Rate. Consequently, that rate directly affects the rate the bank must charge its best customers. This rate is generally referred to as the bank's *prime rate*. When an interest rate quote is 2% "over prime," that means that the quote is based on the rate the bank charges its best customers.

Legislation

Legislation in the last half-century dealing with money, banks, loans, creditors, and consumers has been prolific. For consumers and borrowers, the most significant legislation has been the Consumer Protection Act. Passed by Congress in 1968, and subsequently amended, it includes the Truth in Lending Act (Title I) and the Equal Credit Opportunity Act (Title VII). Other significant legislation includes the Interstate Land Sales Full Disclosure Act, the Fair Housing Act, the Community Reinvestment Act, the Real Estate Settlement Procedures Act, and the Financial Institutions Reform Recovery and Enforcement Act (FIRREA).

Equal Credit Opportunity Act

Congress passed the **Equal Credit Opportunity Act (ECOA)** in 1975 to prevent discrimination in the loan process. ECOA requires lending institutions to make loans on an equal basis to all creditworthy customers without regard to discriminatory factors.

ECOA makes it unlawful for any creditor to discriminate against any loan applicant in any aspect of a credit transaction. Specifically, creditors cannot deny an applicant for the following reasons:

- Applicant's race, color, religion, sex, national origin, marital status, or age (unless the applicant is a minor and therefore does not have the capacity to contract).
- Part of the applicant's income is derived from public assistance.
- The applicant has in good faith exercised any right under the Federal Consumer Credit Protection Act of which the Truth in Lending Act is a part.

In addition, lenders and other creditors must inform all rejected credit applicants in writing within 30 days of the principal reason why credit was denied.

Truth in Lending Act (Regulation Z)

The Board of Governors of the Federal Reserve System is responsible for supervising the **Truth in Lending Act**. In connection with this responsibility, the Fed formulated and issued Regulation Z.

Regulation Z requires lenders to reveal the total cost of loans through a standard measurement referred to as **annual percentage rate or APR**. The APR is not the stated interest rate, but it is the effective rate of interest on the loan. It includes all other loan costs and fees paid by the borrower together with the interest that will be paid on the loan, stated as an annual percentage of the actual amount of the funds to be received by the borrower.

> EXAMPLE—You borrow $10,000 at a stated interest rate of 9% for one year. To do this, you sign a note for $10,000; however, the bank charges a fee of 3 points or 3%, so you actually receive only $9700. After one year, you must pay the bank $10,900 ($10,000 principal plus $900 of interest). Therefore, your annual percentage rate (APR) is 12.37% ($1200/$9700).

Advertising

Regulation Z also applies to advertising the credit terms available in the purchase of a home. The only specific thing that may be stated in the ad is the annual percentage rate, which must be fully spelled out, not abbreviated as "APR." If any other specific credit terms are included in the advertisement, the ad must provide full disclosure.

Disclosure Statement

For most loans, lenders must provide borrowers a disclosure statement with a complete breakdown of all loan charges. If the borrower is pledging a principal residence already owned as security for a loan, the disclosure statement must provide for a **right of rescission** for the loan transaction. The right to rescind the loan must be exercised by the borrower prior to midnight of the third business day following the date the transaction was closed. The three-day right of rescission does not apply when the loan will finance the purchase of a new home or the construction of a dwelling to be used as a principal residence.

Fair Credit Reporting Act

The **Fair Credit Reporting Act** regulates the action of credit bureaus and the use of consumer credit. If a lender refuses to grant credit or make a loan because of derogatory information in a potential borrower's credit report, the lender must make that information available for review and provide the potential borrower with the name and address of the credit bureau that supplied the information. If requested by the borrower, a credit bureau must supply all information included in that person's credit file. A person has the right to have an erroneous credit report corrected. Further, the Act limits access to a person's credit file.

Community Reinvestment Act

The **Community Reinvestment Act** was passed to help prevent redlining and discrimination by lenders. The act is designed to ensure that banks "meet the credit needs of the community" in which they have branches and take in deposits. To comply with the act, financial institutions, which are supervised by federal agencies, must make a reasonable percentage of loans in all areas in which they have a deposit base and must prepare community reinvestment statements that report on various details of their lending activities.

Federal Deposit Insurance Corporation (FDIC)

The **Federal Deposit Insurance Corporation (FDIC)** was established by the Banking Act of 1933. It was designed to stabilize the ailing banking system of the time. In an effort to reestablish public trust, deposits were insured, first up to $50,000 then up to $100,000 and now, through December 31, 2009, to $250,000. All member banks of the Federal Reserve System are required to join the insurance program. Non-member banks can request admission and may, if qualified, join the program.

Federal Home Loan Bank System / Office of Thrift Supervision

The **Federal Home Loan Bank (FHLB)** was organized in 1932 to bring stability to the savings and loan associations. These institutions, typically called "building and loans" in those days, were primarily formed to use their association members' savings deposits to fund residential construction loans. Prior to the establishment of FHLB, these savings and loans had little supervision. Bankruptcies and closings took a significant toll on American families.

The FHLB provided central credit-clearing facilities and established rules and regulations for members. The amount of interest paid on savings was not regulated by FHLB until the 1966 Interest Rate Adjustment Act. This act gave FHLB the power to set maximum rates that could be paid on savings deposits. A major function was to provide a market for the member institutions' securities. Members were allowed to borrow money from their district bank with no collateral for up to one year. Long-term loans, such as real estate financing funded by the institutions, required collateral.

Some difficulties arose from savings and loans that had long-term, low fixed-rate mortgages in their portfolio backed by interest-sensitive deposits. As the high-yield money market securities became popular, billions of dollars in savings were removed from the savings and loans and placed in highly competitive private money market funds. This issue, combined with the slowdown of the real estate market in the mid- to late 1980s, caused many savings and loans to face serious problems. Many savings and loan associations went out of business or were shut down by regulators and, typically, those that survived changed their charters to become thrift associations or savings banks. In 1989, the **Office of Thrift Supervision** replaced the Federal Home Loan Bank as the agency responsible for regulating all federally charted savings associations.

20.2 SOURCES OF REAL ESTATE FINANCING

Sources of real estate financing include everything from commercial banks, savings and loan associations, and pension funds, to your mother-in-law and next-door neighbor. Banks, savings and loans, pension funds, life insurance companies, and credit unions are typically highly regulated institutions. On the other hand, mortgage bankers and brokers, real estate investment trusts, limited partnership syndications, endowment funds, private loan companies, and individuals are not greatly restricted in their lending operations.

Commercial Banks and Mutual Savings Banks

Commercial banks rely on demand deposits, primarily checking accounts, for their supply of available funds for loans. Historically, commercial banks have not been a source of long-term real estate finance. Their real estate lending activity tends to be short-term, such as construction loans, home improvement loans, and mobile home loans. However, many commercial banks originate single-family home loans through affiliated conduit lenders usually licensed as mortgage bankers.

Mutual savings banks are mostly located in the Midwest and eastern United States. They are organized as mutual companies, where profits are distributed to the depositors through interest or dividends.

Savings and Loans

Savings and loans began with the idea of pooling money for real estate loans. Legend has it that 10 friends each put $1000 in a pot, and then each member drew a number. The person who drew number one was able to use the money first, then number two, number three, and so on. Because savings and loans were first referred to as building and loans, they may well have evolved this way.

According to the Society of Real Estate Appraisers, the first house in the United States to be financed by a savings and loan association was purchased with a $375 mortgage payable at $4.90 per month, of which $1.90 represented interest and $3.00 principal. The Philadelphia house built in 1831 was estimated to have been purchased for $750.

The concept of loaning funds only to members soon faded and loans were made to other qualified borrowers. As this happened, the attitude shifted more to serving the depositor, changing from building and loans to savings and loans. By paying their depositors compound interest, at times on a daily basis, they began to attract a larger number of depositors. Savings and loans, which are also called *thrifts*, began to offer a safe depository for savings as well as high interest rates on their deposits. Eventually, savings and loans were able to offer full banking services to everyone.

Savings and loan associations had more flexibility than other regulated institutions. Through conventional loans, they could make loans in amounts up to and exceeding 100% of appraised value, but they usually only went as high as 80% loan-to-value without some form of private mortgage insurance on the loans. Until the savings and loan crisis in the late 1980s, these thrifts were generally the primary source of financing residential real estate.

Life Insurance Companies

Although the sale of such life insurance products as whole life and term life policies remains an important part of the life insurance business, the primary business of life insurance companies is no longer traditional life insurance but the underwriting of *annuities*—contracts that guarantee a fixed or variable payment over a given period of time. Premiums collected by life insurers are invested primarily in government and corporate bonds although a portion is invested in mortgage loans (mostly commercial). Today, the total financial assets of life insurance companies exceed $4.3 trillion. Of that total, $282.7 billion, or 6.45%, is invested in mortgage loans.

Life insurance companies also invest in mortgage-backed securities and make direct investments in real estate as well as originate and hold loans on commercial properties. Loan originations are usually through company employees working with loan brokers as well as directly with developers and investors and through mortgage bankers, acting as a correspondent for a life insurance company.

Pension and Retirement Programs

In the late 1800s, the American Express Company formed a retirement program for its employees. This pension plan idea found favor with railroad companies and utility companies. Employees set aside a portion of their earnings in a matching funds program with their employers. Money was deposited on a regular basis and withdrawn after retirement, so long-term, secure investments such as real estate loans were very popular. While pension and profit-sharing plans were popular with those who were able to participate, plans were not available to most people.

In 1974, Congress passed the **Employee Retirement Income Security Act (ERISA)**, a complete overhaul of federal pension law. This act made it possible for the smallest company (that is, a sole proprietor) to have a pension or profit-sharing plan. Or, if an individual was an employee of an organization that did not offer a pension plan, then that individual could fund his or her own Individual Retirement Account (IRA). ERISA also provided for the protection of the assets set aside for pension and retirement plans through the establishment of the Pension Benefits Guaranty Corporation (PBGC).

Today, these retirement benefit plans cover 150 million workers and contain assets exceeding $4 trillion. Real estate and commercial real estate loans are very attractive investments for these plans because of the security and high rate of return.

Credit Unions

Credit unions are similar to the original savings and loans: They are operated primarily for the benefit of their members or depositors. The popularity of credit unions comes from their ability to pay higher returns and charge lower rates on money borrowed. Credit unions now provide a complete variety of banking services, including mortgages and short-term home improvement loans.

Mortgage Bankers and Brokers

Generally, a **mortgage banker** borrows money to make loans. This is done by means of a warehouse line of credit, usually made available by a bank or savings and loan. The warehouse line is secured by the loans funded through it. The mortgage banker keeps the loans funded by the warehouse line in the "warehouse" until an investor purchases them or they may be packaged and sold in the secondary market. Once the funded loan has been sold, the mortgage banker repays the warehouse line of credit. The mortgage banker continues to service the loan, which means he or she collects payments and receives a fee for this service, or the servicing may also be sold in the secondary market.

Unlike other lenders, who keep some loans in their own portfolio, mortgage bankers sell all their loans to investors or in the secondary market. Today, mortgage bankers are the primary source of residential loans.

A mortgage banker that represents loan originators, such as banks, life insurance companies, and pension funds, is called a **mortgage correspondent**. The correspondent represents the lender in a local community or territory and is paid a fee for originating, processing, closing, and servicing loans.

A **mortgage broker** originates and processes loans but usually has no funds to loan and acts as an intermediary between the borrower and the lender. Once the borrower has been qualified and the loan processing has begun, the mortgage broker places the loan with an investor, who funds the loan through an escrow. The mortgage broker receives an origination fee from the borrower, which is usually a percentage of the loan amount. The loan servicing can be done by the lender (investor), a third-party servicer, or an escrow or title company.

In Nevada, mortgage bankers and mortgage brokers are required to be licensed by the Commissioner of Mortgage Lending.

20.3 THE SECONDARY MORTGAGE MARKET

The **secondary mortgage market** is simply the purchasing and selling of existing mortgages and trust deeds. It involves lenders selling mortgages to other lenders and investors. What may be called the **primary mortgage market** relates to **loan originators** lending directly to qualified borrowers. While many lenders who originate loans may retain some of them in their own investment portfolios, they undoubtedly sell off most of their loan production in the secondary market.

Loan servicing, which involves collecting payments from the borrower and passing them along to the investor for a fee, may be separated from the sale of the loan or it may be included. Thus, the original lender may continue to collect the payments from the borrower, passing the payments along to the investor after deducting a fee for servicing the loan.

Warehousing agencies are major buyers of mortgage loans. These agencies purchase large numbers of mortgage loans and "pool" the individual loans. They use the loan pools as collateral for their mortgage-backed securities (MBS), or bonds which are then traded in the securities market much like other traded securities. The following are the major warehousing agencies:

- Federal National Mortgage Association (FNMA)
- Government National Mortgage Association (GNMA)
- Federal Home Loan Mortgage Corporation (FHLMC)

Federal National Mortgage Association

The **Federal National Mortgage Association (FNMA)** is commonly known as **Fannie Mae**. Fannie Mae was established in 1938 as a government corporation to provide liquidity in the mortgage system by creating a secondary market for FHA loans. The Federal Housing Authority (FHA) program, which was established in

1934 to help rebuild the economy, was having trouble selling its mortgages to secondary investors on the national level. This meant they could not free up their money to reinvest in more loans. Therefore, Fannie Mae was established to provide stability and standards that would make FHA loans a lower-risk investment. The FHA and its loan programs are discussed at length in the next chapter.

Fannie Mae guaranteed the success of the FHA program by providing a secondary market for the purchase of FHA-insured loans, replenishing necessary investor capital for funding more FHA loans.

Private Corporation

An amendment to the Housing and Urban Development Act of 1968 changed the Fannie Mae organization from a successful government-owned and controlled corporation to a private corporation. All treasury-owned stocks were redeemed, and a matching amount of common stock was offered to the general public. Fannie Mae is now a profit-making organization, with its stock listed on the New York Stock Exchange.

As a government-owned corporation, Fannie Mae was limited to purchasing FHA-insured and VA-guaranteed mortgages. As a privately owned corporation, it may also purchase conventional mortgages, as authorized by Congress in 1970.

Purchasing Mortgages

Fannie Mae buys mortgages on a regular basis through a weekly auction. Mortgage bankers, savings and loans, life insurance companies, and other loan originators are major sellers of mortgages to Fannie Mae. Fannie Mae also sells mortgage-backed securities to investors in order to raise capital for the purchase of mortgage pools. The securities are backed by specific pools of mortgages purchased and held by Fannie Mae. Fannie Mae guarantees payments of all interest and principal to the holder of the mortgage-backed securities. Fannie Mae receives no direct government funding or backing and Fannie Mae securities carry a government guarantee of being repaid.

When Fannie Mae purchases mortgages, a signed servicing agreement allows the loan originator to act, for a fee, as servicing agent. This monthly fee is about one-twelfth of one-half of one percent of the loan balance. This fee creates a considerable income for the originator, depending on the size of his or her portfolio. When Fannie Mae purchases pools of loans, lenders are able to rollover their money and loan it out again, collecting more origination fees and more servicing fees. Fannie Mae has become one of the largest purchasers of mortgages in the secondary market. In 2001, Fannie Mae purchased over 40% of the loans produced in that year. For the year 2008, Fannie Mae purchases of lender-originated issues totaled $332.5 billion. In December 2008, their portfolio of mortgage loans exceeded $787 billion.

Government Sponsorship

Even though Fannie Mae is a privately owned corporation, it is still under government sponsorship. The board of directors has 18 members who serve one-year terms. The President of the United States appoints 5 members and stockholders elect 13. On September 6, 2008, the Federal Housing Finance Agency was appointed as the Conservator for Fannie Mae and succeeded to all its rights, titles, powers, and privileges.

Government National Mortgage Association (GNMA)

The **Government National Mortgage Association (GNMA)** is a government corporation under the control of the Department of Housing and Urban Development (HUD). **Ginnie Mae**, as it is called, administers special assistance programs and works with Fannie Mae in secondary market activities. Ginnie Mae does not purchase mortgages. Its function is to guarantee the payment of principal and interest on a pool of FHA, Farmer's Home Administration (FmHA), or DVA mortgages. Ginnie Mae does this by issuing a security, called a **pass-through certificate**, to the investor in the pool of mortgages. Because Ginnie Mae is a government agency, its guarantee is backed by the full faith and credit of the U.S. government. Typically, securities dealers who trade in Ginnie Mae securities purchase the securities issued.

The Ginnie Mae pass-through certificate is a security interest in a pool of mortgages that provides for a monthly "pass-through" of principal and interest payments directly to the certificate holder.

Federal Home Loan Mortgage Corporation (FHLMC)

The second major player in the secondary mortgage market is the **Federal Home Loan Mortgage Corporation (FHLMC)**, known as **Freddie Mac**. The Emergency Home Finance Act of 1970, which gave Fannie Mae the power to purchase conventional loans, authorized the establishment of a new player in the secondary market. Originally created to provide a secondary mortgage market facility for members of the Federal Home Loan Bank System (Savings and Loan Associations), Freddie Mac's charter has been modified to include all mortgage lenders. Freddie Mac is now a publicly owned corporation similar to Fannie Mae and listed on the New York Stock Exchange. However, like Fannie Mae, the Federal Housing Finance Agency was appointed as the Conservator of Freddie Mac on September 6, 2008. Through the years, Freddie Mac has become the largest purchaser of conventional loans in the secondary market. During 2008, Freddie Mac purchased mortgages totaling $321 billion and retained a portfolio that exceeded $804 billion as of December 2008.

Freddie Mac finances its mortgage purchases through the issuance of **mortgage participation certificates (PCs)**. These guaranteed mortgage securities are sold to the public through securities dealers. Freddie Mac ultimately assumes the risk of borrower default in respect to these securities.

CHAPTER SUMMARY

One important function of the Federal Reserve System (Fed) is the control of the supply and cost of money to member banks. By controlling the supply of money, the Fed can maintain a hold on the rate of inflation or stimulate growth as necessitated by economic conditions. Economic stability is directly linked to the supply and cost of money. As the supply of money increases, an increasing level of economic activity will result. The federal agencies empowered to exercise the control of money are the U.S. Treasury and the Federal Reserve System. Member banks and all nationally chartered commercial banks must join the Federal Reserve System.

Some important legislation dealing with money, banks, loans, and so on includes the Equal Credit Opportunity Act, Regulation Z, the Fair Credit Reporting Act, and the Community Reinvestment Act. The Equal Credit Opportunity Act (ECOA) prevents discrimination in the loan process. Regulation Z requires lenders to reveal the total cost of loans through a standard measurement referred to as APR or annual percentage rate. Regulation Z also applies to advertising the credit terms available in the purchase of a home. The only specific thing that may be stated in the ad is the annual percentage rate, and those words must be fully spelled out. The Fair Credit Reporting Act regulates the action of credit bureaus and the use of consumer credit. If a lender refuses to grant credit or make a loan because of derogatory information in a potential borrower's credit report, the lender must make that information available for review and provide the name and address of the credit bureau that supplied the information. The Community Reinvestment Act helps prevent redlining and discrimination by lenders. Financial institutions must make a reasonable percentage of loans in their community and immediate business area.

The Federal Deposit Insurance Corporation (FDIC) currently insures deposits up to $250,000. All member banks of the Federal Reserve System are required to join the insurance program. Non-member banks can request admission and may, if qualified, join the program. The Federal Home Loan Bank System (FHLB) was organized in 1932 to bring stability to the savings and loan associations. But after many problems with savings and loans in the 1980s, the Office of Thrift Supervision replaced the Federal Home Loan Bank System. Sources of real estate financing include commercial banks and mutual savings banks, savings and loans, life insurance companies, pension and retirement programs, credit unions, and mortgage bankers and brokers.

Commercial banks rely on demand deposits, primarily checking accounts, for their supply of available funds for loans. Historically, commercial banks have not been a source of long-term real estate finance. Mutual savings banks, mostly located in the Midwest and eastern United States, are organized as mutual companies where profits are distributed to the depositors through interest or dividends. Until the savings and loan crisis in the late 1980s, savings and loans (also called thrifts) were generally the primary source of financing residential real estate. The primary business of life insurance companies is now the underwriting of annuities. Premiums collected by life insurers are invested primarily in government and corporate bonds, although a portion is invested in mortgage loans. Mortgage loans made by life insurance companies are primarily very large loans on commercial properties. The Employee Retirement Income Security Act (ERISA) made it possible for the smallest company to have a pension or profit-sharing plan. Or, if an individual was an employee of an organization that did not offer a pension plan, then that individual could fund his or her own Individual Retirement Account (IRA). Real estate and real estate loans are very attractive investments for IRA plans because of the security and high rate of return. Credit unions operate primarily for the benefit of their members or depositors. The popularity of credit unions comes from their ability to pay higher returns and charge lower rates on money borrowed.

A mortgage banker borrows money to make loans. Mortgage bankers sell all their loans to investors or to the secondary market. Mortgage bankers are the major source of residential loans. A mortgage broker processes loans but usually has no funds to loan. Once the borrower has been qualified and the loan processing has begun, the mortgage broker places the loan with an investor, who funds the loan through an escrow. The mortgage broker receives an origination fee from the borrower. Mortgage bankers and mortgage brokers are required to be licensed by the Commissioner of Mortgage Lending.

The secondary mortgage market is simply the purchasing and selling of existing mortgages and trust deeds. It involves lenders selling mortgages to other lenders and investors. Loan servicing involves collecting the payments from the borrower and passing them along to the investor for a fee. Loan servicing may be separated from the sale of the loan or it may be included. Warehousing agencies are major buyers of mortgage loans. These agencies purchase large numbers of mortgage loans in "pools," which they use as collateral for their mortgage-backed securities (MBS), which are then traded in the securities market. These major warehousing agencies are the Federal National Mortgage Association (FNMA), Government National Mortgage Association (GNMA), and Federal Home Loan Mortgage Corporation (FHLMC).

The Federal National Mortgage Association is commonly known as Fannie Mae. FNMA is a privately owned corporation under government sponsorship. Fannie Mae was established to create a secondary market for FHA loans. FNMA buys mortgages on a regular basis through a weekly auction. Mortgage bankers, savings and loans, life insurance companies, and other loan originators are major sellers of mortgages to FNMA. Fannie Mae also sells mortgage-backed securities to investors in order to raise capital for the purchase of mortgage pools. Specific pools of mortgages purchased and held by FNMA back the securities. Fannie Mae guarantees payments of all interest and principal to the holder of the mortgage-backed securities. Fannie Mae has become one of the largest purchasers of mortgages in the secondary market.

The Government National Mortgage Association (GNMA) is a government corporation under the control of the Department of Housing and Urban Development. Ginnie Mae does not purchase mortgages. Its function is to guarantee the payment of principal and interest on a pool of FHA, Farmer's Home Administration (FmHA), or DVA mortgages. Ginnie Mae does this by issuing a pass-through certificate to the investor in the pool of mortgages.

The second major player in the secondary mortgage market is the Federal Home Loan Mortgage Corporation (Freddie Mac). Freddie Mac has become the largest purchaser of conventional loans in the secondary market. Freddie Mac finances its mortgage purchases through the issuance of mortgage participation certificates (PCs).

CHECKING YOUR COMPREHENSION

1. Describe the role of the Federal Reserve and summarize its impact on economic stability and credit conditions.

2. List the prohibitions established by the Equal Credit Opportunity Act.

3. Summarize the purpose of Regulation Z and its affect on advertising credit terms.

4. List the sources of real estate financing and describe their real estate finance role.

5. List the three major secondary market warehousing agencies and describe their role in the secondary market.

REVIEWING YOUR UNDERSTANDING

1. Which of the following does **NOT** describe the borrower's rights under the Equal Credit Opportunity Act?
   a. the fact that the borrower's income is primarily from public assistance cannot affect the lender's decision
   b. if a loan is denied, the reason for the denial must be stated
   c. lenders cannot ask questions concerning pregnancy
   d. past financial problems cannot be the basis for a denial

2. The likely effect of raising interest rates would be a(n):
   a. increase in borrowing
   b. great number of construction starts
   c. stimulation of all production
   d. increase in unemployment

3. Mortgage bankers:
   a. manage real estate loans
   b. do not originate loans
   c. use savings deposits to make loans
   d. have no more obligations when a loan is finalized

4. Interest rates on government-backed residential loans are:
   a. established by negotiation between the borrower and lender
   b. established by FNMA
   c. established by GNMA
   d. established by FDIC

5. The owner's right to rescind within three business days when a consumer loan places a lien on his or her own residence is provided by:
   a. RESPA
   b. the Truth in Lending Act
   c. the Equal Credit Opportunity Act
   d. the Uniform Commercial Code

6. The Federal Reserve could **NOT** take the following action:
   a. raise the reserve requirement of banks
   b. raise taxes
   c. buy government bonds on the open market
   d. raise the discount rate

7. Truth in Lending disclosures would be required in an advertisement stating:
   a. no down payment
   b. $3000 down
   c. 10% annual percentage rate
   d. low, low down

8. Which of the following is a buyer in the secondary mortgage market?
   a. Federal Reserve Banks
   b. Veterans Administration
   c. Federal Housing Administration
   d. Federal National Mortgage Association

9. Which of the following is **NOT** a financial intermediary?
   a. federally chartered commercial bank
   b. Federal Housing Administration
   c. federally chartered savings and loan
   d. private insurance company

10. Which of the following terms does **NOT** belong with the others?
    a. pass-through certificate
    b. tandem plan
    c. mortgage-backed securities
    d. origination fee

11. Truth in Lending is also known as:
    a. Credit Act of 1968
    b. Regulation Z
    c. Federal Usury Law
    d. Fair Housing Act

12. The secondary mortgage market refers to:
    a. second trust deeds
    b. loan made by non-institutional lenders
    c. high-risk loans
    d. the resale mortgage marketplace

13. With regard to real estate financing, the "primary market" can **BEST** be described as:
    a. a market where loans are directly originated
    b. a market for investors of mortgage-backed securities
    c. a source of funds for corporate borrowers
    d. Federal National Mortgage Association loans

14. Which of the following disclosures would be made by an advertiser to comply with Regulation Z (the Truth in Lending Act)?
    a. 7% interest
    b. 7% straight interest
    c. 7% annual interest
    d. 7% annual percentage rate

15. The Federal Truth in Lending Act requires the lender to disclose to the borrower all of the following amounts **EXCEPT:**
    a. the annual rate of interest to be paid
    b. the total amount of finance charges payable during the term of the loan
    c. the amount of discount points paid
    d. total property taxes

16. The term *mortgage correspondent* refers to:
    a. one who writes about mortgages
    b. local lenders representative
    c. the co-owner of a mortgage
    d. the mortgagor

17. Regulation Z, part of the Truth in Lending Act, does which of the following?
    a. regulates the agency relationship between broker and sellers
    b. discloses the annual cost of consumer credit
    c. establishes federal usury rates
    d. insures deposits made in member banks

18. Which of the following costs are **NOT** part of Regulation Z?
    a. service charges
    b. title costs
    c. attorney's fees
    d. discount points

19. A three-day right to rescind originates from:
    a. RESPA
    b. usury law
    c. APR
    d. Regulation Z

20. Why is the APR higher than the interest rate quoted?
    a. APR includes all loan charges
    b. APR reflects the compound interest factors
    c. APR includes the property taxes
    d. APR includes the property insurance

Chapter 21

IMPORTANT TERMS AND CONCEPTS

acceleration clause

adjustable rate mortgage (ARM)

alienation clause

all-inclusive deed of trust

bare legal title

beneficiary

blanket mortgage

Certificate of Eligibility

conforming loans

construction loan

contract for deed

contract for sale

conventional loans

deed of reconveyance

deeds of trust

defeasance clause

entitlement

equitable title

FHA loan

government-backed loans

graduated payment mortgage (GPM)

hard money loan

holder in due course

hypothecation

joint and several liability

loan-to-value ratio (LTV)

maintenance clause

mortgage

mortgage insurance premium (MIP)

mortgagee

mortgagor

negotiable instrument

non-conforming loans

open-end mortgage

package mortgage

participation loan

payee

payor

power of sale clause

prepayment clause

private mortgage insurance (PMI)

promissory note

purchase money mortgage

reverse annuity mortgage (RAM)

satisfaction of mortgage

shared appreciation mortgage (SAM)

subordination clause

trust deeds

trustee

trustor

VA loan

vendee

vendor

wraps

wrap-around mortgage

Real Estate Financing Instruments

After completing this chapter, you should be able to:

- Describe the essential elements and purpose of a promissory note, mortgage, deed of trust, and contract for deed.
- Explain the meaning of conforming and non-conforming loans and summarize the criteria for conforming loans.
- Describe the residential financing program similarities and differences for conventional loans, FHA loans, and VA loans.

INTRODUCTION

If all real estate transfers were dependent on cash payments, the real estate industry would be at a standstill. The need and ability to borrow money to buy real property has been with us for centuries. Some of the lending and mortgage laws in use today come from the thirteenth and fourteenth centuries.

Throughout most of the twentieth century, people in the United States were primarily concerned with acquiring real estate to provide housing for themselves and their families. For most people, paying off their mortgage was an important financial goal. Long-term, fixed rate mortgages were ideal for this purpose. Newer generations have different objectives, however. They are much more mobile and flexible in their living arrangements. Today, in the twenty-first century, people are more likely to look at the purchase of a home as an investment rather than just a place to live and raise their families. A celebratory ceremony to "burn the mortgage" is extremely rare. Today many families choose real estate as a means of investing their excess disposable income.

Housing and commercial real estate have experienced tremendous growth in the past 60 years. This growth would not have been possible without mortgage lending. The result of this is that a plethora of financial arrangements is available for today's real estate investors, whatever their financial objectives. To some people, owning property debt-free gives a great feeling of security. To others, it is poor money management.

21.1 FINANCING INSTRUMENTS

The financing of real property typically involves the use of a promissory note, along with some type of security instrument, such as note and mortgage, note and deed of trust, or contract for deed.

The Promissory Note

A **promissory note** is a promise by the maker of the note to pay a specified amount in accordance with specific terms by a certain date.

The note itself is a contract. It is the borrower's promise to pay. The maker of the note is the **payor** and the lender is called the **payee**. A note is personal property and as a negotiable instrument can be sold. The note creates the obligation to pay. A note without collateralization or security is still a note. This is called an *unsecured note* or *signature note*.

Essentials of a Contract

A note must include the essentials of a contract: competent parties, valid consideration, lawful purpose, be written, be signed, and so on. A note also contains the words *promise to pay*, which create a definite legal obligation. In addition, it contains the date of its origin and accurate due date for payment. A note must set forth the provisions for the repayment of the loan and, if it includes a balloon payment, when it is due. A note must state the interest rate, whether it is simple or compound, and, of course, the maker or borrower must sign the note.

Although a note may contain several copies of the original, the borrower signs only one note. The lender holds the note until the loan is satisfied. The signer should be aware that each signed note would be a negotiable instrument, and, therefore, notes are never signed in duplicate. Because the note is a promise to pay, a lender may sue for damages on the note in case of default.

Negotiable Instrument

Because the note is a **negotiable instrument**, the obligation to pay can be sold by the holder of the note without permission of the payor. When a note is sold to a third party, the purchaser of the note is known as a **holder in due course**. The purchaser has all the rights of the original holder.

It is also possible to have a co-signer (co-maker) on a note. This happens many times with first-time buyers who need additional income from another person to qualify for the purchase of a property. All signers are individually and collectively responsible for the repayment of the note. This is known as **joint and several liability**.

Security Instruments

Mortgages

As a general rule of law, if an obligation to pay (promissory note) is secured by an interest in real property, then a mortgage has been created. Specifically, a **mortgage** is a written instrument by which real property is pledged to secure a debt or obligation, that is, a lien on real property. Whether it was created intentionally or accidentally, a mortgage can be foreclosed only judicially, by filing a lawsuit. **Deeds of trust** are an exception to the general rule of law and can be created if the parties follow all the statutory requirements and if "deeds of trust" are allowed in the specific jurisdiction. However, the lender under a deed of trust must follow the statutory rules, including 90-day notice of the trustee's sale, publication, posting, and so on to effect a valid non-judicial foreclosure. When real property is pledged with a mortgage or deed of trust, the real property has been hypothecated. **Hypothecation** means to pledge property as security without giving up possession.

A **contract for sale** (also known as an *agreement for sale* or *contract for deed* or *land contract*) is also an exception to the general rule and is created when the obligation being secured is the purchase price of the property, and the seller (not a third party) is the payee. In a contract for sale, the seller retains legal title to the property until the buyer has paid the full amount due. Until that time, the buyer holds only equitable title. If a buyer fails to pay the monthly payment (a type of monetary default), a contract for sale may be foreclosed non-judicially. At times, non-monetary defaults can occur, such as a buyer's committing or allowing "waste" or failure to insure the property. When this happens, a lawsuit is required to foreclose on the contract for sale. This is similar to mortgages.

The security instrument used in a real estate transaction, whether a mortgage or deed of trust, will contain certain clauses that identify the terms and conditions of appropriate repayment and/or default and foreclosure action.

A mortgage is a contract that includes a pledge of the property granting someone else rights in the property. Therefore, some of the terminology is similar to that of a deed, such as the granting clause, with the words *grant, sell, bargain*, or *convey*. The mortgage documents will also have a legal description and a covenant of seisin, which states that the mortgagor has the right to convey. The mortgage could also have a provision for the impounding of taxes and insurance by the lender.

Provisions in a Mortgage

Other provisions that may be included in a mortgage include a maintenance clause, prepayment clause, alienation clause, acceleration clause, defeasance clause, and subordination clause.

A **maintenance clause** charges the mortgagor with the responsibility to maintain and preserve the property to protect the mortgagees' interest in the property. Failure to maintain the property is called *waste*.

A **prepayment clause** enables the borrower to prepay the note prior to its due date with or without penalty. It also allows the borrower to make monthly payments greater than the agreed amount. Because an amortized loan calculates interest on the unpaid balance, this can greatly reduce the term of a loan.

> **Example**—A $45,000 loan at 9.5% interest amortized for 30 years has a monthly principal and interest payment of $378.38. If a borrower added just $25.00 to the monthly payment, the loan would be paid off in 22 years.

Lenders may not want their loans repaid significantly ahead of time, particularly in a period of declining interest rates. For this reason, some conventional loans have substantial prepayment penalties, and some allow for a prepayment of 20% of the outstanding loan balance in any given year.

An **alienation clause** is also known as a *due on sale clause*. Because the lender **(mortgagee)** qualified the original borrower **(mortgagor)**, that borrower does not have the right to convey the property without the lender's approval because the lender's security interest could be placed in jeopardy. Any conveyance of title without the lender's express approval could give the lender the right to accelerate the final maturity date and immediately call the entire remaining balance of the note due and payable.

An **acceleration clause** enables the lender to call the loan due and payable in the event of a default. This clause may be evoked because the mortgagor has defaulted by not making payments as agreed or by not complying with provisions of the security instrument.

A **defeasance clause** states that if the debt is paid by the due date, the lien that the lender holds is not valid. Obviously, security is no longer required because the note is paid off. However, because mortgages are recorded against the property, the satisfied mortgage must be removed from the chain of title. This is done by recording a **satisfaction of mortgage**, or in the case of a trust deed, a deed of reconveyance (also called a *"deed of release and reconveyance"*).

Certain mortgages or trust deeds may carry a **subordination clause**. This simply means that the lender will agree to a lesser position of security and allow another person/lender to place a lien in front of the original lender's. This is more common with seller carry-back agreements (purchase money mortgages).

Trust Deeds

Trust deeds are used in Nevada as the principal instrument to secure obligations with real property. Trust deeds are also used by most of Nevada's neighboring states. Lenders prefer trust deeds because it takes a shorter time to foreclose and, if desired by the lender, the lender could elect to treat a deed of trust as a mortgage and foreclose judicially. As in any trust arrangement, three parties are involved: the trustor, the trustee, and the beneficiary.

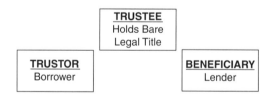

The **trustor** is the borrower, or the mortgagor in a mortgage. The trustor gives bare legal title to the trustee.

The **trustee** acts for both the trustor and beneficiary. The trustee can be a member of the bar association, an escrow agent, or a licensed insurance broker. The trustee holds **bare legal title** to the property, meaning he or she has the power of sale if the borrower defaults. This provision is known as the **power of sale clause**.

The **beneficiary** is the lender or mortgagee and will receive benefits from the action of the trustee or trustor.

The execution of a trust deed is quite simple. The trustor conveys limited legal title to the trustee. Limited legal title is called *"power of sale," "naked title,"* or *"bare title."* The trustee has the power to sell the property and foreclose on the trustor if the trustor does not pay the beneficiary as agreed in the trust deed.

The trustor makes payments to the beneficiary according to the note. When the final payment is made, the beneficiary notifies the trustee that the loan has been paid off. Then, the trustee reconveys the naked title to the trustor. This is accomplished by delivering a **deed of reconveyance** to the trustor.

If the trustor defaults, the beneficiary instructs the trustee to foreclose according to the laws that govern trust deed foreclosure. These rules will be covered in Chapter 23. Recording a trust deed establishes a lien on the property. Recording a deed of reconveyance acknowledges that the lien has been paid off.

Contract for Deed

A **contract for deed**, also called an *"agreement for sale"* or *"land contract,"* enables the seller to finance a buyer by permitting the buyer to make a down payment followed by monthly payments. A contract for deed does not have an accompanying promissory note; it is a single, complete financing and installment sales agreement between a buyer and seller.

A contract for deed should not be considered a mortgage or deed of trust, even though a contract for deed has all the same basic characteristics. These include the pledge of specific property as collateral for the loan, the terms and conditions for the loan's repayment, the statement of the borrower's responsibilities, and consequences of a default. However, legal title is not conveyed until the last payment is made.

Vendor and Vendee

The parties to a contract for deed are known as the **vendor** (seller) and **vendee** (buyer).

The most significant feature of this type of transaction is that the vendor does not deliver a deed to the vendee at the closing. Rather, the vendor promises to deliver the deed in the future when the buyer satisfies the terms of the contract.

Equitable Title

During the period beginning with the buyer and seller signing the contract and the seller signing the deed, the buyer has **equitable title** to the property. With equitable title, the vendee has the right to occupy the property and has all the rights and obligations of ownership. The purchaser's interest can be forfeited in the event of a default.

The concept of equitable title stems from the fact that a buyer can enforce specific performance of the contract in court to get legal title. Meanwhile, the vendor holds legal title in name only and without the full bundle of rights.

The equitable title that a purchaser holds under a contract for deed can be transferred by subcontract or assignment. Equitable title can be sold, given away, or mortgaged, and it passes to the purchaser's heirs and devisees upon the purchaser's death.

21.2 REAL ESTATE LOAN CLASSIFICATIONS

Depending on the needs of the borrower or lender, there are different real estate loan classifications. Some of these include blanket mortgages, open-end mortgages, package mortgages, construction loans, purchase money mortgages, hard money loans, all-inclusive deeds of trust, and adjustable rate mortgages. Although most of the loan classifications are referred to as mortgages, in Nevada they are almost always notes secured by a deed of trust.

Blanket Mortgage

A mortgagor in a **blanket mortgage** pledges more than one property to secure the note. When a developer wishes to develop a large tract of land, he or she pledges all the land as collateral with a *release clause* stating that the lender will release the lot that has been sold with a lump-sum payment so that clear title may pass to the purchaser of the lot.

Open-End Mortgage

An **open-end mortgage** enables a borrower to have a preapproved loan available for future money requirements. These loans are also called *equity loans*. If a developer has a preapproved loan for $500,000, he or she can borrow up to that amount, and as the outstanding loan is paid off, borrow even more. These loan advances are called *"draws."* (Also see *construction loan* later in this chapter.)

Package Mortgage

A **package mortgage** includes a lien on both real and personal property included in the purchase. This enables a buyer to purchase appliances for relatively no money down and at a low rate of interest, although the payment is over a much longer period of time.

Construction Loan

A **construction loan** is also called an *"interim-financing mortgage"* and is a form of an open-end mortgage. This loan finances the cost of materials and labor for a building. The loan is a short-term loan and must be replaced with permanent financing. Because the loan amount is for the entire cost of construction of a building, and a building that does not exist cannot be secured, the money is paid to the contractor in installments as the construction progresses. The periodic payments are referred to as *draws*.

Purchase Money Mortgage or Deed of Trust

Generally, a **purchase money mortgage** or deed of trust is any loan, whatever the source, for all or part of the purchase price for a piece of real property.

Typically, however, the term is most often used to describe a seller carry-back note. This type of purchase money mortgage or deed of trust is created when the seller accepts a note secured by a mortgage or deed of trust on the property he or she is selling as security for his or her equity, which he or she agrees to accept in installment payments. In other words, the seller becomes the bank, lending his or her own equity. This is often done when bank rates are high and the seller can offer a lower rate. With this type of financing, the security can be a mortgage or a trust deed, and the buyer has legal title.

Hard Money Loan

A **hard money loan** is a mortgage given for money received. The mortgagee is usually a private lender. Borrowing based on the equity of owned property is a hard money loan.

Wrap-Around Mortgages

A **wrap-around mortgage** (wrap), or **all-inclusive deed of trust**, is a purchase money transaction subject to, but still including, encumbrances to which it is subordinate. Legal title is actually conveyed and title insurance may also be obtained. An all-inclusive trust deed can be created only when the existing liens are assumable. The seller and buyer allow existing liens to remain in place while selling the property for a higher amount. The buyer now makes payments on the new, higher, wrap loan amount to the seller, who then makes the payments on the smaller original loans.

> **Example**—A property sells for $600,000. The seller's existing loans are a first trust deed with a balance of $236,000 at 8% and a payment of $2360 per month, and a second trust deed with a balance of $64,000, payable at 10%. If the buyer pays $100,000 cash down, the seller's remaining equity of $200,000 can be included in a wrap-around mortgage of $500,000 at 12% annual interest.

$600,000	Sales price	$200,000	Seller's equity
−100,000	Down payment	+300,000	Existing liens
$500,000	Purchase money loan	$500,000	Total wrap loan

The seller is collecting 12% on $500,000 when her equity is only $200,000. Therefore, the seller is making 4% over the first lien (bank money) interest rate of 8% and 2% over the interest rate on the second trust deed. The seller must continue to make the payments to the first and second lien holders.

Adjustable Rate Mortgage (ARM)

An **adjustable rate mortgage (ARM)** results in a sharing between the borrower and lender of risks of a fluctuating interest rate economy. The ARM allows the lender to make interest rate adjustments by referring to a national index, such as the *Wall Street Journal* prime rate, Federal Reserve District Cost of Funds index, U.S. Treasury bills, and so on. Whatever the index, it must be readily available for the borrower's inspection and outside the control of the lender. ARMs generally include caps on the amount and number of interest rate adjustments both annually and over the life of the loan. An ARM is usually assumable and would be unlikely to include a prepayment penalty.

The major advantage of an ARM for the borrower is greater affordability because the interest rate at the inception and perhaps for the first few years of the loan is generally lower than the rate for fixed-rate mortgages.

Graduated Payment Mortgage (GPM)

The **graduated payment mortgage (GPM)** begins with low payments but increases at regular intervals for a set number of years and then levels out for the balance of the term. This way, the buyer can qualify for a higher loan than he or she could on a normal installment fully amortizing loan. For example, payments could increase by $2\frac{1}{2}\%$ a year for 5 years and then remain constant for the balance of the 30-year loan term.

The loan payments in the early years of a GPM can result in negative amortization. Negative amortization occurs when the monthly loan payment is not enough to pay the interest due. The excess is added to the balance owed, which creates an increasing loan balance rather than an amortizing (decreasing) loan balance.

Reverse Annuity Mortgage (RAM)

Under all **reverse annuity mortgage (RAM)** programs, the house is appraised and a loan is made based on a certain percentage of the current value. The loan is paid to the homeowner in the form of a monthly annuity, which provides monthly payments to the owner for the rest of his or her life or the life of the loan. During the loan period, the homeowner owns and lives in the house.

A popular RAM is Fannie Mae's *Home Equity Conversion Mortgage*, which is an FHA-insured reverse mortgage. The program is open to homeowners who are at least 62 years of age, have ownership of their home with significant equity, and wish to use the equity in the home to cover part of their living expenses. The loan is an ARM, and the rates are adjusted either annually or monthly, with caps on increases.

RAMs have gained in popularity as the country's population has grown older. The RAM is designed to enable retired homeowners to use the equity in their homes as a source of additional income, while still retaining ownership.

Shared Appreciation Mortgage (SAM)

In a **shared appreciation mortgage (SAM)**, the lender participates in the appreciation of the property value and in turn accepts a note with a lower rate of interest. For the right to share in a portion of the appreciation, the lender will make the loan at an interest rate that is lower than the market rate of interest for a fixed-term conventional loan. The appreciation of the property is determined at the time the property is sold by comparing the sales price of the property to the original cost.

Participation Loan

With a **participation loan**, the lender participates in the profits generated by a commercial property used to secure the debt. The borrower agrees to the lender's participation in the revenues or net income of the property as an incentive for the lender to make the loan.

21.3 RESIDENTIAL LENDING

There are two major categories of residential loans: **conventional loans** and **government-backed loans**. Government-backed loans include FHA loans and VA loans. An **FHA loan** is one that is *insured* by the Federal Housing Administration. A VA loan is one that is *partially guaranteed* by the Department of Veterans Affairs. A conventional loan is any loan that is not a government-backed loan.

Conforming vs. Non-conforming

The U.S. Congress sets maximum limits on conventional loans purchased by Freddie Mac and Fannie Mae. Currently (2009), this limit is $625,000. Loans for this amount or less that meet Freddie Mac and Fannie Mae underwriting criteria are easily brokered through the secondary mortgage market. These conventional loans are known as **conforming loans**.

Non-conforming loans, also known as *jumbo loans* or *high balance loans*, can also be sold to the secondary mortgage market, although the purchaser will most likely be a non-government entity. Private corporations, usually subsidiaries of large financial institutions, have been formed to purchase these jumbo loans by issuing mortgage-backed securities collateralized by the loans. These private corporations operate in much the same manner as Freddie Mac, Ginnie Mae, or Fannie Mae. Because of the higher risk and smaller pool of funds available for the purchase of these loans, non-conforming loans generally bear a higher interest cost.

Conforming Loan Guidelines

In today's market, conforming loans generally follow the guidelines established by Freddie Mac and Fannie Mae because the vast majority of conventional loans are sold to the secondary mortgage market. Government-backed loans undoubtedly follow the underwriting guidelines of the Federal Housing Authority (FHA) or Department of Veterans Affairs (DVA). Even though a loan originator does not plan to sell loans in the secondary market, the underwriting guidelines provide a uniform set of criteria for the properties and borrowers' qualifications.

Maximum Mortgage Limits

Maximum mortgage limits for conforming loans are established by geographic area and are periodically revised. A mortgage broker or banker can offer advice on the current conforming loan limits in a particular area. In 2008, in Nevada, the Freddie Mac and Fannie Mae loan limits ranged from $417,000 for single-family original loan amounts on a one-unit dwelling to $801,950 for a four-unit dwelling. Maximum VA entitlements are available in amounts up to 25% of the maximum Freddie Mac loan limit, or for 2008, $104,250 for one-unit to $200,488 for a four-unit dwelling.

Underwriting Guidelines

Underwriting guidelines should always consider certain areas of review, regardless of whether they are promulgated by Fannie Mae or just the lender. These areas are called the four C's of lending: *credit, capacity, character,* and *collateral*.

A review of these areas should answer these questions:

Credit—Has the applicant used credit responsibly in the past? Does the applicant have an acceptable credit history?

Capacity—Does the applicant have sufficient financial resources to repay his or her existing debts and the proposed additional debt?

Character—Traditionally described as an applicant's "desire" or "willingness" to repay the debt. Character is more difficult to measure because it is a subjective evaluation.

Collateral—Is adequate property being used as security for the loan?

Loan–to-Value Ratio

The **loan-to-value ratio (LTV)** quantifies the collateral risk the lender takes and conversely, the equity the borrower risks losing. It is often considered the most important underwriting ratio. It is calculated, simply:

$$\frac{\text{Mortgage Amount}}{\text{Lesser of Sales Price or Appraised Value}} = \text{LTV}$$

The important thing to understand about LTV is that the higher the LTV, the less equity is at stake for the borrower. This has a significant impact on the borrower's repayment attitude if his or her financial circumstances change for the worse.

During the 1980s, lenders involved in the secondary market developed two additional LTV ratios that acknowledged the complex changes taking place in the industry. *Combined loan-to-value (CLTV)* for Fannie Mae and *total loan-to-value (TLTV)* for Freddie Mac take into consideration any secured lien junior to the proposed mortgage. This ratio compares the total amount of all mortgages and/or home equity financing, regardless of the source, to the lesser of the sales price or appraised value. The second ratio applies only to special situations where a potential borrower has previously arranged a home equity credit line but has not drawn on it. In these situations, the home equity line of credit must be included in the calculation of CLTV or TLTV, but several differing conditions can be applied that will increase the limits for CLTV or TLTV for borrowers with good credit scores, resulting in a ratio called the *home equity combined LTV (HCLTV)* for Fannie Mae and *home equity total LTV (HTLTV)* for Freddie Mac.

Lenders are able to make many more loan programs available to borrowers with much greater flexibility because of these expanded ratios that are now acceptable to Fannie Mae and Freddie Mac.

Acceptable Properties

As defined by Fannie Mae and Freddie Mac, acceptable properties to be used as collateral for these loans are determined by type of property ownership for conventional loan eligibility:

Principal residence—A one- to four-family property that is the primary residence of at least one of the borrowers. The borrower must occupy the property, take title to the property, and execute the note and deed of trust. The maximum loan-to-value ratio is usually 95%.

Second home—A single-family property that the borrower occupies in addition to his or her principal residence. (Note: A two- to four-family property is not an eligible property for second-home status.) When the property is classified as a second home, rental income may not be used to qualify the borrower. Maximum loan-to-value ratio is usually 80–90%.

Investment property—A one- to four-family property that the borrower does not occupy. This definition is used whether or not the property produces income. The maximum loan-to-value ratio is usually 70–80%.

Private Mortgage Insurance (PMI)

Since the advent of lending at loan-to-value ratios exceeding 80%, particularly by financial institutions, the mortgage insurance business has thrived. Today, nearly all lenders who grant conventional loan requests in excess of an 80% total loan-to-value will require some type of **private mortgage insurance (PMI)**. The FHA requires mortgage insurance on all of its loans and is more restrictive, because of its lower loan limits, than PMI. FHA volume is less volatile than PMI volume. Thus, in the 1990s, private mortgage insurance increased dramatically, and by 2000, PMI accounted for 62% of the mortgage insurance market.

Mortgage insurance insures the part of the purchase price or refinance that is not covered by the down payment (if there is one) and an 80% loan. PMI companies have many different products available. Regardless, a premium is calculated and charged to the borrower, usually as an addition to the monthly mortgage payment. The borrower can usually cancel mortgage insurance when his or her equity reaches 20%. Additionally, a federal law, the Homeowners' Protection Act of 1998, mandates that lenders automatically cancel private mortgage insurance when the borrower's mortgage balance reaches 78% of the original purchase price.

Maximum Allowable Contributions

Under Fannie Mae and Freddie Mac guidelines for conforming loans, maximum allowable borrower contributions depend on the loan-to-value ratio and the occupancy type. Any costs normally paid by the borrower are included as allowable contributions, even if paid by the seller. These costs could include an origination fee, discount points, credit report, appraisal fees, one-half escrow, American Land Title Association (ALTA) premiums, recording fees, prepaid interest, taxes, insurance, and the like. The seller can pay part or all of the borrower's contributions, as long as the total doesn't exceed the maximum allowable as follows:

Loan-to-Value Ratio	+	Occupancy Type	=	Maximum Percentage of Borrower's Contributions That Can Be Paid by Seller
Greater than 90%	+	Principal residence	=	3% of the lesser of the sales price or appraised value
90% or less	+	Principal residence	=	6% of the lesser of the sales price or appraised value
80% or less (or the combined LTV is 90% or less)	+	Second home	=	6% of the lesser of the sales price or appraised value
Any LTV is fine, as long as the loan is fixed rate	+	Investment property	=	2% of the lesser of the sales price or appraised value

Other Costs

The buyer or seller may also pay other costs. These other costs could include a one-time up-front mortgage insurance premium or the first year's premium for a renewable mortgage insurance policy. However, any costs that are normally the responsibility of the purchaser are considered contributions if the seller pays them. Therefore, an adjustment may be required to the property's sales price or appraised value (whichever is less).

FHA Loans

The Federal Housing Administration (FHA) is part of the U.S. Department of Housing and Urban Development (HUD). The FHA does not make loans; it insures loans made by approved lenders and sets minimum requirements for properties and borrowers.

FHA loans are available to any legal resident of the United States whose income is sufficient to make the mortgage payment, who has an acceptable credit history, and who has sufficient funds to close the transaction.

FHA Guidelines

The FHA has many different insurance programs that are generally based on the type of property and loan being sought. By far the most popular and most familiar to the public is Section 203(b). Some parameters for FHA loans follow:

- FHA loans are available to anyone who is financially qualified.
- The buyer's credit history may have some blemishes.
- Eligible properties can be from one to four units and must be owner-occupied.
- Although this does not have to come entirely from the buyer, a 3% minimum cash investment is required.
- Generally, the FHA permits a borrower to carry more debt in total than most conventional lenders.

The FHA establishes the maximum loan amount. The maximum dollar amount allowed increases when housing costs for an area support higher limits. In Nevada, these limits are set by county. In some instances, certain specific areas within a particular county may be designated as "high cost areas." As of June 2008, the limits for single-family residences in Washoe, Clark, and Churchill counties were $403,750, $400,000, and $271,050, respectively.

Loan-to-value limits require that the amount of any insured mortgage not exceed 97.65% of the appraised value of the property (or 98.75% if the value is $50,000 or less). The allowable mortgage is computed by applying the appraised value or sales price, whichever is less, times the appropriate percentage from this list:

- Owner-occupied principal residences / values more than $125,000 = 97.15% of the sales price.
- Owner-occupied principal residences / values more than $50,000 but less than $125,000 = 97.65% of the sales price.

- Owner-occupied principal residences / values less than $50,000 = 98.75% of the sales price.

Interest rate and discount points charged to borrowers are not regulated by the FHA, but once a borrower is approved, he or she must be re-approved if the interest rate is increased by more than 1% or if the amount of discount points increases.

The FHA does not set a maximum interest rate for FHA loans. The loan can be at any interest rate agreed upon between the buyer and seller, subject to lender availability.

If a borrower wishes to "buy-down" the interest rate on the loan by paying the lender points upfront, then the cost of the buy-down plus any origination points paid by the seller cannot exceed 6% of the loan amount, or the loan amount will be decreased by the amount that exceeds 6%, resulting in a higher down payment.

FHA-insured loans have no prepayment penalty. Most lenders require 30 days' notice of a mortgagor's intention to pay off a loan. FHA loans are assumable only after qualification of the new borrower.

For insuring the loan, the FHA charges the borrower a **mortgage insurance premium (MIP)**. Part of the MIP, which is currently 1.5% of the loan amount, is paid upfront when the loan transaction closes. When the seller pays the upfront premium, it must be paid in cash. The borrower may pay the upfront premium in cash at closing, or the premium may be financed by adding it to the loan amount. The other part of the MIP is a monthly charge for an annual premium, currently 0.5% of the loan amount. Premiums on mortgage loans with terms of 15 years or less may be significantly lower depending on the size of the down payment. The annual mortgage insurance premiums are cancelled automatically after 60 months or when the principal balance reaches 78% of the lower of a current appraised value or the initial sales price. If the loan is paid in full within the first 60 months, there may be a refund of the upfront mortgage insurance premium. The borrower must apply to receive a refund.

The only acceptable properties for FHA-insured loans are owner-occupie-done- to four-family units.

Veterans Administration (VA) Loans

The Veterans Administration (VA) was created in 1930 as an independent agency of the federal government.

In 1944, Congress passed the GI Bill of Rights (or Serviceman's Readjustment Act). Its purpose was to help returning veterans adjust to civilian life by creating VA benefit programs to encourage lenders to offer eligible veterans long-term, low down payment mortgages at reasonable interest rates. To accomplish this, the VA agreed to guarantee the loans and protect the lender from loss in the event of foreclosure.

The VA, which was absorbed by the Department of Veterans Affairs (DVA) when it became a Cabinet post in 1989, does not loan money; it guarantees a portion of the loans made to veterans by lenders under the VA programs. Even though the VA is now known as the DVA, the loans themselves are still commonly referred to as *VA loans.*

VA Loan Defined

A **VA loan** is a real estate mortgage available to qualified veterans for the purpose of buying or refinancing real estate for personal residential use only. A veteran must own and occupy the property being mortgaged with VA financing. A veteran may purchase a two- to four-family dwelling but must occupy one of the units as his or her primary residence. A veteran's spouse can meet the owner occupancy requirement.

The advantages of VA financing include the following:

- No down payment.
- Interest rates negotiable between borrower and lender.
- Liberal qualifying guidelines.
- Assumable by qualified purchaser with no change in interest rate.
- No prepayment penalty.
- Use of partial eligibility.
- Refinance eligible.
- Seller can pay 100% of closing costs and the seller can pay up to 4% of purchase price toward prepaids.

Maximum Loan Amount and Maximum Term

The Veterans Benefit Improvement Act of 2004, among other changes, increased the maximum VA loan guaranty amount on loans over $144,000 by indexing the maximum guaranty amount to 25% of the conventional conforming loan limit established by Fannie Mae and Freddie Mac. As of January 1, 2006, this loan limit was set at $417,000, resulting in a maximum guaranty entitlement of $104,250.

For VA loans, the maximum term is 30 years.

Interest Rates and Discounts

Interest rates are negotiated by the veteran with the lender. The DVA has guidelines for acceptable interest rates. If the negotiated interest rate is higher than the guideline, an *interest rate buy-down* may be necessary.

The veteran or the seller can pay the *discount points* necessary to increase the yield on the loan to the lender. However, the discount points cannot be financed in the loan amount. This includes refinances and "rate reduction" refinances.

Eligible Properties

Qualified veterans may use the funds from VA home loans for any of the following purposes:

- Owner-occupied, one- to four-family dwellings that have been completed for at least one year, including condominiums, cooperatives, and mobile homes.
- Owner-occupied, one- to four-family dwellings completed within the past year that were not inspected may qualify when completed upon submission of the following:

a. Copy of purchase agreement.

b. Builder's "plans and specifications" accompanied by a signed statement certifying that the dwelling was completed in compliance with same.

c. Statement from builder or seller (not veteran) agreeing to bear the expense of a "compliance" inspection.

- Home improvements and repairs.
- Purchase of an existing home.
- Purchase and repair or modification of an existing home.
- Refinance of an existing mortgage loan.

DVA Appraisals

Appraisals are done for the DVA in accordance with their guidelines. When an appraisal is completed, a Certificate of Reasonable Value (CRV) is issued to the veteran. CRVs are valid for six months (12 months on properties proposed for construction). The maximum loan amount and term of the loan for the particular property are determined by the appraised value set forth on the Certificate of Reasonable Value.

A veteran may pay more for a home than stated on the CRV if he or she signs a statement acknowledging that the price is more than shown on the CRV and that the difference is being paid by the veteran from his or her own, unfettered funds.

DVA Funding Fee

The DVA charges a funding fee on all loans. The funding fee can range from 2% to 3.35%.

The veteran or seller may pay the funding fee. If paid by the veteran, it may be added to the loan amount and financed over the life of the mortgage. However, the maximum loan amount, including funding fee, on a zero-down purchase transaction still may not exceed $417,000.

Qualifying for a VA Loan

The DVA requires that a veteran qualify for a VA loan under two methods: the residual method and the ratio method.

The *residual method* determines how much money a veteran will have left after paying all expenses including taxes and insurance, maintenance, utilities, debts, state and federal income tax, Social Security, and so on. The amount of money needed varies by geographical location, family size, and size of mortgage.

The *ratio method* calculates "housing expense plus debt" as a percentage of income with the stipulation that it should not exceed 41%. Very strong, compensating factors must be evident for a VA loan to be approved if the "total obligations" ratio exceeds 41%.

Entitlement

Entitlement is the maximum amount the DVA will guarantee a lender in the event of default. It bears a relationship to "maximum mortgage" but is not the same thing.

If a veteran has never used his or her housing benefits, the veteran is automatically eligible for a mortgage equal to four times entitlement. Entitlement was increased to $36,000 for both refinances and purchases as of March 1, 1988. It was increased to $50,750 for purchase transactions on December 20, 1999, but only when the purchase price exceeds $144,000. In 2006, a veteran's basic entitlement was still $36,000, although that amount can be increased up to $104,250 for certain loans in excess of $144,000. Lenders will generally loan up to four times a veteran's available entitlement without a down payment, provided that the veteran has the income and credit history to qualify.

If a veteran previously used his or her benefits but sold the home and either paid off the loan in full or sold it on an assumption to another veteran who substituted his or her entitlement, then the first veteran's entitlement is restored to the current basic entitlement amount.

Requirements for Restoration of Entitlement

1. Deed must transfer.
2. Loan must be paid in full.
3. The mortgage company must notify the DVA that the loan has been paid in full before entitlement can be restored.

Requirements for Substitution of Entitlement When House Is Sold by Assumption

1. Purchaser must be a veteran.
2. Veteran purchaser must have as much loan guaranty entitlement available to use as was used by the original veteran purchaser.
3. Veteran purchaser must be willing to substitute his or her entitlement for the original veteran purchaser.
4. Veteran purchaser must meet the underwriting requirements of the DVA. The DVA does the processing of the assumption.

The **Certificate of Eligibility** determines a veteran borrower's maximum entitlement. If a veteran has previously used his or her entitlement and it has not been restored, a down payment may be required. Typically, veteran borrowers make no down payment.

CHAPTER SUMMARY

The financing of real property typically involves the use of a promissory note, along with some type of security instrument, such as a note and mortgage, a note and deed of trust, or a contract for deed. A promissory note is a promise by the maker of the note to pay a specified amount in accordance with specific terms by a certain date. The maker of the note is the payor and the lender is called the payee. A note is personal property and as a negotiable instrument can be sold. A note must include the essentials of a contract. A note also contains the words *promise to pay*, the date of origin, and the due date. A note must set forth the provisions for the repayment of the loan, must state the interest rate, and must be signed by the maker or borrower. Because the note is a negotiable instrument, the obligation to pay can be sold by the holder of the note without permission of the payor. When a note is sold to a third party, the purchaser of the note is known as a holder in due course. The purchaser has all the rights of the original holder. It is also possible to have a co-signer on a note. All signers are individually and collectively responsible for the repayment of the note. This is known as joint and several liability.

A mortgage is a written instrument by which real property is pledged to secure a debt or obligation, that is, a lien on real property. Whether it was created intentionally or accidentally, a mortgage can be foreclosed only judicially by filing a lawsuit. Deeds of trust are an exception to the general rule of law and can be created if the parties follow all the statutory requirements. A contract for sale or agreement for sale is also an exception to the general rule and is created when the obligation being secured is the purchase price of the property, and the seller is the payee. In a contract for sale, the seller retains legal title to the property until the buyer has paid the full amount due. Until that time, the buyer holds only equitable title.

The security instrument used in a real estate transaction, whether a mortgage or deed of trust, will contain certain clauses that identify the terms and conditions of appropriate repayment and/or default and foreclosure action. Provisions that may be included in a mortgage include a maintenance clause, prepayment clause, alienation clause, acceleration clause, defeasance clause, and subordination clause. These clauses are described in detail in the body of this chapter's text.

There are many different types of mortgages described in the body of this chapter's text. This summary will not include descriptions of all these mortgages. An open-end mortgage enables a borrower to have a preapproved loan available for future money requirements. An adjustable rate mortgage (ARM) results in a sharing of risks of a fluctuating interest rate economy between the borrower and lender. An ARM allows the lender to make interest rate adjustments by referring to a national index. A graduated payment mortgage (GPM) begins with low payments but increases at regular intervals for a set number of years and then levels out for the balance of the term. A participation loan is one where the lender participates in the profits generated by a commercial property used to secure the debt. The borrower agrees to the lender's participation in the revenues or net income of the property as an incentive for the lender to make the loan.

Trust deeds are used in Nevada as the principal instrument to secure obligation with real property as collateral. Lenders prefer trust deeds because it takes a shorter time to foreclose. As in any trust arrangement, there are three parties involved: the trustor, the trustee, and the beneficiary. The trustor is the borrower, or the mortgagor in a mortgage. The trustor gives bare legal title to the trustee. The trustee holds bare legal title to the property. He or she has the power of sale if the borrower defaults. The beneficiary is the lender or mortgagee and will receive benefits from the action of the trustee or trustor.

The execution of a trust deed involves the following steps: The trustor conveys limited legal title to the trustee. The trustor makes payments to the beneficiary according to the note. When the final payment is made, the beneficiary notifies the trustee that the loan has been paid off. Then, the trustee reconveys the naked title to the trustor by delivering a deed of reconveyance to the trustor. If the trustor defaults, the beneficiary instructs the trustee to foreclose according to the laws that govern trust deed foreclosure. The primary difference between a trust deed and a mortgage is the time and process involved in foreclosure.

A contract for deed enables the seller to finance a buyer by permitting the buyer to make a down payment followed by monthly payments. A contract for deed does not have an accompanying promissory note; it is a single, complete financing and installment sales agreement between a buyer and seller. The parties to a contract for deed are known as the vendor (seller) and vendee (buyer). The most significant feature of this type of transaction is that the vendor does not deliver a deed to the vendee at the closing. Rather, the vendor promises to deliver the deed in the future when the buyer has satisfied the terms of the contract. During the period, the buyer has equitable title to the property.

There are two major categories of residential loans: conventional loans and government-backed loans, which are FHA loans and VA loans. An FHA loan is one that is insured by the Federal Housing Administration. A VA loan is one that is partially guaranteed by the Department of Veterans Affairs. A conventional loan is any loan that is not a government-backed loan.

Non-conforming loans can also be sold to the secondary mortgage market, although the purchaser will most likely be a non-government entity. Conforming loans will generally follow the guidelines established by Freddie Mac and Fannie Mae because the vast majority of conventional loans are sold to the secondary mortgage market. Government-backed loans follow the underwriting guidelines of the Federal Housing Authority (FHA) or Department of Veterans Affairs (DVA). Maximum mortgage limits for conforming loans are established by geographic area and are periodically revised.

Underwriting guidelines should always consider certain areas of review, regardless of whether they are promulgated by Fannie Mae or just the lender. Known as the C's of lending, the areas to review are: credit, capacity, collateral, and character. The loan-to-value ratio (LTV) quantifies the collateral risk the lender takes and conversely, the equity the borrower risks losing. It is often considered the most important underwriting ratio. The higher the LTV, the less equity is at stake for the borrower. Nearly all lenders who grant conventional loan requests in excess of an 80% total LTV will require some type of private mortgage insurance. Mortgage insurance insures the part of the purchase price or refinance that is not covered by the down payment (if there is one) and an 80% loan. Under Fannie Mae and Freddie Mac guidelines for conforming loans, maximum allowable borrower contributions depend on the loan-to-value ratio and the occupancy type.

The Federal Housing Administration (FHA) is part of the U.S. Department of Housing and Urban Development (HUD). The FHA does not make loans; it insures loans made by approved lenders and sets minimum requirements for properties and borrowers. FHA loans are available to any legal resident of the United States whose income is sufficient to make the mortgage payment, who has an acceptable credit history, and who has sufficient funds to close the transaction. The guidelines for FHA loans are described fully in the body of the text.

The Department of Veterans Affairs (DVA) does not loan money; it guarantees a portion of the loans made to veterans by lenders under the VA programs.

Even though the VA is now known as the DVA, the loans themselves are still commonly referred to as VA loans. A VA loan is a real estate mortgage available to qualified veterans for the purpose of buying or refinancing real estate for personal residential use only. A veteran must own and occupy the property being mortgaged with VA financing. A veteran may purchase a two- to four-family dwelling but must occupy one of the units as his or her primary residence. A veteran's spouse can meet the owner occupancy requirement.

CHECKING YOUR COMPREHENSION

1. Summarize the essential elements and purpose of a:
   - Promissory note
   - Mortgage
   - Deed of trust
   - Contract for deed

2. List and define the major clauses that could be in a mortgage or deed of trust.

3. Explain the meaning of the following real estate loan classifications:
   - Blanket mortgage
   - Open-end mortgage
   - Package mortgage
   - Construction loan
   - Purchase money mortgage
   - Hard money loan
   - Wraps

4. Summarize the criteria for conforming loans.

5. List the similarities and differences for the following residential financing programs:
   - Conventional loans
   - FHA loans
   - VA loans

REVIEWING YOUR UNDERSTANDING

1. In a trust deed or mortgage, the clause that permits the mortgagee to declare the entire unpaid sum due upon a default by the mortgagor or trustor is called the:
   a. judgment clause
   b. acceleration clause
   c. forfeiture clause
   d. escalator clause

2. A power of sale clause would **MOST** likely be found in which of the following?
   a. mortgage
   b. promissory note
   c. trust deed
   d. listing contract

3. The guarantee on a $184,000 VA loan with no down payment would be:
   a. $36,000
   b. $46,000
   c. $50,750
   d. $92,000

4. An FHA mortgage loan is obtained through which of the following?
   a. a qualified lending institution
   b. any government agency
   c. the Federal Deposit Insurance Corporation
   d. the Federal Housing Authority

5. Loan discount points related to a purchase money mortgage insured by the FHA can be charged to:
   a. the borrower
   b. the broker
   c. the seller
   d. either the buyer or the seller

6. When the mortgagee is the seller the type of mortgage is called a:
   a. conventional mortgage
   b. trust deed
   c. purchase money mortgage
   d. government-insured mortgage

7. The loan **MOST** likely to change its interest rate over its life is a(n):
   a. straight note
   b. ARM
   c. construction loan
   d. second mortgage

8. A defeasance clause would **MOST** likely be found in a(n):
   a. mortgage or trust deed
   b. promissory note
   c. listing contract
   d. offer to purchase

9. Written evidence of a personal promise to repay borrowed money is called a:
   a. mortgage
   b. security instrument
   c. note
   d. trust deed

10. Interest rates on conventional and FHA loans are:
    a. established by negotiation between the borrower and lender
    b. established by Fannie Mae
    c. established by Ginnie Mae
    d. established by the FDIC

11. An existing first mortgage loan **MAY** be changed to a junior lien by:
    a. a court order
    b. satisfaction of the first mortgage loan
    c. a subordination agreement signed by the mortgagee
    d. recording another mortgage

12. A release clause provides for the release of:
    a. brokers from liability
    b. parcels of land from blanket mortgages or trust deeds
    c. leases
    d. listing agreements

13. Trustor is to beneficiary as:
    a. vendor is to vendee
    b. mortgagor is to mortgagee
    c. grantor is to grantee
    d. creditor is to debtor

14. The term *hard money* refers to a:
    a. loan with an extremely high rate of interest
    b. loan that was difficult to obtain
    c. cash loan, as opposed to seller financing
    d. well-secured loan

15. A mortgage that is subordinate to another mortgage but includes the amount of the first mortgage in its balance is a(n):

    a. blanket mortgage

    b. wrap-around mortgage

    c. purchase money mortgage

    d. open-end mortgage

16. A mortgagee might consider making an FHA or VA loan rather than a conventional loan because of the:

    a. lower risk

    b. higher interest

    c. longer investment period

    d. federal tax benefits

17. Both FHA and VA loans cover:

    a. ten-unit apartments with owner occupied units

    b. business and home loans

    c. farm and business loans

    d. single-family and multi-family residences

18. A disadvantage of a conventional loan when compared to a government-insured or -guaranteed loan is **MOST** likely to be a:

    a. lower interest

    b. longer term

    c. greater down payment

    d. longer processing period

19. Real estate has been placed as security for a loan; however, the borrower retains possession. This is:

    a. capitalization

    b. hypothecation

    c. amortization

    d. dedication

20. Conventional loans are:

    a. FHA loans

    b. not secured by a government agency

    c. VA loans

    d. secured by a government agency

Chapter

22

IMPORTANT TERMS AND CONCEPTS

amortized loan	credit	legal rate
back-end ratio	direct reduction loan	partially amortized loan
balloon payment	discount	PITI
bankruptcy	discount point	point
budget loans	income ratio	usury
budget mortgage	installment loans	verifications of deposit
capacity	interest	verifications of employment
character	interest-only loans	
collateral	interest rate buy-downs	yield

CHAPTER OBJECTIVES

After completing this chapter, you should be able to:

- Describe the procedures and criteria for qualification for residential financing.
- Discuss interest and discount points.
- Describe the different types of loan repayment plans.
- Solve real estate financing math problems.

Qualifying Borrowers; Interest and Discount Points

22.1 QUALIFYING BORROWERS

Why bother qualifying borrowers in the first place? If a loan is not repaid appropriately, then the lender can just take the property back and resell it or hold on to it as an investment. The answer is simply that lenders are in the money business, not the real estate business. Probably the last thing a lender wants is to take back a property. Going through the foreclosure and redemption process is expensive and time-consuming. In most cases, the lender will lose money through the cost of time and resources devoted to the foreclosure process.

Many years ago, when 25% or greater down payments were common, qualifying the borrower was important but not as important as it is today. With a large down payment, the borrower has more equity, hence a larger cushion for the lender in a depreciating market, and is less likely to default. Over time, with the political expediency of everyone owning their own home, required down payments decreased to 20%. In recent years, lenders have been making high loan-to-value ratio conventional and government-backed loans that require little, if any, down payment. With no equity in the property, borrowers have little incentive to make their mortgage payments when financial troubles arise. A real estate market in a down cycle can actually produce real estate values that are less than the remaining loan balances.

Because most loans are sold to the secondary market, there must be standards of qualifying that will demonstrate the borrower's willingness and capacity to pay. Lenders generally evaluate these areas through the use of qualifying guidelines called *ratios*. Two ratios most often used are monthly *mortgage payments to income ratio*, called the **income ratio**, and *obligations to income ratio*, generally referred to as the **back-end ratio**. These ratios are used to determine a borrower's capacity or ability to pay. In general, Fannie Mae and Freddie Mac require an income ratio of 28% or less and a back-end ratio of 36% or less. The Federal Housing Administration (FHA) uses the same qualifying procedure as conventional lenders except that they will accept higher ratios

(29% and 41%), but the ratios must include the cost of mortgage insurance. The Department of Veterans Affairs (DVA) uses a more complicated two-phase qualifying procedure: (1) the residual income method and (2) application of qualifying income ratio. Residual income is the amount of gross income left after deducting income and Social Security taxes and/or retirement plan contributions to arrive at net take-home pay, then deducting housing expenses and fixed obligations (long-term debt, alimony, child support, and so on). Under DVA guidelines, the qualifying income ratio is determined by taking the monthly housing expenses (principal, interest, taxes, and insurance) plus long-term debts and dividing this total by net take-home pay. If the ratio is 41% or less, the borrower will qualify. If the ratio is above 41%, then the underwriter must look at other compensating factors.

Borrower's Income

In determining a borrower's qualifying income, what do lenders include? Obviously, a borrower's earned income is the primary basis for determining income levels in qualifying a borrower. The income may be in the form of salaries and wages, commissions, bonuses, self-employment income, rents, alimony, child support payments, Social Security, and pension distributions. Wages from part-time employment are also included if there is a consistent pattern. Overtime earnings may also be considered if borrowers can demonstrate the overtime's consistency and dependability. Income claimed in the borrower's loan application will be subject to verification by the lender, so the borrower should be prepared to provide copies of all important documents (W-2 forms, 1099s, income tax returns, and so on) in addition to signing verification of employment and verification of deposit forms.

Borrower's Expenses

A borrower's expenses can be separated into two categories: housing expenses and monthly expenses. The following table shows examples of each type of expense.

Housing Expenses	Monthly Expenses
Principal and interest payment	Social Security
Taxes and insurance	State and local taxes
Mortgage insurance	Long-term debts
Association dues, if there is a homeowners' association	Child support and/or alimony
Maintenance and utilities	

For conventional loans, lenders may use IRS forms or copies of income tax returns to determine amounts of Social Security and income taxes withheld. The FHA and DVA publish charts for use by lenders in calculating taxes, insurance, maintenance, and utilities.

Debts

Debts are treated differently depending on the type of loan. According to the guidelines, debts are considered "long-term" if their repayment period will be longer than the following:

> *DVA*—All debts that require more than 6 months are considered long-term.
>
> *Conventional*—All debts that require more than 10 months are considered long-term.
>
> *FHA*—All debts that require more than 12 months are considered long-term.

Generally speaking, most other debt is not counted in the qualifying ratios because it can be repaid in a short period of time. However, credit card balances that are beyond the borrower's ability to repay within the previously mentioned time frames will be counted in the calculation of long-term debt.

A real estate salesperson should have a clear understanding of the qualifying guidelines and the qualifying process. The final decision, however, is up to the underwriter at the lender's office. A loan officer is better qualified to advise a buyer if an increased down payment or adjustment needs to be made in the qualifying package.

Meeting with the Lender

During an interview with the lender, a borrower will be asked to provide loan account numbers, loan balances, income tax returns, and money to pay for credit reports and an appraisal. The borrower also will be asked to sign VOEs, or **verifications of employment**, and VODs, **verifications of deposit**, which are sent by the lender to the borrower's employer(s) and bank(s) for verification of the information supplied by the borrower. In today's real estate market, mortgage lenders do a great deal of marketing and advertising aimed at potential borrowers. Therefore, many of today's buyers enter the real estate market with a loan qualification already in hand. Much of this marketing is done via the Internet, which results in significant savings in time and resources for all of the parties involved. A potential buyer may have already supplied the mortgage lender with the necessary income and expense documentation and credit reports, leaving only the qualification of the subject property to be accomplished.

The type and source of income is important, but the lender will also be concerned with the stability of the income. Factors to be considered will include employment and income history, job changes, type of job, and age of the borrower. A consistent employment history of at least two years is generally required, although a recent change in employment is not considered negatively if it is a promotion or a better job. A self-employed individual will usually be asked to provide copies of his or her tax returns for the past two years and, if appropriate, balance sheets and profit and loss statements as well. If a borrower is going to retire within a year or two, then the lender will want to know what kind of retirement income the borrower will have and whether it will be sufficient to make the payments on the loan.

Underwriting the Loan

The overwhelming majority of residential real estate loans written today are intended for sale in the secondary market. As a result, most lenders follow the core underwriting guidelines of Fannie Mae and Freddie Mac, as published in their separate *Seller/Servicer Guides*, or of such government programs as the FHA or VA. These industry standards were developed from ongoing statistical analyses of millions of loan applications from around the country, and they are exceedingly accurate in their predictive ability from a national perspective. The objective in underwriting loans is to avoid delinquencies. These guidelines provide uniformity and ease of use for the entire industry (even for lenders who do not intend to sell loans in the secondary market) in effectively achieving that objective.

Today's technology has made it possible to underwrite a loan in a matter of a few minutes. However, each loan represents a separate risk, and that risk must be analyzed and reviewed on an individual basis. While the use of technology through improved data management and statistical analysis has enabled the industry to process an unprecedented number of loans, the traditional areas for review are still paramount to the loan decision. These four areas are **credit, capacity, character,** and **collateral**.

Credit Analysis

Credit reporting agencies play a major role in the analysis and evaluation of a borrower's credit. Payment history as well as all types of credit granted are commonly included in a credit report. Lenders will obtain credit reports from all three credit-reporting agencies (TransUnion, Experian, and Equifax) and use the credit reports to analyze the applicant's ability and desire to pay. The credit agencies will also supply the lender with a *credit score* or *FICO score* that attempts to objectively determine the probability of repayment of the debt by the applicant.

When the applicant has had a mortgage payment in the past, that payment history will play a large part in the final analysis.

A **bankruptcy** in an applicant's history will not automatically disqualify the loan applicant. A bankruptcy that occurred three to five years ago would be evaluated based on the circumstances surrounding the applicant at the time he or she originally filed for bankruptcy. Also, the credit history since the applicant emerged from bankruptcy would be given consideration.

Capacity

Capacity is the ability to pay the debt or loan being contemplated. Capacity depends on the borrower's income. The level and type of income will be thoroughly evaluated by the loan underwriters. Generally, the underwriters will not be as concerned with the applicant's specific position or industry, or whether he or she is a salaried or hourly employee, but whether the applicant maintains the same level of income regardless of its source.

During the 1980s and 1990s, economic events changed the approach to evaluating earnings and employment history. Numerous changes in employment consistent with the same career path are considered a positive characteristic. "Job stability" today is used to define a consistent income level and employment in related lines of work, rather than having the same job for years on end. However, employment changes without advancement or significant pay increases may still be indicative of future financial instability.

Character

Character is also referred to as *desire* or *willingness to pay*. Lenders have different ways of approaching this task; some do it formally and some do it informally. Although prior payment history and credit scores are helpful, review of this area is basically subjective and must be considered in context with the other areas mentioned previously.

Collateral

In the final analysis, the lender must protect himself or herself and his or her investors by securing the loan with the borrower's property. The property that will be collateral for the loan must be adequate to insure that the lender will be able to recover his or her investment in the event of a default by the borrower. To evaluate the collateral, the lender will obtain an appraisal, which is an opinion or estimate of the property's market value, from a licensed or certified appraiser. Appraisals and the appraisal process are discussed in Chapter 24.

The loan underwriters use the appraisal to determine whether the subject property conforms to the lender's property standards, is in marketable condition, and is of sufficient value to support the loan request.

22.2 INTEREST AND DISCOUNT POINTS

Interest is the cost or money paid for the use of someone else's money. A lender looks at interest as money earned (income) from an investment (a loan). The amount of interest a lender charges depends on the demand for loans and competition among lenders, as well as the risk assumed. The greater the investor's (lender's) risk, the higher the interest rate will be. Risk, of course, involves not only the size of the loan but the quality of the collateral or security and the borrower's credit history.

Most real estate loans are based on simple interest. The formula to calculate simple interest is:

Interest = Principal × Rate × Time

Interest is normally paid in arrears because it accrues or is earned through the passage of time. Borrowers pay for the period of time they have used the money.

EXAMPLE—Based on the simple interest formula, the interest for a $1500 loan at 9% interest for one year is $135.

$$P \times R \times T = I$$
$$\$1500 \times .09 \times 1 = \$135$$

To find the monthly interest, divide by 12 ($135 ÷ 12), which results in $11.25 for the first month's interest.

Legal Rate and Usury

If the rate is left off of an obligation or omitted from a judgment, Nevada law provides for a **legal rate** of 12% interest.

Usury is charging interest at a higher rate than allowed by law. Nevada does not have a usury limit on interest rates.

Discount Points

Loans are made to yield a profit to the lender and provide a source of funds to the borrower. As discussed previously, the borrower's cost of using the funds is called *interest*. The amount of return a lender receives on his or her loan is called *yield*. **Yield** is calculated by dividing the annual interest income by the amount invested in the loan. A **point** is 1% of the loan amount. A **discount** is a charge made by lenders to increase the effective rate of interest (yield) from the stated interest rate on the note. The points paid for the discount are paid by the borrower at loan closing or can be deducted from the loan proceeds at funding. By actually funding less than the loan amount, the lender increases his or her yield over the loan's stated interest rate. A borrower can choose from a wide variety of loan programs that offer varying interest rates and discount points.

> **EXAMPLE**—If a borrower pays 3 points for a 30-year loan of $250,000 at a stated interest rate of 6%, the actual yield to the lender is 6.287%. Because the stated interest rate does not change, the lender would fund only $242,500, keeping the difference and increasing his or her yield.

As a rule of thumb:

- One discount point is equal to raising the yield on a 30-year loan by $\frac{1}{8}$ of a percent.
- Eight points equal a 1% change in yield.

Interest Rate Buy-Downs

Interest rate buy-downs are slightly different from discount points. In this case, the stated interest rate is actually reduced prior to origination. The same process occurs, but the borrower signs a note at a lower interest rate, and the lender funds the entire amount of the original principal. There are several variations, some resulting in temporary reductions in the mortgage payment for the borrower.

> **EXAMPLE**—A home builder may have originally obtained a lender's commitment for financing the sale of the homes in her subdivision at 6.25% to 6.5%, but the market has changed. The builder may now agree to pay the 2 to 3 points to the lender to enable her to sell out her inventory at the current market rate of 6%.

22.3 LOAN REPAYMENT PLANS

Loan repayment plans include interest-only loans, amortized loans, budget loans, partially amortized installment loans, and direct reduction loans.

Interest-Only Loans

Loans that require periodic payment of the interest only are referred to as straight loans, bullet loans, term loans, and **interest-only loans**. The annual interest is calculated and divided into the agreed upon number of payments (12, 4, 2, and so on). The final payment is called a *balloon payment*, which combines the final interest payment with the total principal amount due.

> EXAMPLE—A seller carried back a $10,000 loan at 8.5% interest only for five years. The maturity date is the "call date" or "stop." The monthly payment would be:
>
> $$\$10,000 \times .085 = \$850.00 \div 12 = \$70.83$$
>
> The borrower would make 59 monthly payments of $70.83 and one of $10,070.83.
>
> Because there was no principal reduction during the term of the loan, the amount of monthly interest never changed.

Amortized Loans

An **amortized loan** is the most common type of real estate loan. This type of loan has an installment payment of principal and interest calculated for a certain period of time. The principal and interest payment remains constant throughout the life of the loan. The payment reduces the loan balance by varying amounts relative to the decreasing interest charge. In the beginning, the payment is primarily interest, while the principal portion increases with each subsequent payment until the end of the life of the loan, when the payment will be primarily principal. Because they are repaid in installments, amortized loans are generally referred to as **installment loans**.

Budget Loans

In Nevada, it is common to find that the installment payment must include a prorated amount for property taxes and insurance, which is held in trust by the lender for the payment of the property taxes and insurance. The prorated amount is generally $\frac{1}{12}$ of the estimated taxes and insurance. This type of payment is referred to as **PITI** (principal, interest, taxes, and insurance), and the loans requiring this type of payment are sometimes called **budget loans** because the borrower is forced to put away money in trust for the payment of property taxes and insurance. This trust account may be referred to as an impound account or reserve account.

Partially Amortized Installment Loans

A **partially amortized loan** is used to obtain a lower monthly payment by restricting the length of the loan. The installment payment may be calculated based on a 20-year amortization, but the note may actually be due in five years. This results in a lower monthly payment for five years with a balloon payment due at the end of the period. A **balloon payment** is a note's final installment payment, which is greater than the preceding payments and pays the note in full.

> EXAMPLE—A $150,000 loan at 8.5% amortized for 20 years with a 7-year call would require 83 payments of $1,292.58 and one of $124,127.95.

These partially amortized loans are used when lenders are not willing to loan money for long periods of time.

Direct Reduction Loans

A **direct reduction loan** calls for a constant principal reduction plus the interest due on the unpaid balance. If a borrower were required to make a $100 principal reduction plus 9% interest payment on a $1200 loan, he or she would pay as follows:

1st payment: $1200 × .09 = $108 ÷ 12 = $9.00 = $109.00

2nd payment: $1100 × .09 = $ 99 ÷ 12 = $8.25 = $108.25

3rd payment: $1000 × .09 = $ 90 ÷ 12 = $7.50 = $107.50

… and so on until the loan is paid off. These types of loans are rarely used in real estate lending; they are more commonly used by banks in making short-term working capital loans.

22.4 FINANCING MATH

When completing interest math problems, remember the computation formula Interest (I) = Principal (P) × Rate (R) × Time (T). The T formula can also help in solving financing math problems. The T formula follows, with components placed in the "T" to assist you in solving the subsequent problems:

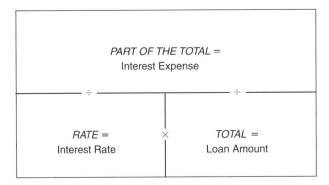

EXERCISE 1—If a person borrowed $26,500 for 20 years at 15% interest per annum, using a straight note, she would pay interest of (select one answer from the following list):

a. $62,200

b. $79,500

c. $95,400

d. $33,300

TELL ME WHY

This problem is a simple calculation of interest to be paid by the borrower. The principal amount, $26,500, will be due at the end of the note's term, in this case 20 years, so there are no installments of principal to be paid until the note is due. Therefore, the interest to be paid is calculated:

$26,500 at 15% = $3975 per annum (year)

$3975 × 20 (the term of the loan) = $79,500

EXERCISE 2—Simple interest was calculated at 8.5% per annum on a loan of $1968 for 3 years, 10 months, and 20 days. The interest was **most** nearly (select one answer from the following list):

a. $589

b. $607

c. $650

d. $668

TELL ME WHY

Again, a simple interest calculation: the annual interest on the loan, $1968 at 8.5% is $1968 × .085 = $167.28.

Three years' interest: $167.28 × 3	=	$501.84	
10 months' interest: ($167.28/12) × 10	=	139.40	
20 days' interest: ($167.28/365) × 20	=	9.17	
Total for the period		$650.41	

EXERCISE 3—If one month's interest paid on a mortgage is $200 and the principal balance is $30,000, what is the annual rate of interest (select one answer from the following list)?

a. 6%

b. 6.67%

c. 7.25%

d. 8%

TELL ME WHY

In this problem, you know that the amount of interest for one month is $200 and the principal balance is $30,000; therefore, using your interest formula, R × $30,000 = $200 for one month. The annual rate is determined:

$200 × 12 = $2400 annually

$2400/$30,000 = .08 or 8%

CHAPTER SUMMARY

Because most loans are sold to the secondary market, there must be standards of qualifying that will demonstrate the borrower's willingness and capacity to pay. Lenders generally evaluate these areas through the use of qualifying guidelines called ratios. Two ratios most often used are monthly mortgage payments to income ratio, called the income ratio, and obligations to income ratio, generally referred to as the back-end ratio.

Several criteria must be considered in qualifying a borrower for residential financing. A borrower's earned income is the primary basis for determining income levels in qualifying a borrower. A borrower's expenses can be separated into two categories: housing expenses and monthly expenses. Second, debts are treated differently depending on the type of loan. Debts are considered "long-term" if their repayment period will be longer than the following: VA—all debts that require more than 6 months; conventional—all debts that require more than 10 months; FHA—all debts that require more than 12 months. Next, the overwhelming majority of residential real estate loans written today are intended for sale in the secondary market. As a result, most lenders follow the core underwriting guidelines of Fannie Mae and Freddie Mac, or of such government programs as the FHA or DVA. Finally, the traditional areas for review are still paramount to the loan decision. These four areas are credit, capacity, character, and collateral.

Credit reporting agencies play a major role in the analysis and evaluation of borrowers' credit. The credit agencies will supply the lender with a credit score or FICO score that attempts to objectively determine the probability of the applicant repaying the debt. A bankruptcy in a loan applicant's history will not automatically disqualify the applicant.

Interest is the cost or money paid for the use of someone else's money. A lender looks at interest as income from an investment. The greater the lender's risk, the higher the interest rate will be. Most real estate loans are based on *simple interest*, which is rent paid only for the amount of the debt still outstanding. The formula to calculate simple interest is I = P × R × T. Interest is normally paid in arrears. If the rate is left off of an obligation or omitted from a judgment, Nevada law provides for a legal rate of 12% interest. Usury is charging interest at a higher rate than allowed by law. Nevada does not have a usury limit on interest rates.

The amount of return a lender receives on a loan is called yield. A point is 1% of the loan amount. A discount is a charge made by lenders to increase the yield from the stated interest rate on the note. The points paid for the discount are paid by the borrower at loan closing or can be deducted from the loan proceeds at funding. Interest rate buy-downs are slightly different from discount points. In this case, the stated interest rate is actually reduced prior to origination. The same process occurs, but the borrower signs a note at a lower interest rate, and the lender funds the entire amount of the original principal.

Loans that require periodic payment of the interest only are referred to as straight loans, bullet loans, term loans, and interest-only loans. The annual interest is calculated and divided into the number of payments agreed upon. The final payment is called a "balloon payment."

An amortized loan is the most common type of real estate loan. This type of loan has an installment payment of principal and interest calculated for a certain period of time. The principal and interest payment remains constant throughout the life of the loan. Amortized loans are generally referred to as installment loans. In Nevada, it is common to find that the installment payment includes a prorated amount for property taxes and insurance, which is held in trust by the lender. This type of payment is referred to as PITI (principal, interest, taxes, and insurance), and the loans requiring this type of payment are sometimes called budget loans. A partially amortized loan is used to obtain a lower monthly payment by restricting the length of the loan. The installment payment may be calculated based on a 20-year amortization, but the note may actually be due in five years. This results in a lower monthly payment for five years with a balloon payment due at the end of the period.

A direct reduction loan calls for a constant principal reduction plus the interest due on the unpaid balance.

CHECKING YOUR COMPREHENSION

1. Describe the procedures and criteria for qualifying a buyer for a residential loan.

2. Explain the terms *interest* and *discount points.*

3. Explain the meaning of usury and the legal rate of interest.

4. Describe the following loan repayment plans:
   - Interest-only loan
   - Amortized loan
   - Partially amortized loan
   - Budget loan
   - Direct reduction loan

REVIEWING YOUR UNDERSTANDING

1. The effect on yield resulting from the payment of one discount point is:
   a. 1% divided by the term of the loan
   b. 1%
   c. one-fourth of 1%
   d. one-eighth of 1%

2. A discount point is equal to 1% of the:
   a. mortgage loan
   b. sales price
   c. listing price
   d. full cash value

3. If each percentage in interest yield is equal to eight points, then to increase the yield from 6¼% to 6⅝%, the borrower would have to pay:
   a. 2 points
   b. 3 points
   c. 4 points
   d. 5 points

4. A lot has 50 feet of frontage by 180 feet deep. The buyer had only $15,000 cash. The lot cost was $173 per front foot, and the house cost was $75,950. He secured a mortgage for the balance. If his interest was 6.5% per annum, payable semiannually, what was the amount of this first semiannual interest payment?
   a. $2468
   b. $4524
   c. $2262
   d. $4937

5. On February 1, a mortgagor makes a $638 monthly payment on her mortgage, which has an interest rate of 10%. The mortgagee allocates $500 to the payment of interest. What is the principal balance due on the mortgage on February 2?
   a. $60,000
   b. $59,862
   c. $63,662
   d. $63,850

6. Discounts and loan origination fees:

   a.   are both measured in points

   b.   describe exactly the same thing

   c.   can be paid by the borrower (buyer)

   d.   both a and c

7. If a loan applicant has a gross monthly income of $5000, mortgage payments (PITI) of $1400, and long-term monthly debts of $350, the applicant's monthly payment or front-end ratio is:

   a.   15%

   b.   28%

   c.   35%

   d.   41%

8. Which of the following is considered a negative for credit scoring purposes?

   a.   credit score of 800

   b.   an average number of current credit accounts

   c.   no history of bankruptcy

   d.   a former collection account paid in full

9. Capacity to pay is best defined as the:

   a.   total of the applicant's assets

   b.   applicant's willingness to repay loans

   c.   applicant's ability to repay debts

   d.   applicant's current mortgage activity

10. During the processing of a loan, a loan officer correlates the characteristics of the applicant, the loan being considered, and the appraised value of the property in making a decision to grant the loan. The most important aspect the loan officer must consider is:

    a.   the property's rental value

    b.   the degree of risk

    c.   the location of the property

    d.   assessment value for property taxes

11. A mortgage loan payable in monthly installments that are sufficient to pay the principal in full during the term of the loan is called a(n):

    a.   straight loan

    b.   purchase money mortgage

    c.   amortized loan

    d.   conventional loan

12. The loan on a property is 60% of its appraised value. If the interest rate is 8% per year and the first semiannual interest payment is $5280, what is the appraised value of the property?

    a. $110,000

    b. $132,000

    c. $220,000

    d. $211,200

13. An $1800 loan is repaid with a $600 payment every six months plus 9% annual interest. What is the total interest paid?

    a. $81

    b. $162

    c. $216

    d. $243

14. A $7000 loan in a straight note earns $210 in 90 days. The annual percentage return is:

    a.   9%

    b.   11%

    c.   12%

    d.   14%

15. The rate of interest that is stated in the note is known as the:

    a.   legal rate

    b.   usury rate

    c.   contract rate

    d.   variable rate

16. A loan that is repaid in one single lump-sum payment at the end of the loan's life is known as a:

    a. straight loan

    b. budget loan

    c. package loan

    d. direct reduction loan

17. The rate of interest that is charged when there is an absence of an express agreement between the parties is known as:

    a. 10%

    b. contract rate

    c. legal rate

    d. usury

18. Money paid for the use of money is:

    a. rent

    b. interest

    c. principal

    d. taxes

19. Increasing the points on a loan in the absence of any economic change would have what effect on the loans?

    a. increase the risk

    b. reduce the interest rate

    c. increase the payments

    d. shorten the loan term

20. In an amortized loan, what occurs each month?

    a. The interest and principal payments each increase.

    b. The interest decreases and the principal portion increases.

    c. The interest increases and the principal decreases.

    d. The amount of principal and interest in each payment remain the same.

IMPORTANT TERMS AND CONCEPTS

certificate of sale

deed in lieu of
    foreclosure

deed of reconveyance

default

deficiency judgment

delinquencies

equitable period of
    redemption

equity of redemption
    period

forbearance

forcible detainer action

foreclosure

HOPE for Home-
    owners Act of 2008

judicial foreclosure

land contract

lis pendens

non-judicial foreclosures

notice of default

novation

period of reinstatement

power of sale clause

satisfaction of mortgage

sheriff's deed

sheriff's sale

short sale

statutory period of
    redemption

trustee deed

CHAPTER OBJECTIVES

After completing this chapter, you should be able to:

- Explain the difference between assuming a loan and buying subject to a loan.
- Summarize the primary types of loan defaults.
- Discuss the alternatives to a loan foreclosure.
- Describe the judicial foreclosure process.
- Describe the non-judicial foreclosure process.
- Describe the land contract forfeiture process.

Loan Satisfaction, Assumptions, Defaults, and Foreclosure

23.1 LOAN SATISFACTION AND ASSUMPTIONS

Borrowers can be relieved of their obligation to repay their mortgage by simply making all of the payments due under the contract, in which case the loan is paid off, or by having someone else assume their debt.

Loan Satisfaction

Loans are generally paid off in one of three ways. Either a borrower makes all of the payments required, in which case the obligation of the note is extinguished, or the property is sold and the loan is repaid through the sale escrow or assumed by the buyer with the seller relieved of all liability, or the proceeds of a new loan are used to pay off the existing loan through a refinance. In either case, the borrower will receive a **satisfaction of mortgage** (for a mortgage) or **deed of reconveyance** (for a deed of trust), which are documents that can be recorded to remove the related lien from the property records. In the case of a refinance or sale, the document will probably be delivered to the escrow company so that all documents can be recorded in the proper sequence. When a loan is simply paid off, the document should be recorded and/or delivered to the borrower by the loan servicing agent or reconveyance trustee.

Loan Assumptions and Assumption and Releases

A loan assumption can be used to transfer the liability for an existing loan to a buyer. A real estate loan can be assumed when a new borrower is approved by the lender and a formal assumption agreement is executed. In this manner, the original borrower (the seller) can be relieved of responsibility for the existing loan, provided that release of liability is given and the new borrower formally assumes the loan. However, a formal assumption can still result in liability for both parties.

To formally assume a loan, the new buyer and the seller need to apply to the lender, who may approve the new borrower and grant the assumption. The new borrower must formally assume the loan and the original borrower must obtain a release of liability. **Novation** is a formal assumption in which a new borrower is substituted for the original maker of the note. Unless there is a complete novation, both parties could still be liable under a formal assumption. Complete novation is similar to a new loan except the original mortgage or deed of trust remains in place and the current principal balance stays the same. The new borrower assumes all financial responsibility and the original borrower is relieved of all responsibility.

Subject To

A property may be purchased "subject to" the existing loan(s) of record. In this case, the buyer does not agree to assume primary liability for these debts. Instead, the seller continues to be obligated to repay these loans, even though the buyer will be making payments directly to the lender(s). The seller remains responsible for any deficiency. Realistically, the buyer will continue to make the payments in order to retain the property. Because the loans are secured by the property, if the buyer fails to make the payments, the lender will proceed against the property through foreclosure. Thus, the distinction between an "assumption" and "subject to" is important only when the foreclosure results in a deficiency. To obtain a deficiency judgment, the lender would only proceed against the maker of the note (the seller) for any unrecovered costs in a separate court action which must be initiated within 90 days of a foreclosure sale.

23.2 DEFAULTS

A **default** is a breach of one or more of the terms and conditions that the borrower agreed to in the loan and security agreements. The agreements may contain acceleration clauses that enable a lender to declare the full amount of the unpaid balance due should a default occur. Because the property is offered as security for the loan, lenders have the right to claim the property and sell it to get their money back. Lenders typically do not want the property, but in many cases, they have no choice but to take the property and sell it following a foreclosure action to recover their investment.

Types of Defaults

There are different types of defaults that can occur depending on the terms of the instrument used to secure the loan.

Delinquencies

Delinquencies are the most common form of default. **Delinquencies** are past due payments. Most loan agreements state that payments are due on or before a specified date. If payment is not made on time, the loan is technically in default. Today's standardized loan documents typically allow for a grace period of 15 days, then a late payment charge is assessed on the sixteenth day. This late payment charge is usually a percentage of the payment. Lenders who have originated loans backed by Ginnie Mae must make payment to Ginnie Mae on the second day of each month, whether they have received payment or not. Delinquencies that are not resolved within 60 days are a genuine concern for the lender or investor, as this typically begins the foreclosure process.

Property Taxes

Property taxes take priority over other liens; therefore, unpaid property taxes create a default, because the lender's security position is jeopardized.

Most lenders will structure impound accounts, and the taxes are prorated over a 12-month payment plan. Tax bills are sent to the lender, who pays the taxes. A lender may or may not allow a borrower to pay taxes directly. All loan agreements include a clause that specifies the borrower's responsibility to pay property taxes.

Hazard Insurance

Failing to keep an appropriate policy of hazard insurance in force is also considered a default. The lender's security must be protected against loss from fire or other perils; therefore, provisions for the continued coverage of the properties are necessary. Lenders are named as co-insured along with the borrower. Lenders require only fire and extended coverage. Homeowners generally get a homeowner's policy, which provides the coverage required by the lender and gives the homeowner some personal liability coverage as well. If a borrower lets his or her insurance policy lapse, the lender has a right to secure a policy to protect the lender's interest and charge the borrower.

Poor Property Maintenance

Borrowers are responsible for protecting the security of the lender, which means maintaining property in a reasonable manner. Defaults due to poor property maintenance can apply to one's own residence, as well as any investment property. It is not easy to judge the extent of the "waste" that would create a default. It is, however, a condition of the loan agreement and can be considered a default if it becomes critical; however, lenders will not usually commence foreclosure proceedings in the case of a non-monetary default.

23.3 FORECLOSURE ALTERNATIVES

Typically, lenders do not want to own the property. In most cases, by the time lenders complete the foreclosure process, repossess the property, clean up the property, market it, and finally sell it, they will show a net loss. Therefore, most lenders will work with borrowers whose loans are delinquent due to situations beyond the borrower's control, such as loss of a job or a serious illness. Lenders would rather work with borrowers to get payments back on schedule than have a frustrated owner abandon the property. Abandoned houses are often subjected to lack of maintenance, vandalism, and uninvited guests. This situation leaves lenders with little to recoup their losses.

Forbearance

Obviously, most defaults are the result of delinquent payments. As the loan becomes a problem loan, the lender may contact the borrower to see if it is necessary to restructure payments. An arrangement that effectively forestalls or delays foreclosure action is called **forbearance**. Partial payment or forbearance on the part of lenders comes from the days of the Depression. Lenders may be urged by the FHA and Fannie Mae to exercise forbearance during periods of widespread unemployment and tight money. Sometimes loans are recast and extended for longer periods of time. Lenders may ask for more collateral or add co-signers to a loan. However the payments and interest due may be restructured, the lender must proceed with caution. If a lien that is junior to the lender's exists, then a modification resulting in a more difficult situation for the borrower (such as a higher interest rate) can place the subject note in a junior position unless the junior lien holder agrees to the modification. Additionally, the rules surrounding the statute of limitations are somewhat complex but should definitely be taken into consideration when any forbearance or partial payment plan is being contemplated.

Short Sale

Under certain circumstances, a lender may agree to a short sale of a property as an alternative to foreclosure. A **short sale** is a situation in which the lender agrees to accept a payoff-in-full amount that is less than the outstanding balance of the loan. A general decline in real estate values where the property is located often results in short sales. A short sale requires the approval of the lender and includes:

- A bona fide sale to a third party.
- A borrower/seller that has been current on the loan payments and has maintained the property.

The short-sale amount is usually the net sales proceeds from the sale of the property that is accepted by the lender as payment in full of the outstanding indebtedness. A short sale usually results in a greater return to the lender than proceeding with a foreclosure and subsequent sale of the property. A short sale usually results in reduced or no consequences to the borrower in regard to credit ratings; however, there may be other consequences depending on the type of loan paid off. For example, the DVA requires that the amount of shortfall be paid in full before the borrower can obtain another VA loan.

Deed in Lieu

A deed in lieu of foreclosure is used when an owner and lender wish to avoid the time-consuming and expensive process of foreclosure. A **deed in lieu of foreclosure** is a mutual agreement in which the borrower is released from liability under the terms of the loan in exchange for a quitclaim deed or a regular grant deed. The deed in lieu is not as damaging to the borrower's credit history as a foreclosure. The deed in lieu may also avoid the possibility of a deficiency judgment. Deficiency judgments are discussed in more detail in the following sections of this chapter. It should be noted, however, that new loan applications ask borrowers if they have ever executed a voluntary deed in lieu of foreclosure. Although the deed in lieu of foreclosure is expedient and efficient, it may not be used to avoid including the asset in a bankruptcy filing. There needs to be some verification that the borrower was solvent at the time of the voluntary transfer.

HOPE for Homeowners Act of 2008

Included within the provisions of the Federal Finance Regulatory Reform Act of 2008 is a measure designed to provide some degree of relief to homeowners (this act is estimated to affect as many as 400,000 homeowners) who are threatened with the loss of their homes because they cannot afford the payments, generally because of resets on adjustable rate mortgages during difficult economic times. The HOPE program was promulgated to assist borrowers and avoid additional pressure on the economy occasioned by borrowers losing their homes during real estate/credit crunch (recession) that started in 2007. The HOPE program is effective from October 1, 2008 through September 30, 2011. The program authorizes the FHA to insure up to $300 billion of 30-year fixed-rate refinance loans up to 90% of appraised value. Conditions of the program include having the existing lender agree to write down, or accept payoff, of a loan to 90% of the property's current appraised value. The existing mortgage has to have been originated on or before January 1, 2008 with an existing mortgage payment, as of March 1, 2008, that exceeds 31% of the borrower's gross monthly income. Additionally, the borrower must not have created an intentional default, cannot have an ownership interest in other residential real estate, cannot have been convicted of fraud in the past ten years, and must not have provided materially false information at the time the existing loan was obtained. The borrower will pay a 3% up-front mortgage insurance premium and a 1.5% annual premium. A key component in the HOPE program is for the federal government to share in the recapture of any equity at the time of sale ranging from 50% to 100% depending on the number of years since the HOPE loan was originated.

Home Affordable Modification Program

The Home Affordable Modification Program was announced in March 2009 in an effort to slow the rate of mortgage foreclosures caused by the decline in home values, credit crisis, and economic slow-down of 2007, 2008, and 2009. The program is designed to encourage more lenders to offer borrowers more-affordable payback terms. The program guidelines combine lender incentives and borrower assistance. A bill being considered in Congress in March 2009 would give bankruptcy judges the power to reduce the interest rate and principle on a home mortgage. Supporters of the legislation regard the additional bankruptcy judge's power as an integral part of the Home Affordable Modification Program.

23.4 FORECLOSURE

To foreclose means to exclude from, deprive of the right, or shut out. **Foreclosure** is a procedure that removes an owner's property rights. When real property is pledged as security for a loan, the process of selling that property as a result of the borrower's default is called foreclosure. The borrower's property is sold to satisfy his or her debt.

History of Foreclosure

From the 1400s and under English common law, when landowners who borrowed money did not make the payment by "law day," the property became the lender's property. Law day is the date that the payment is due. This foreclosure process was known as title theory. Faced with losing their land, the landowners appealed to the king, who turned the problem over to the lord chancellor, who was responsible for administering justice. Under certain circumstances, the lord chancellor granted the landowners a period of time to come up with the money and protect their property rights. This time was referred to as the *equitable period of redemption*. These days, the **equitable period of redemption** is the period of time from the filing of the notice of default to the date of the sale.

If a debt was not paid during the equitable period of redemption, the lord chancellor and/or court of equity gave the lender the right to claim the forfeited collateral. This resulted in a decree of foreclosure, which became known as *strict foreclosure*. At the end of the equitable period of redemption, the lien holder was directed to sell the property, pay off the debt, and hope that some of the equity could be saved for the landowner. In addition to these measures, there was also a period after the sale during which the landowner could redeem the property, called the **statutory period of redemption**. This process of foreclosure under old medieval laws is similar to today's mortgage foreclosure process.

Judicial or Non-Judicial Foreclosure

The foreclosure process for a mortgage requires a judicial foreclosure. Under a **judicial foreclosure**, it is necessary to commence a lawsuit in state court, serve all interested parties with summons and complaints, and wait for a hearing date before a judge. Because this process involves the court system, there may be numerous delays (particularly if the borrower contests the action), and then once a judgment is obtained, a **sheriff's sale** is scheduled. After the sheriff's sale, the debtor has one year in which to redeem the property. The borrower may redeem the property after a foreclosure sale by paying the full amount due plus the costs and expenses incurred by the lender to conduct the sale.

If the lender takes a deed of trust, the process is much simpler. It is much faster and less expensive to proceed by way of non-judicial foreclosure, often referred to as a trustee's sale. A notice of default is filed, and after 90 days, the trustee can sell the property at auction.

Process of Judicial Foreclosure

The following list shows the steps for a judicial foreclosure. These actions must be initiated by the lender, or more likely by the lender's attorneys:

1. File a notice of **lis pendens** (notice of legal action).
2. File a foreclosure suit in superior court in the appropriate county, requesting an order for the sheriff to sell the property.
3. Invoke the acceleration clause in the note under the right of irrevocable acceleration.
4. Notify all persons with an interest in the property of the court action and serve them with a summons and complaint.
5. The court will issue a writ of execution and the county sheriff must then schedule a sheriff's sale.
6. The property is auctioned and sold to the highest bidder.

During this process, from the date of filing the complaint to the date of the sale, the owner can redeem the property by paying the entire loan amount plus interest due and court costs. This is the owner's **equity of redemption period**.

Once the property has been sold to the highest bidder, the borrower still has a period to redeem by law. In Nevada, this period lasts one year and is referred to as the statutory period of redemption. To redeem the property, the borrower must repay the entire balance of the loan, plus costs and interest.

The successful bidder at a judicial foreclosure receives a **certificate of sale**, which he or she holds until after the statutory period of redemption. At that time, the bidder receives a sheriff's deed and may take possession of the property. If, however, the borrower continues to occupy the subject property, the successful bidder and holder of the **sheriff's deed** must evict the borrower. Eviction of the borrower is accomplished by filing an expedited court proceeding called a forcible detainer action.

Deficiency Judgment

Lenders who take the security back due to default may still collect on the note, should the security not be sufficient to repay the debt. This is done in the form of a **deficiency judgment**. The name of this judgment refers to the fact that the sale of the security did not generate enough money to satisfy the debt, leaving an unpaid balance.

The instruments that were used to create the lien were:

1. A promissory note or promise to pay.
2. A mortgage or trust deed, which is a pledge of the real property as security for the promissory note.

Upon application of the mortgagee within six months after the date of the foreclosure sale and after a required court hearing, the court shall award a deficiency judgment to the mortgagee. The judgment will be awarded by the court if the sheriff reports a deficiency in the proceeds from the sale and that a balance remains due the mortgagee. Before awarding the deficiency judgment the court will take evidence presented by either party concerning the fair market value of the property sold as of the date of the foreclosure sale.

After all debts and costs are paid, any leftover funds belong to the defaulted mortgagor (the borrower).

Foreclosure under a Trust Deed

Non-judicial foreclosures are available when a trust deed has been used as the security instrument. This is because of the naked or bare legal title transferred to the trustee by the **power of sale clause**. When a borrower defaults, the beneficiary (lender) notifies the trustee of the default and requests that the trustee foreclose using the power of sale clause. As discussed earlier, the time required to foreclose is considerably less than in a judicial foreclosure.

Process of Non-Judicial Foreclosure

The steps for a non-judicial foreclosure are provided in the following list:

1. **Notice of default** and intent to sell is filed. This gives notice of the intended sale. A deed of trust cannot be accelerated unless judicially foreclosed as a mortgage. The intended sale cannot be scheduled for a period of at least 90 days beginning with the date of filing the notice of default.

2. The trustee must include the time and place of the pending sale in the notice.

3. The sale must be advertised in a newspaper once a week for three consecutive weeks.

4. The notice of the sale must be provided to each trustor and any other person entitled to notice by personal service or by registered or certified mail to the trustor's last known address.

5. The sale cannot take place until at least the ninety-first day after the notice of default is filed.

6. The property is auctioned and sold to the highest bidder, who immediately receives title and possession.

During a 35-day period from the notice of default, a borrower may reinstate the loan by making up all back payments plus costs and bringing the loan current, but he or she is not required to pay off the entire loan balance. The 35-day period is known as the **period of reinstatement**.

There is no statutory period of redemption following the sale; therefore, the bidder receives a **trustee deed** and possession with no waiting period, as the defaulted owner or borrower has lost all property rights. As is the case with a judicial foreclosure, if the borrower continues to occupy the subject property, the successful bidder and holder of the trustee's deed must evict the borrower. Eviction of the borrower is accomplished by filing an expedited court proceeding called a **forcible detainer action**.

The procedures for obtaining the deficiency judgment are the same as previously described for a mortgage foreclosure.

Real estate salespeople should be very careful when advising their clients on matters regarding the legal ramifications of foreclosing on mortgages and trust deeds. A licensee can be held liable for the consequences of any misinformation, as well as practicing law without a license.

Government Loan Foreclosures

FHA and VA loans have special foreclosure procedures that are summarized in the following sections.

FHA Foreclosures

FHA foreclosures begin with the filing of a notice of default. This notice of default must be sent to the local FHA office within 60 days of the default. In some cases, FHA counselors may attempt to negotiate a forbearance agreement between the mortgagor and the mortgagee. If the borrower's problems cannot be resolved, the mortgagee must file a default status report with the FHA, then initiate foreclosure action. If necessary, the lender bids on the property for the unpaid principal balance plus interest, costs, and expenses, then takes title and presents the FHA with an insurance claim. The FHA may pay the claim in cash or in government bonds. In some cases, the lender assigns the defaulted mortgage to the FHA before final foreclosure, and the FHA pays off the lender. Although the FHA may spend some money to fix up these repossessed properties, in most cases, the FHA resells the property in an "as is" condition solely to help recoup its losses.

VA Foreclosures

VA foreclosures are handled differently. VA loans are guaranteed by the government. When a VA loan goes into default, the lender must notify the local DVA office within three months. The DVA may, at its option, bring the loan current by advancing funds to the lender. This "advance" then takes priority over the lender's lien position because of the subrogation rights granted to the DVA as a guarantor. The veteran pays an up-front fee for this guarantee. However, if a deficiency arises, the defaulted veteran is liable for any advances or costs incurred by the DVA. The DVA will then attempt to work out an arrangement with the veteran, which may include counseling, mediation, and forbearance.

In the case of a foreclosure sale, the lender is usually the only bidder at the auction. Assuming the lender gets the property back, the lender will submit a claim to the local DVA office for its losses. At this point, the DVA has the option to pay the claim and take title to the property, or let the lender retain title to the property and pay only the difference between the determined property value at the time of foreclosure and the loan balance. When a property is seriously deteriorated, the DVA is more likely to choose the latter option.

Private Mortgage Insurance

Conventional loans that have private mortgage insurance (PMI) require the lender to notify the insuring company within 10 days of a default. The insurer will instruct the lender on how it wishes to proceed. At a foreclosure sale, the mortgagee is the original bidder, and if successful, the mortgagee notifies the insurer within 60 days after the legal action is complete. The insurer may then pay the mortgagee, take title, and resell the property, or pay the mortgagee an agreed upon amount and let him or her sell the property to recover any unpaid balance.

Land Contract Forfeitures

A **land contract** is also known as an *agreement for sale* or a *contract for deed*. The land contract is an executory contract, in as much as the terms have not been fulfilled. The buyer receives equitable title and the seller retains legal title until the debt has been paid in full. The parties to a land contract are known as the vendor (seller) and vendee (buyer). The agreement for sale does not include a note. The promise to pay and the terms of the agreement are all contained in the one instrument. If the vendee defaults on the obligation, the vendor is required to regain possession of the real property collateral through judicial foreclosure procedures.

CHAPTER SUMMARY

Loans are generally paid off in one of two ways. Either a borrower makes all of the payments required, or the proceeds of a new loan are used to pay off the existing loan through a refinance or sale of the property. In either case, the borrower will receive a satisfaction of mortgage or deed of reconveyance. When recorded, these documents remove the related lien from the property records.

A loan assumption can be used to transfer the liability for an existing loan to a buyer. A real estate loan can be assumed when a new borrower is approved by the lender and a formal assumption agreement is executed. In this manner, the original borrower (the seller) can be relieved of responsibility for the existing loan. Novation is a formal assumption in which a new borrower is substituted for the original maker of the note.

A property may be purchased "subject to" the existing loan(s) of record. In this case, the seller continues to be obligated to repay these loans, even though the buyer will be making payments directly to the lender(s). The seller remains responsible for any deficiency.

A default is a breach of one or more of the terms and conditions that the borrower agreed to in the loan and security agreements. Delinquencies are the most common form of default. Delinquencies are past due payments.

Property taxes take priority over other liens; therefore, unpaid property taxes create a default, because the lender's security position is jeopardized.

Failing to keep an appropriate policy of hazard insurance in force is also considered a default. If a borrower lets his or her insurance policy lapse, the lender has a right to secure a policy to protect his or her interest and charge the borrower. Failing to keep the property reasonably maintained can also create a default.

Most lenders will work with borrowers whose loans are delinquent due to situations beyond the borrower's control. Alternatives to foreclosure include forbearance and a deed in lieu of foreclosure.

Forbearance is a payment arrangement that effectively forestalls or delays foreclosure action. Lenders may recast the loan, extend the loan for a longer period of time, ask for more collateral, or add co-signers to a loan.

A deed in lieu of foreclosure is used when an owner and lender wish to avoid the long process of foreclosure. A deed in lieu of foreclosure is a mutual agreement in which the borrower is released from liability under the terms of the loan in exchange for a quitclaim deed or a regular grant deed. The deed in lieu is not as damaging to the credit history of the borrower as a foreclosure.

Foreclosure is a procedure that removes an owner's property rights. When real property is pledged as security for a loan, the process of selling that property as a result of the borrower's default is called foreclosure. The borrower's property is sold to satisfy his or her debt.

The equitable period of redemption is the period of time from the filing of the notice of default to the date of the sale. The statutory period of redemption is the period after the sale during which the landowner can redeem the property.

The foreclosure process for a mortgage requires a judicial foreclosure. Under a judicial foreclosure, it is necessary to commence a lawsuit in state court, serve all interested parties with summons and complaints, and wait for a hearing date before a judge. Once a judgment is obtained, a sheriff's sale is scheduled. After the sheriff's sale, the debtor has one year in which to redeem the property.

The successful bidder at a judicial foreclosure receives a certificate of sale, which he or she holds until after the statutory period of redemption. At that time, the bidder receives a sheriff's deed and may take possession of the property.

Lenders who take the security back because of default may still collect on the note, should the security not be sufficient to repay the debt. This is done in the form of a deficiency judgment.

Non-judicial foreclosures are available when a trust deed has been used as the security instrument. When a borrower defaults, the beneficiary (lender) notifies the trustee of the default and requests that the trustee foreclose using the power of sale clause. The time required to foreclose is considerably less than in a judicial foreclosure. There is no statutory period of redemption; therefore, the bidder receives a trustee deed and possession with no waiting period, while the defaulted owner or borrower has lost all property rights.

The 35-day period from the notice of default is known as the period of reinstatement. During this time, a borrower may reinstate the loan by making up all back payments plus costs and bringing the loan current. The trustee sale cannot be held until the ninety-first day after the proper filing of the notice of default.

FHA foreclosures begin with the filing of a notice of default. If necessary, the lender bids on the property for the unpaid principal balance plus interest, costs, and expenses, then takes title and presents the FHA with an insurance claim. The FHA may pay the claim in cash or in government bonds.

When a VA loan goes into default, the lender must notify the local DVA office within three months. The DVA may, at its option, bring the loan current by advancing funds to the lender. This "advance" then takes priority over the lender's lien position because of the subrogation rights granted to the DVA as a guarantor. In the case of a foreclosure sale, the lender is usually the original bidder at the auction. Assuming the lender gets the property back, the lender will submit a claim to the local DVA office for its losses. At this point, the DVA has the option to pay the claim and take title to the property, or let the lender retain title to the property and pay only the difference between the determined value of the property at the time of foreclosure and the loan balance.

Conventional loans that have private mortgage insurance (PMI) require the lender to notify the insuring company within 10 days of a default. The insurer will instruct the lender on how it wishes to proceed.

A land contract is an executory contract. The buyer receives equitable title and the seller retains legal title until the debt has been paid in full. In case of default, the vendor is required to regain possession of the real property collateral through judicial foreclosure.

CHECKING YOUR COMPREHENSION

1. Describe the meaning and potential obligations under:
   * Assumption of a loan
   * Assumption of a loan with novation
   * Acquiring a property subject to a loan

2. Summarize the meaning of the terms *forbearance* and *deed in lieu of foreclosure.*

3. Describe the judicial foreclosure process, including the time frames and the mortgagor's post-foreclosure rights.

4. Describe the non-judicial foreclosure process, including time frames and the trustor's post-foreclosure rights.

REVIEWING YOUR UNDERSTANDING

1. When a buyer takes title to real property "subject to" the existing mortgage, he or she:
   a. becomes responsible to the existing mortgagee for the mortgage balance due
   b. does not become responsible to the mortgagee for the existing mortgage balance
   c. assumes the same interest rate and terms as the sellers
   d. releases the sellers from all original obligations

2. The term applied to the transfer of all responsibility for an existing mortgage from the seller to the buyer is:
   a. hypothecation
   b. prior appropriation
   c. novation
   d. partition

3. A borrower can be relieved of primary responsibility for a mortgage by finding a buyer who is willing to:
   a. take subject to the loan
   b. assume the loan
   c. subordinate the loan
   d. give a wrap-around mortgage

4. Which of the following **MOST** accurately describes the major purpose of a deed of trust?
   a. secure the payment of a note
   b. convey a title to the trustee
   c. provide for equity of redemption
   d. prevent assumption

5. The acceleration clause provides for which of the following?
   a. equity of redemption
   b. prepayment penalty
   c. right of lender to require immediate payment of principal balance when borrower is in default
   d. alienation by borrower

6. A deficiency judgment **MAY** be available to the:
   a. mortgagee
   b. mortgagor
   c. trustee
   d. trustor

7. All of the following statements are true, **EXCEPT**:
   a. land contracts may be foreclosed judicially
   b. the parties to a land contract are the vendor and vendee

c. the promise to pay and the security
    agreement are included in one
    document

d. the buyer under a land contract receives
    full legal title at the close of escrow

8. In Nevada, the statutory redemption period
   after a judicial foreclosure is:
   a. 1 month
   b. 3 months
   c. 6 months
   d. 1 year

9. Failure to meet a mortgage obligation
   when due is known as:
   a. duress
   b. deficiency
   c. default
   d. defeasance

10. After the statutory redemption period, the
    holder of the certificate of sale receives a:
    a. treasurer's deed
    b. grant deed
    c. general warranty deed
    d. sheriff's deed

11. Which of the following liens has the high-
    est priority to mortgage foreclosure sale
    proceeds?
    a. mortgage lien
    b. income tax lien
    c. real property tax lien
    d. mechanic's lien

12. A deed in lieu of foreclosure conveys a title
    to which of the following?
    a. lender
    b. borrower
    c. trustee
    d. mortgagor

13. Under Nevada law, the trust deed conveys
    the power of sale to the:
    a. trustor
    b. trustee
    c. beneficiary
    d. lender

14. The type of sale that results from a judicial
    foreclosure is:
    a. trustee's sale
    b. sheriff's sale
    c. treasurer's sale
    d. beneficiary's sale

15. The successful bidder at a mortgage fore-
    closure receives a:
    a. certificate of purchase
    b. certificate of sale
    c. certificate of redemption
    d. certificate of foreclosure

16. When a property is purchased and the seller
    remains contingently responsible for the sell-
    er's mortgage loan, the purchase has been:
    a. financed subject to the seller's mort-
        gage loan
    b. financed with novation of the seller's
        mortgage
    c. financed through an assumption of the
        mortgage debt
    d. financed with a new mortgage loan

17. In a judicial foreclosure, the period from
    the notice of default to the date of the fore-
    closure sale is known as:
    a. period of reinstatement
    b. equity of redemption
    c. statutory redemption
    d. recess period

18. In Nevada, a trustee's sale under a deed of
    trust can be held:
    a. 60 days after the date of the notice
    b. 61 days after the date of the notice
    c. 90 days after the date of the notice
    d. 91 days after the date of the notice

19. The statutory redemption period after a
    trustee's sale is:
    a. 90 days
    b. 6 months
    c. 30 days, if the property has been
        abandoned
    d. none

Chapter

24

IMPORTANT TERMS AND CONCEPTS

amenity

annual net income

anticipation

appraisal

appreciation

assemblage

assessed value

balance

book value

capitalization rate

change

compaction

competition

competitive market analysis (CMA)

conformity

contribution

cost

cost approach

demand

depreciation

economic obsolescence

effective annual gross income

functional obsolescence

gross rent multiplier (GRM)

highest and best use

income approach

increasing and decreasing returns

insurable value

integration, equilibrium, and disintegration

loan value

market data approach

market value

percolation test

physical deterioration

plottage

price

progression

reconciliation

regression

replacement cost

reproduction cost

scarcity

subjective value

substitution

supply and demand

transferability

Uniform Standards of Professional Appraisal Practice (USPAP)

utility

value

Real Estate Appraisal

After completing this chapter, you should be able to:

- Define the terms *value*, *cost*, and *price*, and list the four characteristics of value.
- Define market value and differentiate it from subjective value, loan value, assessed value, insurable value, and book value.
- Describe the factors that influence value.
- List and describe the economic principles used by an appraiser when completing an appraisal.
- Describe the three approaches to value.
- Calculate the answers to yield and profit and loss problems.

24.1 CHARACTERISTICS AND TYPES OF VALUE

For students of real estate, the knowledge of appraising and its uses will be one of the most valuable skills you can learn. Understanding the concepts and principles of appraising is key to your success in real estate, whether as a licensee or as an investor.

Definitions

An **appraisal** is an estimate or opinion of value as of a specified date based on analysis of factual data. Appraising is not a science. It is sometimes referred to as an art, but you will do well to remember that it is an opinion of value that is good for that day only.

Value means the exchange of present worth for future benefits to the owner of the property. Most property is purchased with the expectation of **appreciation**, which is an increase in value.

Cost is the historical expenditure for the purchase, construction, or improvement of a property. Cost has nothing to do with present value.

Price is the amount asked and the amount paid for property. The listing price is the amount asked for property. The sale or purchase price is the amount paid for property. Many different influences affect price, such as:

- Being forced to sell.
- The terms of the contract.
- Selling the property to relatives.
- Being willing to sell only at the listing price.

Here is an example of the difference between value, cost, and price: A three-bedroom home was built in 1945 for $9500 (cost). The house sold in 1960 for $35,000 (purchase price). The property has been well maintained, is in a good residential location, and in 2008, its value is $235,000. Value, cost, and price are almost never equal.

Characteristics of Value

There are four principal characteristics of value: *demand*, *utility*, *scarcity*, and *transferability*. To help you remember them, use the acronym DUST:

D   **Demand** is the need or desire to possess something and having the money to fulfill that need.

U   **Utility**, or usefulness, is the capacity to satisfy human needs and desires. For example, a shopping center in the middle of an isolated desert would not be very useful or create the same desire for ownership as it would in a growing section of a city.

S   **Scarcity** reflects the theory of supply and demand. More scarcity in relation to the demand results in an increase in value. If there is an overabundance of supply in relation to demand, the value will decrease.

T   **Transferability**. Title that cannot be freely transferred or is restricted has little value as a purchase. For example, a life tenant can transfer only the life estate, which has a reduced value, because all property rights go to the remainder or reversionary estates upon the termination of the life estate.

Types of Value

Depending on the purpose of the appraisal, there are many types of value. The most common are market value, subjective value, loan value, assessed value, insurable value, and book value.

Market Value

Market value is an unemotional, objective price at which a seller would sell and a willing buyer would purchase, with neither party under abnormal pressure to act. Market value is also described as *the highest price a property will bring on the open market*, allowing for a reasonable time to sell. In real estate, this is the most commonly used type of value.

Subjective Value

Subjective value represents the emotional value of a property's worth to a person, regardless of cost. The value is created by the amenities or because it fulfills the desires of the individual. (An **amenity** is a condition of agreeable living or a beneficial influence resulting from the location.)

Loan Value

Loan value is the value used for establishing the amount of mortgage or trust deed loan to be made. Normally, this value would be less than market value.

Assessed Value

Assessed value is the value put on the property by the county assessor for the purpose of computing ad valorem property taxes. Although *ad valorem* means "according to value" in Latin, the valuation determined by the county assessor for real property taxes seldom represents market value.

Insurable Value

Insurable value is used to determine the amount of insurance needed to meet co-insurance clause requirements.

Book Value

Book value is not used in appraising. Book value is a bookkeeping entry used for the purposes of depreciation in the calculation of income tax. It represents cost and capital improvements less depreciation.

24.2 FACTORS INFLUENCING VALUE

Value is influenced by factors that can be grouped into four main classifications: *physical characteristics*, *social standards*, *economic trends*, and *political regulations*.

Physical Characteristics

Climatic conditions. The more favorable the climate, the more valuable the property. Before the development of air-conditioning, the hot climate of certain areas of Nevada negatively affected property value.

Size of lot, width, depth, and shape. Corner lots are important for commercial use, but may not increase the value of residential lots.

Topography. Rolling hills are desirable for residential property. Flat, level land is necessary for industrial, business, and commercial properties.

Soil conditions. Type of soil is important for agriculture, but for high-rise buildings, the amount of compaction is important. **Compaction*** is a state in which soil particles are forced close together, reducing pore space. Another necessary quality of good soil is its drainage ability, which is determined by a percolation test. A **percolation test** determines the speed at which standing water is absorbed by the soil. It is important to identify the type of soil when

*Source: *Real Estate Dictionary: Pocket Guide for Professionals* by Charles Jacobus and Nora Olmos (Cincinnati: South-Western, 2004).

building because it can affect the size, depth, and construction of foundations.

Action of the sun. This is particularly important in commercial properties. Property on the south and west sides of the street is preferable because in warmer climates people walk on the shady side of the streets. The afternoon sun also has a detrimental effect on window displays. However, in the modern era of air-conditioned shopping malls, this is no longer an important factor.

Any *physical hazards* that limit ingress, egress, or use of the property are negative factors in value.

Social Standards

Social influences on a community or area that can affect market values follow.

Population growth and population density. An increase in a community's population results in more living units per acre of land, including the development of condominium units and other common-interest developments, which generally increases the market value of land. Another result of increased population density is the desire of some community members to live in the suburbs, which will increase the demand for and value of suburban housing.

Proximity of schools, shopping centers, churches, and transportation is an important aspect of property value, as is the availability of cultural or sports centers.

Population mobility is the ability of the population to easily travel throughout the community due to a transportation system, such as a mass transit system.

Recreational opportunities at the individual property or in the immediate neighborhood or regional areas, such as parks, swimming pools, or tennis courts, all affect an area's market values.

Situs (people's desire for a given area) is probably the most important influence on a person's choice of property.

Economic Trends

Economic trends also play an important role in the value of property. Some aspects of economic trends follow.

Natural resources. An area without natural resources is not very valuable. Resources that affect property value include water, mineral deposits, rich soil for agriculture, and timber.

Employment opportunities. When unemployment increases and the economy becomes distressed or depressed, there is normally a decrease in the value of property. On the other hand, when a major business moves into the area, employment will increase, and this new business will have a ripple effect on other businesses in the area, enhancing the value of property.

Fluctuating interest rates and inflation also influence value. In the early 1980s, high interest rates coupled with inflation nearly brought the real estate market to a standstill.

Tax rates not only are a concern to residential owners but are also a deciding influence in the location of new businesses.

Wage scales coupled with the cost of living in an area are a vital factor in the value of property.

Availability of credit is of prime importance in determining value for market value appraisals. The lack or cost of credit reduces demand, with a resulting decrease in values.

Political Regulations

Political regulations can be instrumental factors in value. A few important regulations follow.

Zoning. A residential zone now best suited to commercial zoning because of area growth would be greatly enhanced in value if the zoning were changed.

Building codes, followed strictly, will be an asset to the value of the property.

Police and fire protection. These two city services are essential to the maintenance of property values.

The area's commitment to solving community problems, such as mass transportation, traffic, and pollution, is of great interest to potential property owners. Attitudes toward solution of community problems can have either a positive or negative effect on property values.

24.3 ECONOMIC PRINCIPLES OF VALUE

The following economic principles will help you to understand the purpose, techniques, and procedures of valuation used by an appraiser in making an appraisal.

Highest and best use is the most profitable use for which land can be used at the time of appraisal, that is, the use that will bring the greatest return. The highest and best use is not necessarily the present use. It is determined by analysis of the community, neighborhood, site, and improvements. Highest and best use is the primary consideration in the determination of market value.

Substitution sets the maximum value of a property by the cost of equally desirable and valuable substitute property in the same area.

Conformity means that a property achieves maximum value when the property reasonably conforms to the neighborhood. This includes both social and economic conformity. Conformity should not be confused with monotonous uniformity. However, maximum value is obtained when homes in a neighborhood are similar in size, construction quality, and age.

Balance is *not* achieved when a property in a given neighborhood is over- or underdeveloped. Balance is particularly important when appraising income properties. This principle implies that balance between net return on investment and expenses of labor, capital, management, and land have been met.

Anticipation is value created by expectation of benefits to be collected in the future. A person buys income property in anticipation of appreciation. Investors buy raw land in anticipation of directional growth in the city.

Change is a continuous process. Value is based on present and future changes. This includes both social and economic changes. When valuing real estate, economic, social, and physical changes of the past and future must be considered.

Competition ensues when a business is profitable in a given area. The free market economy and the concept of supply and demand allow competitive development in an area that is providing a positive yield on the investment. If too much competition is attracted to the area, losses in profits will result. In valuing investment properties, the limitation on profits from competition must be considered.

The principle of **increasing and decreasing returns** means that as long as money, labor, and management costs invested to improve a property increase return, the law of increasing return applies and value rises. If additional funds spent do not produce a positive return, the law of decreasing return applies and value lowers (see previous discussion of *balance*).

Contribution is the same principle as increasing and decreasing returns, except that it applies to only a portion of the property. One example would be when an owner adds a swimming pool to an apartment complex in order to increase income through higher rent rates.

The principle of **supply and demand** affects real estate values as it does with any other marketable object. The principle states that values rise as demand increases or supply decreases. Values generally fall when supply increases or demand decreases.

Regression exists when there are properties of different values in a neighborhood. The better property is adversely affected by the poorer properties.

Progression is the opposite of regression and exists when there is a poorer property among more expensive properties. In this instance, the lower-valued home will increase in value.

Integration, equilibrium, and disintegration are the three stages of a neighborhood life cycle. Integration is the development stage, when the value of a property is increasing. Equilibrium is the static period, when the property reaches its maximum value. Disintegration is the period during which the neighborhood declines and the value goes down.

Plottage is the process of putting several parcels together as one larger parcel to achieve the highest and best use and an increase in value. The process of consolidating the separate parcels into one larger parcel is known as **assemblage**.

Depreciation

Depreciation is a decrease in value. There are three types of depreciation applied in appraising: *physical deterioration*, *functional obsolescence*, and *economic obsolescence*.

Physical Deterioration

Physical deterioration is the loss of value due to normal wear and tear or to postponed maintenance. Physical deterioration can be either curable or incurable. Considering the economic life of the building helps to decide whether it would pay to fix the problem. *Economic life* is the estimated useful life of a building. If it is feasible to do the maintenance, the deterioration is *curable*. If the cost to fix the problem is prohibitive, the deterioration is considered *incurable*. Examples of physical deterioration include cracks in walls or ceilings, settling of foundation, termites, fixtures that need replacing, or worn carpeting.

Functional Obsolescence

Functional obsolescence is due to obsolete equipment or outdated architecture or floor plans. Functional obsolescence can be curable or incurable, depending on the economic life of the building and the expense of remodeling. Examples of functional obsolescence are out-of-date plumbing, inadequate electrical wiring to handle modern appliances, one bathroom in a three- or four-bedroom home, no air-conditioning or central heating, no family room, and so on.

Economic Obsolescence

Economic obsolescence is caused by an influence outside the property over which the property owner has no control. Economic obsolescence is usually incurable. Examples include a prison too close to a residential neighborhood or noise from an airport. A new freeway can result in businesses along the old highway losing value.

24.4 THREE APPROACHES TO VALUE

Three approaches to value include:

1. *Market data approach*, also known as *comparative analysis report*
2. *Cost approach*, also called *appraisal by summation*
3. *Income approach*

As we cover each of these approaches in detail, you will understand their particular uses.

Market Data Approach

The **market data approach** is similar to the approach used by licensees or investors when listing residences. As a licensee, you will continually use this approach even though you will not be making a formal appraisal. The licensee completes a **competitive market analysis (CMA)** using recent sales data on properties sold and the listing prices for comparable properties on the market to assist a seller in determining the listing price.

The market data approach, also known as the *sales comparison approach*, reflects recent market trends. However, the appraiser considers comparables only from actual sales, whereas the licensee also considers listing prices for comparable properties on the market when completing a CMA. In doing a sales comparison analysis, the subject property is compared with similar properties in the area that have recently sold. Most appraisers use three comparable sales when completing an estimate of value using the market data approach. The following information is compared and the value is adjusted up or down:

- Date of sale.
- Age of the building.
- Location of the neighborhood.
- Lot size and terrain.
- Square footage, number of rooms, and so on.

If a property is in some way inferior to the subject property, add the estimated difference to the comparable sales price. If the comparable property is better than the subject property, subtract the estimated difference from the comparable sales price. Figure 24.1 shows an example of the adjustment to comparable sales prices that is made when completing a market data approach appraisal.

Single-Family Homes

The market data approach is considered the most reliable of the three approaches to value, especially when the subject property is in a location where there are comparable resales. The market data approach would not be applicable for single-family homes in a new subdivision where there are still properties available from the homebuilder. The market data approach is also used to establish land value.

Cost Approach

The **cost approach**, also called *appraisal by summation*, estimates today's cost of all improvements, minus all factors of depreciation, plus the valuation of the land using the market data approach.

There are two choices for estimating values. One is the **reproduction cost**, which estimates the cost by using the original materials and technologies. The second method is called **replacement cost**, which estimates cost based on using today's materials and technologies.

Steps in the Replacement Cost Approach Method

1. Estimate the value of the land, plus site improvements such as a driveway, a walkway, or landscaping.
2. Estimate the replacement cost of building. There are three methods that can be used:
   - *Square foot cost method.* Multiply the cost per square foot of a recently constructed comparable building by the square footage of the building.
   - *Unit in place method.* Estimate the cost of each part of the structure, such as the cost of the walls, roof, and plumbing. The replacement cost is the sum of the estimated cost of each part of the structure.
   - *Quantity survey method.* Itemize and estimate the cost, including labor and overhead, of all raw materials needed to replace the structure.

FIGURE 24.1   Market Data Approach Appraisal

Assume that the subject property is a medium quality, 25-year-old, three-bedroom home, that has a two-car garage. The square footage of the home is 1,300 square feet. The appraiser locates three similar homes that have recently sold in the neighborhood at fair market prices. All have identical square footage and number of rooms.

Comparables

Data	Comparable A	Comparable B	Comparable C
Price paid	$173,900	$171,500	$166,000
Location	better than subject property	equal to subject property	equal to subject property
Lot size	equal to subject property	larger than subject property	smaller than subject property
Overall condition	better than subject property	equal to subject property	worse than subject property

Dollar Adjustment Factors per the Opinion of the Appraiser

Location difference	$1,000
Lot size difference	$1,500
Overall condition difference	$3,000

Adjustments

Data	Comparable A	Comparable B	Comparable C
Price paid	$173,900	$171,500	$166,000
Location	−1,000	0	0
Lot size	0	−1,500	+1,500
Overall condition	−3,000	0	+3,000
Price comparables would have sold for if they were like the subject home	$169,900	$170,000	$170,500

3. Estimate all types of depreciation:
   - Physical
   - Functional obsolescence
   - Economic obsolescence

   The appraiser's depreciation estimate is often the most difficult aspect of the cost approach to valuation.

4. Deduct the total depreciation from the estimated cost of building.
5. Add the estimated land value to the depreciated value of building to get the property value.

Example of Replacement Cost Approach

Land Valuation:	
Size of lot 100 × 135 @ $500 per front foot	$ 50,000
Plus site improvements: driveway, landscaping, etc.	$ 8000
Total Land Valuation	$ 58,000
Building Valuation:	
2300 sq. ft. @ $75 per sq. ft.	$ 172,500
Less Depreciation:	
Physical Depreciation	
curable	
exterior painting	$ 3500
interior painting	$ 1600
incurable (none)	
Functional Obsolescence	
curable, additional wiring and outlets	$ 4000
Economic Obsolescence	
(none)	0
Total Depreciation	($ 9100)
Value of Building: (after depreciation)	$ 163,400
Value of Property According to Replacement Cost Approach:	$221,400

The appraiser will generally rely most on the cost approach when valuing special-purpose buildings such as schools, churches, and public buildings. The cost approach is also the most reliable when valuing single-family homes in a new subdivision with little or no comparable sales. In general, the cost approach is the most reliable when there are few comparable sales and the subject property is not income producing.

Income Approach

Income is the third approach to value. As the title for this approach implies, this approach is used for income property. The **income approach** assumes that income from property establishes value. The value is computed by converting the right to the future operating income to the valuation amount using a **capitalization rate**. This approach is used primarily for apartments, commercial sites, and shopping centers.

Steps Involved in an Income Approach Appraisal

1. Estimate the annual income.
2. Deduct the estimated vacancy rate and bad debt expense (5% is often used as a rule of thumb). The result will be the **effective annual gross income**.

3. Deduct annual operating expenses. The result will be the **annual net income**. Do not include any mortgage payments or mortgage interest under operating expenses.

4. Arrive at a capitalization rate. The capitalization rate is the rate of return or yield on investment. Use a comparable building's net income, divided by sales price of that building to get a capitalization rate.

5. Use the net income divided by the capitalization rate to get the value of the subject property. Use the T math formulas for capitalization problems. For capitalization problems, the T formula is sometimes referred to as IRV. Both formulas are set forth in Figure 24.2.

FIGURE 24.2 T Math Formulas

IRV Formula	T Formula
I	INCOME PART
R V	% RATE YIELD TOTAL YIELD

The following table demonstrates how to use the capitalization rate to determine property value.

Gross Annual Income Estimate (rent)	$ 75,000
Less Vacancy—estimated at 5%	(3750)
Effective Annual Gross Income	$ 71,250
Expenses	
Real Estate Taxes	$ 9500
Insurance	1000
Janitor	6000
Utilities	15,000
Repairs	1000
Painting	1200
Maintenance	1500
Legal/Accounting	750
Management	3750
	(39,700)
ANNUAL NET INCOME	$ 31,550

If the capitalization rate is 10%, the property would be valued at $315,500 ($31,550 divided by 10% = $315,500).

The higher the risk, the greater the capitalization rate. The capitalization rate needs to reflect the recapture of the original investment, provide for the repayment of any borrowed capital, and give investors an acceptable rate of return on their investment.

24.5 RECONCILIATION AND THE APPRAISAL REPORT

Reconciliation (formerly called *correlation*), which reconciles the three approaches to value, is the last step in the appraisal process. In each appraisal, all three approaches to value are figured, even though one would be more appropriate than the others. Each approach would produce a different value. Each approach is then analyzed and assigned a weighing factor by the appraiser. Appraisers use their judgment as to which approach is the most relevant.

The Appraisal Report

Depending on the complexity of the appraisal, one of three different kinds of appraisal reports can be used. The *appraisal letter* is used for a simple, straightforward appraisal. The *appraisal form* or *checklist* is used for most single dwellings or small business properties. A sample appraisal form is presented in Figure 24.3. A large project will be reported in the form of a *narrative report*, which will be lengthy, detailed, and expensive. However, a narrative report will provide necessary detailed data, charts, and so on that are essential in large transactions.

24.6 GROSS RENT MULTIPLIER

Gross rent multiplier (GRM) is used as a rule of thumb for a quick estimate of value based on the relationship of comparable sales prices to the comparables' monthly rental income. It is *not* an approach to value. The GRM is often used as a substitute for the income approach for single-family rental units because there is very little information on single-family rentals.

Formula

This formula is used for calculating the GRM:

> **Step 1.** Comparable sales price ÷ Comparable monthly rental income = GRM
>
> **Step 2.** Monthly rental income for the subject property × GRM = Value

To establish the GRM for a given neighborhood, compare at least four rentals. Study the example in Figure 24.4.

24.7 LICENSING AND PROFESSIONAL ASSOCIATIONS

The Financial Institutions Reform, Recovery, and Enforcement Act of 1989 (FIRREA) established the requirement that all "federally related real estate appraisals" be performed only by appraisers *licensed or certified* by the state in which the real estate is located.

Appraiser Classifications

The three appraiser classifications are described in the following list. All three of the classifications have specific education, examination, and experience requirements.

FIGURE 24.3 Uniform Residential Appraisal Form

File #

The purpose of this summary appraisal report is to provide the lender/client with an accurate, and adequately supported, opinion of the market value of the subject property.

SUBJECT

Property Address		City		State	Zip Code

Borrower · Owner of Public Record · County

Legal Description

Assessor's Parcel # · Tax Year · R.E. Taxes $

Neighborhood Name · Map Reference · Census Tract

Occupant ☐ Owner ☐ Tenant ☐ Vacant · Special Assessments $ · ☐ PUD · HOA $ ☐ per year ☐ per month

Property Rights Appraised ☐ Fee Simple ☐ Leasehold ☐ Other (describe)

Assignment Type ☐ Purchase Transaction ☐ Refinance Transaction ☐ Other (describe)

Lender/Client · Address

Is the subject property currently offered for sale or has it been offered for sale in the twelve months prior to the effective date of this appraisal? ☐ Yes ☐ No

Report data source(s) used, offering price(s), and date(s).

CONTRACT

I ☐ did ☐ did not analyze the contract for sale for the subject purchase transaction. Explain the results of the analysis of the contract for sale or why the analysis was not performed.

Contract Price $ · Date of Contract · Is the property seller the owner of public record? ☐Yes ☐No Data Source(s)

Is there any financial assistance (loan charges, sale concessions, gift or down payment assistance, etc.) to be paid by any party on behalf of the borrower? ☐ Yes ☐ No
If Yes, report the total dollar amount and describe the items to be paid.

NEIGHBORHOOD

Note: Race and the racial composition of the neighborhood are not appraisal factors.

Neighborhood Characteristics	One-Unit Housing Trends	One-Unit Housing	Present Land Use %
Location ☐ Urban ☐ Suburban ☐ Rural	Property Values ☐ Increasing ☐ Stable ☐ Declining	PRICE / AGE	One-Unit %
Built-Up ☐ Over 75% ☐ 25–75% ☐ Under 25%	Demand/Supply ☐ Shortage ☐ In Balance ☐ Over Supply	$ (000) (yrs)	2-4 Unit %
Growth ☐ Rapid ☐ Stable ☐ Slow	Marketing Time ☐ Under 3 mths ☐ 3–6 mths ☐ Over 6 mths	Low	Multi-Family %
Neighborhood Boundaries		High	Commercial %
		Pred.	Other %

Neighborhood Description

Market Conditions (including support for the above conclusions)

SITE

Dimensions · Area · Shape · View

Specific Zoning Classification · Zoning Description

Zoning Compliance ☐ Legal ☐ Legal Nonconforming (Grandfathered Use) ☐ No Zoning ☐ Illegal (describe)

Is the highest and best use of the subject property as improved (or as proposed per plans and specifications) the present use? ☐ Yes ☐ No If No, describe

Utilities	Public	Other (describe)		Public	Other (describe)	Off-site Improvements—Type	Public	Private
Electricity	☐	☐	Water	☐	☐	Street	☐	☐
Gas	☐	☐	Sanitary Sewer	☐	☐	Alley	☐	☐

FEMA Special Flood Hazard Area ☐ Yes ☐ No FEMA Flood Zone · FEMA Map # · FEMA Map Date

Are the utilities and off-site improvements typical for the market area? ☐ Yes ☐ No If No, describe

Are there any adverse site conditions or external factors (easements, encroachments, environmental conditions, land uses, etc.)? ☐ Yes ☐ No If Yes, describe

IMPROVEMENTS

General Description	Foundation	Exterior Description materials/condition	Interior materials/condition
Units ☐ One ☐ One with Accessory Unit	☐ Concrete Slab ☐ Crawl Space	Foundation Walls	Floors
# of Stories	☐ Full Basement ☐ Partial Basement	Exterior Walls	Walls
Type ☐ Det. ☐ Att. ☐ S-Det./End Unit	Basement Area sq. ft.	Roof Surface	Trim/Finish
☐ Existing ☐ Proposed ☐ Under Const.	Basement Finish %	Gutters & Downspouts	Bath Floor
Design (Style)	☐ Outside Entry/Exit ☐ Sump Pump	Window Type	Bath Wainscot
Year Built	Evidence of ☐ Infestation	Storm Sash/Insulated	Car Storage ☐ None
Effective Age (Yrs)	☐ Dampness ☐ Settlement	Screens	☐ Driveway # of Cars
Attic ☐ None	Heating ☐ FWA ☐ HWBB ☐ Radiant	Amenities ☐ Woodstove(s) #	Driveway Surface
☐ Drop Stair ☐ Stairs	☐ Other Fuel	☐ Fireplace(s) # ☐ Fence	☐ Garage # of Cars
☐ Floor ☐ Scuttle	Cooling ☐ Central Air Conditioning	☐ Patio/Deck ☐ Porch	☐ Carport # of Cars
☐ Finished ☐ Heated	☐ Individual ☐ Other	☐ Pool ☐ Other	☐ Att. ☐ Det. ☐ Built-in

Appliances ☐Refrigerator ☐Range/Oven ☐Dishwasher ☐Disposal ☐Microwave ☐Washer/Dryer ☐Other (describe)

Finished area **above** grade contains: Rooms Bedrooms Bath(s) Square Feet of Gross Living Area Above Grade

Additional features (special energy efficient items, etc.)

Describe the condition of the property (including needed repairs, deterioration, renovations, remodeling, etc.).

Are there any physical deficiencies or adverse conditions that affect the livability, soundness, or structural integrity of the property? ☐ Yes ☐ No If Yes, describe

Does the property generally conform to the neighborhood (functional utility, style, condition, use, construction, etc.)? ☐ Yes ☐ No If No, describe

Uniform Residential Appraisal Report

File #

There are comparable properties currently offered for sale in the subject neighborhood ranging in price from $ to $.

There are comparable sales in the subject neighborhood within the past twelve months ranging in sale price from $ to $.

SALES COMPARISON APPROACH

FEATURE	SUBJECT	COMPARABLE SALE # 1		COMPARABLE SALE # 2		COMPARABLE SALE # 3	
Address							
Proximity to Subject							
Sale Price	$		$		$		$
Sale Price/Gross Liv. Area	$ sq. ft.	$ sq. ft.		$ sq. ft.		$ sq. ft.	
Data Source(s)							
Verification Source(s)							
VALUE ADJUSTMENTS	DESCRIPTION	DESCRIPTION	+(-) $ Adjustment	DESCRIPTION	+(-) $ Adjustment	DESCRIPTION	+(-) $ Adjustment
Sale or Financing Concessions							
Date of Sale/Time							
Location							
Leasehold/Fee Simple							
Site							
View							
Design (Style)							
Quality of Construction							
Actual Age							
Condition							
Above Grade	Total Bdrms. Baths	Total Bdrms. Baths		Total Bdrms. Baths		Total Bdrms. Baths	
Room Count							
Gross Living Area	sq. ft.	sq. ft.		sq. ft.		sq. ft.	
Basement & Finished Rooms Below Grade							
Functional Utility							
Heating/Cooling							
Energy Efficient Items							
Garage/Carport							
Porch/Patio/Deck							
Net Adjustment (Total)		☐ + ☐ -	$	☐ + ☐ -	$	☐ + ☐ -	$
Adjusted Sale Price of Comparables		Net Adj. % Gross Adj. %	$	Net Adj. % Gross Adj. %	$	Net Adj. % Gross Adj. %	$

I ☐ did ☐ did not research the sale or transfer history of the subject property and comparable sales. If not, explain

My research ☐ did ☐ did not reveal any prior sales or transfers of the subject property for the three years prior to the effective date of this appraisal.

Data source(s)

My research ☐ did ☐ did not reveal any prior sales or transfers of the comparable sales for the year prior to the date of sale of the comparable sale.

Data source(s)

Report the results of the research and analysis of the prior sale or transfer history of the subject property and comparable sales (report additional prior sales on page 3).

ITEM	SUBJECT	COMPARABLE SALE # 1	COMPARABLE SALE # 2	COMPARABLE SALE # 3
Date of Prior Sale/Transfer				
Price of Prior Sale/Transfer				
Data Source(s)				
Effective Date of Data Source(s)				

Analysis of prior sale or transfer history of the subject property and comparable sales

Summary of Sales Comparison Approach

Indicated Value by Sales Comparison Approach $

RECONCILIATION

Indicated Value by: Sales Comparison Approach $ Cost Approach (if developed) $ Income Approach (if developed) $

This appraisal is made ☐ "as is," ☐ subject to completion per plans and specifications on the basis of a hypothetical condition that the improvements have been completed, ☐ subject to the following repairs or alterations on the basis of a hypothetical condition that the repairs or alterations have been completed, or ☐ subject to the following required inspection based on the extraordinary assumption that the condition or deficiency does not require alteration or repair:

Based on a complete visual inspection of the interior and exterior areas of the subject property, defined scope of work, statement of assumptions and limiting conditions, and appraiser's certification, my (our) opinion of the market value, as defined, of the real property that is the subject of this report is $, as of , which is the date of inspection and the effective date of this appraisal.

Freddie Mac Form 70 March 2005 Page 2 of 6 Fannie Mae Form 1004 March 2005

FIGURE 24.3 Continued.

Uniform Residential Appraisal Report

File #

ADDITIONAL COMMENTS

COST APPROACH TO VALUE (not required by Fannie Mae)

Provide adequate information for the lender/client to replicate the below cost figures and calculations.

Support for the opinion of site value (summary of comparable land sales or other methods for estimating site value)

ESTIMATED ☐ REPRODUCTION OR ☐ REPLACEMENT COST NEW	OPINION OF SITE VALUE .... = $
Source of cost data	Dwelling Sq. Ft. @ $ .... =$
Quality rating from cost service Effective date of cost data	Sq. Ft. @ $ .... =$
Comments on Cost Approach (gross living area calculations, depreciation, etc.)	
	Garage/Carport Sq. Ft. @ $ .... =$
	Total Estimate of Cost-New .... = $
	Less Physical | Functional | External
	Depreciation =$( )
	Depreciated Cost of Improvements................ =$
	"As-is" Value of Site Improvements................ =$
Estimated Remaining Economic Life (HUD and VA only) Years	Indicated Value By Cost Approach .... =$

INCOME APPROACH TO VALUE (not required by Fannie Mae)

Estimated Monthly Market Rent $ X Gross Rent Multiplier   = $ Indicated Value by Income Approach

Summary of Income Approach (including support for market rent and GRM)

PROJECT INFORMATION FOR PUDs (if applicable)

Is the developer/builder in control of the Homeowners' Association (HOA)? ☐ Yes ☐ No   Unit type(s) ☐ Detached ☐ Attached

Provide the following information for PUDs ONLY if the developer/builder is in control of the HOA and the subject property is an attached dwelling unit.

Legal name of project

Total number of phases   Total number of units   Total number of units sold

Total number of units rented   Total number of units for sale   Data source(s)

Was the project created by the conversion of an existing building(s) into a PUD? ☐ Yes ☐ No If Yes, date of conversion

Does the project contain any multi-dwelling units? ☐ Yes ☐ No Data source(s)

Are the units, common elements, and recreation facilities complete? ☐ Yes ☐ No If No, describe the status of completion.

Are the common elements leased to or by the Homeowners' Association? ☐ Yes ☐ No If Yes, describe the rental terms and options.

Describe common elements and recreational facilities

Freddie Mac Form 70   March 2005   Page 3 of 6   Fannie Mae Form 1004   March 2005

397

FIGURE 24.3 Continued.

Uniform Residential Appraisal Report

File #

This report form is designed to report an appraisal of a one-unit property or a one-unit property with an accessory unit; including a unit in a planned unit development (PUD). This report form is not designed to report an appraisal of a manufactured home or a unit in a condominium or cooperative project.

This appraisal report is subject to the following scope of work, intended use, intended user, definition of market value, statement of assumptions and limiting conditions, and certifications. Modifications, additions, or deletions to the intended use, intended user, definition of market value, or assumptions and limiting conditions are not permitted. The appraiser may expand the scope of work to include any additional research or analysis necessary based on the complexity of this appraisal assignment. Modifications or deletions to the certifications are also not permitted. However, additional certifications that do not constitute material alterations to this appraisal report, such as those required by law or those related to the appraiser's continuing education or membership in an appraisal organization, are permitted.

SCOPE OF WORK: The scope of work for this appraisal is defined by the complexity of this appraisal assignment and the reporting requirements of this appraisal report form, including the following definition of market value, statement of assumptions and limiting conditions, and certifications. The appraiser must, at a minimum: (1) perform a complete visual inspection of the interior and exterior areas of the subject property, (2) inspect the neighborhood, (3) inspect each of the comparable sales from at least the street, (4) research, verify, and analyze data from reliable public and/or private sources, and (5) report his or her analysis, opinions, and conclusions in this appraisal report.

INTENDED USE: The intended use of this appraisal report is for the lender/client to evaluate the property that is the subject of this appraisal for a mortgage finance transaction.

INTENDED USER: The intended user of this appraisal report is the lender/client.

DEFINITION OF MARKET VALUE: The most probable price which a property should bring in a competitive and open market under all conditions requisite to a fair sale, the buyer and seller each acting prudently, knowledgeably and assuming the price is not affected by undue stimulus. Implicit in this definition is the consummation of a sale as of a specified date and the passing of title from seller to buyer under conditions whereby: (1) buyer and seller are typically motivated; (2) both parties are well informed or well advised, and each acting in what he or she considers his or her own best interest; (3) a reasonable time is allowed for exposure in the open market; (4) payment is made in terms of cash in U.S. dollars or in terms of financial arrangements comparable thereto; and (5) the price represents the normal consideration for the property sold unaffected by special or creative financing or sales concessions* granted by anyone associated with the sale.

*Adjustments to the comparables must be made for special or creative financing or sales concessions. No adjustments are necessary for those costs which are normally paid by sellers as a result of tradition or law in a market area; these costs are readily identifiable since the seller pays these costs in virtually all sales transactions. Special or creative financing adjustments can be made to the comparable property by comparisons to financing terms offered by a third party institutional lender that is not already involved in the property or transaction. Any adjustment should not be calculated on a mechanical dollar for dollar cost of the financing or concession but the dollar amount of any adjustment should approximate the market's reaction to the financing or concessions based on the appraiser's judgment.

STATEMENT OF ASSUMPTIONS AND LIMITING CONDITIONS: The appraiser's certification in this report is subject to the following assumptions and limiting conditions:

1. The appraiser will not be responsible for matters of a legal nature that affect either the property being appraised or the title to it, except for information that he or she became aware of during the research involved in performing this appraisal. The appraiser assumes that the title is good and marketable and will not render any opinions about the title.

2. The appraiser has provided a sketch in this appraisal report to show the approximate dimensions of the improvements. The sketch is included only to assist the reader in visualizing the property and understanding the appraiser's determination of its size.

3. The appraiser has examined the available flood maps that are provided by the Federal Emergency Management Agency (or other data sources) and has noted in this appraisal report whether any portion of the subject site is located in an identified Special Flood Hazard Area. Because the appraiser is not a surveyor, he or she makes no guarantees, express or implied, regarding this determination.

4. The appraiser will not give testimony or appear in court because he or she made an appraisal of the property in question, unless specific arrangements to do so have been made beforehand, or as otherwise required by law.

5. The appraiser has noted in this appraisal report any adverse conditions (such as needed repairs, deterioration, the presence of hazardous wastes, toxic substances, etc.) observed during the inspection of the subject property or that he or she became aware of during the research involved in performing this appraisal. Unless otherwise stated in this appraisal report, the appraiser has no knowledge of any hidden or unapparent physical deficiencies or adverse conditions of the property (such as, but not limited to, needed repairs, deterioration, the presence of hazardous wastes, toxic substances, adverse environmental conditions, etc.) that would make the property less valuable, and has assumed that there are no such conditions and makes no guarantees or warranties, express or implied. The appraiser will not be responsible for any such conditions that do exist or for any engineering or testing that might be required to discover whether such conditions exist. Because the appraiser is not an expert in the field of environmental hazards, this appraisal report must not be considered as an environmental assessment of the property.

6. The appraiser has based his or her appraisal report and valuation conclusion for an appraisal that is subject to satisfactory completion, repairs, or alterations on the assumption that the completion, repairs, or alterations of the subject property will be performed in a professional manner.

FIGURE 24.3 Continued.

Uniform Residential Appraisal Report

File #

APPRAISER'S CERTIFICATION: The Appraiser certifies and agrees that:

1. I have, at a minimum, developed and reported this appraisal in accordance with the scope of work requirements stated in this appraisal report.

2. I performed a complete visual inspection of the interior and exterior areas of the subject property. I reported the condition of the improvements in factual, specific terms. I identified and reported the physical deficiencies that could affect the livability, soundness, or structural integrity of the property.

3. I performed this appraisal in accordance with the requirements of the Uniform Standards of Professional Appraisal Practice that were adopted and promulgated by the Appraisal Standards Board of The Appraisal Foundation and that were in place at the time this appraisal report was prepared.

4. I developed my opinion of the market value of the real property that is the subject of this report based on the sales comparison approach to value. I have adequate comparable market data to develop a reliable sales comparison approach for this appraisal assignment. I further certify that I considered the cost and income approaches to value but did not develop them, unless otherwise indicated in this report.

5. I researched, verified, analyzed, and reported on any current agreement for sale for the subject property, any offering for sale of the subject property in the twelve months prior to the effective date of this appraisal, and the prior sales of the subject property for a minimum of three years prior to the effective date of this appraisal, unless otherwise indicated in this report.

6. I researched, verified, analyzed, and reported on the prior sales of the comparable sales for a minimum of one year prior to the date of sale of the comparable sale, unless otherwise indicated in this report.

7. I selected and used comparable sales that are locationally, physically, and functionally the most similar to the subject property.

8. I have not used comparable sales that were the result of combining a land sale with the contract purchase price of a home that has been built or will be built on the land.

9. I have reported adjustments to the comparable sales that reflect the market's reaction to the differences between the subject property and the comparable sales.

10. I verified, from a disinterested source, all information in this report that was provided by parties who have a financial interest in the sale or financing of the subject property.

11. I have knowledge and experience in appraising this type of property in this market area.

12. I am aware of, and have access to, the necessary and appropriate public and private data sources, such as multiple listing services, tax assessment records, public land records and other such data sources for the area in which the property is located.

13. I obtained the information, estimates, and opinions furnished by other parties and expressed in this appraisal report from reliable sources that I believe to be true and correct.

14. I have taken into consideration the factors that have an impact on value with respect to the subject neighborhood, subject property, and the proximity of the subject property to adverse influences in the development of my opinion of market value. I have noted in this appraisal report any adverse conditions (such as, but not limited to, needed repairs, deterioration, the presence of hazardous wastes, toxic substances, adverse environmental conditions, etc.) observed during the inspection of the subject property or that I became aware of during the research involved in performing this appraisal. I have considered these adverse conditions in my analysis of the property value, and have reported on the effect of the conditions on the value and marketability of the subject property.

15. I have not knowingly withheld any significant information from this appraisal report and, to the best of my knowledge, all statements and information in this appraisal report are true and correct.

16. I stated in this appraisal report my own personal, unbiased, and professional analysis, opinions, and conclusions, which are subject only to the assumptions and limiting conditions in this appraisal report.

17. I have no present or prospective interest in the property that is the subject of this report, and I have no present or prospective personal interest or bias with respect to the participants in the transaction. I did not base, either partially or completely, my analysis and/or opinion of market value in this appraisal report on the race, color, religion, sex, age, marital status, handicap, familial status, or national origin of either the prospective owners or occupants of the subject property or of the present owners or occupants of the properties in the vicinity of the subject property or on any other basis prohibited by law.

18. My employment and/or compensation for performing this appraisal or any future or anticipated appraisals was not conditioned on any agreement or understanding, written or otherwise, that I would report (or present analysis supporting) a predetermined specific value, a predetermined minimum value, a range or direction in value, a value that favors the cause of any party, or the attainment of a specific result or occurrence of a specific subsequent event (such as approval of a pending mortgage loan application).

19. I personally prepared all conclusions and opinions about the real estate that were set forth in this appraisal report. If I relied on significant real property appraisal assistance from any individual or individuals in the performance of this appraisal or the preparation of this appraisal report, I have named such individual(s) and disclosed the specific tasks performed in this appraisal report. I certify that any individual so named is qualified to perform the tasks. I have not authorized anyone to make a change to any item in this appraisal report; therefore, any change made to this appraisal is unauthorized and I will take no responsibility for it.

20. I identified the lender/client in this appraisal report who is the individual, organization, or agent for the organization that ordered and will receive this appraisal report.

FIGURE 24.3 Continued.

Uniform Residential Appraisal Report
File #

21. The lender/client may disclose or distribute this appraisal report to: the borrower; another lender at the request of the borrower; the mortgagee or its successors and assigns; mortgage insurers; government sponsored enterprises; other secondary market participants; data collection or reporting services; professional appraisal organizations; any department, agency, or instrumentality of the United States; and any state, the District of Columbia, or other jurisdictions; without having to obtain the appraiser's or supervisory appraiser's (if applicable) consent. Such consent must be obtained before this appraisal report may be disclosed or distributed to any other party (including, but not limited to, the public through advertising, public relations, news, sales, or other media).

22. I am aware that any disclosure or distribution of this appraisal report by me or the lender/client may be subject to certain laws and regulations. Further, I am also subject to the provisions of the Uniform Standards of Professional Appraisal Practice that pertain to disclosure or distribution by me.

23. The borrower, another lender at the request of the borrower, the mortgagee or its successors and assigns, mortgage insurers, government sponsored enterprises, and other secondary market participants may rely on this appraisal report as part of any mortgage finance transaction that involves any one or more of these parties.

24. If this appraisal report was transmitted as an "electronic record" containing my "electronic signature," as those terms are defined in applicable federal and/or state laws (excluding audio and video recordings), or a facsimile transmission of this appraisal report containing a copy or representation of my signature, the appraisal report shall be as effective, enforceable and valid as if a paper version of this appraisal report were delivered containing my original hand written signature.

25. Any intentional or negligent misrepresentation(s) contained in this appraisal report may result in civil liability and/or criminal penalties including, but not limited to, fine or imprisonment or both under the provisions of Title 18, United States Code, Section 1001, et seq., or similar state laws.

SUPERVISORY APPRAISER'S CERTIFICATION: The Supervisory Appraiser certifies and agrees that:

1. I directly supervised the appraiser for this appraisal assignment, have read the appraisal report, and agree with the appraiser's analysis, opinions, statements, conclusions, and the appraiser's certification.

2. I accept full responsibility for the contents of this appraisal report including, but not limited to, the appraiser's analysis, opinions, statements, conclusions, and the appraiser's certification.

3. The appraiser identified in this appraisal report is either a sub-contractor or an employee of the supervisory appraiser (or the appraisal firm), is qualified to perform this appraisal, and is acceptable to perform this appraisal under the applicable state law.

4. This appraisal report complies with the Uniform Standards of Professional Appraisal Practice that were adopted and promulgated by the Appraisal Standards Board of The Appraisal Foundation and that were in place at the time this appraisal report was prepared.

5. If this appraisal report was transmitted as an "electronic record" containing my "electronic signature," as those terms are defined in applicable federal and/or state laws (excluding audio and video recordings), or a facsimile transmission of this appraisal report containing a copy or representation of my signature, the appraisal report shall be as effective, enforceable and valid as if a paper version of this appraisal report were delivered containing my original hand written signature.

APPRAISER

Signature_____
Name _____
Company Name _____
Company Address_____
_____
Telephone Number _____
Email Address_____
Date of Signature and Report_____
Effective Date of Appraisal _____
State Certification #_____
or State License # _____
or Other (describe) _____ State # _____
State _____
Expiration Date of Certification or License _____

ADDRESS OF PROPERTY APPRAISED
_____

APPRAISED VALUE OF SUBJECT PROPERTY $ _____

LENDER/CLIENT
Name _____
Company Name _____
Company Address_____
_____
Email Address _____

SUPERVISORY APPRAISER (ONLY IF REQUIRED)

Signature _____
Name_____
Company Name _____
Company Address_____
_____
Telephone Number _____
Email Address _____
Date of Signature _____
State Certification #_____
or State License # _____
State _____
Expiration Date of Certification or License _____

SUBJECT PROPERTY
☐ Did not inspect subject property
☐ Did inspect exterior of subject property from street
  Date of Inspection _____
☐ Did inspect interior and exterior of subject property
  Date of Inspection _____

COMPARABLE SALES
☐ Did not inspect exterior of comparable sales from street
☐ Did inspect exterior of comparable sales from street
  Date of Inspection _____

FIGURE 24.4   Gross Rent Multiplier Example

		Properties			
	Subject	A	B	C	D
Sales Price	???	$60,000	$65,000	$62,000	$64,000
Monthly Rent	$475	$ 475	$ 500	$ 480	$ 490
GRM		126	130	129	131

In this example, if 130 were used as the GRM, the value would be $61,750 (130 × $475 = $61,750).

The *licensed residential appraiser* classification applies to the appraisal of non-complex one- to four-residential units having a transaction value less than $1 million, and complex one- to four-residential units having a transaction value less than $250,000.

The *certified residential appraiser* classification applies to the appraisal of one- to four-residential units without regard to transaction value.

The *certified general appraiser* classification applies to the appraisal of all types of real property.

The Appraisal Foundation

Established in 1987, the Appraisal Foundation is a non-profit corporation that is recognized by Congress as the main source of appraisal standards and qualifications. FIRREA requires that state appraiser licensing and certification qualifications, plus appraisal standards, meet or exceed those of the Appraisal Qualification Board of the Appraisal Foundation.

Affiliations

Appraisal organizations affiliated with the Appraisal Foundation include the American Association of Certified Appraisers, American Society of Farm Managers and Rural Appraisers, Appraisal Institute, International Association of Assessing Officers, International Right of Way Association, National Association of Independent Fee Appraisers, and National Association of Master Appraisers. For more information on the Appraisal Foundation, visit its website at www.appraisalfoundation.org.

Professional Standards of Practice

The major appraisal associations have been leaders in establishing standards of appraisal practice as well as defining ethical conduct by members of the profession. In 1987, representatives from nine appraisal groups published the **Uniform Standards of Professional Appraisal Practice (USPAP)**. The standards have been amended several times since 1987 and cover real estate, personal property, and business appraisal, as well as other topics. The standards are interpreted and amended by the Appraisal Standards Board of the Appraisal Foundation.

24.8 MATH PROBLEMS

Percentage of Yield

This is the "T" formula covered earlier in this chapter. In this instance, the Part is the *Net Income,* the Rate or Percentage is the *Yield* or *Rate of Return,* and the Total is the *Cost* or *Value.*

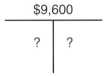

To practice finding the yield or rate of return, use the following exercises. The first one is done for you.

EXERCISE 1: An investor received $9600 net income, which cost him $120,000. What is his rate of return?

Step 1: The $9600 is part of the total. Place it on the top.

$$\frac{\$9{,}600}{?\ |\ ?}$$

Step 2: The total is $120,000. Place it in the lower-right side.

$$\frac{\$9{,}600}{?\ |\ \$120{,}000}$$

Step 3: Divide the number on top ($9600) by the number on bottom ($120,000).

$$\$9600 \div \$120{,}000 = 0.08$$

Step 4: Convert decimal answer to percentage.

$$0.08 = 8\%   \text{The investor's rate of return is 8\%.}$$

EXERCISE 2: A man paid $540,000 for an apartment complex that returns a monthly net income of $4500. What is the annual rate of return of his investment?

Step 1: Multiply monthly net income by 12 to get annual net income.

Step 2: Divide the annual net income by the amount of the investment.

Step 3: Convert your answer to a percentage.

EXERCISE 3: An apartment complex has an annual gross income of $22,800 and a total monthly expense of $900. The owner enjoys a 15% return on her investment. What is her investment?

Step 1: Multiply monthly expense by 12 to get annual expense.

Step 2: Subtract annual expense from annual gross to get annual net.

Step 3: Divide the annual net by the decimal equivalent of the rate of the return.

Profit and Loss Problems

When dealing with a problem that involves percentage of profit, you must first find the amount of profit before you can solve the problem. Then simply divide the cost into the profit to find the percentage of profit.

Profit is expressed as a percentage of cost. If the sales price is $50,000 and the owner's cost when he purchased it was $30,000, what was his percentage of profit?

This is the T formula covered earlier. In this instance, the part is the *profit*, the rate is the *percentage of profit*, and the total is the *original cost*.

```
         PART OR
         PROFIT
      _____
         %     |
      PROFIT | COST
             |
```

Practice Problems

EXERCISE 1: Mr. Jones listed his property for $40,000. If his cost was 80% of the listed price, what will be his percentage of profit if he sells it for the listed price?

Step 1: Compute the cost by multiplying the sales price of $40,000 by 80%. The answer of $32,000 is the original cost and goes in the lower-right part of the T diagram.

Step 2: Compute the profit by subtracting the cost from the sales price ($40,000 less $32,000 equals $8000). The profit of $8000 goes on the top.

Step 3: Divide the item on top by the total cost on the lower-right side of the T diagram to get the percentage of profit.

EXERCISE 2: A house was sold for $60,000, which was 95% of the listing price. If the seller's cost of the property was $43,200, what is her percentage of gross profit before commission and expense?

EXERCISE 3: Elaine buys a house at 20% below the listed price and later resells it at the original list price. What was her percentage of profit?

EXERCISE 4: A property was sold at $77,500. Of this sales price, 30% represents profit. What was the seller's cost?

Step 1: Multiply sales price by the decimal equivalent of 70%. (If 30% of sales price is profit, 70% of sales price is cost.)

CHAPTER SUMMARY

An appraisal is an estimate or opinion of value as of a specified date based on analysis of factual data. Value means the exchange of present worth for future benefits to the owner of the property. Most property is purchased with the expectation of appreciation, which is an increase in value. Cost is the historical expenditure for the purchase, construction, or improvement of a property.

Cost has nothing to do with present value. Price is the amount asked and the amount paid for property.

There are four principal characteristics of value: demand, utility, scarcity, and transferability. The most common types of value are market value, subjective value, loan value, assessed value, insurable value, and book value.

Market value is the highest price a property will bring on the open market, allowing for a reasonable time to sell. In real estate, this is the most commonly used type of value. Subjective value represents the emotional value of a property's worth to a person, regardless of cost. Loan value is the value used for establishing the amount of mortgage or trust deed loan to be made. Assessed value is the value put on the property by the county assessor for the purpose of computing "ad valorem" property taxes. Insurable value is used to determine the amount of insurance needed to meet co-insurance clause requirements. *Book value* is an accounting term and is based on historical cost.

Value is influenced by four main factors: physical characteristics, social standards, economic trends, and political regulations. Physical characteristics include climatic conditions, size and shape of lot, topography, soil conditions, action of the sun, and physical hazards. Social standards include population growth, population density, population mobility, proximity, recreational opportunities, and situs. Situs is people's desire for a given area. Economic trends include natural resources, employment opportunities, fluctuating interest rates, inflation, tax rates, wage scales, and availability of credit. Political regulations can be instrumental factors in value. A few important regulations include zoning, building codes, police and fire protection, and the attitude toward solution of community problems.

Economic principles of value assist an appraiser in making an appraisal. These principles are described fully in the body of this chapter's text. Some of the principles include conformity, substitution, balance, progression, and regression.

Depreciation is a decrease in value. There are three types of depreciation applied in appraising: physical deterioration, functional obsolescence, and economic obsolescence. Physical deterioration is the loss of value due to normal wear and tear, or to postponed maintenance. Physical deterioration can be either curable or incurable. Functional obsolescence is due to obsolete equipment or outdated architecture or floor plan. Functional obsolescence can be curable or incurable, depending on the economic life of the building and the expense of remodeling. Economic obsolescence is caused by an influence outside the property over which the property owner has no control. Economic obsolescence is usually incurable.

The three approaches to value are the market data approach, the cost approach, and the income approach. The market data approach reflects recent market trends and is similar to the approach used by licensees or investors when listing residences. The market data approach is also known as the sales comparison approach; however, the appraiser considers comparables from actual sales only, whereas the licensee considers listing prices for comparable properties on the market when completing a competitive market analysis. The market data approach is considered the most reliable of the three approaches to value when appraising a single-family home.

The cost approach, also called appraisal by summation, estimates today's cost of all improvements, minus all factors of depreciation, plus the valuation of the land using the market data approach. There are two choices for estimating values in the cost approach. One is the reproduction cost, which estimates the cost based on using the original materials and technologies. The second method is called replacement cost, which estimates cost based on today's materials and technologies. The cost approach is the most reliable when there are few comparable sales and the subject property is not income producing.

The income approach assumes that income from property establishes value. The value is computed by converting the right to the future operating income to the valuation amount using a capitalization rate. This approach is used for income property.

Reconciliation is the last step in the appraisal process, which reconciles the three approaches to value. In each appraisal, all three approaches to value are figured, producing three different values. Each approach is then analyzed and assigned a weighing factor by the appraiser. The appraiser uses his or her judgment as to which approach is the most relevant.

Three different kinds of appraisal reports can be used depending upon the complexity of the appraisal: the appraisal letter, the appraisal form or checklist, or a narrative report.

Gross rent multiplier (GRM) is used as a rule of thumb for a quick estimate of value based on the relationship of comparable sales prices to the comparables' monthly rental income. It is not an approach to value.

All "federally related real estate appraisals" may be performed only by appraisers *licensed or certified* by the state in which the real estate is located. The three major appraiser classifications are licensed residential appraiser, certified residential appraiser, and certified general appraiser. All three of the appraiser classifications have specific education, examination, and experience requirements. The Appraisal Foundation serves as the main source of appraisal standards and qualifications. The Uniform Standards of Professional Appraisal Practice (USPAP) cover real estate, personal property, and business appraisal, as well as other topics.

CHECKING YOUR COMPREHENSION

1. List and describe the four characteristics of value.

2. Define market value and compare it to subjective value and book value.

3. List and describe the economic principles used by an appraiser when completing an appraisal.

4. Describe how an estimate of value is determined under each of the following:
   • Market data approach
   • Cost approach
   • Income approach

5. Summarize the calculation methods of using a gross rent multiplier and explain why it is not considered an approach to value by an appraiser.

REVIEWING YOUR UNDERSTANDING

1. Which method would **MOST** likely be used by licensees in estimating the value of single-family residences?
   a. income approach
   b. cost approach
   c. market data approach
   d. gross rent multiplier

2. An appraiser, using the cost approach to value, has the most difficulty in determining the:
   a. cost new
   b. cost basis
   c. net income
   d. accumulated depreciation

3. A property has a net income of $30,000. An appraiser decides to use a 12% capitalization rate rather than 10%. This will result in:
   a. a 2% increase in appraised value
   b. a $50,000 increase in appraised value
   c. a $50,000 decrease in appraised value
   d. no change in the appraised value

4. Certain data must be utilized by an appraiser in computing value through an income approach. Which of the following is **NOT** required for this process?
   a. annual net income
   b. accrued depreciation
   c. annual gross income
   d. capitalization rate

5. The market data approach to value is normally used in estimating the value of:
   a. an oil refinery
   b. a hotel
   c. a gas station
   d. vacant land

6. Razing a hotel to build an office building is **MOST** likely an example of the principle of:
   a. highest and best use
   b. conformity
   c. progression
   d. substitution

7. With fixed rents and a capitalization rate of 8%, an increase in taxes of $4000 would result in the value of a property:
   a. decreasing by $5000
   b. decreasing by $50,000
   c. remaining unchanged
   d. increasing by $50,000

8. Loss of value due to negligent care of the property is called:
   a. physical deterioration
   b. depreciation
   c. functional obsolescence
   d. accrued depreciation

9. The principle of supply and demand predicts:
   a. a price increase when supply increases
   b. demand decreasing when supply increases
   c. demand increasing when price decreases
   d. price decreasing when demand increases

10. Land and improvements must be appraised separately when using the:
    a. cost approach
    b. market comparison
    c. gross rent multiplier
    d. income approach

11. An appraiser received figures from a CPA on past rent receipts and operating expenses. The appraiser should:

    a. use the figures provided to determine the net income

    b. adjust the figures provided for future occurrences

    c. use the figures provided but add depreciation as an expense

    d. use the figures provided only after their verification

12. Which of the following is **NOT** considered in the market data approach to value?

    a. sales price of comparable properties

    b. terms of sale of comparable properties

    c. location of each comparable property

    d. acquisition cost to present owner

13. In using the market comparison approach, the appraiser assumes:

    a. Anticipated future income is more important than present income.

    b. No two properties are identical.

    c. The cost to reproduce now is more important than the original cost.

    d. Risk will affect the capitalization rate.

14. Using all three methods of appraisal and assigning different weights to each method is known as:

    a. averaging

    b. reconciliation

    c. bond of investment method

    d. the Ellwood method

15. A duplex whose rents total $1250 is in an area of a smaller duplex in similar condition that rents for $440 per unit and just sold for $132,000. Using this information, the larger duplex would have a value of:

    a. $150,000

    b. $167,500

    c. $187,500

    d. $192,500

16. The market comparison method has the **LEAST** validity:

    a. when used for commercial property

    b. when there have been few sales

    c. in a period of rapid change

    d. when applied to raw land

17. What is the function of a real estate appraiser?

    a. to set market value

    b. to determine market value

    c. to estimate market value

    d. to establish the cost

18. A loss in value because of lesser-value homes being built in an area would be an example of the principle of:

    a. change

    b. contribution

    c. regression

    d. conformity

19. Market value is **BEST** defined as:

    a. assessed value less depreciation

    b. the maximum price a willing informed buyer would pay to a willing informed seller

    c. average sale price for similar properties in the current market

    d. utility value of the property to the owner

20. Functional obsolescence would **NOT** be caused by:

    a. surplus utility

    b. eccentric design

    c. lack of heating and cooling

    d. the proximity of a nuisance

Chapter 25

IMPORTANT TERMS AND CONCEPTS

active participation

adjusted gross income

advance rentals

boot

capital asset

capital gain or loss

capital improvements

cost recovery

depreciation

dwelling unit

earned income

effective rate

gross income

home mortgage
   interest deduction

itemized deductions

leveraging

marginal rate

material participation

net cash flow

nonresidential rental
   property

passive income

passive loss limitation

personal residence gain
   exclusion

portfolio income

principal residence

repair

residential rental
   property

risk

Section 1031

security deposits

speculation

Starker case

tax-deferred exchange

taxable income

tenant-in-common (TIC)
   investment

unadjusted basis

CHAPTER OBJECTIVES

After completing this chapter, you should be able to:

- Explain basic real estate investment principles including the concepts of risk versus speculation, leverage, and cash flow.
- Describe the computation of taxable income for the individual taxpayer.
- Summarize the major income tax considerations for rental real estate.
- Explain the purpose and computation of the depreciation deduction.
- Describe the passive loss limitation on deductions from a passive activity.
- Summarize the income tax benefits related to the sale of real property, including the tax advantages of home ownership and the tax-deferred exchange of property.

Investing in Real Estate and Income Tax Aspects of Real Estate

25.1 REAL ESTATE INVESTMENT PRINCIPLES

Investing in real estate requires a long-term perspective. The real estate market is cyclical in nature, resulting in periodic highs and lows. There is a vast difference between investing and speculating. *Investing* is committing capital to a business in order to earn a financial return or profit. *Speculating* is entering into a transaction where the profits are subject to chance; to buy or sell with the hope of profiting through the fluctuations in price.

A thorough discussion of investing in real estate is beyond the scope of this textbook. However, any student of real estate should be familiar with some of the basic principles. Probably the most important concept to understand is this: Have a plan! Planning is a common principle for every successful business, but more often than not it is ignored or overlooked when it comes to real estate. If you really want to succeed with an investment in real estate, then you will want to:

1. Learn about the business
2. Research the market
3. Develop a plan for success
4. Acquire an investment according to your plan
5. Monitor and manage your investment to achieve your goals

Risk vs. Speculation

Risk is a major consideration in all real estate investments. Even the purchase of a home you intend to occupy involves some degree of risk. Investment real estate or **speculation** in real estate involves a high degree of risk. As with most investments, buying low and selling high is a primary objective. Market conditions, financing, liquidity, staying power, and the ability to control the property are all important considerations in evaluating the risk of a real estate investment. Suffice to say that "rolling the dice" is not a sound approach to real estate investing.

Speculating in real estate is much more complicated than merely assuming a higher degree of risk. Speculation is gambling on the fluctuations in prices. This may seem to be a simple concept in a cyclical market: You buy property when prices are down and sell when they go up. But it is definitely not something for the uninitiated. Bad things sometimes happen to good investments. As a speculator, you are relying on someone or something else to change or happen, the occurrence of which will have, you hope, a positive effect on your investment. The key word is *hope*. This is similar to buying a lottery ticket—you *hope* your number comes up.

Leveraging

Leveraging means borrowing money from another source to supplement your own funds in completing the acquisition of a piece of property. Leverage can dramatically increase your return on an investment, while spreading some of the risk to others. Leverage can be a mortgage or a limited partnership or just another investor. For example, if an investor has $100,000 to invest, he can buy a particular piece of property for $100,000, and if he sells the property in two years for $125,000, the investor has made 12.5% per annum on his investment, but has had no access to those funds for two years. Utilizing some leverage, the same property can be acquired with an $80,000 mortgage at say, 8%, if he keeps his $80,000 in the bank at 4%, then the net interest cost is 4% (ignoring any income tax effects) and the return on the $20,000 actually invested is 46.5%. Looking at it from a different perspective, if you can buy a property for 10% down, and market values are increasing at a 3% rate, then your 10% investment will earn 30%.

Sources of Funding

The primary source for leverage funding is real estate lenders. There is an excess of funding available for real estate investments. Many kinds of financial institutions, mortgage bankers, mortgage brokers, sellers, private individuals, and the like are available as sources of funds for financing real estate investments. Because investing in real estate also includes your personal residence, government-backed loans are a great source of leverage. Some FHA or DVA programs will go as high as 95% or even 100% on the leverage. A more thorough understanding of real estate lending and financing may be found in Chapters 21 and 22.

Short-Term Benefits

Investing in real estate should involve a long-term perspective. There are, however, some short-term benefits that can accrue to the investor, such as cash flow and tax benefits. Cash flow should be determined at the time you evaluate the investment opportunity. As part of your due diligence process, you should review the rental income schedule and related property expenses so that you can reasonably determine the amount of cash flow from the property. Cash flow is easily determined as follows:

Gross income − Operating expenses and loan payments = Net cash flow

In determining the taxable income from your investment, you will be able to deduct all of the operating expenses from the rental income received, as well as take a depreciation deduction (now referred to as **cost recovery** by the Internal Revenue Service) for a pro-rata amount of the cost of the buildings and improvements.

This is usually a significant tax benefit, very often turning taxable income into a tax loss. These tax losses can be used to offset other sources of income in an individual's tax return, thereby providing another tax benefit.

In the meantime, the rents you have received have been used to pay the mortgage, which increases your equity. Your property's market value should be appreciating so that when it is time to sell the property, you will realize a significant profit. This profit or gain will be taxable; however, it will be taxed as a capital gain, for which currently the maximum rate is 15%.

25.2 INCOME TAX AND REAL ESTATE

As the cost of government climbs, the federal income tax remains a major personal obligation. Included in the income tax laws are certain opportunities for individuals to reduce or defer their income tax obligations. The federal income tax code, rules, and regulations are complicated and constantly changing. Therefore, real estate agents and brokers should not provide tax advice to their clients and customers, but should refer them to a professional tax accountant or attorney.

However, real estate agents should have a basic understanding of tax laws in order to alert clients and customers to the potential tax risks or savings opportunities and to know when to recommend that they seek professional advice. To appreciate the income tax benefits related to the ownership of real estate, the agent must understand the basic concepts and tax rates for individual income taxes.

Basic Concepts

Taxable income for the individual taxpayer is computed as follows:

Gross Income

Less

Deductions for Adjusted Gross Income

Equals

Adjusted Gross Income

Less

Itemized Deductions or Standard Deduction and Personal Exemptions

Equals

Taxable Income

Gross Income

Gross income includes earned income, portfolio income, passive income, and capital gains and losses.

- **Earned income** includes wages, salaries, income from a business or profession, and other earned income. Generally, everything an individual receives as payment for personal services must be included in gross income.

- **Portfolio income** is income that is a return on invested capital, such as interest and dividends.
- **Passive income** is income from a business in which the owner does not materially participate. Rental real estate is generally classified as a passive activity.
- A **capital gain or loss** is a gain or loss on the sale of a capital asset. As a general rule, everything a taxpayer owns for personal and investment purposes is a capital asset.

Adjusted Gross Income

To determine **adjusted gross income**, a taxpayer subtracts amounts specifically authorized by the Revenue Code from gross income. Among the items currently authorized for deduction are: IRA, SEP, Simple, and qualified plan contributions; health savings account contributions; employment-related moving expenses; self-employed health insurance deduction; one-half of self-employment tax; student loan interest deduction; alimony paid; and tuition and fees deduction.

Currently, a taxpayer's adjusted gross income affects the extent to which he or she can withhold itemized deductions for medical expenses, casualty and theft losses, charitable contributions, and other miscellaneous items. These particular deductions are limited to amounts in excess of specific percentages of an individual's adjusted gross income.

Itemized Deductions

Itemized deductions may include personal expenses for the following:

1. Medical and dental
2. Taxes
3. Interest
4. Gifts to charity
5. Casualty and theft losses
6. Job expenses and other miscellaneous deductions

Although a thorough discussion of itemized deductions is beyond the scope of this textbook, keep in mind that many rules and regulations limit the amount of the previously mentioned personal expenses that may be included in the itemized deduction.

Taxpayers are entitled to a standard deduction amount. The amount of the deduction varies according to the filing status of the taxpayer and is adjusted annually by a cost-of-living adjustment. If the total of a taxpayer's itemized deductions exceeds the amount of the standard deduction, then he or she may use the higher amount. The deduction is then subtracted from the figure for adjusted gross income.

Personal and dependent exemptions are also subtracted from adjusted gross income to determine taxable income. The amount of these exemptions is adjusted annually to reflect increases in the cost of living. Currently, deductions for personal exemptions are reduced or eliminated for taxpayers at higher income levels. For 2008, the personal exemption was $3500, but was phased out when adjusted gross income exceeded $289,000 for single persons and $372,000 for married persons filing a joint return.

Tax Rates

In 2008, there were six basic individual tax rates: 10%, 15%, 25%, 28%, 33%, and 35%. The 35% rate applies to taxable income in excess of $357,700.

There are eight different rates used to calculate a corporation's federal income tax. These rates range from 15% for taxable incomes under $50,000 to 39% for income between $100,000 and $335,000. For larger profitable corporations, the rates blend to produce an effective rate of 34% if the corporation makes up to $10 million or 35% if it makes $18,333,333 or more.

The difference between corporate and individual tax rates influences the selection of the entity to hold a real estate investment. There are many entities available—individual, corporation, partnership, limited partnership, and so on. This choice can significantly affect the investor's return on the investment, and therefore, often requires the assistance of legal and accounting professionals. A discussion of the income tax aspects related to the selection of an entity for holding a real estate investment is included in Chapter 9.

The **marginal rate** is the rate of tax on the next dollar of income, whereas the **effective rate** is the average tax rate on all of the individual's taxable income. For example, if a married taxpayer filing jointly had taxable income of $320,000 before receiving additional income of $10,000, the marginal rate on the additional income would be 33%, meaning that $0.33 of the next $1.00 of the couple's income represents taxes they must pay, whereas the effective rate (average rate) of the couples' income would be 27%. The marginal tax rate is used to determine the benefit of tax-deductible expenses.

25.3 RENTAL REAL ESTATE

Accounting for the income and expenses of a rental property may be done on a cash basis or an accrual basis. As a taxpayer, you must elect one method or the other; however, almost all individual taxpayers use the cash basis. On the cash basis, rental income is reported in the year in which payment is received, and expenses are reported in the year they are actually paid. On the accrual basis, rental income is reported in the year in which the taxpayer is entitled to receive payment, less an allowance for uncollectible rentals, and expenses are accrued when they are due rather than when paid.

Advance Rentals vs. Security Deposits

A taxpayer should always distinguish between advance rentals and security deposits. **Advance rentals** are income when received. They are reported in the year received, whether the taxpayer is reporting on a cash or accrual basis. **Security deposits** are deposited with the landlord solely as security for the tenant's performance of the terms of the lease, and are usually not taxed when received. If the tenant breaches the lease, the landlord is entitled to apply the sum as rent, at which time the deposit is reported as income. If the landlord and the tenant both agree that a security deposit is to be used as a final rent payment, it is advance rent and included as rental income when received.

Improvements by a Tenant

A landlord does not realize taxable income when a tenant improves the leased premises, provided the improvements are not a substitute for rent payments. Furthermore, when the landlord takes possession of the improvements at lease termination, income is not realized. However, because the landlord has no tax basis in the improvements, they may not be depreciated.

Operating Expenses

All expenses incurred by the real property owner in the operation of the property are deductible from the rental income. For cash basis taxpayers, normal operating expenses are deductible in the year the expenses are paid. Examples of normal operating expenses include:

- Utilities
- Interest on mortgages and loans
- Insurance
- Property and sales taxes
- Gardening and cleaning expenses
- License and city fees
- Repairs and maintenance
- Management fees
- Advertising and rental commissions

Interest

Interest on mortgages and other debt specifically related to the rental property is deductible as an operating expense. Of course, any portion of these loan payments that is a principal reduction may not be included as an operating expense.

Repair vs. Capital Improvement

Taxpayers frequently have difficulty distinguishing between a repair and a capital improvement. It is important to differentiate between the two, because maintenance and repair expenses are not treated in the same way as costs for capital improvements and replacements. Only maintenance and incidental repair costs are deductible against rental income. Improvements that add value, prolong the life of the property, or adapt it to new uses are capital improvements. Capital improvements may not be deducted currently, but may be depreciated.

A **repair** keeps the real property in good operating condition. For example, repairs include painting, fixing gutters or floors, fixing leaks in plumbing or roofs, plastering, and replacing broken windows.

Capital improvements include carpeting, window coverings, new roofs, new plumbing or electrical systems, building additions, and major repairs such as a new driveway, refurbishing stucco, or new landscaping.

25.4 DEPRECIATION

The principal tax advantage for owners of investment real property is depreciation. The property must be a "capital asset" under Sec. 1231 of the Internal Revenue Code, which means a capital asset used in a trade or business. Therefore, you may not depreciate your personal residence. The depreciation deduction often allows net positive cash flow to be enjoyed by the taxpayer without any current tax liability.

Depreciation is the annual deduction allowed for recovering the taxpayer's cost of the investment property. The depreciation deduction is allowable on the portion of the cost allocated to the buildings and improvements, as these are subject to wear and tear, decay, and obsolescence. The cost of land is not depreciable.

For real property acquired after May 1993, taxpayers must use the Modified Accelerated Cost Recovery System (MACRS). Assets are classified based on their stipulated recovery period. The recovery period for residential rental property placed in service after December 31, 1986, is 27.5 years. The recovery period for nonresidential rental property is 39 years for property placed in service after May 12, 1993. The recovery period is 31.5 years for nonresidential property placed in service after December 31, 1986, but before May 13, 1993. Real estate acquired prior to January 1, 1987, is subject to different recovery periods. Because this is a complex area of the tax code, it is a good idea to review the proper asset classifications and recovery periods with your professional tax advisor when planning your investment strategy.

Residential and Nonresidential Rental Property

Residential rental property is a building or structure in which 80% or more of the gross rental income is rental income from dwelling units. A **dwelling unit** is a house or apartment used to provide living accommodations. A dwelling unit does not include hotel units, motel units, and other establishments where more than half the units are used on a transient basis.

Nonresidential rental property is real property that is not residential rental property.

Depreciation Deduction Computation

The computation of the depreciation deduction for real property uses the mid-month convention, which requires that the depreciation for the first year a property is placed in service will be based on both of the following:

a. The number of months the property was in service
b. For property placed in service during a month it will be treated as placed in service in the middle of the month

An example of the depreciation calculation for a nonresidential building placed in service in June 2008 is as follows:

Total cost	$1,000,000
Less land cost	(200,000)
Building cost	800,000

The recovery period is 39 years and the annual depreciation is $20,513 ($800,000 divided by 39). Depreciation in the year 2008 would be for 6.5 months or $11,111 according to the mid-month convention.

25.5 PASSIVE LOSS LIMITATION

Passive activities generally include any business or investment activity in which the taxpayer does not materially participate. The rental of real or personal property is generally a rental activity under the passive activity loss rules, but exceptions apply. The passive activity laws were intended to discourage tax-shelter investments, but their reach goes beyond tax shelters to cover all real estate investors and persons who invest in businesses as silent partners, or who are not involved full time in the business.

The passive activity rules prevent an investor from deducting what the law defines as a passive loss from earned income such as salary, self-employment income, or portfolio income such as interest, dividends, or retirement income. Such losses are deductible only from income from other passive activities.

Real Estate Professionals

Rental income and losses are automatically treated as passive unless earned or incurred by a real estate professional, or the rentals are considered by law to be business activity. Even if rental income or loss is earned by a professional or is considered business income, the passive loss restrictions still apply unless the taxpayer materially participates in the activity.

The exception for real estate professionals allows income or loss from the rental real estate to be reported as non-passive. Therefore, if all the requirements are met, a real estate professional could reduce earned income, such as commissions, by the amount of any losses from rental real estate. There are two tests that must be met to be classified as a *real estate professional*. First, more than half of the personal services you perform in trades or businesses were performed in real property trades or businesses in which you materially participated; and second, you performed more than 750 hours of services in real property trades or businesses in which you materially participated.

Material participation generally applies only to trades or businesses in which you have an ownership interest greater than 5%. In addition, there are seven tests under which a taxpayer can then qualify to meet the material participation requirement. These tests typically deal with the number of hours of participation accumulated during the year in a particular activity. The taxpayer needs to meet only one of the seven tests to qualify as a material participant. If the taxpayer meets one of the tests, the taxpayer is considered to have materially participated in that activity, and the income and loss from the business activity is considered non-passive for that year.

Rental Real Estate Passive Loss Allowance

The owner of rental real estate may deduct up to $25,000 of loss from the rental real estate against non-passive income, such as salaries and wages, if the owner actively participates in the management of the rental real estate, and is not a real estate professional.

Active participation is a lower level of involvement than material participation. The owner can have an agent manage his or her property and still meet the active participation test. The taxpayer must show that he or she participates in management decisions, such as selecting tenants, setting rental terms, and reviewing expenses. The IRS may not recognize the taxpayer's activity as meeting the test if the activity is only affirmation of the manager's decisions. The taxpayer must have at least a 10% interest in the rental real estate to qualify for the loss allowance. Limited partners are not considered active participants and do not qualify for the allowance.

Computing the Allowance

The $25,000 allowance is computed as follows: First, match income and loss from all of the rental real estate activities in which the active participation test is met. A net loss from these activities is then applied to net passive income, if any, from other sources to determine the amount of the rental real estate loss that can reduce other non-passive income.

> **EXAMPLE**—Rob Rental has an $80,000 salary, $10,000 income from a limited partnership (passive income), and $30,000 loss from rental real estate in which he actively participated. The $30,000 loss is first reduced by the $10,000 limited partnership income. The $20,000 remaining balance of the rental real estate loss is deductible from the salary income due to the rental real estate allowance.

The rental real estate loss allowance is phased out when the taxpayer has modified adjusted gross income over $100,000. For every dollar of income over $100,000, the loss allowance is reduced by $0.50. When the modified adjusted gross income reaches $150,000, the allowance is completely phased out.

A taxpayer's other sources of income in a particular tax year determine which classification (passive or non-passive) is more advantageous.

> **EXAMPLE**—If Tom had income from an apartment complex of $50,000, it would automatically be considered passive and could be reduced only by passive losses. Therefore, if Tom were also an owner in a business entity with an allocated operating loss of $30,000, it could only be used to reduce the apartment complex operating profit in Tom's tax return if it were classified as a passive loss, which requires that Tom not materially participate in the activities of the business entity.

The major factor in determining the characterization of the income from business entities is whether the taxpayer materially participates. As previously stated, material participation must be determined on an annual basis. The taxpayer must be able to prove the level of participation by keeping an appointment book, calendar, or log of the days and time spent in the operation. The IRS will not recognize time spent as an investor as *participation* unless the taxpayer can show involvement in daily operations or management of the activity.

25.6 INCOME TAX AND THE SALE OF REAL PROPERTY

Investing in real estate provides a significant tax break, because frequently the sale of real property at a gain is taxed at capital gain rates. A capital gain or loss results from the sale of a **capital asset**, which generally includes all assets owned as an investment or for personal purposes. Examples include stocks, bonds, a personal residence, household furnishings, cars, precious metals, and assets used in a trade or business. However, the capital gain tax rate is not available for all property sales, because the capital gain rate availability depends on the taxpayer's purpose for holding the property. For example, business inventory and property held for sale to customers is not considered a capital asset.

A capital gain occurs when the sale price of a capital asset exceeds the adjusted cost basis of the asset sold. When capital assets are sold at a gain, the applicable tax rate depends on the period of time the taxpayer held the property before sale. The favorable capital gains tax rate applies only to long-term capital gains, which require a holding period of more than one year. The maximum tax rate applicable to long-term capital gains is 15%, whereas the rate applicable to ordinary income was as high as 35% in 2006. The 20% rate difference enhances investment returns when the investment strategy emphasizes capital appreciation over current income.

Computing Capital Gains and Losses

Capital gains or losses are computed as follows:

1. Amount Realized or Total Selling Price $_____
2. Cost or Other Unadjusted Basis $_____
3. Plus: Improvements $_____
4. Minus: Accumulated Depreciation $_____
5. Adjusted Basis (2 plus 3 minus 4) $_____
6. Selling Expenses $_____
7. Total Cost (5 plus 6) $_____
8. Gain or Loss (Subtract 7 from 1) $_____

Amount Realized

The amount realized is the total selling price. It includes cash, the fair market value of additional property received, and any liabilities that the buyer agrees to pay. A buyer's note (purchase money mortgage) is included in the selling price at fair market value. This is generally the discounted amount that a bank or other party will pay for the note. The selling price includes the amount of the unpaid mortgage. This is true whether or not the taxpayer is personally liable on the debt, and whether or not the buyer assumes the mortgage or merely takes the property subject to the mortgage. The full amount of the unpaid mortgage is included, even if the value of the property is less than the unpaid mortgage.

Unadjusted Basis

The cost or **unadjusted basis** is the original cost of the property, if it was purchased. There are different rules for determining unadjusted basis when the property was received by gift, inheritance, or tax-deferred exchange. For property purchased, the unadjusted basis is the cash paid plus the value of any property given to the seller. If a mortgage is assumed or the property is bought subject to a mortgage, the amount of the mortgage is part of the unadjusted basis. Purchase expenses are also included, such as real estate commissions, title insurance recording fees, escrow fees, and survey costs. When a buyer pays part of the purchase price by providing services, the value of the services is included in the unadjusted basis to the extent of the taxable compensation.

Permanent improvements and additions made to the property are also added to the unadjusted basis. Examples include adding a room or a fence, putting in new plumbing or wiring, and paving a driveway. Ordinary maintenance and repairs are not considered improvements and do not increase the cost basis, but if the property is rental real estate, they would be deducted as operating expenses. The cost of repairing real estate after a casualty such as a fire or storm would also be added to the cost basis. However, the uninsured loss from the casualty and any insurance awards will reduce the cost basis.

The unadjusted basis is reduced for the amount of depreciation that was allowed or allowable during the ownership period. Selling expenses are added to the adjusted basis to determine the net cost that is deducted from the selling price to arrive at the capital gain or loss. Examples of selling expenses are real estate commissions, escrow fees, title insurance, and recording fees.

To obtain the benefit of the 15% capital gains rate, the taxpayer must hold the capital asset more than one year before selling. When the asset is held for more than one year, the gain or loss on the sale is classified as long-term.

25.7 INCOME TAX ADVANTAGES OF HOME OWNERSHIP

Home ownership is the cornerstone of the American dream. Historically, a home has been a taxpayer's most valuable asset, both financially and emotionally. The tax law gives home ownership numerous tax benefits, including the home mortgage interest deduction and the personal residence gain exclusion.

Home Mortgage Interest Deduction

A taxpayer can generally deduct interest expense as an itemized deduction. The interest must be paid during the tax year on the types of debt related to the acquisition of a residence or a home equity loan, as long as the debt is secured by a qualified residence. A *qualified residence* is a taxpayer's principal residence or one other home. Interest expenses related to other personal debts, such as the purchase of a car, are not deductible.

A taxpayer can deduct interest on debt that is incurred in acquiring, constructing, substantially improving, or refinancing a qualified residence. This type of debt is referred to as *acquisition indebtedness.* Acquisition indebtedness is limited to $1 million and can be incurred in the purchase of a maximum of two residences. Therefore, if the taxpayer has a principal residence and two other residences, such as a beach house and a mountain cabin, only the debt related to the principal residence and one of the other two residences can qualify as home acquisition indebtedness. For the interest to be deductible as home acquisition interest, the debt must be secured by the real property acquired.

Home Equity Loans

Interest paid is also deductible on up to $100,000 of home equity loans. For the interest to be deductible, the home equity loan cannot exceed the fair market value of the residence, reduced by any acquisition indebtedness. The purpose of the funds related to the home equity loan is usually not relevant when determining whether interest paid on it is deductible. For example, the fact that the proceeds from a home equity loan are used to finance the purchase of a new car does not affect interest deductibility. However, if the debt proceeds are used to purchase tax-exempt municipal bonds, the interest expense would not be deductible.

Points

Points paid in arranging financing are generally treated as prepaid interest that must be deducted over the period of the loan. However, there is an exception for points paid on a loan to buy, build, or improve the principal residence. The points on such loans are deductible in the year paid if these tests are met:

1. The loan is secured by the principal residence.
2. Charging points is an established business practice in the geographic area where the loan is made.
3. The points charged do not exceed the points generally charged in the area.
4. The amount of points is computed as a percentage of the loan and specifically labeled on the closing statement as "points," "loan origination fees," or "loan discount."
5. The points are paid directly to the lender.

Points withheld from the principal of a loan used to buy a principal residence are treated as if they were paid directly to the lender, as long as the taxpayer has made a down payment, escrow deposit, or earnest money deposit at or before closing. The down payment, escrow deposit, or earnest money deposit must be at least equal to the amount of the points withheld. If the loan is used to improve the principal residence, the points are not immediately deductible if withheld from the loan principal. To claim the full deduction in the year of payment, the taxpayer must pay the points with funds that have not been obtained from the lender. Otherwise, the deduction must be spread over the loan term.

Points paid by a seller are deductible by the buyer in the year of acquisition. The seller's payment is treated as an adjustment to the purchase price that the seller gives to the buyer and turned over to the lender to pay the points. The buyer must reduce the cost basis of the home for the points paid by the seller.

The IRS does not allow a current deduction for points on a refinancing of debt secured by a qualified residence. The points must be deducted ratably over the loan period, unless part of the new loan is used for home improvements. For example, if a taxpayer paid points of $3600 when refinancing a 30-year mortgage on the principal residence, a deduction of only $120 per year would be allowed.

Also, if points are paid for a mortgage debt secured by a second home or a vacation home, the points can be deducted over the life of the loan only. When a taxpayer is deducting points over the term of the loan because a full first-year deduction is not allowed, the taxpayer may deduct the unamortized balance in the year the mortgage ends (such as when the loan is refinanced).

Personal Residence Gain Exclusion

One of the major tax benefits of home ownership is the gain exclusion available on the sale of a principal residence. A taxpayer can exclude up to $250,000 of gain from the sale of the taxpayer's home as long as the property is owned and used as the principal residence by the taxpayer for at least two of the five years before sale. Married taxpayers filing jointly may exclude a gain up to $500,000.

The gain exclusion is not a once-in-a-lifetime benefit. If the taxpayer meets the ownership-and-use test for a principal residence, he or she can claim the exclusion even if the exclusion was previously claimed for a different residence, provided that the sales are more than two years apart.

If a taxpayer claims the exclusion on a sale and within two years of the first sale sells another principal residence, the exclusion may not be claimed on the second sale, even if the taxpayer met the ownership-and-use tests for that residence. There is an exception if the second sale was due to a change in employment, health reasons, or unforeseen circumstances. In those cases, a prorated exclusion is allowed.

Principal Residence

A **principal residence** is not restricted to single-family homes, but may include a house, mobile home, houseboat, co-op, or condominium apartment used as the taxpayer's main home. An investment in a retirement community does not qualify as a principal residence, unless the taxpayer receives equity in the property. Your main home is the one you live in most of the time.

Spouses

If a married couple has owned and lived in their principal residence for at least two years during the five-year period ending on the date of sale, they may claim an exclusion of up to $500,000 of the gain on a joint return. The up-to-$500,000 exclusion may be claimed on a joint return provided that during the five-year period ending on the date of sale:

1. *Either* spouse owned the residence for at least two years.
2. *Both* spouses lived in the house as their principal residence for at least two years.
3. *Neither* spouse claimed the exclusion on a sale of a principal residence within the two-year period ending on the date of the sale.

If tests one and three are met, but only one spouse meets test two, the exclusion limit on a joint return is $250,000.

Hot Markets

Sellers of a principal residence in hot, upscale real estate markets will have to pay capital gains tax on any profit above the $250,000/$500,000 limits. Because the exclusion is available once every two years, whether or not it has been used before, some homeowners may decide to sell before their gains exceed the limits. That way, additional gain on their replacement residence could also qualify for the exclusion in another two years.

25.8 TAX-DEFERRED EXCHANGE OF PROPERTY

A **tax-deferred exchange** is a transaction in which "like-kind" property is traded. *Like-kind* means exchanging business or income property for other business or income property, or exchanging personal property for personal property. A strong motivation for exchanging property is the ability to defer capital gains income tax on the transaction.

Section 1031

Section 1031 of the Internal Revenue Code states that no gain or loss will be recognized if property held for productive use in a trade or business or for investment is exchanged for property of like kind to be held for similar purposes. Payment of any capital gains tax is deferred until the time the replacement property is sold.

Unlike property can be included in an exchange to balance the equity in the trade. However, a capital gains tax will be due from the recipient of the unlike property. Unlike property received in a tax-deferred exchange is called **boot**.

Starker Case

The 1979 Supreme Court decision on the **Starker Case** has had a lasting effect on tax-deferred exchanges. Before this decision, it was thought that the exchange of properties had to take place all at once in order to qualify as tax-deferred. The key outcome of this case was that simultaneous conveyance is not a requirement for a tax-free exchange. The essential facts of the Starker Case are as follows:

> On April 1, 1967, T.J. Starker and his son and daughter-in-law entered into an exchange agreement with the Crown Zellerbach Corporation by which the Starkers agreed to convey timberland to Crown that was valued by the parties at $1.5 million. In return, Crown agreed to transfer property of equal value to the Starkers over a five-year period. The Starkers deeded their timberland to Crown and during the next two and a half years, the Starkers designated sufficient properties of equal value to conclude the transaction.
>
> For their 1967 income tax returns, all three Starkers reported the transaction as a tax-deferred exchange. The Internal Revenue Service disagreed and required the Starkers to pay income taxes as if the transaction were an outright sale. The Starkers paid the taxes and filed for refunds in the U.S. District Court.

The Starkers won their case, but the IRS declared it would not abide by the court's decision. Several years later, the IRS defined what would be allowable. The rule is that the properties in the exchange must either have simultaneous closings, or "the property to be traded for must be identified within 45 days of the closing of the first property, proceeds held in trust, and the identified property must be closed within 6 months." This includes the 45-day identity period.

IRS Rules for 1031 Tax-Deferred Exchanges

* There must be an *exchange* between parties.
* *Must be like-kind*: Farms, ranches, stores, offices, warehouses, hotels, motels, shopping centers, industrial, apartments, bare land, and rental houses are all like-kind. Like-kind property is "any . . . property held for productive use in a trade or business for investment."
* *Cannot be non-like-kind*: Non-like-kind property includes real estate contracts (installment sales), personal residence, vacation homes, personal property, stock-in-trade (developer property), stocks, bonds, and interest in partnership. These items cannot be exchanged. Personal residences and vacation homes can be converted to investments.
* *Time requirements*: Target properties must be identified within 45 days; the "clock" starts the day the first escrow closes. It is not necessary to have earnest money on the target property. The exchange period ends 180 days after the clock starts (including the 45-day identification period). There are no exceptions, no extensions, and Saturdays, Sundays, and holidays count. An exchangor must have a qualified intermediary and the exchange documents must be in place before the first escrow closes. A qualified intermediary acts as an exchange facilitator. In Nevada, a qualified intermediary must be licensed by the Nevada Division of Financial Institutions.
* *Identification rules*: The identification criteria must be written, signed, and delivered to the qualified intermediary. The exchangor must abide by either the *three-property rule* or the *200% rule*. The *three-property rule* says that the exchangor can identify three properties of any value. The *200% rule* says that

the exchangor can identify any number of properties, as long as the combined fair market value does not exceed 200% of the relinquished property.

- *Related parties*: There is a two-year holding period on exchanges between related parties. Related parties includes certain blood relatives, most corporation or partnership interests, and most agents of the exchangor.

- *Actual or constructive receipt of funds*: Funds must be in "substantially limited access." The exchangor or his or her agent cannot receive exchange funds. Certain restrictions apply as to how and when funds are to be used or released to the exchangor.

- *Full tax-deferred exchange*: All capital gain taxes will be deferred if fair market value, equity, and mortgage values are all equal.

- *Partial tax-deferred exchange*: Any value that decreases is considered "boot" and subject to taxation, but only to the extent of the boot. This is a popular type of exchange, which is often used to retain some cash.

- *Future construction*: A "build to suit" exchange can apply to new construction or remodels. The 45-day/180-day time limit applies, however, so the project must be completed within the six-month timeframe. A qualified intermediary will hold title to the property until the construction is complete.

- *Other rules* cover interest or growth factor, direct deeding, financing, residential conversions, multiple owners, partnerships, and reverse exchanges.

1031 Tenant-in-Common Investment

It is important to remember that timing is critical; the IRS strictly interprets the 45-day and 180-day rules, and identifying a replacement property may be difficult. The fair market value and equity of the replacement property must be equal to or greater than the property being sold in order to avoid receiving any boot. If a specific property cannot be located quickly, the exchangor may want to consider a **tenant-in-common (TIC) investment**. Essentially, this is buying an undivided interest in a development or other commercial property with other investors who are also tenants-in-common.

The IRS has guidelines and specific criteria that must be followed by the sponsors of these investments, but they do provide a source of qualifying like-kind rental real estate investments for 1031 tax-deferred exchanges. They will be marketed and sold through registered securities broker-dealers. The important distinction here is that these investments are not partnership interests. Partnership interests are personal property and do not qualify for 1031 tax-deferred exchanges. These are sophisticated investments that are available and can be beneficial to someone looking for a replacement property. However, exchangors are well-advised to get their accountants and lawyers involved at an early stage, because 45 days is not really a great deal of time.

CHAPTER SUMMARY

Investing is committing capital to a business in order to earn a financial return or profit. Speculating is entering into a transaction where the profits are subject to chance. Risk is a major consideration in all real estate investments. Investment real estate or speculation in real estate involves a high degree of risk. Leveraging means borrowing money from another source to supplement your own funds in completing the acquisition of a piece of property. The primary source for leverage funding is real estate lenders.

Taxable income for an individual taxpayer is computed as follows: gross income − deductions for adjusted gross income = adjusted gross income − itemized deductions or standard deduction and personal exemptions = taxable income.

Gross income includes earned income, portfolio income, passive income, and capital gains and losses. To determine adjusted gross income, a taxpayer subtracts amounts specifically authorized by the Revenue Code from gross income. Currently, a taxpayer's adjusted gross income affects the extent to which he or she can withhold itemized deductions.

Accounting for the income and expenses of a rental property may be done on a cash basis or an accrual basis. Taxpayers must elect one method or the other. Almost all individual taxpayers use the cash basis.

A taxpayer should always distinguish between advance rentals and security deposits. Advance rentals are income when received. They are reported in the year received, whether the taxpayer is reporting on a cash or accrual basis. Security deposits are deposited with the landlord solely as security for the tenant's performance of the terms of the lease, and are usually not taxed when received. A landlord does not realize taxable income when a tenant improves the leased premises.

All expenses incurred by the real property owner in the operation of the property are deductible from the rental income. Interest on mortgages and other debt specifically related to the rental property is deductible as an operating expense.

A repair keeps the real property in good operating condition. Capital improvements include carpeting, window coverings, new roofs, new plumbing or electrical systems, and major repairs. Only maintenance and incidental repair costs are deductible against rental income.

The principal tax advantage for owners of investment real property is depreciation. Depreciation is the annual deduction allowed for recovering the depreciable cost of the investment property. The property must be a capital asset used in a trade or business. A personal residence may not be depreciated.

Residential rental property is a building or structure in which 80% or more of the gross rental income is rental income from dwelling units. Nonresidential rental property is real property that is not residential rental property.

Passive activities generally include any business or investment activity in which the taxpayer does not materially participate. The rental of real or personal property is generally a rental activity under the passive activity loss rules, but exceptions apply. The passive activity rules prevent an investor from deducting what the law defines as a passive loss from earned income or portfolio income. Such losses are deductible only from income from other passive activities.

Rental income and losses are automatically treated as passive unless earned or incurred by a real estate professional, or the rentals are considered by law to be business activity. Even if rental income or loss is earned by a professional or is considered business income, the passive loss restrictions still apply unless the taxpayer materially participates in the activity.

The owner of rental real estate may deduct up to $25,000 of loss from the rental real estate against non-passive income, if the owner actively participates in the management of the rental real estate, and is not a real estate professional.

Investing in real estate provides a significant tax break, because frequently the sale of real property at a gain is taxed at capital gain rates. A capital gain or loss results from the sale of a capital asset, which generally includes all assets owned as an investment or for personal purposes. A capital gain occurs when the sale price of a capital asset exceeds the adjusted cost basis of the asset sold. When capital assets are sold at a gain, the applicable tax rate depends on the period of time the taxpayer held the property before sale. The favorable capital gains tax rate applies only to long-term capital gains, which require a holding period of more than one year.

The amount realized is the total selling price. The cost or unadjusted basis is the original cost of the property, if it was purchased. There are different rules for determining unadjusted basis when the property was received by gift, inheritance, or tax-deferred exchange.

The tax law gives home ownership numerous tax benefits, including the home mortgage interest deduction and the personal residence gain exclusion.

The home mortgage interest deduction allows a taxpayer to deduct interest expense as an itemized deduction. The interest must be paid during the tax year on the types of debt related to the acquisition of a residence or a home-equity loan, as long as the debt is secured by a qualified residence. A qualified residence is a taxpayer's principal residence or one other home.

A taxpayer can deduct interest on debt that is incurred in acquiring, constructing, substantially improving, or refinancing a qualified residence. This type of debt is referred to as acquisition indebtedness.

Interest paid is also deductible on up to $100,000 of home equity loans. For the interest to be deductible, the home equity loan cannot exceed the fair market value of the residence, reduced by any acquisition indebtedness.

The **personal residence gain exclusion** allows a taxpayer to exclude up to $250,000 of gain from the sale of the taxpayer's home as long as the property is owned and used as the principal residence by the taxpayer for at least two of the five years before sale. Married taxpayers filing jointly may exclude a gain up to $500,000.

A tax-deferred exchange is a transaction in which "like-kind" property is traded. Section 1031 of the Internal Revenue Code states that no gain or loss will be recognized if property held for productive use in a trade or business or for investment is exchanged for property of like kind to be held for similar purposes. Payment of any capital gains tax is deferred until the time the replacement property is sold.

Unlike property can be included in an exchange to balance the equity in the trade. However, a capital gains tax will be due from the recipient of the unlike property. Unlike property received in a tax-deferred exchange is called boot. The IRS rules for 1031 tax-deferred exchanges are described in the body of this chapter.

CHECKING YOUR COMPREHENSION

1. Explain the basic real estate principles, including:
   - Risk versus speculation
   - Leveraging
   - Cash flow

2. Diagram the computation of taxable income for the individual taxpayer.

3. Summarize the major income considerations, including depreciation, for rental real estate.

4. Describe the passive loss limitation on deductions from a passive activity and the rental real estate passive loss allowance.

5. Describe the following:
   - Computing capital gains and losses
   - Personal residence gain exclusion
   - Tax-deferred exchange

REVIEWING YOUR UNDERSTANDING

1. A leveraged investment describes:
   a. a low-risk investment
   b. an equity investment
   c. use of other people's money
   d. collateralized equity

2. Net cash flow equals:
   a. gross income
   b. operating expenses and loan payments
   c. gross income less operating expenses
   d. gross income less operating expenses and loan payments

3. In depreciating a residential property, an accountant would base the depreciation life for income tax purposes on:
   a. age life tables
   b. the observed condition of the property
   c. 27½ years
   d. 31½ years

4. The deduction a homeowner has for tax purposes is:
   a. property taxes
   b. insurance cost
   c. depreciation
   d. maintenance expense

5. The cost basis of a home would be affected by:
   a. extensive repairs
   b. interest paid
   c. amortization of the loan
   d. a room addition

6. A tax-deferred exchange requires properties to be:
   a. residential
   b. of equal value
   c. of equal equities
   d. of like kind

7. To be depreciated, real property **MUST** be:
   a. owned in fee simple
   b. improved
   c. paid for
   d. your residence

8. Mary, a single individual, may exclude up to $250,000 of capital gain on the sale of her residence if:
   a. she has owned it for one year
   b. the residence was her principal residence for two of the preceding five years
   c. she does not have a second residence as a vacation home
   d. she has not sold a residence within the past five years

9. On their tax returns, taxpayers may deduct interest expense on indebtedness related to a first and second home. The maximum combined amount of debt for which interest expense can be deducted is:
   a. $500,000
   b. $1 million
   c. $2 million
   d. $2.5 million

10. Which of the following items would be taxed in a tax-deferred exchange?
    a. like-for-like real property
    b. boot
    c. assuming a mortgage of equal value
    d. salvage value

11. The period of time over which a property will yield a return of the investment over and above the ground rent due for the land is called:
    a. highest and best use
    b. straight line
    c. economic life
    d. appreciation increment

12. The highest price which a property should bring in a competitive and open market under the conditions existing on a certain date is:
    a. economic life
    b. market value
    c. marginal value
    d. market price

13. Loan points paid by a borrower to obtain a new owner-occupied residential loan are:
    a. deductible as a cost of sale for the seller
    b. deductible by the borrower
    c. a tax credit for the buyer
    d. a tax deduction for the seller

14. A passive investor in a real estate syndicate could be called a:
    a. beneficiary
    b. trustee
    c. limited partner
    d. general partner

15. Portfolio income is **BEST** described as:
    a. real estate investments actively managed
    b. real estate held for less than one year
    c. yield from investments, including stocks, bonds, and commercial paper
    d. all securities and real estate investments

16. A property is valued at $200,000, using a 6% capitalization rate. If an investor wants an 8% return, he would be willing to pay only:
    a. $150,000
    b. $225,000
    c. $270,000
    d. $290,000

17. An apartment building has six units. Two pay $400 per month, two pay $275 per month, and the remaining two pay $200 each. If the monthly operating expenses are $635, compute the property's net annual income:
    a. $28,740
    b. $16,200
    c. $13,380
    d. $7,740

18. Samantha Turner, the owner of a commercial building, estimates the depreciation of the physical plant at $15,000, the furniture and fixtures at $8000, and the machinery at $7500. If she is in the 40% tax bracket, her tax savings would be:
    a. $1220
    b. $12,200
    c. $30,500
    d. $18,300

19. The term *tax shelter* is generally associated with:
    a. real property tax
    b. income tax
    c. sales tax
    d. personal property tax

20. A commercial property was purchased for $85,000 and has depreciated to $28,000 book value. If it is sold for $75,000, there is a:
    a. $10,000 taxable loss
    b. $18,800 taxable gain
    c. $28,200 taxable gain
    d. $47,000 taxable gain

Chapter 26

IMPORTANT TERMS AND CONCEPTS

business broker

business broker permit

business brokerage

license status-current

license status-active

license status-inactive

license status-inactive renewed

license status-inactive not renewed

property management

property management permit

real estate broker

real estate broker-salesperson

real estate brokerage

real estate salesperson

sales agent or time share agent

CHAPTER OBJECTIVES

After completing this chapter, you should be able to:

- Describe the requirements for licensure and the exemption from licensure.
- List the three general real estate licenses and the requirements for obtaining each license.
- Describe the various classifications of license status.
- Summarize the post-licensing and continuing education requirements for license renewal.
- List and summarize other licenses, permits, and certifications issued by the Real Estate Division.

Nevada Licensing Law

INTRODUCTION

All 50 states, including Nevada, require that individuals representing others in real estate transactions for compensation be licensed. Licensing is required to ensure that the public is represented by competent individuals and to protect the public from fraud and other dishonest acts. Nevada licensing requirements are set forth in Chapter 645 of the Nevada Revised Statutes, which are summarized in the following sections.

26.1 LICENSE REQUIREMENTS

It is unlawful for any person, corporation, partnership, or limited liability company to engage in business as a real estate broker, broker-salesperson, or salesperson or to do any act for which a real estate license is required without first obtaining a real estate license.

According to Nevada statutes, a **real estate broker**, broker-salesperson, or salesperson is any person, partnership, limited liability company, or corporation who for another and for compensation participates in any of the following:

a. Sells, exchanges, options, purchases, rents, or leases, or negotiates or offers, attempts, or agrees to negotiate the sale, exchange, option, purchase, rental, or lease of, or lists or solicits prospective purchasers, lessees, or renters of, any real estate or the improvements thereon or any modular home, used manufactured homes, used mobile homes, or other housing offered or conveyed with any interest in real estate.

b. Engages in or offers to engage in the business of claiming, demanding, charging, receiving, collecting, or contracting for the collection of an advance fee in connection with any employment undertaken to promote the sale or lease of business opportunities or real estate by advance fee listing advertising or other offerings to sell, lease, exchange, or rent property.

c. Engages in or offers to engage in the business of property management.

d. Engages in or offers to engage in the business of business brokerage.

In addition, any person who, for another and for compensation, aids, assists, solicits, or negotiates the procurement, sale, purchase, rental, or lease of public lands is required to be licensed.

License Exemption

The requirement for licensing does not apply to the following:

1. Exemptions for property management activities:
   a. Any owner or lessor of property, or any regular employee of such a person, who performs any of the acts that require a real estate license, with respect to the property in the management of or investment in the property. Management means activities that tend to preserve or increase the income from the property by preserving the physical desirability of the property or maintaining high standards of service to tenants. The term does not include sales activities.
   b. Any employee of a real estate broker while engaged in the collection of rent for or on behalf of the broker.
   c. Any person performing the duties of a property manager for a property, if the person maintains an office on the property and does not engage in property management with regard to any other property.
   d. Any person engaged in property management for a common-interest community.
   e. Any person performing the duties of a property manager for a property used for residential housing that is subsidized by a governmental agency.

2. Exemptions for sales activities:
   a. Attorney at law in his or her normal duties.
   b. Person acting under a court order, such as a bankruptcy trustee.
   c. Trustee selling under a deed of trust.
   d. Bank or any related banking institution for property acquired for development, through foreclosure or when it is in their best interest.
   e. A corporation for its corporate property.
   f. Any person or entity when buying or selling mining claims only.
   g. Any officer or employee of a governmental agency in the conduct of the officer's or employee's official duties.
   h. Any person who is employed by a licensed real estate broker to accept reservations on behalf of a person engaged in the business of the rental of lodging for 31 days or less, if the employee does not perform any tasks related to the sale or other transfer of an interest in real estate.

26.2 TYPES OF LICENSES

The following are the three types of general real estate licenses:

- Real estate broker
- Real estate broker-salesperson
- Real estate salesperson

A broker may be licensed as a sole proprietorship, but the brokerage must register with the county clerk's office and can register only one fictitious name. Alternatively, a brokerage may be licensed as a corporation, limited liability company, or partnership. If the brokerage is a business entity, then the brokerage must have a designated broker who is one of the following:

1. An officer of the corporation and the designation must be verified by the president and secretary of the corporation.
2. A manager or member of the limited liability company and the designation must be verified by at least two members of the limited liability company.
3. A partner of the partnership and the designation must be verified by at least two partners.

A **real estate broker-salesperson** is any person who holds a real estate broker's license, but who, as an employee or as an independent contractor, for compensation or otherwise is associated with a licensed real estate broker in the capacity of a salesperson or registered owner-developer as a sales manager. A **real estate salesperson** is any person who, as an employee or as an independent contractor, is associated with a licensed real estate broker or registered owner-developer to do or to deal in any acts or transactions for which a real estate license is required.

Other licenses, permits, and certificates issued by the Real Estate Division are covered in section 26.4 of this chapter.

Real Estate License Application

Applications for a real estate broker license must be in writing, signed by the applicant, and notarized. Applicants must be at least 18 years old and must be U.S. citizens. Non-citizens must provide proof of the right to work in the United States. The application must tell whether the applicant has ever been charged with or convicted of a criminal offense. The application must also disclose whether the applicant has ever been refused a license or had a license revoked or suspended. Applicants pay an examination fee and a license fee. Applicants must also submit fingerprints and allow the Division to investigate the applicant's background prior to receiving a license. The application must also include:

1. A certificate of completion for the required pre-licensing education.
2. Proof of a passing (75%) grade on the state licensing examination.
3. A statement regarding the current status of any child support or if not, current approval from the imposing court.
4. Occupation history for the two years preceding the application.

5. Current residence address and the residence address for the preceding three years.

6. The required fees.

An applicant for a Nevada real estate license cannot be a current felon, unless the felony conviction is more than three years old, or restitution was made three years ago, or the applicant has been off probation for three years, whichever of the three is the latest.

The Nevada Real Estate Division or Commissioners cannot assist in the completion of the application. Further, the Division can request proof of the applicant's honesty, truthfulness, and good reputation. A copy of the required application and the amount of required fees can be obtained from the Division website, at www.red.state.nv.us.

Education, Experience, and Testing

The applicant must have taken 90 hours of instruction that includes 45 hours of principles and practices of real estate and 45 hours in federal and state law and ethics. The principles and practice 45 hours consist of:

• 21 hours of brokerage and laws of agency.

• 12 hours of valuation and economics.

• 12 hours of finance.

The 45 hours of federal and state law and ethics consist of:

• 25 hours of ownership, transfer, and use of property.

• 18 hours of Nevada Revised Statutes.

• 2 hours of applied practice and statutory disclosures.

The applicant must have passed the final examination at the school where the applicant completed the required pre-license course. The applicant must also pass the Nevada state examination, which is in two parts: the national portion with 80 questions and the state-specific part with 40 questions. A Nevada broker-salesperson and broker must have 64 college units in the following subjects:

• 15 college units in real estate courses, such as real estate business, real estate finance, and real estate economics.

• 6 college units in Nevada law; the initial 90-hour course meets this requirement.

• 3 college units in Nevada broker management; real estate experience cannot replace this course.

• 3 college units in real estate appraisal.

• 37 college units in any subject.

The Nevada Real Estate Division will grant 16 college units for every two years as a full-time real estate agent in the United States.

An applicant who completes the Nevada broker test before the experience and college education requirements are met can be licensed as a Nevada real estate salesperson immediately. The applicant has one year to complete the college unit educational requirement and to receive a broker-salesperson license, without retaking the Nevada broker test. If the college units are not obtained in one year, the licensee will continue as a real estate salesperson.

An applicant cannot receive a real estate broker license until the real estate experience requirement has been met. The experience required to obtain a broker license is two of the previous four years, full-time experience in real estate. Full-time means 30 hours a week for 48 weeks in a year. The experience can be completed anywhere in the United States or, on a case-by-case basis, outside the country.

License Period

An original license for a real estate broker, broker-salesperson, or salesperson is issued for a 12-month period. During the initial 12-month period, a 30-hour post-licensing classroom course must be completed. The curriculum must contain at least 15 modules that include the following:

1. Real estate contracts
2. Listing process
3. Communications, technology, and records management
4. Buyer representation
5. Professional conduct
6. Advertising
7. Proceeds of sale, cost sheets
8. Agency relationships
9. Land
10. Regulatory disclosures
11. Property management
12. Escrow, title, and closing
13. Financing
14. Negotiations
15. Tax opportunities and liabilities

After the initial license period, each subsequent license will be issued for a 24-month period.

License Status

The status of a Nevada real estate license can be classified as follows:

- Current
- Active
- Inactive
- Inactive renewed
- Inactive not renewed

Current

A current license indicates that fees to the Nevada Real Estate Division have been paid.

Active

An active license indicates that fees to the Nevada Real Estate Division have been paid and the license is placed with a Nevada broker or Nevada owner-developer. The active licensee can sell real estate for a commission while working for the Nevada real estate broker or owner-developer. If the licensee leaves the current broker or owner-developer within 10 days, the broker or owner-developer may do either of the following:

- Authorize the licensee to hand-carry his or her license to the Division.
- Deliver or send by certified mail the license to the Division.

Inactive

An inactive license indicates that fees to the Nevada Real Estate Division have been paid, but the license has been held by the Division for 30 days or less. A Nevada licensee cannot sell real estate for a commission while the license is inactive and held by the Division. An inactive licensee may return to active status with no additional requirements if the licensee associates with a new Nevada broker within 30 days and pays a fee to the Division.

Inactive Renewed

An inactive renewed license indicates that fees to the Nevada Real Estate Division have been paid, but the license has been held by the Division for more than 30 days. A Nevada licensee cannot sell real estate for a commission while the license is inactive and has been held by the Division for more than 30 days. An inactive renewed licensee may return to active status as follows:

a. When the license has been on inactive renewed status for less than two years, the licensee must complete the required continuing education and associate with a Nevada broker or owner-developer.

b. When the license has been on inactive renewed status for more than two years, the licensee must complete the required continuing education and 15 additional hours of continuing education, take a test assigned by the Division with a passing score of 75%, associate with a Nevada broker or owner-developer, and pay a fee to the Division.

Inactive Not Renewed

An inactive license that has not been renewed indicates that the Nevada licensee does not have a current Nevada real estate license. When a Nevada non-current licensee does not become current within one year, the licensee will apply as an initial applicant if he or she desires to be licensed as a real estate broker,

broker-salesperson, or salesperson. The requirements for a licensee to return to active status within the one year period are as follows:

- Pay a two-year license fee and a penalty of $95 for a broker or broker-salesperson and $75 for a salesperson.
- Complete the required continuing education.
- Associate with a new Nevada broker.

26.3 CONTINUING EDUCATION

After the initial renewal, Nevada requirements for license renewal mandate 24 hours of continuing education every two years. The 24 hours must consist of a minimum of three hours of contracts, three hours of agency, three hours of Nevada law, and three hours of ethics. Additional required topics are:

- For brokers and broker-salespersons, a minimum of three hours of Nevada broker management.
- For licensees with a property management permit, a minimum of three hours of property management.
- For licensees with a business broker permit, a minimum of three hours in business brokerage.

Only three hours of personal development classes can be taken in a renewal period. After the initial post-licensing 30-hour course, classroom or distance learning is allowed for license renewal credit. A course provider of continuing education must keep attendance and other educational records for a minimum of four years.

Educational Requirements Based on License Status

The educational requirements to transfer from inactive status to active status vary depending on when and how long a license has been inactive. The various requirements are as follows:

1. A licensee has been active or the licensee has been inactive for less than two years and none of the inactive time was during the first-year licensing period. The 24 hours of continuing education, including the 12 hours of required courses, must be completed to remain active or transfer from inactive status to active status.

2. A licensee has been inactive for more than two years and none of the inactive time was during the first-year licensing period. The 12 hours of required courses must be completed, plus an additional 36 hours in general real estate topics must be completed to transfer from inactive status to active status.

3. A licensee is inactive for less than two years, and part of the period is during the first year of licensing. The licensee must complete the 30-hour post-licensing classroom course and the 12 hours of required courses, plus 6 hours in general real estate–related topics to transfer from inactive to active status.

4. A licensee is inactive for more than two years, and part of the period is during the first year of licensing. The licensee must complete the 30-hour post-licensing classroom course and the 12 hours of required courses, plus 12 hours in general real estate–related topics to transfer from inactive to active status.

26.4 OTHER LICENSES, PERMITS, AND CERTIFICATES

Other licenses, permits, and certificates issued by the Real Estate Division are as follows:

- Sales agent license.
- Property management permit.
- Business broker permit.
- Cooperative broker certificate.
- Owner-developer registration.
- Community association management certificate.

The owner-developer registration and community association management certificate are covered in Chapter 5.

Sales Agent

A Nevada sales agent license, also referred to as a time share agent license, is issued by the Real Estate Division to qualified individuals for a two-year period. An applicant must complete the following:

- Written application.
- 14 hours of instructions in time shares and ethics.
- The Nevada sales agent examination with a grade of 75% or better.

After licensure and while working for a Nevada broker, a sales agent can sell only time shares. The sales agent is required to complete six hours of continuing education in law and ethics during every two-year renewal period.

Property Management Permit

A property management permit must be obtained from the Real Estate Division before a real estate broker, broker-salesperson, or salesperson is allowed to engage in property management, as defined in the Nevada Revised Statutes. An applicant for a permit must complete the following:

- Written application.
- 24 hours of classroom instruction in property management.
- The 50-question Nevada state test with a grade of 75% or better.

A Nevada broker who desires to offer property management services must obtain a property management permit or designate a Nevada broker-salesperson to manage the property management section of the brokerage. The designee must have a property management permit and must have two years of active experience conducting property management activities within the immediate past four years. A real estate salesperson with a property management permit who is conducting property management activities must work for a real estate broker or designated broker-salesperson with a property management permit.

A property management permit is attached to the Nevada real estate license and expires at the same time as the license expires. The permit can be renewed when the real estate license is renewed and requires that three hours of property management continuing education be completed.

Business Broker Permit

A business broker permit must be obtained from the Real Estate Division before a real estate broker, broker-salesperson, or salesperson is allowed to engage in business brokerage, as defined in the Nevada Revised Statutes. An applicant for a permit must complete the following:

- Written application.
- 24 hours of classroom instruction in business brokerage.
- The 50-question Nevada state test with a grade of 75% or better.

A Nevada broker who desires to offer business brokerage services must obtain a business broker permit or designate a Nevada broker-salesperson to manage the business brokerage section of the brokerage. The designee must have a business broker permit and two years of active experience conducting business brokerage activities within the immediate past four years. A real estate salesperson with a business broker permit when conducting business brokerage activities must work for a real estate broker or designated broker-salesperson with a business broker permit.

A business broker permit is attached to the Nevada real estate license and expires at the same time as the license expires. The permit can be renewed when the real estate license is renewed and requires that three hours of business brokerage continuing education be completed.

Cooperative Broker Certificate

A cooperative broker is someone from outside of Nevada who meets both of the following requirements:

- Has a real estate broker license to sell real estate issued by another state.
- Desires to cooperate with a Nevada broker to sell Nevada real estate.

The cooperative broker cannot be a Nevada resident. Also, the cooperative broker must pay a non-refundable fee and complete a written application that includes the following:

- A copy of the current license issued in the other state.
- A history of employment for the past 10 years.
- Information on the Nevada broker with whom they wish to cooperate.
- A history of any disciplinary, criminal, or other legal proceedings involving the real estate salesperson or broker-salesperson who will be working for the applicant.
- A list of other cooperative agreements currently in effect with the Nevada broker.
- A photograph of the applicant.

- A copy of the license of the real estate salesperson or broker-salesperson who will be working for the applicant.
- A statement of consent to the cooperative agreement by the Nevada broker.

The Nevada real estate broker must verify the cooperative broker application, and the Nevada Real Estate Division or Commissioners cannot assist in preparing the application.

A cooperative certificate is issued for a one-year period. During the period:

- The Nevada broker oversees all work performed and monies involved in the transaction under the certificate.
- The cooperative broker must carry the certificate and may authorize assistance from one of his or her licensees.
- Cooperative brokers are governed by the Nevada Revised Statutes and Administrative Code.

A client of the cooperative broker that holds a valid certificate may collect from the Nevada Education, Research and Recovery Fund if wrongdoing occurred (see Chapter 27).

The cooperative broker may work with more than one Nevada broker, but the cooperative broker must obtain a certificate for each Nevada broker with whom he or she cooperates.

CHAPTER SUMMARY

Nevada statutes define the actions that require a real estate salesperson, broker-salesperson, or broker license. The three types of general real estate licenses are real estate broker, real estate broker-salesperson, and real estate salesperson. To receive a real estate license, the applicant must be a U.S. citizen or provide proof of the right to work in the United States, be at least 18 years old, and provide background history. In addition, the applicant must have taken 90 classroom hours and passed the school and the state exam. The licensing requirements, exemptions, and qualification should be studied in full in this chapter's text.

The Nevada real estate examination consists of 120 multiple-choice questions (80 national and 40 Nevada-specific). Students must receive at least a 75% grade on both the national and state portions of the exam to pass. Once an applicant has passed the state examination, he or she has one year to activate the license.

An initial license is issued for a one-year period. During the initial 12-month period, the licensee must complete a 30-hour post-licensing classroom course. After the initial license period, each subsequent license will be issued for a 24-month period.

The status of a Nevada real estate license can be classified as current, active, inactive, inactive renewed, or inactive not renewed. The status of the real estate license will affect the continuing education required to renew and activate a license.

After the initial renewal of a license, Nevada requirements for license renewal mandate 24 hours of continuing education every two years, with 12 hours to be completed in specified topics.

The Real Estate Division also issues a sales agent license, property management permit, business broker permit, cooperative broker certificate, owner-developer registration, and community association management certificate.

CHECKING YOUR COMPREHENSION

1. Summarize what activities require a real estate license and some situations in which a real estate license is not required.

2. List the general real estate licenses and summarize the education and experience requirements.

3. List and describe the various license status classifications.

4. How often must a salesperson license or broker license be renewed? List the continuing education requirements.

5. List and describe the other licenses, permits, and certifications issued by the Division.

REVIEWING YOUR UNDERSTANDING

1. Each brokerage is operated by a(n):
   a. licensed broker
   b. licensed broker-salesperson
   c. associate broker
   d. independent broker

2. In real estate, to qualify as an independent contractor, a salesperson must meet all of the following conditions, **EXCEPT**:
   a. be a licensed real estate agent
   b. receive all income as a result of sales commissions
   c. follow the brokerage requirements for floor time, attendance at sales meetings, and so on
   d. have a written contract giving the agent's status as an independent contractor

3. A real estate license for which the fees have been paid but the license has been held by the Real Estate Division for more than 30 days is an:
   a. inactive license
   b. inactive not renewed license
   c. inactive renewed license
   d. active license

4. A salesperson can be compensated for an act within the scope of the real estate law by:
   a. another salesperson
   b. his or her own broker
   c. another broker
   d. his or her principal

5. A licensee who acts as the broker for a corporation is a(n):
   a. broker-salesperson
   b. designated broker
   c. associate broker
   d. principal broker

6. When a license is issued to a corporation, who is entitled to act as the designated broker(s)?
   a. the corporation president
   b. one officer of the corporation
   c. all officers of the corporation
   d. the sales manager of the corporation

7. A licensed real estate broker from another state who desires to sell Nevada real estate must:
   a. obtain a Nevada real estate license
   b. obtain a sales agent license
   c. obtain a non-resident broker license
   d. obtain a cooperative broker certificate

8. Which of the following people would be required to have a real estate license?
   a. an owner-developer selling new homes in his or her subdivision
   b. an attorney-in-fact selling property for a principal
   c. a trustee selling under a court order
   d. an attorney-at-law taking a listing

9. If your license expires, it is:
   a. automatically reinstated for 30 days
   b. automatically reinstated for six months
   c. automatically reinstated for one year
   d. terminated, but can be reinstated within one year

10. The primary purpose of the real estate licensing statute is to:
    a. have trained professionals
    b. protect brokers against incompetent salespeople
    c. avoid cutthroat competition
    d. protect the public

11. An inactive not renewed licensee must complete all of the following to become current within one year, **EXCEPT**:
    a. payment of a two-year license fee and a penalty
    b. complete the required continuing education
    c. pass the Nevada state examination
    d. associate with a new Nevada broker

12. A real estate licensee who desires to engage in business brokerage must obtain a business broker permit. To obtain the permit, a licensee must comply with all of the following, **EXCEPT**:
    a. pass the Nevada state test
    b. complete 90 hours of classroom instruction in business brokerage
    c. complete 24 hours of classroom instruction in business brokerage
    d. file a written application

13. An original real estate license is issued for a 12-month period and during that period the licensee must complete how many hours of post-licensing classroom education?
    a. 24 hours
    b. 30 hours
    c. 45 hours
    d. post-licensing education is not required

14. An unlicensed secretary in a real estate office can:
    a. solicit listings by phone
    b. collect rent for the broker's property management clients
    c. negotiate an offer to purchase
    d. quote prices on the phone

15. When a salesperson with a broker's license is employed by a real estate broker, the salesperson may use which of the following designations:
    a. D.B.W.F.
    b. broker-salesperson
    c. affiliate broker
    d. assistant broker

16. The Real Estate Division's right to license real estate agents comes from the:
    a. Administrator
    b. Nevada Revised Statutes
    c. Governor
    d. Nevada Association of REALTORS

17. Which of the following is **NOT** required for a real estate salesperson license in Nevada?
    a. 90 hours of education
    b. 90 days, residency
    c. passing an examination
    d. minimum age

18. A licensed salesperson referred a buyer to an out-of-state broker who agreed to pay a commission for the referral. The licensed salesperson would be paid by:
    a. the buyer
    b. his or her broker
    c. the out-of-state broker
    d. the seller

19. Full-time experience in real estate means:
    a. 20 hours a week for 48 weeks in a year completed in Nevada only
    b. 30 hours a week for 48 weeks in a year completed in Nevada only
    c. 30 hours a week for 48 weeks in a year completed anywhere in the United States
    d. 20 hours a week for 48 weeks completed anywhere in the United States

20. After the initial license period, each subsequent license is issued for:
    a. 12 months
    b. 24 months
    c. 36 months
    d. 48 months

27

IMPORTANT TERMS AND CONCEPTS

Administrator

Administrative Code

advance fee

broker absence

blind ad

Chapter 645

commingled

Commissioner

conversion

Nevada Revised
Statutes

promptly

Real Estate
Commission

Real Estate Division

Real Estate Education,
Research and
Recovery Fund

team or group

trust account

unlicensed activity

CHAPTER OBJECTIVES

After completing this chapter, you should be able to:

- Summarize the duties and responsibilities of the Administrator of the Real Estate Division and the Real Estate Commission.

- Summarize the regulations related to the operation of a brokerage.

- List the improper conduct that allows the Commission to suspend or revoke a license.

- Describe the process for resolution of a complaint and the potential penalties that can be assessed by the Real Estate Commission.

- Summarize the purpose and operation of the Real Estate Education, Research and Recovery Fund.

Nevada Real Estate Broker and Salesman Statute and Administrative Code: Chapter 645

INTRODUCTION

A person involved in real estate activities is subject to Chapter 645 of the Nevada Revised Statutes and the Nevada Administrative Code, entitled Real Estate Brokers and Salesmen. The **Administrative Code** is authorized by statutes and allows the Real Estate Commission or the Administrator with the approval of the Commission to interpret the law and develop Code that clarifies Chapter 645 of the Statutes.

Chapter 645 of the Nevada Revised Statutes contains 13 sections as follows:

1. General Provisions
2. Administration
3. Regulation of Practices
4. Advance Fees
5. Licenses
6. Property Managers
7. Qualified Intermediaries for Tax-Deferred Exchanges of Property
8. Disciplinary Actions
9. Expiration and Renewal of Licenses
10. Real Estate Education, Research and Recovery Fund
11. Business Brokers
12. Brokerage Agreements Involving Commercial Real Estate
13. Unlawful Acts; Penalties

Information on licensing is covered in Chapter 26.

27.1 REAL ESTATE DIVISION

Chapter 645 of the Nevada Revised Statutes authorizes the Real Estate Division of the Department of Business and Industry sets forth the duties and responsibilities of the Administrator, Real Estate Division, and Real Estate Commission.

Administrator

The **Administrator** is appointed by the Director of the Nevada Department of Business and Industry. The Administrator shall possess a broad knowledge of generally accepted real estate practice and be reasonably well informed on laws governing real estate agency contracts. Further, the Administrator cannot have a real estate license with or a personal and/or financial interest in a real estate firm or brokerage.

Duties of the Administrator

The Administrator heads the Real Estate Division on behalf of the Division of Business and Industry. In addition to running the Real Estate Division, the Administrator also:

- Investigates wrongdoing in Nevada real estate.
- Arranges hearings for licensees with the Nevada Real Estate Commission.
- Arranges hearings for non-licensees before a Nevada District Attorney or the Nevada Attorney General.
- May issue fines from $100 to $1000 and require nine hours of continuing education.
- Issues certificates for a cooperative broker.
- Issues registrations for owner-developers.
- Issues the year-end certification of the Nevada Real Estate Education, Research and Recovery Fund.

Real Estate Division

The **Real Estate Division** administers the provisions of Chapter 645 of the Statutes subject to the supervision of the Director of the Department of Business and Industry. The Division must have a principal and at least one branch office. When the principal office is located in the southern district of Nevada, one branch office must be located in the northern district of the state. If the principal office is located in the northern district, a branch office must be in the south. The Division consists of:

- Customer service and licensing department.
- Education department.
- Investigating department.
- Administrative department.
- Support staff.

An employee of the Division cannot have a real estate license with or a personal or financial interest in a real estate firm or brokerage. All records of the Division are open to the public, except:

- Broker, broker-salesperson, and salesperson examinations.
- Criminal and financial records of licensees, applicants, or owner-developers, unless these records are ordered by a court to be open to the public.

The Nevada Attorney General acts as the legal advisor to the Division and will defend the Division against any action brought against it.

Duties of the Division

The duties of the Real Estate Division include the following:

- Administer the provisions of Chapter 645 of the Nevada Revised Statutes and Administrative Code.
- Complete day-to-day activities such as issuing and renewing licenses, collecting fines against licensees, investigating real estate activities by licensees, and examination of the broker and owner-developer office.
- Prepare and distribute forms for duties owed by a licensee when acting for (1) only one party to a real estate transaction, (2) more than one party to a real estate transaction, (3) a real estate broker who assigns different licensees affiliated with his or her brokerage, or (4) separate parties to a real estate transaction.
- Prepare a booklet concerning certain disclosures required in the sale of residential property and the Sellers Real Property Disclosure Form. The format and content of the booklet must be approved by the Nevada Real Estate Commission. Copies of the booklet and form are to be available to licensees for distribution to buyers and sellers.

Real Estate Commission

The **Real Estate Commission** is composed of five members who are appointed by the Governor. Members serve three-year terms with a maximum of two consecutive membership terms. If due to a resignation or other departure, the Governor appoints a replacement member and that member serves for less than 18 months, that appointment will not count as a term. A term period begins on July 1 and ends on June 30. The membership of the Commission shall consist of two Commissioners each from the southern and northern districts of Nevada counties with no more than two Commissioners from any one Nevada county. The four requirements to be a member of the Nevada Real Estate Commission are as follows:

1. A citizen of the United States.
2. A resident of the state of Nevada for not less than five years.
3. Actively engaged in business as a Nevada broker for at least three years preceding appointment, or as a Nevada broker-salesperson for at least five years preceding appointment.
4. Take a constitutional oath of office and an oath that he or she is legally qualified under the previously mentioned provisions.

At the first meeting of the fiscal year, the Commissioners elect a President, Vice President, and Secretary to serve for the fiscal year. The Commission must hold a minimum of two meetings each year with one meeting each in the northern and southern districts. The President can call a meeting at any time with three working days, notice, and any two Commissioners can call a meeting with three working days, notice. A quorum, which is three members, is required for an official meeting. Commissioners are paid not more than $150 per day while attending a meeting, plus any travel expenses.

Duties of the Commission

The Real Estate Commission duties are as follows:

- Act in an advisory capacity to the Real Estate Division.
- Adopt regulations establishing standards for the operation of licensees' offices and for their business conduct and ethics, including provisions of the Nevada Administrative Code, Chapter 645.
- Conduct hearings against Nevada licensees. A Nevada licensee may appeal the decision of the Commission to an appellate or district court.

Deposit and Use of Money

The Division deposits all monies collected in the state general fund except:

a. Fees received from the sale of publications, which must be retained by the Division to pay the costs of printing and distribution.
b. Fees received for examinations, which must be retained by the Division to pay the costs of administering the examinations.
c. Fees received from licensees for their contributions to the Real Estate Education, Research and Recovery fund.

Except for amounts collected for item (c) above, any surplus of the fees retained by the Division must be deposited with the State Treasurer for credit to the state general fund. Money for the support of the Division must be provided by direct legislative appropriation and be paid out on claims as other claims against the State are paid.

27.2 REGULATION

Chapter 645 of the Nevada Revised Statutes and the Administrative Code covers the general operation of a brokerage and the authority of the Commission to suspend or revoke a real estate license.

General Operation of a Brokerage

The regulations covering the general operation of a brokerage are covered in the following sections.

Place of Business

A real estate brokerage office must comply with the following:

1. A broker shall establish an office in a location that is easily accessible to the public. If the broker chooses to establish an office in a private home or in conjunction with another business, a separate room or rooms for conducting the real estate business shall be set aside. A broker's office must comply with local zoning requirements.

2. The broker's license and the licenses of all broker-salespersons and salespersons associated with the broker must be conspicuously displayed in the place of business. If the real estate broker maintains more than one place of business within Nevada, an additional license must be issued to the broker for each branch office and the broker's license along with the licenses of all broker-salespersons and salespersons associated with the broker at that office must be conspicuously displayed at the branch office location.

3. A sign must be erected and maintained in a conspicuous place upon the premises of the broker's place of business. The name of the broker or the name under which the broker conducts business, as set forth in the license, must be clearly shown on the entrance signage. The entrance signage must be readable from the nearest public sidewalk, street, or highway unless the brokerage is located in an office building, hotel, or apartment house. In that instance, the signage must be posted on the building directory or on the exterior of the entrance to the business. Upon request by the Division, the broker shall furnish a photograph of the sign as proof of compliance with the Statutes and Code.

4. Brokers must, within 10 days, notify the Real Estate Division in writing of a change of name or business location, or of a change of association of any broker-salesperson or salesperson licensee.

Branch Office

A real estate broker must obtain a license for each branch office and must comply with the following:

1. The branch office must be managed by a licensed Nevada broker or broker-salesperson who has two of the previous four years' full-time experience as a real estate licensee. A Nevada branch office may have a Nevada trust account, and the branch manager must be a signatory on the branch trust account. The branch manager has the same responsibilities and obligations as the real estate broker.

2. The branch office signage requirements at the entrance are the same as the real estate broker's main office.

Teaching Responsibility

Every real estate broker shall teach the licensees associated with the broker the fundamentals of real estate or time-sharing practice, or both, plus the ethics of the profession. The teaching curriculum shall include the meaning of deceitful, fraudulent, and dishonest dealings. This includes that it is illegal to give or accept any fee, rebate, or kickback from any of the following:

- Lending institution
- Insurance company
- Appraiser
- Inspector
- Title insurance company
- Escrow company
- Contractor
- Attorney
- Other person involved in a real estate transaction

It is not illegal for the payment or acceptance of a fee that is approved by a client, payable on or before the close of escrow, specified in the documentation of the real estate transaction, and with an aggregate value of $100 or less. The fee must be to or from a client and a Nevada real estate licensee per transaction.

Broker Supervision and Control

The broker shall supervise the activities of all licensees associated with the broker, the activities of the employees, and the operation of the brokerage. Supervision includes, without limitation, establishing policies, rules, procedures, and systems that allow the broker to review, oversee, and manage the following:

a. The real estate transactions performed by a licensee who is associated with him or her.
b. Documents that may have a material effect upon the rights or obligations of a party to a real estate transaction.
c. The filing, storage, and maintenance of the documents.
d. The handling of money received on behalf of a real estate broker.
e. The advertising of any service for which a real estate license is required.
f. The familiarization by the licensee of the requirements of federal and state law governing real estate transactions, including without limitation prohibitions against discrimination.

When the broker establishes the supervision system, the number of licensees, employees, and branch offices should be considered. A system for the monitoring of the supervision policies, rules, procedures, and systems must be established and a broker-salesperson is allowed to assist in its administration. The assignment of a broker-salesperson to assist does not relinquish the overall responsibility of the broker.

Agent Employment

Real estate licensees may associate with the real estate broker as an employee or independent contractor. A written agreement between the broker and real estate licensee must be signed by both parties and dated when the licensee is retained as an independent contractor. The independent contractor agreement must include the material aspects of the relationship, including, without limitation, the supervision by the real estate broker of the licensee's activities for which a real estate license is required. The brokerage policies and rules also must be signed and dated by the broker and licensee.

Broker Absence

A broker shall not be absent from his or her business for 30 days or more if he or she is the only broker in his or her office unless he or she inactivates his or her license or otherwise notifies the Real Estate Division in advance. Failure to observe the requirement is grounds for suspension. If a broker will be absent from his or her business for 30 days or more, he or she must designate an office manager. The designated office manager must be a real estate broker-salesperson with at least two years' active experience within the immediately preceding four years, or the arrangements for the designated manager must be approved by the Division.

Deposits and Trust Accounts

All deposits accepted by every real estate broker or owner-developer that is retained pending consummation or termination of the transaction must be accounted for in the full amount at the time of the consummation or termination. When a real estate salesperson or broker-salesperson associated with the broker or owner-developer receives any money on behalf of the broker or owner-developer he or she shall promptly turn over all such money to the broker or owner-developer. **Promptly** means by the next business day, excluding holidays and weekends.

Unless otherwise provided in writing by all parties to a transaction, the broker must promptly deposit funds entrusted to the broker in a neutral trust account in Nevada. Again, promptly means no later than the next business day. If authorized in writing, the funds can be deposited in the escrow company that is handling the transaction. In addition, the real estate broker may pay to any seller or the seller's authorized agent the whole or any portion of the special deposit received by the broker; however, the broker will remain personally responsible and liable for the full deposit at all times.

Funds deposited in the broker's trust account cannot be **commingled** with the personal funds of the broker. The use of funds by the broker for other than their stated purpose is illegal and is known as **conversion**.

A Nevada real estate broker who does not engage in property management activities is not required to have a trust account. Nevada brokers with a property management permit must have two trust accounts, one for property management operations and one for security deposits. All Nevada trust accounts must:

- Name the brokerage as the trustee.
- Give the name of the bank that holds the trust account and the account number to the Nevada Real Estate Division.
- Allow the Real Estate Division to check the trust accounts with or without the real estate broker being present.

The real estate broker is required to maintain records of all money deposited into the trust account, and those records are to clearly indicate the following:

- Date and from whom the money was received.
- Date the money was deposited.
- Dates of any withdrawals.
- For whom the money was deposited and to whom the money belongs.

The real estate broker shall balance each separate trust account at least monthly. In addition, the broker shall provide to the Division on a form it provides an annual accounting that shows an annual reconciliation of each separate trust account. All trust account records and money are subject to inspection and audit by the Division and its authorized representatives.

Records and Document Preparation

The following list is a summary of record retention, filing, and inspection availability requirements.

- A broker must keep records of each transaction for five years from termination of the transaction.
- All transactions must be numbered consecutively.
- The Division may inspect records and documents at any reasonable time.

The following list is a summary of document preparation requirements.

1. Upon execution of any transaction document, the broker, broker-salesperson, or salesperson must deliver, as soon as practical, a legible copy to each party signing the document. A salesperson or broker-salesperson must provide any paperwork to the broker with whom he or she is associated within five calendar days after that paperwork is executed by all parties.
2. Documents cannot contain forged information (any changes must be initialed by both or all parties).
3. Sales contracts must be in writing.
4. Listings may be oral or written, but when written the listing must contain an ending date. All exclusive listings must be written and contain the Nevada Duties Owed form, and they cannot contain an automatic extension. The listing contract becomes enforceable when signed by the seller and a licensed agent associated with the brokerage.
5. All offers, oral or written, must be presented, regardless of price. The offers must be presented promptly and contain the Nevada Duties Owed, Nevada Confirmation of Brokerage Representation, and the Consent to Act if the broker is acting as a dual agent. The offeree must sign and date the offer and indicate the offeree's acceptance or rejection.

Licensee Advertising

Advertising includes, without limitation, any unsolicited printed material and any broadcast made by radio, television, or electronic means, including unsolicited e-mail, the Internet, billboards, and signs. It also includes business cards, stationery, forms, and other documents used in a real estate transaction.

A salesperson, broker-salesperson, or broker acting as an agent must not advertise property in a manner that implies that no salesperson or broker is taking part in the offer for sale, lease, or exchange. Such an ad is called a **blind ad**. All Nevada advertisements must contain the name of the Nevada brokerage involved in the sale, lease, or exchange.

Any salesperson, broker-salesperson, or broker advertising their own property for sale, lease, or exchange must disclose their status as a real estate licensee and as the property owner in the advertisement. The advertisement should disclose the status of the seller as "owner/licensee" and must not read as "owner/REALTOR." Further, the signage or advertisement should not have on the same sign or in the same ad the statement "for sale by owner" along with the name of the involved Nevada brokerage.

Advertising Requirements

The designated broker supervises all advertising. A licensee must ensure that all advertising contains accurate claims and representations. A salesperson or broker must not misrepresent the facts or create misleading impressions. For example, a licensee must not use the term *acre* unless referring to an area of land measuring 43,560 square feet.

Before placing a sign giving notice that property is being offered for sale, lease, rent, or exchange, a licensee must secure the written consent of the property owner and no more than one sign can be placed in the seller's yard.

Brokerage Name

The name of a brokerage firm under which a real estate broker does business or which a real estate broker-salesperson or salesperson is associated must be clearly identified with prominence in any advertisement. In determining whether the name of the brokerage firm is identified with prominence, the Division shall consider, without limitation, the style, size, and color of the type or font used and the location of the name of the brokerage firm as it appears in the advertisement.

A broker shall not operate under a fictitious name unless a certificate has been filed with the county clerk of each county in which the business is being or intended to be conducted. The information to be included in the certificate is prescribed by Chapter 602 of the Nevada Revised Statutes. The certificate issued by the county clerk must be filed with the Real Estate Division before commencing business as a real estate broker. If a broker changes or assumes a fictitious name, a certified copy of the certificate issued by the county clerk must be filed with the Division within 10 days of the county clerk issuing the certificate. The Division will not issue more than one license or register more than one owner-developer under the same name.

When advertising under the name of a franchise, a broker shall incorporate in a conspicuous way the real, fictitious, or corporate name under which the broker is licensed to engage in business. In addition, the advertisement shall include the following statement: "Each office is independently owned and operated."

Team or Group Advertising

A licensee may use the terms *team* or *group* to advertise and promote real estate services if those terms do not constitute the unlawful use of a trade name, if the terms are not deceptively similar to a name under which any other person is lawfully doing business, and if all of the following are true:

- The team or group is composed of more than one licensee.
- The team or group members are employed by the same broker.
- The team or group name contains the last name of at least one of the members of the team or group.
- The advertising otherwise complies with statutes and rules.

Telephone Canvassing

The federal government established the Do Not Call registry in December 2002 with joint enforcement by the Federal Trade Commission and Federal Communications Commission beginning in June 2003. Further, the state of Nevada has adopted Do Not Call statutes that are more restrictive than the federal laws and are therefore the controlling law in Nevada. The laws were originally enacted to regulate telemarketing firms. However, they regulate all individuals and companies utilizing the telephone for sales purposes. Prior to launching a telephone campaign, licensees should check their brokers' Do Not Call policies to ensure that they and the brokerage are in compliance with state and federal regulations.

Commissions

All commissions earned from a real estate transaction must be paid to the real estate brokerage, and the escrow company must have the Nevada real estate broker's license number to pay the commissions. A Nevada real estate brokerage that receives commissions can share those commissions with the following:

- Licensees associated with the Nevada brokerage.
- Other Nevada brokerages that cooperated in the real estate transaction.
- Brokerages outside Nevada that have a cooperative certificate.
- Brokerages outside Nevada with a referral agreement.

Any dispute about a real estate commission between the brokerage and client is a civil matter and will not be heard by the Nevada Real Estate Commission. The dispute is between the brokerage and the client, and a licensee associated with the broker cannot bring any action against the brokerage client. A Nevada brokerage doing commercial real estate can file a complaint for a legal action for commissions.

Advance Fees

An **advance fee,** as defined in the Statutes, is a fee received by the real estate brokerage before the completion of the real estate transaction. A licensee who charges or collects an advance fee shall within three months furnish to the client an accounting of the use of that money. The Real Estate Division may also demand an accounting from the brokerage. An agreement for an advance fee must:

a. Be in writing.

b. Contain a definite and complete description of the services to be rendered.

c. Specify the total amount of the fee involved and clearly state when the fee is due.

d. Not imply or purport to guarantee that the real property involved will be purchased, sold, rented, leased, or exchanged as a result of the services rendered.

e. Specify the date of full performance of the services contracted for.

f. Not imply or purport to represent to purchasers and prospective purchasers in the advertising or promotional services offered that a buyer for the property is immediately or soon available.

g. Provide that a full refund will be made to the customer if the services for which the advance fee is being received are not substantially or materially provided to the customer.

Suspension or Revocation of License

The Real Estate Commission can suspend, revoke, or deny the renewal of a real estate license for improper conduct set forth in Chapter 645 of Nevada Revised Statutes and Administrative Code. The Commission can consider any conduct that took place before a licensee became licensed that was unknown to the Division when the license was issued that would have been grounds for denial of a license had the Division been aware of the conduct. The following list is a partial summary of the types of improper conduct listed in these regulations:

1. Pursued a course of material misrepresentation or made a false promise likely to influence, persuade, or induce.

2. Accepted other than cash as earnest money unless that fact is communicated to the owner before offer acceptance by the owner or that fact is shown in the receipt for the earnest money.

3. Represented or attempted to represent a real estate broker other than the broker with whom he or she is associated.

4. Paid a commission, compensation, or a finder's fee to any person performing the services of a broker, broker-salesperson, or salesperson that has not secured a real estate license as required by Chapter 645. This does not preclude payments to a broker who is licensed in his state of residence.

5. Accepted compensation as a licensee for the performance of any of the acts that require a real estate license from any person other than the licensed broker to whom he or she is licensed.

6. Failed, within a reasonable time, to account for, timely deposit, or to remit any monies coming into the licensee's possession that belong to others.

7. Accepted, gave, or charged any undisclosed commission, rebate, or direct profit on expenditures made for a client.

8. Induced any party to a contract to break the contract for the purpose of substituting a new contract if the substitution is motivated by the personal gain of the licensee.

9. Willfully used any trade name, service mark, or insigne of membership in any real estate organization without the legal right to do so.

10. Failed to keep a trust account or other record of funds deposited with the licensee relating to a real estate transaction, to balance trust accounts at least monthly, and to submit to the Division the annual accounting.

11. Commingled the money or property of the licensee's principal with the licensee's own, or converted the money or property to the licensee or another.

12. Failed to maintain for review and audit by the Division a complete record of each brokerage agreement and property management agreement entered into by the licensee.

13. A conviction of, or the entry of a plea of guilty, guilty but mentally ill, or nolo contendere to:

    a. A felony relating to the practice of the licensee, property manager, or owner-developer.

    b. Any crime involving fraud, deceit, misrepresentation, or moral turpitude.

14. Failure to include a fixed date of expiration in any written brokerage agreement or failure to leave a copy of such a brokerage agreement or any property management agreement with the client.

15. Gross negligence or incompetence in performing any act for which a real estate license is required.

16. Any other conduct that constitutes deceitful, fraudulent, or dishonest dealings.

When determining whether a licensee has been guilty of gross negligence or incompetence, or conduct that constitutes deceitful, fraudulent, or dishonest dealing, the Real Estate Commission will consider, among other things, whether the licensee:

1. Has done his or her utmost to protect the public against fraud, misrepresentation, or unethical practices related to real estate or time shares.

2. Has ascertained all pertinent facts concerning any time share or property for which he or she accepts an agency.

3. Has attempted to provide specialized professional services concerning a type of property or service that is outside his or her field of experience or competence without the assistance of a qualified authority unless the facts of such lack of experience or competence are fully disclosed to his or her client.

4. Has disclosed, in writing, his or her interest or contemplated interest in any property or time share with which he or she is dealing. The disclosure must include, but is not limited to, a statement of:

    a. Whether he or she expects to receive any direct or indirect compensation.

    b. His or her affiliation with or financial interest in any person or company that furnishes services related to the property.

c. If he or she is managing the property, his or her interest in or financial arrangement with any person or company that provides maintenance or other services to the property.

d. If he or she refers one of his or her clients or customers to another person or company, such as a contractor, title company, attorney, engineer, or mortgage banker, his or her expectation of a referral fee from that person or company.

e. If he or she receives compensation from more than one party in a real estate transaction, full disclosure to and consent from each party to the real estate transaction. A licensee shall not accept compensation from more than one party in a real estate transaction, even if otherwise permitted by law, without full disclosure to all parties.

5. Has kept informed of current statutes and regulations governing real estate, time shares, and related fields in which he or she attempts to provide guidance.

6. Has breached his or her obligation of absolute fidelity to his or her principal's interest or his or her obligation to deal fairly with all parties to a real estate transaction.

7. Has ensured that each agreement for the sale, lease, or management of property or time shares is contained in a written agreement that has been signed by all parties and that his or her real estate broker and each party to the real estate transaction has a copy of the written agreement.

8. Has obtained all changes of contractual terms in writing and whether such changes are signed or initialed by the parties concerned.

9. Understands and properly applies federal and state statutes relating to the protection of consumers.

10. Has acquired knowledge of all material facts that are reasonably ascertainable and are of customary or express concern and has conveyed that knowledge to the parties to the real estate transaction.

11. Has impeded or attempted to impede any investigation of the Division by:

a. Failing to comply or delaying his or her compliance with a request by the Division to provide documents.

b. Failing to supply a written response, including supporting documentation, if available.

c. Supplying false information to an investigator, auditor, or any other officer of the Division.

d. Providing false, forged, or altered documents.

e. Attempting to conceal any documents or facts relating to a real estate transaction.

Unlicensed Activity

A person who acts as a broker, broker-salesperson, salesperson, property manager, or business broker or who advertises in a manner indicating that he or she is licensed as such, without actually being licensed as prescribed by the Statutes, is subject to prosecution before any state court. The Real Estate Division, which may assist in presenting the law or facts upon any trial, may file the complaint. The district attorney of each county shall prosecute all violations for unlicensed activity in their county unless the violations are prosecuted by the Attorney General. The Administrator of the Real Estate Division may request that the Attorney General, in lieu of the district attorney, prosecute an unlicensed activity violation.

Injunctions

Whenever the Real Estate Division believes from evidence satisfactory to it that any licensee has violated or is about to violate any of the provisions of Chapter 645 of the Nevada Revised Statutes, any order, license, permit, decision, demand, or requirement, or any part or provision thereof, the Division may bring an action in district court of the State of Nevada to enjoin such person from continuing such violation or engaging therein or doing any act or acts in furtherance thereof. An order or judgment may be entered awarding a preliminary or final injunction, but no preliminary injunction or temporary restraining order shall be granted without at least five days' notice.

Complaint, Hearing, and Judicial Review

Before the Real Estate Commission can suspend, revoke, or deny the renewal of a real estate license, permit, or registration, the Administrator presents the licensee with the written complaint of the charges and allows the licensee the opportunity for a hearing before the Commission. The Commission shall hold the hearing within 90 days of the filing of the complaint, and the respondent must be given at least 30 days' notice in writing of the date, time, and place of the hearing along with a copy of the complaint and copies of all communications, reports, affidavits, or depositions in possession of the Division and relevant to the complaint. The licensee has 30 days after service of the notice and other documents to file a written answer to the complaint. The licensee may be represented by legal counsel. The case is heard and decided by the Real Estate Commission. When the decision is in favor of the licensee, it is final. If desired and if legal grounds exist, the Commission's final decision that is not in favor of the licensee may be appealed by filing an action for judicial review.

Administrative Fines

After a hearing, any licensee who has violated any provision of Chapter 645 of the Nevada Revised Statutes or Administrative Code may be assessed an administrative fine in an amount not to exceed $10,000 for each violation.

27.3 REAL ESTATE EDUCATION, RESEARCH AND RECOVERY FUND

The **Real Estate Education, Research and Recovery Fund** (Recovery Fund) has been created as a special revenue fund for the benefit of any person (except for another licensee) aggrieved by any fraud, misrepresentation, or deceit by a licensee in a real estate transaction. The fund pays only for actual direct out-of-pocket losses arising out of the real estate transaction in which the licensee:

- Performed acts that required a real estate license.
- Engaged in fraud, misrepresentation, or deceit.

A person with a real estate license may not recover from the Recovery Fund for damages that are related to a transaction in which the licensee acted in his or her capacity as a licensee.

Distribution

The distribution of monies from the Fund is limited to actual damages suffered, up to a maximum of $25,000 per judgment. The Fund has no more responsibility to pay losses resulting from acts of one licensee once the fund has paid $100,000 in damages for multiple transactions on behalf of the licensee.

Time Limits

To collect from the Recovery Fund, the judgment creditor files a verified petition in the court in which the final judgment was entered. The petition requests an order from the court directing payment out of the Recovery Fund in an amount equal to the unpaid actual damages. The petition must be filed no more than one year after the termination of all proceedings in connection with the judgment, including reviews and appeals.

Petition and Hearing

The petition shall include a copy of the judgment, complaint upon which the judgment was entered, and the writ of execution that was returned unsatisfied. The petition to the court with its required attachments must be served upon the Administrator and the judgment debtor, and affidavits of service must be filed with the court.

At the hearing, the aggrieved person must show that he or she has obtained a proper judgment against the licensee and has complied with the requirements of the Recovery Fund and has taken every possible legal avenue to collect the judgment and found that the licensee does not have enough assets to satisfy the entire judgment. If the aggrieved person has collected any funds from the licensee in a city court, the court must be informed. The aggrieved must also show that he or she is not a spouse or representative of the licensed person. The Administrator may answer and defend any action against the Recovery Fund.

If the court is satisfied with the efforts of the aggrieved person, the court will direct the Administrator to make a payment from the Fund on behalf of the licensee. When the Administrator has paid from the Recovery Fund any money to the aggrieved person, the Administrator is subrogated to all other rights of the aggrieved person to the extent of the amount paid. Any amount and interest recovered by the Administrator on the judgment must be deposited in the State Treasury for credit to the Recovery Fund.

License Termination

If the Administrator pays money from the Fund on behalf of a licensee, the license is automatically suspended. The licensee is not eligible to obtain a new license until he or she has repaid the Recovery Fund with interest at the rate of 2% over the prime rate as determined each January 1 and July 1.

Licensee Contributions and Fund Balance

The Real Estate Education, Research and Recovery Fund is funded by real estate licensees who are required to pay to the Recovery Fund $40 upon issuance of a new license and $40 upon renewal of the license. An owner-developer is not required to pay into the Recovery Fund nor is the Fund responsible to pay on a judgment against an owner-developer.

If on June 30 of any year the Recovery Fund balance exceeds $300,000, the excess must be set aside and used by the Administrator, after approval of the Commission, for education and research. The interest and income earned on the money in the Fund, after deducting any applicable charges, is credited to the Recovery Fund.

CHAPTER SUMMARY

The Administrator is in charge of the Real Estate Division. In addition to other duties, the Administrator investigates wrongdoing in Nevada real estate, arranges hearings for licensees with the Nevada Real Estate Commission, and issues the year-end certification of the Nevada Real Estate Education, Research and Recovery Fund. The Real Estate Division consists of the Customer Service and Licensing, Education, Investigating, and Administrative departments. The Real Estate Commission is composed of five members appointed by the Governor. The Commission acts in an advisory capacity to the Division, adopts regulations, and conducts hearings against Nevada licensees.

A real estate brokerage office must comply with the following: A brokerage must have an office in a location that is easily accessible to the public. The broker's license and the licenses of all broker-salespersons and salespersons associated with the broker must be conspicuously displayed in the place of business. There must be a sign erected and maintained in a conspicuous place upon the premises of the broker's place of business. The name of the broker or the name under which the broker conducts business, as set forth in the license, must be clearly shown on the entrance signage. The broker must notify the Division in writing of a change of name or business location, or of a change of association of any broker-salesperson or salesperson licensees.

Each branch office must obtain a license and must be managed by a licensed broker or broker-salesperson.

The teaching responsibilities and broker supervision and control obligations of the real estate broker are lengthy and detailed and should be studied in the body of this chapter's text.

A broker shall not be absent from his or her business for 30 days or more if he or she is the only broker in the office unless the broker inactivates his or her broker license or otherwise notifies the Division in advance. All deposits accepted by every real estate broker that are retained pending consummation or termination of the transaction must be accounted for in the full amount. When a real estate salesperson or broker-salesperson receives any money on behalf of the broker, such money shall be promptly turned over to the broker. Promptly means by the next business day. Unless otherwise provided in writing by all parties to a transaction, the broker must promptly deposit funds entrusted to him or her in a neutral escrow account in Nevada. Funds deposited in the broker's trust account cannot be commingled with the personal funds of the broker. The illegal use of funds by the broker for other than their stated purpose is called "conversion."

A Nevada real estate broker who does not engage in property management activities is not required to have a trust account. Nevada brokers with a property management permit must have two trust accounts. The real estate broker is required to maintain records of all money deposited into the trust account, and the trust account is to be balanced monthly. The broker shall provide to the Real Estate Division, on a form it provides, an annual accounting that shows a reconciliation of each separate trust account.

A broker must keep records of each transaction for five years from termination of the transaction. The Division may inspect records and documents at any reasonable time. A summary of document preparation requirements is included in the body of this chapter's text.

The broker supervises all advertising. A salesperson or broker-salesperson must not advertise property in a manner that implies that no salesperson or broker is taking part in the offer for sale, lease, or exchange. Such an ad is called a "blind ad."

Any salesperson, broker-salesperson, or broker advertising the salesperson's or broker's own property must disclose in the advertisement the salesperson's or broker's status as a salesperson or broker, and as the property owner.

The name of a brokerage firm under which a real estate broker does business or which a real estate broker-salesperson or salesperson is associated must be clearly identified with prominence in any advertisement. A broker shall not operate under a fictitious name unless a certificate has been filed with the county clerk of each county in which the business is being or is intended to be conducted. Along with other requirements listed in this chapter's text, a licensee may use the terms *team* or *group* to advertise and promote real estate services if those terms do not constitute the unlawful use of a trade name.

All commissions earned from a real estate transaction must be paid to the real estate brokerage, and the brokerage can share the commission with licensees associated with the brokerage, other brokerages who cooperated in the transaction, or brokerages outside Nevada that have a cooperative certificate or a referral agreement. Any dispute about a real estate commission between the brokerage and client is a civil matter and will not be heard by the Nevada Real Estate Commission.

An advance fee is a fee received by the real estate brokerage before the completion of the real estate transaction. A licensee who charges or collects an advance fee shall within three months furnish to the client an accounting of the use of that money. The requirements for an advance fee agreement are included in the body of this chapter's text.

There are 16 types of improper conduct listed in Chapter 645 of the Statutes that allow the Real Estate Commission to suspend, revoke, deny, or refuse to renew a real estate license. A summary of such improper actions is included in the body of this chapter's text.

A person who acts as a broker, broker-salesperson, salesperson, property manager, or business broker or who advertises in a manner indicating that he or she is licensed as such, without actually being licensed as prescribed by the Statutes, is subject to prosecution before any state court.

Before the Real Estate Commission can suspend, revoke, or deny the renewal of a real estate license, permit, or registration, the Administrator presents the licensee with the written complaint of the charges and allows the licensee the opportunity for a hearing before the Commission.

After a hearing, any broker or salesperson who has violated any provision of Chapter 645 of the Nevada Revised Statutes or Administrative Code may be assessed an administrative fine in an amount not to exceed $10,000 for each violation.

The Real Estate Education, Research and Recovery Fund is a special revenue fund for the benefit of any person (except for another licensee) aggrieved by any fraud, misrepresentation, or deceit by a licensee in a real estate transaction.

CHECKING YOUR COMPREHENSION

1. List the duties and responsibilities of the Real Estate Division.

2. Describe the composition of the Real Estate Commission and its duties.

3. Summarize the regulations related to the operation of brokerages, including:
   - Place of business
   - Branch offices
   - Teaching responsibilities
   - Broker supervision and control
   - Agent employment
   - Broker absence
   - Deposits and trust accounts
   - Records and document preparation

- Licensee advertising
- Commissions
- Advance fees

4. Describe the improper conduct that can result in a complaint, the process for the resolution of a complaint, and the potential penalties.

5. Summarize the purpose and operation of the Real Estate Education, Research and Recovery Fund.

REVIEWING YOUR UNDERSTANDING

1. Blind ads do **NOT**:
   a. provide the name of the owner
   b. provide the property address
   c. give the listing price of the property
   d. indicate that the advertiser is an agent

2. The **MAXIMUM** amount of money that may be paid from the Recovery Fund for any one licensee is:
   a. $25,000
   b. $50,000
   c. $90,000
   d. $100,000

3. Brokers must keep records of transactions for a period of:
   a. three years from the inception of a transaction
   b. five years from the inception of a transaction
   c. three years from the termination of a transaction
   d. five years from the termination of a transaction

4. Engaging in the sale of real estate when a license is required but in fact acting without a license is:
   a. a misdemeanor
   b. not subject to action by the Real Estate Commission because the party is not licensed
   c. subject to prosecution before any state court
   d. subject to action before the Real Estate Commission

5. Which of the following people would be unable to file a claim for money from the Real Estate Education, Research and Recovery Fund?
   a. a buyer in a subdivision
   b. a seller of a residence
   c. a mortgagor
   d. a licensee

6. The Real Estate Commission is required to do all of the following, **EXCEPT**:
   a. adopt regulations establishing standards for the operation of licensees' offices
   b. act in an advisory capacity to the Real Estate Division
   c. manage the Real Estate Division
   d. conduct hearings against Nevada licensees

7. A Nevada Real Estate Commissioner is:
    a. appointed by the state legislature
    b. appointed by the Governor
    c. elected by popular vote
    d. appointed by the Secretary of State

8. When the real estate broker is absent from his or her business for more than 30 days, all of the following are true, **EXCEPT**:
    a. a broker-salesperson with at least two years' active experience within the immediately preceding four years may be appointed the designated office manager
    b. a salesperson with at least two years' active experience within the immediately preceding four years may be appointed as a designated office manager
    c. if the broker is the only licensed broker in the office, he or she must inactivate the broker license or notify the Real Estate Division in advance of the more than 30-day absence
    d. a broker-salesperson with less than two years' active experience may be appointed as the designated office manager but only when the arrangements are approved by the Real Estate Division

9. A real estate salesperson advertising his or her own property for sale should disclose his or her status as a licensee as follows:
    a. owner/licensee
    b. owner/REALTOR
    c. for sale by owner/name of brokerage
    d. for sale by owner is the only required disclosure

10. The Real Estate Commission consists of:
    a. seven members
    b. six members
    c. five members
    d. four members

11. Who may accept commission from an out-of-state broker?
    a. the referring salesperson
    b. the referring broker
    c. a property manager with a property management permit
    d. any individual who made the referral

12. A broker, in dealing with the public, may **NOT**:
    a. keep silent about a material fact in the transaction
    b. take an option
    c. accept a commission from both buyer and seller
    d. negotiate different commissions with different owners

13. A broker receives an oral offer over the telephone. The broker shall:
    a. refuse to present it until it is in writing
    b. refuse to present it unless he has earnest money
    c. present the oral offer
    d. tell the buyer that oral offers are illegal

14. A suit by a principal against a broker who failed to follow instructions will probably result in:
    a. loss of broker's license
    b. fine and/or jail
    c. money damages
    d. exoneration, since a broker is not required to obey instructions (the broker only has to procure a buyer)

15. A sales licensee can receive compensation from the:
    a. seller
    b. buyer
    c. employing broker
    d. listing broker

16. When a commission dispute arises between two licensees from different companies, their recourse would be to:
    a. appeal to the Real Estate Commission
    b. not allow a closing until their dispute was settled
    c. seek relief through civil action
    d. appeal to the Administrator of the Real Estate Division

17. When a broker moves his office, how long does he have to notify the Real Estate Division?
    a. 6 months
    b. 10 days
    c. immediately
    d. 30 days

18. A real estate broker is required to have all of the following, **EXCEPT**:
    a. a trust account
    b. day-to-day control of the business
    c. use of the brokerage name in advertising
    d. a broker manager at each branch office

19. The use of funds received by the broker in trust for other than their stated purpose is known as:
    a. conversion
    b. commingling
    c. diversion
    d. cooperative

20. A salesperson or broker-salesperson must provide any paperwork to the broker with whom he or she is associated within:
    a. five calendar days after the paperwork is executed
    b. five business days after the paperwork is executed
    c. seven calendar days after the paperwork is executed
    d. five calendar days after the close of the transaction

Chapter

28

IMPORTANT TERMS AND CONCEPTS

area measurement   perimeter   surface area formula

cubic area formula   proper fractions   T formula

improper fractions   rectangle   triangle

percentage   square

CHAPTER OBJECTIVES

After completing this chapter, you should be able to:

- Apply the T formula to solve real estate math problems.
- Calculate the answers to commission problems.
- Solve area and volume problems.

Real Estate Math

28.1 MATH REVIEW

Real estate licensees have to know how to compute math problems that involve fractions, decimals, and percentages. You will need to be familiar with the formulas for area, volume, and perimeter. In the business of real estate, you will figure commissions, profit, loss, capitalization, taxes, principal and interest, depreciation, and appreciation. This brief review of the basics and tips in understanding some simple formulas should make the math easier.

Fractions

In fractions, the top number is the numerator; the bottom number is the denominator.

$$\frac{\text{Numerator}}{\text{Denominator}}$$

Proper fractions are less than one whole unit. That is, the numerator is smaller than the denominator.

Example—Proper Fractions

$$\frac{1}{4} \quad \frac{3}{5} \quad \frac{6}{10}$$

Improper fractions equal a whole number or more. The numerator is equal to or greater than the denominator. A whole number is a number without a fraction. For example, $10/10$ or $15/15$ equals the whole number 1. An improper fraction needs to be reduced to a mixed number, which is a whole number with a fraction.

Example—Improper Fractions Converted to Mixed Numbers

$$\frac{7}{4} = 1\frac{3}{4} \quad \frac{5}{2} = 2\frac{1}{2}$$

To add fractions, convert all of the fractions to the lowest common denominator and then add the numerators as follows.

EXERCISE: What is the sum of $\frac{1}{2} + \frac{3}{4} + \frac{1}{8}$?

Step 1: Convert to the lowest common denominator.

$$\frac{1}{2} + \frac{3}{4} + \frac{1}{8} = \frac{4}{8} + \frac{6}{8} + \frac{1}{8}$$

Step 2: Add the numerators; the denominator remains the same.

$$\frac{4}{8} + \frac{6}{8} + \frac{1}{8} = \frac{11}{8}$$

Step 3: Convert improper fractions to mixed numbers, if necessary.

$$\frac{11}{8} = 1\frac{3}{8}$$

Percentages

Percentage problems will be the most common math problems used in everyday real estate transactions.

Remember that percent means *parts per 100*, with 100 as the total. For example, 50% means 50 parts per 100. To change a percentage to a decimal, divide by 100. The simple rule is to move the decimal point two places to the left. To change a decimal to a percentage, move the decimal point two places to the right.

Example—Converting Percentage to Decimal

75% = 0.75

Example—Converting Decimal to Percentage

0.10 = 10%

EXERCISE: Change the following percentages to decimals.

5% = _____   25% = _____   120% = _____

EXERCISE: Change the following decimals to percentages.

0.875 = _____   0.35 = _____   0.06 = _____

To change a percentage to a fraction, place the percentage (as the numerator) over 100 (as the denominator) to create the fraction, and then reduce the fraction to its lowest common denominator.

Example—Converting Percentage to Fraction

$$25\% = \frac{25}{100} = \frac{1}{4}$$
$$70\% = \frac{70}{100} = \frac{7}{10}$$
$$250\% = \frac{250}{100} = 2\frac{1}{2}$$

To change a fraction to a percentage, simply reverse the process previously mentioned by first converting the fraction to a decimal. Then multiply by

100, changing the number to a percentage. To convert a fraction to a decimal, divide the numerator by the denominator.

Example—Converting Fraction to Percentage

$$\frac{1}{4} = 0.25 = 25\%$$

$$\frac{3}{5} = 0.60 = 60\%$$

Decimals

Adding and Subtracting Decimals

When adding or subtracting decimals, the most important thing to remember is to line up the decimal points.

```
   2.50        or in %       8.75%
   3.75                     25.00%
+ 10.325                  + 10.25%
 ------                    -------
 16.575                     44.00%
```

Multiplying and Dividing Decimals

To multiply decimals, follow the standard procedure used for multiplying whole numbers and then determine the correct placement of the decimal. To do this, count the number of places in the numbers to be multiplied. Then count off the same number of places in the answer and place the decimal there.

Example—Multiplying Decimals

```
   0.52        1.02%
 ×0.12        ×3%
 ------       -----
   104        3.06%
    52
 ------
 0.0624
```

If you are dividing by a decimal number, you will first have to change it to a whole number. To do this, simply move the decimal point of the divisor to the right until it becomes a whole number. Then, move the decimal point of the dividend the same number of places to the right, adding zeros as necessary. Place the decimal point in the quotient directly above the point in the dividend.

Example—Dividing Decimals

$$6 \div 12.12 = 600 \div 1212$$

28.2 WORD PROBLEMS AND THE T FORMULA

The math involved in word problems is not complex and requires you only to add, subtract, multiply, and divide. Many students, however, have difficulty translating a word problem into a math problem. For a helpful tip on understanding word problems, use the following guide:

The word *of* usually means "multiply."

The word *is* implies the word "equals."

The **T formula** will be used throughout this book to solve different types of problems. The T formula is an aid in solving word problems and works as follows:

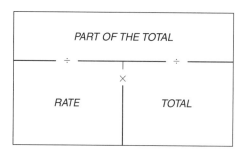

There are always three factors in a percentage problem. Two factors will be stated in the problem, and the third unknown factor will be the answer to the problem.

- If the two factors known are below the line, multiply to find the part.
- If one known factor is above the line, and the second known factor is below the line, divide the one above the line by the one below to find the missing factor.

A word of caution: If the rate is given as a percentage or a fraction, it must be changed to a decimal before the problem can be solved.

Commission Problems

For commission problems, the following additional information should be considered when applying the **T** formula.

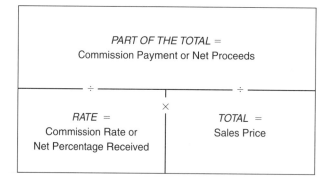

Practice Problems

EXERCISE 1: Broker Sam Seller receives $4900 commission. His listing stated he was to receive a 7% commission. What was the sale price of the home?

COMMISSION = $4900	
RATE = 0.07	TOTAL = ?

Divide the item on top, $4900, by the rate, 0.07, which results in the answer of $70,000.

EXERCISE 2: What would the gross commission be if a $65,000 home was sold and the seller paid the broker a 7% commission?

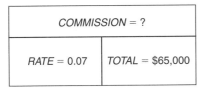

Multiply the total sales price, $65,000, by the rate, 0.07, which results in a commission of $4550.

EXERCISE 3: What is the broker's commission rate if she receives a commission of $3450 on a $57,000 sale?

COMMISSION = $3450	
RATE = ?	TOTAL = $57,000

Divide the commission, $3450, by the total sales price, $57,000, which results in a rate of 0.06, or 6%.

EXERCISE 4: The owner lists a property with a broker at a price that will net the seller $56,000 after paying a 7% commission. What is the listed price (rounded)?

Whenever you are given a net figure, it will be a part of something larger, called the gross amount. In this problem, the seller wants to net $56,000. That means that the net plus the commission is 100% (gross amount). If the commission is 7%, the net must be 93%. To find the gross amount, you simply divide the net amount by 0.93.

28.3 AREA PROBLEMS

The principles for solving area problems and six practice problems are presented in the following sections.

Measurements

16½ feet = 1 rod, perch, pole

320 rods = 1 mile

5280 feet = 1 mile

1760 yards = 1 mile

43,560 square feet = 1 acre

208.71 × 208.71 feet = 1 square acre

Surface Area

A **rectangle** is a four-sided area that has sides at right angles to each other. A **square** is a rectangle with equal sides. A **triangle** is a three-sided figure.

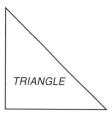

Surface Area of a Rectangle or Square = Width × Length

Remember, when solving an area problem all units of measure must be the same.

feet × feet = square feet

or

yards × yards = square yards

Surface Area of a Right Triangle = $\frac{1}{2}$ Base (or Width) × Height (Length)

Volume

To compute volume, multiply the *width × length × depth* (or height). Volume is generally referred to as cubic feet or cubic yards.

feet × feet × feet = cubic feet

yards × yards × yards = cubic yards

Conversions between Feet and Yards

The principles for converting units of measure for surface area and volume area computations are covered in the following sections.

Surface Area Conversions

To convert square yards to square feet, multiply the square yards by 9. Nine is used because there are 9 square feet in a square yard (3 feet × 3 feet = 9 square feet).

To convert square feet to square yards, divide the square feet by 9.

Volume Area Conversions

To convert cubic yards to cubic feet, multiply the cubic yards by 27. Twenty-seven is used because there are 27 cubic feet in a cubic yard (3 feet × 3 feet × 3 feet = 27 cubic feet).

To convert cubic feet to cubic yards, divide the cubic feet by 27.

Perimeter

Perimeter means the "distance around" the property. If you have a piece of property that is 65 ft. × 100 ft., you would add all four sides, or multiply both dimensions by two and add the sums.

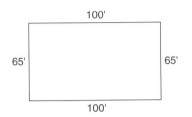

$$100 \times 2 = 200$$
$$65 \times 2 = \underline{130}$$
$$330 \text{ feet}$$

or

$$100 + 100 + 65 + 65 = 330 \text{ feet}$$

Perimeter will be in linear feet, yards, rods, or miles. Linear measurement is the distance from one point to another.

Calculating the Area of an Irregular Lot

When listing a parcel of land, it is necessary to know how to find the number of square feet or acres in the parcel. Because the sides are not all right angles, it takes a little more understanding to find the correct measurements. To calculate the area of the following parcel of land, you must section it into rectangles and triangles, calculate each separately, then add them together.

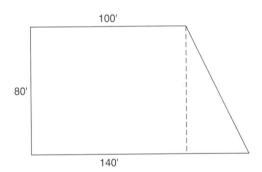

The formula for finding the *area of a rectangle* is simply to multiply the length by the width:

$$80 \times 100 = 8000 \text{ square feet}$$

The formula for finding the *area of a right triangle* is the height × ½ of the base. That is the same as multiplying the height and base and then dividing by 2.

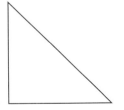

$$80 \times 20 = \begin{array}{r} 1600 \\ + 8000 \\ \hline 9600 \text{ square feet} \end{array}$$

Area Practice Problems

1. What is the area of a lot 60' × 100'? _____

2. Find the area of a right triangle that measures 25' × 50'. _____

3. A man has a lot 83' wide and 114' deep. How many square feet are contained in this lot? _____

4. Find the volume of a room that is 12' × 20' with an 8' ceiling. _____ (This type of problem would be used to figure needs for air conditioning or heating.)

5. What is the depth of a lot that is 60' wide and contains 800 square yards? _____

6. How many acres are in a lot that is 200' wide by 326.7' deep? _____

CHAPTER SUMMARY

Real estate licensees will figure commissions, profit, loss, capitalization, taxes, principal and interest, depreciation, and appreciation. Therefore, licensees need to be comfortable with fractions, decimals, percentages, and the formulas for area, volume, and perimeter.

Proper fractions are less than one whole unit. The numerator is smaller than the denominator. Improper fractions equal a whole number or more. The numerator is equal to or greater than the denominator. To add fractions, convert all of the fractions to the lowest common denominator and then add the numerators.

Percent means *parts per 100*. To change a percentage to a decimal, divide by 100. To change a decimal to a percentage, move the decimal point two places to the right.

To change a fraction to a percentage, simply reverse the process above by first converting the fraction to a decimal and then multiplying by 100, changing it to a percentage. To convert a fraction to a decimal, divide the numerator by the denominator.

When adding or subtracting decimals, the most important thing to remember is to line up the decimal points. Multiplying decimals is the same as multiplying whole numbers except for the correct placement of the decimal. To do this, count the number of places in the numbers to be multiplied. Then count off the same number of places in the answer and place the decimal there. If you are dividing a whole number into a decimal, put the decimal in the same place in the answer. If you are dividing by a decimal number, first change it to a whole number.

When solving word problems, the T formula may prove helpful. There are always three factors in a percentage problem. Two factors will be stated in the problem, and the third unknown factor will be the answer to the problem. If the two known factors are below the line, multiply to find the part. If one known factor is above the line and the second known factor is below the line, divide the one above the line by the one below to find the missing factor.

A rectangle is a four-sided shape that has sides at right angles to each other. A square is a rectangle with equal sides. A triangle is a three-sided figure.

$$\text{Surface Area of a Rectangle or Square} = \text{Width} \times \text{Length}$$

$$\text{Surface Area of a Right Triangle} = \frac{1}{2} \text{ Base (or Width)} \times \text{Height (Length)}$$

$$\text{Volume} = \text{Width} \times \text{Length} \times \text{Depth}$$

Perimeter means the "distance around" the property. To find the perimeter of a rectangular or square lot, add all four sides, or multiply each dimension by two and add the sums.

To calculate the area of an irregular lot, section it into rectangles and triangles, calculate each separately, and then add them together.

CHECKING YOUR COMPREHENSION

1. Draw the T diagram and place the components of the T in their proper places.

2. Explain how the T formula assists in solving word problems.

PRACTICAL APPLICATION

1. If the commission on a sale of a property was $5525, and the purchase price was $85,000, what percent commission was charged?

2. The seller wanted a net of $50,000 for his home after paying a commission of 7%. What would be the listing price?

3. Tim earns a 6% commission on the first $75,000 of sales for the month and 3% for all sales over that amount. If Tim sold houses totaling $162,100 for the month, how much more would Tim have earned at a straight 6% commission?

4. Find the area of this lot: _____

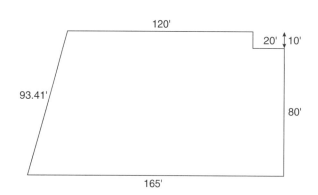

REVIEWING YOUR UNDERSTANDING

1. Susanna sells a lot for $45,400. She netted $41,428 after paying a broker's commission. What was her rate of commission? (*Hint:* Before you find the rate of commission, you must find the amount of commission.)
   a. 8.50%
   b. 8.75%
   c. 9.00%
   d. 9.60%

2. A broker splits the commission with her salespeople by paying three-fifths of the total commission. If one of her salespeople sold a property for $125,000 at a 7% commission, how much did the salesperson receive?
   a. $4625
   b. $4375
   c. $1457
   d. $5250

3. A seller paid $32,000 for a house. He wants to sell it at a 20% profit after paying a broker a 5% commission. What is the selling price (rounded)?
   a. $33,684
   b. $36,096
   c. $36,480
   d. $40,400

4. Sharon receives a commission at 6% on the first $50,000 and 3% on the excess over $50,000. If Sharon received $3895 of commission, what was the sales price?
   a. $35,733
   b. $64,917
   c. $79,833
   d. $129,833

5. A seller wants to net $11,600 from the sale of his house after he pays the cost of the sale, which includes a 5½% brokerage fee and 6½% for the closing costs. What must the sales price be for the seller to net $11,600?
   a. $13,000
   b. $12,992
   c. $13,182
   d. $13,300

6. A rectangular lot is worth $193,000. The value is $4.40 per square foot for the lot. If the lot is 200' deep, what is the width?
   a. 100'
   b. 220'
   c. 600'
   d. 890'

7. Monthly rent on a warehouse was set at $1.75 per cubic yard. Assuming the warehouse is 36' × 200' and it is 12' high, what would be the annual rent?

   a. $5600

   b. $50,400

   c. $67,200

   d. $151,200

8. How many half-acre lots can be obtained from a parcel of land 660 feet by 1,320 feet after removing 15% for streets?

   a. 17

   b. 20

   c. 34

   d. 40

9. A triangular lot measures 350 feet along the street and 425 feet in depth on the side that is perpendicular to the street. If a broker sold the lot for $1.50 per square foot and his commission rate was 9%, what was the amount of commission earned?

   a. $20,081.25

   b. $13,387.50

   c. $18,423.17

   d. $10,040.62

10. If a half-acre lot has a frontage of 75 feet, what is its depth?

   a. 290 feet

   b. 272 feet

   c. 189 feet

   d. 346 feet

Appendix A
Practice State Examination

PART I: NEVADA EXAMINATION CONTENT

Introduction

The State of Nevada salesperson and broker examinations contain 120 test questions that will be used to determine your score (80 national examination questions, plus 40 Nevada state–specific questions). The test may also contain 10 pretest questions mixed in throughout the examination. Because PSI Exams, Inc., who administers the Nevada examinations, provides a score to you immediately after you take the State of Nevada examination, they need to know how test questions perform before they are used to calculate your score. For this reason,

PSI must pretest questions in order to evaluate question reliability. If a pretest question is included in your examination, it will not be counted in the calculation of your score. Pretest questions are not identified and you should answer all questions as if each counted toward your score. This will provide PSI with reliable evaluation of the questions. The following test outlines show the approximate number of questions on the state test for each major category, along with a reference to the chapter in this text where the subject is covered.

National Test Outline

	Chapter
I. Property Ownership (Sales person: 7 questions, Broker: 7 questions)	
A. Classes of Property	2
B. Land Characteristics and Property Descriptions	1 & 3
C. Encumbrances	6
D. Types of Ownership	8
II. Land Use Controls and Regulations (Salesperson: 7 questions, Broker: 7 questions)	
A. Government Rights in Land	2
B. Public Controls Based in Police Power	4
C. Private Controls	6
III. Valuation and Market Analysis (Salesperson: 7 questions, Broker: 6 questions)	
A. Value	24
B. Methods of Estimating Value (Applicability, Key Elements)	24
C. Competitive Market Analysis	24

	Chapter
D. Transactions Requiring Formal Appraisal	24
IV. Financing (Salesperson: 8 questions, Broker: 7 questions)	
A. General Concepts	20
B. Types of Loans	21
C. Sources of Loan Money	20
D. Government Programs	21
E. Mortgages/Deeds of Trust	21 & 23
F. Financing/Credit Laws	20
V. Laws of Agency (Salesperson: 10 questions, Broker: 10 questions)	
A. Law, Definition, and Nature of Agency Relationships	13
B. Common Types of Agency Agreements in Real Estate	13 & 14
C. Agency Duties	13
D. Disclosure of Agency (General, Detailed Requirements in State Portion)	13 & 14
E. Commission and Fees	13 & 14

VI. **Mandated Disclosures (Salesperson: 6 questions, Broker: 7 questions)**

   A. Property Condition Disclosure Forms   13

   B. Need for Inspection and Obtaining/Verifying Information   13

   C. Material Facts   13

VII. **Contracts (Salesperson: 10 questions, Broker: 10 questions)**

   A. General Knowledge of Contract Law   17

   B. Offers/Purchase Agreements   17

   C. Counteroffers/Multiple Counteroffers   17

   D. Leases as Contracts   10

   E. Rescission and Cancellation Agreements/Other Contract Terminations   17

VIII. **Transfer of Property (Salesperson: 7 questions, Broker: 6 questions)**

   A. Title Insurance   12

   B. Deeds   11

   C. Escrow or Closing   12 & 18

   D. Tax Aspects   25

   E. Special Processes (e.g., Probate, Foreclosures) **(Broker Only)**   11

IX. **Practice of Real Estate (Salesperson: 10 questions, Broker: 10 questions)**

   A. Fair Housing Laws   16

   B. Advertising and Misrepresentation   13 & 27

   C. Agent Supervision **(Broker Only)**   27

   D. Ethical Issues   13, 16, & 27

   E. Broker/Salesperson Agreements   13

X. **Real Estate Calculations (Salesperson: 5 questions, Broker: 6 questions)**

   A. General Math Concepts   28

   B. Property Tax Calculations (not Prorations)   6

   C. Lending Calculations   22

   D. Calculations for Transactions   28

   E. Calculations for Valuations   24

   F. Mortgage Calculations   22

XI. **Specialty Areas (Salesperson: 3 questions, Broker: 4 questions)**

   A. Property Management and Landlord/Tenant   19

   B. Subdivisions   5

   C. Commercial Property/ Income Property   25

   D. Business Opportunities **(Broker only)**   13 & 26

Nevada State–Specific Outline

Chapter

I. **Commission Duties and Pwers (Salesperson: 4 questions, Broker: 4 questions)**

   A. Determining Misconduct, Investigations, Hearings, and Appeals   27

   B. Sanctions, License Suspension, Revocation, and Grounds for Discipline   27

   C. Inspection of Records **(Broker Only)**   27

II. **Licensing (Salesperson: 5 questions, Broker: 6 questions)**

   A. Types of Licensing and Activities Requiring a License   26

   B. Coperative Certificates **(Broker Only)**   26

   C. Property Management Permits

Chapter

   D. License Renewal, Changes in License, Terminations, and Reasons for Denial   26

   E. Licensing Process and Requirements   26

   F. Branch Offices and License Display **(Broker Only)**   27

   G. Other Situations Affecting License, Including: Felony Conviction, Failure to Pay Child Support, and Non-Compliance   26

III. **Standards of Conduct (Salesperson: 16 questions, Broker: 13 questions)**

   A. Advertising   27

   B. Property Disclosures, Including: Seller's Real Property Disclosure,   5 & 13

PART 2: NEVADA PRACTICE EXAMINATION

National Portion of Nevada Test

I. Property Ownership

1. Which of the following is **NOT** an encumbrance on real property?

   a. Lease

   b. Easement

   c. Homestead right

   d. Restrictive covenant

2. Which of the following is **NOT** an appurtenance?

   a. Easement rights

   b. Mineral rights

   c. Water rights

   d. Trade fixtures

3. The physical characteristics of land include:

   a. indestructibility

   b. homogeneity

   c. improvements

   d. supply

4. How many acres would be contained in the following legal descriptions? NW¼, SE¼, N½, SE¼, and the SW¼, SE¼, S½, N¼ of Section 21:

   a. 0.078 acres

   b. 15 acres

   c. 40 acres

   d. 10 acres

5. What would a landlocked property owner **MOST** likely ask the court for?

   a. An easement by prescription

   b. An easement in gross

   c. An easement by necessity

   d. Adverse possession of servient tenement

6. A metes and bounds description **MUST**:
   a. cover an area larger than 10 acres
   b. be in areas not included in the rectangular survey system
   c. commence and finish at the same identifiable point
   d. always use north as the basis for directions

7. Which of the following is **NOT** a characteristic of a fee simple estate?
   a. Indefinite duration
   b. Free of encumbrances
   c. Transferable with or without consideration
   d. Transferable by will or intestate succession

II. Land Use Controls and Regulations

8. Which of the following restrictive covenants is **MOST** likely to be enforceable?
   a. Prohibits sales to blacks
   b. Prohibits resales for 20 years
   c. Prohibits use for anything other than single-family dwellings
   d. Absolutely prohibits any resales

9. Restrictive covenants are enforced by:
   a. the district attorney
   b. the lender
   c. the planning commission
   d. legal action by other owners

10. Which of the following is **NOT** done under the police power?
    a. Control land use
    b. Control rents
    c. Collect taxes
    d. Condemn as unfit for occupancy

11. Taking property for public use by utilizing the condemnation process is under the:
    a. police power of the state
    b. power of eminent domain
    c. power of adverse possession
    d. dedication rights of the state

12. The property of a person who dies intestate and has no heirs will escheat to the:
    a. U.S. government
    b. state government
    c. county government
    d. city government

13. Failure to assert a right within a reasonable period may cause the court to determine that the right to assert it is lost due to:
    a. laches
    b. novation
    c. rescission
    d. reformation

14. Which of the following is **NOT** a classification of real estate under zoning regulations?
    a. Industrial
    b. Residential
    c. Commercial
    d. Rental

III. Valuation and Market Analysis

15. Razing a hotel to build an office building is **MOST** likely an example of the principle of:
    a. highest and best use
    b. conformity
    c. progression
    d. change

16. The appraisal on a quality single-family residence would be **LEAST** influenced by:
    a. projected rental income
    b. its location
    c. recent comparable sales
    d. its floor plan

17. What is the function of a real estate appraiser?
    a. To set market value
    b. To determine market value
    c. To estimate market value
    d. To establish the cost

18. A loss in value because of lesser-value homes being built in the area would relate to the principle of:
    a. change
    b. contribution
    c. regression
    d. conformity

19. Market value is **BEST** defined as:
    a. assessed value less depreciation
    b. the maximum price a willing informed buyer would pay to a willing informed seller
    c. average sale price for similar properties in the current market
    d. utility value of the property to the owner

20. An element that does **NOT** create value is:
    a. demand
    b. cost
    c. transferability
    d. utility

21. Depreciation is divided into three types: physical deterioration, functional obsolescence, and:
    a. curable obsolescence
    b. economic obsolescence
    c. substitution obsolescence
    d. neo-obsolescence

IV. Financing

22. A property has a first note and deed of trust for $20,000 and a second note and deed of trust for $10,000. The first is in default and the lender agrees to take back a quitclaim deed. What is the position of the $10,000 second?
    a. The quitclaim deed eliminated the second.
    b. The second must be paid before a quitclaim can be given on the first.
    c. The second is now in first position.
    d. The $10,000 is still in second position.

23. Naked legal title **BEST** describes the interest of:
    a. trustee under a trust deed
    b. trustee in an agreement for sale
    c. trustee in a mortgage
    d. beneficiary to owner

24. After a Deed of Trust foreclosure sale, which of the following is true?
    a. A deed of reconveyance is given to the trustor.
    b. The note is marked *paid* and returned to the trustor.
    c. A trustee's deed is given to the new owner.
    d. The trust deed is returned to the trustor.

25. A mortgage loan payable in equal monthly installments that are sufficient to pay the principal in full during the term of the loan is called a(n):
    a. straight loan
    b. purchase money mortgage loan
    c. amortized loan
    d. conventional loan

26. A defeasance clause would **MOST** likely be found in a(n):
    a. mortgage or trust deed
    b. promissory note
    c. listing contract
    d. offer to purchase

27. A disadvantage of a conventional loan compared with a government insured or guaranteed loan is **MOST** likely to be a:
    a. lower interest rate
    b. longer term
    c. greater down payment
    d. longer processing period

28. The secondary mortgage market refers to:
    a. secondary financing
    b. loans made by non-institutional lenders
    c. high-risk loans
    d. the resale mortgage marketplace

29. "Regulation Z," Truth in Lending, does which of the following?
    a. Regulates the agency relationship between broker and sellers
    b. Discloses the annual cost of consumer credit
    c. Establishes federal usury rates
    d. Insures deposits made in member banks

V. Laws of Agency

30. A broker's authority includes:
    a. everything necessary to effectuate a sale
    b. all acts of the broker that are in the owner's best interest
    c. powers as a general agent
    d. only that authority granted or implied

31. The holder of a general power of attorney, in dealing with real property of his principal, could **NOT**:
    a. buy it
    b. sell it
    c. lease it
    d. give an exclusive right to sell listing

32. Which of the following is **TRUE?**
    a. All agency agreements must be in writing.
    b. Because agency is a contract, it must have consideration.
    c. A salesperson cannot create an agency relationship.
    d. An agency relationship can be created by the actions of a salesperson.

33. The duties of an agent to a principal do **NOT** include:
    a. loyalty
    b. obedience
    c. accountability
    d. guarantees

34. Dual agency is **BEST** described as:
    a. working with buyers and sellers
    b. selling an MLS listing
    c. representing buyers and sellers
    d. working with a buyer but collecting a fee from a seller

35. Commission sharing is an agreement between:
    a. broker and seller
    b. broker and buyer
    c. salespersons within an office
    d. cooperating brokers

36. Commission amounts are determined by:
    a. local custom
    b. negotiation
    c. multiple listing service
    d. the Real Estate Division

37. A licensed real estate broker operating a residential brokerage is usually which type of agent?
    a. General
    b. Special
    c. Universal
    d. Limited

38. If the principal dies or becomes incapacitated, which of the following will occur?
    a. Fee payment is accelerated
    b. Any purchase agreements in effect are cancelled
    c. Agency is terminated
    d. Expieration of the listing becomes indefinite

39. Which of the following is required for a valid agency relationship?
    a. Mutual consent
    b. Compensation
    c. Written agreement
    d. Brokerage license

VI. Mandated Disclosures

40. A buyer gives a post-dated check with an offer. The broker should:
    a. wait to see if the check is good before presenting the offer
    b. treat the check as any other check
    c. inform the seller as to the form of the deposit
    d. refuse to accept the offer

41. A broker, in dealing with the public, may **NOT:**
    a. keep silent a material fact in the transaction
    b. take an option
    c. accept a commission from both buyer and seller
    d. negotiate different commissions with different owners

42. In regard to the party the agent is **NOT** representing, which of the following is included in the agent's responsibilities?
    a. The agent has no responsibilities to the party she is not representing.
    b. The agent must give advice and counsel to the party.
    c. The agent must disclose material defects about the property.
    d. The agent must provide truthful information about the principal.

43. A salesperson, while listing a home, notices evidence of termite infestation. The salesperson would:
    a. inform the seller only
    b. inform the seller and disclose to buyer
    c. say nothing
    d. tell his/her broker

44. If a residence was built before this date, potential purchasers must be given a leaflet regarding possible lead paint contamination. What is the date?
    a. 1978
    b. 1988
    c. 1976
    d. 1990

45. An owner offers property on an "as is" basis. If the owner's agent has knowledge of a latent defect, the agent and owner must:
    a. repair the problem
    b. disclose the defect
    c. maintain confidentiality
    d. back out of the pending sale

VII. Contracts

46. Which of the following contracts does **NOT** have to be in writing to be enforceable?
    a. Promise to pay a debt to another.
    b. One-year lease starting immediately.
    c. Six-month lease starting in seven months.
    d. Contract for sale of real property valued at less than $500.

47. A voidable contract is:
    a. unenforceable
    b. illegal
    c. void
    d. valid until voided

48. A written agreement whereby the seller agreed to convey title to a house for $80,000 and the buyer agreed to purchase the house for $80,000 with the sale to be completed within 30 days is:
    a. an express unilateral executory contract
    b. an express bilateral executory contract
    c. an express bilateral executed contract
    d. a valid bilateral implied executory contract

49. Equitable title under a purchase contract would refer to:
    a. seller's interest
    b. buyer's interest
    c. broker's interest
    d. buyer's and seller's interest

50. An offer that fails to specify a definite period for acceptance:
    a. must be accepted immediately or it lapses
    b. cannot be accepted because it lacks definiteness
    c. is valid for a reasonable period of time
    d. remains valid for the statutory limit

51. A contract could **BEST** be described as a(n):
    a. written agreement between competent parties to do or refrain from doing a legal act
    b. offer and acceptance between parties to do a legal act
    c. written offer and acceptance between parties to do or not to do some legal act
    d. offer and acceptance between competent parties upon consideration to do or not do some legal act

52. A salesperson was presenting the buyer's offer to the seller and at the same time the buyer calls the salesperson to cancel his offer. What is the status of the buyer's offer?
    a. The buyer cannot back out.
    b. The buyer would owe the salesperson a commission.
    c. The offer is void.
    d. The buyer is bound to the seller's decision.

53. Failure to meet the requirement set forth in a contract is a:
    a. waiver
    b. breach
    c. novation
    d. reformation

54. Smith enters into a binding contract to buy Lot 3 in subdivision X from Brown. Before closing, Brown receives a higher offer for the lot and refuses to convey it, offering Smith instead an adjacent similar lot. What can happen now?
    a. Brown can return Smith's deposit and cancel the contract.
    b. Smith must accept the similar lot.
    c. Smith can sue for specific performance under the contract and force Brown to convey Lot 3.
    d. Smith must meet the higher price in order to get the lot.

55. A contract was ambiguous in that numbers written as words differed from the numerals. Which of the following statements is true?
    a. Words take precedence over numerals.
    b. Numerals take precedence over words.
    c. The contract is void.
    d. The contract is voidable.

VIII. Transfer of Property

56. A valid deed does **NOT** require a:
    a. signature of the grantee
    b. statement of consideration
    c. legal description of the property
    d. grantor with legal capacity

57. "To have and to hold" **MOST** likely would be included in a(n):
    a. habendum clause
    b. alienation clause
    c. mortgage
    d. legal description

58. A seller who will defend the title he is giving only against others who claim an interest through or under him would give a:
    a. general warranty deed
    b. special warranty deed
    c. bargain and sale deed
    d. quitclaim deed

59. Title is transferred by deed at the time:
    a. of delivery and acceptance
    b. the deed is executed
    c. of recording
    d. stated within the deed

60. A single taxpayer may exclude up to $250,000 of capital gain on the sale of her residence if:
    a. the taxpayer was over 62 years of age and had not previously used the exclusion.
    b. the residence had been the principal residence for two of the past five years.
    c. the taxpayer reinvested the sales proceeds in a new residence within 24 months.
    d. there are no special requirements for the exclusion of capital gain on a residence because such gains are not taxable.

61. Which of the following actions would **NOT** prevent a claim of adverse possession?
    a. Physically barring entry of adverse user.
    b. Ousting the adverse user.
    c. Ordering the adverse user to desist.
    d. Giving the adverse user express permission to use the property.

62. Standard coverage in a title insurance policy does **NOT** insure against:
    a. forged documents
    b. incompetent grantor
    c. questions of survey
    d. improperly delivered deed

IX. Practice of Real Estate

63. A broker is instructed not to show a property while the owner, who is white, is away. While the owner is out of town, a black couple requests to be shown the property. The broker should:
    a. show the property
    b. refuse to show the property
    c. ask HUD for an exception to the Fair Housing Act
    d. inform the prospects that the home is not available

64. A broker wants to advertise a property in a black neighborhood in a paper aimed at black readership. To do so, the broker **MUST:**
    a. indicate compliance with the fair housing laws
    b. also advertise in a paper (or papers) of general circulation
    c. include the Equal Housing Opportunity logo in the ad
    d. identify the location in the ad

65. The practice of making a profit by telling owners a particular minority group is moving into the neighborhood, thus inducing the owners to sell is called:
    a. blockbusting
    b. racial steering
    c. redlining
    d. puffing

66. A developer, when selling homes, would be advertising illegally if he advertised:
    a. for "singles only"
    b. to persons of a specific national origin
    c. for persons with a "poor credit history"
    d. to persons of a specific political party

67. A salesperson knows that the buyer's closing costs on a specific sale transaction are likely to be $1,500. The buyer wants to make an offer but is concerned about coming up with enough money for the down payment and closing costs. In order to help the buyer decide to make the offer, the salesperson says that the seller usually pays all the closing costs. This comforts the buyer and she makes the offer, only to find out about the $1,500 in closing costs that she is going to have to pay. What ethical or legal violation, if any, has the salesperson most likely committed?
    a. Modifying the listing agreement without the buyer's authorization.
    b. Misrepresenting to the seller the amount of the buyer's down payment.
    c. Underestimating closing costs to induce the buyer to make an offer.
    d. Misrepresenting the buyer's ability to repay a note to the seller.

68. A broker has just received a full price offer on one of her own listings. Minutes later, she receives an identical offer from another office. How should she proceed with the presentation of the offers?
    a. Present them in the order they were received.
    b. All offers should be presented at the same time.
    c. Present the first offer but inform the owner about the duplicate offer.
    d. Recommend acceptance of the first offer as the primary offer and the second offer as a backup offer.

69. Fraud is:
    a. deception not intended to harm
    b. deception intended to harm
    c. the same as misrepresentation
    d. similar to puffing

70. A real estate salesperson advises her buyer-client to take title to the house the married couple acquired as joint tenants. The salesperson:
    a. is required to make the recommendation
    b. in giving such advice is completing her professional obligation
    c. could be held liable for the unlawful practice of law
    d. did nothing wrong

71. When a broker secures a listing, which of the following actions would **NOT** require the owner's approval?
    a. Assigning the listing to another brokerage firm.
    b. Assigning the listing to another salesperson.
    c. Placing a sign on the property.
    d. Advertising the property for sale.

72. A broker should **NOT** tell a prospective purchaser:
    a. about property defects she was told about by a neighbor
    b. about zoning that makes the present use nonconforming
    c. that people of a different race live next door
    d. that the area has been designated for urban renewal

X. Real Estate Calculations

There are approximately five real estate math questions on the Nevada examination. Please review Part 3: Real Estate Mathematics to prepare for the Real Estate Calculations included on the examination.

XI. Specialty Areas

78. Regarding a lease assignment, the:
    a. assignee becomes primarily liable under the lease and the assignor is released
    b. assignor remains primarily liable under the lease
    c. assignee becomes primarily liable under the lease and the assignor retains secondary liability
    d. assignee is liable only to the assignor and the assignor is liable to the lessor

79. Carla leases a building and installs shelves, cabinets, a refrigerator, and other articles for use in her business. Therefore:
    a. Carla can remove the equipment installed before her lease expires.
    b. Carla must leave them for landlord's benefit.
    c. Carla can remove them at any time.
    d. The landlord must pay Carla for any articles left.

80. What is the purpose of the management agreement?
    a. To define the scope of responsibilities and authorities of the manager
    b. To create an opportunity for the manager to earn additional income through solicitation and acceptance of gratuities from suppliers of goods and services
    c. To hire the manager to find a buyer for the property
    d. To delegate to the manager the authority to purchase adjacent properties

NEVADA PRACTICE EXAMINATION

State-Specific Portion of Test

I. Commission Duties and Powers

1. Engaging in the sale of real estate when a license is required but in fact acting without a license is:
    a. a misdemeanor
    b. not subject to action by the Real Estate Commission because the party is not licensed
    c. subject to prosecution before any state court
    d. subject to action before the Real Estate Commission

2. The Real Estate Commission is required to do all the following **EXCEPT:**
    a. adopt regulations establishing standards for the operation of licensees' offices
    b. act in an advisory capacity to the Real Estate Division
    c. manage the Real Estate Division
    d. conduct hearings against Nevada licensees

3. The Real Estate Commission consists of:
   a. 7 members
   b. 6 members
   c. 5 members
   d. 4 members

4. The Real Estate Commission is headed by the:
   a. Administrator
   b. President
   c. Commissioner
   d. Governor

II. Licensing

5. A real estate license for which the fees have been paid, but the license has been held by the Real Estate Division for more than 30 days is an:
   a. inactive license
   b. inactive not renewed license
   c. inactive renewed license
   d. active license

6. The primary purpose of real estate licensing is to:
   a. have trained professionals
   b. protect brokers against incompetent salespeople
   c. avoid cutthroat competition
   d. protect the public

7. A licensed real estate broker from another state that desires to sell Nevada real estate must:
   a. obtain a Nevada real estate license
   b. obtain a sales agent license
   c. obtain a non-resident broker license
   d. obtain a cooperative brokers certificate

8. If your license expires, it is:
   a. automatically reinstated for 30 days
   b. automatically reinstated for six months
   c. automatically reinstated for one year
   d. terminated, but can be reinstated within one year

9. Full-time experience in real estate means:
   a. 20 hours a week for 48 weeks in a year completed in Nevada only
   b. 30 hours a week for 48 weeks in a year completed in Nevada only
   c. 30 hours a week for 48 weeks in a year completed anywhere in the United States
   d. 20 hours a week for 48 weeks completed anywhere in the United States

III. Standard of Conduct

10. The use of funds received by the broker in trust for other than their stated purpose is known as:
    a. conversion
    b. commingling
    c. diversion
    d. cooperative

11. Who may accept commission from an out-of-state broker?
    a. The referring salesperson
    b. The referring broker
    c. An unlicensed property manager
    d. Any individual who made the referral

12. A salesperson runs an ad in the local paper promoting a broker's listing. Which of the following is **TRUE?**
    a. The salesperson's name must appear.
    b. The broker's name must be larger in size than the salesperson's.
    c. The brokerage name must appear in the ad.
    d. The broker's telephone number must appear in the ad.

13. The term "commingling" means:
    a. the same office acting as buyer's broker and seller's broker for the same property
    b. seeking clients at social events
    c. mixing funds held for other persons with one's own money
    d. an office finding a buyer for another office's listing

14. "**R**" submits a purchase agreement to "**T**" who accepts it and makes minor changes. Then "**R**" dies. What is the status of the contract?
    a. Valid subject to approval of heirs.
    b. Binding to the heirs.
    c. Void because the changes were not initialed by the purchaser.
    d. Unenforceable because a new contract should have been written.

15. A *valid* contract could be unenforceable because of:
    a. lack of contractual capacity
    b. statute of limitations
    c. the absence of consideration
    d. an illegal purpose

16. Verbal testimony will be admitted as evidence for all of the following, **EXCEPT:**
    a. clarification of a contractual ambiguity
    b. showing a later modification to a written contract
    c. showing that fraud induced the contract
    d. showing that the contract means other than what it clearly says

17. The premium for title insurance is paid:
    a. monthly with the mortgage payment
    b. on an annual basis
    c. upon issuance of the title policy
    d. by the original subdivider for all subsequent issuances

18. A salesperson or broker-salesperson must provide any paperwork to the broker with whom he or she is associated within:
    a. within 5 calendar days after the paperwork is executed
    b. within 5 business days after the paperwork is executed
    c. within 7 calendar days after the paperwork is executed
    d. within 5 calendar days after the close of the transaction

19. A salesperson acting for the seller offers buyers a lower sales price without consulting the seller. The salesperson:
    a. has violated the law due to not obtaining authorization to lower the price
    b. has done nothing wrong
    c. is now acting for both parties
    d. has done the opposite of "puffing"

20. A "for sale" sign that has a licensee's name in 10 point print with the brokerage name in 14 point print:
    a. is in compliance with the law
    b. is violating the law
    c. is not regulated by signage rules
    d. needs to be in red ink

21. A real estate salesperson advised a prospective buyer that the property the buyer was considering was scheduled for annexation into the city limits. This disclosure constituted which of the following?
    a. Disloyalty to principal
    b. Misrepresentation
    c. Required disclosure to buyer
    d. Violation of disclosure of information by agent

22. Which of the following may a broker disclose to a prospective purchaser without permission?
    a. Why the seller must sell now.
    b. Why the property is not desirable.
    c. What the owner actually will accept.
    d. What the owner originally paid.

23. A property is purchased based on fraudulent statements by the listing broker. The purchase contract, which has not closed escrow, is **MOST** likely:

    a. void

    b. valid

    c. voidable

    d. illegal

24. A broker receives an oral offer over the telephone. The broker shall:

    a. refuse to present it until it is in writing

    b. refuse to present it unless he has earnest money

    c. present the oral offer

    d. tell the buyer that oral offers are illegal

25. The person who signs to show acceptance of the sales contract is the:

    a. offeror

    b. offeree

    c. grantor

    d. grantee

IV. Agency/Brokerage

26. Is it possible for a licensee to collect a commission from both parties to a transaction?

    a. The rules and regulations prohibit this.

    b. It is unethical.

    c. It is possible with full disclosure to both parties and with their written consent.

    d. It creates a dual agency, which is illegal.

27. In order to collect a commission in court, a licensee **MUST** prove:

    a. the listing was in effect at the time of closing

    b. the purchase contract was approved by the broker

    c. he was licensed when the claim was made

    d. the listing was signed by the broker

28. A commission is earned by a broker when the:

    a. escrow is paid

    b. funds are disbursed at settlement

    c. broker finds a ready, willing, and able buyer

    d. seller is paid

29. Nevada law requires which of the following to appear on the face of an exclusive listing contract?

    a. Expiration date

    b. Street address

    c. Annual taxes

    d. Mortgage balance

30. A valid exclusive right to sell listing contract:

    a. requires the seller to sell the property as per the terms of the listing contract

    b. requires the seller to pay the broker a commission if the broker performs in accordance with the terms of the listing contract

    c. allows the seller to sell the property without paying a commission

    d. is the same as an open listing

31. A contract in which a property owner employs a broker to market the property creates an agency relationship between which of the following:

    a. buyer and seller

    b. buyer and broker

    c. broker and seller

    d. broker, seller, and buyer

32. Which of the following is **TRUE?**

    a. All agency agreements must be in writing.

    b. Because agency is a contract, there must be consideration.

    c. A salesperson cannot create an agency relationship for his or her broker.

    d. None of the above.

33. An "exclusive right to represent a buyer" contract:
    a. is illegal in Nevada
    b. must be in writing
    c. can be drawn up only by a broker
    d. is a guarantee of commission

34. A broker's "client" is:
    a. the same thing as a "customer"
    b. the principal in a transaction
    c. anyone who contacts the broker
    d. an agent

35. A person holding a broker-salesperson license may:
    a. sell real estate only in Clark County
    b. operate his own brokerage firm
    c. manage a branch office of a brokerage
    d. there is no such license

36. A licensed salesperson may receive a commission from:
    a. his/her broker
    b. directly from the home seller
    c. directly from the home buyer
    d. from a loan officer

37. A form that informs a client of services owed to her by a licensee is:
    a. consent to act
    b. duties owed
    c. seller property disclosure
    d. purchase contract

38. A form that designates which party a licensee is representing is:
    a. duties owed
    b. confirmation regarding relationship
    c. consent to act
    d. no such form exists

V. Special Topic

39. The maximum amount of money that may be paid for any one licensee from the Recovery Fund is:
    a. $25,000
    b. $30,000
    c. $75,000
    d. $100,000

40. All of the following are true for a domestic well, **EXCEPT:**
    a. water right permit not required
    b. pumpage cannot exceed a daily maximum of 1,800 gallons
    c. water cannot be furnished by a water district
    d. subject to forfeiture or revocation

PART 3: REAL ESTATE MATHEMATICS

INTRODUCTION

The Nevada practice examination in Part 2 does not include real estate math. However, in the actual test, approximately 5 math questions are included in the salesperson test and 6 questions are included in the broker test. Explanations of math calculations are presented in the following chapters:

- Math Review   Chapter 28
- Word Problems and the   Chapter 28
  "T" Formula
- Area Problems   Chapter 28
- Commission Problems Math   Chapter 28
- Legal Descriptions Math   Chapter 3
- Real Property Tax Math   Chapter 6
- Proration Math   Chapter 18
- Closing Statements   Chapter 18
- Income Approach to Value   Chapter 24
  Math
- Profit and Loss Problems Math   Chapter 24
- Financing Math   Chapter 22

REAL ESTATE MATH PRACTICE QUESTIONS

The following real estate math questions will prepare you for the Nevada Real Estate Examination.

1. A nine percent (9%) straight loan at 75% of a property's appraised value earned first year's interest of $9,840. What was the property's valuation?
   a. $82,000
   b. $96,840
   c. $109,333
   d. $145,777

2. A duplex that rents for $550 is in an area with a smaller duplex in similar condition that rents for $240 per unit and just sold for $67,200. Using this information, the larger duplex would have a value of:
   a. $67,200
   b. $70,000
   c. $77,000
   d. $77,500

3. Adam owns a property free and clear valued at $30,000, on which he plans to build a building and lease it at an annual rent of $65,000. Operating expenses are estimated to be $11,000 per year. If an 8% net return is expected on the total investment, what will be the cost of the improvements?
   a. $435,750
   b. $595,000
   c. $645,000
   d. $675,000

4. Gina's home was recently appraised at $105,000. It has depreciated 30% in the three years since it was purchased. What was the original cost?
   a. $ 80,769
   b. $136,500
   c. $139,650
   d. $150,000

5. Mike bought a house for $60,000. Six months later he had to move and sold it for $54,600. His percentage loss is calculated by using which of the following:
   a. $5,400 divided by $54,600
   b. $5,400 divided by $60,000
   c. $60,000 divided by $54,600
   d. $54,600 divided by $60,000

6. Sheila borrows 80% of the appraised value of a house. If the interest on the amount borrowed is $7,012.50 each year at an annual rate of 8¼%, what is the appraised value of the house?
   a. $85,000
   b. $103,125
   c. $106,250
   d. $101,250

7. A bank agrees to lend an amount equal to 66% of its appraised value at an interest rate of 9% annum. The first year's interest is $1,800. What is the appraised value, rounded to the nearest $100?
   a. $13,200
   b. $20,000
   c. $30,300
   d. $58,800

8. A commercial property is estimated to generate $5,500 in monthly net income. Using a capitalization rate of 11%, what would the appraiser's opinion of value be?
   a. $726,000
   b. $50,000
   c. $600,000
   d. $60,500

9. In constructing his financial report, Alan Smithee estimates that his real estate holdings have appreciated by 18% since purchase. If the original value was $585,000, what would Alan's balance sheet show now?

   a. $479,700
   b. $526,500
   c. $585,000
   d. $690,300

10. A broker writes a contract on a $100,000 property with a 5% earnest deposit. Thirty days later, the buyers give the broker an additional $10,000 toward the home. What is the balance due at closing from the buyers if they secure an 80% loan to value mortgage?

   a. $2,500
   b. $5,000
   c. $10,000
   d. $15,000

11. Ronny sold a house for $129,500. The buyer's lender required a 20% down payment and a 2% origination charge on the mortgage. The buyer also had $750 in closing costs. What is the total amount the buyer will need to close?

   a. $25,900
   b. $27,972
   c. $28,490
   d. $28,722

12. A property was assessed at $22,000 and the asking price was $67,500. It was sold for $63,400 and the lender's appraised value was $65,500. The loan to value ratios will be based upon which amount?

   a. $22,000
   b. $63,400
   c. $65,500
   d. $67,500

13. The loan on a property is 65% of its appraised value. If the interest rate is 7¾% and the monthly interest payments are $210.80, what is the appraised value?

   a. $27,273
   b. $32,640
   c. $50,215
   d. $38,900

14. A seller accepts an offer to purchase in the amount of $395,000. After the seller has paid a brokerage fee of 5.5%, paid off a loan of $300,000, and paid various settlement fees totaling 4% of the sale price, what are the seller's net proceeds?

   a. $373,275
   b. $73,275
   c. $58,344
   d. $57,475

15. Rosalyn Harris bought a house for $120,000. She put 20% down and borrowed the rest on a mortgage. At the end of the first year, her principal had been paid down by $480 and the property values in that neighborhood had risen by 5%. Rosalyn's equity at the end of that first year was:

   a. $23,512
   b. $30,480
   c. $96,000
   d. $6,000

16. The Valmonts receive two offers on their property, which is listed for $140,000. Gary Farber offers to pay $138,000 cash for the house. Annette Adams offers $141,000, putting 20% down, if the Valmonts will pay three points to her lender for the mortgage loan the buyer needs. What is the difference between the two offers?

   a. $384
   b. $1,128
   c. $2,000
   d. $3,000

17. A buyer is to assume a seller's existing loan with an outstanding balance of $20,000 as of the date of closing. The interest rate is 9% and payments are made in arrears with the last payment made on October 1. Closing is set for October 11. What will be the entry in the seller's closing statement?

    a. $150 debit
    b. $150 credit
    c. $50 credit
    d. $50 debit

18. A buyer assumed a seller's existing 11%, $80,000 first deed of trust on the settlement date of June 13. The seller made the monthly payment on June 1 with interest in arrears. Which of the following is a **CORRECT** settlement entry for the interest?

    a. $439.92 seller's credit
    b. $293.28 buyer's debit
    c. $439.92 seller's debit
    d. $293.28 seller's debit

19. On June 6 an escrow closed. The annual taxes were $775 and the water bill of $86 for the current year was paid in full on January 1. If these payments are prorated, what amount will be returned to the seller?

    a. $373
    b. $418
    c. $490
    d. $508

20. For the purchase of a house, a buyer assumes the seller's loan balance of $43,000 with 9.5% interest in arrears. If the September 1 payment has been made and the closing is scheduled for September 20, how much credit for interest is the buyer entitled to at closing?

    a. $114
    b. $216
    c. $227
    d. $340

21. A property is sold on July 15. The prepaid annual insurance is $750 and the annual water bill of $90 was prepaid on January 1. If these payments are prorated, what amount will be returned to the seller?

    a. $350
    b. $387
    c. $403
    d. $455

22. Mr. Warner's annual insurance premium was due April 1. He paid a $625 premium for the coming year on that date. If he sells his house on August 15 of this year, what prorated amount will be returned to him?

    a. $234
    b. $392
    c. $417
    d. $625

23. A sale is closed on February 13. The buyer is assuming the seller's mortgage, which has an outstanding balance of $28,000 as of the date of closing. The annual interest rate is 7¾% and is paid in arrears. What would be the interest proration appearing in the buyer's closing statement if the last payment was made on February 1?

    a. $180.83 debit
    b. $72.24 debit
    c. $72.24 credit
    d. $253.19 credit

24. A property is sold for $100,000, with 5% paid with the offer as a good faith deposit and an additional $10,000 paid 20 days later. How much does the buyer pay at closing?

    a. $10,000
    b. $15,000
    c. $80,000
    d. $85,000

25. Tina earns a 6% commission on the first $75,000 of sales for the month and 3% for all sales over that amount. If Tina sold houses totaling $162,100 for the month, how much more would she have earned at a straight 6% commission?
    a. $810.50
    b. $1,113.00
    c. $2,613.00
    d. $9,726.00

26. An owner lists a lot for sale with a broker to net $27,500 after paying the broker a 7% commission. At what price would the broker have to sell the property to receive a 7% commission?
    a. $29,425
    b. $29,569
    c. $31,350
    d. $32,125

27. A seller paid $32,000 for a house and now wants to sell it at 20% profit after paying a broker a 5% commission. What is the selling price?
    a. $34,689.24
    b. $35,096.00
    c. $36,480.00
    d. $40,421.05

28. An office rents for $665 a month and measures 20 by 42 feet. The advertised annual rent per square foot for this space would be
    a. $9.50
    b. $8.40
    c. $7.92
    d. $12.00

29. Two brokers agreed to split a 4½% commission on a 50-50 basis on the sale of a property for $162,500. The listing salesperson agreed to a 50-50 split with his employing broker. The salesperson would be paid a commission of
    a. $8,125.00
    b. $4,875.00
    c. $3,656.25
    d. $1,828.13

30. A property described as the N½ of the NW¼ of the NW¼ contains:
    a. 10 acres
    b. 20 acres
    c. 40 acres
    d. 160 acres

31. A deposit receipt said, "Seller to take back a second trust deed securing a note for $11,400 payable $240.00 or more per month, including interest at 7% per annum from March 15, 2009." If the first payment date on the second trust deed note is April 15, 2009, how much of the regular payment will go to the reduction of principal?
    a. $90.25
    b. $149.75
    c. $154.50
    d. $173.50

32. An investor was going to have a building constructed at a cost of $300,000. He had a tenant who was willing to lease the property for $5,000 a month on a long-term lease. He calculated that the expenses would amount to $12,000 per year. The desired rate of return was 12%. How much could he afford to pay for the land?
    a. $80,000
    b. $100,000
    c. $104,000
    d. $110,000

33. A woman purchased a property at 20% less than the listed price and later sold the property for the original listed price. What was the percentage of profit?
    a. 10%
    b. 20%
    c. 25%
    d. 40%

34. Cameron owns a 30-unit apartment building next to a loud nightclub. Cameron loses $400 net income per month because of the loud noise. Many appraisers suggest using a 12% capitalization rate for this type of property in that neighborhood. Cameron's property suffers a loss in value of approximately:

a. $4,800

b. $48,000

c. $40,000

d. $2,400

35. A woman bought two 60-foot lots for $18,000 net each and divided them into three lots of equal frontage, which she sold for a price of $15,000 each. Her percentage of gross profit was most nearly:

a. 15%

b. 20%

c. 25%

d. 40%

36. A parcel of vacant land measuring 110 yards by 220 yards would contain how many acres?

a. 2½

b. 5

c. 10

d. 40

37. A seller wants to net $11,600 from the sale of his house after he pays the cost of the sale, which includes a 5½% brokerage fee and 6½% for the closing costs. What must the sales price be for the seller to net $11,600?

a. $13,000

b. $12,992

c. $13,182

d. $13,300

38. If real property in your area is assessed at 35% of taxable value and is taxed at $2.75 per $100 of assessed value, the tax on a property with a taxable value of $130,000 would be:

a. $12,512.50

b. $3,575.00

c. $2,502.50

d. $1,251.25

39. A property with a taxable value of $120,000 is assessed at 35%. If the tax rate is $4.55 per $100 of assessed value, the property taxes would be:

a. $1,911

b. $2,322

c. $3,822

d. $5,460

40. An owner-occupied residential property with a taxable value of $45,000 is assessed for tax purposes at the prescribed rate, and the tax rate is $ 2.50 per $100 of assessed value. The tax on the property would be:

a. $1,125.00

b. $393.75

c. $11,250.00

d. $39,375.00

Appendix B
Practice State Examination: Answer Key

NATIONAL PORTION OF NEVADA TEST

I. Property Ownership

1. c	2. d	3. a	4. d	5. c
6. c	7. b			

II. Land Use Controls and Regulations

8. c	9. d	10. c	11. b	12. b
13. a	14. d			

III. Valuation and Market Analysis

15. a	16. a	17. c	18. c	19. b
20. b	21. b			

IV. Financing

22. c	23. a	24. c	25. c	26. a
27. c	28. d	29. b		

V. Laws of Agency

30. d	31. a	32. d	33. d	34. c
35. d	36. b	37. b	38. c	39. a

VI. Mandated Disclosures

40. c	41. a	42. c	43. b	44. a
45. b				

VII. Contracts

46. b	47. d	48. b	49. b	50. c
51. d	52. c	53. b	54. c	55. a

VIII. Transfer of Property

56. a	57. a	58. b	59. a	60. b
61. c	62. c			

IX. Practice of Real Estate

63. b	64. b	65. a	66. b	67. c
68. b	69. b	70. c	71. b	72. c

X. Real Estate Calculations

See Real Estate Mathematics.

XI. Specialty Areas

78. c	79. a	80. a

STATE-SPECIFIC PORTION OF TEST

I. Commission Duties and Powers

1. c	2. c	3. c	4. b

II. Licensing

5. c	6. d	7. d	8. d	9. c

III. Standards of Conduct

10. a	11. b	12. c	13. c	14. c
15. b	16. d	17. c	18. a	19. a
20. a	21. c	22. b	23. c	24. c
25. b				

IV. Agency/Brokerage

26. c	27. c	28. c	29. a	30. b
31. c	32. d	33. b	34. b	35. c
36. a	37. b	38. b		

V. Special Topic

39. d	40. d

REAL ESTATE MATHEMATICS

1. d	2. c	3. c	4. d	5. b
6. c	7. c	8. c	9. d	10. b
11. d	12. b	13. c	14. d	15. b
16. a	17. d	18. d	19. c	20. b
21. b	22. b	23. c	24. d	25. c
26. b	27. d	28. a	29. d	30. b
31. d	32. b	33. c	34. c	35. c
36. b	37. c	38. d	39. a	40. b

Appendix C
Reviewing Your Understanding: Answer Key

Chapter 1:

1. c	2. a	3. c	4. b	5. b
6. a	7. d	8. c	9. b	10. c
11. d	12. b	13. a	14. b	15. d
16. a	17. c	18. a	19. d	20. b

Chapter 2:

1. a	2. b	3. d	4. d	5. a
6. b	7. c	8. d	9. c	10. c
11. c	12. d	13. b	14. b	15. c
16. d	17. b	18. c	19. b	20. d

Chapter 3:

Practical Application:

1. Section 33
2. 3 miles
3. a. 5 miles
   b. 3 miles
4. 11,520 acres
5. $300,000
6. 12 lots

Reviewing Your Understanding:

1. b	2. b	3. a	4. b	5. a
6. c	7. c	8. d	9. c	10. d
11. a	12. c	13. c	14. b	15. c
16. d	17. b	18. b	19. c	20. b

Chapter 4:

1. c	2. c	3. a	4. c	5. b
6. d	7. c	8. c	9. b	10. d
11. d	12. c	13. b	14. b	15. b
16. a	17. c	18. b	19. d	20. d

Chapter 5:

1. a	2. a	3. c	4. c	5. a
6. a	7. d	8. c	9. c	10. a
11. c	12. c	13. d	14. b	15. d
16. d	17. a	18. b	19. d	20. c

Chapter 6:

Practical Application:

1. D

2. D

3. C

Reviewing Your Understanding:

1. a	2. a	3. c	4. d	5. d
6. c	7. b	8. b	9. c	10. b
11. c	12. a	13. c	14. c	15. b
16. a	17. a	18. b	19. c	20. c

Chapter 7:

1. b	2. d	3. c	4. b	5. a
6. b	7. a	8. d	9. c	10. d
11. a	12. b	13. b	14. a	15. b
16. d	17. b	18. c	19. a	20. c

Chapter 8:

1. d	2. a	3. c	4. b	5. b
6. b	7. d	8. c	9. a	10. c
11. d	12. a	13. d	14. c	15. b
16. b	17. c	18. c	19. a	20. b

Chapter 9:

1. d	2. d	3. c	4. b	5. c
6. c	7. d	8. c	9. a	10. b
11. b	12. d	13. c	14. d	15. c
16. d	17. c	18. d	19. a	20. b

Chapter 10:

1. d	2. b	3. c	4. b	5. c
6. b	7. a	8. d	9. c	10. c
11. d	12. b	13. b	14. a	15. a
16. c	17. a	18. a	19. a	20. c

Chapter 11:

1. d	2. d	3. d	4. a	5. b
6. a	7. c	8. b	9. b	10. c
11. c	12. d	13. d	14. c	15. c
16. c	17. a	18. b	19. a	20. d

Chapter 12:

1. b	2. b	3. c	4. d	5. c
6. c	7. b	8. a	9. c	10. c
11. d	12. c	13. a	14. c	15. a
16. d	17. c	18. d	19. d	20. c

Chapter 13:

1. a	2. c	3. c	4. d	5. b
6. d	7. d	8. b	9. a	10. c
11. d	12. b	13. a	14. b	15. d
16. a	17. c	18. b	19. d	20. a

Chapter 14:

1. d	2. b	3. c	4. a	5. c
6. d	7. d	8. c	9. a	10. b
11. c	12. c	13. b	14. c	15. c
16. d	17. a	18. b	19. a	20. c

Chapter 15:

1. b	2. d	3. c	4. d	5. a
6. b	7. b	8. d	9. c	10. d
11. d	12. a	13. b	14. a	15. c
16. d	17. d	18. c	19. c	20. c

Chapter 16:

1. d	2. a	3. c	4. b	5. d
6. a	7. a	8. a	9. b	10. c
11. c	12. b	13. a	14. c	15. c
16. b	17. d	18. b	19. b	20. c

Chapter 17:

1. d	2. c	3. b	4. b	5. c
6. a	7. b	8. a	9. b	10. d
11. b	12. c	13. d	14. b	15. b
16. b	17. c	18. b	19. b	20. d

Chapter 18:

1. d	2. c	3. b	4. d	5. d
6. b	7. d	8. a	9. b	10. a
11. a	12. a	13. a	14. a	15. a
16. b	17. b	18. b	19. d	20. a

Chapter 19:

1. c	2. d	3. a	4. d	5. a
6. c	7. a	8. b	9. d	10. b
11. d	12. b	13. d	14. a	15. c
16. a	17. a	18. b	19. d	20. b

Chapter 20:

1. d	2. d	3. a	4. a	5. b
6. b	7. b	8. d	9. b	10. d
11. b	12. d	13. a	14. d	15. d
16. b	17. b	18. c	19. d	20. a

Chapter 21:

1. b	2. c	3. b	4. a	5. d
6. c	7. b	8. a	9. c	10. a
11. c	12. b	13. b	14. c	15. b
16. a	17. d	18. c	19. b	20. b

Chapter 22:

1. d	2. a	3. b	4. c	5. b
6. d	7. b	8. d	9. c	10. b
11. c	12. c	13. b	14. c	15. c
16. a	17. c	18. b	19. b	20. b

Chapter 23:

1. b	2. c	3. b	4. a	5. c
6. a	7. d	8. d	9. c	10. d
11. a	12. c	13. a	14. b	15. b
16. b	17. c	18. b	19. d	20. d

Chapter 24:

1. c	2. d	3. c	4. b	5. d
6. a	7. b	8. a	9. c	10. a
11. b	12. d	13. b	14. b	15. c
16. b	17. c	18. c	19. b	20. d

Chapter 25:

1. c	2. d	3. c	4. a	5. d
6. d	7. b	8. b	9. b	10. b
11. c	12. b	13. b	14. c	15. c
16. a	17. c	18. b	19. b	20. d

Chapter 26:

1. a	2. c	3. c	4. b	5. b
6. b	7. d	8. d	9. d	10. d
11. c	12. b	13. b	14. b	15. b
16. b	17. b	18. b	19. c	20. b

Chapter 27:

1. d	2. d	3. d	4. c	5. d
6. c	7. b	8. b	9. a	10. c
11. b	12. a	13. c	14. c	15. c
16. c	17. b	18. a	19. a	20. a

Chapter 28:

1. b	2. d	3. d	4. c	5. c
6. b	7. c	8. c	9. d	10. a

Glossary

15-day notice notifies the owner and prime contractor for the work of improvement on a multifamily or single-family residence of the intent to lien 15 days before recording a notice of lien

90-day clause provides for the listing broker to be compensated if a buyer was procured during the period of the listing contract and subsequently agreed to purchase the property within the 90-day period

100 percent brokerage the salesperson receives all of the commission collected by the brokerage; however, the salesperson must pay a monthly fee to the brokerage and sometimes a transaction fee as well

abstract of title summary of all conveyances and legal proceedings affecting title to a parcel of real estate

acceleration clause enables the lender to call the loan due and payable in the event of a default

accord and satisfaction occurs when the parties voluntarily agree to complete the contract, even though all of the terms and conditions have not been met

accountability one of the broker agent's fiduciary duties; the responsibility to account for any trust funds received by the broker

accretion slow buildup of land by natural forces such as wind or water

accrual basis a method of accounting whereby revenue is recognized when it is earned and expenses are recorded when they are due rather than when paid

accurate legal description a description recognized by law; a description by which property can be definitely located by reference to government surveys or approved recorded maps

acknowledgement the formal declaration by a person executing an instrument that he or she is freely signing it

acre-foot volume of water equal to an area of one acre with a depth of one foot (43,560 cubic feet) and equal to 325,850 gallons

active participation a lower level of involvement than material participation

actual damages the estimated money equivalent for loss or injury sustained

actual notice knowledge one has gained based on what has been actually seen, heard, read, or observed

ad valorem tax property tax, which means "according to value"; each piece of property is taxed according to its assessed value

adjustable rate mortgage (ARM) borrower and lender share risks of a fluctuating interest rate economy

adjusted gross income a federal income tax amount that is determined by subtracting amounts specifically authorized by the Internal Revenue Code from gross income

Administrator appointed by the Director of the Nevada Department of Business and Industry; heads the Real Estate Division

Administrative Code authorized by Nevada Revised Statutes and allows the Real Estate Commission or the Administrator with the approval of the Commission to interpret the law and develop Code that clarifies Chapter 645 of the Statutes

advance fees fees received by the real estate brokerage before the completion of the real estate transaction

advance rentals rents received in advance of the period for which they are paid

adverse possession a method of acquiring property based on open and notorious possession, under a claim of right, color of title, continuous use for five years, and the payment of taxes

affidavit of completion of forfeiture a written statement recorded by a vendor that terminates a buyer's interest when the buyer defaults on a land contract

agency a relationship between a principal and an agent arising out of a brokerage agreement whereby the agent is engaged to do certain acts on behalf of the principal in dealings with a third party

agency coupled with an interest an irrevocable agency in which the agent has an interest in the property as part or all of his compensation

agent one who represents another called a principal and who has authority to act for the principal in dealing with third parties

agricultural lease a lease by owners of agricultural land with tenants who entered one of two types of agreements: cash rent or sharecropping

air lots air-specific elevation boundaries over a parcel of land

air rights allow the owner the right to reasonable use of the airspace for light and air

alienation the act of transferring real property from one person to another

alienation by descent the transfer of property after death in accordance with the laws of descent when a person dies intestate

alienation by will the transfer of property after death pursuant to the terms of the decedent's valid will

alienation clause in a deed of trust or mortgage, a provision that if the secured property is sold or transferred, the lender has the option of accelerating the loan and declaring the entire unpaid balance immediately due and payable; also called a "due on-sale" clause

all-inclusive deed of trust *see* wrap-around mortgage

allodial system establishes absolute ownership, which means there is no obligation to pay rent or services

alluvion surface land gained by accretion

amenity a condition of agreeable living or a beneficial influence resulting from the location

American Land Title Association (ALTA) association of land title companies throughout the country

Americans with Disabilities Act (ADA) the first comprehensive American civil rights law for people with disabilities; affects every employer, business, and public service, including real estate

amortized loan the liquidation of a financial obligation on an installment basis, which includes both principal and interest

annual net income gross income less costs and expense for a one year period

annual percentage rate (APR) the cost of credit as determined in accordance with Regulation Z of the Federal Truth in Lending Act

anticipation value created by expectation of benefits to be collected in the future

appraisal an estimate or opinion of value as of a specified date based on analysis of factual data

appraiser may either be staff appraisers working for county assessors, banks, or the government, or they may work as independent fee appraisers

appraising an important division of the real estate business Appraisals are necessary for many purposes, including determining insurance value, assessed value, condemnation value, and so on

appreciation an increase in property value

appurtenances rights, privileges, or improvements that belong to and pass with a property

appurtenant easement attached to the land and if the property is sold, the easement is transferred to the new owner

Articles of Incorporation a document filed in the state in which a corporation is formed that establishes a corporate entity

Articles of Organization a document filed with the Office of the Secretary of State of the State of Nevada to form a Nevada limited liability company

asbestos mineral fiber found in rocks, which is fire resistant and extremely durable

assemblage the process of combining two or more parcels into one

assessed value the value put on the property for the purpose of computing *ad valore*m property taxes

asset something of value; a useful item of property, owned by a person

assignee third party to the contract

assignment a transfer to another of any property or right; the transfer of one's entire interest in property

assignor the original party to the contract

associate broker has the same privileges and responsibilities as licensed sales agents

avulsion a sudden loss of land, which may occur as a result of a sudden shift in a riverbed, volcanic action, an earthquake, or another cause

back-end ratio a loan qualifying ratio based on total living expenses

balance the principle that implies a balance between net return on investment and expenses of labor, capital, management, and land

balloon payment a note's final installment payment, which is greater than the preceding payments and pays the note in full

bankruptcy insolvency; a legal process wherein one is declared bankrupt and the estate of the bankrupt is managed under court supervision for the creditors' benefit

bare legal title the trustee has the power of sale if the borrower defaults

bargain and sale deed a deed that contains no covenants, but does imply that the grantor owns the property being conveyed

base lines imaginary lines that are east-west lines parallel to the latitudinal lines

bench mark brass marker embedded in a road or permanently attached to a tree or iron post to give the elevation based on the official datum

beneficiary one for whose benefit a trust is created; the lender in a deed of trust arrangement

bequest the transfer of personal property through a will

bilateral contract two-sided contract, with each side making a promise of performance that is binding upon both parties; most real estate contracts are bilateral contracts

blanket mortgage mortgagor pledges more than one property to secure the note

blind ad advertising property in a manner that implies that no salesperson or broker is taking part in the offer for sale, lease, or exchange

blind trust a trust in which the beneficiary is not disclosed

blockbusting illegal practice of inducing panic selling in a neighborhood for profit, based on the introduction of minority homeowners into a neighborhood

book value an accounting term for the cost of real estate less depreciation recorded for accounting and tax purposes

boot unlike property paid in a tax deferred exchange

breach of contract occurs when either party defaults on the contract; rescission, damages, liquidated damages, or suit for specific performance are actions that may result from a breach of contract

broker absence a broker shall not be absent from his or her business for 30 days or more if he or she is the only broker in his or her office unless he or she inactivates his or her license or otherwise notifies the Real Estate Division in advance

brokerage the business of bringing buyers and sellers together in the marketplace for a fee called a commission

brokerage agreement an oral or written contract between a client and a broker in which the broker agrees to accept valuable consideration from the client or another person for assisting, soliciting, or negotiating the sale, purchase, option, rental, or lease of real property, or the sale, exchange, option, or purchase of a business; the term does not include a property management agreement

Brown v Board of Education the US Supreme Court decision in this case outlawed segregation in schools and marked the beginning of the end of the era of legalized segregation

brownfields a property, the expansion, redevelopment, or reuse of which may be complicated by the presence or potential presence of a hazardous substance, pollutant, or contaminant

budget loan when the borrower is forced to put away money in trust for the payment of the property taxes and insurance

budget mortgage features loan payments that include principal, interest, taxes, and insurance (often called PITI)

buffer zone strip of land that separates one land use from another

bundle of rights property rights that include the rights of control, possession, quiet and peaceful enjoyment, disposition, and encumbrance

business the tangible assets and goodwill of an existing enterprise

business broker a person who, while acting as a real estate broker, real estate broker-salesperson, or real estate salesperson for another and for compensation or with the intention or expectation of receiving compensation; (1) sells, exchanges, options, or purchases a business; (2) negotiates or offers, attempts or agrees to negotiate the sale, exchange, option, or purchase of a business; or (3) lists or solicits prospective purchasers of a business

Business Broker Permit issued by the Nevada Real Estate Division to a real estate broker, broker-salesperson, or salesperson and required before engaging in business brokerage

business brokerage a Nevada broker that offers services for the sale or purchase of a business

business trust a trust created by a trust instrument under which property, including the operation of a business or professional services entity, is held, managed, and controlled by a trustee for the benefit of the beneficiaries

caissons small parcels of land that serve as support foundations

capacity competent party; a person considered legally capable of entering into a binding contract

capacity (in connection with the granting of credit) ability to pay a debt or loan being contemplated

capital asset generally includes all assets owned as an investment or for personal purposes, for example, stocks, bonds, a personal residence, household furnishings, cars, precious metals, and assets used in a trade or business

capital gain or loss gain or loss on the sale of a capital asset

capital improvements include carpeting, window coverings, new roof, new plumbing or electrical systems, building additions, and major repairs such as a new driveway, refurbishing stucco, or new landscaping

capitalization rate the percentage rate or rate of interest considered a reasonable return on the investment

cash basis a method of accounting whereby revenue and expenses are recognized when cash is received or disbursed

cash rent a lease between an agricultural landowner and a tenant, whereby the tenant pays the landowner a specified amount of money in advance in exchange for the right of the tenant to use the agricultural land to plant, maintain, and harvest a crop upon the land

caveat emptor a Latin phrase meaning "let the buyer beware"; the legal maxim stating that the buyer must examine the goods or property and buy at his or her own risk

caveat venditor a Latin phrase meaning "let the seller beware"

cease and desist orders an order issued by a legal authority to discontinue a certain action

Certificate of Eligibility determines a veteran borrower's maximum entitlement

Certificate of Occupancy a government-issued document that states a structure meets local zoning and building code requirements and is ready for use

Certificate of Purchase a document issued to the successful bidder at a sale held by the county treasurer for delinquent property taxes

certificate of sale a document issued to the highest bidder at a judicial foreclosure sale

chain of title a series of conveyances, encumbrances, and other instruments affecting the title from the time original patent was granted, or as far back as records are available; a history of the recorded ownership of real estate and claims against title to real estate

change a principle in valuation that considers economic, social, and physical changes

Chapter 645 the chapter of the Nevada Revised Statutes and Administrative Code entitled Real Estate Brokers and Salesmen

character desire or willingness to pay a debt or loan being contemplated

chattel real a leasehold estate

Civil Rights Act of 1866 guarantees property rights to all citizens regardless of race

Civil Rights Act of 1964 prohibited discrimination in programs receiving federal financial assistance, but had little impact in the housing market

clandestine drug laboratory a facility that uses chemicals and equipment in the manufacture of illegal substances; meth lab

client a person (principal) who has entered into a brokerage agreement with a broker or a property management agreement with a broker

closing costs expenses paid by the buyer and seller to complete the transaction

clouds on title a claim or document that affects title to real estate; the actual cloud may ultimately prove invalid, but its existence mars the title

CLUE report an insurance industry report based on a national database of claims and inquiries

cluster zoning zoning that changes street patterns and reduces the size of individual lots, but provides for the same number of residences with more open recreational space and less traffic congestion than on a regular grid pattern of subdivision

Code of Ethics articles that pertain to the REALTOR's relation to clients, other real estate agents, and the public

coinsurance clause the insurer and the insured share the insurance risk; calculated on the policy amount and the percentage of the actual insured values

collateral security pledged for the payment of a loan

color of title that which appears to be a good title but, in fact, is not; for example, a forged deed

commercial banks banks specializing in checking and savings accounts and short-term loans

commercial facilities facilities "that are intended for nonresidential use" by a private entity and "whose operations affect commerce"

commercial property insurance covers most types of commercial buildings

commingled the mixing of clients' or customers' funds with an agent's personal funds

commission an agent's compensation for performing the duties of his or her agency agreement

commission sharing brokerage a percentage of the commission amount collected by the brokerage is paid to the salesperson; the commission sharing percentages generally range from 50 to 70 percent, depending on the experience and volume of production by the licensed salesperson

common elements all portions of a common interest community other than units

common interest communities a development with common elements, including cooperatives, condominiums, planned unit developments, and time-shares

common law based on tradition, customs, and usage; generally unwritten in statute or code; was developed in England and transferred to the United States with the early colonists

Common Promotional Plan any offering, sale, or lease of subdivided land by a developer or a group of developers acting in concert; the land is contiguous or is known, designated, or advertised as a common unit or development or by a common name

Community Manager Certificate a certificate that must be obtained from the Real Estate Division before an individual is allowed to manage a Common Interest Community

community property co-ownership wherein husband and wife are treated as equal partners with each owning a one-half interest

community property with rights of survivorship allow a married couple to receive benefits under the federal tax code for community property while avoiding probate

Community Reinvestment Act an act passed by Congress to help prevent redlining and discrimination by lenders and to ensure that banks "meet the credit needs of the community" in which they have branches and take in deposits

comprehensive development plan a development plan that provides housing, recreation, and commercial development in one self-contained development or in urban high-rise facilities where individuals can live, work, and play within the same area

compaction a process in which soil particles are forced closely together

Comprehensive Environmental Response, Compensation, and Liability Act (CERCLA) the law that was enacted by Congress in 1980 in response to the environmental and public health hazards imposed by improper disposition of hazardous waste

Community Reinvestment Act an act by Congress to help prevent redlining and discrimination by lenders

competition the appraisal principle that states that excess profits generate competition; if too much competition is attracted to an area, losses in profits will result

Competitive Market Analysis a comparison of prices of recently sold homes that are similar to a seller's home

comprehensive development plan provides housing, recreation, and commercial development in one self-contained development or in urban high-rise facilities where individuals can live, work, and play within the same area

concurrent ownership or co-ownership ownership by two or more persons at the same time

condemnation the act of taking private property for public use by a political subdivision through the exercise of the power of eminent domain

condominiums a system of individual ownership of units in a multifamily structure, combined with an undivided interest in the common areas of the structure and the land

confidentiality a part of the agent's fiduciary duty to treat information from the client with confidence

Confirmation Regarding Agency Relationship a state mandated form to be obtained by a licensee that confirms the real estate agent relationship with the seller, buyer, or both the seller and buyer

confiscation right of government to seize property without compensation in the interest of national security

conforming loan a conventional loan that follows Fannie Mae and Freddie Mac residential loan uniform documentation and qualification parameters

conformity appraisal principle sating that a property achieves maximum value when the property reasonably conforms to the neighborhood

Consent to Act a form that must be reviewed, considered and approved or rejected by both parties to a transaction when there is multiple representation

consideration the inducement to contract; is something of value, such as money, property, personal services, or the promise to perform a specific action; consideration makes a contract enforceable

construction loan an open-end mortgage loan that finances the cost of materials and labor for a building; short-term loan that must be replaced with permanent financing

constructive eviction termination of a rental agreement by the landlord's noncompliance

constructive notice notice is given by a recorded document because a person could have discovered certain facts upon reasonable investigation, and a "reasonable man" in the same situation would have conducted such an investigation

contract legally enforceable agreement between competent parties who agree to perform or refrain from performing certain acts for a consideration

contract for deed also called an *agreement for sale* or *land contract*, enables the seller to finance a buyer by permitting the buyer to make a down payment followed by monthly payments

contract for sale a real estate installment sales arrangement whereby the buyer may use, occupy, and enjoy the property; however, no deed is delivered by the seller until the entire contract price has been paid

contract rent the rental price stated on the lease agreement

contract rescission the canceling of a contract by either mutual consent of the parties or legal action

contribution the same principle as increasing and decreasing returns, except that it applies to only a portion of the property

conventional (or formal) will a will that is normally prepared by an attorney and properly witnessed according to statute

conventional life estate a fee simple estate granted for the life of an individual

confidentiality the part of the agent's fiduciary duty to treat information from the client with confidence

conventional loan a loan that is made that is not federally insured or guaranteed

conversion use of funds by the broker for other than their stated purpose is illegal

cooperating broker a broker that the listing broker agrees to pay a portion of the commission if the broker procures the buyer; generally referred to as the selling broker

Cooperative Brokers Certificate an out-of-state person who has a real estate broker license to sell real estate issued by a state other than Nevada and who desires to cooperate with a Nevada broker to sell Nevada real estate

cooperatives generally organized as corporations, with the tenants owning the stock

corporation a legal entity formed and authorized by law to act as an individual person with rights and liabilities distinct from those of the persons comprising it

corrective deed a document used to correct an error in a previously recorded deed

cost the historical expenditure for the purchase, construction, or improvement of a property

cost approach also called *appraisal by summation*, estimates today's cost of all improvements, minus all factors of depreciation, plus the valuation of the land using the market data approach

cost recovery the recovery of cost through depreciation for accounting and tax purchases

covenants agreements written into deeds and other instruments promising performance or non-performance of certain acts

Covenants, Conditions, and Restrictions (CC&Rs) document that itemizes deed restrictions that uniformly affect all of the subdivision; also called the Uniform Declaration of Restrictions

credit the reputation of a person or firm for the paying of bills when due; in a closing statement, the money is received by the person in whose statement it appears; a credit is also given in the closing statement for monies paid against an expense obligation in the transaction

credit report a report reflecting the credit-worthiness of a borrower by showing past credit history

credit unions similar to the original savings and loans; operated primarily for the benefit of their members or depositors

cubic area formula to compute, multiply the width by length by depth or height

curtesy the legal right of a widower to a portion of his deceased wife's real property

customer third party to whom the seller sells or agrees to sell

damages the estimated money equivalent for loss or injury sustained

datum point of reference to which heights and depths are referred

deal fairly one of the duties of a licensee, wherein a licensee must be honest and truthful with all parties to a transaction

debit means that the item will be paid for by the person in whose closing statement it appears

debit and credit statement type of settlement statement used for commercial transaction settlements and residential settlements not covered by RESPA

declaration of homestead a recorded notice by the owner that establishes the homestead exemption on the owner's principal residence

dedication the voluntary conveyance of private land to the public

deed a written instrument that when properly executed by the grantor and delivered to the grantee conveys title for the real estate described

deed in lieu of foreclosure mutual agreement in which the borrower is released from liability under the terms of the loan in exchange for a quitclaim deed or a regular grant deed

deed of reconveyance instrument used to reconvey title to a trustor under a trust deed once the debt has been satisfied

deed of trust a security instrument transferring title to property to a third person (trustee) as security for a debt or other obligation owed by the borrower (trustor) to the lender (beneficiary)

deed restriction clauses in a deed restricting or limiting future uses of the property

default breach of one or more of the terms and conditions that the borrower agreed to in the loan and security agreements

defeasance clause a mortgage clause that states the mortgage is defeated if the accompanying note is repaid on time; in a lease the clause may terminate the lease upon the occurrence of specified events, such as destruction of the premises or condemnation

defeasible qualified fees that can be terminated if certain conditions are met or not met

denominator the bottom number of a fraction

deficiency judgment a judgment against the defaulting mortgagor for the difference between the indebtedness and the sale price through a foreclosure sale

delinquency past due payment

demand the need or desire to possess something and having the money to fulfill that need

demise the transfer of a leasehold interest

Department of Housing and Urban Development (HUD) provides assistance for housing and community development; insures mortgages and promotes and enforces equal housing opportunity

depreciation decrease in value

depreciation (cost recovery) the annual deduction allowed for recovering the taxpayer's cost of the investment property

derivative title all ownership belonging to individuals or legal entities and derived from the government's original title

designated broker a Nevada real estate broker designated to act as the responsible individual for a real estate brokerage formed as a corporation, limited liability company, or partnership

developer (1) the owner of subdivided land who, on his or her own behalf or through an agent or subsidiary, offers it for sale or (2) the principal agent of an inactive owner

devise the transfer of real property by will

devisee one who receives real property under a will

devisor the person who wills the property

direct reduction loan a constant principal reduction plus the interest due on the unpaid balance

discharge of contract when performance of the agreed upon actions has been completed, the contract is *discharged*

disclaimer deed a deed executed by one spouse that denies any interest in the property of the other spouse

disclosure the agent's duty to keep the principal informed of all facts or information that could materially affect a transaction

discount a charge made by lenders to increase the effective rate of interest (yield) from the stated interest rate on the note

discount point   charges made by lenders to adjust the effective rate of interest on a loan; one point is equal to 1 percent

distraint   forcing the tenant to pay rent or other financial obligations by seizing the leased premises and/or personal property inside the leased premises

dominant tenement   landowner who benefits from the easement

dower   old English law, wherein any property bought during marriage belongs to the husband, but husband and wife share the use of the property

down zoning   occurs when a property zoned for higher-density uses is rezoned for lower-density uses

dual agency   a national common law concept that occurs when a broker represents the opposing principals (buyer and seller) at the same time; the concept of dual agency is not used anywhere in the Nevada Revised Statute title Real Estate Brokers and Salesmen

Duties Owed by a Nevada Real Estate Licensee   a state mandated form that a licensee is required to provide the client and each unrepresented party

dwelling insurance   covers losses from fire, lightning, and internal explosion for residential properties

dwelling unit   a structure or part of a structure that is used as a home, residence, or sleeping place by one person who maintains a household or by two or more persons who maintain a common household

earned income   includes wages, salaries, income from a business or profession, and other earned income

easement   interest that entitles one party to some limited use of another party's land

easement in gross   right to use the land of another

economic characteristics of real estate   the four main categories that describe real estate in economic terms: scarcity, improvements, fixed investments, and situs

economic obsolescence   caused by an influence outside the property over which the property owner has no control

economic rent   the amount that a property would bring at current market if it were not under prior contract

effective annual gross income   total income after deductions for vacancies and bad debts

effective rate   the average tax rate on all of the individual's taxable income

egress   exit

electromagnetic field   the area created by the movement of electrical current

electronic will   a will written, created, and stored in an electronic record

emblements   growing crops

eminent domain   government's right to take private property for public use without the owner's consent, after paying the owner fair compensation

eminent domain   taking property for the public welfare by paying fair market value for it

Employee Retirement Income Security Act (ERISA)   federal law that provides for the protection of assets set aside for pension and retirement plans through the establishment of the Pension Benefits Guaranty Corporation

encroachment   intrusion upon another person's property without a right to use it

encumbrance   a claim upon real property; any impediment to a clear title

enforceable   a valid contract with all of the essential elements present that is binding on all parties and can be enforced through a court of law

entitlement   the maximum amount the DVA will guarantee a lender in the event of default

entity taxation   the business entity is a taxpayer; the basic difference between a corporation and a partnership

Environmental Impact Statement   a document that gathers information that will demonstrate the positive or negative impact of a proposed project on the physical, economic, and social environment of the area

Equal Credit Opportunity Act (ECOA)   federal law prohibiting discrimination in the extension of credit

Equal Housing Opportunity poster   a poster required to be displayed in brokerages, mortgage companies, and new home sites; failure to display the poster may be considered as evidence of discriminatory practices

equitable period of redemption   the period of time from the filing of the notice of default to the date of the sale

equitable title   the vendee has the right to occupy the property and has all the rights and obligations of ownership

equity of redemption period   the right to redeem property during the foreclosure period

erosion   gradual wearing away of land through processes of nature

escheat   reversion of property to the state upon the death of an owner who has no will or heirs able to inherit

escrow company   orders loan payoffs, prepares escrow instructions, takes signatures, disburses funds, and arranges for the recording of documents

escrow instructions   documents in which buyers and sellers hire escrow companies to work on their behalf

estate   the degree, quantity, nature, and extent of the interest that a person has in real property

estate at sufferance   the lowest type of estate a person can hold

estate at will   use of the property at the will of the landlord; either party can terminate the lease at any time since there is no set termination date

estate for years   a lease that extends for a definite term

estate in remainder the interest that takes effect after the termination of a prior estate, such as a life estate

estate in reversion the interest that reverts to the grantor after the termination of a prior estate such as the expiration of a lease or the death of a life tenant

estate *pur autre vie* a life estate pur autre vie grants a life estate to one person that expires on the death of another person

estoppel agency an agency that cannot be denied when a broker allows a seller or buyer to create the illusion that the broker is his or her agent

eviction the act of depriving a person of possession of land that he or she has held pursuant to the judgment of the court of competent jurisdiction

exceptions limitations on the title, such as easements, mineral rights or deed restrictions, or other encumbrances on the property

exclusive agency listing a written agreement giving one agent the exclusive right to sell property for a specified period of time, but reserving the right of the owner to sell the property himself or herself without liability for the payment of a commission

exclusive right to represent buyer agreement listing used to located properties on behalf of the buyer; buyer brokerage agreement

exclusive right to sell listing a written agreement giving one agent the exclusive right to sell property for a specified period of time; the agent may collect a commission if the property is sold by anyone, including the owner, during the term of the listing agreement

executed contract a contract in which all of the terms and conditions have been fulfilled

executory contract contract that is not yet finished (unperformed) and therefore incomplete

exempt domestic well a well that serves one home does not require water-right permitting when the pumpage does not exceed a daily maximum of 1,800 gallons and water cannot be furnished by an entity such as a water district or municipality

exempt sales lot sales that are exempt from the requirements for the developer to register the subdivision in accordance with the Nevada Revised Statutes and Administrative Code

express contract an oral or written contract in which the parties state the contract's terms and express their intentions in words

extended coverage policy that includes all of the coverage of a standard policy, plus additional insurance against anything an inspection of the property might disclose, discrepancies or conflicts in boundaries, unrecorded liens, encumbrances, leases, and not having legal access

Fair Credit Reporting Act regulates the action of credit bureaus and the use of consumer credit

Fair Housing Act of 1968 bans discrimination on the basis of race, color, religion, and national origin in most types of housing transactions In 1974, the 1968 Act was amended to include the ban on discrimination on the basis of sex

Fair Housing Amendments Act of 1988 added the protected classes of handicap and familial status

familial status one or more individuals (under the age of 18) living with either a parent or legal guardian, or a designee holding written permission of a parent or legal guardian for the child or children to live with him or her

Fannie Mae *see* FNMA

Federal Deposit Insurance Corporation (FDIC) a federal insurance program that insures deposits in banking institutions up to $100,000; the amount increases to $250,000 through December 31, 2009

federal flood insurance insurance coverage for losses to real and personal property resulting from the inundation of normally dry areas

Federal Home Loan Bank System (FHLB) now known as the Office of Thrift Supervision, it is the regulatory and supervisory agency for federally chartered savings and thrift institutions

Federal Home Loan Mortgage Corporation (FHLMC) the second major player in the secondary mortgage market is the Federal Home Loan Mortgage Corporation (FHLMC), known as Freddie Mac; the Emergency Home Finance Act of 1970 gave Fannie Mae the power to purchase conventional loans and authorized the establishment of a new player in the secondary market

Federal National Mortgage Association (FNMA) commonly known as Fannie Mae, it was established in 1938 as a government corporation to create a secondary market for FHA loans

Federal Reserve System (FED) the federal central banking system of the United States under the control of a central board of governors (Federal Reserve Board); it is responsible for controlling and regulating the nation's monetary policy and money supply

fee simple conditional also known as *fee tail*, is a fee simple with a restriction to the right of inheritance, such as limiting the right of inheritance to a fixed line of succession, such as "to the first-born son in each generation"; fee simple conditional is not legal in Nevada

fee simple determinable a fee simple estate in which the property automatically reverts to the grantor upon the occurrence of a specified event or condition

fee simple estate also known as *fee*, or *fee simple absolute*, it gives the owner the greatest interest possible and is of indefinite duration

fee simple on condition subsequent a qualified fee estate subject to conditions on the grantee, often recognized by the negative restriction or the words "but if"

feudal system   all the land belongs to the sovereign king (or queen) and everyone owes rent or services to a superior

FHA loan   one that is *insured* by the Federal Housing Administration

fiduciary relationship   relationship created between the principal (client) and the agent and is one of trust and confidence

fief   an estate held as a condition of service to another

finder's fee   fee paid to a person for introducing or arranging an introduction between the parties to a transaction involving the rental of an apartment unit

fixtures   an item that was once tangible, personal property that has been attached to and made a part of the land or improvements

forbearance   an arrangement that effectively forestalls or delays foreclosure action

forcible detainer action   expedites eviction of the borrower

foreclosure   procedure that removes an owner's property rights; when real property is pledged as security for a loan, the process of selling that property as a result of the borrower's default is called foreclosure

forfeiture clause   the loss of money or anything of value due to failure to perform under a contract

foundation   the substructure for a superstructure; includes footings, foundation walls, columns, and pedestals

fractional interest   an undivided interest in improved or unimproved land and lots or parcels of any size created for sale or lease

fractional section   the sections where township corrections are made are confined to sections 1, 2, 3, 4, 5, 6, 7, 18, 19, 30, and 31; there are 11 fractional sections in a township

fraudulent misrepresentation   deceitful practice or material misstatement known to be false and done with intent to deceive

Freddie Mac   *see* FHLMC

freehold   an estate of ownership of real property of uncertain duration

freehold estate   real property ownership estate of uncertain duration

fructus industrials   annual crops; these crops are considered personal property

fructus naturals   perennial crops; these crops are considered real property

functional obsolescence   loss of value from all causes within the property, except those due to physical deterioration

general agent   one who represents the principal in a specific range of matters, such as all real estate

general partnership   an association of two or more persons (natural or legal) who share in the management and operation of the business, as well as the profits and losses

general warranty deed   a deed with covenants whereby the grantor agrees to protect the grantee against any claimant

Ginnie Mae   *see* GNMA

government checks   24-mile squares established by Guide Meridians and Standard Parallels; each contains 16 townships

Government National Mortgage Association (GNMA)   government corporation under the control of the Department of Housing and Urban Development (HUD), also called Ginnie Mae; it administers special assistance programs in secondary market activities

government rights   include police power, taxation, eminent domain, and escheat

government-backed loan   residential mortgage loans that are insured or guaranteed by federal agencies

graduated lease   a lease that provides for agreed upon rent increases

graduated payment mortgage (GPM)   begins with low payments but increases at regular intervals for a set number of years and then levels out for the balance of the term

grantee   the person named in a deed who acquires ownership

granting clause   transfers property rights along with the grantor's covenants (promises); the wording related to the covenants varies depending upon the type of deed

grantor   the seller or giver in the sale or gift of real property

gross income   includes earned income, portfolio income, passive income, and capital gains and losses

gross lease   a simple lease used in most houses and apartment complexes

gross rent multiplier (GRM)   used as a rule of thumb for a quick estimate of value based on the relationship of comparable sales prices to the comparables' monthly rental income; *not* an approach to value

ground lease   a long-term lease for the use of land

groundwater   all water under the surface of the earth except water flowing in underground streams with definite and ascertainable beds and banks

guide meridians   survey line running north and south that corrects for the earth's curvature

habendum clause   the "to have and to hold" clause that defines or limits the quantity of the estate granted in the deed

handicapped person   one who has "a physical or mental impairment which substantially limits one or more of such person's major life activities," and who has a record of having such an impairment or being regarded as having such an impairment

hard money loan mortgage given for money received

hereditament anything capable of being inherited, both real and personal property

highest and best use the most profitable use for which land can be used at the time of appraisal; the use that will bring the greatest return

hold harmless clause a clause in commercial leases that transfers all liability for the leased premises to the tenant

holder in due course third-party purchaser of a note; has all the rights of the original holder

holographic will a handwritten will that is signed and dated by its maker; cannot be typed, but can be a preprinted form that was filled in by hand; requires no witness

home mortgage interest deduction itemized interest expense deduction allowed on an individual taxpayer's return

home warranty contract a warranty on resale homes that covers mechanical items

homeowners' association (HOA) manages the common elements of a condominium development and ensures compliance with the HOA rules and the development's deed restrictions

homeowners' insurance multiline policy that combines property and casualty coverage in the same policy

homestead exemption law that exempts the homestead of any person 18 years of age or over, married or single, who resides in the state and is the head of the household, from forced sale by creditors

HOPE for Homeowners Act of 2008 an act of Congress designed to provide relief to homeowners who are threatened with the loss of their homes

HUD-1 statement closing statement required by RESPA to be used for most residential real estate closings

hypothecation to pledge property as security without giving up possession

impairment a substantial limitation of one or more major life activities to be covered by the Americans with Disabilities Act

implied agency when the buyer assumes by an agent's actions that the agent is working for the buyer

implied contract agreement of the parties is demonstrated by their acts or conduct

improper fraction a fraction that equals a whole number or more

improved lot or parcel a lot or parcel featuring a residential, commercial, or industrial building

improvements additions to raw lands such as buildings, streets, sewers, and so on

inchoate incomplete rights in property

income approach an appraisal technique used on income producing properties; assumes that income from property establishes value

income ratio a ratio used to qualify borrowers for a mortgage loan; computed by dividing the monthly mortgage payments by monthly gross income

increasing and decreasing returns principle of value; if funds spent on improving a property increase return, the law of increasing return applies; if they do not produce a positive return, the law of decreasing return applies

indefeasible fee fee simple estate; cannot be annulled, forfeited, or terminated without the action of the owner, as long as the owner is not doing anything to interfere with the rights of others or the government

index lease a lease that allows for periodic increases in base rental fees based on a predetermined guideline

ingress entrance to landlocked property

in-house sale brokerage transaction in which one sales associate obtains the listing and also finds the buyer, or a second associate with the same brokerage procures the buyer

innocent-purchaser defense a defense to owner liability under CERCLA when a landowner can demonstrate that at the time of acquisition there was "no reason to know" that the property was contaminated

inquiry any call to the insurance agent about an actual or potential loss that would be covered by a homeowner's policy

inquiry notice the expected examination of public records and visual inspection for claims and the extent of those clams by anyone acquiring a property right or interest

installment loan a loan that allows payment over an extended period of time

insulation materials placed in walls and ceilings that is rated by R-factor for its ability to resist heat transfer

insurable value used to determine the amount of insurance needed to meet co-insurance clause requirements

insurance underwriting process used by the insurance company to ascertain the types of risks it will accept through the issuance of an insurance policy

intangible assets incorporeal or invisible assets—*without a body*

integration, equilibrium, and disintegration integration is the development stage, when the value of a property is increasing; equilibrium is the static period, when the property reaches its maximum value; disintegration is the period during which the neighborhood declines and the value goes down

interest the charge or cost for the use of money

interest rate buy-down a reduction of the interest rate stated on the note by payment of points at the time of loan funding

interest-only loan loan that require periodic payment of the interest only; often referred to as a straight loan

Interstate Land Sales Full Disclosure Act regulates the sale or lease when developers of 25 or more unimproved lots in a subdivision sell or lease to citizens of another state as part of a Common Promotional Plan

intestate dying without a will

intestate succession the transfer of property to the surviving heirs of an individual who dies intestate

investor one who acquires property to obtain a profit

involuntary alienation transfer of property ownership without the consent of the owner; accomplished by operation of the law

irrigation grandfathered rights grandfathered water rights established in 1980 applicable to farming for cash crops

itemized deductions personal expenses that can be deducted on an income tax return when computing taxable income

joint and several liability enforceable on the makers as a group and upon each maker individually

joint tenancy type of ownership in which in the case of death, the survivor automatically acquires ownership of the property

Jones v Mayer 1968 landmark case banning discrimination based on race in the sale of housing

judgment a court of competent jurisdiction's final determination of a matter presented to it; the final decision by a court in a lawsuit, motion, or other matter

judicial foreclosure foreclosure action taken through the filing of a lawsuit

laches loss of the right to make a claim due to a delay in asserting one's rights

land includes the surface of the earth plus everything attached to the earth by nature, the space above the earth (air rights), and below the surface (mineral rights)

land contract also known as an *agreement for sale* or a *contract for deed*, it is an executory contract, in as much as the terms have not been fulfilled

land developers improve lots by adding buildings and then selling the developed lots

land trust a real estate trust wherein the person who creates the trust, the trustor, is also its beneficiary; a trust created solely for the ownership, operation, and management of real estate interests

landlord the owner of the property, who subordinates the rights of possession

latent defects a hidden or concealed defect that cannot be discovered by ordinary observation or inspection

lawful purpose one of the four requirements for a valid contract

lead-based paint paint that has a lead component and that is extremely harmful and may be deadly to children

lead-based paint disclosure required disclosure by sellers or lessors of residential properties built before 1978

leasehold the interest a lessee has in a lease; a personal property interest

leasehold estate an estate that is less than freehold and lasts a certain duration of time

leasehold policy provides protection to a tenant or a lender to the tenant against defects in the lessor's title

lease-purchase a simple lease for a specified period of time, after which or during which the lessor agrees to sell and the lessee has the option to purchase at an agreed price and terms

legal life estate the life estate created by state laws; the only legal life estate applicable to Nevada is the homestead exemption

legal rate the rate of interest allowed by law when an obligation or court ordered judgment does not state a rate of interest on the obligation due; the legal rate of interest in Nevada is 12%

lender's policy provides protection against defects in the title pledged as security in a mortgage or trust deed note and insures the lender of his or her security position

lessee a tenant; the person who is entitled to possession of property under a lease

lessor a landlord; the property owner who executes a lease

leveraging borrowing money from another source to supplement your own funds in completing the acquisition of a piece of property

license personal, non-assignable authorization to enter and perform certain acts on another's land

license status-active the fees to the Nevada Real Estate Division have been paid and the license is placed with a Nevada broker or Nevada owner-developer

license status-current fees to the Nevada Real Estate Division have been paid

license status- inactive fees to the Nevada Real Estate Division have been paid, but the license has been held by the Division for 30 days or less

license status inactive renewed fees to the Nevada Real Estate Division have been paid, but the license has been held by the Division for more than 30 days

license status inactive not renewed the Nevada licensee does not have a current Nevada real estate license; the fees to the Nevada Real Estate Division have not been paid

lien claim or charge against a property as security for the payment of a debt or obligation

life insurance companies a source for large loans on commercial properties

life tenant a person who holds a freehold interest (life estate) in property for his/her lifetime or for the lifetime of another designated person

limited liability company (LLC) a form of business organization, combining the most favorable attributes of a partnership and a corporation and consisting of members or managers that is governed by its operating agreement

limited partnership a group of passive investors who, as a class of limited partners, join with a general partner who manages the investment or business enterprise

lis pendens recorded legal document that gives constructive notice that an action affecting a particular piece of property has been filed in a state or federal court

listing broker the real estate broker who procured the listing

listing a written employment contract between principal and agent, authorizing agent to perform services for the principal involving real estate

littoral rights the lawful claim of a landowner to use and enjoy the water of a lake or sea bordering the land, but can only own the land to the water's edge of the nearest high water mark

livery of seisin a mid-seventeenth century ceremony for the transfer of real property ownership

living trust also known as an intervivos trust, it is created and takes effect during the trustor's lifetime; a living trust relieves the trustor of the responsibility of handling the estate

loan originator individuals or entities in the primary mortgage market who lend directly to the qualified borrower

loan servicing collecting payments from the borrower and passing them along to the investor for a fee, may be separated from the sale of the loan or it may be included

loan value value used for establishing the amount of mortgage or trust deed loan to be made

loan-to-value ratio the collateral risk the lender takes and conversely, the equity the borrower risks losing

lot reservation an expression of interest by a prospective purchaser in buying a subdivided or unsubdivided lot, unit, or parcel at some point in the future; a subsequent affirmative action must be made by the prospective purchaser to create a contractual obligation to purchase

loyalty a requirement that an agent place his principal's interest above his or her own

maintenance clause charges the mortgagor with the responsibility to maintain and preserve the property to protect the mortgagees' interest in the property; failure to maintain the property is called *waste*

major life activities to be covered under the Americans with Disabilities Act there must be an impairment that substantially limits a person's life activities such as walking, speaking, breathing, seeing, hearing, learning, working, or independently caring for oneself

Manufactured Home Parks Landlord and Tenant Act applies to the rental of mobile home lots (not the mobile homes themselves)

map and plat description or lot and block description a system of describing land in urban areas

marginal rate the rate of tax on the next dollar of income

MARIA an acronym related to testing whether an item is a fixture or personal property

market data approach similar to the approach used by licensees or investors when listing residences

market value an unemotional, objective price at which a seller would sell and a willing buyer would purchase, with neither party under abnormal pressure to act

marketable title title that is reasonably free from risk of legal dispute over possible defects

Master Plan a comprehensive long-term general plan that cities and counties in Nevada are required to complete and adopt

master planned community development consisting of two or more separately platted subdivisions and is subject to either (1) a master declaration of covenants, conditions, or restrictions; (2) restrictive covenants that clearly indicate a general scheme for improvement or development of real property; or (3) a master owner's association that governs or administers the development

material facts facts that would be likely to affect a person's decision to determine whether to enter into a particular transaction; any information that will influence the judgment or decision of the customer

material participation a measure of a taxpayer's involvement in a business or investment activity related to the federal income tax passive loss limitations

mechanic's lien or materialmen's lien a lien created by state law in favor of persons who have performed work or furnished material in the erection or repair of a building

meeting of the minds a complete understanding between the interested parties

membership camping a campground for which a membership (license) is sold; in Nevada memberships cannot be sold until the Administrator has approved the site

meridians imaginary lines that are north-south lines parallel to the longitudinal lines

metes and bounds description oldest form of legal descriptions used in the United States

mill money equal to 1/10 cent

misrepresentation false statement or concealment of a material fact made to someone entitled to the information, by which that person responds with action and thereby suffers damage

mold a growth produced on damp or decaying organic matter or on living organisms; a fungus; certain molds have been identified as major contributors to illness

monetary encumbrance a lien; a claim or charge against a property as security for the payment of a debt or obligation

monuments an iron pipe, stone, tree or other fixed point used in making a survey

mortgage a written instrument by which real property is pledged to secure a debt or obligation; a lien on real property

mortgage banker a person who makes loans with their own funds, then sells the loans to investors

mortgage broker processes loans but usually has no funds to loan; someone who brings borrowers and lenders together

mortgage correspondent mortgage banker that represents loan originators, such as banks, life insurance companies, and pension funds

mortgage insurance premium (MIP) the premium charged for insuring an FHA loan

mortgage participation certificate (PC) guaranteed mortgage securities are sold to the public through securities dealers

mortgagee one to whom a mortgagor gives a mortgage to secure a loan or performance of an obligation; the lender under a mortgage

mortgagor one who gives a mortgage on his or her property to secure a loan or ensure performance of an obligation; the borrower under a mortgage

Mt. Diablo Base Line and Meridian intersection of the Base Line and Principal Meridian that establishes the point of beginning for a government survey in Nevada; the actual intersection of the Mt. Diablo base line and meridian is on Mt. Diablo, near Walnut Creek, California

Multiple Listing Service (MLS) organization of member brokers who agree to share listing information and commissions

multiple representation representation of more than one party in a real estate transaction that may be undertaken only upon the licensee's full disclosure to each party that he or she is acting for more than one party in that transaction and with each party's subsequent consent to multiple representation in writing; *see* Consent to Act

mutual assent *see* meeting of the minds

mutual savings banks organized as mutual companies, where profits are distributed to the depositors through interest or dividends

navigable waterways the landowner owns the land to the water's edge at the high water mark, but none below the water; the Colorado River, the Virgin River, and Winnemucca Lake are the only navigable waterways in Nevada

negligence when an agent fails to exercise a degree of reasonable caution that would be exercised by a person of ordinary prudence under all existing circumstances in view of probable danger or injury

negligence per se conduct that may be declared and treated as negligence without any argument or proof as to the particular surrounding circumstances, either because it is in violation of a statute or because it is so palpably opposed to the dictates of common prudence that it can be said without hesitation that no careful person would have been guilty of such conduct

negligent misrepresentation statement contrary to fact resulting from failure to exercise reasonable care in obtaining or communicating information; the licensee could be held liable

negotiable instrument an instrument signed by a maker or drawer, containing an unconditional promise to pay a certain sum of money, which can be passed freely from one person to another; often a promissory note or bank draft

net cash flow the number of dollars remaining each year after collecting rents and paying operating expenses and mortgage payments

net lease a commercial lease wherein the tenant pays a base rent plus maintenance, property taxes, and insurance

net listing listing that provides that the agent may retain as compensation for his or her services all sums received over and above a stated net price to the owner

Nevada Revised Statutes Nevada laws enacted by legislation

nonconforming loans also known as *jumbo loans* or *high balance loans*, can also be sold to the secondary mortgage market, although the purchaser will most likely be a nongovernment entity

nonconforming use building or land use that does not conform to the zoning ordinance

nonjudicial foreclosure foreclosure and sale of property without resorting to court action

nonmonetary encumbrance affects the physical condition or use of property; includes deed restrictions, easements, and encroachments

non-navigable waterways the landowner owns the land beneath the surface of the water to the center of the streambed at the low water mark

nonresidential property real property that is not residential rental property

notice of default a notice that is recorded in the county recorder's office stating that a trust deed is in default and that the holder has chosen to have the property sold

novation formal assumption in which a new borrower is substituted for the original maker of the note or a new party is substituted for an original party to a contract

nuncupative will an oral will usually done in the last minutes of a person's life

obedience a requirement that an agent obey all legal instructions given by the principal

offer a proposal to make a contract

offeree a person to whom an offer is made

offeror a person who makes an offer

Office of Thrift Supervision replaced the Federal Home Loan Bank Board; organization that authorizes institutions to make adjustable mortgage loans

oil or gas lease a lease that generally requires a flat fee for the exploration for gas and oil and a royalty if any is found

open listing an authorization given by a property owner to a real estate agent in which the agent is given the nonexclusive right to secure a purchaser; open listings may be given to any number of agents without liability to compensate any except the one who first secures a buyer ready, willing, and able to meet the terms of the listing or who secures the acceptance by the seller of a satisfactory offer

open-end mortgage a mortgage containing a clause that permits the mortgagor or trustor to borrow additional money without rewriting the mortgage or deed of trust

operating agreement an agreement between members of a limited liability company that is similar to the bylaws and shareholders' agreement of a corporation or the partnership agreement of a partnership

option clause a lease clause giving the tenant the option to renew the lease or to purchase the property

option to purchase an agreement to enter into a contract to purchase at the option of the lessee, and at a specified time during the lease

option to renew a lease clause that gives the tenant the right to extend the lease for a specified period of time

original title title to real estate owned by the country or state

owner-developer registration a registration with the Real Estate Division that allows the owner-developer to employ licensed real estate salesperson to sell single-family residences owned by the owner-developer that have not been previously sold and that are located in the area of the current registration

owner's policy a title insurance policy designed to protect the fee owner

package mortgage a security instrument that includes real property and the personal property on the premises

parol evidence rule in a court of law, a contract must stand on the written word; no oral explanation is acceptable, except to clarify a written ambiguity

part performance allows the enforcement of an oral contract covered by the Statute of Frauds where one party to the oral contract has substantially performed

partially amortized loan loan that begins with amortized payments but ends with a balloon payment

participation loan loan where the lender participates in the profits generated by a commercial property used to secure the debt

partition action a legal action by which co-owners seek to sever their concurrent ownership; the physical division of property between co-owners, usually through court action

partnership an association of two or more persons to unite their property, labor or skill, or any one or combination thereof, in prosecution of some joint business, and to share the profits in certain proportions; an agreement of two or more individuals jointly to undertake a business enterprise

passive income income from a business in which the owner does not materially participate

passive loss limitation a federal income tax provision that prevents an investor from deducting passive losses from earned income

pass-through certificate a security interest in a pool of mortgages that provides for a monthly "pass-through" of principal and interest payments directly to the certificate held; guaranteed by Ginnie Mae

patent the instrument used when an original title is conveyed by a state or federal government to an individual

payee lender

payor maker of the note

pension and retirement programs a source for real estate loans

per stirpes method of distributing property to heirs whereby the descendant of a deceased heir receives that heir's inheritance

percentage a part of a whole expressed in hundredths

percentage lease a commercial lease in which the tenant pays a percentage of the gross income received by the tenant, in addition to rent

percolation test determines the speed at which standing water is absorbed by the soil

perimeter the "distance around" the property; that is, add all four sides, or multiply both dimensions by 2 and add the sums

period of reinstatement 35-day period from the notice of default when a borrower may reinstate the loan

periodic estates a leasehold estate that continues indefinitely for successive periods of time, until terminated by proper notice; when the periods are one month in duration, it is often called a month-to-month lease

Permanent School Fund assets remaining from the original school trust lands that are required by the Nevada state constitution to be managed or disposed of to generate revenue for the Fund

personal property   any property that is not real property

personal residence gain exclusion   a gain exclusion from taxable income from the sale of a personal residence that has been the taxpayer's primary residence for two of the past five years

Phase One Environmental Analysis   the first phase of an environmental assessment; a review by competent professionals who have expertise in evaluating the presence of hazardous substances and other hazards and who are familiar with the liability implications

physical characteristics of real estate   three main categories that describe real estate in physical terms: immobility, indestructibility, and non-homogeneity

physical deterioration   the loss of value due to normal wear and tear or due to postponed maintenance

PITI   type of payment (principal, interest, taxes, and insurance)

planned community   a real estate development that includes real estate owned by an association created for the purpose of managing, maintaining, or improving the property, and in which the owners of units are mandatory members and required to pay association assessments

Planned Unit Development   high-density, single-family structures that utilize the land area to the greatest possible extent

Planning Commission   the commission of a municipality or county that hears petitions for zoning changes and makes recommendations to the city council or county board of supervisors

plat   survey that shows the location and boundaries of individual properties, dedicated streets, parks, and so on

Plessy v. Ferguson   infamous ruling, which held that the enforcement of racial segregation of private or public facilities did not violate the U.S. Constitution as long as the separate facilities were equal

plottage   the process of putting several parcels together as one larger parcel to achieve the highest and best use and an increase in value

point   1 percent of the loan amount paid to the lender or the lender's agent at the time the loan is made

point of beginning   indicates the place where the surveyor begins to describe the parcel in terms of the distance and direction from that point

police power   government's right to enact and enforce laws for the common good

portfolio income   income that is a return on invested capital, such as interest and dividends

potable water   water that can be safely and agreeably used to drink

power of attorney   an instrument authorizing a person to act as the agent of the person granting it

power of sale clause   clause in a deed of trust that allows the trustee to conduct a foreclosure sale without first going to court

prepayment clause   enables the borrower to prepay the note prior to its due date without penalty

prescription   method of acquiring an easement by continuous, open, hostile, and notorious use for a period of 10 years without the consent of the owner

price   the amount asked and the amount paid for property; the listing price is the amount asked for property

price fixing   set commission for all real estate brokerages; a violation of the Sherman Anti-Trust Act

primary mortgage market   a market in which lenders originate loans and make funds available to borrowers

principal   someone who engages the services of an agent (also called *client*)

principal meridian   a survey line running due north and south, as established by the rectangular survey system

principal residence   not restricted to single-family homes, but may include a house, mobile home, houseboat, co-op, or condominium apartment used as the taxpayer's main home; the home that a taxpayer lives in most of the time during the tax year

prior appropriation   water rights doctrine that applies to arid regions of the country, which is often translated to mean "first in time, first in use"

priority of liens   liens with the highest priority are superior to junior liens; real estate taxes have the highest priority followed by special assessments; priority of other liens is established by date recorded except for mechanic's liens

private mortgage insurance (PMI)   insurance for lenders against mortgage foreclosure losses

probate   a legal process by which a court determines the assets of the estate and who will inherit the property of the deceased person

procuring cause   direct or proximate cause

profit or profit a prendre   type of easement; a right to remove soil, minerals, fruit, timber, or some product of the land with compensation to the surface owner of the land

progression   opposite of regression; exists when there is a poorer property among more expensive properties

promissory note   a promise by the maker of the note to pay a specified amount in accordance with specific terms by a certain date

promptly   means the next business day, excluding holidays and weekends

proper fraction   less than one whole unit—the numerator is smaller than the denominator

property   the rights of ownership; the right to use, possess, enjoy, and dispose of a thing in every legal way and to exclude everyone else from interfering with these rights

property assessment a site analysis of the site and surrounding properties for indications of environmental hazards

property development includes subdividers who take raw land, do the initial planning for its best use by subdividing it into lots, and after approval of the plan by the proper authorities, do the initial development of the streets, sewers, sidewalks, and so on

property management agreement a written contract between a client and a broker in which the broker agrees to accept valuable consideration from the client or another person for providing property management for the client

property management permit issued by the Real Estate Division to a real estate broker, broker-salesperson, or salesperson before acting as the designated property manager within the state of Nevada

property management trust account a bank account for holding property management trust funds in two separate accounts in accordance with Nevada Revised Statutes for such accounts; one trust account must be used solely for rental operating activities and the other trust account must be used solely for security deposits

property management the physical, administrative, or financial maintenance and management of real property, or the supervision of such activities for a fee, commission, or compensation or valuable consideration, pursuant to a property management agreement

Property Management Permit must be obtained from the Real Estate Division before a real estate broker, broker-salesperson, or salesperson is allowed to engage in property management

property manager a person engaged in property management who, as an employee or independent contractor, is associated with a licensed real estate broker, whether or not for compensation

Property Report a report issued by the Real Estate Administrator in accordance with the Nevada Revised Statutes, which authorizes a developer to offer to sell all of or an interest in a subdivision

proration allocating taxes, insurance, rents, and interest at settlement to determine the amount of money to be charged or credited to the buyer or seller

protected class a class of people that by law are protected from discrimination

public accommodation a place of public use or operation by government or private entities that must comply with the ADA

puffing an agent making an exaggerated statement of opinion, without intending to deceive, such as, "This site has the most beautiful view in the city"

punitive damages amounts over the actual damages suffered as compensation for the breach of the contract

purchase money mortgage also known as deed of trust, it refers to any loan, whatever the source, for all or part of the purchase price for the purchase of real property

qualified fee estate a fee simple estate subject to certain limitations imposed by its grantor

quantum meruit a legal theory used to establish the compensation rate when there is no express agreement or when the agreement fails but the court finds it would be inequitable not to give the broker a commission

quitclaim deed a deed to relinquish any interest in property that the grantor may have, but implying no warranties; a deed that transfers only whatever right, title, or interest, if any, the grantor owns, without implying any warranties

R factor a rating system for insulation material; determines the level of insulation provided by a substance

radon a colorless, odorless, tasteless, radioactive gas that is present in the environment as a byproduct of the natural decay of uranium in the earth

range lines a strip of land six miles wide, determined by a government survey, running in a north-south direction but measuring in an east-west direction

ratified agency created when a seller or buyer accepts the benefits of an agent's prior and unauthorized actions *after the fact*

ready, willing, and able purchasers who have made up their minds to buy a given parcel of property and are financially able to do so according to the price and terms agreed upon with the seller

real estate land and the improvements or tenements attached to it by nature or by man

real estate broker a person licensed by the state of Nevada acting as a sole proprietorship in conducting a real estate brokerage business or a business entity licensed as a corporation, limited liability company, or partnership that must have a designated broker

real estate broker-salesperson any person who holds a real estate broker's license, but who, as an employee or as an independent contractor for compensation or otherwise, is associated with a licensed real estate broker in the capacity of a salesperson or registered owner-developer as a sales manager

real estate brokerage engaged in the business of bringing buyers and sellers together for the purpose of completing real estate transactions with a licensed real estate broker

Real Estate Commission composed of five members who are appointed by the governor whose duties are to act in an advisory capacity to the Real Estate Division, adopt regulations, and conduct hearings against Nevada licensees

Real Estate Division administers the provisions of Chapter 645 of the Statutes subject to the supervision of the Director of the Department of Business and Industry

Real Estate Education, Research and Recovery Fund created as a special revenue fund for the benefit of any person, except for another licensee, aggrieved by any fraud, misrepresentation, or deceit by a licensee in a real estate transaction

Real Estate Investment Trust (REIT)   a means of pooling investor money by using the trust form of ownership and featuring single taxation of profits; IRS rules require a minimum of 100 investors and distribution of 95% of profits to investors annually

real estate purchase contract   a contract binding on all parties that sets out all the details of a sale, states the agreement of buyer and seller, and dictates the contents of the deed

real estate salesperson   any person who, as an employee or as an independent contractor, is associated with a licensed real estate broker or registered owner-developer to do or to deal in any acts or transactions for which a real estate license is required

Real Estate Settlement Procedures Act (RESPA)   enacted by Congress in 1974 to ensure that borrowers were provided with more abundant and timelier information on the nature and costs of the settlement process

real property   ownership rights in land and its improvements

real property classifications   the five general classifications used in zoning: residential, commercial, industrial and manufacturing, agricultural and raw land, and special purpose

reasonable accommodation   any modification or adjustment that will enable a qualified employee or occupant with a disability to enjoy equal opportunity to use a dwelling or perform essential job functions

reasonable care and diligence   a requirement that an agent exhibit competence and expertise, keep clients informed, and take proper care of entrusted property

reasonable modification   barrier removal and modifications required to ensure equal opportunity for access to individuals with disabilities

reasonable use   water doctrine that declares that users must show beneficial use of water

receipt for property report   signed by each purchaser of any subdivision property before execution of any contract for the sale of any subdivision property

reconciliation   the last step in the appraisal process, whereby the appraiser reconciles the three approaches to value, arriving at his or her estimate

recording acts   law that provides for the placing of documents in the public records

rectangle   four-sided shape whose sides are at right angles to each other

rectangular survey or government survey   system of land description developed by the federal government

redlining   mortgage credit discrimination based upon the density of minorities in a geographic area

regression   when there are properties of different values in a neighborhood, the better property is adversely affected by the poorer properties

Regulation Z   regulation pursuant to the Truth-in-Lending Act requiring credit institutions to inform borrowers of the true cost of obtaining credit

release   unintentional or intentional, chronic or sudden, small or major releases of hazardous substances to the environment or people's exposure to these substances

remainderman   the third person with the remainder interest

rent   the consideration paid under a leasehold estate for the use and possession of real property

rental real estate passive loss allowance   owner's deduction of up to $25,000 of loss from rental real estate against earned income if the owner actively participates in the management of the rental property

repair   keeps the real property in good operating condition; repairs include painting, fixing gutters or floors, fixing leaks in plumbing or roofs, plastering, and replacing broken windows

replacement cost   estimated cost based on using today's materials and technologies

reproduction cost   estimated cost of using the original materials and technologies

rescission   legal remedy of canceling, terminating, or annulling a contract and restoring the parties to their original positions

reservations   uses that the grantor withholds from the title being conveyed for personal use

Residential Landlord Tenant Act   a Nevada statute that applies statewide to almost all residential units

residential rental property   a building or structure in which 80 percent or more of the gross rental income is rental income from dwelling units

retroactive liability   a property owner can be responsible for actions years earlier than passage of CERCLA regardless of whether the prior actions were standard practices of the time or had received approval

reverse annuity mortgage (RAM)   the lender makes monthly payments to a homeowner who repays in a lump sum upon the homeowners death or sale of the home

reversionary rights   the interest a person has in property upon the termination of the preceding estate; the right to retake possession of a leased property at some future time

right of rescission   a borrower's right to cancel a contract within three business days

rights of others   private, nongovernmental limitations on the bundle of rights such as deed restrictions

riparian rights   grants owners of land located along a stream, river, or lake— generally non-navigable waters— rights to the land beneath the surface of the water

risk the degree or possibility of loss on an investment

roof the outside covering of the top of a building or structure

rooftop lease used to rent the airspace above a piece of real estate

sale and leaseback leases used after a person has developed a building and wants his or her working capital available for other developments

sale clause a clause in residential leases that allows the tenant or landlord to terminate the lease in the event the subject property is sold

sales agent or time share agent an individual who has qualified and been issued a sales agent license that allows the individual to only sell time shares, while working for a Nevada broker

sandwich lease lease held by a lessee who becomes a lessor by subletting; typically, the sandwich leaseholder is neither the owner nor the user of the property

satisfaction of mortgage certificate from the lender stating that the loan has been repaid; can be recorded to remove the related lien from the property records

savings and loans a primary source of residential real estate loans

scarcity an economic characteristic of real estate; shortage of land in a geographical area where there is a great demand for land

secondary mortgage market purchase and sale of existing mortgages and trust deeds

section a square mile of land, as established by government survey, containing 640 acres

Section 1031 a section of the Internal Revenue Code for deferring capital gains taxes by exchanging one like kind property for another

security deposits deposited with the landlord solely as security for the tenant's performance of the terms of the lease; usually not taxed when received

Seller's Real Property Disclosure Form a form prescribed by the Real Estate Division for the proper disclosure by the seller of material facts related to any residential resale

senior housing housing intended for and solely occupied by persons 62 years of age or older, or at least one person in 80 percent of the households is 55 years or older

servient tenement land on which the easement runs

severalty taking title as sole owner, either as a natural person or a legal person

sharecropping a lease between an agricultural landowner and a tenant, whereby the landowner provides the land and may also provide equipment in return for the tenant's planting, maintaining, and harvesting a crop; proceeds are then divided (not necessarily equally) between the tenant and the landowner

shared appreciation mortgage (SAM) lender participates in the appreciation of the property value and in turn accepts a note with a lower rate of interest

sheathing a 4-foot by 8-foot plywood or other wood exterior covering placed over exterior studding

sheriff's sale a sale ordered by the court in which a sheriff or county official has the legal right to sell a distressed or foreclosed property

Sherman Anti-Trust Act federal laws that condemn contracts, culmination, and conspiracies in restraint of trade and monopolizing, attempts to monopolize, and combinations and conspiracies to monopolize trade

short sale a transaction where the lender agrees to accept a payoff-in-full amount that is less than the outstanding balance of the loan

single agency practice of representing either the buyer or seller, but never both; if a broker intends to be a single agent, he or she must take special care regarding the licensees within the office

situs area preference, or the people's choice of a given area

special agent is authorized to represent the principal in one specific transaction, such as in a listing, but is not given the power to bind the principal

special assessments improvements that enhance the value of property, such as curbs, sidewalks, streets, sewers, and streetlights

Special Improvement Districts generally formed by counties, cities, and towns for specific projects within the district and to provide a source of funding for eligible improvements

special use permit given by approval of the Planning Commission for a property owner to develop a property in the public interest, as long as it does not interfere with the intent of the existing zoning

special warranty deed a deed in which the grantor warrants or guarantees the title only against defects arising during his or her ownership of the property and not against defects existing before the time of ownership

specific performance contract performance according to the precise terms agreed upon

speculation a transaction where the profits are subject to chance; to buy or sell with the hope of profiting through the fluctuations in price

spot zoning zoning change is requested for an individual piece of property, as opposed to a change for an area

square a rectangle with equal sides

standard coverage used in residential conveyance and limited to insurance against forged documents of incorrect marital status, documents signed by incompetent parties, unmarketable property due to defect of title, and an improperly delivered deed

standard parallels lines that are "1st or 2nd Standard Parallel, North or South," and so on, according to the distance from the base line

Starker case 1979 Supreme Court decision that has had a lasting effect on tax deferred exchanges

State Enabling Act laws that allow the admission as a state in the United States of America

State Engineer the appointed administrative head of the Nevada Division of Water Resources

State Land Office the "real estate" agency of the state of Nevada

Statement of Record any person or broker proposing to sell any subdivision, lot, or parcel in Nevada must file the Statement of Record with the Nevada Real Estate Division on a form furnished by the Division

Statute of Frauds a state law that provides that certain contracts must be in writing in order to be enforceable in the courts; established in England in 1677 and adopted in full or in part by all 50 states

statutory law law created by the enactment of legislation

statutory period of redemption period after the sale during which the landowner could redeem the property

steering illegal practice of directing certain persons into or out of areas that are or are not racially integrated

straw person individual or entity that briefly holds title to real estate and then transfers the interest at one time to the group of owners that now includes the new owner

strict liability CERCLA laws apply regardless of whether intent to pollute or knowledge of the situation was present

stucco one of the most common materials used because it is flexible and inexpensive

subagent person appointed by the broker agent to assist in the performance of the assignment

subchapter S corporation a corporation that, for federal tax purposes only, is taxed similarly to a partnership; the corporate entity is disregarded for most federal tax purposes, and the shareholders are generally taxed as individual partners

subdividers take raw land, do the initial planning for its best use by subdividing it into lots, and, after approval of the plan by the proper authorities, do the initial development of the streets, sewers, sidewalks, and so on

subdivision any land or tract of land in another state, in Nevada, or in any foreign country from which a sale is attempted, which is divided or proposed to be divided over any period into 35 or more lots, parcels, units, or interests, including but not limited to undivided interests, which are offered, known, designated, or advertised as a common unit by a common name or as a part of a common promotional plan of advertising and sale

subjective value emotional value of a property's worth to a person, regardless of cost

sublease a lease from a lessee to another lessee; the new lessee is a sublesee or subtenant

sublessee the tenant in a sublease, who makes rent payments to the sublessor who in turn pays the lessor according to the original lease

sublessor the original lessee, who becomes the sublessor in a sublease

subordination clause the lender will agree to a lesser position of security and allow another person/lender to place a lien in front of the original lender's

subrogation substitution of one person in the place of another with reference to a lawful claim, such as when an insurance company pays a claim and then has the right to collect from the party causing the loss

substitution principle of value wherein the maximum value of a property in the marketplace tends to be set by the cost of purchasing an equally desirable substitute property

subsurface rights the right of the owner to use land below the earth's surface

Superfund also known as Comprehensive Environmental Response, Compensation, and Liability Act of 1980 (CERCLA), it was created to provide the authority and a source of funding for cleaning up hazardous materials released into the environment

Superfund Amendments and Reauthorization Act (SARA) contains provisions defining who is liable to pay for the cleanup of contamination caused by past activities

supply and demand an economic principle related to the desire and ability to acquire land related to the scarcity of land suitable for a desired purpose

surface area formula the formula for computing square feet or square yards of a rectangle or triangle

surface water water that sits or flows above the earth, including lakes, oceans, rivers and streams

"T" formula math formula for solving word problems

tack or tacking adding successive periods of continuous occupation to qualify for title by adverse possession

tangible assets corporeal and visible assets that _have a body_

Tax Equity and Fiscal Responsibility Act 1982 act that provides that licensed real estate agents may be classified as independent contractors exempt from classification as employees by the Internal Revenue Service

taxable income the amount for federal income tax purposes computed as follows: gross income less deductions for adjusted gross income less itemized or standard deductions less personal exemptions equals taxable income

taxable value the value of real property consisting of (1) the full cash value of the land and (2) the replacement cost new less depreciation of the improvements, with the rate of depreciation set by statute; the computed value is used for determining the assessed value for the computation of real property taxes in Nevada

taxation the government's right to levy taxes against real and personal property in order to provide city, county, and state governmental services for the benefit of the people

tax-deferred exchange transaction in which "like-kind" property is traded; *like-kind* means exchanging business or income property for other business or income property, or exchanging personal property for personal property

team or group a licensee may use the terms "team" or "group" to advertise and promote real estate services if those terms do not constitute the unlawful use of a trade name and if the team or group is composed of more than one licensee, employed by the same broker and contains the last name of at least one of the members of the team or group and the advertising otherwise complies with statutes and rules

temporary absence when a designated broker is unable to act within 24 hours

tenancy by the entirety type of ownership existing only between husband and wife; not used in Nevada

tenant one who possesses real estate by any kind of title, either in fee, for life, for years or at will; a tenant who has the temporary use of real estate that belongs to another

tenant-in-common investment (TIC) the purchase of an undivided interest in a development or other commercial property that qualifies as like-kind property in a Section 1031 exchange

tenants in common ownership by two or more persons who hold an undivided interest in real property, without right of survivorship; the interests need not be equal

tenements everything of a permanent nature attached to the land

termite a type of insect that eats wood

testamentary trust similar to a living trust, except that it is set up in a will and takes effect upon the maker's death

tiers horizontal rows of townships running in an east-west direction, but measuring in a north-south direction

"time is of the essence" clause the parties will perform within the limits specified; any party not doing so is considered in breach of contract

time-shares a form of joint ownership of property where numerous owners share title and enjoy use or occupation of the property according to a specific schedule

title gives evidence of the quality, right, and interest in real property, which allows a government, individual, individuals, or legal entity to retain possession of the property

Title Commitment/Preliminary Title Report a statement of current condition of title for a parcel of land; obligates the title insurance company to issue a policy of title insurance when curative requirements have been satisfied

title insurance insurance policy written by a title company to protect a property owner against loss if the title is defective or not marketable

topography nature of the surface of the land; the characteristics of the land in terms of elevation, slope, and orientation

Torrens system a legal system for the registration of land ownership; verifies ownership of land and the status of title, including any encumbrances except tax liens

township a territorial subdivision that is six miles long and six miles wide and that contains 36 sections, each one mile square

township lines east-west lines that run parallel to the base line every six miles

trade fixtures items that are the personal property of a tenant or owner and that are used to carry on his or her business

transferability ability to transfer a good or service to another person

treasurer's deed a document that conveys title to property purchased at a tax sale

triangle a three-sided figure

trust an entity created to own assets, including real and personal property, for the benefit of a person, persons, or another entity

trust account a bank account in which funds received from a client or customer for a specific purpose are not commingled with the personal funds of the broker

trust deed deed given by a borrower to a trustee to be held pending fulfillment of an obligation, which is usually repayment of a loan to a beneficiary; a deed of trust

trustee one who holds property in trust for the benefit of one or more beneficiaries; in a deed of trust, the person who holds bare legal title in trust

trustee deed the deed issued by the trustee after the foreclosure and sale of property under a deed of trust

trustor one who conveys his or her property to a trustee to be held on the behalf of a beneficiary

Truth in Lending Act a federal statute that requires certain disclosures when extending or advertising credit

unadjusted basis the original cost of the property, if it was purchased

underground storage tanks registration is required for all tanks containing regulated substances (all petroleum products) that are not already listed as hazardous "wastes"

unending liability liability for a problem on a site does not end with the transfer of property, but extends as long as the problem exists

Unenforceable a contract that is void is not enforceable in a court of law; a valid contract whose enforcement is barred by the statute of limitations or the doctrine of laches

Uniform Commercial Code   code that requires that the sale of personal property with value in excess of $500 be in writing

Uniform Standards of Professional Appraisal Practice (USPAP)   mandatory requirements for certain federally related real estate appraisals

unilateral contract   one-sided contract in which one party makes a promise in order to induce a second party to perform

unit   a portion of a condominium designated for separate ownership or boundaries

universal agent   someone empowered to perform any act that can be lawfully authorized to an agent; usually established by a power of attorney

unlicensed activity   a person who acts as a broker, broker-salesperson, or salesperson or who advertises in a manner indicating that he or she is licensed as a broker, broker-salesperson, or salesperson without actually being licensed

urea-formaldehyde foam insulation   thermal insulation material that is pumped into the spaces between the walls of a building, where it hardens to form a solid layer of insulation

usury   charging interest at a higher rate than allowed by law

utility   the capacity to satisfy human needs and desires

VA loan   real estate mortgage available to qualified veterans for the purpose of buying or refinancing real estate for personal residential use only

valid   contract is valid if it contains all of the essential elements of capacity, mutual assent, consideration; and lawful purpose; a valid contract is legal, enforceable, and binding on all parties

value   exchange of present worth for future benefits to the owner of the property

variable lease   a lease that provides that the rent may increase during the term of the lease including an index lease and a graduated lease

vendee   buyer in a contract for deed (land contract)

vendor   seller in a contract for deed (land contract)

verification of deposit (VOD)   confirmation to the lender by the borrower's bank of the amounts on deposit

verification of employment (VOE)   confirmation to the lender by the borrower's employer of employment information

void   to have no force or effect; does not exist; an agreement missing one of the essential elements of a contract

voidable   contract that seems valid and enforceable on the surface, but may be voided by one of the parties

voluntary alienation   the transfer of ownership with the consent of the owner

water rights   the right to use water on or below or bordering a parcel of land

water table   the natural level at which water will be located, be it above or below the surface of the ground

wetlands   areas that are inundated or saturated by surface water or groundwater at a frequency and duration sufficient to support, and that under normal circumstances do support, a prevalence of vegetation typically adapted for life in saturated soil conditions

wood frame construction   the most frequent method of construction for single-family homes; wood frame is less expensive, is easier to heat and cool, and offers a variety of architectural styles

wrap-around mortgage   purchase money transaction subject to, but still including, encumbrances to which it is subordinate; legal title is actually conveyed and title insurance may also be obtained

writ of attachment   legal process of seizing the real or personal property of a defendant in a lawsuit and holding it in the custody of the court as security for satisfaction of a judgment

writ of execution   an order directing the proper officer of the court to seize property to satisfy a judgment or carry out any other such judgment or decree

yield   annual interest income divided by the amount invested in the loan

zoning changes   may be initiated by a property owner or by the local government; requires a petition and formal hearing before the Planning and Zoning Commission

zoning variance   a minor change in zoning for one specific property without changing the character of the zoned area

Index